USING COMPUTERS IN THE
LAW OFFICE

BASIC

USING COMPUTERS IN THE
LAW OFFICE

BASIC

Matthew S. Cornick, J.D.
Clayton State University

DELMAR
CENGAGE Learning·

Australia • Brazil • Japan • Korea • Mexico • Singapore • Spain • United Kingdom • United States

Using Computers in the Law Office—Basic
Matthew S. Cornick

Vice President, Careers & Computing:
Dave Garza

Director of Learning Solutions: Sandy Clark

Senior Acquisitions Editor: Shelley Esposito

Senior Product Development Manager:
Larry Main

Senior Product Manager: Melissa Riveglia

Editorial Assistant: Diane Chrysler

Vice President, Marketing: Jennifer Ann Baker

Marketing Director: Deborah Yarnell

Senior Market Development Manager:
Erin Brennan

Senior Brand Manager: Kristin McNary

Senior Production Director: Wendy Troeger

Production Manager: Mark Bernard

Senior Content Project Manager:
Betty L. Dickson

Art Director: Riezebos Holzbaur Group

Senior Technology Project Manager: Joe Pliss

Media Editor: Deborah Bordeaux

Cover Credits: Binary code with abstract light
pattern: ©imagewerks/Getty Images

Supreme Court building:
©Tetra Images/Getty Images

Cover Design: Studio Montage/Melissa Welch

For product information and technology assistance, contact us at
Cengage Learning Customer & Sales Support, 1-800-354-9706

For permission to use material from this text or product,
submit all requests online at **www.cengage.com/permissions.**
Further permissions questions can be e-mailed to
permissionrequest@cengage.com

Library of Congress Control Number: 2012950773

ISBN-13: 978-1-4390-5706-3

ISBN-10: 1-4390-5706-0

Delmar
5 Maxwell Drive
Clifton Park, NY 12065-2919
USA

Cengage Learning is a leading provider of customized learning solutions with office locations around the globe, including Singapore, the United Kingdom, Australia, Mexico, Brazil, and Japan. Locate your local office at: **international.cengage.com/region**

Cengage Learning products are represented in Canada by Nelson Education, Ltd.

To learn more about Delmar, visit **www.cengage.com/delmar**

Purchase any of our products at your local college store or at our preferred online store **www.cengagebrain.com**

Notice to the Reader

Printed in the United States of America
1 2 3 4 5 6 7 16 15 14 13 12

BRIEF CONTENTS

CONTENTS

CHAPTER **3**

Spreadsheet Software | 166

CHAPTER **4**

Legal Timekeeping and Billing Software | 262

CHAPTER 5

Database Management Systems | 322

CHAPTER 6

The Electronic Courthouse, Automated Courtroom, and Presentation Graphics | 410

PREFACE

I should make a confession. There was a time (many years ago) when I believed that I could be successful in the law office without knowing much about computers. That was then. This is now. Let me state this as plainly as I can: A successful legal professional *must* know how to use a computer and the applications commonly used in a law office. With the advent of all things "e"—email, e-discovery, e-filing, and so on—it is essential that you gain the skills this text seeks to impart. The 21st century is well under way and computer literacy is a basic competency in law offices. *Using Computers in the Law Office—Basic*, is designed to give students both theoretical understanding and practical experience with common law-office computer applications. These include widely used applications, such as Microsoft Word, Excel, Access, PowerPoint, Adobe Acrobat, HotDocs, and Tabs3. I hope that students will learn not only the specific uses of these programs, but also that they should not doubt their abilities or fear the prospect of working with computers.

TO THE STUDENT

If I could give you only one piece of advice, it would be this: *be patient*. Do not rush through the Hands-On Exercises. I can tell you from personal experience that haste is a sure path to mistakes and frustration. If you are a novice to these applications, I hope (and expect) that you will find you can do far more than you ever thought possible.

If I could give you a second piece of advice, it would be to *keep learning*. Technology is always evolving. Never more so than today, knowledge is power. For years, I have been telling my students that the surest way to make themselves invaluable to their employers is to know how to do something the employer does not know. Learn the skills emphasized throughout this text and then keep learning, and your success is almost a certainty.

ORGANIZATION OF THE TEXT

This textbook is organized into six chapters. The first chapter introduces students to computers with a discussion of the importance of computers to the legal field and a review of computer hardware and software terms. The objective is to give students a rudimentary understanding of basic computer terminology and systems on which the rest of the book can build.

The next five chapters represent the heart of the book. They cover word processing, PDF creation, document assembly, spreadsheets, timekeeping and billing, databases, and the electronic courthouse/automated courtroom and presentations. Each topic is presented in a clear and organized manner and includes many examples of how the relevant software is actually used by paralegals in legal organizations.

LEARNING FEATURES

Chapter features include the following:

- **Chapter objectives** open each chapter to focus the student's attention on the main elements of the chapter.
- **Internet sites** are referenced, and useful and relevant ones are listed near the end of each chapter.
- **Key terms** are boldfaced in the body of the text, and definitions appear in the margin for easy review and reference. (A comprehensive glossary appears at the end of the book.)
- **Numerous illustrations,** including screen shots, legal documents, tables, and other graphics, are included throughout the text.
- **Test Your Knowledge exercises** are included in each chapter.
- **On the Web Exercises** are included in each chapter.
- **Questions and Exercises** are included in each chapter to challenge students to apply the information learned in the chapter.
- An **Ethics Question** is included for each chapter.
- **Hands-On Exercises** are included for most chapters to give students actual experience on a computer.

HANDS-ON EXERCISES

Hands-On Exercises are included for 7 different applications. These exercises assume that the student has access to a computer and to application software, but no prior computer experience is necessary to complete the tutorials.

The Hands-On Exercises include step-by-step instructions that guide the student through the application. There are literally hundreds of screen shots to guide the student and act as reference points. All of the Hands-On Exercises are completely interactive, allowing the student to gain hands-on experience with the software. In addition, all of the Hands-On Exercises are specifically related to legal organizations and legal applications, so the student not only learns how to operate the computer and software, but also learns how to use them in the legal environment.

Full tutorials are included for the following applications:

- Microsoft Word 2010 and 2007
- Adobe Acrobat 9 Pro
- HotDocs 10
- Microsoft Excel 2010 and 2007
- Tabs3 (v.15) (ON THE DISK)
- Microsoft Access 2010 and 2007
- Microsoft PowerPoint 2010 and 2007

EDUCATIONAL SOFTWARE

To help students complete some of the Hands-On Exercises, data files are provided on the disk included with the text:

- Adobe Acrobat
- Access
- Excel
- HotDocs
- PowerPoint
- Word Processing

Access to the following demonstration software is included with the text via the Premium Website. Use the Access Code included on the Premium Website card included with your text to activate your free online access. Please visit http://www.CengageBrain.com to create your account, log in, and access the Premium Website.

Please note that many of the programs expire and will not work after a certain number of days elapse from when the program was first loaded; other limitations may also apply to certain demonstration software.

- **Adobe Acrobat Professional** is a registered trademark of Adobe Systems Incorporated. Adobe Acrobat Professional expires 30 days after it is first installed.
- **HotDocs.** HotDocs 10 is a registered trademark of HotDocs, Ltd. HotDocs expires 120 days after it is first installed.
- **Tabs3.** Tabs3 is a registered trademark of Software Technology, Inc. Tabs3 does not expire; however, the following features are disabled: run data file integrity check, run reindex data files, run advance current reporting month, run credit card authorization.

Access to Microsoft applications (Word; Excel; Access; PowerPoint) is not included with the text.

SUPPLEMENTAL TEACHING AND LEARNING MATERIALS

CourseMate

Paralegal CourseMate

Using Computers in the Law Office—Basic, has a Paralegal CourseMate available.

Paralegal CourseMate includes:

- an interactive eBook, with highlighting, note-taking, and search capabilities
- interactive teaching and learning tools, including:
  - Quizzing
  - Case studies
  - Chapter objectives
  - Chapter resources
  - Flashcards
  - Web links
  - Crossword puzzles
  - PowerPoint® presentations
  - And more!
- Engagement Tracker, a first-of-its-kind tool that monitors student engagement in the course

Go to cengagebrain.com to learn more about this resource. To access CourseMate materials you have purchased, go to login.cengagebrain.com.

Premium Website

The Premium Website includes resources for instructors and students. The card in the main text includes an access code for this book's Premium Website. Go to login.cengagebrain.com to access the downloadable software demos and updates to the text.

Instructor's Manual

The Instructor's Manual provides comprehensive teaching support. The Instructor's Manual contains the following:

- Chapter Objectives
- Teaching suggestions and class discussion ideas
- Answers to exercises in the text
- Testbank and answer key
- Sample grading rubrics

Instructor Resources

Spend less time planning and more time teaching. With Delmar Cengage Learning's Instructor Resources to Accompany Using Computers in the Law Office—Basic, preparing for class and evaluating students have never been easier!

This invaluable instructor CD-ROM allows you "anywhere, anytime" access to all of your resources.

- The **Instructor's Manual** contains various resources for each chapter of the book.
- The **Computerized Testbank** in ExamView makes generating tests and quizzes a snap. With many questions and different styles to choose from, you can create customized assessments for your students with the click of a button. Add your own unique questions and print rationales for easy class preparation.
- Customizable **PowerPoint® Presentations** focus on key points for each chapter. (PowerPoint® is a registered trademark of the Microsoft Corporation.)

You can also access these materials online at login.cengage.com, using your SSO (single sign on) login. Additional materials (including CourseMate) can also be accessed via SSO.

WebTutor™ WebTUTOR

The WebTutor™ supplement allows you, as the instructor, to take learning beyond the classroom. This online courseware is designed to complement the text and benefit students and instructors alike by helping to better manage your time, prepare for exams, organize your notes, and more. WebTutor™ allows you to extend your reach beyond the classroom.

WebPage

Please visit our website at http://www.paralegal.delmar.cengage.com/, where you will find valuable information on Delmar Cengage Learning products.

Supplements At-A-Glance

Supplement:	What it is:	What's in it:
Paralegal CourseMate **CourseMate**	Online interactive teaching and learning tools and an interactive eBook. Go to login.cengage.com to access.	Interactive teaching and learning tools, including: • Quizzing • Case Studies • Chapter Objectives • Chapter Resources • Flashcards • Weblinks • Crossword Puzzles • PowerPoint® Presentations • Interactive eBook • Engagement Tracker
Premium Website	Resources for instructor and students. Access card included with textbook. Go to login.cengage.com.	• Downloadable software demo links • Updates to the text
Instructor Companion Site	Resources for the instructor, posted online at Cengage Single Sign On.	• Instructor's Manual with Chapter Objectives, teaching suggestions, answers to text questions, testbank, answer key, and grading rubrics. • PowerPoint® presentations
Instructor Resources CD-ROM	Resources for the instructor, available on CD-ROM and via SSO.	• Instructor's Manual with Chapter Objectives, teaching suggestions, answers to text questions, testbank, and answer key. • Computerized Testbank in ExamView, with many questions and styles to choose from to create customized assessments for your students • PowerPoint® presentations
WebTUTOR™ **WebTUTOR**	WebTUTOR™ supplemental courseware is the best way to use the Internet to turn everyone in your class into a front-row student. It complements Cengage Learning paralegal textbooks by providing interactive reinforcement that helps students grasp complex concepts. WebTUTOR™ allows you to know quickly what concepts your students are or aren't grasping.	• Automatic and immediate feedback from quizzes and exams • Online exercises that reinforce what students have learned • Flashcards • Greater interaction and involvement through online discussion forums

ACKNOWLEDGMENTS

This book was made possible by many individuals. This book required an enormous amount of work from a superb team of talented professionals. To all of you, many thanks.

REVIEWERS

Special thanks go to the reviewers of the text for their ideas and suggestions:

Sally Bisson
College of St. Mary
Omaha, NE

Anne Murphy Brown
Ursuline College
Pepper Pike, OH

Katherine Currier
Elms College
Chicopee, MA

Darren Defoe
Andover College
South Portland, ME

Donna Donathan
Marshall University
Huntington, WV

Barry Goodson
Columbia Southern University
Orange Beach, AL

Jonathan Kaiser
Tacoma Community College
Tacoma, WA

Wesley Marion
Ivy Tech Community College of Indiana
Lafayette, IN

Susan McCabe
Kellogg Community College
Battle Creek, MI

Elizabeth McCowan
Pellissippi State Technical Community College
Knoxville, TN

Tonya Morse
Institute of Business and Medical Careers, Inc.
Fort Collins, CO

Mary Mullin
Cerritos College
Norwalk, CA

Jessica Neilson
Highline College
Des Moines, WA

Mary Carol Parker
Maryville University
St. Louis, MO

Beth Pless
NE Wisconsin Technical College
Green Bay, WI

Donna Schoebel
Capital University Law School
Columbus, OH

Marc Vallen
University of Hartford
West Hartford, CT

Delmar Cengage Learning

I am deeply indebted to my editors at Cengage Delmar Learning. Shelley Esposito is my Acquisitions Editor; she asked me to take on this project and was always there when I needed her. Melissa Riveglia, the Senior Product Manager, had the unenviable task of making sure all the T's were crossed and the I's dotted. So many other folks had the responsibility of double-checking the accuracy of the text and the Hands-On Exercises. This project would not have been possible without their support and encouragement.

My Family

I am so grateful to my family. By necessity, writing is a solitary task and there have been more than a few missed dinners and vacations not taken in the past two years. I love you all very much and appreciate your patience and encouragement. This is for you.

DEDICATION

For Renda, Peter, and Julia

Please note that the Internet resources are of a time-sensitive nature and
URL addresses may often change or be deleted.

CHAPTER 1

Overview of Computers in the Law Office

CHAPTER OBJECTIVES

After completing this chapter, you should be able to do the following:

1. Identify how computers are being used in legal organizations.
2. Identify the various computer-system components.
3. Distinguish among the various forms of computer software.
4. Understand the concept of metadata.
5. Recognize the ethical issues raised by the use of computers in the law office.

Computers are an important part of our society. They are used in nearly every facet of our lives, including our jobs, to automate services and products; our health, to enhance medical treatment; our government, to maintain, organize, and analyze information; our education, to help children read and write; our financial institutions, to track and maintain our banking, credit, and investment-related information; our entertainment, including the Internet, movies, music, and the arts; and our transportation, to control the electronic systems in cars and public transportation systems such as subways.

Just as the use of computers in our society has grown, so has the use of computers in the practice of law. The application of computers in large, medium, and small law firms, corporate law departments, and government offices has increased dramatically over the past few decades. It is imperative for paralegals entering the job market to have an understanding of computers, because computers and computer skills (1) allow a paralegal to be more productive and efficient, (2) can give an attorney and paralegal a competitive advantage in court, (3) simplify complicated tasks, and (4) allow the user to stay competitive in the job market.

INTRODUCTION TO COMPUTERS AND THE LAW

Prior to the early 1980s, computers had little effect on the practice of law. A few extremely large firms used them for "back-office" functions such as accounting or billing, but other than that, computers were not used much in legal organizations. A legal professional's tools of the trade were pen, legal pad, law books, typewriter, and copy machine. After the introduction of personal computers in the mid-1980s, all of that began to change. Now computers are involved in nearly every facet of a legal professional's job. Virtually all legal professionals use a desktop, laptop, and/or handheld computer with DVD drives, Internet and email access, and a printer. It is now possible—indeed, often required—to stay in contact with colleagues no matter where they are.

A computer revolution has taken place in the legal industry. An industry that started out rejecting technology has now embraced it. Much of the rise in computer use in legal organizations is due to the increased power, decreased cost, and increased ease of use and efficiency of computers, all of which contribute to the competitive advantage that they give the user. Computers are being used for everything from word processing, timekeeping, and billing to legal research on the Internet to web-site management. This holds true for all types and sizes of law firms, whether a solo practitioner, a thousand-attorney global law firm, or a corporate or government legal department. In prior years, solo practitioners and small law offices lagged far behind larger law offices when it came to technology. This is generally no longer true. Technology is no longer a tool just for the large law firm. The cost of technology has decreased so much that even solo practitioners, small law offices, and legal aid offices can afford state-of-the-art computers.

Computers are used to organize documents, not just in large cases involving tens of thousands of documents, but in smaller cases as well. Computers are used to communicate with clients, often via email, and to exchange documents. Attorneys take depositions of witnesses by using videoconferencing. Laptop computers are used in the courtroom to search for documents, track exhibits, and make presentations to juries. Laptop or handheld computers are used in the courtroom to conduct legal research right at the counsel table. Later in this chapter, we will discuss some more recent and emerging technologies.

The Internet has had a profound impact on the practice of law and on how paralegals perform their jobs. The **Internet** is one of the world's largest computer networks; actually, it is a "network of networks." It connects hundreds of millions of computers around the world and allows them to share information. Legal organizations and paralegals in particular can send and receive electronic messages, research both legal and nonlegal information, send documents, and do much more. The pervasive use of the Internet is clearly driving some of the need for paralegals to have good computer skills.

Internet
One of the world's largest computer networks; actually a "network of networks." It allows hundreds of millions of users around the world to share information.

Computers are also being used by courts in a variety of ways. Many courts allow parties to file documents electronically, using the Internet, and allow attorneys and paralegals online access to the courts' computer systems. Courts use computers to track currently pending cases. Such systems can automatically set scheduling deadlines for each case and alert judges to scheduling concerns or problems, particularly for criminal cases in which defendants have the right to a speedy trial. In some courts, court reporters can store information electronically, within seconds of it being presented, so that it can be displayed immediately for jurors, judges, and parties to view the information.

In short, all types of legal organizations and legal professionals, including paralegals, are using computers on a daily basis in a variety of ways. Given this overwhelming move toward technology use and computerization, all types of legal organizations are looking for legal professionals who not only have good legal skills, but also have the skills to use the organization's computer systems with little additional training.

ELEMENTARY COMPUTER CONCEPTS

This text is not concerned with imparting technical and scientific information on how a computer operates; rather, its focus is on how paralegals can use computers in a practical way to carry out their duties. Nevertheless, it is necessary to cover some basic computer concepts as background for users. The following sections introduce most of the terms and concepts that a paralegal will encounter on the job.

SYSTEM COMPONENTS

A **computer** is an electronic device that accepts, processes, outputs, and stores information. Information that is entered into a computer is called **input**. Information that comes out of a computer is called **output**. **Hardware** is the actual physical components of a computer system. **Software** refers to instructions that make the computer hardware function. A computer system works together with peripheral devices, such as auxiliary storage and input, output, and communication devices (hardware), to accomplish the information-handling tasks. The system contains a central processing unit and a main memory.

Central Processing Unit

The **central processing unit (CPU)** organizes and processes information. It is the "brain" of the computer. It performs logical operations—in accordance with the operating system software—and coordinates and communicates with auxiliary storage devices and input, output, and communication devices (see Exhibit 1–1).

At the heart of the CPU is the **processor chip** (see Exhibit 1–1). One or more processor chips perform the actual arithmetic computations and logic functions. The speed of the processor, and thus of the computer, is determined by how many bits or bytes of information the chip can process at a time and how fast it acts to process the information. The more bits that can be processed in one cycle, the faster the computer will be. For example, a processor that processes 64 bits at a time is considerably faster than one that processes only 16 bits. How fast a computer works to process information is also characterized in **gigahertz (GHz)**, which refers to the "clock speed" of a computer. The faster the clock speed is, the faster the computer processes information.

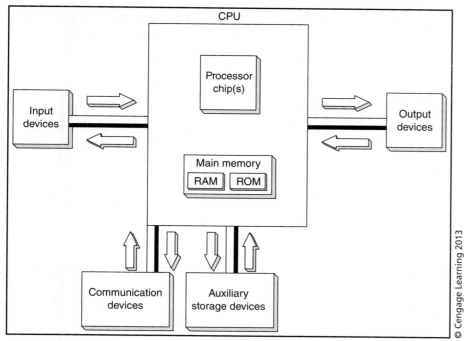

© Cengage Learning 2013

EXHIBIT 1–1
Central processing unit (CPU)

---

computer
An electronic device that accepts input data, processes data, outputs data, and stores data electronically; types include desktop, laptop, handheld, tablet, and file server.

input
Data or information that is entered or transferred into a computer (including by keyboard, mouse, scanner, voice, etc.).

output
Information or computer results that are produced or transmitted from a computer to a user as a result of the computer's operations (including to monitor, printer, etc.).

hardware
The physical equipment of a computer system, as opposed to programs or software.

software
Computer programs that instruct the computer hardware how to function and perform tasks.

central processing unit (CPU)
The part of a computer that contains the processor chip and main memory. The CPU organizes and manipulates information, in addition to coordinating with peripheral devices.

processor chip
The part of the computer that performs the actual arithmetic computations and logic functions.

gigahertz (GHz)
Measure of the clock speed of a computer.

Main Memory

The function of the **main memory** is to hold or store information that the computer is processing. This is accomplished through memory chips. **Memory chips**, like processor chips, are made up of tiny electronic circuits, but instead of processing information, they store or hold information. Main memory comes in one of two types: read-only and random-access.

Read-Only Memory

Read-only memory (ROM) is permanent, unchanging memory that a computer uses internally to operate itself. It is permanently installed by the manufacturer and cannot be changed or altered; hence the name "read-only." A computer reads ROM, but you cannot enter information into ROM or change the data in it. The data contained in ROM are not lost when the computer is turned off. Practically speaking, you never even become aware that ROM exists.

Random-Access Memory

Random-access memory (RAM) is temporary memory that is used when the computer is turned on. Unlike ROM, it is erased when the computer is turned off. RAM is used to temporarily store programs "on the computer screen" when the programs are loaded. For example, when a person is using a word-processing program, that program is in RAM. As words are typed into the word processor, the words are also stored in RAM. To save the information when the computer is turned off, the user must save the information from RAM to an auxiliary storage device such as a hard disk. An auxiliary storage device stores data so it can be retrieved later. One of the most frustrating experiences in computer use occurs when one is working with information in RAM and power is interrupted, such as when the lights flicker from an interruption in power transmission. When power to the computer is lost, even if just for a fraction of a second, the computer turns off and any information in RAM is lost. (This quickly teaches users the value of frequent saves, which transfer information from RAM to more permanent **storage**.)

The number of bytes of information a computer can hold is measured in kilobytes (K), megabytes (MB), gigabytes (GB), terabytes (TB), or petabytes (PB) (see Exhibit 1–2).

PERIPHERAL DEVICES

Peripheral devices are pieces of equipment that are connected to a computer to perform specific functions. They include auxiliary storage devices, input devices, output devices, and communication devices.

Kilobyte (K)	=	One thousand bytes	(1,000)
Megabyte (MB)	=	One million bytes	(1,000,000)
Gigabyte (GB)	=	One billion bytes	(1,000,000,000)
Terabyte (TB)	=	One trillion bytes	(1,000,000,000,000)
Petabyte (PB)	=	One quadrillion bytes	(1,000,000,000,000,000)

EXHIBIT 1–2
Storage capacities

© Cengage Learning 2013

---

main memory
The part of the CPU that stores information that the computer is processing. Main memory consists of read-only memory and random-access memory.

memory chips
Parts of a computer that store or hold information.

read-only memory (ROM)
A part of main memory that contains permanent information a computer uses to operate itself. ROM can be read, but cannot be written to.

random-access memory (RAM)
A part of main memory that is temporary and volatile in nature; it is erased every time the computer's power is turned off. Application programs and data are loaded into RAM when the computer is processing the data.

storage
Retention of electronic information for future use (using storage devices such as hard disks, CD-ROMs, DVDs, flash drives, and other media).

peripheral devices
Pieces of equipment that are connected to a computer to perform specific functions, such as storing information (auxiliary storage devices), inputting information (input devices), outputting information (output devices), and communicating with other computers (communication devices).

Auxiliary Storage Devices

An **auxiliary storage device** is used to permanently store information. Auxiliary storage devices and RAM are sometimes confused with one another, because they both use megabytes and gigabytes to refer to their respective **storage capacities**, and they both store information, albeit for different purposes. RAM is where information is stored temporarily, while the user is working with it, and is erased every time the computer is turned off. In contrast, an auxiliary storage device stores information permanently.

Hard Disk For permanent storage, most personal computers contain a rigid magnetic disk or **hard disk drive**. Hard disks are very reliable and have fast **access times**. They can also read and write data. It is possible, however, for them to crash if they are handled roughly (e.g., if the computer is dropped) or if they are defective or old. When a crash occurs, some or all of the information on the hard disk is lost or destroyed. Crashing often causes physical damage to the surface of the disk, making data retrieval difficult even for experts. Sometimes, it seems that hard drives crash for no reason at all. This alone is a good reason to get in the habit of backing up your data on a regular basis.

At least one hard disk drive is usually mounted inside the computer; usually a small light turns on when information is either accessed from or saved to the drive. Most hard disks are permanently sealed and are fixed inside the drive; thus, they cannot be removed. Large-capacity hard disks are standard equipment on most computers produced today. Many people use external hard drives for backup purposes; these auxiliary devices are literally freestanding hard disk drive units.

Removable Drives A large amount of data can be stored using **removable drives**. Removable drives include zip drives and flash drives. Zip drives are about the size of an audio cassette and are relatively slow; they are a somewhat dated technology. Flash drives have largely replaced them. Flash drives, thumb drives (so called because they are about the size of a human thumb), or sticks are extremely small and portable, and are also fairly fast. A flash drive simply plugs into a computer's USB port and is immediately accessible by the computer once it has been loaded. Flash drives are typically used to move large files from one system to another. Many MP3 players also use this technology.

Magnetic Tape In a **magnetic tape system**, data are written to and stored on a spool of magnetic tape. The magnetic tape can be stored either on large tape reels or in tape cartridges.

Magnetic tape systems store data sequentially. (This is similar to a VHS tape: if you want to access a particular section of the tape, you typically have to fast-forward or rewind the tape to the desired section.) For this reason, access times are quite slow. This is why magnetic tape is usually used only for making backup copies of information residing on other storage devices. However, although their access times are slow, they have large capacities, up to a terabyte or more.

Optical Storage Devices Using laser beams, **optical storage devices** can record data on and retrieve data from small plastic disks, such as CDs and DVDs. Optical storage devices can store hundreds of megabytes of data on a single disk. This has allowed manufacturers to store everything from music and video/multimedia presentations to large software programs on a single disk. The space saving made possible by these technologies has been immensely beneficial to law offices, which often must keep large numbers of records for long periods of time.

auxiliary storage device
A device that stores information so that it can be retrieved for later use. Auxiliary storage devices retain data after power to the computer has been turned off. Auxiliary storage devices include flash drives, hard disk drives, and others.

storage capacity
The maximum amount of data that can be stored on a device.

hard disk drive
A reliable and fast auxiliary storage device that stores data on a rigid magnetic disk; may be built into the computer (internal) or a freestanding peripheral device (external).

access time
The amount of time it takes to transfer data between a storage device and RAM.

removable drive
A small portable device that stores a large amount of data; often used to transfer information between computers.

magnetic tape system
Storage device that records data on magnetic tape.

optical storage devices
Devices that use laser beams to write data onto small plastic disks. Optical storage devices can record hundreds of megabytes of data on a single disk.

Input Devices

Input devices are used to enter information into a computer. Input devices include the mouse, keyboards, scanners (including bar code and imaging scanners), voice recognition devices, digital cameras, and others.

Computer Keyboard   Most computer keyboards are similar to the keyboard of an ordinary typewriter, with a few additions. They are made up of alphanumeric keys, function keys, cursor movement keys, special keys, and a numeric keypad. Keyboards are inexpensive and come in a variety of types and styles.

Scanners   A scanner has the ability to bring hard-copy documents into a computer. Many scanners look like small office copiers. Scanners shine light on the document and translate the reflected light into digital signals that a computer can recognize and store. The scanner allows the image of a document, such as a photograph or a microfilm frame, to be put into a computer; this is called imaging.

More specifically, **imaging** refers to the ability to scan a document into a computer so the user can see the exact image of the original document on the computer. Imaging is similar to taking a photograph of a document: you can see the image of the document, but you cannot change it or edit the text. To edit the text of a document, you would need optical character recognition software (see below).

With document imaging, the paper is handled only once, when it is scanned into the computer. Document images can be reviewed, copied, sorted, and filed electronically. Document imaging gives users immediate access to documents, saves storage space, and keeps originals from being lost or damaged. Imaging software allows law offices to track and manage scanned images. Imaging and OCR technologies are used quite frequently in litigation support to track and search for documents in litigation.

Scanners can also translate the text of a document into an electronic format so that the text can then be electronically searched or manipulated with a word processor. This is called **optical character recognition (OCR)**. Using a scanner and OCR software, users can "read" printed material into a computer so the text of the document can be searched (like searching in Westlaw or LexisNexis databases) or brought into a word processor for text editing. In OCR, the scanner reflects light onto the printed text, compares the shapes of the letters in the text to the letters in the scanner/computer memory, and writes the information into the computer. Through the use of OCR technology, it is possible to scan printed information into a computer much faster than a keyboard operator could enter the information. Large OCR scanners can scan thousands of pages of text into a computer in a relatively short time.

However, if the printed text that is being scanned does not exactly match the letters in the scanner's memory, an error will occur, and the right letter will not be entered. This potential for inaccuracy can be a problem. Even if a document is scanned in with 99 percent accuracy, that can still leave plenty of errors in the scanned version of the document. For example, if a user scans in a 10,000-word document, that would leave 100 errors in the document. The accuracy rating drops dramatically if a document is not clear or has nonstandard type. OCR scanners can be very useful, but accuracy must be checked carefully.

Imaging and optical character recognition are similar yet different. Imaging allows the user to see the document in its original state, but the user cannot search for words using imaging. Optical character recognition allows the user to search for words and word patterns, but not to see the exact image of the original document, only the text it contained.

Some law firms use **bar code scanner** systems to track documents in litigation. This is the same technology used in nearly all retail stores. Once a bar code is applied to a document, the bar code scanner or reader can read the special lines on the bar codes and recognize which document it identifies.

Many multifunction devices are currently on the market that combine OCR scanning, imaging, faxing, copying, and printing. The prices of all of these technologies have decreased significantly in recent years, making these useful devices extremely popular.

Mouse The cursor on a monitor is moved with a **mouse**. This input device is approximately the same size as the palm of your hand. As the mouse is moved, it transmits to the computer a signal that correspondingly moves the cursor in the same direction. For example, if the mouse is moved to the right, the cursor moves to the right, and so on. There are a variety of other devices that perform functions similar to those of a mouse. These include trackballs, trackpoints, and touch pads.

Speech Recognition The ability of a computer to understand spoken words is called **speech recognition**. The user speaks into a microphone that is connected to the computer. Using sophisticated software, the computer is able to interpret the speech and translate it into computer commands and into text for use with word processors, email, and other software. Typically, speech recognition software leads the user through exercises that are designed to teach the software the nuances of that particular person's voice.

Voice input systems have a number of advantages. Most people can speak faster and more naturally than they can write or type, and they need little or no training to use such a system. It also frees the hands to perform other tasks. Speech recognition systems are very popular in offices where they augment or take the place of some secretarial functions such as transcribing dictation. Some users also prefer to use speech recognition instead of typing, as it increases their productivity.

Although speech recognition accuracy is quite good—typically greater than 95 percent—it is still absolutely necessary to proofread the text created by the software. For this reason, among others, many legal organizations do not make much use of speech recognition technology.

Digital Cameras and Camcorders Digital cameras and camcorders allow the user to take photographs or full-motion video and sound and download or transfer them directly into a computer. The software accompanying these devices also allows the user to easily edit, enhance, and view the information. Many legal organizations are using these devices to cut and paste data directly into presentation graphics programs for displaying evidence to juries. Many legal organizations are rediscovering the old adage that "a picture is worth a thousand words." Video evidence can be extremely persuasive to juries and factfinders.

Output Devices

Output devices provide a user with the data that a computer has generated or stored. Like input devices, they come in many different types. The type you select depends on the application you are using.

Computer output is displayed on a **monitor**. It is important to recognize that the quality of the picture on the monitor is in part determined by the **video adapter card**, which acts as an interface between the monitor and the computer. The number of colors that a color monitor can display also depends on the video adapter card. Because of the graphical nature of the Internet and the rise in multimedia and video, manufacturers now produce graphics accelerators, video card memory, and other hardware to make graphics appear on the monitor faster.

---

bar code scanner
Device that reads the special lines of bar codes. Can be used to track documents in litigation, or physical objects such as office furniture and equipment.

mouse
An input device used to move the cursor on the monitor. The cursor moves in the same direction as the mouse is moved.

speech recognition
The ability of a computer to understand spoken words.

output device
Peripheral device that provides a user with the data a computer has generated, accessed, or manipulated.

monitor
Screen that displays computer output.

video adapter card
Piece of hardware that acts as an interface between the monitor and the computer.

Much data is still output on paper (sometimes called hard copy) with a printer. Nearly all computers now come with a sound card and speakers. A **sound card** enhances the sounds that come out of the computer and/or enables speakers attached to a computer to function.

A portable projector allows a user to display the image from a computer to an audience. Portable projectors are often used in trials in conjunction with laptop computers to display presentations and computer-generated evidence to juries.

Communication Devices

A communication device, such as a modem, allows computers to exchange information. Such a device is technically both an input and an output device, as it can receive data from other computers (input) and also send data to other computers (output).

A **modem** allows computers in different locations to communicate using a telephone line. Although a modem acting through a dial-up connection allows users to exchange information with each other over long distances, this type of connection is very slow compared to other types of technology. This is particularly true regarding most World Wide Web sites on the Internet, which are graphically based. Cable, T1, and DSL are alternatives to standard analog phone lines and modems, and are increasingly popular because of the much speedier communication they enable. These and other technologies are making standard modems obsolete. The main advantages that dial-up connections have over cable, T1, and DSL are their much lower cost and almost universal availability. However, these advantages seldom compensate for the extended time required for information transfer via dial-up.

A **cable modem** is a data modem that is designed to work over cable television lines (increasingly, these lines are fiber-optic). The primary advantage of cable modems over dial-up modems is their much faster data-transmission speed, made possible by cable's far greater bandwidth.

DSL (Digital Subscriber Line) is a type of digital phone line that is hundreds of times faster than a dial-up connection. This type of connection also allows data and voice to be transmitted on the same line.

Wireless Modem   Many mobile phones and handheld computers now use **wireless modems** to connect to the Internet. A wireless modem typically is either built into the device or slides into an open slot on a laptop or handheld computer; in either case, it allows the user to access email, the Internet, and other mobile devices without hardwired connections.

Videoconferencing   **Videoconferencing** is a private broadcast between two or more remote locations, with live image transmission, display, and sound. This technology uses data communications to conduct long-distance, face-to-face meetings. Because of the huge amounts of sound and image data transferred with this technology, it requires audiovisual equipment and special communication lines. Videoconferencing is very useful in a legal organization for meeting with clients, interviewing job candidates, meeting with co-counsel, taking depositions, and other applications.

Voice over Internet Protocol   **Voice over Internet Protocol (VoIP)** allows users to make telephone calls using a broadband Internet connection instead of a regular (analog) phone line. Most VoIP service providers allow the user to call anyone who has a telephone number, including local, long-distance, mobile, and international numbers. VoIP allows a user to make a call directly from a computer, a special VoIP phone, or a traditional telephone using an adapter. Cost savings over long-distance telephone charges can be substantial, because most VoIP providers charge a flat fee for unlimited call time. Some systems can support multiparty conference calls, and can integrate voice mail and faxes with email.

A major disadvantage is VoIP's dependence on electrical power: if the power goes out, so do the phones, unless there is a backup system. VoIP is also dependent on proper operation of both the broadband connection and the network; if they go down, so do the phones.

Communication Devices in Legal Organizations Most legal organizations have long since moved from slower, dial-up modems to faster communication technologies such as cable, DSL, and T1. This is primarily due to the overwhelming use of the Internet in law offices and the need for fast connections to email.

LOCAL AND WIDE AREA NETWORKS

Networks connect a multitude of computers and allow them to work together. Law offices may use local area and/or wide area networks.

Local Area Networks

Computers started as single-user systems. A **single-user system** can accommodate only one person at a time and is not linked to other systems or computers. A **local area network (LAN)** is a multiuser system that links computers that are in close proximity for the purpose of communication. Two primary reasons for installing a LAN are to share data and software among multiple computers and to share peripheral devices such as printers, optical storage devices, and communication devices (see Exhibit 1–3).

Consider how a LAN could be used in a law office. Suppose a law office has 20 staff members who need access to each other's word-processing files, docket control data, and time and billing information, and who also need to communicate via email with one another. Using stand-alone computers, the staff members would not be able to share information effectively. However, using a LAN, each staff member has access to all the information residing on any computer in the network. Another advantage is that different types of computers (e.g., IBM-compatible machines, Apple Macintosh machines, and others) can be linked together to share data in many LAN configurations.

Nearly all legal organizations now have a LAN, and most software that is purchased for legal organizations is a networked version of a single-user program. Primary network software used in a legal organization typically includes word processing, database management, spreadsheets, timekeeping and billing, accounting, calendar/docket control/case management, electronic mail, document management, litigation support, client files/records, and specialized legal-specific programs. With a network, attorneys and paralegals who are traveling can connect to the network and exchange messages, access files, and do other tasks.

There are different types of LANs, including client/server and peer-to-peer networks.

Client/Server Networks **Client/server networks** use a server or servers to enhance the functionality of the other computers on the network. Network servers are computers that meet the needs of the other computers on the network, which are called *workstations* or *clients* (see Exhibit 1–3). The server stores program files and data files, and hosts email and remote access platforms used by the workstations, among other possible applications. Some servers are dedicated, meaning that they

---

single-user system
A computer that can accommodate only one person at a time and is not linked to other systems or computers.

local area network (LAN)
A multiuser system linking computers that are in close proximity for the purpose of communication.

client/server network
A network that uses a server (or servers) to enhance the function and meet the needs of the other computers on the network.

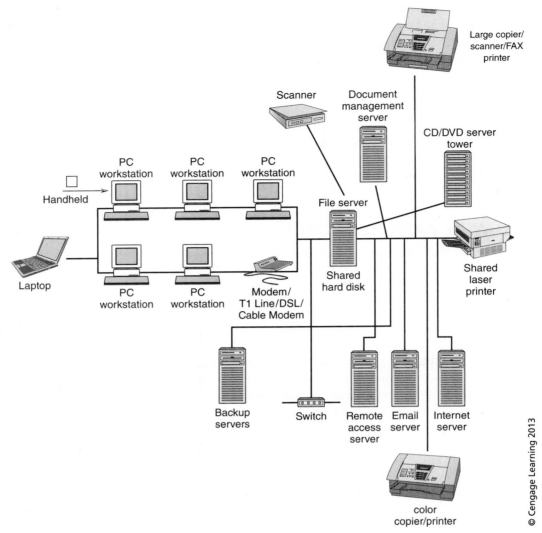

EXHIBIT 1–3

A local area network (LAN) allows users to share hardware and software.

cannot be used for any other purpose. Other servers, depending on how the LAN is configured, are nondedicated, meaning that they can also be used as workstations. Most LANs in legal organizations are the client/server type.

Servers are generally high-powered machines with large memories that can support or even perform some of the computing functions of many workstations. Servers can be devoted to specific network operating functions and can be connected together on the network. For example, a legal organization could have separate electronic mail servers, file servers, print servers, web servers, and remote access servers (for giving staff access to the office network from remote locations such as a staff member's house, hotel room, or a courtroom).

In years past, most networks were hardwired. Today, an alternative to hardwired networks that require cables is **wireless networking.** Wireless networks are extremely popular in law offices, because they nearly eliminate the necessity to install long cable runs throughout an office.

Peer-to-Peer Networks **Peer-to-peer networks** do not use a server; instead, each computer on the network acts both as a server and a client. Because the computers

wireless networking
System that allows computers on the network to communicate with each other using wireless antennas coordinated through a wired access point.

peer-to-peer network
A computer network in which each computer acts both as a server and a client.

are performing two tasks—running an application program, such as a word processor, and acting as a server—they are not as fast as the workstations on a client/server network. However, they still offer the ability to share printers, files, and other resources. Peer-to-peer networks are less expensive, because they do not require a separate server.

Web-Based Networks: Internet, Intranet, and Extranet

Many legal organizations have expanded their networks to include intranets and extranets. An **intranet** is an internal network designed to provide and disseminate information to internal staff; most such systems use a web browser and mimic the look and feel of the World Wide Web. In much the same way as the Internet provides information to the public, an intranet provides information to internal users. An intranet can be walled off from the Internet to provide security from Internet users. An intranet is part of a legal organization's networked computer system and in some cases the organization has a server dedicated to supporting the intranet. Information that a legal organization typically places on an intranet includes office policies and procedures, links to law-related websites, training materials, contact lists, and access to the firm's extranet. The use of intranets is growing substantially in legal organizations.

An **extranet** is a network designed to provide, disseminate, and share confidential information with clients. A client with a web browser can tap into the legal organization's extranet, after going through security and identification/password protections, to access his or her case plans, documents, case strategies, billing information, and other information. This is also extremely helpful when a law office must communicate with multiple clients or co-counsel on one case. Exhibit 1–4 notes the similarities and differences between intranets and extranets.

Wide Area Networks

Wide area networks take up where LANs stop. A **wide area network (WAN)** is a multiuser system linking computers that may be located thousands of miles apart. Large law firms that have offices located across the country or across the world can use WANs to allow their offices to communicate with each other as if they were next door. LANs and WANs can also be used together. A law firm's offices located in New York and Los Angeles may each have a LAN, but be connected to each other using a WAN. LANs and WANs allow law offices to share information in the same location, across town, or across the globe.

Networks in Legal Organizations

LANs, WANs, intranets, and extranets are now commonly found in legal organizations. As technology continues to expand, so will the use of all types of networks in the legal industry. Although it is not necessary for a paralegal to have detailed knowledge of the ins and outs of office networks, it is helpful to have a general overview of how they function, because of the importance of networks to the practice of law in the 21st century.

INTRODUCTION TO COMPUTER SOFTWARE

Computer hardware is useless without computer software to make it operate. Computer software (i.e., a computer program) is a set of step-by-step instructions that direct a computer how to function and perform tasks. Three basic types of software are available: operating system software, utility software, and application software.

The **operating system software (program)** instructs the computer hardware how to operate its internal circuitry and how to communicate with input, output,

intranet
An internal network designed to provide and disseminate information to internal staff; most mimic the look and feel of the World Wide Web.

extranet
A secure web-based site that allows clients to access information about their cases and collaborate with the legal professionals who are providing legal services to them.

wide area network (WAN)
A multiuser system linking computers that may be located thousands of miles apart.

operating system software (program)
A set of instructions that tell the computer how to operate its own circuitry and manage its components; also controls how the computer communicates with input, output, and auxiliary storage devices. Allows the user to manage the computer.

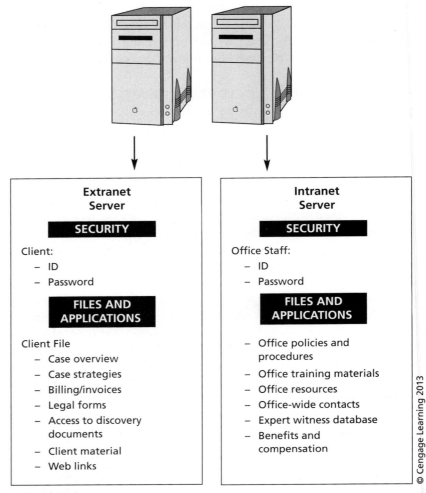

EXHIBIT 1–4
Extranet and intranet

and auxiliary storage devices; this program also allows the user to manage the computer. Operating system software ties the computer hardware and software together. Using operating system software, users can delete old or unwanted files, obtain a directory of the files on a disk, and manage the resources of a computer. Some type of operating system software comes free with nearly all computers.

Utility software helps users with the housekeeping and maintenance tasks that a computer requires. Thousands of utility programs are available. Utility programs can back up a hard disk, recover data that have been accidentally deleted, protect computers from viruses, and carry out many other tasks.

Application software instructs the computer to perform a specific function or task, such as word processing. Practically speaking, when people use the word *software*, they are usually referring to application software. A word-processing program, a spreadsheet program, and a database program are all examples of application software, because they each tell the computer how to perform a specific task or set of tasks.

Relax, You've Done This Before: Specific Law Office Uses of Computer Software

Take comfort in the fact that most paralegal students are already competent in and comfortable with performing basic computer functions. You may have used a software

---

utility software
Instructions that help users with the housekeeping and maintenance tasks a computer requires; helps manage either the hardware or software aspects of a computer.

application software
Instructions (programs) that tell the computer to perform a specific function or task, such as word processing.

program to "clean" your computer by removing unwanted files. That is an example of a utility program. It is likely that you have prepared documents (e.g., a term paper) using a word-processing program. That is an example of application software. It follows, then, that you probably already have many of the essential skills required to use a computer in a modern law office.

Software Licensing

Most software is purchased subject to a **license agreement**. The license agreement sets out the terms under which the person or group is allowed to use the software; it specifies the purchaser's rights to and restrictions on use of the software. Some license agreements are based on the number of computers that the software can be loaded on, whereas others are based on the number of people who can use the software. Use of software in a manner that violates the license agreement, such as loading software onto additional computers beyond the number of licenses that have been purchased, can constitute copyright infringement. The licensor may revoke a violator's license(s) and/or may bring a civil suit against the violator.

license agreement
Contract setting out the user's rights and restrictions on how a piece of software can be used.

Operating System Software

When the computer is turned on, or "booted up," the operating system is loaded into RAM. The operating system is necessary to the basic functioning of a computer; the computer cannot even turn itself on properly without such a system.

Operating systems are usually unique to each type of computer. For example, an Apple Macintosh computer uses a different operating system than do IBM-compatible computers. The manufacturer of a computer usually supplies the operating system, though this is not always the case. Some computer manufacturers now offer a choice of the operating system to be used.

Duties of the Operating System   The operating system is a cross between a traffic officer who directs the flow of data between the computer and different input, output, and auxiliary storage devices and a housekeeper who organizes and maintains the system. Operating systems manage main memory; control input, output, and auxiliary storage devices (including addition of new devices and deletion of old ones); manage the CPU; give the user tools with which to perform maintenance on the computer; and manage the computer's files. From a user's viewpoint, file management is one of the most important things the operating system software does. File management includes copying files, deleting files, and renaming files, as well as maintaining and accessing stored files.

The Windows Operating System   **Windows** is a graphical operating system developed by Microsoft for IBM-compatible computers. Every few years Microsoft updates Windows to add more features.

All versions of Windows use a graphical user interface (GUI). The graphical interface allows users to enter commands and work with programs using a mouse, pull-down menus, and icons (pictures that appear on the screen to represent applications or documents) instead of requiring users to learn a complicated and exacting command structure. Windows is also a multitasking environment that allows users to run several programs at the same time.

Tens of thousands of programs are currently available for the Windows operating system. It is the predominant operating system for IBM-compatible computers, and it commands most of the computer software market share in the United States. Windows applications have similar menus and appearances, and

Windows
A graphical operating system developed by Microsoft for IBM-compatible computers. Various versions of Windows include Windows XP, Windows Vista, and Windows 7.

can share information quite easily. This similarity among programs allows users to learn programs more quickly than if they had to learn a new command structure for each program. More than 95 percent of all legal organizations use some version of the Windows operating system. Microsoft Windows, in its various versions, dominates the legal market for computer operating systems.

Network Operating Systems   Local area networks require special **network operating systems** to handle communications among the computers on a network. Regular operating systems such as Windows XP and Windows 7 may work with file server networks. However, more complex client/server networks require network operating systems such as Windows NT or Novell Netware.

Utility Software

Utility software helps manage either the hardware or the software aspects of a computer. Some utility programs come as part of the operating system; others are separate programs. There is a huge amount of utility software, including utilities that compress files, back up files, and protect a computer from viruses or other "malware."

Compression Utilities   **Compression utilities**, such as WinZip, reconfigure (compress) a file so that it takes up less room when it is saved or transmitted. This is particularly important when one is sending or receiving extremely large files (files containing graphics or video are often huge, and can take a long time to download or upload). Many large files that are downloaded from the Internet are routinely compressed.

Backup Utilities   **Backup utility** programs create a copy of a user's hard disk or other storage device. The backup copy can be restored if the hard disk is damaged or lost. Some backup utilities allow users to schedule specific times to back up their files (for example, every Wednesday and Friday, or every morning at 2:00 a.m.).

Antivirus and Antispyware Utilities   **Antivirus and antispyware utilities** attempt to prevent viruses and spyware programs from getting into a computer system, and also locate and remove any viruses that do manage to get into the computer. Because new viruses and spyware appear almost daily, many antivirus software manufactures allow users to update their software from the Internet. Exhibit 1–5 lists some important things that users can do to prevent or lessen the chance of getting a computer virus or spyware. Once a virus or spyware gets onto a user's computer system, it can be extremely difficult to completely remove it (depending on the program). The best solution is to prevent it from attaching to or "infecting" the computer in the first place.

Application Software

Thousands of different kinds of application software (applications or apps) have been developed. This text focuses on the application programs that are widely used in legal organizations, including word processing, PDF creation and document assembly (Chapter 2), spreadsheets (Chapter 3), timekeeping and billing (Chapter 4), databases, case management and docket control (Chapter 5), and presentation graphics/trial software (Chapter 6). Following is a brief description of several other types of application software used in legal organizations.

---

network operating system
System that handles communication tasks between the computers on a network.

compression utility
Program that reorganizes a file so that the file takes up less room when it is saved. Many large files that are downloaded from the Internet are routinely compressed to reduce the time needed for the download.

backup utility
Program that creates a copy of a user's hard disk or other storage device. The backup copy can be restored if the hard disk is damaged or lost.

antivirus and antispyware utilities
Programs that attempt to prevent virus and spyware programs from getting into the computer system; most also function to locate and remove any viruses or spyware that do manage to get into the computer.

- Make backup copies of data on a regular schedule.
- Do not borrow DVDs or CD-ROMs from others; buy and use your own.
- Use passwords on your computer system.
- Turn your computer off when you are not using it.
- Do not let other people install programs on your computer or use your computer without expressly telling you how they will use it.
- Avoid downloading games, shareware, and other information from the Internet or other sources if you are not certain that the site is reputable and virus-free.
- Do not loan or pass your software programs on to others.
- Install antivirus and antispyware programs and run them frequently.
- Update your antivirus and antispyware programs regularly.
- Do not open files that are attached to emails unless you know the sender of the email and that the attached file is safe. An email scanner, which may be part of your antivirus/antispyware program package, is an excellent first line of defense.
- Read license agreements and installation instructions carefully to avoid installing spyware.
- Try to restrict your Internet surfing to known, reputable sites.

© Cengage Learning 2013

EXHIBIT 1–5
How to protect your electronic data from a computer virus

Project Management
Project management software uses the computer to track the sequence and timing of the separate activities of a larger project or task. Complex projects or jobs consist of many smaller activities that must be completed before the overall project is finished. Some activities must be performed in a certain sequence, whereas others must be completed concurrently. Project management software tracks all of this information. For example, a paralegal might use a project manager to track all the tasks that must be completed before a case is ready for trial.

> **project management software**
> Application program that allows the user to track the sequence and timing of the separate activities of a larger project or task.

Accounting
Accounting software uses a computer to track and maintain the financial data and records of a business. Accounting information is crucial to any business or organization. It is required for income tax purposes, to obtain loans, to help in the operation and control of an organization, and more. Computerized accounting programs are often less time-consuming to use, introduce fewer errors, and usually produce final reports better and faster than manual methods. Accounting software used by a legal organization might include a general ledger, accounts payable, accounts receivable, payroll, and trust accounting.

Document Management
Document management software organizes, controls, distributes, and allows for extensive searching of electronic documents, typically in a networked environment. Document management software allows a legal organization to file documents electronically so that they can be found by anyone in the organization, even when there are hundreds of users spread across offices located throughout the country. Document management software goes far beyond the file management capabilities built into operating system software. It is the electronic equivalent of a file room with rows and rows of filing cabinets. As the legal community moves to the "paperless office," each legal organization will most likely have to use a document management program to manage electronic files. Document

> **document management software**
> Program that organizes, controls, distributes, and allows for extensive searching of electronic documents, typically in a networked environment.

management software also provides extensive searching capabilities and allows users to add a profile of every document, which can be easily searched on later.

Application Service Providers and Internet-Based Programs

application service provider (ASP)
A company that provides software or a service application through the Internet directly to the user's computer.

An **application service provider (ASP)** is a company that supplies software or a service application through the Internet directly to the user's computer. The software is not retained on the user's computer, but instead resides on the software company's computer/server at a remote location and is "rented" to the user as needed. This is sometimes referred to as *hosted software*. The advantages of ASPs are that the user does not have to purchase the software, install the software, upgrade the software, or maintain the software in any way. The user still has access to the software 24 hours a day, 7 days a week, globally, wherever there is an Internet connection.

Two of the best known ASPs in the legal industry are Westlaw and LexisNexis. Other common law-office ASP applications include timekeeping and billing, document management, and litigation support.

HOW COMPUTERS CAN HELP THE PARALEGAL

A paralegal's job is information intensive. A paralegal using a computer can both gather and organize data many times faster than one using manual methods.

The Internet

The availability of the Internet has had a profound impact on how legal professionals practice law and how paralegals do their jobs. The Internet is used in countless ways by paralegals: sending and receiving electronic mail (email); sending instant messages; conducting factual and legal research; accessing listservs, blogs, and newsgroups to gather information and communicate with groups of people; maintaining a legal organization's website; purchasing legal-related services; and gaining continuing education.

Electronic Mail Paralegals use email to exchange information and documents via the Internet with clients, attorneys, other paralegals, courts, co-counsel, vendors, and many others in a manner that is quick, convenient, and cost-effective. Many courts now accept electronic filing of documents in lieu of hard copy, so email is used to submit documents to many court clerks.

Instant Messaging Instant messaging allows users who are connected to the Internet to communicate immediately with one another. Using instant messaging, paralegals or attorneys in court can communicate in real time with colleagues at their office for assistance, legal research, or other needs that may affect the outcome of a case or a hearing.

General and Factual Research Paralegals use the Internet for a wide variety of research, including:

- Conducting background information research on parties to cases
- Locating expert witnesses throughout the world
- Finding newspaper, online, and technical articles related to cases
- Locating the current whereabouts of people for service of process
- Researching information about witnesses
- Discovering financial information about corporations, including accessing Securities and Exchange Commission filings
- Finding public records about people or businesses
- Finding co-counsel in another jurisdiction

Legal Research   Many paralegals perform legal research. In the past, the only option for legal research was the law library with its law books, periodicals, statutes, indexes, and digests. Nowadays, legal research can be conducted for free using the Internet. Sites such as www.findlaw.com and hundreds of others provide access to federal and state cases and statutes, provide a portal to other legal research sites on the Internet, and generally offer a wealth of free legal-related information. Fee-based computer-assisted legal research sites, including Westlaw and LexisNexis, allow users to electronically search the full text of cases, statutes, and documents.

Listservs and Electronic Mailing Lists   Listservs are like electronic mailing lists. They send email messages to people whose names are on a list. They are a simple way for groups of people to communicate with one another through email. There are thousands of listservs on the Internet. Paralegals use these to communicate with other paralegals, to communicate with other legal professionals who practice in their legal specialty, and to communicate with others who have similar interests in other areas. Examples include:

> *Law Tech*—for legal professionals who want to discuss legal technology issues (see www.abanet.org)
>
> *Legal Assistant Today*—specifically for paralegals who want to share information about paralegal issues, ideas, and experiences or who have questions about practice issues (see www.legalassistanttoday.com)

To find more listservs about the practice of law or the paralegal profession, you can use an Internet browser and a general search engine to search for "legal assistant listservs," "paralegal listservs," or whatever specific topic you are interested in.

Blogs   A blog (originally short for "weblog") is a website with information contained in posts that are arranged in reverse chronological order. Blogs resemble diary or journal entries, and they may contain links to other websites or articles. There are many law-related blogs (sometimes referred to as "blawgs") on the Internet, including blogs on specific areas of law, such as immigration or tax.

Litigation Support Software

Many paralegals are involved in litigation support tasks. This means that they help attorneys organize, store, retrieve, and summarize the information that is gathered for the conduct of a lawsuit. During the course of any lawsuit, numerous documents and pieces of information are gathered, and must be organized for use at the time of trial or in support of settlement negotiations. For example, suppose your case has 10,000 documents associated with it, and you are requested to find all the documents that refer to a person named John Doe. Manual methods, such as looking through all 10,000 documents, could take weeks. Computerized litigation support software automates this process so that you can do such a search in seconds. In addition, using the Internet or an extranet, your firm can make litigation support databases available to staff, clients, or co-counsel, so that they can access the information from remote locations such as other offices, a courthouse, or a client's office. Litigation support software is crucial in large cases, but even small cases can benefit from this technology.

Collecting and Organizing Data: Database Management Software

Paralegals are often required to collect and organize data. For example, a paralegal might be asked to prepare a list of the names of witnesses and their probable testimony in a case; generate a list of all the documents in a case; prepare a chronological listing of major events in a case; or put together a current list of all the cases being handled by the firm, including name of client, adverse party, case number, court, and name of the presiding judge.

A *database management system* is a computer program that stores, searches, sorts, and organizes data. Database management systems allow users to manipulate information in many different formats. For example, a paralegal can easily create a current case list database that shows all active cases for the firm in alphabetical order. Once the data are entered, users can produce many different types of reports in many different formats without having to reenter the data. In our example, the paralegal could then use the same current-case database to produce a list of all the firm's cases in a specific court or before a particular judge or to produce a numerical listing by case number of all the firm's cases. Databases are covered in detail in Chapter 5.

Performing Mathematical Calculations: Spreadsheet Software

Paralegals may be required to perform mathematical calculations as part of their jobs. The calculations might be relatively simple, such as adding up the amount of damages a party has asked for in a case or preparing a case budget for a client; or more complicated, such as calculating principal and interest payments in a real estate transaction, analyzing statistics for trends, or calculating lost wages in a workers' compensation case.

A spreadsheet program calculates and manipulates numbers. Spreadsheet programs allow numerical data to be added, subtracted, multiplied, and divided automatically. They also allow users to edit, copy, and move numerical data; perform complex calculations quickly and accurately; graph numerical data automatically; save and retrieve information; and recalculate totals if any numbers in the spreadsheet change. Spreadsheet programs are easy to use and can greatly expedite work with numerical data.

Performing Timekeeping and Billing Functions: Timekeeping and Billing Software

In some law firms, paralegals record and track attorney and paralegal time and then send out bills to clients based on the amount of time spent on a case. Using a word processor for timekeeping and billing functions is tedious and time-consuming. Manual billing methods are so slow, in fact, that billings done manually tend to be generated infrequently, and in many cases bills are late getting to clients. Both of these consequences hurt the cash flow of a law office. In addition, bills prepared manually are more likely to contain errors, as numerous calculations must be performed for many bills.

When set up correctly, computerized legal timekeeping and billing programs are simple and easy to use. Information, such as the client's name, address, and billing rates, is entered into the system once. Then, as an attorney or paralegal spends time on a case, the time is entered into the system. If all entries are accurate, at the end of a billing period—one week, two weeks, one month, etc.—the computer automatically calculates and generates invoices, so they are produced and mailed on time with no calculation errors. This is covered in detail in Chapter 4.

Tracking Appointments and Deadlines: Computerized Docket Control and Case Management Software

Some paralegals must track appointments, deadlines, hearings, and other important dates to ensure that events get scheduled and then are not forgotten. This function is referred to as *docket control*, or sometimes as *case management*.

Although scheduling and tracking appointments and deadlines in a legal organization may seem at first glance like unimportant or merely clerical tasks, controlling an attorney's schedule and legal docket is, in fact, critical to his or her practice. Every year, thousands of ethical complaints are filed against attorneys. A primary reason clients file ethical complaints against their attorneys is the attorneys' failure to properly follow up on client matters. Many legal malpractice claims are also filed every year for the same reason. The importance of an effective docket control system in a legal organization should not be underestimated.

Although the terms *docket control* and *case management* are sometimes used interchangeably, there is a difference. Docket control software is fairly limited in nature, and primarily tracks appointments and deadlines in legal matters. Case management programs typically control the docketing of a case, but they usually also help the legal professional track and control the entire case, not just the scheduling aspects. Many case management programs include the ability to track a client's name, address, and telephone numbers; make notes about each phone conversation a legal professional has with the client; track appointments and deadlines by case; automatically schedule deadlines by type of case (typically where court rules mandate deadlines); perform conflict-of-interest searches when new cases are entered; produce letters and notices depending on the type of case; and more.

Presentation Graphics/Trial Software

High-quality, professional presentations can be created using presentation graphics software. Paralegals use presentation graphics programs to prepare charts, tables, video clips, evidence, and other information for juries and factfinders; to present information to clients; and to present information to colleagues, such as an in-house training program, a marketing plan for the law office, a proposed budget, or a new initiative. Each page of a presentation can contain many elements, including color, images of documents, text, charts, shapes, video, clip art, photos, and sound. Presentation graphics programs can produce the information on paper, overhead transparencies, 35-mm slides, or electronic on-screen presentations. This is covered in detail in Chapter 6.

LEGAL TECHNOLOGY TRENDS

Legal technology is continuing to move forward. Following are some general technology trends that are significantly changing how legal professionals will be performing their jobs in the future.

Mobile Computing, Instant Wireless Access, and Remote Access

Laptop, tablet, netbook, and handheld computers (also called personal digital assistants or PDAs), along with mobile phones and other wireless technologies, are changing the way legal professionals communicate. All of these technologies are being merged in small, extremely powerful, fully connected mobile machines. These machines, no matter what you call them, operate as mobile phones, allow the user to send and receive email, have instant-messaging features, act as pagers, access the Internet, act as PDAs (including calendaring, note-taking, and address book functions), send and receive faxes, allow the user to edit and send documents, and synchronize with a user's desktop system. Small laptops or netbooks can store millions of pages of documents electronically, fully access online legal databases such as Westlaw and LexisNexis on the go, and remotely access law-firm and service provider databases nearly globally. Mobile printers, mobile scanners, and wireless hotspots where users can connect to networks and the Internet allow legal professionals to access nearly all the same information and tools as if they were sitting at a desk in the office. This kind of mobile and immediate access to information will continue to change and drive the way legal professionals practice law.

Electronic Discovery

Electronic discovery is the process of producing litigation documents in an electronic format. The Federal Rules of Civil Procedure and many state court rules now require electronic discovery. This fact is forcing legal organizations to develop internal systems that can produce, store, search, and handle the production of electronic information in a variety of formats and across multiple computing platforms (desktops, servers, laptops, PDAs, etc.). Electronic discovery will continue to have a profound impact on the practice of law for many years to come, especially as more and more courts and legal professionals make effective use of it.

Electronic Filing

electronic filing
Supplying electronic versions of legal documents to a court, via the Internet or other electronic means, when the court does not require the hard copy of the document.

With **electronic filing**, courts accept (and may even require) electronic versions of legal documents to be submitted, via the Internet or other electronic means, instead of requiring a hard copy of the document. Although this might sound easy, in reality it can be quite complicated. Issues concerning standardization, control, security, and the establishment of hardware and software systems to support electronic filing have all had to be overcome. Nevertheless, many states, courts, federal agencies, and other regulatory bodies have successfully implemented electronic filing, and many others are currently entering the implementation stage.

The Paperless Office

paperless office
Firm in which all hard-copy documents are converted into electronic form(s) for storage, processing, and distribution.

Just as courts have been working to implement electronic filing and require electronic discovery, many law offices have begun to implement the **paperless office**. This refers to converting all information into an electronic form for storage, processing, distribution, and use. Typically, this is done by scanning all hard-copy documents that come into the office and saving all computer-generated documents electronically without a hard copy. Some advantages of the paperless office include: (1) significant reduction in paper usage and copying costs, (2) reduction of storage and lease space (the cost of office lease space now far exceeds the cost of electronic storage space), (3) increased portability, (4) increased collaboration (because digital information can be shared by multiple users via a network or the Internet), and (5) quicker search and retrieval of documents than with manual methods. As with electronic filing, there are implementation issues regarding the paperless office, including putting the hardware and software systems in place to support it, training staff, and other issues. Some law offices have fully implemented this concept and many others are taking steps toward this goal.

Cloud Computing

cloud computing
The ability to use one computer to access information stored on a different computer or server.

In recent years there has been much talk of "the cloud" and "cloud" computing. **Cloud computing** refers to the ability to use one computer to access information stored on a different computer or server. Although the term *cloud computing* may be relatively new, the concept is as old as the Internet. For example, Westlaw is a form of cloud computing. So is web-based email such as Google's Gmail.

Cloud computing has affected law offices in several ways. One is the use of hosted software applications. These are software applications that are not downloaded onto the user's computer; rather, users access the software via the Internet. This allows each user to store information on the host's computers, ensures that the user is always using the latest version of the software, and eliminates the need to download and install applications. Another use of the cloud is as a place to store documents and other data. This raises ethical issues: How secure are the data stored with a third party, and what is the law firm's liability for any breaches of confidentiality? There are more questions than answers as the law struggles to keep up with emerging technologies.

That said, there are several principles legal professionals should follow when working in the cloud environment:

1. Encryption—look for the lock icon to indicate use of Secure Sockets Layer (SSL), an industry-standard encryption technology used for Internet commerce
2. Server security—there must be evidence that a competent third party has audited the service provider's security
3. Client security—legal professionals need to be sure that their computers are properly secured (firewalls, current antivirus protection, etc.)
4. Password security—make sure all users have good passwords

Social Media

What is social media? Definitions may vary, but **social media** may generally be defined as online platforms that enable people to communicate easily to share information and resources, including text, audio, video, and images. Examples include blogs and well-known websites such as Facebook, Twitter, LinkedIn, Foursquare, and Wikipedia. Social media allows a community of users to create the content that is then viewed and commented on by other users. For legal professionals, social media is the new frontier. On the one hand, social media provides a vast source of original material (Facebook status updates, photographs, tweets, etc.). Nevertheless, this new frontier is not without its challenges, both practical and ethical.

Practical challenges include:

- The need to authenticate the material discovered on social media. It is necessary to prove that the comments made on a Facebook page were actually made by the person alleged to have made them.
- It may not be possible to get the material from the social media provider. Companies like Facebook and Twitter may be governed by the Stored Communications Act (18 U.S.C. § 2701), which prevents certain Internet companies from responding to formal discovery requests. Case law in this area is still evolving, but a leading case in this area as of this writing is *Crispin v. Christian Audigier*, 717 F. Supp. 2d 965 (C.D. Cal. 2010). In this case, the Court ruled that whether an Internet company is compelled to comply with a subpoena depends on the user's privacy settings. For example, if the Facebook user sets the privacy settings so that only invited "friends" have access to the user's page and "wall posts" (essentially an electronic bulletin board), that material is deemed private and is not subject to formal discovery. However, if the privacy settings allow the general public to view the material, the Internet company/host would have to comply with the discovery request. In any event, any material sent as a private message would not be subject to a formal discovery request sent to the Internet company/host. A better option may be to try to get the information directly from the user.

Ethical challenges include:

- Legal professionals have the duty to maintain the confidences and secrets of clients as well as information relating to the representation of a client. In several instances, an attorney has been sanctioned for a blog post that revealed information about a case or expressed the attorney's less-than-temperate opinions of a judge.
- Legal professionals also have the duty to act competently and diligently on behalf of a client. Recently, family law attorneys have been using social media sites such as Facebook as a source of incriminating information. Legal

social media
Online platforms that enable people to communicate easily to share information and resources, including text, audio, video, and images.

professionals who do not know how to use social media, or who fail to do so, are not acting ethically. Furthermore, diligent representation requires attorneys to help their clients avoid legal problems in the first place. Thus, it could be argued that law firms should work with clients to help them create and implement social media policies to teach their employees the dangers posed by careless use of social media.

The Automated Courtroom

Many courts have installed sophisticated electronic equipment in their courtrooms, including evidence display systems and real-time court reporting. An evidence display system is a computerized system that shows evidence, via monitors, to the judge, jurors, counsel, and the public simultaneously. It also displays this information to the court reporter and clerks.

The master controls are located at the judge's bench so that he or she can control all monitors, sound systems, and cameras in the courtroom. The attorneys and/or judge can use the evidence display system to display properly admitted evidence in the courtroom, whether by means of video images, animation, photographic images, hard copy, or other media.

Many evidence display systems also support videoconferencing. For example, with the judge's approval, an out-of-state witness can testify at a trial without actually being present in the courtroom. It may also be possible to receive real-time text of the transcript in addition to the audio and video feeds.

Another type of courtroom technology is real-time court reporting. A witness's testimony is transcribed by a court reporter within a few seconds and can be displayed on the courtroom monitors or given to the judge, jurors, or attorneys on a real-time basis. This gives parties instant written and electronic access to witness testimony and can eliminate the need to read back a witness's testimony when there is a question.

LEGAL ETHICS AND COMPUTER TECHNOLOGY

At first it may appear that legal ethics and computers have little to do with one another. In fact, the opposite is true. In addition to known, existing ethical issues (which do not disappear with computerization), many legal ethical issues arise specifically from the proliferation of computers and computer use in legal organizations. Many of these ethical concerns revolve around two key issues: competence or negligence of a legal professional and client confidentiality.

Attorney Competence

Attorneys have a duty to perform legal services in a competent manner. Computers, though incredibly helpful, can also be a vehicle for incompetence and legal malpractice. Computer-related legal malpractice and ethical breaches can take place in a variety of ways:

- Legal research performed with a computer may be inadequate and less than thorough.
- New documents are prepared using previously saved word-processing documents, but are inadequately proofread and contain old information (from the previous client).
- Typographical errors are made (especially when the person preparing the document relies on a spell checker rather than intelligent proofreading).
- Improper computerized forms or templates are used.

- A user generally fails to understand how a computer or a piece of software works, and thus fails to anticipate or discover an error.
- Automated legal or spreadsheet software is used with formula errors, logic errors, or lack of oversight or proofreading/review by the supervising attorney or other legal professionals.

Attorneys are responsible for their work product. It does not matter whether it was prepared by or with the assistance of a computer: If the end product has errors in it or is incompetently prepared, the attorney is still ultimately responsible for the work product. If the error or incompetent work product causes harm to the client, the attorney may be subject to attorney discipline charges and a legal malpractice claim.

Client Confidentiality

Attorneys have a duty to safeguard and keep confidential all client-related information, including information that is contained on computers. Every state has rules requiring attorneys to maintain the confidentiality of client information, no matter where that information resides.

This represents an enormous responsibility, given the technological advances in society generally and in legal organizations in particular. Although computers yield tremendous benefits to legal organizations in terms of efficiency, productivity, and delivery of high-quality legal services to clients, they also create substantial ethical and security issues. The threat of confidential client information being released either by mistake or by intrusion is very real, and can happen in a wide variety of ways, including:

- Interception of electronic mail by a third party (whether inadvertent or intentional)
- Interception of word-processing documents and other attachments to electronic mail by outsiders
- A breach of legal organization computer security, such as:
  - passwords not being appropriately maintained
  - computer hackers gaining access to confidential legal organization computers via the Internet or other online means
  - computer viruses deleting, accessing, or corrupting confidential client information
  - laptop and handheld computers holding confidential client information being stolen or inadvertently left for third parties to find
  - computer disks holding confidential client information being left or misplaced for third parties to find
  - computer hardware and storage devices not being sufficiently cleaned, so that client data are not destroyed before outdated equipment is disposed of

General Law Office Security

Law office computer systems in general are vulnerable to ordinary security threats, such as theft, sabotage, and natural disasters. It is important for all legal organizations to maintain adequate security measures, including having security and alarm systems to protect computer equipment from being stolen or damaged.

Passwords **Passwords** are codes entered into a computer system or software that act as a key and allow the user to access the system and the information it contains. Passwords are very important and are usually a good first line of defense against intrusion into a computer system, but they are not invulnerable.

password
Code entered into a computer system or software that acts as a key, allowing the user to access the system and the information it contains.

It is important to choose strong passwords. Hacker software programs on the Internet contain tens of thousands of common passwords that can be used to break into a computer system. Here are some rules for selecting and using strong passwords:

- Passwords should be a minimum of eight characters.
- They should be non-dictionary words.
- They should combine uppercase and lowercase characters.
- They should use at least one symbol (e.g., $ or :).
- They should use at least one number.
- They should be changed every 90 days.
- They should not contain or be based on personal information such as birthdates, names of family members, or other easily attainable pieces of information.

An example of a strong password would be something such as: RD10$Tk# or XP358LIN!.

Access Rights

Access Rights   All network operating systems for LANs and WANs and even some sophisticated application programs allow an administrator to limit the access rights of users. **Access rights** determine which computer directories, programs, or functions a user can get to and use, and are usually granted on a need-to-know basis. Users should be given only the access rights they absolutely need to have—never more than they need. For example, if John needed to use only general word-processing and litigation support files, his access rights could be limited to only those files and directories; he would thus not be able to access other directories and programs.

Limiting users' access rights limits the number of people who can access computer files, information, and programs, so the exposure of the legal organization is less than it would be if everyone were given access to everything. It is important that access rights be closely controlled and monitored regularly.

Backing Up

Backing Up   **Backing up** refers to making a copy of a computer file or program. Backups are absolutely necessary in the event the legal organization's file server or other storage device crashes; files are accidentally deleted; files become corrupted; the computer system becomes infected with a virus or other malware; or fire, theft, or a natural disaster occurs. If a legal organization has a good plan for regular, timely backup of its data, and a disaster does happen, the data can be restored with no loss of information.

Backing up data is easier than ever before. A number of hardware tools are available for performing backups, including high-capacity, highly reliable data backup units; secondary servers that back up data throughout the day or at the end of the day; and DVDs or CDs that duplicate information (typically used in smaller offices). Also, there are Internet-based companies that will back up a legal organization's data automatically at predetermined times.

Whatever method is chosen, it is important that the information be maintained securely offsite, that backup be done regularly, and that the backup be reliable and usable. Legal organizations should verify on a regular basis that their backups are actually working; a good way to do this is by restoring some of the saved data to make sure it is usable.

The Dangers of Metadata

The Dangers of Metadata   **Metadata** is electronically stored information that may identify the origin, date, author, usage, comments, or other information about an electronic file. Metadata is often described as "data about data." For example, in Microsoft Office files (such as Word or Excel files), you can see metadata that identifies the original author of a document, company name, subject, previous authors, date created, date last modified, editing time, and other information. You can see this for yourself by simply loading a file and clicking on File Properties. Metadata is usually not visible when a document is printed, but if one knows where to look it is often easy to find.

Other, more dangerous metadata includes things like the comments and tracked changes in a Word document. In several instances, Word files were produced and tracked changes or comments were enabled to show the various stages of revisions of the document, including who saw the document and when and exactly what changes were made to the document. This kind of metadata allows subsequent users to infer things about the thinking of original creators.

Subsequent chapters will detail the specific dangers posed by metadata for specific law office computer applications and how best to mitigate those dangers.

Electronic Mail

Electronic mail is an incredibly popular means of communication. Millions of Americans use email and collectively we send hundreds of millions of messages each day. Although it is extremely convenient, email can pose a large security risk due to a lack of privacy and security. The problem is that email sent over the Internet is not secure; it may pass through many other networks before it gets to the intended recipient. As it passes through the networks, others have the potential to see or read the message. Email can be encrypted to ensure that no one except the intended recipient can read the contents of the message while it is in transit. **Encryption** runs the message through an encoder that uses an encrypting key to alter the characters in the message. Unless a person has the correct encryption (decryption) key needed to decode it, the message appears unreadable.

There are many other security issues with email, including sending email to the wrong person, sending email to distribution lists (many email recipients) by mistake, and much more. These problems can become quite acute and complicated when the message contains confidential client information. Unless encryption or similar methods are used, it is safest not to send confidential client information via email, given the potential for abuse. These issues are discussed further later in this text.

Viruses   Email also presents a threat because computer viruses can be attached to emails. A **computer virus** is a computer program that is destructive in nature. When the attachment containing the virus is opened, the virus is brought or allowed into the receiver's computer system. Users should never open an attachment from an unknown source. Most legal organizations run antivirus programs that prevent or at least alert users to potential viruses. However, because hackers are constantly updating their technology, legal organizations must regularly update their antivirus programs at least weekly (preferably daily), using the Internet. Most software suppliers issue patches and updates to their programs to respond to new threats. In addition to updating virus definitions regularly, many software companies update their programs to include new security measures. Users should regularly update their operating systems and application programs and take advantage of the latest security measures they provide.

Spyware   **Spyware** is a general term used for software that tracks your movement on the Internet for advertising and marketing purposes, collects personal information about the user, or changes the configuration of the user's computer without the user's consent. Spyware commonly gets onto a user's computer when the user downloads or installs a program. Spyware may be included with the program software, although that information may be buried in the licensing agreement—or the user may not be warned about it at all. Whenever you install programs on your computer, it is

---

encryption
Process of running a message through an encoder that uses an encrypting key to alter the characters in the message. Unless the person wanting to read the message has the encryption key needed to decode it, the message appears unreadable.

computer virus
A destructive computer program that may be designed to delete data, corrupt files, or do other damage; may also be self-replicating, using an "infected" computer to transmit itself to other computers.

spyware
A general term for software that tracks a user's movement on the Internet for advertising and marketing purposes, collects personal information about the user, or changes the configuration of the user's computer without the user's consent.

important to carefully read the disclosures, the license agreement, and the privacy statement. A number of antispyware programs are available that can detect and remove installed spyware.

Computer Hackers and Firewalls   Nearly all legal organizations now provide access to the Internet for their staff. Many of these organizations use DSL, T1, cable modems, or other communication technologies that are "always connected" to the Internet. Computer hackers can use such connections to access the office computer system unless there is a firewall that cuts off this access. A **firewall** allows users from inside an organization to access the Internet but keeps outside users from entering a computer or the organization's LAN.

Mobile Computing and Wi-Fi Dangers   The security threats associated with mobile computers and wireless networks are substantial. Because laptop computers now rival the power and versatility of desktop computers, they can contain literally tens of thousands of client records. The potential for harm to a client cannot be exaggerated. One way to protect data on laptops and handheld computers is to install a power-on password. With a **power-on password**, the computer immediately prompts the user to enter a password after the machine has been turned on, but before the computer has completely booted the operating system software. If the user does not know the password, the system will not start and the computer will be unusable. Nearly all laptops and handhelds have this feature, but it must be activated. This type of system is very effective in the event a computer is stolen.

Encryption software can also be loaded onto a laptop. If the user loses the laptop or it is stolen, the data on the laptop remains safe because it cannot be accessed without the encryption key.

Wi-Fi computing allows users to access wireless LANs. A Wi-Fi–enabled device allows a user to connect to the Internet when in proximity to an access point (sometimes referred to as *hotspots*). The problem is that in crowded and public spaces, there are increased security risks, including easier anonymous hacking, inadvertent transmission diversion, and intentional hijacking of signals and access points. For example, using a Wi-Fi connection in a hotel may let the person in the next room hack into your computer through its own wireless connection. It would be better, in these circumstances, to use an ethernet or other hardwired system.

"Delete" Is Not Permanent   Many users mistakenly believe that when a file is "deleted," it is permanently deleted. This is usually not the case. Simply erasing or deleting does not permanently delete files even if you have emptied the recycle bin. In many instances, files can be retrieved by hackers and others from hard drives, flash drives, and CD-ROMs even after the files have been deleted. It is critical to physically destroy a storage device such as a flash drive or CD-ROM to ensure that the data on it cannot be retrieved. In addition, in Windows, deleted files are typically not deleted at all, but are sent to the recycle bin, so it is important to empty that utility from time to time.

Disaster Recovery Plans

A **disaster recovery plan** is a plan of action that can be followed in case a disaster (whether of natural or human origin) befalls the legal organization. For example, what would happen if a legal organization suffered a total loss to its computer systems from a fire, hurricane, flood, earthquake, tornado, bomb, power failure, theft, hard disk crash, or virus? Disaster recovery plans are prepared in advance of a disaster

---

firewall
Security measure that allows users from inside an organization to access the Internet but keeps outside users from entering the computer or LAN.

power-on password
Password that the computer immediately prompts the user to enter after the machine has been turned on, but before the computer has completely booted the operating system software. If the user does not know the password, the system will not start and the computer will be unusable.

disaster recovery plan
A prewritten plan of action to be followed if a disaster befalls the legal organization.

(typically multiple plans are prepared for different types of disasters) when there is plenty of time to think through alternative courses of action, anticipate problems, and design appropriate solutions.

Disaster recovery plans include a wide variety of information, such as who will be in charge, what services are the most vital, what steps will be taken first, what each department will require in terms of resources (computers, software, data, etc.), how to contact vendors, and how to contact employees. Many organizations make offsite data and backup storage an integral part of disaster recovery planning.

SUMMARY

A few years ago, it was important for a paralegal entering the job market to have computer skills. Now it is imperative. Computer use in law offices has grown substantially and will continue to grow in the future. Computers are currently used in the legal field for a wide variety of purposes.

A computer is an electronic device that accepts, processes, outputs, and stores information. Information that is entered into a computer is called input. Information that comes out of a computer is called output. Hardware is the actual, physical components of a computer system. Software refers to instructions to the computer hardware that make the computer function. Computers can be used to help paralegals perform many of their functions, including communicating with clients and other legal professionals using electronic mail; drafting documents using word-processing software; collecting and organizing data using database management software; performing mathematical calculations using spreadsheet software; performing timekeeping and billing functions using timekeeping and billing software; tracking appointments and deadlines using docket control and case management software; providing litigation support using litigation support software; preparing electronic discovery requests using electronic discovery software; conducting legal and factual research using the Internet and fee-based online services; and creating presentations with presentation graphics software.

Every computer has a system unit, which contains the CPU and main memory. The CPU, which is the "brain" of the computer, organizes and processes information in addition to coordinating functions of peripheral devices. The main memory is made up of ROM, which is permanent memory, and RAM, which is volatile memory.

Auxiliary storage devices, such as hard disks and optical storage devices, store information so that it can be retrieved later. Removable drives such as flash or "thumb" drives are small and portable, but can still hold up to several gigabytes of information.

Input devices enter information into a computer. Scanning and imaging both refer to importing a picture of a hard-copy document into a computer. Making an image of a document is similar to taking a photograph of the document. A related functionality is optical character recognition. When a user scans a document into a computer using OCR, the result is a file that contains the text of the document, which can be edited or manipulated with a word processor or other application.

Output devices provide the user with the data that the computer has generated or received. They include monitors, printers, portable projectors, and soundboards.

Communication devices allow computers to exchange information with other users via the Internet and other channels. Communication technology uses dial-up modems, cable modems, DSL and T1 lines, wireless modems, VoIP, and videoconferencing, among others.

A local area network is a multiuser system that links mainframes or computers that are in close proximity for the purpose of communication. LANs can be either client/server or peer-to-peer networks. A wide area network is a multiuser system that links computers that may be located thousands of miles apart.

Operating system software instructs the computer hardware how to operate its circuitry and how to communicate with input, output, and auxiliary storage devices. It allows the user to manage the computer. Microsoft Windows is the most common operating system in the legal environment.

Utility software helps to manage the hardware and software of a computer. Popular utility programs include antivirus and antispyware programs.

Legal organizations use many types of application programs, and the list grows longer every day. Document management software organizes, controls, distributes, and allows for extensive searching of electronic documents, typically in a networked environment. An application service provider is a company that provides software or a service application through the Internet directly to the user's computer.

Current and future technology trends that will affect the way legal professionals provide services to clients include mobile computing and instant wireless access, automated courtrooms, electronic filing of court documents, the paperless office, cloud computing, the use of social media, and heightened security and confidentiality concerns.

Many security and ethical issues surround the use of technology in legal organizations. The underlying principle is that legal professionals must safeguard and keep client information confidential. Current security concerns include passwords, access rights to files, data backup, release of client information, security surrounding electronic mail, viruses, spyware, firewalls, mobile computing problems with lost or stolen laptops or handhelds, disaster recovery, and metadata. Metadata is electronically stored information that may identify the origin, date, author, usage, comments, or other information about a file.

KEY TERMS

access rights
access time
antivirus and antispyware utilities
application service provider (ASP)
application software
auxiliary storage device
backing up
backup utility
bar code scanner
cable modem
central processing unit (CPU)
client/server network
cloud computing
compression utility
computer
computer virus
disaster recovery plan
document management software
DSL (Digital Subscriber Line)
electronic filing
encryption
extranet
firewall
gigahertz (GHz)
hard disk drive

hardware
imaging
input
input devices
Internet
intranet
license agreement
local area network (LAN)
magnetic tape system
main memory
memory chips
metadata
modem
monitor
mouse
network operating system
operating system software (program)
optical character recognition (OCR)
optical storage devices
output
output device
paperless office
password
peer-to-peer network

peripheral devices
power-on password
processor chip
project management software
random-access memory (RAM)
read-only memory (ROM)
removable drive
single-user system
social media
software
sound card
speech recognition
spyware
storage
storage capacity
utility software
video adapter card
videoconferencing
Voice over Internet Protocol (VoIP)
wide area network (WAN)
Windows
wireless modem
wireless networking

INTERNET SITES

Internet sites for this chapter include:

GENERAL LEGAL ASSISTANT/LEGAL SITES ON THE INTERNET

ORGANIZATION	PRODUCT/SERVICE	WORLD WIDE WEB ADDRESS
American Bar Association	Products/services for legal professionals	www.abanet.org
National Federation of Paralegal Associations	Products/information for paralegals	www.paralegals.org
National Association of Legal Assistants	Products/information for paralegals	www.nala.org
International Paralegal Management Association	Products/information for paralegals	www.paralegalmanagement.org
Legal Assistant Today magazine	Magazine for paralegals	www.legalassistanttoday.com
Technolawyer.com	Email newsletter on legal technology issues	www.technolawyer.com
American Bar Association, Legal Technology Resource Center	Legal technology issues	www.lawtechnology.org
Findlaw's Legal Technology Center	Legal technology issues	www.technology.findlaw.com

COMPUTER HARDWARE

ORGANIZATION	PRODUCT/SERVICE	WORLD WIDE WEB ADDRESS
AMD	Microprocessors	www.amd.com
Apple	Hardware/software for Apple computers	www.apple.com
Blackberry	PDAs and smartphones	www.rim.net
Cisco	Network operating system peripherals	www.cisco.com
Dell Computers	Computer hardware/software	www.dell.com
Hewlett-Packard	Computer hardware/peripherals	www.hp.com
Iomega Corp.	Removable drives/storage devices	www.iomega.com
Intel	Microprocessors	www.intel.com
Lenovo	Computer hardware	www.lenovo.com
NEC	Computer hardware/software	www.nec.com
Toshiba	Computer hardware/peripherals	www.toshiba.com

COMPUTER SOFTWARE

ORGANIZATION	PRODUCT/SERVICE	WORLD WIDE WEB ADDRESS
Business Software Alliance	Antipiracy information	www.bsa.org
LexisNexis	Research databases and document assembly software	www.lexisnexis.com
Microsoft	Computer software	www.microsoft.com
Mozilla	Browser software	www.mozilla.com
Network Associates	Antivirus/spyware software	www.mcafee.com
Novell	Network operating systems	www.novell.com
Software and Information Industry	Antipiracy information	www.siia.com
Symantec Corp.	Antivirus and other application programs	www.symantec.com
Worldox	Document management software	www.worldox.com

TEST YOUR KNOWLEDGE

1. Why is it imperative for paralegals to have an understanding of computers?

2. True or False: The Internet has only had a mild impact on practicing paralegals, because many of their day-to-day activities have not changed.

3. Distinguish between intranets, extranets, and the Internet.

4. True or False: Manual billing systems are typically slow and impede a legal organization's cash flow.

5. In the legal field, another name for a calendaring system software is _____.

6. Name two ways in which computer technology affects an attorney's ethical duties.

7. True or False: The central processing unit is the "brain" of a computer.

8. The memory that is cleared when a user turns the machine off is called __rAM__.

9. Name three auxiliary storage devices.

10. Differentiate between imaging and optical character recognition.

11. What is VoIP?

12. Why are software access rights important?

13. What is an alternative to backing up software using hardware components such as tape backup and secondary servers?

14. Define metadata.

15. What are some of the ethical dangers of mobile computing?

16. What is the federal statute that governs whether an Internet company may comply with a formal discovery request?

Store Communications Act

imaging — scanning doc. in
opt. ch. — image is translated to text so it can be edited.

ON THE WEB EXERCISES

1. Using the Internet and a general search engine, such as www.yahoo.com or www.google.com, or using one or more of the websites listed at the end of this chapter, research one of the following topics and write a one- to two-page paper on the topic. Update the information contained in this chapter and give a general overview of the topic.
   - Automated courtroom
   - Videoconferencing
   - Electronic filing
   - The paperless office

2. Using the Internet and a general search engine, such as www.yahoo.com or www.google.com, identify at least one free source of online access to your state's statutes.

3. Identify a minimum of five potential security threats that could affect a law office. For each, identify ways in which a legal organization can mitigate the threat.

4. Using a general search engine on the Internet, such as www.google.com or www.yahoo.com, write a one-page summary of what metadata is. If possible, list examples of how mistakes or problems arise from the use of metadata for unintended purposes.

5. As a paralegal in a small law office, you have been asked for your input regarding replacing your current IBM-compatible computer, which is now outdated. Go to www.pcmagazine.com, www.pcworld.com, http://practice.findlaw.com, www.dell.com, www.gateway.com, www.toshiba.com, and www.compaq.com and research the following:
   a. What common microprocessors are being used
   b. How much RAM is usually included with the machines
   c. How much hard disk storage is typically being included
   d. What types and sizes of monitors are common
   e. What common peripherals (such as CD-ROM or DVD burners) are sold with the computers
   f. What choices you have among handheld, laptop, tablet, or desktop machines

   What would you choose, and why?

6. Using the Internet, determine what is the largest-capacity flash drive you can find and what it costs. Approximately how many hard-copy pages of documents could be stored on the flash drive by an employee who decided to steal documents from your law firm?

7. As a paralegal in a corporate legal department, you are responsible for tracking hundreds of real estate transactions throughout the United States every year. Keeping the paperwork organized and on track is beginning to overwhelm you. Because you work with attorneys and corporate staff all over the country, it would be nice to be able to forward electronic versions of real estate records, title searches, and other records. Because many of the documents are in hard-copy format, you would have to convert the documents to images. Using www.lawofficecomputing.com, www.lawtechnology.org, www.technolawyer.com, and www.practice.findlaw.com, write a short paper on imaging. Answer the following questions:
   a. How much do high-speed scanners cost?
   b. How accurate is imaging?
   c. Do many legal organizations use imaging?
   d. In the end, would you recommend the move to imaging?

8. As a paralegal in a solo practitioner's office, you have approached the attorney about purchasing handheld computers for both of you so that you can communicate more easily with each other and with clients. The attorney is concerned about security regarding handheld computers. He would like to know answers to the following questions:
   a. If the device gets lost, can just anyone pick it up and have access to the information (and if so, are there any precautions that can be taken to reduce this risk)?
   b. How secure is information when using wireless services such as wireless email?
   c. Assuming that the security issues can be solved, what are the latest features being offered in these devices?

9. Microsoft is continually updating its Windows operating system software and Office application programs. Go to its website at www.microsoft.com and comment on the latest version(s) of the program that it is releasing.

10. Go to www.facebook.com and www.twitter.com and read the privacy policies. What options are available on these platforms, and how do they differ?

QUESTIONS AND EXERCISES

1. Are you surprised to see the extent to which paralegals use computers in their jobs? What conclusions can you draw regarding the paralegal computer user?

2. Knowing that some legal research can be done free of charge on the Internet, and that other information is best found using a fee-based system, what approach would you use in conducting legal research?

3. You work as a paralegal for a small law firm that handles collection matters. The firm is currently representing a furniture store that loaned money to a number of customers who now have disappeared. Unless you find the whereabouts of the customers, the furniture store will not be able to collect its money. What computer resource would you use to try to find the customers, and why?

4. What policies and procedures could be put in place to limit an employee's ability to download and subsequently successfully use large amounts of client data when the employee leaves a law firm to practice elsewhere?

5. Write a two-page memorandum regarding the ethical rules in your state regarding a law firm's duty to safeguard client information that is stored electronically. What are the rules that might apply? Are there any exceptions for accidental disclosure?

ETHICS QUESTION

A client of your firm is engaged in complex litigation. She has just purchased the latest must-have mobile Wi-Fi device. The client plans on using this device for email and voice communication. What ethical issues are raised by this scenario?

The available CourseMate for this text has an interactive eBook and interactive learning tools, including flash cards, quizzes, and more. To learn more about this resource and access free demo CourseMate resources, go to www.cengagebrain.com, and search for this book. To access CourseMate materials that you have purchased, go to login.cengagebrain.com.

CHAPTER 2

Word Processing, PDF File Creation, and Document Assembly

CHAPTER OBJECTIVES

After completing this chapter, you should be able to do the following:

1. Explain how legal organizations and paralegals use word processors.
2. Describe major features found in word-processing programs.
3. Identify what a PDF file is and how PDF files are created.
4. Explain what document assembly is and how it works.
5. Discuss ethical problems related to word processing.

INTRODUCTION

This chapter introduces the fundamentals of word processing, Portable Document Format (PDF) file creation, and document assembly. **Word-processing software** is used to edit, manipulate, and revise text to create documents. It is one of the most widely used types of application software in legal organizations. Paralegals use word processors to prepare memos, correspondence, form letters, discovery documents, and many other legal documents.

Portable Document Format (PDF) is a file format developed by Adobe Systems for sharing files; it works independently of the application that was used to create the file or the operating system of the computer on which the file was created. The PDF file format is the de facto standard for digital document distribution, including for filing documents electronically with courts.

Document assembly software creates powerful standardized templates and forms. Once a template or form has been set up, users respond to a series of questions and prompts to fill in data. The document assembly program then merges the form or template with the answers and builds a new, completed document. Many legal organizations incorporate document assembly into their practices, particularly in areas for which well-structured forms and templates have been created and are routinely used.

CENTRALIZED AND DECENTRALIZED WORD PROCESSING

Legal organizations use various approaches to word processing, including centralized, decentralized, or a combination of both.

word-processing software
Program used to edit, manipulate, and revise text to create documents.

Portable Document Format (PDF)
A file format developed by Adobe Systems, Inc., for sharing files independently of the application that created the file or the computer's operating system.

document assembly software
Powerful computer program that creates standardized templates and forms.

Centralized Word Processing

With a **centralized word-processing system**, a legal organization has a separate word-processing department where correspondence, memorandums, and other documents in the office are input (typed). For example, a large firm with a centralized word-processing system might require its litigation, tax, and corporate law departments to send all their major word-processing projects to the word-processing department.

Most word-processing departments, sometimes called word-processing centers, have trained staff that do nothing but type in documents and data. Usually, the firm uses a standardized form for requesting services from this department. When a document has been input and printed, it is then sent back to the originating party for correction and for distribution. Such centralized word-processing departments are most often found in large firms.

Decentralized Word Processing

With a **decentralized word-processing system**, individuals perform word processing for themselves, for another person, or for a small group. For example, it is common for paralegals, law clerks, legal secretaries, and attorneys to perform some or all of their own word processing. Many law firms are now able to place relatively inexpensive personal computers on the desks of most staff, thus creating a decentralized system. In the past, attorneys rarely, if ever, did their own typing or word processing. Now it is very common.

Today, many small law firms use a decentralized word-processing system. Even large firms, which have traditionally used centralized word processing, may now use a combination of the two systems. It is common for large firms to maintain a word-processing center while still allowing legal professionals to do some of their own word processing.

LEGAL WORD-PROCESSING PROGRAMS: MICROSOFT WORD VS. COREL WORDPERFECT

The leading word-processing program for legal organizations is Microsoft Word, but some firms prefer to use Corel WordPerfect. Microsoft offers several versions of Word, which are all popular in the legal field: Word 2010, Word 2007 and Word 2003. Word 2007 implemented a major change in the Word interface. Word 2007 and Word 2010 use a "ribbon" (see Exhibit 2–1) packed with tools that the user can change based on what the user is doing. The newer versions of Word also include a "quick access toolbar" that the user can customize (see Exhibit 2–1). Word 2007 introduced the Office button, which provided quick access to a series of common commands (such as New, Open, Close, Save, Save As, and Print). Word 2010 replaces the Office button with the File tab. See Exhibit 2–1A. One of the major differences between the newer versions and earlier versions of Word is that the drop-down menus that have been a staple of Word were eliminated. Word 2003, like earlier versions of Word, uses an interface that includes drop-down menus and a static toolbar.

Another major change beginning with Word 2007 is that the file format in which documents are saved was revised. The default file format in Word 2007 is ".docx" (e.g., "letter.docx"). For many years, Word saved documents with the ".doc" file extension (e.g., "letter.doc"). Word 2007 and Word 2010 offer users the option of saving documents in the older ".doc" file format, but at the cost of sacrificing some options that are not available or do not work in the older file format.

All Microsoft Office 2010 applications, including Word 2010, introduced yet another new feature, the File tab. The File tab replaces the Office button used in the 2007 versions. Microsoft describes the File tab as the place "you do everything *to* a file that you don't do *in* a file." In other words, this is where you access the Open, Save, and Print features (among many others). See Exhibit 2–1A. Extensive hands-on exercises, which can be done in Word 2010 or Word 2007, appear at the end of this chapter.

See Exhibits 2–2 and 2–2A for quick reference guides to Word.

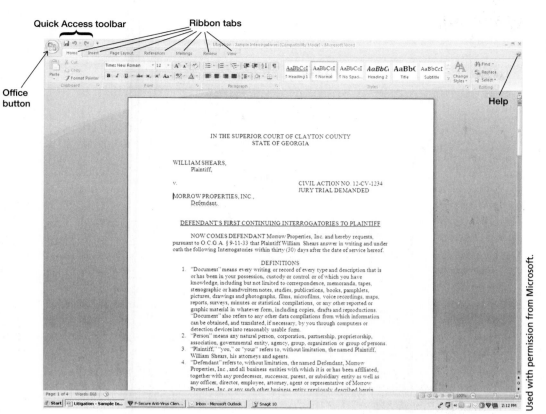

EXHIBIT 2–1
Microsoft Word 2007

Used with permission from Microsoft.

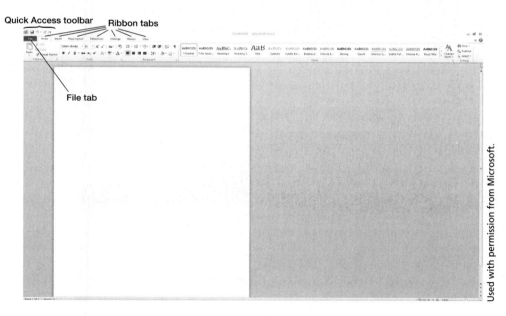

EXHIBIT 2–1A
Microsoft Word 2010

Used with permission from Microsoft.

LEGAL WORD-PROCESSING FUNDAMENTALS

Legal organizations use a variety of basic and advanced word-processing features and techniques. These include basic editing functions, such as copying, pasting, deleting, inserting, formatting text, and printing, among others. Legal organizations also make great use of some basic functions such as page numbering, footnoting, and tables. It is not uncommon for legal documents to be in the hundreds of pages, for a single footnote to run across several pages in a document, or for a table to be extremely complex. Legal organizations also use advanced word-processing features such as tables of authorities, macros, and merges. A number of these features are covered in this chapter.

Word 2007 Quick Reference Guide

HOME RIBBON

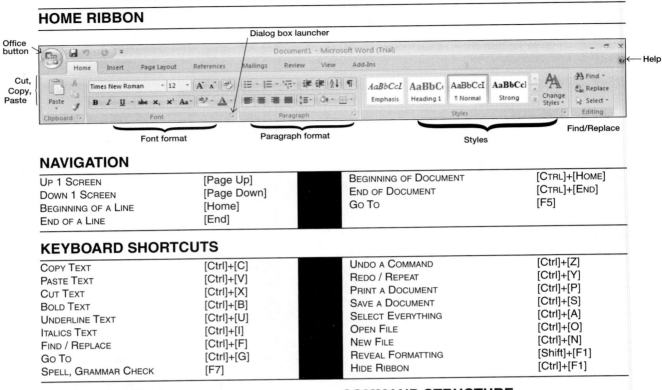

NAVIGATION

UP 1 SCREEN	[Page Up]	BEGINNING OF DOCUMENT	[CTRL]+[HOME]
DOWN 1 SCREEN	[Page Down]	END OF DOCUMENT	[CTRL]+[END]
BEGINNING OF A LINE	[Home]	GO TO	[F5]
END OF A LINE	[End]		

KEYBOARD SHORTCUTS

COPY TEXT	[Ctrl]+[C]	UNDO A COMMAND	[Ctrl]+[Z]
PASTE TEXT	[Ctrl]+[V]	REDO / REPEAT	[Ctrl]+[Y]
CUT TEXT	[Ctrl]+[X]	PRINT A DOCUMENT	[Ctrl]+[P]
BOLD TEXT	[Ctrl]+[B]	SAVE A DOCUMENT	[Ctrl]+[S]
UNDERLINE TEXT	[Ctrl]+[U]	SELECT EVERYTHING	[Ctrl]+[A]
ITALICS TEXT	[Ctrl]+[I]	OPEN FILE	[Ctrl]+[O]
FIND / REPLACE	[Ctrl]+[F]	NEW FILE	[Ctrl]+[N]
GO TO	[Ctrl]+[G]	REVEAL FORMATTING	[Shift]+[F1]
SPELL, GRAMMAR CHECK	[F7]	HIDE RIBBON	[Ctrl]+[F1]

WORD FEATURE	COMMAND STRUCTURE
ATTACH DOCUMENT TO AN EMAIL	Office Button, Send, Email
CHANGE CASE OF TEXT	Home, Font, Change Case
CLEAR ALL FORMATTING OF TEXT	Home, Font, Clear Formatting
CLIP ART FROM INTERNET (INSERTING)	Insert, Illustrations, Clip Art, Clip Art on Office Online
CLIP ART / FILES / CHARTS, SHAPES (INSERTING)	Insert, Illustrations
COMPARE DOCUMENTS	Review, Compare
FIND / REPLACE	Home, Editing, Find / Replace
FONT CONTROL	Home, Font
FOOTNOTES / ENDNOTES	References, Footnotes, Insert Footnotes
HEADER / FOOTER	Insert, Header & Footer, Header or Footer
INDENT TEXT	Home, Paragraph, Dialog Box Launcher
LINE SPACING CHANGES	Home, Paragraph, Line Spacing
MACROS	View, Macros
MAIL MERGE	Mailings, Start Mail Merge
MARGINS, PAPER ORIENTATION	Page Layout, Page Setup, Margins
SHADING	Home, Paragraph, Shading
STYLES	Home, Styles
TABLES (INSERTING)	Home, Insert, Tables
TABS	Home, Paragraph, Dialog Box Launcher, Indents and Spacing, Tabs
TRACK CHANGES	Review, Tracking, Track Changes
NEW DOCUMENT	Office Button, New
OPEN (EXISTING) DOCUMENT	Office Button, Open
SAVE A DOCUMENT	Office Button, Save
PRINT AND PRINT PREVIEW	Office Button, Print
TABLE OF AUTHORITIES	References, Table of Authorities

EXHIBIT 2–2

Word 2007 Quick Reference Guide

Word 2010 Quick Reference Guide

HOME RIBBON

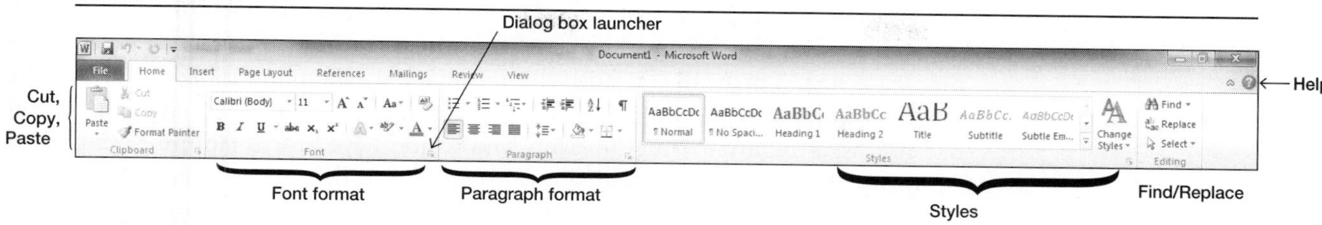

Dialog box launcher

Cut, Copy, Paste — Help

Font format | Paragraph format | Styles | Find/Replace

NAVIGATION

Up 1 Screen	[Page Up]	Beginning of Document	[Ctrl]+[Home]
Down 1 Screen	[Page Down]	End of Document	[Ctrl]+[End]
Beginning of a Line	[Home]	Go To	[F5]
End of a Line	[End]		

KEYBOARD SHORTCUTS

Copy Text	[Ctrl]+[C]	Undo a Command	[Ctrl]+[Z]
Paste Text	[Ctrl]+[V]	Redo / Repeat	[Ctrl]+[Y]
Cut Text	[Ctrl]+[X]	Print a Document	[Ctrl]+[P]
Bold Text	[Ctrl]+[B]	Save a Document	[Ctrl]+[S]
Underline Text	[Ctrl]+[U]	Select Everything	[Ctrl]+[A]
Italics Text	[Ctrl]+[I]	Open File	[Ctrl]+[O]
Find / Replace	[Ctrl]+[F]	New File	[Ctrl]+[N]
Go To	[Ctrl]+[G]	Reveal Formatting	[Shift]+[F1]
Spell, Grammar Check	[F7]	Hide Ribbon	[Ctrl]+[F1]

WORD FEATURE / COMMAND STRUCTURE

Word Feature	Command Structure
Attach Document to an Email	Office Button, Send, Email
Change Case of Text	Home, Font, Change Case
Clear all Formatting of Text	Home, Font, Clear Formatting
Clip Art from Internet (Inserting)	Insert, Illustrations, Clip Art, Clip Art on Office Online
Clip Art / Files / Charts, Shapes (Inserting)	Insert, Illustrations
Compare Documents	Review, Compare
Find / Replace	Home, Editing, Find / Replace
Font Control	Home, Font
Footnotes / Endnotes	References, Footnotes, Insert Footnotes
Header / Footer	Insert, Header & Footer, Header or Footer
Indent text	Home, Paragraph, Dialog Box Launcher
Line Spacing Changes	Home, Paragraph, Line Spacing
Macros	View, Macros
Mail Merge	Mailings, Start Mail Merge
Margins, Paper Orientation	Page Layout, Page Setup, Margins
Shading	Home, Paragraph, Shading
Styles	Home, Styles
Tables (Inserting)	Home, Insert, Tables
Tabs	Home, Paragraph, Dialog Box Launcher, Indents and Spacing, Tabs
Track Changes	Review, Tracking, Track Changes
New Document	Office Button, New
Open (Existing) document	Office Button, Open
Save a document	Office Button, Save
Print and Print Preview	Office Button, Print
Table of Authorities	References, Table of Authorities

Used with permission from Microsoft.

EXHIBIT 2–2A
Word 2010 Quick Reference Guide

Whole-Paragraph Functions

Automatic Paragraph Numbering Most word processors have an automatic paragraph numbering feature that allows users to have paragraphs and lists of information numbered automatically by the software. This feature is used extensively in legal organizations because information is routinely presented in a hierarchical format (e.g., 1, 2, 3 or A, B, C). With the automatic paragraph numbering feature, the program will automatically renumber a list when you add or delete material. If you had not used the numbering function, you would have had to renumber the whole list manually each time you added information to or deleted material from the list. For example, notice in Exhibit 2–3 that the headings "A. Introduction" and "B. Jurisdiction" are in a hierarchical format, as is the list with items "1)," "2)," and "3)." If, for example after "A. Introduction," you created a new topic, "B. Venue," the program would automatically renumber "Jurisdiction" to be "C. Jurisdiction."

In addition to improving accuracy, this feature saves huge amounts of time for legal organizations, because motions and briefs can be extremely long and complex and have many levels of hierarchical information. Users can even set up custom paragraph numbering schemes, including setting custom margins to comply with local court rules and employing a variety of numbering formats and sublevels (including numeric, alphanumeric, alphabetical, and others).

style
A named set of formatting characteristics that users can apply to text.

Styles A **style** is a named set of formatting characteristics that users apply to text. Using styles, users can quickly apply multiple formatting to text. For example, notice the different styles used in Exhibit 2–3. The style applied to "A. Introduction" and "B. Jurisdiction" is titled "Heading 2." Any material styled "Heading 2" is bolded, underlined, set in small caps, and automatically numbered. Instead of having to go to

EXHIBIT 2–3

Word processing: Header, footer, Styles, footnotes, Auto Number, Automatic Page Numbering in Word 2007

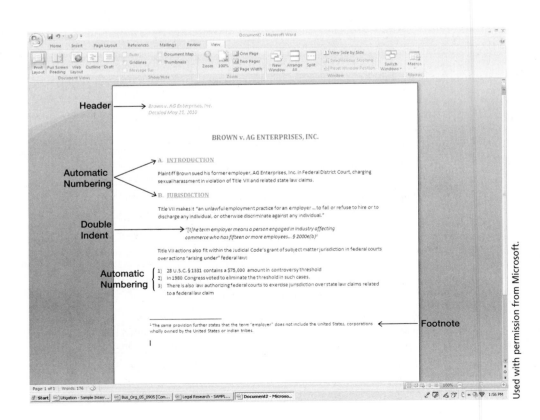

Used with permission from Microsoft.

each section heading and then enter the font command and the automatic numbering command, you can simply use the Style command to have all the formatting automatically applied, all at once.

Styles can also be automatically changed and updated. Suppose that the user who created Exhibit 2–3 has 40 section headings and now needs to change the format of all of these headings so that they are not underlined. If the user had not used the Style feature, he or she would have had to go to each of the 40 headings and manually make the desired changes. Using the Style feature, the user can simply invoke the Style command, click on "Heading 2," use the Select All feature to automatically select all text with the "Heading 2" style, and then make the desired changes. The format of all "Heading 2" text is then automatically updated.

The Style feature is particularly helpful in long and complex documents that have recurring elements and where consistency is important. Styles are covered in detail in Lesson 6 of the Hands-On Exercises for Word 2010 and Word 2007, found at the end of this chapter.

Headers and Footers

Headers and Footers A **header** is a title or heading that appears at the top of each page of a document. A **footer** is text that appears at the bottom of each page of a document. For example, a footer may indicate the current page number and the total number of pages of the document. The program can automatically calculate both the current page number and the total number of pages using an automatic page numbering feature.

Automatic Page Numbering

Automatic Page Numbering An **automatic page numbering** feature automatically calculates the appropriate page number for each page of a document. In most word processors, you can specify where the page number should be placed on the page (e.g., centered at the bottom of the page in a footer or in the upper right corner of the header). With the automatic page numbering feature, new page numbers are automatically recalculated and inserted when text is added to, moved or reformatted, or deleted from a page.

Double Indenting

Double Indenting Text is indented an equal distance from the left and right margins by using **double indenting**. Paralegals and attorneys use the double-indent feature frequently when including quotations from primary authorities. To use the double-indent feature, go to where the double indent should start, enter the Double Indent command, and type in the appropriate text. The text is automatically indented the same distance from the left and right margins.

Footnotes and Endnotes

Footnotes and Endnotes A **footnote** is material that is printed at the bottom of a page on which a numbered reference appears in text. An **endnote**, like a footnote, has a numbered reference in the text, but instead of appearing at the bottom of a page, the note material appears at the end of a chapter or document. Footnotes and endnotes are easy to produce with a word processor. Most word processors have an automatic footnote feature that tracks the current footnote number and formats the page(s) so that the note text is printed (or at least started) at the bottom of the page on which the reference number appears. To enter a footnote, simply go to the place in the text that is to be referenced and execute the Insert Footnote command (within the References tab/ribbon). This command automatically enters the correct footnote number and brings up a special footnote screen in which the user types the text of the footnote. Word processors automatically number the notes, and renumber them as necessary when notes are added or deleted.

---

header
A title or heading that appears at the top of each page of a document.

footer
Text that appears at the bottom of each page of a document.

automatic page numbering
Word-processor feature that automatically numbers the pages of a document for the user; also renumbers pages as material is moved, added, or deleted.

double indenting
Word-processor feature (also found in other types of programs) that indents text an equal distance from the left and right margins.

footnote
Material that is printed at the bottom of a page; marked in text by a numbered referent.

endnote
Material that is printed at the end of a chapter or document; marked in text by a numbered referent.

Footnotes and endnotes are heavily used in law-office word processing, especially in legal briefs. Because lawyers and legal assistants must cite the law when making an argument, footnotes and endnotes containing citations are common—and may be quite lengthy.

Electronic Distribution of Documents

Any modern law office must be able to distribute documents, including word-processing documents, in electronic form. For example, it is commonplace in many legal organizations to attach Microsoft Word documents to emails sent to corporate clients. This allows clients to see and make revisions to legal work. Most legal organizations are also now filing documents electronically with court clerks. Most courts use the Portable Document Format as the standard format for documents filed electronically. PDF can be a secure format when recipients are prohibited from editing the document. As long as the recipient has a PDF viewer, the recipient can view the file on a different type or version of computer than the one on which the document was created. Some word processors can export to a PDF file from within the word-processing program. Users can also purchase a separate program, such as Adobe Acrobat, to convert word-processing and other documents to PDF files. PDF file creation is covered in more detail later in this chapter.

Printing

Even with the prevalence of electronic document distribution, the ability to print hard copies of documents is still important. Word processors are extremely flexible when it comes to printing documents. Users can print single pages, whole documents, specific pages (e.g., pages 67 to 74), color, one- or two-sided pages, and much more. Many legal organizations have moved to digital printing, using multifunction printers that can print, copy, scan, add tabs, collate, and staple. Most word processors also have a "print layout" view or a Print Preview command that allows the user to see exactly how the document will look when printed.

Tables

The table feature in a word processor allows you to create a table of information using rows and columns. You can then quickly organize information into columns and rows without using tabs. Exhibit 2–4 shows a basic table. Grid lines divide the table into rows and columns (although you can adjust the settings so the lines are not displayed). Tables can include text, numbers, and even formulas.

Tables are very easy to set up in most word processors. You simply enter the Table command and tell the program how many rows and columns to start with. You can also change the size of the columns or rows, add and delete columns or rows, split columns or rows, add color, add graphics, and include calculations. Tables are frequently used in legal word processing for many purposes. Tables are covered in detail in Lesson 4 of the Hands-On Exercises for Word 2010 and Word 2007, found at the end of this chapter.

macro
Word-processor feature that records the user's keystrokes, saves those keystrokes, and then allows the user to play those keystrokes back.

Macros

A **macro** records a user's keystrokes, saves those keystrokes, and then allows the user to play those keystrokes back. For example, you might create a macro for the legal organization's name or to close a letter. Notice in the first screen of Exhibit 2–5 that the user has created a macro entitled "PleadSignBlock." When it was created,

SCHEDULE FOR FALL 2014 SCHOOL OF TECHNOLOGY PARALEGAL

Due Date: ____________

MAX ENR	COURSE PREFIX	SEC	DAY/TIME	LAB HRS.	INSTRUCTOR	ROOM #	Special Needs
44	PARA 1101	1	M 1:30-4:15		M. BURGAR	T220	
50	PARA 1101	2	M 6:00-8:45		M. CORRY	T220	
30	PARA 1101	3	T 6:00-8:45		S. RICHT	T212	
50	PARA 1103	1	W 6:00-8:45		S. SCHNEIDER	T220	
30	PARA 1103	2	R 6:00-8:45		L. COHEN	T215	
50	PARA 1103	3	S 9:00-3:15 ALTERNATE SATURDAYS		K. FISHER	T220	
20	PARA 1105	1	M 6:00-8:45		C. BAILEY	TBA	
20	PARA 1105	2	T 6:00-8:45		S. RICHT	TBA	
20	PARA 1105	3	W 6:00-8:45		T. WOLFE	TBA	
20	PARA 1105	4	R 1:30-4:15		K FISH	T220	
20	PARA 1105	5	R 6:00-8:45		TBA	TBA	
50	PARA 1107	1	T 6:00-8:45		C. ZEITNER	T220	
30	PARA 1107	2	R 6:00-8:45		M. SHAPIRO	TBA	
30	PARA 1109	1	M 6:00-8:45		S. RICHT	TBA	
50	PARA 1109	2	T 1:30-4:15		S. RICHT	T220	
30	PARA 1109	3	T 6:00-8:45		G. VARTASH	TBA	
30	PARA 1113	1	M 6:00-8:45		M. BURGAR	TBA	
30	PARA 1113	2	T 6:00-8:45		TBA	TBA	
50	PARA 1221	1	R 6:00-8:45		K. FISH	T220	
30	PARA 1223	1	W 6:00-8:45		TBA	TBA	
30	PARA 1225	1	W 6:00-8:45		R. ROLLO	TBA	

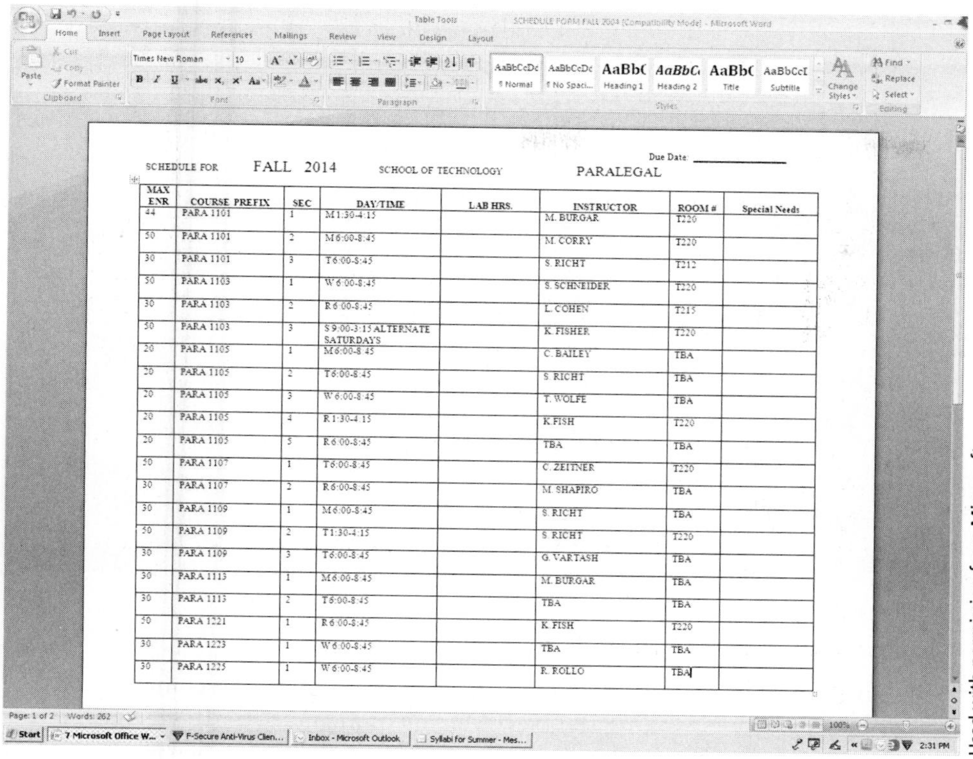

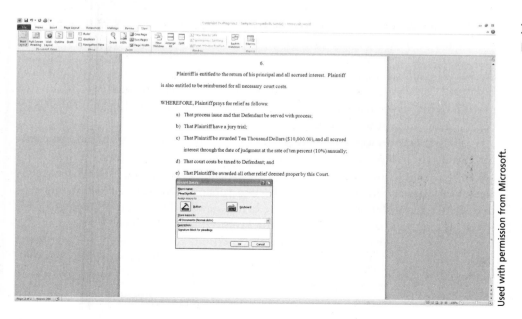

EXHIBIT 2–4
A table in Word 2007

the macro recorded the keystrokes that produce the standard signature block for a pleading. From then on, you never have to retype that signature block. At the end of a pleading, such as the second screen of Exhibit 2–5, you simply run the macro: the macro does the rest by quickly and sequentially replaying the recorded keystrokes.

Macros can also be created to perform word-processing commands or even series of commands (e.g., applying a style, then applying a double indent). Macros increase productivity, efficiency, and accuracy, because users do not have to keep

6.

Plaintiff is entitled to the return of his principal and all accrued interest. Plaintiff is also entitled to be reimbursed for all necessary court costs.

WHEREFORE, Plaintiff prays for relief as follows:

a) That process issue and that Defendant be served with process;

b) That Plaintiff have a jury trial;

c) That Plaintiff be awarded Ten Thousand Dollars ($10,000.00), and all accrued interest through the date of judgment at the rate of ten percent (10%) annually;

d) That court costs be taxed to Defendant; and

e) That Plaintiff be awarded all other relief deemed proper by this Court.

EXHIBIT 2–5
Macro in Word 2010

EXHIBIT 2–5
(*continued*)

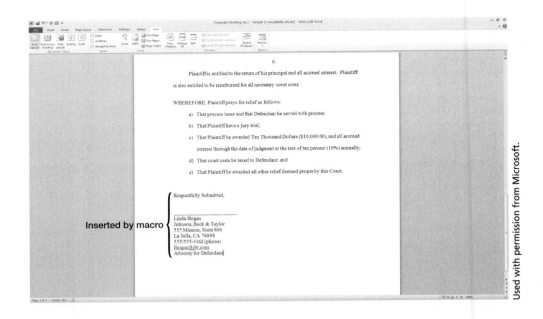

keying in repetitive material or going through long sequences of commands. Macros can be created by invoking the New Macro command; with the recording feature, the user's keystrokes and commands are recorded in the order in which they are executed, and then saved under whatever file name the user has assigned to the macro. To play the macro, the user simply invokes the Play Macro command and enters the name of the macro or clicks on the name in a list. (For even quicker access, macros that are used frequently can be assigned to a keyboard stroke combination, such as Ctrl-Alt-P; this means the user need not even go to the Macros menu or take hands off the keyboard.)

Macros are an extremely handy and time-saving feature. Macros are covered in detail in Lesson 12 of the Hands-On Exercises for Word 2010 and Word 2007, found at the end of this chapter.

Comments, Comparing Documents, and Track Changes

Word processors allow groups of people to collaborate effectively using a number of features and tools, including comments, compare documents, and track changes. The **comment** feature allows a user to annotate and make notes or comments in a document without actually changing it. Notice in Exhibit 2–6 that the reviewer has inserted a comment, which includes questions, in the user's document. The original user can then make changes and delete the comment or respond to the reviewer by editing the comment with his or her own opinion.

A **compare documents** feature allows you to compare two separate word-processing files. Most word processors can do this in a couple of ways, including allowing simultaneous viewing of the two files or by producing a third document that shows the differences between the two versions. Notice in Exhibit 2–7 that two similar but different documents are being viewed. The second document adds some verbiage to paragraph 1 (Term of Employment), but other than that it is substantially similar to the first. Using this method, you can view two documents at the same time to find the differences. You can also set the word processor to synchronize the documents so that they scroll side by side as you move through the documents.

comment
Word-processor feature that allows a user to annotate and create notes in a document without changing the text of the document.

compare documents
Word-processor feature that allows a user to compare and contrast two documents, either side by side or by blacklining (usually through the creation of a third document showing differences).

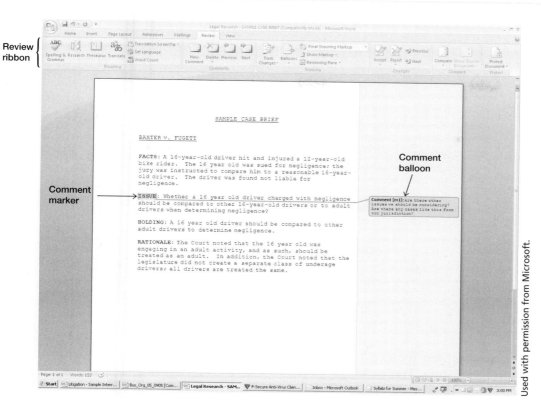

EXHIBIT 2–6

Adding a comment to a document in Word 2007

Used with permission from Microsoft.

Another way to compare documents is to have the word processor "blackline" the documents. With this feature, the word processor creates a new document showing what the second document added to or deleted from the first document.

Legal organizations find the Compare Documents feature to be very useful in many situations. The Compare Document feature is covered in detail in Lesson 8 of the Hands-On Exercises for Word 2010 and Word 2007, found at the end of this chapter.

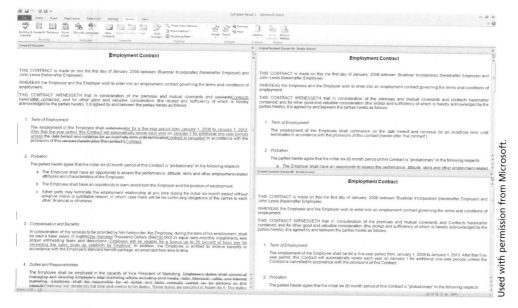

EXHIBIT 2–7

Comparing documents: Simultaneous viewing and blacklining in Word 2010

Used with permission from Microsoft.

EXHIBIT 2–8

Track Changes in
Word 2010

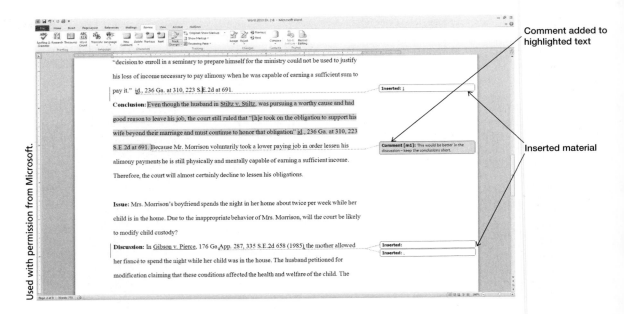

Comment added to
highlighted text

Inserted material

Another way for users to use word processors collaboratively is to use the Track Changes feature. **Track changes** allows reviewers to make changes to a document that later can be either accepted or rejected by the user. For example, suppose an attorney asks a paralegal to write a draft of a pleading. The paralegal drafts the pleading; then the attorney turns on the Track Changes feature and makes changes right in the document itself (see Exhibit 2–8). Notice in Exhibit 2–8 that you can see all the changes the attorney made, with inserted and deleted material flagged. You could accept all of the changes at once, reject all of the changes at once, or go through the changes one by one and accept or reject them separately.

In some instances documents are reviewed by multiple people, including attorneys, co-counsel, and clients. Most word processors can accommodate reviews by multiple parties by assigning different colors to each reviewer. The user can then easily determine who made each change. Track changes is covered in detail in Lesson 9 of the Hands-On Exercises for Word 2010 and Word 2007, found at the end of this chapter.

Table of Authorities

Most word processors have automated features for creating a table of authorities (commonly referred to as a TOA or TA). A **table of authorities** is a section in a legal document or brief that lists the cases, statutes, and other authorities referenced in that legal document or brief. A table of authorities is similar to a table of contents except that it lists cases and other reference materials, along with the page numbers on which they appear in the document. Tables of authorities are typically created by marking all of the case citations and other authorities and then generating the table itself near the beginning of the document (see Exhibit 2–9).

The Table of Authorities feature in a word processor is very important because manual creation of a TOA is an extremely time-consuming process, particularly if revisions are made after the table has been generated. With the automated feature, even if changes are made to a document after a table of authorities has been created, the user can regenerate the table; that is, the program will automatically recreate the table with all of the new items and page numbers. Tables of authorities are covered in detail in Lesson 11 of the Hands-On Exercises for Word 2010 and Word 2007, found at the end of this chapter.

track changes
Word-processor feature that allows reviewers to make or recommend changes to a document; these changes can later be either accepted or rejected by the original author.

table of authorities
Automated word-processor feature that allows the program to generate an accurate list of case and statute citations (authorities), along with the page number(s) on which each cite appears.

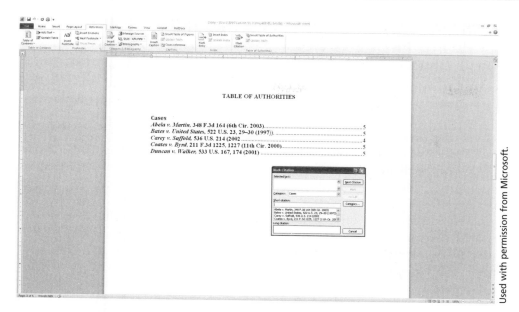

Used with permission from Microsoft.

EXHIBIT 2–9

Table of authorities in Word 2010

Revealing Hidden Codes

When text is typed into a word processor, all the user sees on the screen is the actual text. However, most word processors have a command that allows the user to see the "invisible" codes that indicate things such as word spaces, boldfacing, and margin changes.

Revealing the hidden codes makes it easier to delete, edit, or change the formatting of a document (see Exhibit 2–10). For example, in Exhibit 2–10, when the Reveal Formatting feature is turned on, you can plainly see that the word "COMPLAINT" has formatting codes of "Font: Times New Roman, 12 pt., and Underline." If you wanted to delete one of these formatting codes, you could use a reveal codes command to go to the spot in the document where the code is and then delete it in the Reveal Formatting view. Reveal codes commands are helpful when trying to determine what formatting codes were previously entered in a document. (It can be the quickest and easiest way to discover why the word processor keeps doing something to a document other than what you thought you told it to do!)

Microsoft Word calls this feature "Reveal Formatting." Revealing hidden codes and formatting is included in Lesson 5 of the Hands-On Exercises for Word 2010 and Word 2007, found at the end of this chapter.

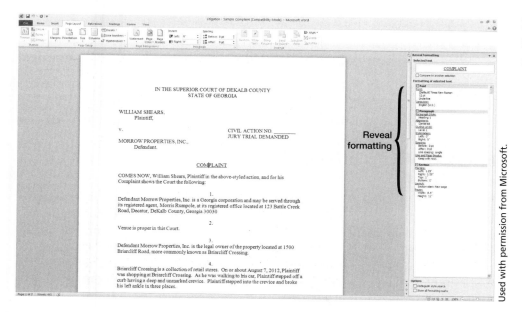

Used with permission from Microsoft.

EXHIBIT 2–10

Styles and formatting revealed in Word 2010

MERGING AND DOCUMENT ASSEMBLY IN WORD PROCESSORS

merging
The process of combining a form with a list of variables to automatically produce a document; sometimes called document generation.

primary file
A file that contains the information that remains the same (the constant) in a document that is used more than once; usually referred to as a *form* or *template* in a merge document.

secondary file
The file that contains the information that varies (the *variable*) in a merge document.

Merging, sometimes called *document generation* or *document assembly*, is the process of combining an existing form with a list of variables to automatically produce a new document. For instance, if you want to send the same letter to a number of clients, but you want each letter to be personalized, you can use the Merge feature found in most word processors to do this quickly. The body of each letter remains the same; the only information that changes is the name and address of the client. The information that remains the same in each letter (in this example, the body of the text) is called a *constant*. The information that changes in each letter (here, the name and address of the client) is called a *variable*.

The first step in the merge process is to create the primary file. The **primary file** (also called a *main document*) contains the constant information and is usually referred to as a *form* or *template* in a merge document. The second step is to create the list of names and addresses. This is called the secondary file. The **secondary file** (also called a *data file*) contains the variable information in a merge document. In this example, the secondary file contains the names and addresses of the clients. The third step is to merge or combine the primary file with the secondary file, thus creating a separate letter for each client, using the Merge command. The final step is to print the document(s).

Another way to use a merge file is to create a primary file or template and then enter information into the form as you go along, without using a secondary file at all. This is helpful for creating short, mundane forms such as letters, memos, and so forth. Once the primary file is created, use the merge command to retrieve it. Then, as you go along, fill in each variable that changes. Finally, when the document has been filled in, print it. Merge files greatly reduce the time it takes to perform repetitive tasks.

Many of the letters, pleadings, and other documents that law offices produce are essentially forms. In many instances, although the client names change from case to case, the letters and documents produced are generally the same. Merge files allow you to save these forms, so that later you can simply retrieve them and quickly fill in the blanks. Merging is covered in detail in Lessons 7 and 10 of the Hands-On Exercises for Word 2010 and Word 2007, found at the end of this chapter.

In addition to word processors with merge/document assembly capabilities, there are also separate document assembly programs that work together with a word processor to perform this function. Document assembly programs typically have more features and capabilities than word processors. Many legal organizations use document assembly programs to further automate production of correspondence, pleadings, contracts, and other legal documents. These programs are covered later in this chapter.

WORD-PROCESSING FILE FORMATS

Most word processors, including Microsoft Word, can save documents in multiple file formats. Word 2007, for example, can save files in several formats, including Word 2007, Word 97-2003, plain text, Rich Text Format, Web Page, and others.

MICROSOFT WORD ONLINE TRAINING AND WORD TEMPLATES

Microsoft provides free online training courses for Microsoft Word on its website. More than 20 courses are available for each version. To find the online training courses, use a general search engine (such as www.google.com or www.yahoo.com) and use the search terms "Microsoft Word 2010 Courses" or "Microsoft Word 2007 Courses."

The Microsoft website also provides a wide variety of free Word templates. In Word 2007, the online templates can be accessed by selecting the Office button, selecting New, and then clicking on any of the available templates. In Word 2010, the online templates can be accessed by clicking the File tab, selecting New, and then clicking on any of the available templates.

PDF FILE CREATION

As noted earlier, many courts now allow—and in fact require—legal organizations to file documents electronically. Most courts use PDF as the standard for filing documents electronically. The federal courts in particular have standardized filing around the PDF format. Thousands of attorneys have filed documents for millions of cases using the federal courts' Case Management and Electronic Case File system.

The PDF standard was created by Adobe Systems. PDF can be made a secure format, meaning that recipients cannot edit the document and that the look and format of the document are locked. For electronic filing of documents with a court, this is crucial.

Another advantage of PDF is that as long as the recipient has a PDF viewer (which is free), the recipient can view the file on a different type of computer than the one on which the document was created. Thus, if a court system used a UNIX-based operating system and an attorney used an Apple Macintosh computer, it would not matter. As long as the attorney saved the document to be filed as a PDF, the court could still use and access the document, even though it was created on a computer with a completely different operating system.

Adobe Acrobat

Adobe Acrobat is a PDF conversion utility. Acrobat can convert many types of files to PDF. Adobe Acrobat has several versions, which may be confusing. Acrobat has a Reader program that can be downloaded for free from the Internet. However, to create PDF files, you need either the Standard or Professional version of Adobe Acrobat.

Adobe Acrobat is an output program; it is essentially a glorified digital printer. As a matter of fact, when Acrobat is downloaded, it adds an option to your list of available printers; images may now be sent to the PDF printer. This can be useful for saving images from web pages (receipts, travel information, etc.). Also, even though Acrobat is essentially a print utility, you can "print" a copy of something as a PDF without actually creating a hard copy; instead, you can just save a copy of a document as a PDF.

Acrobat is not used to create documents. That task is left to programs such as Word and Excel. However, Acrobat may be used to convert a digital photograph or other image to a PDF file. When you download Acrobat, it automatically installs (depending on the version of Windows on the computer) a new toolbar, or new buttons on your existing toolbars, that enables you to easily convert documents, pictures, and other images to PDFs.

Creating a PDF from a Microsoft Word File

There are a number of ways to convert documents and other images to PDFs. For example, suppose that you have a file in Word that you would like to convert to a PDF file. Notice in Exhibit 2–11 that when Adobe Acrobat was installed it created a new menu item in Word, entitled "Adobe PDF." The first step in converting the Word document to PDF is to select "Convert to Adobe PDF" from the Adobe PDF menu items on the Word menu line (see Exhibit 2–11, screen 1). Acrobat asks you to enter the name of the new PDF file that is being created. Acrobat then converts the file and opens it in the Adobe Acrobat program (see Exhibit 2–11, screen 2). Alternatively, you can load Acrobat first and identify the file to be converted, in this case the Word file; then Acrobat will convert it and load the converted file into Acrobat. Acrobat can also convert multiple files into one PDF file. The conversion progress is typically easy and straightforward.

EXHIBIT 2–11

Converting a Word file to a
PDF in Adobe Acrobat

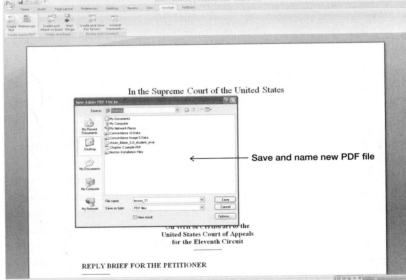

Save and name new PDF file

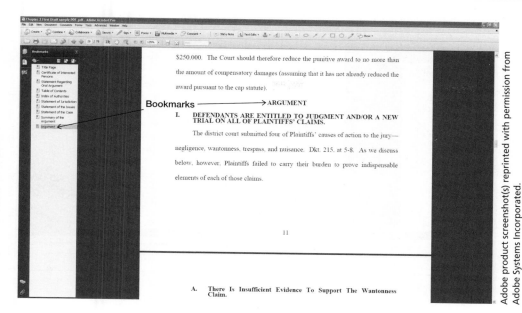

EXHIBIT 2–12
Bookmarks in Adobe Acrobat

Creating a PDF from Internet Content

Adobe Acrobat can be used to capture—and, if desired, print—web pages. Without Acrobat, you would have to use a "screen shot" captured by clicking the Print Screen key. However, this often results in a less-than-satisfactory image. Acrobat provides a far better and more useful end product.

To create a PDF from a web page, you have several options. Perhaps the easiest is to "print" a PDF. To do this, just click on the Print button and choose "PDF Printer"; then save the document as a PDF. Another option is to use the Acrobat buttons now embedded on the toolbar.

Acrobat has a number of features, including the Bookmark feature. A *bookmark* is a navigation link to a specific location in the PDF file. Notice in Exhibit 2–12 that to the left of the page, under the Bookmarks tab, there is a series of bookmarks, including "Table of Authorities," "Argument," "Conclusion," and so on. When the user clicks on the Argument bookmark, the user is immediately taken to that section of the document. This is a quick and convenient way to navigate in PDF files. Interestingly, if Microsoft Word users use the Style feature to create their documents, including using Headings in the Style feature, Acrobat can convert all of these headings directly to bookmarks.

Using Acrobat, users have tremendous control over how a PDF file will look. Users can assign custom page numbers, include headers or footers, insert multimedia links, create fill-in electronic forms, and much more.

Adobe Acrobat has many features, including the ability to create and insert notes and comments (see Exhibit 2–13). Using this feature, people can collaborate using Acrobat even if they do not all use the same word processor. Notice also in Exhibit 2–13 that the user has clicked on the Pages tab and that page views of the document are being displayed to the left.

Adobe Acrobat allows users to attach a digital signature to a PDF file. A digital signature not only validates the PDF file, but also validates with Acrobat the identity of the person signing it. Using digital signatures is another security feature: once a document is digitally signed, the recipient cannot alter the PDF file. Some courts require all PDF files to have a digital signature.

By default, new PDF files are *not* secure. This means that anyone receiving the PDF file can open, view, print, or make changes to that file. However, Acrobat offers a number

EXHIBIT 2–13

Notes and page view in Adobe Acrobat

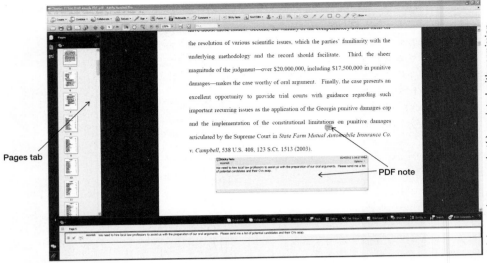

of security features that allow the creator to completely lock down a PDF file. For example, Exhibit 2–14 shows that the user has the option to restrict printing and editing of the documents and to choose its security settings. This enables the user to "lock" the PDF file so that unless the recipient has the password, the recipient cannot print or change the PDF file. However, Adobe Acrobat can export a PDF file to Microsoft Word as long as the user who created the original PDF file allows it by turning this feature on.

With all these features, and the considerable security protections it provides, Adobe Acrobat is an incredibly powerful tool for information sharing. It will most likely remain an important part of word processing and document distribution, for legal organizations, courts, and clients, for the foreseeable future.

DOCUMENT ASSEMBLY PROGRAMS

Document assembly software creates powerful standardized templates and forms. Users create forms and templates and then respond to a series of questions and prompts. The document assembly program then merges the selected template or

EXHIBIT 2–14

Adobe Acrobat security features

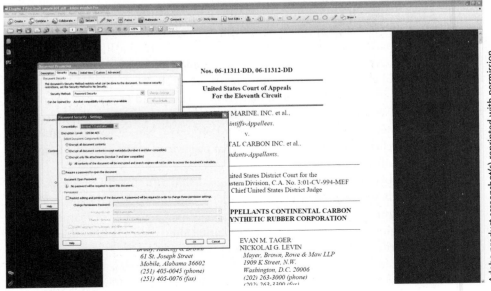

form with the answers and builds a completed document. Document assembly programs work best, and are most useful, when the user has well-structured templates and forms that must be completed often and in a routine manner.

Word processors have some document assembly functions, but stand-alone document assembly programs are much more powerful. Text templates are based on text documents (e.g., a simple will or articles of incorporation) and are initially created with the user's word-processing program. Form templates create forms (e.g., an IRS tax form or credit application). At most law firms, text templates are much more common than form templates.

Suppose that a law firm routinely drafts employment contracts for a large client. Instead of using a word processor to slowly edit the document for every new employee the client hires, the law firm would like to use a document assembly program to automate the process.

Exhibit 2–15 shows a template for an employment agreement, which was built in a document assembly program. The document assembly program is running inside of the user's word processor; notice the special document assembly toolbar in Exhibit 2–15. Notice also that a number of variables are listed in Exhibit 2–15, including <Employee Name>, <Agreement Date>, <Job Title>, and others.

A *variable* is something that will change in the document. Notice that the variable <Employee Name> in Exhibit 2–15 is included more than once in the document. The beauty of a document assembly program is that once the text for the variable <Employee Name> has been entered (e.g., "Cynthia Jones"), the computer automatically fills it in anywhere the variable <Employee Name> appears. This software also allows the form to correctly enter "he" or "she" depending on the gender of the employee.

Once a template has been built, the user executes the template in the document assembly program (creates a custom document from a generic form). The document assembly program takes the answers the user gives and opens a new word-processing document. The next step is for the user to answer the questions the template asks. When all of the questions have been answered, the finished template document is displayed in the user's word-processing program so that the finished document can be edited as needed.

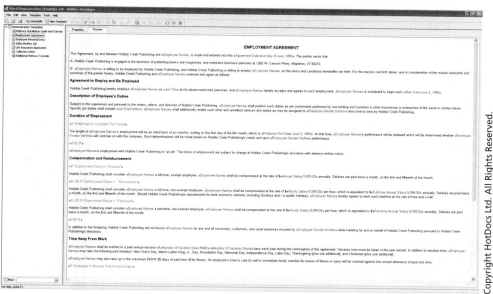

EXHIBIT 2–15

Document assembly program: Employment agreement—Completed template

Document assembly programs are extremely powerful and have many advanced features that make them great time-savers in many legal organizations. You will have the opportunity to assemble a text template and create a new text template in the HotDocs Hands-On Exercises at the end of this chapter (HotDocs 10).

ETHICAL CONSIDERATIONS

Although word processing has done wonders for the legal profession in terms of efficiency and ease of use, it has a downside that raises important ethical issues. Word processors can make users lazy. For instance, users may misspell words because they assume that the spell checker will catch any errors. Users can use poor grammar because the grammar checker will fix it. Users do not have to start from scratch to prepare a will or other legal documents because form wills, templates, and other documents that can easily be modified are available on the computer or on the Internet. Users do not have to go back and do legal research over and over again every time a new legal document is filed, because they can copy legal research from one client's documents to another's.

Finally, even if a document's content is poor, users can make it look pretty with fancy fonts, justified margins, tables, and many other features. And that is the problem: potential lack of content. An attorney has an ethical duty to provide competent representation. Lawyers and paralegals must make sure that their word-processing documents are competently and thoroughly prepared. That is, they should not only look good, but also be proofread well, contain up-to-date and accurate cites, and be the best documents the attorney or paralegal can produce.

The following are a few common ethical issues related to the use of word processors.

Leaving Metadata in Documents

As you may recall from Chapter 1, *metadata* is electronically stored information that may identify the origin, date, author, usage, comments, or other information about a file. It is important that a legal organization delete or remove the metadata from any document before that document leaves the firm.

In Word 2007, a user can inspect all parts of a document for metadata. If metadata is discovered in the document, the user can choose to remove it. In addition, Adobe Acrobat now has strong security enhancements that can remove metadata from PDF files and permanently delete the redacted information.

It should be noted that while legal organizations do not want documents going out of the office with metadata still present in them, some courts have held that in the context of discovery (production of documents during the discovery stage of a lawsuit), opposing parties are entitled to metadata. Note here the major difference between documents prepared by attorneys for their clients (e.g., word-processing documents), where security is of the utmost importance, and discovery documents produced by clients for the opposing parties in a case. In the latter, some courts have said that the parties have the right to see the metadata, including the origin of documents and other information. This is another reason to make sure, as an important matter of practice, that a word-processing document has no metadata attached to it before it leaves the legal organization.

Old Client Data Left in New Document

It is common, when preparing a new document, to retrieve an old document and use it as the basis of the new one. For instance, when preparing a new real estate contract, the user might pull up an old real estate contract from a few months ago as a place to start. The trouble is that it is easy to leave the old data (i.e., old property description, old client names, old prices, wrong pronouns) in the new document. This problem is a strong argument for both excellent proofreading and the creation and use of fill-in templates or forms.

Typographical Errors That Spell Checkers Will Not Catch

Some typographical errors will not be caught by a spell checker; they can be picked up only by careful proofreading of the document. Common errors of this sort include insertion or retention of the wrong case facts, and misuse of a correctly spelled word. For example, a complaint should demand a jury *trial*, not a jury *trail*. In one well-publicized case, a paralegal mistakenly left out the last three zeros on a mortgage used to secure a $92,885,000 loan to a company that eventually went into bankruptcy. Because of the mistake, the company the paralegal worked for had only a $92,885 lien. Going by the provisions of the mortgage, that left $92,792,115 unsecured.

It is absolutely critical that all documents be carefully proofread even if the user is using a word processor, and a spell checker, and a grammar checker. Some mistakes can be caught only by the user. Supervising attorneys cannot afford to become careless about these matters, no matter how good or trustworthy the paralegal is.

Improper Form Selected; Leaving in or Deleting Wrong Paragraphs

It is very easy to select the wrong form when creating new documents. Unfortunately, this can have a devastating impact. Another very common error is to either leave in inappropriate material or delete a wrong paragraph from the form. If you are using a form, it is important to know and understand every paragraph in the form so you can make appropriate decisions about what stays and what goes.

Not Following Court Rules

Many courts have document preparation rules, especially regarding the kind of font or typeface to be used, the font size, margin widths, and paper sizes. It is important that these rules be followed exactly. In one case, a corporate legal department repeatedly filed appellate briefs using a 10-point Times New Roman font instead of the 12-point Courier required by court rules. The law department did this because another court rule limited briefs to 30 pages, and they could get in 50 percent more verbiage using the smaller font. The court finally dismissed the appeal because the law office did not follow the court's rules.

Preparing Legal Documents without the Supervision of an Attorney (Unauthorized Practice of Law)

Most states have a criminal statute that prohibits a layperson from practicing law. In addition to criminal laws, there are also ethical prohibitions that proscribe a nonlawyer from practicing law. Simply put, paralegals cannot draft legal documents, such as wills, briefs, motions, pleadings, or contracts, without the supervision of an attorney. Paralegals routinely draft these types of documents; the distinction is that they do so properly, under the direction and supervision of a member of the bar. The attorney is ultimately responsible for the legal documents.

What happens if an attorney does not look at a document a paralegal has prepared using a word processor or document assembly program? Assume that the paralegal has been working hard on a motion and has taken cases and arguments from past documents prepared by the supervising attorney, but the document is due by 5:00 p.m. and there is no time for the attorney to review it. This is how unauthorized practice of law issues regarding word processing and drafting documents arise in real life.

The reason for the rule is that legal documents affect the legal rights of clients and parties and therefore require the attention of an attorney. As long as a paralegal is actively working under the supervision of an attorney, and the attorney maintains a relationship with the client, the paralegal may interview witnesses or prospective clients, perform legal research, draft pleadings and briefs, and investigate the facts of cases without being accused of the unauthorized practice of law. However, the moment the paralegal prepares a legal document on her own, without the review of an attorney, a breach of the rule has most likely occurred.

No matter how routine the legal document is, always have an attorney review it. Never let an attorney approve your work without reading it. If the attorney says, "I don't have time to review it; I'll sign it and you just send it out, I trust you," bring the document back at another time or find a tactful way to suggest to the attorney that the document must be approved in the correct way.

Overlooking Prudent Practices

Competent representation of a client requires more than just competence regarding knowledge of the law and the quality of the legal services provided. It requires competence in all aspects of the law office, including the following areas.

Use Full-Function Spell and Grammar Checkers
Certainly, you should not rely on the spell checker/grammar checker to do your only review of documents. However, you should by all means use these functions on every document you prepare. There is nothing more embarrassing than finding obvious typographical or grammatical errors in a document that has gone out—particularly when it has been sent out under the signature of your supervising attorney. Never assume that the automatic spell/grammar checking that occurs as you type your document (where problems are flagged by being underlined with colored squiggly lines) is enough. *It is not.* It is extremely easy to fail to see these errors when drafting. Always go back and run the full-function spell/grammar checker to make sure you have not missed any obvious mistakes.

Always Validate Cases/Citations and Factual References
Before a paralegal cites a case or references a fact in a legal document that he is unsure about, it is imperative that he double-check and validate the case or fact to make sure it is still good law or that the "fact" actually happened. Never throw something into a word processor with the thought that you will get back to it and verify it—what happens if you forget? The answer is that the client can be harmed, the attorney's reputation can be harmed, your reputation certainly will be harmed, and serious ethical ramifications could arise for your supervising attorney or the law office. Do not take the chance; always double-check your work.

Password-Protect Confidential Word-Processing Documents That Will Be Emailed
It is always a good idea, out of an abundance of caution, to password-protect confidential documents that will be emailed through an Internet provider or sent over large networks. Most word-processing programs have the capability to do this; for example, Microsoft Word can password-protect word-processing files. It is very easy to do and does not cost anything. It is just one more layer of protection to maintain the confidentiality of client or case-related data.

SUMMARY

Word processors are computer programs that are used to edit, manipulate, and revise text to create documents. A law office with a centralized word-processing system has a separate word-processing department that inputs all documents for an organization, as opposed to a decentralized word-processing system in which individuals perform word processing for themselves or a small group. The primary word-processing program in law offices is Microsoft Word, though some still use Corel WordPerfect.

Modern legal organizations use a variety of word-processing functions and features, including, among others, automatic paragraph numbering, styles, footnotes and endnotes, tables, macros, comments, multiple-document comparisons, track changes, creation of tables of authorities, and document merging.

Creating Portable Document Format (PDF) files is an important part of document generation for many

legal organizations because many jurisdictions require word-processing documents to be filed electronically in this format. Adobe Acrobat is the most popular program used for converting files into PDFs.

Document assembly software creates powerful templates for form documents. Once the user answers the questions in the template, the answers are then merged with the template and a new, final document is output. Document assembly software is extremely sophisticated and serves many functions in legal organizations.

When preparing legal documents, it is important for users to carefully review their work to ensure that old information is not left in documents, metadata is deleted, research is updated and current, and there are no typographical errors.

KEY TERMS

automatic page numbering
centralized word-processing system
comment
compare documents
decentralized word-processing system
document assembly software
double indenting

endnote
footer
footnote
header
macro
merging
Portable Document Format (PDF)

primary file
secondary file
style
table of authorities
track changes
word-processing software

INTERNET SITES

Internet sites for this chapter include:

ORGANIZATION	PRODUCT/SERVICE	INTERNET ADDRESS
LexisNexis	HotDocs document assembly program	www.hotdocs.com
Corel Corporation	WordPerfect	www.corel.com
Findlaw.com	Online legal forms	www.findlaw.com
Microsoft	Microsoft Word	www.microsoft.com/word
ProDoc	ProDoc document assembly program	www.prodoc.com
Adobe Systems, Inc.	Adobe Acrobat PDF file creation	www.adobe.com
Nitro PDF, Inc.	Free PDF creator software	www.primopdf.com

TEST YOUR KNOWLEDGE

1. What does "PDF" stand for?
2. Compare and contrast centralized and decentralized word processing.
3. True or False: The automatic paragraph numbering feature numbers the pages in a document.
4. True or False: A style is a named set of formatting characteristics that users apply to text.
5. Text that is indented an equal distance from the left and right margin is called _____.
6. True or False: A word-processing feature that combines a primary and secondary file is called a macro. *merge feature*

7. A word-processing feature that allows the reviewer to make annotations in the document without actually changing the document is called a _____. *comment feature*
8. Distinguish between primary and secondary merge files.
9. What standard document type do most courts use to allow attorneys to file documents electronically? *PDF*
10. True or False: Word-processing merge files have exactly the same features as stand-alone document assembly programs.

ON THE WEB EXERCISES

1. Using the "Internet Sites" listed in this chapter and a general Internet search engine (such as www.google.com or www.yahoo.com), research the current versions of Microsoft Word. Prepare a summary of the differences, similarities, and reviews of the products. Which product would you rather use in the legal environment and why?
2. Using the "Internet Sites" listed in this chapter and a general Internet search engine (such as www.google.com or www.yahoo.com), research the Case Management and Electronic Filing System for the U.S. federal courts. Write a two-page summary of your findings, including how it works, what the standard is, and other relevant information about the system.
3. Using the "Internet Sites" listed in this chapter and a general Internet search engine (such as www.google.com or www.yahoo.com), find a word-processing template for a simple last will and testament for your state. How hard or easy was it to find? Were you able to find fee-based forms, free forms, or both?

4. Using http://forms.lp.findlaw.com, find a recent United States Supreme Court opinion under "Cases and Codes." Copy and paste the opinion into your word processor. How easy was this to do? Can you manipulate and edit the document? Describe why using the Internet and your word processor in this way might be an important feature for a legal organization.
5. Using the "Internet Sites" listed in this chapter and a general Internet search engine (such as www.google.com or www.yahoo.com), research document assembly programs. What programs did you find? What features do they have? What are their advantages? How are they different from the merge capabilities in word processors? Do they have any disadvantages?
6. Using the "Internet Sites" listed in this chapter and a general Internet search engine (such as www.google.com or www.yahoo.com), research what a PDF file is and what advantages PDFs have over other file formats.

QUESTIONS AND EXERCISES

1. Contact a law office, legal organization, paralegal, or attorney you know and ask what word processor they use and why. Ask what features they like about it, what features they wish they had, whether the program is fulfilling their basic needs, and whether they are looking to change word processors. Also, ask who does word processing at the firm, and if there is a centralized or decentralized system. Type a one-page summary of your conversations.

2. Word processors have developed over time to include hundreds of features and functions. Write a short paper on the top 10 functions or features that you use when you do word processing. Explain what each function is and why you use it.

3. On your own computer, open any word-processing document in your word processor. Point and click on File and then on Properties. What metadata was included in the "Properties" section of the document?

4. In Microsoft Word, open a new document and do the following:

   a. Type the following phrases: This is secret text no one should see. This is text that is open to the public.

   b. Turn on Track Changes by going to "Tools" on the menu bar and then clicking on "Track Changes."

   c. Now, using the delete key, delete the sentence "This is secret text no one should see." Notice that to the right it now shows the text is deleted.

   d. Point and click with your mouse on the down arrow next to "Final Showing Markup" in the "Tracking" item on the Review toolbar. Then click on "Final." Notice that you cannot see "This is secret text no one should see." Assume for the purposes of this exercise that you sent this document to the opposing party in a case.

   e. Now, assume that you are the opposing party in the case. Select the down arrow next to "Final" in the "Tracking" item on the Review toolbar and select "Original." Notice that you can perfectly see "This is secret text no one should see." Point and click with your mouse on the down arrow next to "Original" in the "Final Showing Markup" item on the Review toolbar and select "Original Showing Markup." You can now see all of the changes in the document.

   What confidentiality issues might arise with use of the Track Changes feature? Suggest some ways to avoid these problems.

ETHICS QUESTION

Your firm represents a wife in a divorce case. She wants to know what issues are covered in a separation agreement, so she asks you for a sample of a separation agreement. You do not have a "blank" separation agreement, but your computer contains dozens of examples. What ethical issues are raised by this scenario?

The available CourseMate for this text has an interactive eBook and interactive learning tools, including flash cards, quizzes, and more. To learn more about this resource and access free demo CourseMate resources, go to www.cengagebrain.com, and search for this book. To access CourseMate materials that you have purchased, go to login.cengagebrain.com.

HANDS-ON EXERCISES

> **FEATURED SOFTWARE**
> Microsoft Word 2010
> Microsoft Word 2007
> Adobe Acrobat
> HotDocs

WORD PROCESSING HANDS-ON EXERCISES

 ## *READ THIS FIRST!*

1. Microsoft Word 2010
2. Microsoft Word 2007

I. DETERMINING WHICH TUTORIAL TO COMPLETE

To use the Word Processing Hands-On Exercises, you must already own or have access to Microsoft Word 2010 or Microsoft Word 2007. If you have one of the programs but do not know the version you are using, it is easy to find out (e.g., whether your version is Word 2010, Word 2007, or some other version of Word). For Word 2007, click on the Office button, and then click on "Word Options" and look under the title "Resources." For Word 2010, click on the File tab, then click on "Help." You must know the version of the program you are using and select the correct tutorial version or the tutorials will not work correctly. For example, if you have Word 2010 but try to use the Word 2007 tutorial, the tutorial will not work correctly.

II. USING THE WORD PROCESSING HANDS-ON EXERCISES

The Word Processing Hands-On Exercises in this section are easy to use and contain step-by-step instructions. They start with basic word-processing skills and proceed to intermediate and advanced levels. If you already have a good working knowledge of your word processor, you may be able to proceed directly to the intermediate and advanced exercises. To truly be ready for word processing in a legal environment, you must be able to accomplish the tasks and exercises in the advanced exercises.

III. ACCESSING THE HANDS-ON EXERCISE FILES ON THE DISK THAT COMES WITH THE TEXT

Some of the intermediate and advanced Word Processing Hands-On Exercises use documents on the disk that comes with the text. On some computers, to access the files all you need to do is put the disk in the drive and close the drive; the directory will automatically be loaded. If the directory does not automatically load, follow the directions in this section.

To access these files, put the disk into your computer. Select "Start," then "My Computer"; then select the appropriate drive and double-click on the Word-Processing Files folder. To access the exercise files, double-click on the appropriate folder. You should then see a list of word-processing files that are available for each lesson. These files are also available on the Premium Website. To access them, go to your

CengageBrain account and click on the link for Premium Website for Cornick's Using Computers in the Law Office—Basic. A new window will open. Under Book Level Resources, click the link for Data Files: Word, then click the link to the desired lesson. When prompted, click Open.

IV. INSTALLATION QUESTIONS

If you have installation questions regarding loading the word-processing file from the data disk, you may contact Technical Support at http://cengage.com/support.

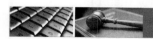 **HANDS-ON EXERCISES**

MICROSOFT WORD 2010 FOR WINDOWS

Number	Lesson Title	Concepts Covered
BASIC LESSONS		
Lesson 1	Typing a Letter	Using word wrap, Tab key, cursor keys, underline, bold, italic, and saving and printing a document.
Lesson 2	Editing a Letter	Retrieving a file, block moving/deleting, and spell/grammar checking.
Lesson 3	Typing a Pleading	Centering, changing margins, changing line spacing, adding a footnote, double indenting, and automatic page numbering.
Lesson 4	Creating a Table	Creating a table, entering data in a table, using automatic numbering, adjusting columns in a table, and using the Table Auto Format command.
INTERMEDIATE LESSONS		
Lesson 5	Tools and Techniques	Editing an employment policy, using the Format Painter tool, revealing formatting, using Beginning of Document command, clearing formatting, changing case, using Search and Replace, using Go To command, creating a section break, and changing the orientation of the page to Landscape.
Lesson 6	Using Styles	Using, modifying, and creating styles to maintain consistent and uniform formatting of documents.
Lesson 7	Creating a Template (office letterhead/letter)	Finding ready-made templates in Word, creating a new office letterhead and letter template, filling in/completing a template, and adding a command to the Quick Access toolbar.
Lesson 8	Comparing Documents (multiple versions of an employment contract)	Comparing documents using the simultaneous viewing method and merging the documents into a separate, annotated, blacklined document.
Lesson 9	Using Track Changes	Turning on Track Changes, making revisions, and then accepting and rejecting revisions.

(continued)

HANDS-ON EXERCISES

Number	Lesson Title	Concepts Covered
ADVANCED LESSONS		
Lesson 10	Creating a Mail Merge Document	Creating and entering a list of recipients for a mail merge, creating a mail merge document, and merging the list with the document.
Lesson 11	Creating a Table of Authorities	Finding and marking cases in a reply brief, and then generating an actual table of authorities for the brief.
Lesson 12	Creating a Macro (pleading signature block)	Creating and executing a pleading signature block macro.
Lesson 13	Drafting a Will	Using Word to draft a will.

GETTING STARTED
Introduction

Throughout these lessons and exercises, information you need to type into the program will be designated in several different ways:

- Keys to be pressed on the keyboard are designated in brackets, in all caps, and in bold (e.g., press the **[ENTER]** key).
- Movements with the mouse pointer are designated in bold and italics (e.g., **point to File and click**).
- Words or letters that should be typed are designated in bold (e.g., type **Training Program**).
- Information that is or should be displayed on your computer screen is shown in bold, with quotation marks (e.g., "**Press ENTER to continue.**").
- Specific menu items and commands are designated with an initial capital letter (e.g., click Open).

OVERVIEW OF MICROSOFT WORD 2010

Here are some tips on using Microsoft Word 2010 that will help you complete these exercises.

I. General Rules for Microsoft Word 2010

A. *Word Wrap.* You do not need to press the **[ENTER]** key after each line of text as you would with a typewriter.

B. *Double-Spacing.* If you want to double-space, do not hit the **[ENTER]** key twice. Instead, change the line spacing by **clicking on the Home Ribbon tab, then clicking on the Line Spacing icon in the Paragraph group and selecting 2.0** (see Word 2010 Exhibit 1).

C. *Moving through Already Entered Text.* If you want to move the mouse pointer to various positions within already entered text, **use the cursor (arrow) keys or point and click.**

D. *Moving the Pointer Where No Text Has Been Entered.* You cannot use the cursor keys to move the pointer where no text has been entered. Said another way, you cannot move any further in a document than where you have typed

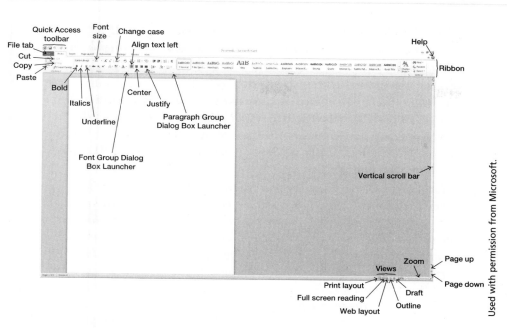

WORD 2010 EXHIBIT 1
Word 2010 screen

Used with permission from Microsoft.

text or pressed the [**ENTER**] key. You must use the [**ENTER**] key or first type text.

E. *Saving a Document.* To save a document, ***click the File tab in the upper left corner of the screen and then click Save*** (see Word 2010 Exhibit 1).

F. *New Document.* To get a new, clean document, ***click the File tab, then click New, and then double-click on "Blank document"*** (see Word 2010 Exhibit 1).

G. *Help.* To get help, press [**F1**] or ***click on the ? icon in the upper right corner of the screen*** (see Word 2010 Exhibit 1).

II. Editing a Document

A. *Pointer Movement*

One space to left	[**LEFT ARROW**]
One space to right	[**RIGHT ARROW**]
Beginning of line	[**HOME**]
End of line	[**END**]
One line up	[**UP ARROW**]
One line down	[**DOWN ARROW**]
One screen up	[**PAGE UP**]
One screen down	[**PAGE DOWN**]
Beginning of document	[**CTRL**]+[**HOME**]
End of document	[**CTRL**]+[**END**]

B. *Deleting Text*

Delete the text under the pointer or to the right	[**DEL**]
Delete the text to the left of the pointer	[**BACKSPACE**]
Delete the whole word to the left of the pointer	[**CTRL**]+[**BACKSPACE**]
Delete the whole word to the right of the pointer	[**CTRL**]+[**DEL**]

C. *Delete Blocked Text.* ***Drag the mouse pointer to select or highlight text,*** and press [**DEL**], or ***drag the mouse pointer and then from the Home Ribbon tab, select the Cut icon from the Clipboard group*** (see Word 2010 Exhibit 1).

HANDS-ON EXERCISES

Another way to select or highlight text is ***to press the [SHIFT] key and keep it depressed while you use the cursor keys to mark/highlight the desired text.***

D. *Undoing/Undeleting Text.* If you delete text and immediately want it back, ***click the Undo icon on the Quick Access toolbar.*** This can also be done by pressing **[CTRL]+[Z]**. Press **[CTRL]+[Z]** or ***click the Undo icon*** until your desired text reappears. The Undo feature works on many other activities in Word, but not all. So, if something goes wrong, at least try pressing **[CTRL]+[Z]** to undo whatever you did.

E. *Moving Text.* ***Drag the mouse pointer to highlight or select the text. Then, from the Home Ribbon tab, select the Cut icon from the Clipboard group*** (see Word 2010 Exhibit 1)***, move the mouse pointer to where the text should be moved, and from the Home Ribbon tab, select Paste from the Clipboard group.*** Another way to do this is to ***drag the mouse pointer to highlight the area and then right-click.*** This brings up a menu that includes the Cut, Copy, and Paste commands. Yet another way to do this is to use the drag-and-drop method: ***Drag the mouse pointer to highlight the area, release the mouse button, click the highlighted area, drag the text to the new location, and release the mouse button.***

F. *Copying Text.* ***Drag the mouse pointer to highlight or select the area. From the Home Ribbon tab, click the Copy icon from the Clipboard group*** (see Word 2010 Exhibit 1). ***Then, move the mouse pointer to where the text should be copied, and from the Home Ribbon tab, click Paste.*** Another way to do this is to use the drag-and-drop method: ***Drag the pointer to highlight the area, release the mouse button, click the highlighted area, drag the text to the new location while pressing [CTRL], and release the mouse button.*** The text is then copied to the new location.

III. Formatting

A. *Centering Text.* ***Move the pointer to the line with the text that should be centered. From the Home Ribbon tab, click the Paragraph Group Dialog Box Launcher icon*** (see Word 2010 Exhibit 1). ***In the Indents and Spacing tab, click on the down arrow key next to Alignment and select Centered, then click on OK and begin typing.*** If the text has already been typed, move the pointer to the paragraph where the text is and then issue the command. Alternatively, ***from the Home Ribbon tab, click the Center icon in the Paragraph group*** (see Word 2010 Exhibit 1).

B. *Bold Type.* To type in bold, ***from the Home Ribbon tab, click the Font Group Dialog Box Launcher icon*** (see Word 2010 Exhibit 1), ***and then, in the Font tab, click Bold under Font Style. Then, click on OK.*** Alternatively, ***from the Home Ribbon tab, click the Bold icon in the Font group.*** Another way is to press **[CTRL]+[B]**.

C. *Underlining.* To underline, ***from the Home Ribbon tab, click the Font Group Dialog Box Launcher icon*** (see Word 2010 Exhibit 1). ***Then, in the Font tab, click the down arrow under Underline style, select the underline style you would like, and then click OK.*** Alternatively, ***from the Home Ribbon tab, click the Underline icon in the Font group.*** Another way is to press **[CTRL]+[U]**.

D. *Margins.* Margins can be set by ***clicking the Page Layout ribbon tab and then clicking on Margins from the Page Setup group.***

E. *Line Spacing.* Line spacing can be changed by **clicking the Home Ribbon tab and then clicking the Line Spacing icon in the Paragraph group** (see Word 2010 Exhibit 1).

F. *Justification.* Move the pointer to the line where the text should be justified. Then, **from the Home Ribbon tab, click the Paragraph Group Dialog Box Launcher icon** (see Word 2010 Exhibit 1). **In the Indents and Spacing tab, click the down arrow key next to Alignment and select Justified; then click on OK and begin typing.** If the text has already been typed, move the cursor to the paragraph where the text is and then issue the command. Alternatively, **from the Home Ribbon tab, click the Justify icon in the Paragraph group** (see Word 2010 Exhibit 1).

G. *Header/Footer.* **From the Insert ribbon tab, click on Header or Footer from the Header & Footer group.**

H. *Hard Page Break.* To force the addition of a new page in the current document by using the Hard Page Break command, press **[CTRL]+[ENTER]** or **from the Insert ribbon tab, click Blank Page from the Pages group.** Page breaks also occur automatically when the current page is full of text.

I. *Indent.* **From the Home Ribbon tab, click the Paragraph Group Dialog Box Launcher icon** (see Word 2010 Exhibit 1). **In the Indents and Spacing tab under Indentation, click the up arrow next to Left or Right to set the indentation amount; then click on OK and begin typing.** Alternatively, **from the Home Ribbon tab, point to the Decrease Indent or Increase Indent icon in the Paragraph group.**

IV. Other Functions

A. *Printing.* To print, **click the File tab and then click Print** (see Word 2010 Exhibit 1).

B. *Spell Check.* To turn on the spell-checking function, **from the Review ribbon tab, click Spelling & Grammar in the Proofing group.** Additionally, a red squiggly line will appear under each word that is not recognized. If you **right-click the word,** the program will suggest possible spellings.

C. *Open Files.* To open a file, **click the File tab then click Open** (see Word 2010 Exhibit 1).

D. *Tables.* **From the Insert ribbon tab, click Table from the Tables group.** You can move between cells in the table by pressing the **[TAB]** and the **[SHIFT]+[TAB]** keys.

▶ BASIC LESSONS

LESSON 1: TYPING A LETTER

This lesson shows you how to type the letter shown in Word 2010 Exhibit 2. It explains how to use the word wrap feature; the **[TAB]** key; the cursor (or arrow) keys; the underline, bold, and italics features; the save document function; and the print document function. Keep in mind that if at any time you make a mistake in this lesson, you may press **[CTRL]+[Z]** to undo what you have done. Also remember that any time you would like to see the name of an icon on the ribbon tabs, just **point to the icon for a second or two** and the name will be displayed.

WORD 2010 EXHIBIT 2
Letter

October 1, 2013

Steven Matthews
Matthews, Smith & Russell
P.O. Box 12341
Boston, MA 59920

Subject: Turner v. Smith
            Case No. CV-13-0046

Dear Mr. Matthews:

In line with our recent conversation, the deposition of the defendant, Jonathan R. Smith, will be taken in your office on **November 15 at 9:00 a.m.** Please find enclosed a *"Notice of Deposition."*

I expect that I will be able to finish this deposition on November 15 and that discovery will be finished, in line with the Court's order, by December 15.

I will be finishing answers to your interrogatories this week and will have them to you by early next week.

If you have any questions, please feel free to contact me.

Kindest regards,

Mirabelle Watkinson
For the Firm

MW:db
Enclosures (as indicated)
cc

1. Open Windows. When it has loaded, *double-click on the Microsoft Office Word 2010 icon on the desktop* to open Word 2010 for Windows. Alternatively, *click the Start button, point to Programs or All Programs, and then click on the Microsoft Word 2010 icon* (or *point to Microsoft Office and then click Microsoft Office Word 2010*). You should now be in a clean, blank document. If you are not in a blank document, *click the File tab, click New, and then double-click Blank document.*

2. At this point you cannot move the pointer around the screen by pushing the cursor keys (also called arrow keys). Text must first be entered before the pointer can be moved using the cursor keys. The pointer can only move through text. *On the Home Ribbon tab, click the Paragraph Group Dialog Box Launcher. In the "Paragraph" window, click the down arrow below "Line spacing" and select "Single." Make sure the "Before" and "After" spacing are both 0 point. Then, click OK.*

3. Press the [ENTER] key four times. (Watch the status line in the lower left-hand corner of the screen, which tells you what page of your document you are on.)

4. Type the date of the letter as shown in Word 2010 Exhibit 2. Notice as you type the word "October" that Auto Text may anticipate that you are typing "October" and give you the following prompt: **"October (Press ENTER to Insert)."** You can either press the **[ENTER]** key and let Auto Text finish typing the word for you, or you can ignore it and continue typing the word yourself.

5. Press the **[ENTER]** key three times.

6. Type the inside address as shown in Word 2010 Exhibit 2. Press the **[ENTER]** key after each line of the inside address. When you finish the line with "Boston, MA 59920," press the **[ENTER]** key three times.

7. Press the **[TAB]** key one time. (Word automatically sets default tabs every five spaces.) The pointer will move five spaces to the right.

8. Type **Subject:** and then press the **[TAB]** key. *On the Home Ribbon tab, click on the Underline icon in the Font group* (it looks like a "U"). Alternatively, you can press **[CTRL]+[U]** to turn the underline feature on and off, or *point to the Font Group Dialog Box Launcher* (see Word 2010 Exhibit 1) and select the Underline style. Then, type **Turner v. Smith**. *On the Home Ribbon tab in the Font group, click the Underline icon* to turn the underline feature off.

9. Press the **[ENTER]** key one time.

10. Press the **[TAB]** key three times and then type **Case No. CV-13-0046.**

11. Press the **[ENTER]** key three times.

12. Type the salutation **Dear Mr. Matthews:**

13. Press the **[ENTER]** key twice.

14. Type **In line with our recent conversation, the deposition of the defendant, Jonathan R. Smith, will be taken in your office on.** *Note:* You should not press the **[ENTER]** key at the end of the line. Word will automatically "wrap" the text down to the next line. Be sure to press the **[SPACEBAR]** once after the word "on."

15. *Turn on the Bold feature by clicking the Bold icon* (a capital "B") *in the Font group in the Home Ribbon tab* (see Word 2010 Exhibit 1). Alternatively, you can press **[CTRL]+[B]** to turn bold on and off. Type **November 15 at 9:00 a.m.** Turn off the Bold feature either by pressing **[CTRL]+[B]**, or by *clicking the Bold icon in the Font group in the Home Ribbon tab.* Press the **[SPACEBAR]** twice.

16. Type **Please find enclosed a** and then press **[SPACEBAR]**.

17. *Turn on the Italics feature by clicking the Italics icon* (it looks like an "I") *in the Font group in the Home Ribbon tab* (see Word 2010 Exhibit 1). Alternatively, you can press **[CTRL]+[I]** to turn italics on and off. Type **Notice to Take Deposition.** Turn off the Italics feature either by pressing **[CTRL]+[I]** or by *clicking the Italics icon in the Font group in the Home Ribbon tab.*

18. Press the **[ENTER]** key twice.

19. Type the second paragraph of the letter and then press the **[ENTER]** key twice.

20. Type the third paragraph of the letter and then press the **[ENTER]** key twice.

21. Type the fourth paragraph of the letter and then press the **[ENTER]** key twice.

22. Type **Kindest regards,** and then press the **[ENTER]** key four times.

23. Type **Mirabelle Watkinson** and then press the **[ENTER]** key.

24. Type **For the Firm** and then press the **[ENTER]** key twice.

25. Finish the letter by typing the author's initials, enclosures, and copy abbreviation (cc) as shown in Word 2010 Exhibit 2.

HANDS-ON EXERCISES

26. To print the document, **click the File tab, click Print, and then click on Print.**

27. To save the document, **click the File tab and then click Save.** Then, type **Letter1** next to **"File Name."** **Click Save** to save the letter to the default directory. (*Note:* In Lesson 2, you will edit this letter, so it is important that you save it.)

28. **Click the File tab and then click Close** to close the document, or to exit Word 2010, **click the File tab and then click Exit** to exit the program.

This concludes Lesson 1.

LESSON 2: EDITING A LETTER

This lesson shows you how to retrieve and edit the letter you typed in Lesson 1. It explains how to retrieve a file, perform block moves and deletes, and spell-/grammar-check your document. Keep in mind that if at any time you make a mistake in this lesson, you may press **[CTRL]+[Z]** to undo what you have done. Also remember that any time you would like to see the name of an icon on the Ribbon tab, just **point to the icon for a second or two** and the name will be displayed.

1. Open Windows. When it has loaded, **double-click on the Microsoft Office Word 2010 icon on the desktop** to open Word 2010 for Windows. Alternatively, **click the Start button, point to Programs or All Programs, and then click on the Microsoft Word 2010 icon** (or **point to Microsoft Office and then click Microsoft Office Word 2010**). You should now be in a clean, blank document. If you are not in a blank document, **click the File tab, click New, and then double-click Blank document.**

2. In this lesson, you will begin by retrieving the document you created in Lesson 1. To open the file, **click the File tab and click Open.** Then type **Letter1** and **click Open.** Alternatively, **scroll using the horizontal scroll bar until you find the file, click on it, and then click Open.**

3. Notice in Word 2010 Exhibit 3 that some changes have been made to the letter. You will spend the rest of this lesson making these changes.

4. Use your cursor keys or mouse to go to the salutation line, "Dear Mr. Matthews:" With the pointer to the left of the "M" in "Mr. Matthews," press the **[DEL]** key 12 times until "Mr. Matthews" is deleted.

5. Type **Steve**. The salutation line should now read "Dear Steve:"

WORD 2010 EXHIBIT 3
Corrections to a letter

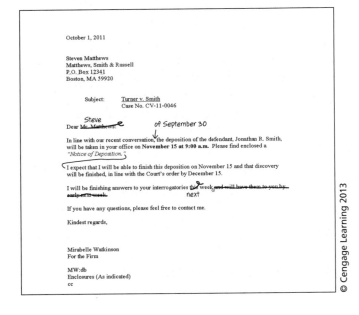

6. Using your cursor keys or mouse, *move the pointer to the left of the comma following the word "conversation" in the first paragraph.* Press the **[SPACEBAR]**, then type **of September 30**. The sentence now reads:

   In line with our recent conversation of September 30, the deposition of the defendant ...

7. The next change you will make is to move the second paragraph so that it becomes part of the first paragraph. Although this can be accomplished in more than one way, this lesson uses the Cut command.

8. Using your cursor keys or mouse, *move the pointer to the beginning of the second paragraph of Word 2010 Exhibit 2.*

9. *Click and drag the mouse pointer* (hold the left mouse button down, and move the mouse) *until the entire second paragraph is highlighted, and then release the mouse button.*

10. *From the Home Ribbon tab, click the Cut icon in the Clipboard group* (see Word 2010 Exhibit 1). An alternative is to right-click anywhere in the highlighted area, and then *click Cut.* The text is no longer on the screen, but it is not deleted—it has been temporarily placed on the Office Clipboard.

11. Move the pointer to the end of the first paragraph. Press the **[SPACEBAR]** twice. If the pointer appears to be in italics mode, *from the Home Ribbon tab, click the Italics icon in the Font group,* or press **[CTLR]+[I]** to turn the Italics feature off.

12. *From the Home Ribbon tab, click Paste from the Clipboard group* (see Word 2010 Exhibit 1). Notice that the text has now been moved. Also, you may notice that a small icon in the shape of a clipboard has appeared where you pasted the text. *Click the down arrow of the Paste Options icon.* Notice that you are given the option to keep the source formatting or change the formatting so that the text matches the destination formatting (i.e., the formatting of the place you are copying it to). In this example, both formats are the same, so it does not matter, but if the text you are copying is a different format, you may or may not want to change it to the destination format. Press the **[ESC]** key to make the Paste Options menu disappear.

13. Move the pointer to the line below the newly expanded first paragraph, and use the **[DEL]** key to delete any unnecessary blank lines.

14. Using your cursor keys or mouse, *move the pointer to what is now the second paragraph and place it to the left of the "t" in "this week."*

15. Use the **[DEL]** key to delete the word **"this,"** and then type **next**.

16. We will now delete the rest of the sentence in the second paragraph. *Drag the pointer until* "**and will have them to you by early next week.**" *is highlighted.* Press the **[DEL]** key. Type a period at the end of the sentence.

17. You have now made all of the changes that need to be made. To be sure the letter does not have misspelled words or grammar errors, we will use the Spelling and Grammar command.

18. *Click on the Review Ribbon tab and then click Spelling & Grammar in the Proofing group.*

19. If an error is found, it will be highlighted. You have the choice of ignoring it once, ignoring it completely, accepting one of the suggestions listed, or changing or correcting the problem yourself. Correct any spelling or grammar errors. When the spell and grammar check is done, *click OK.*

20. To print the document, *click on the File tab, click Print, and then click on Print.*

HANDS-ON EXERCISES

21. To save the document, ***click the File tab and then select Save As.*** Type **Letter2** in the "File name" box, ***and then click Save*** to save the document in the default directory.

22. ***Click the File tab and then click Close*** to close the document, or ***click the File tab and then click Exit*** to exit the program.

This concludes Lesson 2.

LESSON 3: TYPING A PLEADING

This lesson shows you how to type a pleading, as shown in Word 2010 Exhibit 4. It expands on the items presented in Lessons 1 and 2. It also explains how to center

WORD 2010 EXHIBIT 4
A pleading

IN THE DISTRICT COURT OF
ORANGE COUNTY, MASSACHUSETTS

JIM TURNER,

        Plaintiff,

vs.   Case No. CV-13-0046

JONATHAN R. SMITH,

        Defendant.

<u>NOTICE TO TAKE DEPOSITION</u>

COMES NOW the plaintiff and pursuant to statute[1] hereby gives notice that the

deposition of Defendant, Jonathan R. Smith, will be taken as follows:

      Monday, November 15, 2013, at 9:00 a.m. at the law offices of Matthews,

      Smith & Russell, 17031 W. 69th Street, Boston, MA.

Said deposition will be taken before a court reporter and is not expected to take more than

one day in duration.

_____
Mirabelle Watkinson
Attorney for Plaintiff

_____
[1] Massachusetts Statutes Annotated 60-2342(a)(1).

---

text, change margins, change line spacing, add a footnote, double-indent text, and use automatic page numbering. Keep in mind that if at any time you make a mistake, you may press **[CTRL]+[Z]** to undo what you have done.

1. Open Windows. When it has loaded, ***double-click the Microsoft Office Word 2010 icon on the desktop*** to open Word 2010 for Windows. Alternatively, ***click the Start button, point to Programs or All Programs, and then click the Microsoft Word 2010 icon*** (or ***point to Microsoft Office and then click Microsoft Office Word 2010***). You should now be in a clean, blank document. If you are not in a blank document, ***click the File tab, click New, and then double-click on Blank document.*** Remember, any time you would like to see the name of an icon on the ribbon tabs, just ***point to the icon for a second or two*** and the name will be displayed.

2. You will be creating the document shown in Word 2010 Exhibit 4. The first thing you will need to do is to change the margins so that the left margin is 1.5 inches and the right margin is 1 inch. To change the margins, ***click the Page Layout ribbon tab and then click Margins in the Page Setup group. Next, click Custom Margins at the bottom of the drop-down menu. In the Page Setup window, change the left margin to 1.5 inches and the right margin to 1 inch. Then, click OK.*** Also, ***on the Home Ribbon tab, click the Paragraph Group Dialog Box Launcher. In the "Paragraph" window, click the down arrow below Line Spacing and select Single. Make sure the Before and After spacing are both 0 point. Then, click OK.***

3. Notice in Word 2010 Exhibit 4 that there is a page number at the bottom of the page. Word will automatically number your pages for you.

4. ***Click the Insert ribbon tab, and then click Page Number in the Header & Footer group*** (see Word 2010 Exhibit 5).

5. ***Next, point to Bottom of Page*** (see Word 2010 Exhibit 5) and notice that a number of options are displayed. ***Click the down arrow in the lower right*** for additional options (see Word 2010 Exhibit 5). Notice that many page-number options are available. ***Scroll back up to the top of the option list and click the second option, Plain Number 2.***

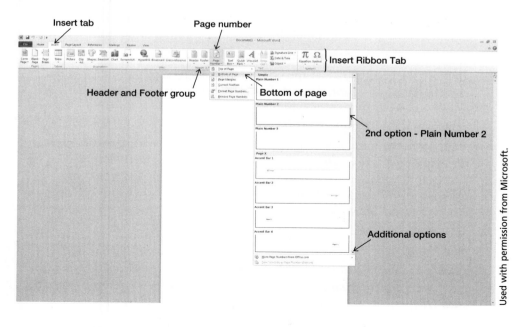

Insert tab   Page number

Insert Ribbon Tab

Header and Footer group   Bottom of page

2nd option - Plain Number 2

Additional options

WORD 2010 EXHIBIT 5
Adding a page number

HANDS-ON EXERCISES

6. Your pointer should now be in the area marked "Footer." Specifically, your pointer should be to the left of the number 1. Type **Page** and then press **[SPACEBAR]**.

7. *Click the Home Ribbon tab. Then, click the vertical scroll bar* (see Word 2010 Exhibit 1) *or use the [UP ARROW] key to go back to the beginning of the document.*

8. *Double-click just below the header.*

9. On the first line of the document, *from the Home Ribbon tab, click the Center icon in the Paragraph group.* Type **IN THE DISTRICT COURT OF**. Press the **[ENTER]** key. Type **ORANGE COUNTY, MASSACHUSETTS.**

10. Press the **[ENTER]** key five times. *From the Home Ribbon tab, click the Align Text Left icon in the Paragraph group.*

11. Type **JIM TURNER,** and press the **[ENTER]** key twice.

12. Press the **[TAB]** key three times and type **Plaintiff,** then press the **[ENTER]** key twice.

13. Type **vs.** Then, press the **[TAB]** key six times, and type **Case No. CV-13-0046**.

14. Press the **[ENTER]** key twice.

15. Type **JONATHAN R. SMITH,** and press the **[ENTER]** key twice.

16. Press the **[TAB]** key three times and type **Defendant.** Press the **[ENTER]** key four times.

17. *From the Home Ribbon tab, click the Center icon in the Paragraph group.*

18. *From the Home Ribbon tab, click the Bold icon and the Underline icon, both found in the Font group.* Type **NOTICE TO TAKE DEPOSITION**. *Click the Bold and Underline icons* to turn them off.

19. Press the **[ENTER]** key three times. *From the Home Ribbon tab, click the Align Text Left icon in the Paragraph group.*

20. *From the Home Ribbon tab, click the Line Spacing icon from the Paragraph group* (see Word 2010 Exhibit 1), *and then click on 2.0.* This will change the line spacing from single to double.

21. Type **COMES NOW the plaintiff and pursuant to statute**. Notice that a footnote follows the word *statute* in Word 2010 Exhibit 4.

22. With the pointer just to the right of the "e" in "statute," *from the References Ribbon tab, click Insert Footnote from the Footnotes group.* The cursor should now be at the bottom of the page in the footnote window.

23. Type **Massachusetts Statutes Annotated 60-2342(a)(1).**

24. To move the pointer back to the body of the document, simply *click to the right of the word "statute" (and the superscript number 1) in the body of the document.* Now, continue to type the rest of the first paragraph. Once the paragraph is typed, press the **[ENTER]** key twice.

25. To double-indent the second paragraph, *from the Home Ribbon tab, click the Paragraph Group Dialog Box Launcher* (see Word 2010 Exhibit 1). The "Paragraph" window should now be displayed. *Under Indentation, add a 0.5" left indent and a 0.5" right indent using the up arrow icons* (or you can type it in). *Click OK in the "Paragraph" window.*

26. Type the second paragraph.

27. Press the **[ENTER]** key twice.

28. *From the Home Ribbon tab, click the Paragraph Group Dialog Box Launcher and, under Indentation, change the left and right indents back to 0. Then, click OK.*

29. Type the third paragraph.

30. Press the **[ENTER]** key three times.

31. The signature line is single spaced, so *from the Home Ribbon tab, click the Line Spacing icon from the Paragraph group, and then click 1.0.* This will change the line spacing from double to single.

32. Press **[SHIFT]+[-]** (the key to the right of the zero key on the keyboard) 30 times to draw the signature line. Press the **[ENTER]** key. *Note*: If Word automatically inserts a line across the whole page, press **[CTRL]+[Z]** to undo the Auto Correct line. Alternatively, you can *click the down arrow in the Auto Correct Options icon* (it looks like a lightning bolt and should be just over the line that now runs across the page) and *select Undo Border Line.*

33. Type **Mirabelle Watkinson**, and then press the **[ENTER]** key.

34. Type **Attorney for Plaintiff**.

35. To print the document, *click the File tab, click Print, and then click Print.*

36. To save the document, *click the File tab and then select Save As.* Type **Pleading1** in the "File name" box *and then click Save* to save the document in the default directory.

37. *Click the File tab and then Close* to close the document, or *click the File tab, and then Exit* to exit the program.

This concludes Lesson 3.

LESSON 4: CREATING A TABLE

This lesson shows you how to create the table shown in Word 2010 Exhibit 6. It expands on the items presented in Lessons 1, 2, and 3 and explains how to change a font size, create a table, enter data into a table, add automatic numbering, adjust column widths, and use the Table AutoFormat command. Keep in mind that if at any time you make a mistake, you may press **[CTRL]+[Z]** to undo what you have done.

1. Open Windows. When it has loaded, *double-click the Microsoft Office Word 2010 icon on the desktop* to open Word 2010 for Windows. Alternatively, *click the Start button, point to Programs or All Programs, and then click the Microsoft Word 2010 icon* (or *point to Microsoft Office and then click on Microsoft Office Word 2010*). You should be in a clean, blank document.

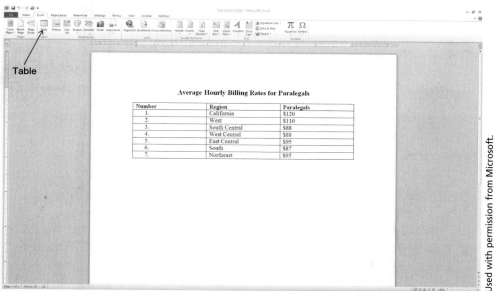

WORD 2010 EXHIBIT 6
Creating a table

Used with permission from Microsoft.

If you are not in a blank document, *click the File tab, click New, and then double-click Blank document.*

2. *From the Home Ribbon tab, click the Center icon in the Paragraph group, and then click the Bold icon in the Font group.*

3. *From the Home Ribbon tab, click the Font Size icon in the Font group* and change the font size to 14 either by typing **14** in the box or by *choosing 14 from the drop-down menu.* Alternatively, you can both turn on bold and change the font size by *clicking the Font Group Dialog Box Launcher from the Home Ribbon tab* (see Word 2010 Exhibit 1).

4. Type **Average Hourly Billing Rates for Paralegals** (see Word 2010 Exhibit 6). Press the **[ENTER]** key once, and then *click the Font Size icon and change the type back to 12 point. Click the Bold icon* to turn bold off.

5. Press the **[ENTER]** key once.

6. *From the Insert Ribbon tab, click Table.* Notice that a number of columns and rows of boxes are displayed. This allows you to graphically depict your table.

7. *Point within the Table menu so that three columns are highlighted, and then point and click so that eight rows are highlighted* (e.g., 3 x 8 Table). Notice that as you point, the table is temporarily shown in your document. This is called a *live preview.* When you click on the cell that is three columns over and eight cells down, the table (as opposed to the live preview) will be displayed permanently in your document.

8. The blank table should now be displayed and the cursor should be in the first column of the first row of the table. *If the cursor is not in the first column of the first row, click in this cell to place the cursor there. Click on the Bold icon on the Home Ribbon tab.* Type **Number** and then press the **[TAB]** key once to go to the next cell in the table.

9. *Click on the Bold icon.* Type **Region** and then press the **[TAB]** key once to go to the next cell in the table. (*Note*: If you need to go back to a previous cell, you can either use the mouse or the cursor keys, or you can press **[SHIFT]+[TAB]**. Also, if you accidentally hit the **[ENTER]** key instead of the **[TAB]** key, you can either press the **[BACKSPACE]** key to delete the extra line, or you can press **[CTRL]+[Z]** to undo it.

10. *Click on the Bold icon.* Type **Paralegals** and then press the **[TAB]** key to go to the next cell.

11. We will now use the automatic paragraph numbering feature to number our rows. *From the Home Ribbon tab, click on the Numbering icon in the Paragraph group* (see Word 2010 Exhibit 1—it is the icon that has the numbers 1, 2, 3 in a column, with a short line next to each number). Notice that the number 1 was automatically entered in the cell. *From the Home Ribbon tab, point on the down arrow next to the Numbering icon in the Paragraph group.* Under Numbering Library, look at the different formats that are available. The default format is fine, so press **[ESC]** to make the menu disappear.

12. Press the **[TAB]** key to go to the next cell.

13. Type **California** and then press the **[TAB]** key to go to the next cell.

14. Type **$120** and then press the **[TAB]** key to go to the next cell.

15. *From the Home Ribbon tab, click on the Numbering icon in the Paragraph group,* and then press the **[TAB]** key to go to the next cell.

16. Continue entering all of the information shown in Word 2010 Exhibit 6 into your table.

17. ***Put the pointer in the uppermost left cell of the table and drag the pointer to the lowest cell at the right of the table to completely highlight the table. Then, from the Home Ribbon tab, click on the Align Text Left icon in the Paragraph group.*** Now the whole table is left aligned.

18. ***Put the pointer on the vertical column line that separates the Number column and the Region column, and then drag the line to the left*** (see Word 2010 Exhibit 6). Notice that by using this technique you can completely adjust each column width as much as you like. Press **[CTRL]+[Z]** to undo the column move, because the current format is fine.

19. ***Click on any cell in the table.*** Notice that just above the Ribbon tab, new options are now shown; under the new heading Table Tools, two more tabs (Design and Layout) appear. ***Click on the Design Ribbon tab.*** Notice that the Ribbon tab now shows six table styles. ***Point (don't click) on one of the tables;*** notice that the Live Preview feature shows you exactly what your table will look like with this design. ***Click on the down arrow in the Table Styles group*** and browse to see many more table styles. ***Click on a table style that you like.*** The format of the table has been completely changed.

20. To print the document, ***click on the File tab, click on Print, and then click on Print.***

21. ***To save the document, click on the File tab and then select Save As.*** Type **Table1** in the "File name" box, ***and then click on Save*** to save the document in the default directory.

22. ***Click on the File tab and then on Close*** to close the document, or ***click on the File tab and then on Exit*** to exit the program.

This concludes Lesson 4.

▶ INTERMEDIATE LESSONS

LESSON 5: TOOLS AND TECHNIQUES

This lesson shows you how to edit an employment policy (from the data disk supplied with this text), use the Format Painter tool, reveal formatting, clear formatting, change the case of text, use the Find and Replace feature, use the Go To command, create a section break, and change the orientation of a page from Portrait to Landscape. This lesson assumes that you have completed Lessons 1 through 4 and that you are generally familiar with Word 2010.

1. Open Windows. When it has loaded, ***double-click on the Microsoft Office Word 2010 icon on the desktop*** to open Word 2010 for Windows. Alternatively, ***click on the Start button, point the pointer to Programs or All Programs, and then click on the Microsoft Word 2010 icon*** (or ***point to Microsoft Office and then click on Microsoft Office Word 2010***). You should be in a clean, blank document. If you are not in a blank document, ***click on the File tab, click on New, and then double-click on Blank document.***

2. The first thing you will do is to open the "Lesson 5" file from the disk supplied with this text. Ensure that the disk is inserted in the disk drive, ***click on the File tab, and then click on Open.*** The "Open" window should now be displayed. ***Click on the down arrow to the right of the white box next to*** "Look in:" ***and select the drive where the disk is located. Double-click on the***

Word-Processing Files folder. Double-click on the Word 2010 folder. Double-click on the "Lesson 5" file.

3. The file entitled "World Wide Technology, Inc. alcohol and drug policy" should now be displayed on your screen. In this lesson, you will be editing this policy for use by another client. The next thing you need to do is to go to section 3, "Definitions," and change the subheadings so that they have all have the same format. You will use the Format Painter tool to do this.

4. Use the cursor keys or the mouse and the horizontal scroll bars to scroll to section 3, "Definitions" (see Word 2010 Exhibit 7). Notice that the first definition, "Alcohol or alcoholic beverages," is bold and in a different font from the rest of the definitions in section 3. You will use the Format Painter feature to quickly copy the formatting from "Alcohol or alcoholic beverages" to the other four definitions in section 3.

5. *Click anywhere in the text* **"Alcohol or alcoholic beverages:"** This tells the Format Painter feature the formatting you want to copy.

6. *From the Home Ribbon tab, click on the Format Painter icon in the Clipboard group.* It looks like a paintbrush (see Word 2010 Exhibit 7.) Remember, if you hover your mouse pointer over an icon for a second or two, the name of the icon will appear.

7. Notice that your mouse pointer now turns to a paintbrush. *Drag the pointer* (hold the left mouse button down and move the mouse) *until the heading* **"Legal drugs:"** *is highlighted* (see Word 2010 Exhibit 7), *and then let go of the mouse button.* Notice that the paintbrush on your cursor is now gone. *Click the left mouse button once anywhere in the screen to make the highlight go away.* Notice that **"Legal drugs"** now has the same formatting as **"Alcohol or alcoholic beverages."** The Format Painter command is a quick way to make formatting changes.

8. You will now use the Format Painter command to copy the formatting to the remaining three definitions, with one additional trick. *Click anywhere in the text* **"Legal drugs."**

9. Next, *from the Home Ribbon tab, double-click on the Format Painter icon in the Clipboard group.* (Your pointer should now have a paintbrush attached

WORD 2010 EXHIBIT 7
The Format Painter tool

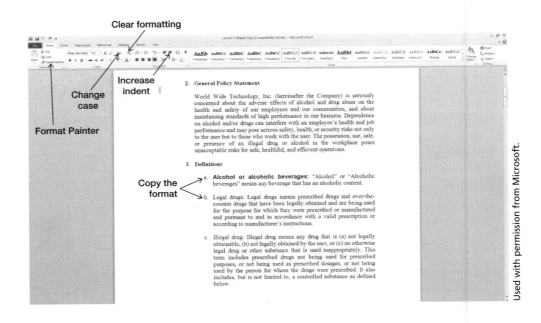

to it.) The double-click tells Format Painter that you are going to copy this format to multiple locations, instead of just one location. This is a great time-saving feature if you need to copy formatting to several places, because it keeps you from having to click the Format Painter icon each time you copy the same formatting to a new location.

10. *Drag the pointer until the heading* "**Illegal drug:**" *is highlighted, and then let go of the mouse button.* Notice that the paintbrush is still attached to your pointer.

11. *Drag the pointer until the heading* "**Controlled substance:**" *is highlighted, and then let go of the mouse button.*

12. *Drag the pointer until the heading* "**Prescription drug:**" *is highlighted, and then let go of the mouse button.*

13. To turn the Format Painter off, press the **[ESC]** button on the keyboard. *Click the left mouse button once anywhere in the document to make the highlight go away.* Notice that all of the headings are now uniform.

14. You will now learn to use the Reveal Formatting command. *Click on the heading* "**Prescription drug:**"

15. Press **[SHIFT]+[F1]** on the keyboard. Notice that the Reveal Formatting task pane has opened on the right side of the screen. The Reveal Formatting task pane lists all format specifications for the selected text. The items are divided into several groups, including Font, Paragraph, Bullets and Numbering, and Section. You can make formatting changes to the text directly from the Reveal Formatting task pane by simply clicking on the format setting you want to change (the links are shown in blue, underlined text). For example, *click on the blue underlined word* "**Font**" *in the Reveal Formatting task pane.* Notice that the "Font" window opens. You can now select a new font if you so desire. The Reveal Formatting task pane allows you to quickly see all formatting attached to specific text and, if necessary, to change it.

16. *Click on Cancel in the Font window.* To close the Reveal Formatting task pane, *click on the "x" (the Close button) at the top of the Reveal Formatting task pane.* It is just to the right of the words "**Reveal Formatting.**" The Reveal Formatting task pane should now be gone.

17. Press **[CTRL]+[HOME]** to go to the beginning of the document.

18. You will now learn how to use the Clear Formats command. Notice under the heading "**1. Objectives**" that the sentence "**The objectives of this policy are as follows:**" is in bold and italics; this is a mistake. *Drag the pointer until this text is highlighted.*

19. *From the Home Ribbon tab, click on the Clear Formatting icon in the Font group* (see Word 2010 Exhibit 7). This icon looks like an eraser next to a capital "A" and a lowercase "a". *Click the left mouse button once anywhere in the sentence to make the highlight go away.* Notice that all of the formatting is now gone. The Clear Formats command is a good way to remove all text formatting quickly and easily.

20. To move the text to the right so it is under "**1. Objectives,**" *from the Home Ribbon tab, click three times on the Increase Indent icon in the Paragraph group* (see Word 2010 Exhibit 7). This is the icon with a right arrow and some lines on it. The line should now be back in its place.

21. You will now learn how to use the Change Case command. Press **[CTRL]+[HOME]** on the keyboard to go to the beginning of the document.

22. *Drag the pointer until* "**World Wide Technology, Inc.**" *in the document's title is highlighted.*

23. *From the Home Ribbon tab, click on the Change Case icon in the Font group. Click on UPPERCASE.* Notice that the text is now in all capitals. *Click anywhere in the document to make the highlighting disappear.*

24. *Drag the pointer until the subtitle* "alcohol and drug policy" *is highlighted. From the Home Ribbon tab, click on the Change Case icon in the Font group. Click on* "Capitalize Each Word." Notice that the text is now in title case. *Click the left mouse button once anywhere in the document to make the highlighting go away.* The Change Case command is a convenient way to change the case of text without having to retype it.

25. Notice that the "*A*" in *and* in **"Alcohol And Drug Policy"** is now capitalized, and that a green squiggly line is underneath the word "And". This tells you that Word believes there is a grammar error. *Point and right-click on the word "And" in the title. A menu will be displayed. Click on* "**and**" (this is what Word is suggesting the correction should be). The word **"and"** in the title is now lower case.

26. Press **[CTRL]+[HOME]** on the keyboard to go to the beginning of the document.

27. You will now learn how to use the Find and Replace command. *From the Home Ribbon tab, click on the Replace icon in the Editing group.* Alternatively, you could press **[CTRL]+[H],** and then click on Replace.

28. In the "Find and Replace" window, in the white box next to **"Find what,"** type **World Wide Technology, Inc.** Then, in the white box next to **"Replace with,"** type **Johnson Manufacturing.** *Now, click on the Replace All button in the "Find and Replace" window.* The program will respond by stating that it made four replacements. *Click on OK.*

29. *Click on the Close button in the "Find and Replace" window to close the window.* Notice that World Wide Technology, Inc. has now been changed to Johnson Manufacturing.

30. You will now learn how to use the Go To command. The Go To command is an easy way to navigate through large and complex documents. Press **[F5].** Notice that the "Find and Replace" window is again displayed on the screen, but this time the Go To tab is selected. In the white box directly under **"Enter page number,"** type **7** from the keyboard and then *click on Go To in the Find and Replace window.* Notice that page 7, "REASONABLE SUSPICION REPORT," is now displayed. (*Note:* If the "Find and Replace" window blocks your ability to see the text of the document, point at the blue box in the "Find and Replace" window and drag the window lower so you can see the document text). *Click on Close in the "Find and Replace" window.*

31. Suppose that you would like to change the orientation of only one page in a document from Portrait (where the length is greater than the width) to Landscape (where the width is greater than the length). In this example, you will change the layout of only the REASONABLE SUSPICION REPORT to Landscape while keeping the rest of the document in Portrait orientation. To do this in Word, you must enter a section break.

32. Your cursor should be on page 7 just above **"Johnson Manufacturing REASONABLE SUSPICION REPORT."** *From the Page Layout ribbon tab, click on Breaks in the Page Setup group.*

33. *Under Section Breaks, click on Next Page.*

34. In the lower right of the screen, *click on the Draft icon* (see Word 2010 Exhibit 7). Press the **[UP ARROW]** key two times. Notice that a double-dotted line that says **"Section Break (Next Page)"** is now displayed.

35. The Word 2010 interface allows you to switch views by clicking on one of the view layouts in the lower right of the screen (see Word 2010 Exhibit 7). Print and Draft are two of the most popular layouts. In addition, the Zoom tool just to the right of the Draft view allows you to zoom in or out of your document.

36. With the section break in place, you can now change the format of the page from Portrait to Landscape without changing the orientation of previous pages.

37. *With the cursor on the* "**Johnson Manufacturing REASONABLE SUSPICION REPORT**" *page, from the Page Layout ribbon tab, click on Orientation in the Page Setup group. Click on Landscape.* Notice that the layout of the page has changed.

38. *Click on the Print Layout icon in the lower right of the screen* (see Word 2010 Exhibit 7).

39. To confirm that the layout has changed, *click on the File tab, then point to Print.* On the left side of the screen you can see that the layout is now Landscape (the width is greater than the length). Press the **[PAGE UP]** key until you are back to the beginning of the document. Notice that all of the other pages in the document are still in Portrait orientation.

40. To print the document, *click on the File tab, click on Print, and then click on Print.*

41. To save the document, *click on the File tab, click Save As, and then click on "Word 97-2003 Document." Under Save in, select the drive or folder* you would like to save the document in. Then, next to File Name, type **Done— Word 2010 Lesson 5 Document** and *click on Save* to save the document.

42. *Click on the File tab, and then click on Close* to close the document, or *click on the File tab, and then on Exit* to exit the program.

This concludes Lesson 5.

LESSON 6: USING STYLES

This lesson gives you an introduction to styles. Styles are particularly helpful when you are working with long documents that must be formatted uniformly.

1. Open Windows. When it has loaded, *double-click on the Microsoft Office Word 2010 icon on the desktop* to open Word 2010 for Windows. Alternatively, *click on the Start button, point to Programs or All Programs, and then click on the Microsoft Word 2010 icon* (or *point to Microsoft Office and then click on Microsoft Office Word 2010*). You should now be in a clean, blank document. If you are not in a blank document, *click on the File tab, click on New, and then double-click on Blank document.*

2. The first thing you will do is to open the "Lesson 6" file from the disk supplied with this text. Ensure that the disk is inserted in the drive, *click on the File tab, and then click on Open.* The "Open" window should now be displayed. *Click on the down arrow to the right of the white box next to Look in: and select the drive where the disk is located. Double-click on the Word-Processing File folder. Double-click on the Word 2010 folder. Double-click on the "Lesson 6" file.*

3. The text "SARBANES-OXLEY ACT OF 2002" should now be displayed on your screen (see Word 2010 Exhibit 8). In this lesson you will use styles to add uniform formatting to this document. In the Home Ribbon tab, notice the Styles group. *Click on any text on the page.* Notice in the Styles group on the Home Ribbon tab that the "Normal" box is highlighted in yellow (see Word 2010 Exhibit 8). Currently, all text in the document is in the Normal style.

WORD 2010 EXHIBIT 8
Styles

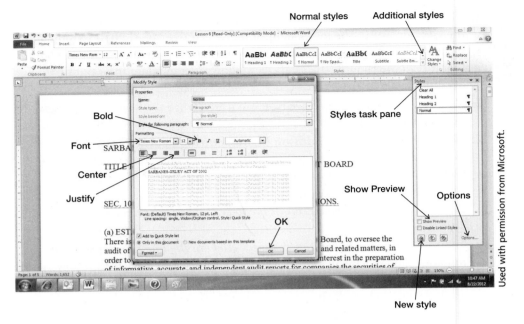

4. Using your cursor keys or the horizontal scroll bar, scroll down through the document. Notice that all of the paragraphs are left-aligned and that the right edge of all the paragraphs is jagged (e.g., not justified).

5. *From the Home Ribbon tab, click on the Styles Group Dialog Box Launcher.* Notice that the Styles task pane now appears on the right side of the screen (see Word 2010 Exhibit 8). In the Styles task pane, *if the white box next to "Show Preview" is not marked, click on the box so a green check mark appears* (see Word 2010 Exhibit 8). Notice that a few styles in the Styles task pane are currently being displayed (e.g., Heading 1, Heading 2, and Normal). Also notice that the Normal style has a blue box around it, indicating that your cursor is on text with the Normal style. Finally, notice that there is a paragraph sign after each of these heading names, indicating that these are paragraph styles.

6. Notice at the bottom of the Styles task pane the word "**Options**" in blue; *click on Options.* The "Styles Pane Options" window should now be displayed.

7. *In the "Styles Pane Options" window, under Select styles to show, click the down arrow next to In current document and click on All styles. Then, in the "Styles Pane Options" window, click on OK.*

8. Notice that the Styles task pane is now full of additional styles. These are all of the styles that are automatically available in Word 2010. *Click on the down arrow in the Styles task pane* to see the full list of styles.

9. To return to the list of just a few styles, *click on Options in the lower right of the Styles task pan. Under Select styles to show, click on the down arrow and click on In current document. Then, in the "Styles Pane Options" window, click on OK.*

10. Notice that the short list of styles is again displayed. To access a longer list of styles from the Styles group on the Home Ribbon tab, *click on the down arrow in the Styles group.* If you select the More icon (the icon that shows a down arrow with a line over it) in the Styles group, you can see all of the styles at one time. Press the **[ESC]** key to close the list.

11. Styles are extremely useful. Assume now that you would like to have all of the text in the document justified. *Point and right-click on Normal in the Styles task pane. Then, point and left-click on Modify.* The "Modify Style" window

should now be displayed (see Word 2010 Exhibit 8). Using the "Modify Style" window, you can completely change the formatting for any style.

12. ***Click on the Justify icon in the "Modify Style" window to change the Normal style from left-aligned to fully justified*** (see Word 2010 Exhibit 8).

13. ***Click on the down arrow in the "Font" box in the "Modify Style" window and click on Arial*** (you may have to scroll through some fonts to find it). ***Next, click on the OK button in the "Modify Style" window.*** Notice that Word quickly changed the alignment of all of the text to fully justified and changed the font to Arial.

14. ***Drag the pointer until the full title of the document is highlighted*** (SARBANES-OXLEY ACT OF 2002 TITLE I—PUBLIC COMPANY ACCOUNTING OVERSIGHT BOARD).

15. ***Click on Heading 1 in the Styles task pane.***

16. ***Point and right-click on Heading 1 in the Styles task pane and select Modify. Then, click on the Center icon. Click the OK button in the "Modify Style" window.***

17. ***Click the left mouse button anywhere in the title to make the highlight disappear.*** Notice that the text of the title shows as Heading 1 in the Styles task pane.

18. ***Click anywhere in "SEC. 101. ESTABLISHMENT; ADMINISTRATIVE PROVISIONS." Then, click on Heading 2 in the Styles task pane.*** Notice that the heading has now changed.

19. ***Click anywhere in the subheading "(a) ESTABLISHMENT OF BOARD." Then, click on the New Style icon at the bottom of the Styles task pane*** (see Word 2010 Exhibit 8).

20. The "Create New Style from Formatting" window should now be displayed. Under Properties, next to Name, type **Heading 3A**, and then under Formatting, ***click on the Bold icon. Then, click on OK in the "Create New Style from Formatting" window.***

21. Now, go to the following subheadings and format them as Heading 3A by ***clicking on them and selecting Heading 3A from the Styles task pane:***
    (b) STATUS
    (c) DUTIES OF THE BOARD
    (d) COMMISSION DETERMINATION
    (e) BOARD MEMBERSHIP
    (f) POWERS OF THE BOARD
    (g) RULES OF THE BOARD
    (h) ANNUAL REPORT TO THE COMMISSION
    Press **[CTRL]+[HOME]** to go to the beginning of the document. Your document is now consistently formatted. Using styles, your documents can also easily be uniformly changed. For example, if you read in your local rules that subheadings for pleadings must be in 15-point Times New Roman font, you could quickly change the subheadings in your document by modifying the heading styles, rather than highlighting each subheading and changing the format manually.

22. To print the document, ***click on the File tab, click on Print, and then click on Print.***

23. To save the document, ***click on the File tab and click Save As. Then click on "Word 97-2003 Document." Under Save in, select the drive or folder*** you

would like to save the document in. Then, next to File Name, type **Done—Word 2010 Lesson 6 Document** *and click on Save* to save the document.

24. *Click on the File tab, and then on Close* to close the document, or *click on the File tab, and then on Exit* to exit the program.

This concludes Lesson 6.

LESSON 7: CREATING A TEMPLATE

This lesson shows you how to create the template shown in Word 2010 Exhibit 9. It explains how to create a template of a letter, how to insert fields, and how to fill out and use a finished template. You will also learn how to add a command to the Quick Access toolbar. The information that will be merged into the letter will be entered from the keyboard. Keep in mind that if at any time you make a mistake, you may press [CTRL]+[Z] to undo what you have done.

1. Open Windows. When it has loaded, *double-click on the Microsoft Office Word 2010 icon on the desktop* to open Word 2010 for Windows. Alternatively, *click on the Start button, point to Programs or All Programs, and then click on the Microsoft Word 2010 icon* (or *point to Microsoft Office and then click on Microsoft Office Word 2010*). You should be in a clean, blank document. If you are not in a blank document, *click on the File tab, click on New, and then double-click on Blank document.*

2. *Click on the File tab, then click on New, and then under Available Templates click on My templates.*

3. *Click on Template under the Create New field in the lower right of the Templates window* (see Word 2010 Exhibit 10).

4. *Click on Blank Document.* Blank Document should now be highlighted. *Then, click on OK* (see Word 2010 Exhibit 10).

5. You should now have a blank template on your screen. The Windows title should say **"Template1—Microsoft Word"** in the upper middle of the screen. You will now build the template shown in Word 2010 Exhibit 9.

6. Also, *on the Home Ribbon tab, click the Paragraph Group Dialog Box Launcher. In the "Paragraph" window, click the down arrow below Line Spacing and select Single. Make sure the Before and After spacing are both 0 point. Then, click OK.*

WORD 2010 EXHIBIT 9
Office Letter template

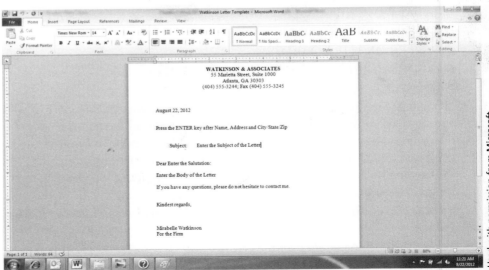

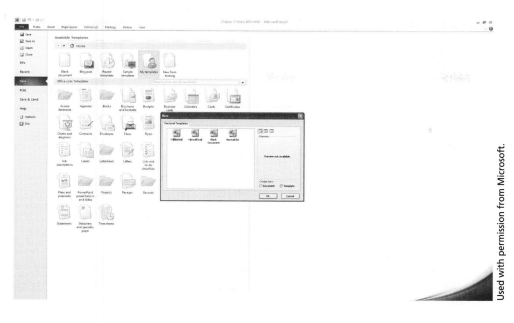

WORD 2010 EXHIBIT 10
Creating a new template

HANDS-ON EXERCISES

7. *From the Home Ribbon tab, click on the Center icon in the Paragraph group. Then, from the Home Ribbon tab, click on the Bold icon in the Font group.*

8. *From the Home Ribbon tab, click on the Font Size icon from the Font group and select 14 from the list. Then, click on the "Font" box and select Times New Roman.*

9. Type **WATKINSON & ASSOCIATES** and then, *from the Home Ribbon tab, click on the Font Size icon and select 12 from the list. Click on the Bold icon from the Font group* to turn off bolding.

10. Press the **[ENTER]** key.

11. Type **55 Marietta Street, Suite 1000** and press the **[ENTER]** key.

12. Type **Atlanta, Georgia 30303** and press the **[ENTER]** key.

13. Type **(404) 555-3244; Fax (404) 555-3245** and press the **[ENTER]** key.

14. *From the Home Ribbon tab, click on the Align Text Left icon in the Paragraph group.*

15. Press the **[ENTER]** key three times.

16. *From the Insert Ribbon tab, click on Quick Parts from the Text group and then click Field.*

17. The "Field" window should now be displayed (see Word 2010 Exhibit 11). The "Field" window has several sections, including Categories and Field Names. Under Categories, (*All*) should be selected.

18. *Click on the down arrow on the Field Names scroll bar until you see the field name Date* (see Word 2010 Exhibit 11). *Click on it.*

19. *From the Field Properties list, click on the third option from the top (the date, the month spelled out, and the year).* Notice that the current date is displayed. This field will always display the date on which the template is actually executed, so if the template is executed on January 1, January 1 will be the date shown on the letter. *Click on OK in the "Field" window.*

20. Press the **[ENTER]** key three times.

21. *From the Insert Ribbon tab, click on Quick Parts from the Text group and then click Field.*

WORD 2010 EXHIBIT 11
Inserting fields in a template

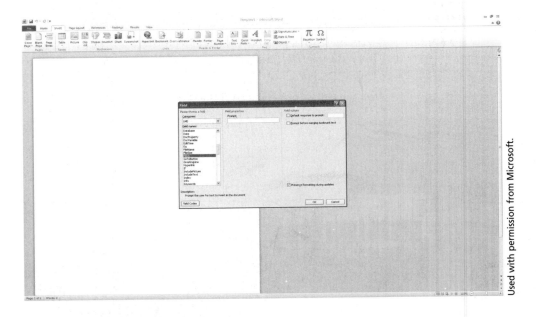

22. *Click on the down arrow on the Field names scroll bar until you see Fill-In in the Field Name area* (see Word 2010 Exhibit 11). *Click on Fill-In.*

23. In the "Prompt:" box under Field Properties, type **"Type the Name and Address of the Recipient."** *Note:* You must type the quotation marks.

24. *Click on OK in the "Field" window.*

25. You will now see a window on your screen that says **"Type the Name and Address of the Recipient."** Type **Press the ENTER key after Name, Address, and City/St/Zip** (see Word 2010 Exhibit 12). *Then, click on OK.*

26. Press the **[ENTER]** key three times.

27. Press the **[TAB]** key.

28. Type **Subject:**.

29. Press the **[TAB]** key.

30. *From the Insert Ribbon tab, click on Quick Parts from the Text group and then click on Field.*

WORD 2010 EXHIBIT 12
Entering a "fill-in" field

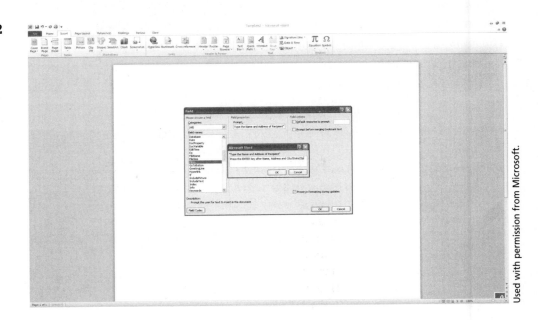

31. *Click on the down arrow on the Field names scroll bar until you see Fill-In in the Field Name area. Click on Fill-In.*

32. In the "Prompt:" box under Field Properties, type **"Type the Subject of the Letter."** *Note:* You must type the quotation marks. *Click on OK.*

33. You will now see a window on your screen that says **"Type the Subject of the Letter."** Type **Enter the Subject of the Letter.** *Click on OK.*

34. Press the **[ENTER]** key three times.

35. Type **Dear,** press the **[SPACEBAR]**; *from the Insert Ribbon tab, click on Quick Parts from the Text group, and then click Field.*

36. *Click on the down arrow on the Field names scroll bar until you see Fill-In in the Field Name area. Click on Fill-In.*

37. In the "Prompt:" box under Field Properties, type **"Salutation."** *Note:* You must type the quotation marks. *Click on OK.*

38. You will now see a window on your screen that says **"Salutation."** Type **Enter the Salutation.** *Then, click on OK.*

39. Type **:** (a colon).

40. Press the **[ENTER]** key twice.

41. *From the Insert Ribbon tab, click on Quick Parts from the Text group and then click Field.*

42. *Click on the down arrow on the Field names scroll bar until you see Fill-In in the Field Name area. Click on Fill-In.*

43. In the "Prompt:" box under Field Properties, type **"Body of Letter."** *Note:* You must type the quotation marks. *Click on OK.*

44. You will now see a window on your screen that says **"Body of Letter."** Type **Enter the Body of the Letter.** *Then, click on OK.*

45. Press the **[ENTER]** key twice.

46. Type **If you have any questions, please do not hesitate to contact me.** Press the **[ENTER]** key three times.

47. Type **Kindest Regards,** and press the **[ENTER]** key four times.

48. Type **Mirabelle Watkinson** and press the **[ENTER]** key once.

49. Type **For the Firm**.

50. *Click on the File tab, then point to Save As and click on Word Template.* (Note: If you do not save this as a Word template, you will not be able to finish the lesson). Then, next to File Name:, type **Watkinson Letter Template.** Word will save the template to a special template folder; if you save it to another folder you will not be able to run the template in the next portion of this exercise. *Next to Save as type:, click on the down arrow button, select Word 97-2003 Template, and then click on Save* to save the document.

51. *Click on the File tab and then on Close.* You are now ready to type a letter using the template.

52. *Click on the File tab, then click on New. Next, under Templates click on My templates.* In the "New" window, under the My Templates tab, *double-click on Watkinson Letter Template.*

53. The template letter is now running. You will see the "Type the Name and Address of the Recipient" field on the screen. You will also see the prompt that reminds you to press the **[ENTER]** key after the name, address, and city/state/zip. Type over this prompt.

54. Type **Steven Matthews, Esq.** and press the **[ENTER]** key.

55. Type **Matthews, Smith & Russell** and press the **[ENTER]** key.

HANDS-ON EXERCISES

56. Type **P.O. Box 12341** and press the **[ENTER]** key.

57. Type **Boston, MA 59920** and then *click on OK.*

58. You will see the Type the Subject of the Letter field on the screen. You will also see the prompt that reminds you to enter the subject of the letter. Type over this prompt.

59. Type **Turner v. Smith, Case No. 13-0046** and then *click on OK.*

60. You will now see the Salutation field on the screen. You will also see the prompt that reminds you to enter the salutation. Type over this prompt.

61. Type **Steve** and then *click on OK.*

62. You will now see the Body of Letter field on the screen. You will also see the prompt that reminds you to enter the body of the letter. Type over this prompt.

63. Type **This will confirm our conversation of this date. You indicated that you had no objection to us requesting an additional ten days to respond to your Motion for Summary Judgment.** *Click on OK.* You are now through typing the letter. The completed letter should now be displayed. (*Note:* If another window displays, prompting you for the name and address of the recipient, simply *click cancel*; the completed letter should then be displayed.)

64. You are now ready to print the document. First, you will create a Quick Print icon on the Quick Access toolbar. Instead of going to the File tab each time to print, you will be able to print a document from the Quick Access toolbar (see Word 2010 Exhibit 12).

65. *Point and right-click anywhere in the ribbon. Click on Customize Quick Access Toolbar.*

66. The "Word Options" window should now be displayed. *Double-click on Quick Print on the left side of the screen (under Popular Commands). Click on Add and then click OK in the "Word Options" window.*

67. Notice that a Quick Print icon is now displayed in the Quick Access toolbar.

68. *Click on the Quick Print icon on the Quick Access toolbar,* or *click on the File tab, click on Print, and then click on Print.*

69. To save the document, *click on the File tab, click Save As, and then click on Word 97-2003 Document. Under Save in, select the drive or folder* you would like to save the document in. Then, next to File Name, type **Done— Word 2010 Lesson 7 Document** *and click on Save* to save the document. *Note*: You just saved the output of your template to a separate file named "Done—Word Lesson 7 Document." Your original template ("Watkinson Letter Template") is unaffected by the Lesson 7 document, and is still a clean template ready to be used again and again for any case.

70. *Click on the File tab, and then on Close* to close the document, or *click on the File tab, and then on Exit* to exit the program.

This concludes Lesson 7.

LESSON 8: COMPARING DOCUMENTS

This lesson shows you how to compare documents by simultaneously viewing two documents and by creating a separate blacklined document with the changes. There will be times in a law office when you send someone a digital file for revision, and find that when the file is returned, the revisions are not apparent. Using these tools in Word 2010, you can see what has changed in the document.

1. Open Windows. When it has loaded, *double-click on the Microsoft Office Word 2010 icon on the desktop* to open Word 2010 for Windows.

Alternatively, *click on the Start button, point to Programs or All Programs, and then click on the Microsoft Word 2010 icon* (or *point to Microsoft Office and then click on Microsoft Office Word 2010*). You should now be in a clean, blank document. If you are not in a blank document, *click on the File tab, click on New, and then double-click on Blank document.*

2. For the purpose of this lesson, we will assume that your firm drafted an employment contract for a corporate client named Bluebriar Incorporated. Bluebriar is in negotiations with an individual named John Lewis, whom they would like to hire as their vice president of marketing. Your firm is negotiating with John Lewis's attorney regarding the terms and language of the employment contract. The file "Lesson 8A" on the disk that came with this text is the original document you sent to John Lewis's attorney. The file "Lesson 8B" on the disk that came with this text is the new file sent to you by John Lewis's attorney.

3. You will now open both of these files from the disk supplied with this text and then compare them side by side. Ensure that the disk is inserted in the drive, *click on the File tab, and then click on Open.* The "Open" window should now be displayed. *Click on the down arrow to the right of the white box next to Look in: and select the drive where the disk is located. Double-click on the Word-Processing Files folder. Double-click on the Word 2010 folder. Double-click on the "Lesson 8A" file.*

4. Follow the same directions to open the "Lesson 8B" file.

5. *From the View ribbon tab, click on View Side by Side in the Window group.* Both documents should now be displayed side by side (see Word 2010 Exhibit 13).

6. Keep pushing the [**DOWN ARROW**] key to scroll down through the document. Notice that both documents scroll simultaneously.

7. From the View ribbon tab, notice that the Synchronous Scrolling icon in the Window group is highlighted (see Word 2010 Exhibit 13). To turn off this feature, you would click on this icon. The Synchronous Scrolling icon toggles Synchronous Scrolling on and off. If you turn off Synchronous Scrolling and wish to turn it back on, simply realign the windows where you want them,

HANDS-ON EXERCISES

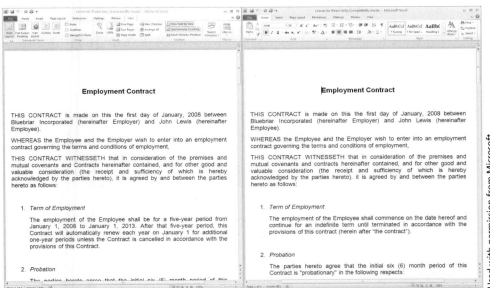

WORD 2010 EXHIBIT 13
Comparing documents side-by-side

and *click on the Synchronous Scrolling icon.* (*Note:* If the View ribbon tab shows the Window group collapsed, *click on the Window Group, and click Synchronous Scrolling.*)

8. You will now learn how to merge the changes into one document. *Click anywhere in Lesson 8A.doc; then click on the File tab and then on Close.*

9. Do the same for Word Lesson 8B.doc.

10. You should now have no documents open.

11. *From the Review ribbon tab, click on Compare in the Compare group. Then, click on Compare.*

12. The "Compare Documents" window should now be displayed (see Word 2010 Exhibit 14). *Under Original document, click on the down arrow, use the Browse feature to find Lesson 8A.doc, and then double-click on it* (see Word 2010 Exhibit 14).

13. *Under Revised document, click on the down arrow, use the Browse feature to find Lesson 8B.doc, and then double-click on it* (see Word 2010 Exhibit 14).

14. Next to **"Label Changes with,"** type **John Lewis' Attorney** and then *click on OK in the "Compare Documents" window.*

15. Notice that a new document has been created that merges the documents (see Word 2010 Exhibit 15). Scroll through the new document and review all of the changes.

16. The Compare feature is extremely helpful when you are comparing multiple versions of the same file. By right-clicking on any of the additions or deletions, you can accept or reject the change. This is called Track Changes, and you will learn how to do this in more detail in the next lesson.

17. To print the document, *click on the Quick Print icon on the Quick Access toolbar, or click on the File tab, click on Print, and then click on Print.*

18. To save the document, *click on the File tab, click Save As, and then click on "Word 97-2003 Document." Under Save in, select the drive or folder* you would like to save the document in. Next to File Name:, type **Done—Word 2010 Lesson 8 Merged Doc** and then *click on Save* to save the document.

WORD 2010 EXHIBIT 14
Comparing documents—
Legal blackline settings

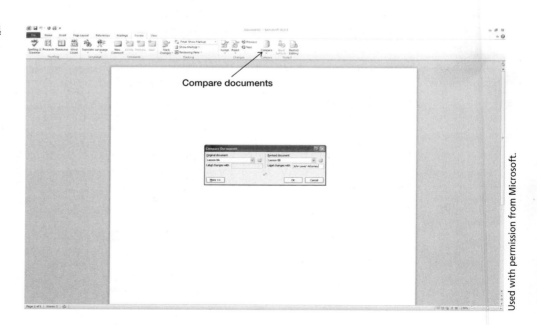

Compare documents

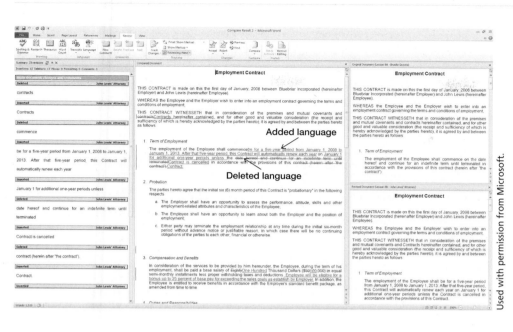

WORD 2010 EXHIBIT 15
Completed blackline
documents

19. *Click on the File tab, and then on Close* to close the document, or *click on the File tab, and then on Exit* to exit the program.

This concludes Lesson 8.

LESSON 9: USING TRACK CHANGES

In this lesson, you will learn how to use the Track Changes feature by editing a will, and then accepting and/or rejecting the changes.

1. Open Windows. When it has loaded, *double-click on the Microsoft Office Word 2010 icon on the desktop* to open Word 2010 for Windows. Alternatively, *click on the Start button, point to Programs or All Programs, and then click on the Microsoft Word 2010 icon* (or *point to Microsoft Office and then click on Microsoft Office Word 2010*). You should now be in a clean, blank document. If you are not in a blank document, *click on the File tab, click on New, and then double-click on Blank document.*

2. The first thing you will do is to open the "Lesson 9" file from the disk supplied with this text. Ensure that the disk is inserted in the drive, *click on the File tab, and then click on Open.* The "Open" window should now be displayed. *Click on the down arrow to the right of the white box next to Look in:, and select the drive where the disk is located. Double-click on the Word-Processing Files folder. Double-click on the Word 2010 folder. Double-click on the "Lesson 9" file.*

3. The text "LAST WILL AND TESTAMENT" should now be displayed on your screen (see Word 2010 Exhibit 16). Notice in Word 2010 Exhibit 16 that several revisions have been made to this document. Your client, William Porter, has asked you to use the Track Changes feature to show your supervising attorney the changes he would like to make. Mr. Porter is rather leery of the legal process and wants to make sure your supervising attorney approves of the changes.

4. *From the Review ribbon tab, click on Track Changes from the Tracking group. Then, click on Track Changes from the drop-down menu* to turn on Track Changes.

WORD 2010 EXHIBIT 16
Using Track Changes

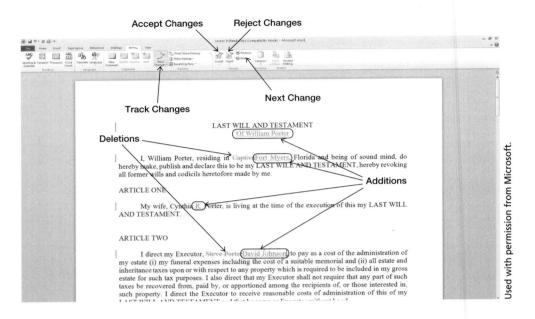

Accept Changes   Reject Changes

Next Change

Track Changes

Deletions

Additions

5. Make the changes shown in Word 2010 Exhibit 16. Everything that should be added is circled, and everything that should be deleted is shown at the right

6. Assume now that you have shown the changes to your supervising attorney. *From the Review ribbon tab, click on Track Changes, and then click on Track Changes on the drop-down menu* to turn off Track Changes (see Word 2010 Exhibit 16). This allows you to make changes to the document without having them show up as revisions.

7. *Point and right-click anywhere on the text, "Of William Porter," which you added just under "LAST WILL AND TESTAMENT."* Notice that a menu is displayed that allows you to accept or reject the insertion, among other actions. *Click on Accept Change.* The revision has now been accepted.

8. *From the Review ribbon tab, click on Next in the Changes group* (see Word 2010 Exhibit 16). This should take you to the next change. *From the Review ribbon tab, click on Accept in the Changes group, then click on Accept and Move to Next* (see Word 2010 Exhibit 16) to accept the change. Notice that one of the options is "Accept All Changes in Document." Do not select it. This is a quick way to accept all changes in a document without going through each one of them.

9. Use the Next feature to continue to go to each change and accept the revisions. The only revision you will *not* accept is changing the executor from Steve Porter to David Johnson; reject this change. Assume that the supervising attorney has learned that Mr. Johnson is terminally ill and most likely will not be able to serve as executor, so the client has decided to keep Steve Porter as the executor.

10. To print the document, *click on the Quick Print icon on the Quick Access toolbar,* or *click on the File tab, click on Print, and then click on Print.*

11. To save the document, *click on the File tab, click Save As, and then click on "Word 97-2003 Document." Under Save in, select the drive or folder* you would like to save the document in. Next to File Name, type **Done—Word 2010 Lesson 9 Document** *and then click on Save* to save the document.

12. *Click on the File tab, and then on Close* to close the document, or *click on the File tab, and then on Exit* to exit the program.

This concludes Lesson 9.

 # ADVANCED LESSONS

LESSON 10: CREATING A MAIL MERGE DOCUMENT

In this lesson, you will create a merge document for an open house that you will send to three clients (see Word 2010 Exhibit 17). First, you will create the data file that will be merged into the letter. You will then create the letter itself; finally, you will merge the two together. Keep in mind that if at any time you make a mistake, you may press [CTRL]+[Z] to undo what you have done.

1. Open Windows. When it has loaded, *double-click on the Microsoft Office Word 2010 icon on the desktop* to open Word 2010 for Windows. Alternatively, *click on the Start button, point to Programs or All Programs, and then click on the Microsoft Word 2010 icon* (or *point to Microsoft Office and then click on Microsoft Office Word 2010*). You should now be in a clean, blank document. If you are not in a blank document, *click on the File tab, click on New, and then double-click on Blank document.*

2. *From the Mailings Ribbon tab, click on Start Mail Merge. Then, from the drop-down menu, select Step by Step Mail Merge Wizard... .* The Mail Merge task pane is now shown on the task pane to the right of your document.

3. The bottom of the Mail Merge task pane shows that you are on step 1 of 6. You are asked to **"Select document type."** You are typing a letter, so the default selection, Letters, is fine. To continue to the next step, *click on Next: Starting document at the bottom of the Mail Merge task pane under Step 1 of 6.*

4. The bottom of the Mail Merge task pane shows that you are on step 2 of 6. You are asked to **"Select starting document."** You will be using the current

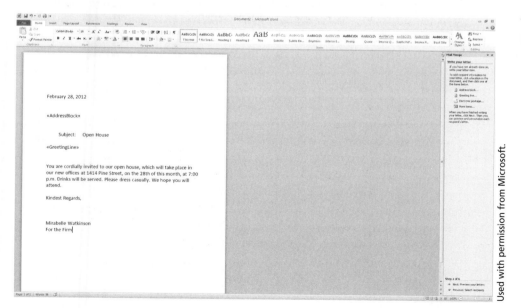

WORD 2010 EXHIBIT 17
Mail merge letter

document to type your letter, so the default selection, Use the current document, is fine. To continue to the next step, *click on Next: Select recipients at the bottom of the Mail Merge task pane under Step 2 of 6.*

5. The bottom of the Mail Merge task pane shows that you are on step 3 of 6. You are asked to **"Select recipients."** You will be typing a new list, so *click on Type a new list.*

6. *Under the Type a new list section of the Mail Merge task pane, click on "Create... ."*

7. The "New Address List" window is now displayed. You will now fill in the names of the three clients to whom you want to send your open house letter.

8. Type the following. (*Note:* You can use the **[TAB]** key to move between the fields, or you can use the mouse.) Only complete the fields below; skip the fields in the "New Address List" window that we will not be using.

TITLE	
First Name	Jim
Last Name	Woods
Company Name	
Address Line 1	2300 Briarcliff Road
Address Line 2	
City	Atlanta
State	GA
ZIP Code	30306
Country	
Home Phone	
Work Phone	
Email Address	

9. When you have entered all of the information for Jim Woods, *click on the New Entry button in the "New Address List" window.*

10. Enter the second client in the blank "New Address List" window.

TITLE	
First Name	Jennifer
Last Name	John
Company Name	
Address Line 1	3414 Peachtree Road
Address Line 2	
City	Atlanta
State	GA
ZIP Code	30314
Country	
Home Phone	
Work Phone	
Email Address	

11. When you have entered all of the information for Jennifer John, ***click on the New Entry button in the "New Address List" window.***

12. Enter the third client in the blank "New Address List" window.

TITLE	
First Name	Jonathan
Last Name	Phillips
Company Name	
Address Line 1	675 Clifton Road
Address Line 2	
City	Atlanta
State	GA
ZIP Code	30030
Country	
Home Phone	
Work Phone	
Email Address	

13. When you have entered all of the information for Jonathan Phillips, ***click on OK in the "New Address List" window.***

14. The "Save Address List" window is now displayed. You need to save the address list so that it can later be merged with the open-house letter. In the "Save Address List" window, next to File Name, type **Open House List** and then ***click on Save in the "Save Address List" window*** to save the file to the default directory.

15. The "Mail Merge Recipients" window is now displayed (see Word 2010 Exhibit 18). ***Click on the "Last Name" field in the "Mail Merge Recipients" window to sort the list by last name*** (see Word 2010 Exhibit 18). Notice that the order of the list is now sorted by last name.

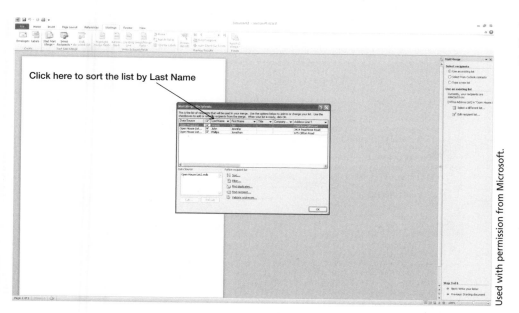

WORD 2010 EXHIBIT 18
Entering mail merge recipients

Used with permission from Microsoft.

16. ***Click on OK in the "Mail Merge Recipients" window.*** You are now back at a blank document with the Mail Merge task pane open to the right. The bottom of the Mail Merge task pane indicates that you are still at step 3 of 6. ***Click on Next: Write your letter at the bottom of the Mail Merge task pane under Step 3 of 6*** to continue to the next step.

17. The bottom of the Mail Merge task pane indicates that you are on step 4 of 6. In the Mail Merge task pane, **"Write your letter"** is displayed. You are now ready to write the letter. ***On the Home Ribbon tab, click the Paragraph Group Dialog Box Launcher. In the "Paragraph" window, click the down arrow below Line Spacing and select Single. Make sure the Before and After spacing are both 0 point. Then, click OK.***

18. Press the **[ENTER]** key four times.

19. Type the current date and press the **[ENTER]** key three times.

20. ***Click on Address Block… in the Mail Merge task pane under the Write your letter option.***

21. The "Insert Address Block" window is now displayed. You will now customize how the address block will appear in the letters.

22. ***In the "Insert Address Block" window, click on "Joshua Randall Jr." Then, click on Insert company name to deselect it, because we did not include company names in our data list*** (see Word 2010 Exhibit 19).

23. ***Under Insert postal address, click on Never include the country/region in the address*** (see Word 2010 Exhibit 19).

24. ***Click on OK in the "Insert Address Block" window.***

25. The words "**<<AddressBlock>>**" are now displayed in your document.

26. Press the **[ENTER]** key three times.

27. Press the **[TAB]** key once and then type **Subject:**.

28. Press the **[TAB]** key and then type **Open House.**

29. Press the **[ENTER]** key twice.

30. ***In the Mail Merge task pane, under "Write your letter," click on Greeting line…*** (see Word 2010 Exhibit 19).

31. The "Insert Greeting Line" window is now displayed. You will now customize how the greeting or salutation will appear in the letter. ***In the "Insert Greeting***

WORD 2010 EXHIBIT 19
Insert address block

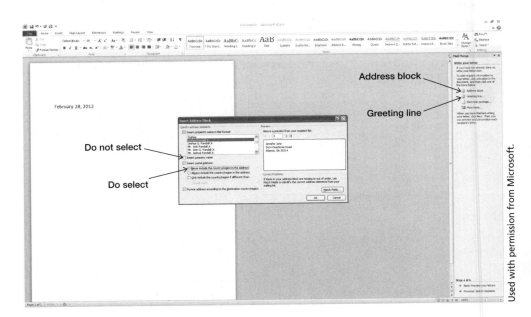

Line" window, click on the down arrow next to "Mr. Randall" and then scroll down and click on "Josh." Click on OK in the "Insert Greeting Line" window.

32. The words "<<GreetingLine>>" are now displayed in your document.

33. Press the [ENTER] key three times.

34. Type **You are cordially invited to our open house, which will take place in our new offices at 1414 Pine, on the 28th of this month, at 7:00 p.m. Drinks will be served. Please dress casually. We hope you will attend.**

35. Press the [ENTER] key twice.

36. Type **Kindest Regards,.**

37. Press the [ENTER] key four times.

38. Type **Mirabelle Watkinson**.

39. Press the [ENTER] key once and type **For the Firm**.

40. You are now done typing the letter. Your letter should look similar to Word 2010 Exhibit 17. The only thing left to do is to merge the recipient list with the form.

41. *Under Step 4 of 6 at the bottom of the Mail Merge task pane, click on Next: Preview your letters* to continue to the next step.

42. Your first letter is now displayed. *In the Mail Merge task pane, under Preview your letters, click on the button showing two arrows pointing to the right to see the rest of your letters.*

43. To continue to the next step, *click on Next: Complete the merge at the bottom of the Mail Merge task pane under Step 5 of 6.*

44. The Mail Merge task pane now will display **"Complete the merge."** *Click on Print... in the Mail Merge task pane under Merge, and then click on OK. At the "Merge to Printer" window, click on OK* to print your letters.

45. *Click on Edit individual letters... in the Mail Merge task pane under Merge.* In the "Merge to New Document" window, *click on OK.* Word has now opened a new document with all of the letters in it. (*Note:* Here you can edit and personalize each letter if you would like.)

46. To save the document, *click on the File tab, click Save As, and then click on "Word 97-2003 Document." Under Save in, select the drive or folder* you would like to save the document in. Then, next to File Name:, type **Open House Letters** *and then click on Save* to save the document.

47. *If they do not close automatically, click on the File tab and then on Close* to close the personalized letters.

48. You should be back at the mail merge letter. *Click on the File tab and click Save As. Then click on "Word 97-2003 Document." Under Save in, select the drive or folder* you would like to save the document in. Then, next to File Name:, type **Open House Mail Merge;** *click on Save* to save the document.

49. *Click on the File tab, and then on Close* to close the document, or *click on the File tab, and then on Exit* to exit the program.

This concludes Lesson 10.

LESSON 11: CREATING A TABLE OF AUTHORITIES

In this lesson, you will prepare a table of authorities for a reply brief (see Word 2010 Exhibit 22). You will learn how to find cases, mark cases, and then automatically generate a table of authorities.

1. Open Windows. When it has loaded, *double-click on the Microsoft Office Word 2010 icon on the desktop* to open Word 2010 for Windows.

WORD 2010 EXHIBIT 20
Marking a citation for inclusion in a table of authorities

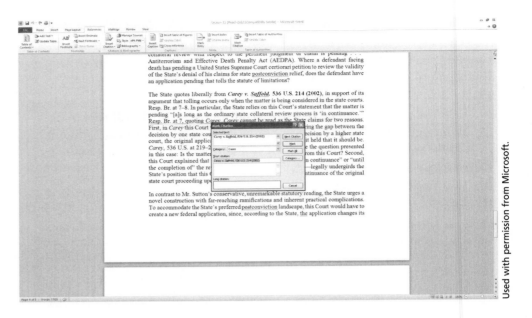

Alternatively, ***click on the Start button, point to Programs or All Programs, and then click on the Microsoft Word 2010 icon*** (or ***point to Microsoft Office and then click on Microsoft Office Word 2010***). You should now be in a clean, blank document. If you are not in a blank document, ***click on the File tab, click on New, and then double-click on Blank document.***

2. The first thing you will do is to open the "Lesson 11" file from the disk supplied with this text. Ensure that the disk is inserted in the disk drive, ***click on the File tab, and then click on Open.*** The "Open" window should now be displayed. ***Click on the down arrow to the right of the white box next to Look in: and select the drive where the disk is located. Double-click on the Word-Processing Files folder. Double-click on the Word 2010 folder. Double-click on the "Lesson 11" file.***

3. The text "***In the Supreme Court of the United States–TED SUTTON, Petitioner v. STATE OF ALASKA, Respondent***" should now be displayed on your screen.

4. In this exercise you will build the case section of the table of authorities for this reply brief. There are five cases to be included and they are all shown in bold so that you can easily identify them. Your first task will be to mark each of the cases so that Word knows they are the cases to be included; then you will execute the command for Word to build the table.

5. If you are not at the beginning of the document, press **[CTRL]+[HOME]** to go to the beginning.

6. You will now mark the cases. ***From the References ribbon tab, click on Mark Citations from the Table of Authorities group.***

7. The "Mark Citation" window should now be displayed (see Word 2010 Exhibit 20). Notice, next to Category:, that Cases is displayed. This indicates that you will be marking case citations. ***Click on the down arrow next to Cases*** to see that you can also mark citations to be included for Statutes, Rules, Treatises, Regulations, and Other Authorities.

8. ***Click on Cases again;*** you will now start marking cases to be included in the TABLE OF AUTHORITIES.

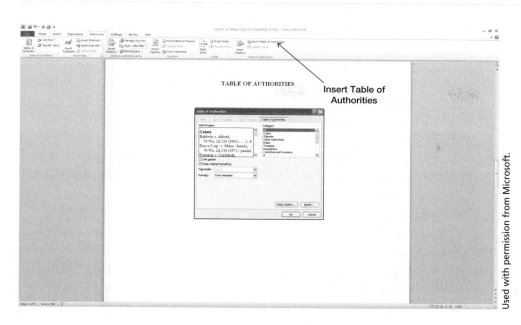

WORD 2010 EXHIBIT 21
Inserting a table of authorities

HANDS-ON EXERCISES

9. *In the "Mark Citation" window, click on Next Citation.* Word looks for terms such as "vs" or "v." when finding citations. The cursor should now be on the "v." in *Ted Sutton v. State of Alaska.* Because this is the caption of the current case, we do not want to mark it. *Note*: If the "Mark Citation" window gets in the way of your seeing the brief, put the pointer on the blue title bar of the "Mark Citation" window and drag it out of your way.

10. *Click on Next Citation in the "Mark Citation" window.* Again, this is the caption of the current case, *Ted Sutton v. State of Alaska,* so we do not want to mark it.

11. *Click again on Next Citation in the "Mark Citation" window.* Word has now found the case *Carey v. Saffold.* We want to mark this case so that it will be included in the table of authorities.

12. *Click once on the* **Carey v. Saffold** *case.*

13. *Drag the pointer to highlight* **"Carey v. Saffold, 536 U.S. 214 (2002)"** *and then click in the white box under Selected text: in the "Mark Citation" window.* The case is automatically copied there (see Word 2010 Exhibit 20).

14. *Click on Mark in the "Mark Citation" window. Note:* When you mark a citation, Word changes your view to the Show/Hide paragraph view. It shows you that you have embedded table of authorities formatting codes in the document. To switch out of Show/Hide view, *from the Home Ribbon tab, click on the Show/Hide icon in the Paragraph group.* (It looks like a paragraph sign.)

15. *Click on Next Citation in the "Mark Citation" window.*

16. *Click once on the "Duncan v. Walker" case.*

17. *Drag the mouse to highlight "Duncan v. Walker, 533 U.S. 167, 174 (2001)" and then click in the white box under Selected text: in the "Mark Citation" window.* The case is automatically copied there.

18. *Click on Mark in the "Mark Citation" window.* Notice under Short Citation in the "Mark Citation" window that the *Carey* and *Duncan* cases are listed. Again, if at any time the "Mark Citation" window prevents you from seeing

the case you need to highlight, just *click on the blue bar at top of the "Mark Citation" window and drag to the left or the right* to move the window out of your way.

19. To switch out of Show/Hide view, *from the Home tab on the ribbon, click on the Show/Hide icon in the Paragraph group.*

20. *Click on Next Citation in the "Mark Citation" window.*

21. *Click once on the* **"Bates v. United States"** *case.*

22. *Drag the pointer to highlight "Bates v. United States, 522 U.S. 23, 29–30 (1997)," and then click in the white box under Selected text: in the "Mark Citation" window.* The case is automatically copied there.

23. *Click on Mark in the "Mark Citation" window.*

24. *Click on Next Citation in the "Mark Citation" window.*

25. *Click once on the "Abela v. Martin" case.*

26. *Drag to highlight "Abela v. Martin, 348 F.3d 164 (6th Cir. 2003)" and then click in the white box under Selected text: in the "Mark Citation" window.* The case is automatically copied there.

27. *Click on Mark in the "Mark Citation" window.*

28. *Click on Next Citation in the "Mark Citation" window.*

29. *Click once on the "Coates v. Byrd" case.*

30. *Drag the mouse to highlight "Coates v. Byrd, 211 F.3d 1225, 1227 (11th Cir. 2000)," and then click in the white box under Selected text: in the "Mark Citation" window.* The case is automatically copied there.

31. *Click on Mark in the "Mark Citation" window.*

32. *Click on Close in the "Mark Citation" window to close it.*

33. *On the Home Ribbon tab, click on the Show/Hide paragraph icon to make the paragraph marks disappear.*

34. Using the cursor keys or the horizontal scroll bar, place the cursor on page 3 of the document two lines under the title **"TABLE OF AUTHORITIES"** (see Word 2010 Exhibit 22). You are now ready to generate the table.

35. *From the References Ribbon tab, click on the Insert Table of Authorities icon in the Table of Authorities group* (see Word 2010 Exhibit 21).

WORD 2010 EXHIBIT 22
Completed table of authorities

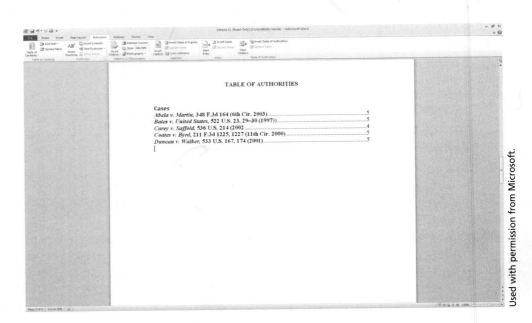

36. *The "Table of Authorities" window should now be displayed* (see Word 2010 Exhibit 21). *Click on Cases under Category and then click on OK.*

37. Notice that the table of authorities has been prepared and completed, and that the cases and the page numbers where they appear in the document have been included (see Word 2010 Exhibit 22).

38. To print the document, *click on the Quick Print icon on the Quick Access toolbar,* or *click on the File tab, click on Print, and then click on Print.*

39. To save the document, *click on the File tab and click Save As, then click on "Word 97-2003 Document." Under Save in, select the drive or folder* you would like to save the document in. Then, next to File Name:, type **Done— Word 2010 Lesson 11 Document** *and click on Save* to save the document.

40. *Click on the File tab, and then on Close* to close the document, or *click on the File tab, and then on Exit* to exit the program.

This concludes Lesson 11.

LESSON 12: CREATING A MACRO

In this lesson you will prepare a macro that will automatically type the signature block for a pleading (see Word 2010 Exhibit 23). You will then execute the macro to make sure that it works properly.

1. Open Windows. When it has loaded, *double-click on the Microsoft Office Word 2010 icon on the desktop* to open Word 2010 for Windows. Alternatively, *click on the Start button, point to Programs or All Programs, and then click on the Microsoft Word 2010 icon* (or *point to Microsoft Office and then click on Microsoft Office Word 2010*). You should now be in a clean, blank document. If you are not in a blank document, *click on the File tab, click on New, and then double-click on Blank document.*

2. The first thing you need to do to create a new macro is to name the macro and then turn on the Record function. *From the View Ribbon tab, click on the down arrow under Macros in the Macros group* (see Word 2010 Exhibit 23).

3. *Click on Record Macro... on the drop-down menu.*

4. The "Record Macro" window should now be displayed (see Word 2010 Exhibit 23). In the "Record Macro" window, under Macro Name:, type **Pleadingsignblock** *and then click on OK* (see Word 2010 Exhibit 23).

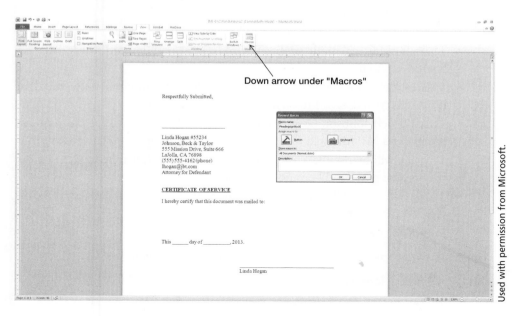

WORD 2010 EXHIBIT 23
Creating a pleading signature block macro

5. Notice that your cursor has a cassette tape on it. The cassette tape on your cursor indicates that Word is now recording all of your keystrokes and commands.

6. Type the information shown in Word 2010 Exhibit 23. When you have completed typing the information, *from the View Ribbon tab, click on the down arrow under Macros in the Macros group* (see Word 2010 Exhibit 23).

7. *Click on Stop Recording on the drop-down menu.*

8. You will now test your macro to see if it works properly. *Click on the File tab and then on Close* to close the document. At the prompt **"Do you want to save the changes to Document?"** *click on Don't Save.*

9. To open a blank document, *click on the File tab, click on New, and then double-click on Blank document.*

10. To run the macro, *from the View Ribbon tab, click on the down arrow under Macros in the Macros group* (see Word 2010 Exhibit 23).

11. *Click on View Macros.*

12. *In the "Macros" window, click on* **Pleadingsignblock** *and then click on Run.* Your pleading signature block should now appear in your document.

13. To print the document, *click on the Quick Print icon on the Quick Access toolbar,* or *click on the File tab, click on Print, and then click on Print.*

14. To save the document, *click on the File tab, click Save As, and then click on "Word 97-2003 Document." Under Save in, select the drive or folder* you would like to save the document in. Then, next to File Name:, type **Done— Word 2010 Lesson 12 Document** *and click on Save* to save the document.

15. *Click on the File tab, and then on Close* to close the document, or *click on the File tab, and then on Exit* to exit the program.

This concludes Lesson 12.

LESSON 13: DRAFTING A WILL

Using the websites at the end of the chapter or a form book from a law library, draft a simple will that would be valid in your state. You will be drafting the will for Thomas Mansell, who is a widower. The will should be dated July 1 of the current year. Mr. Mansell requests the following:

- That his just debts and funeral expenses be paid.
- That his lifelong friend, Dr. Jeff Johnson, receive $20,000 in cash.
- That his local YMCA receive his 100 shares of stock in IBM.
- That all of his remaining property (real or personal) descend to his daughter Sharon Mansell.
- That in the event Mr. Mansell and his daughter die simultaneously, for all of his property to descend to Sharon's son Michael Mansell.
- That Dr. Jeff Johnson be appointed the executor of the will; if Dr. Johnson predeceases Mr. Mansell, that Mr. Joe Crawford be appointed executor.
- That his will be double-spaced and have 1-inch margins; he would like the will to look good and be valid in his state.
- Three witnesses will watch the signing of the will: Shelly Stewart, Dennis Gordon, and Gary Fox.
- John Boesel will notarize the will.

Print out a hard copy of the will and turn it in or email it to your instructor.

This concludes the lessons in the Word 2010 Hands-On Exercises.

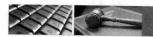

HANDS-ON EXERCISES

MICROSOFT WORD 2007 FOR WINDOWS

Number	Lesson Title	Concepts Covered
BASIC LESSONS		
Lesson 1	Typing a Letter	Using word wrap, Tab key, cursor keys, underline, bold, italics; saving and printing a document
Lesson 2	Editing a Letter	Retrieving a file, block moving/deleting, and spell/grammar checking
Lesson 3	Typing a Pleading	Centering, changing margins, changing line spacing, adding a footnote, double indenting, and automatic page numbering
Lesson 4	Creating a Table	Creating a table, entering data in a table, using automatic numbering, adjusting columns in a table, and using the Table AutoFormat command
INTERMEDIATE LESSONS		
Lesson 5	Tools and Techniques	Editing an employment policy using the Format Painter tool, revealing document formatting, using the Beginning of Document command, clearing formatting, changing case, using Search and Replace, using the Go To command, creating a section break, and changing the orientation of the page to Landscape
Lesson 6	Using Styles	Using, modifying, and creating styles to maintain consistent and uniform formatting of documents
Lesson 7	Creating a Template (office letterhead/letter)	Finding ready-made templates in Word, creating a new office letterhead and letter template, filling in/completing a template, and adding a command to the Quick Access toolbar
Lesson 8	Comparing Documents (multiple versions of an employment contract)	Comparing documents using the simultaneous viewing method and merging the documents into a separate annotated blacklined document
Lesson 9	Using Track Changes	Turning on Track Changes, making revisions, and accepting and rejecting revisions
ADVANCED LESSONS		
Lesson 10	Creating a Mail-Merge Document	Creating and entering a list of recipients for a mail merge, creating a mail-merge document, and merging the list with the document
Lesson 11	Creating a Table of Authorities	Finding and marking cases in a brief and generating an actual table of authorities for the brief
Lesson 12	Creating a Macro (pleading signature block)	Creating and executing a pleading signature block macro
Lesson 13	Drafting a Will	Using Word to draft a will

GETTING STARTED
Introduction

Throughout these lessons and exercises, information you need to type into the program will be designated in several different ways:

- Keys to be pressed on the keyboard are designated in brackets, in all caps, and in bold (e.g., press the **[ENTER]** key). A key combination, where two or more keys are pressed at once, is designated with a plus sign between the key names (e.g., **[CTRL]+[BACKSPACE]**). You should not type the plus sign.
- Movements with the mouse are designated in bold and italics (e.g., ***point to File on the menu bar and click***).
- Words or letters that should be typed are designated in bold (e.g., type **Training Program**).
- Information that is or should be displayed on your computer screen is shown in bold, with quotation marks (e.g., **"Press ENTER to continue."**).

OVERVIEW OF MICROSOFT WORD 2007

The following tips on using Microsoft Word will help you complete these exercises.

I. General Rules for Microsoft Word 2007

A. *Word Wrap*—You do not need to press the **[ENTER]** key after each line of text, as you would with a typewriter.

B. *Double Spacing*—If you want to double-space, do not hit the **[ENTER]** key twice. Instead, change the line spacing (***click on the Home ribbon tab, then click on the Line spacing icon in the Paragraph group and select 2.0).*** See Word 2007 Exhibit 1.

C. *Moving Through Already-Entered Text*—If you want to move the cursor to various positions within already-entered text, use the cursor (arrow) keys, or ***point and click.***

D. *Moving the Pointer Where No Text Has Been Entered*—You cannot use the cursor keys to move the pointer where no text has been entered. Said another way, you cannot move any further in a document than where you have typed text or pressed the **[ENTER]** key. You must use the **[ENTER]** key or first type text.

E. *Saving a Document*—To save a document, ***click the Office button in the upper left corner of the screen and then click Save*** (see Word 2007 Exhibit 1).

F. *New Document*—To get a new, clean document, ***click the Office button, then click New, then double-click on Blank document*** (see Word 2007 Exhibit 1).

G. *Help*—To get help, press **[F1]** or ***click on the ? icon in the upper right corner of the screen*** (see Word 2007 Exhibit 1).

II. Editing a Document

A. Pointer Movement

One space to left	**[LEFT ARROW]**
One space to right	**[RIGHT ARROW]**
Beginning of line	**[HOME]**
End of line	**[END]**
One line up	**[UP ARROW]**

WORD 2007 EXHIBIT 1
Word 2007 screen

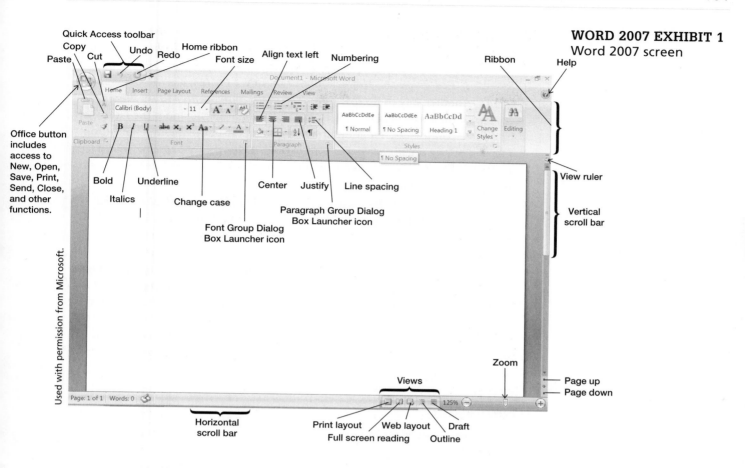

Used with permission from Microsoft.

One line down	**[DOWN ARROW]**
One screen up	**[PAGE UP]**
One screen down	**[PAGE DOWN]**
Beginning of document	**[CTRL]+[HOME]**
End of document	**[CTRL]+[END]**

B. Deleting Text

Delete the text under the cursor or to the right of it	**[DEL]**
Delete the text to the left of the cursor	**[BACKSPACE]**
Delete the whole word to the left of the cursor	**[CTRL]+[BACKSPACE]**
Delete the whole word to the right of the cursor	**[CTRL]+[DEL]**

C. *Delete Blocked Text*—***Drag the mouse pointer to select or highlight text,*** and then press **[DEL]**; or ***drag the mouse pointer to select or highlight text, and then from the Home ribbon tab, select the Cut icon from the Clipboard group*** (see Word 2007 Exhibit 1). Another way to select or highlight text is to press and hold the **[SHIFT]** key while using the cursor keys to mark/highlight the desired text.

D. *Undoing/Undeleting Text*—If you delete text and immediately want it back, ***click the Undo icon on the Quick Access toolbar.*** This can also be done by pressing **[CTRL]+[Z]**. Press **[CTRL]+[Z]** or ***click the Undo icon*** until your desired text reappears. The Undo feature also works on many other activities in Word, but not all. So, if something goes wrong, at least try pressing **[CTRL]+[Z]** to undo whatever you did.

E. *Moving Text*—**Drag the mouse pointer to highlight or select the text. Then, from the Home ribbon tab, select the Cut icon from the Clipboard group** (see Word 2007 Exhibit 1). **Move the cursor to where the text should be inserted, and, from the Home ribbon tab, select Paste from the Clipboard group.** Another way to do this is to **drag the mouse pointer to highlight the area and then right-click.** This brings up a menu that includes the Cut, Copy, and Paste commands. Yet another way to do this is to use the drag-and-drop method: **Drag the mouse pointer to highlight the area, release the mouse button, click the highlighted area, drag the text to the new location, and release the mouse button.**

F. *Copying Text*—**Drag the mouse pointer to highlight or select the area. From the Home ribbon tab, click the Copy icon from the Clipboard group** (see Word 2007 Exhibit 1). **Move the cursor to where the text should be copied, and, from the Home ribbon tab, click Paste.** Another way to do this is to **drag the pointer to highlight the area and then right-click Copy. Then move the cursor to where you want to copy the text and right-click Paste.** Still another way to do this is to use the drag-and-drop method: **Drag the cursor to highlight the area, release the mouse button, click the highlighted area** while pressing **[CTRL]**, **drag the text to the new location, and release the mouse button.** The text is then copied to the new location.

III. Formatting

A. *Centering Text*—**Move the pointer to the line where the text should be centered. From the Home ribbon tab, click the Paragraph Group Dialog Box Launcher icon** (see Word 2007 Exhibit 1). **In the Indents and Spacing tab, click on the down arrow key next to Alignment and select Centered; then click on OK and begin typing.** If the text has already been typed, move the pointer to the paragraph where the text is and then issue the command. Alternatively, **from the Home ribbon tab, click the Center icon in the Paragraph group** (see Word 2007 Exhibit 1).

B. *Bold Type*—To type in bold, **from the Home ribbon tab, click the Font Group Dialog Box Launcher icon** (see Word 2007 Exhibit 1); **in the Font tab, click Bold under Font style. Click on OK.** Alternatively, **from the Home ribbon tab, click the Bold icon in the Font group.** Another way is to press **[CTRL]+[B]**.

C. *Underlining*—To underline, **from the Home ribbon tab, click the Font Group Dialog Box Launcher icon** (see Word 2007 Exhibit 1); **in the Font tab, click the down arrow under Underline style, select the underline style you would like, then click OK.** Alternatively, **from the Home ribbon tab, click the Underline icon in the Font group.** Another way is to press **[CTRL]+[U]**.

D. *Margins*—Margins can be set by **clicking the Page Layout ribbon tab and then clicking on Margins from the Page Setup group.**

E. *Line Spacing*—Line spacing can be changed by **clicking the Home ribbon tab, then clicking the Line Spacing icon in the Paragraph group** (see Word 2007 Exhibit 1).

F. *Justification*—**Move the pointer to the line where the text should be justified.** Then, **from the Home ribbon tab, click the Paragraph Group Dialog Box Launcher icon** (see Word 2007 Exhibit 1). **In the Indents and Spacing tab, click the down arrow key next to Alignment and select Justified; then click** *on OK and begin typing.* If the text has already been typed, move the cursor to the paragraph where the text is and then issue the command. Alternatively, *from the Home ribbon tab, click the Justify icon in the Paragraph group* (see Word 2007 Exhibit 1).

G. *Header/Footer—From the Insert ribbon tab, click Header or Footer from the Header & Footer group.*

H. *Hard Page Break*—To force the addition of a new page in the current document by using the Hard Page Break command, press **[CTRL]+[ENTER]**, or *from the Insert ribbon tab, click Blank Page from the Pages group.* Page breaks also occur automatically when the current page is full of text.

I. *Indent—From the Home ribbon tab, click the Paragraph Group Dialog Box Launcher icon* (see Word 2007 Exhibit 1). *In the Indents and Spacing tab under Indentation, click the up arrow next to Left or Right to set the indentation amount; then click on OK and begin typing.* Alternatively, *from the Home ribbon tab, point to the Decrease Indent or Increase Indent icon in the Paragraph group.*

IV. Other Functions

A. *Printing*—To print, *click the Office button, and then click Print* (see Word 2007 Exhibit 1).

B. *Spell Check*—To turn on the spell-checking function, *from the Review ribbon tab, click Spelling & Grammar in the Proofing group.* Additionally, a red squiggly line will appear under each word that the computer's dictionary does not recognize. If you right-click the word, the program will suggest possible spellings.

C. *Open Files*—To open a file, *click the Office button, and then click Open* (see Word 2007 Exhibit 1).

D. *Tables—From the Insert ribbon tab, click Table from the Tables group.* You can move between cells in the table by pressing the **[TAB]** and the **[SHIFT]+[TAB]** keys.

▶ BASIC LESSONS

LESSON 1: TYPING A LETTER

This lesson shows you how to type the letter shown in Word 2007 Exhibit 2. It explains how to use the word wrap feature; the [TAB] key; the cursor (or arrow) keys; the underline, bold, and italics features; the save document function; and the print document function. Keep in mind that if you make a mistake in this lesson at any time, you may press **[CTRL]+[Z]** to undo what you have done. Also remember that any time you would like to see the name of an icon on the ribbon tabs, just *point to the icon for a second or two* and the name will be displayed.

1. Open Windows. After it has loaded, *double-click on the Microsoft Office Word 2007 icon on the desktop* to open Word 2007 for Windows. Alternatively, *click the Start button, point to Programs or All Programs, then click on the Microsoft Word 2007 icon,* or *point to Microsoft Office and then click Microsoft Office Word 2007.* You should now be in a new, clean, blank document. If you are not in a blank document, *click the Office button, click New, then double-click Blank document.*

WORD 2007 EXHIBIT 2
Letter

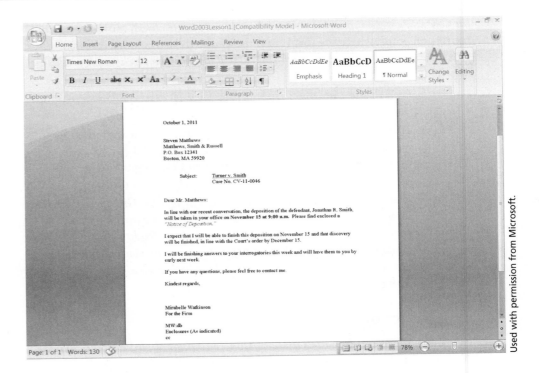

2. At this point you cannot move the pointer around the screen by pressing the cursor keys (also called arrow keys). This is because text must first be entered; the pointer can only move through text, so the cursor keys will not function if no text exists. *On the Home ribbon tab, click the Paragraph Group Dialog Launcher icon. In the "Paragraph" window, click the down arrow below Line spacing and select Single.* Make sure the "Before" and "After" spacing boxes are both 0 point. *Click OK.*

3. Press the [ENTER] key four times. Watch the status line in the lower left-hand corner of the screen, which tells you what page of your document you are on.

4. Type the date of the letter as shown in Word 2007 Exhibit 2. Notice that as you type the word "October," AutoText may anticipate that you are typing "October" and give you the following prompt: **"October (Press ENTER to Insert)."** If you press the [ENTER] key, AutoText will finish typing the word for you. You can also ignore it and just continue typing the word yourself.

5. Press the [ENTER] key three times.

6. Type the inside address as shown in Word 2007 Exhibit 2. Press the [ENTER] key after each line of the inside address. When you finish the line with "Boston, MA 59920," press the [ENTER] key three times.

7. Press the [TAB] key one time (Word automatically sets default tabs every five spaces). The pointer will move five spaces to the right.

8. Type **Subject:** and then press the [TAB] key. *On the Home ribbon tab, click on the Underline icon in the Font group* (it looks like a "U" with a thin line under it). Alternatively, you can press [CTRL]+[U] to turn the underline feature on and off, or *point to the Font Group Dialog Box Launcher icon* (see Word 2007 Exhibit 1) and *select the Underline style.* Then, type **Turner v. Smith**. *On the Home ribbon tab in the Font group, click the Underline icon* to turn the underline feature off.

9. Press the [ENTER] key one time.

10. Press the **[TAB]** key three times, and then type **Case No. CV-11-0046**.

11. Press the **[ENTER]** key three times.

12. Type the salutation **Dear Mr. Matthews:**

13. Press the **[ENTER]** key twice.

14. Type **In line with our recent conversation, the deposition of the defendant, Jonathan R. Smith, will be taken in your office on**. *Note:* You should not press the **[ENTER]** key at the end of a line. Word will automatically "wrap" the text down to the next line. Be sure to press the **[SPACEBAR]** once after the word "on."

15. Turn on the bold feature by *clicking the Bold icon* (a capital "B") *in the Font group in the Home ribbon tab* (see Word 2007 Exhibit 1). Alternatively, you can press **[CTRL]+[B]** to turn bold on and off. Type **November 15 at 9:00 a.m.** Turn off the bold feature either by pressing **[CTRL]+[B]**, or *by clicking the Bold icon in the Font group in the Home ribbon tab*. Press the **[SPACEBAR]** twice.

16. Type **Please find enclosed a** and then press **[SPACEBAR]**.

17. Turn on the italics feature by *clicking the Italics icon* (it looks like an "I") *in the Font group in the Home ribbon tab* (see Word 2007 Exhibit 1). Alternatively, you can press **[CTRL]+[I]** to turn italics on and off. Type "**Notice of Deposition.**" Turn off the italics feature either by pressing **[CTRL]+[I]**, or *by clicking the Italics icon in the Font group in the Home ribbon tab*.

18. Press the **[ENTER]** key twice.

19. Type the second paragraph of the letter and then press the **[ENTER]** key twice.

20. Type the third paragraph of the letter and then press the **[ENTER]** key twice.

21. Type the fourth paragraph of the letter and then press the **[ENTER]** key twice.

22. Type **Kindest regards,** and then press the **[ENTER]** key four times.

23. Type **Mirabelle Watkinson** and then press the **[ENTER]** key.

24. Type **For the Firm** and then press the **[ENTER]** key twice.

25. Finish the letter by typing the author's initials, enclosures, and copy abbreviation (cc) as shown in Word 2007 Exhibit 2.

26. To print the document, *click the Office button, then click Print, then click on OK.*

27. To save the document, *click the Office button and then click Save.* Type **Letter1** next to File name:. *Click Save* to save the letter to the default directory. *Note*: You will edit this letter in Lesson 2, so it is important that you save it.

28. *Click the Office button and then Close* to close the document, or, to exit Word 2007, *click the Office button and then click Exit Word*.

This concludes Lesson 1.

LESSON 2: EDITING A LETTER

This lesson shows you how to retrieve and edit the letter you typed in Lesson 1. It explains how to retrieve a file, perform block moves and deletes, and spell-/grammar-check your document. Keep in mind that if you make a mistake in this lesson at any time, you may press **[CTRL]+[Z]** to undo what you have done. Also remember that any time you would like to see the name of an icon on the ribbon tab, just *point to the icon for a second or two* and the name will be displayed.

1. Open Windows. *Double-click on the Microsoft Office Word 2007 icon on the desktop* to open Word 2007 for Windows. Alternatively, *click the Start button,*

WORD 2007 EXHIBIT 3
Corrections to a letter

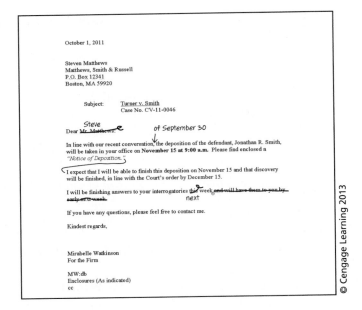

October 1, 2011

Steven Matthews
Matthews, Smith & Russell
P.O. Box 12341
Boston, MA 59920

      Subject: <u>Turner v. Smith</u>
                  Case No. CV-11-0046

          Steve
Dear ~~Mr. Matthews~~:   *of September 30*
In line with our recent conversation, the deposition of the defendant, Jonathan R. Smith,
will be taken in your office on **November 15 at 9:00 a.m.** Please find enclosed a
"Notice of Deposition."
I expect that I will be able to finish this deposition on November 15 and that discovery
will be finished, in line with the Court's order by December 15.

I will be finishing answers to your interrogatories this week ~~and will have them to you by
early next week.~~   *next*

If you have any questions, please feel free to contact me.

Kindest regards,

Mirabelle Watkinson
For the Firm

MW:db
Enclosures (As indicated)
cc

point to Programs or All Programs, then click the Microsoft Word 2007 icon. (You can also *point to Microsoft Office and then click Microsoft Office Word 2007*). You should now be in a new, clean, blank document. If you are not in a blank document, *click the Office button, click New, then double-click Blank document.*

2. In this lesson, you will begin by retrieving the document you created in Lesson 1. To open the file, *click the Office button and click Open.* Then type **Letter1** and *click Open.* Alternatively, *scroll using the horizontal scroll bar until you find the file, then click on it, then click Open.*

3. Notice in Word 2007 Exhibit 3 that some editing changes have been made to the letter. You will spend the rest of this lesson making these changes.

4. Use your cursor keys or mouse to go to the salutation line, "Dear Mr. Matthews:" With the pointer to the left of the "M" in "Mr. Matthews," press the **[DEL]** key 12 times until "Mr. Matthews" is deleted.

5. Type **Steve**. The salutation line should now read "Dear Steve:"

6. Using your cursor keys or mouse, *move the pointer to the left of the comma following the word "conversation" in the first paragraph.* Press the **[SPACEBAR]**, then type **of September 30**. The sentence now reads:

In line with our recent conversation of September 30, the deposition of the defendant, ...

7. The next change you will make is to move the second paragraph so that it becomes part of the first paragraph. Although this can be accomplished in more than one way, this lesson uses the Cut command.

8. Using your cursor keys or mouse, *move the pointer to the beginning of the second paragraph of Word 2007 Exhibit 3.*

9. *Click and drag the cursor* (hold the left mouse button down and move the mouse) *until the entire second paragraph is highlighted, and then release the mouse button.*

10. *From the Home ribbon tab, click the Cut icon in the Clipboard group* (see Word 2007 Exhibit 1). An alternative is to *right-click anywhere in the highlighted area and then click Cut.* The text is no longer on the

screen, but it is not deleted—it has been temporarily placed on the Office Clipboard.

11. Move the pointer to the end of the first paragraph. Press the **[SPACEBAR]** twice. If the pointer appears to be in italics mode, *from the Home ribbon tab, click the Italics icon in the Font group,* or press **[CTLR]+[I]** to turn the italics feature off.

12. *From the Home ribbon tab, click Paste from the Clipboard group* (see Word 2007 Exhibit 1). Notice that the text has now been moved. Also, you may notice that a small icon in the shape of a clipboard has appeared where you pasted the text. Click the down arrow of the Paste Options icon. Notice that you are given the option to keep the source formatting or change the formatting so that the text matches the destination formatting (i.e., the formatting of the place you are copying it to). In this example, both formats are the same, so it does not matter, but if the text you are copying is a different format, you can choose whether or not to change it to the destination format. Press the **[ESC]** key to make the Paste Options menu disappear.

13. Move the pointer to the line below the first paragraph, and use the **[DEL]** key to delete any unnecessary blank lines.

14. Using your cursor keys or mouse, *move the pointer to what is now the second paragraph and place the pointer to the left of the "t" in "this week."*

15. Use the **[DEL]** key to delete the word "this," and then type **next**.

16. We will now delete the rest of the sentence in the second paragraph. *Drag the pointer until "and will have them to you by early next week." is highlighted.* Press the **[DEL]** key. Type a period at the end of the sentence.

17. You have now made all of the necessary changes. To be sure the letter does not have misspelled words or grammar errors, you will use the Spelling and Grammar command.

18. *Point on the Review ribbon tab, then click Spelling & Grammar in the Proofing group.*

19. If an error is found, it will be highlighted. You have the options of ignoring it once, ignoring it completely, accepting one of the suggestions listed, or changing/correcting the problem yourself. Correct any spelling or grammar errors. When the spell and grammar check is done, *click OK.*

20. To print the document, *click on the Office button, click Print, then click on OK.*

21. To save the document, *click the Office button and then select Save As.* Type **Letter2** in the "File name:" box, *then click Save* to save the document in the default directory.

22. *Click the Office button and then click Close* to close the document, or *click the Office button and then click Exit Word* to exit the program.

This concludes Lesson 2.

LESSON 3: TYPING A PLEADING

This lesson shows you how to type a pleading, as shown in Word 2007 Exhibit 4. It expands on the items presented in Lessons 1 and 2. It also explains how to center text, change margins, change line spacing, add a footnote, double-indent text, and use automatic page numbering. Keep in mind that if you make a mistake at any time, you may press **[CTRL]+[Z]** to undo what you have done.

1. Open Windows. *Double-click the Microsoft Office Word 2007 icon on the desktop* to open Word 2007 for Windows. Alternatively, *click the Start button, point to Programs or All Programs, then click the Microsoft Word 2007 icon.*

HANDS-ON EXERCISES

WORD 2007 EXHIBIT 4
A pleading

IN THE DISTRICT COURT OF
ORANGE COUNTY, MASSACHUSETTS

JIM TURNER,

               Plaintiff,

vs.   Case No. CV-11-0046

JONATHAN R. SMITH,

               Defendant.

<u>**NOTICE TO TAKE DEPOSITION**</u>

COMES NOW, the plaintiff and pursuant to statute[1] hereby gives notice that the

deposition of Defendant, Jonathan R. Smith, will be taken as follows:

       Monday, November 15, 2012, at 9:00 a.m. at the law offices of Matthews,

       Smith & Russell, 17031 W. 69th Street, Boston, MA.

Said deposition will be taken before a court reporter and is not expected to take more than

one day in duration.

_____
Mirabelle Watkinson
Attorney for Plaintiff

_____
[1] Massachusetts Statutes Annotated 60-2342(a)(1).

(You can also *point to Microsoft Office and then click Microsoft Office Word 2007*.) You should now be in a new, clean, blank document. If you are not in a blank document, *click the Office button, click New, then double-click on Blank document.* Remember, any time you would like to see the name of an icon on the ribbon tabs, just *point to the icon for a second or two* and the name will be displayed.

2. You will be creating the document shown in Word 2007 Exhibit 4. The first thing you will need to do is change the margins so that the left margin is 1.5 inches and the right margin is 1 inch. To change the margins, *click the Page Layout ribbon tab and then click Margins in the Page Setup group. Next, click Custom Margins at the bottom of the drop-down menu. In the "Page Setup" window in the Margins tab, change the left margin to*

1.5 inches and the right margin to 1 inch. Click OK. Also, *on the Home ribbon tab, click the Paragraph Group dialog launcher. In the "Paragraph" window in the Indents and Spacing tab, click the down arrow below Line spacing and select Single.* Make sure the "Before" and "After" spacing boxes are both 0 point; then *click OK.*

3. Notice in Word 2007 Exhibit 4 that there is a page number at the bottom of the page. Word will automatically number your pages for you.

4. *Click the Insert ribbon tab, then click Page Number in the Header & Footer group* (see Word 2007 Exhibit 5).

5. *Point to Bottom of Page* (see Word 2007 Exhibit 5) and notice that a number of options are displayed. *Click the down arrow in the lower right for additional options* (see Word 2007 Exhibit 5). Notice that many page number options are available. *Scroll back up to the top of the option list and click the second option, Plain Number 2.*

6. Your pointer should now be in the area marked "Footer." Specifically, your pointer should be to the left of the number 1. Type **Page** and then press **[SPACEBAR].**

7. *Click the Home ribbon tab. Then, click the vertical scroll bar* (see Word 2007 Exhibit 1) *or use the [UP ARROW] key to go back to the beginning of the document.*

8. *Point and double-click just below the header.*

9. On the first line of the document, *from the Home ribbon tab, click the Center icon in the Paragraph group.* Type **IN THE DISTRICT COURT OF.** Press the **[ENTER]** key. Type **ORANGE COUNTY, MASSACHUSETTS.**

10. Press the **[ENTER]** key five times. *From the Home ribbon tab, click the Align Text Left icon in the Paragraph group.*

11. Type **JIM TURNER,** and press the **[ENTER]** key twice.

HANDS-ON EXERCISES

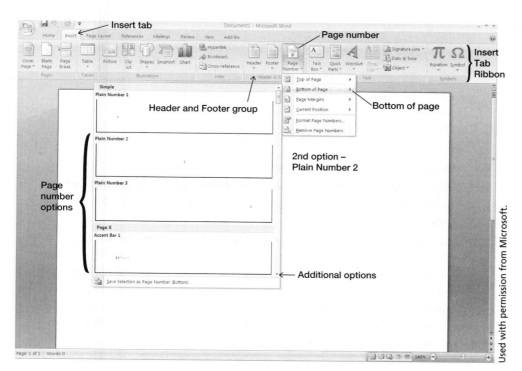

WORD 2007 EXHIBIT 5
Adding a page number

Used with permission from Microsoft.

12. Press the [TAB] key three times and type **Plaintiff,** then press the [ENTER] key twice.

13. Type **vs.** Then press the [TAB] key six times, and type **Case No. CV-11-0046**.

14. Press the [ENTER] key twice.

15. Type **JONATHAN R. SMITH,** and press the [ENTER] key twice.

16. Press the [TAB] key three times and type **Defendant.** Press the [ENTER] key four times.

17. *From the Home ribbon tab, click the Center icon in the Paragraph group.*

18. *From the Home ribbon tab, click the Bold icon and the Underline icon, both found in the Font group.* Type **NOTICE TO TAKE DEPOSITION**. *Click the Bold and Underline icons* to turn them off.

19. Press the [ENTER] key three times. *From the Home ribbon tab, click the Align Text Left icon in the Paragraph group.*

20. *From the Home ribbon tab, click the Line spacing icon from the Paragraph group* (see Word 2007 Exhibit 1), *then click on 2.0.* This will change the line spacing from single to double.

21. Type **COMES NOW, the plaintiff and pursuant to statute**. Notice that a footnote follows the word *statute* in Word 2007 Exhibit 4.

22. With the pointer just to the right of the e in "statute," *from the References ribbon tab, click Insert Footnote from the Footnotes group.* The cursor should now be at the bottom of the page in the footnote window.

23. Type **Massachusetts Statutes Annotated 60–2342(a)(1)**.

24. To move the pointer back to the body of the document, simply *click to the right of the word "statute" and the superscript number 1 in the body of the document.* Now, continue to type the rest of the first paragraph. Once the paragraph is typed, press the [ENTER] key twice.

25. To double-indent the second paragraph, *from the Home ribbon tab, click the Paragraph Group Dialog Box Launcher icon* (see Word 2007 Exhibit 1). The "Paragraph" window should now be displayed. *In the Indents and Spacing tab under Indentation, add a 0.5-inch left indent and a 0.5-inch right indent using the up arrow icons* (or you can type in .5). *Click OK in the "Paragraph" window.*

26. Type the second paragraph.

27. Press the [ENTER] key twice.

28. *From the Home ribbon tab, click the Paragraph Group dialog launcher and, under Indentation, change the left and right indents back to 0. Click OK.*

29. Type the third paragraph.

30. Press the [ENTER] key three times.

31. The signature line is single spaced, so *from the Home ribbon tab, click the Line spacing icon from the Paragraph group, then click 1.0.* This will change the line spacing from double to single.

32. Press [SHIFT]+[-] (the key to the right of the zero key on the top row of the keyboard) 30 times to draw the signature line. Press the [ENTER] key. *Note*: If Word automatically inserts a line across the whole page, press [CTRL]+[Z] to undo the AutoCorrect line. Alternatively, you can *click the down arrow in the Auto Correct Options icon* (it looks like a lightning bolt and should be just over the line that now runs across the page) *and select Undo Border Line.*

33. Type **Mirabelle Watkinson** and then press the [ENTER] key.

34. Type **Attorney for Plaintiff.**

35. To print the document, *click the Office button, click Print, then click OK.*

36. To save the document, *click the Office button and then select Save As.* Type **Pleading1** in the "File name:" box, *then click Save* to save the document in the default directory.

37. *Click the Office button and then click Close* to close the document, or *click the Office button and then click Exit Word* to exit the program.

This concludes Lesson 3.

LESSON 4: CREATING A TABLE

This lesson shows you how to create the table shown in Word 2007 Exhibit 6. It expands on the items presented in Lessons 1, 2, and 3 and explains how to change a font size, create a table, enter data into a table, add automatic numbering, adjust column widths, and use the Table AutoFormat command. Keep in mind that if you make a mistake at any time, you may press **[CTRL]+[Z]** to undo what you have done.

1. Open Windows. *Double-click the Microsoft Office Word 2007 icon on the desktop* to open Word 2007 for Windows. Alternatively, *click the Start button, point to Programs or All Programs, then click the Microsoft Word 2007 icon,* or *point to Microsoft Office and then click on Microsoft Office Word 2007.* You should be in a new, clean, blank document. If you are not in a blank document, *click the Office button, click on New, then double-click on Blank document.*

2. *From the Home ribbon tab, click the Center icon in the Paragraph group, and then click the Bold icon in the Font group.*

3. *From the Home ribbon tab, click the Font Size icon in the Font group* and change the font size to 14 by either typing **14** in the box or *choosing 14 from the drop-down menu.* Alternatively, you can both turn on bold and change

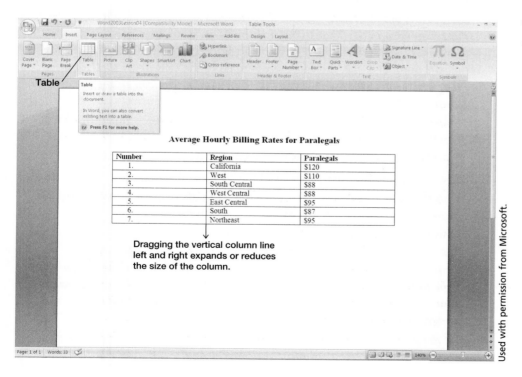

WORD 2007 EXHIBIT 6
Creating a table

the font size by *clicking the Font Group Dialog Box Launcher icon from the Home ribbon tab* (see Word 2007 Exhibit 1).

4. Type **Average Hourly Billing Rates for Paralegals** (see Word 2007 Exhibit 6). Press the **[ENTER]** key once, and then *click the Font Size icon and change the type back to 12 point. Click the Bold icon* to turn bold off.

5. Press the **[ENTER]** key once.

6. *From the Insert ribbon tab, click Table from the Tables group.* Notice that a number of columns and rows of boxes are displayed. This allows you to choose the graphic style of your table.

7. *Point within the Table menu so that three columns are highlighted, then point and click so that eight rows are highlighted* (e.g., 3 x 8 Table). Notice that as you point, the table is temporarily shown in your document. This is called a *live preview*. When you point and click on the cell that is three columns over and eight cells down, the table (as opposed to the live preview) will be displayed permanently in your document.

8. The blank table should now be displayed and the cursor should be in the first column of the first row of the table. If the cursor is not in the first column of the first row, *click in this cell to place the cursor there. From the Home ribbon tab, click on the Bold icon on the Font group.* Type **Number** and then press the **[TAB]** key once to go to the next cell in the table.

9. *Click on the Bold icon.* Type **Region** and then press the **[TAB]** key once to go to the next cell in the table. *Note*: If you need to go back to a previous cell, you can use either the mouse or the cursor keys, or you can press **[SHIFT]+[TAB]**. Also, if you accidentally hit the **[ENTER]** key instead of the **[TAB]** key, you can either press the **[BACKSPACE]** key to delete the extra line, or you can press **[CTRL]+[Z]** to undo it.

10. *Click on the Bold icon.* Type **Paralegals** and then press the **[TAB]** key to go to the next cell.

11. You will now use the automatic paragraph numbering feature to number the rows. *From the Home ribbon tab, click on the Numbering icon in the Paragraph group* (see Word 2007 Exhibit 1—it is the icon that has the numbers 1, 2, 3 in a column, with a short line next to each number). Notice that the number 1 was automatically entered in the cell. *From the Home ribbon tab, point on the down arrow next to the Numbering icon in the Paragraph group.* Under Numbering Library, look at the different formats that are available. The default format is fine, so press **[ESC]** to make the menu disappear.

12. Press the **[TAB]** key to go to the next cell.

13. Type **California** and then press the **[TAB]** key to go to the next cell.

14. Type **$120** and then press the **[TAB]** key to go to the next cell.

15. *From the Home ribbon tab, click on the Numbering icon in the Paragraph group,* and then press the **[TAB]** key to go to the next cell.

16. Continue entering all of the information shown in Word 2007 Exhibit 6 into your table.

17. *Put the pointer in the uppermost left cell of the table and drag the pointer to the lowest cell at the right of the table to completely highlight the table. Then, from the Home ribbon tab, click on the Align Text Left icon in the Paragraph group.* Now the whole table is left-aligned.

18. *Put the pointer on the vertical column line that separates the Number column and the Region column, and then drag the line to the left* (see Word

2007 Exhibit 6). Notice that by using this technique you can completely adjust each column width as much as you like. Press **[CTRL]+[Z]** to undo the column move, because the current format is fine.

19. ***Click on any cell in the table.*** Notice that just above the ribbon tab, new options are now shown; two more tabs, Design and Layout, appear under the new heading "Table Tools." ***Click on the Design ribbon tab.*** Notice that the ribbon tab now shows seven table styles. ***Point (don't click) on one of the tables;*** notice that the Live Preview feature shows you exactly what your table will look like with this design. ***Point and click on the down arrow in the Table Styles group and browse to see many more table styles. Point and click on a table style that you like.*** The format of the table changes completely.

20. To print the document, ***click on the Office button, click on Print, then click on OK.***

21. To save the document, ***click on the Office button and then select Save As.*** Type **Table1** in the "File name:" box, ***then point and click on Save*** to save the document in the default directory.

22. ***Click on the Office button and then on Close*** to close the document, or ***click on the Office button and then on Exit Word*** to exit the program.

This concludes Lesson 4.

 # INTERMEDIATE LESSONS

LESSON 5: TOOLS AND TECHNIQUES

This lesson shows you how to edit an employment policy (from the data disk supplied with this text), use the Format Painter tool, reveal formatting, clear formatting, change the case of text, use the Find and Replace feature, use the Go To command, create a section break, and change the orientation of a page from portrait to landscape. This lesson assumes that you have completed Lessons 1 through 4 and that you are generally familiar with Word 2007.

1. Open Windows. ***Double-click on the Microsoft Office Word 2007 icon on the desktop*** to open Word 2007 for Windows. Alternatively, ***click on the Start button, point the pointer to Programs or All Programs, then click on the Microsoft Word 2007 icon.*** You also may ***point to Microsoft Office and then click on Microsoft Office Word 2007.*** You should be in a new, clean, blank document. If you are not in a blank document, ***click on the Office button, click on New, then double-click on Blank document.***

2. The first thing you will do is open the "Lesson 5" file from the disk supplied with this text. Ensure that the disk is inserted in the disk drive, ***click on the Office button, then click on Open.*** The "Open" window should now be displayed. ***Click on the down arrow to the right of the white box next to Look in: and select the drive where the disk is located. Double-click on the Word Processing Files folder. Double-click on the Word 2007 folder. Double-click on the "Lesson 5" file.***

3. The file entitled "World Wide Technology, Inc. alcohol and drug policy" should now be displayed on your screen. In this lesson, you will be editing this policy for use by another client. The next thing you need to do is to go to section 3, "Definitions," and change the subheadings so that they all have the same format. You will use the Format Painter tool to do this.

4. Use the cursor keys or the mouse and the scroll bars to scroll to section 3, "Definitions" (see Word 2007 Exhibit 7). Notice that the first definition, "Alcohol or alcoholic beverages:," is bold and in a different font from the rest of the definitions in section 3. You will use the Format Painter tool to quickly copy the formatting from "Alcohol or alcoholic beverages:" to the other four definitions in section 3.

5. *Point and click anywhere in the text "Alcohol or alcoholic beverages:"* This tells the Format Painter tool the formatting you want to copy.

6. Next, *from the Home ribbon tab, point and click on the Format Painter icon in the Clipboard group.* It looks like a paintbrush (see Word 2007 Exhibit 7). Remember, if you hover your cursor over an icon for a second or two, the name of the icon will appear.

7. Notice that your cursor now turns to a paintbrush. *Drag the pointer* (hold the left mouse button down and move the mouse) *until the heading "Legal drugs:" is highlighted* (see Word 2007 Exhibit 7), *then let go of the mouse button.* Notice that the paintbrush on your cursor is now gone. *Click the left mouse button once anywhere in the screen to make the highlight go away.* Notice that "Legal drugs:" now has the same formatting as "Alcohol or alcoholic beverages:" The Format Painter command is a quick way to make formatting changes.

8. You will now use the Format Painter command to copy the formatting to the remaining three definitions, with one additional trick. *Click anywhere in the text "Legal drugs:"*

9. Next, *from the Home ribbon tab, double-click on the Format Painter icon in the Clipboard group.* (Your pointer should now have a paintbrush attached to it.) The double-click tells Format Painter that you are going to copy this format to multiple locations, instead of just one location. This is a great

WORD 2007 EXHIBIT 7
The Format Painter tool

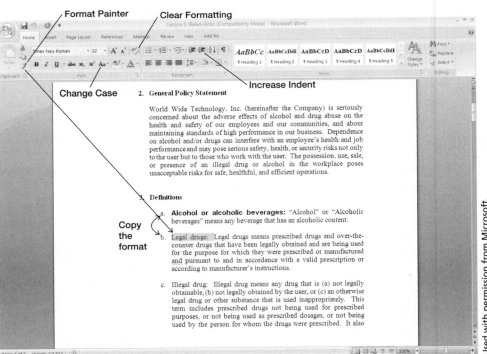

time-saving feature if you need to copy formatting to several places, because it keeps you from having to click the Format Painter icon each time you copy the same formatting to a new location.

10. ***Drag the pointer until the heading "Illegal drug:" is highlighted, then let go of the mouse button.*** Notice that the paintbrush is still attached to your pointer.

11. ***Drag the pointer until the heading "Controlled substance:" is highlighted, then let go of the mouse button.***

12. ***Drag the pointer until the heading "Prescription drug:" is highlighted, then let go of the mouse button.***

13. To turn the Format Painter off, press the **[ESC]** button on the keyboard. ***Click the left mouse button once, with the cursor anywhere in the document, to make the highlight go away.*** Notice that all of the headings are now uniform.

14. You will now learn to use the Reveal Formatting command. ***Click on the heading "Prescription drug:"***

15. Press **[SHIFT]+[F1]** on the keyboard. Notice that the Reveal Formatting task pane opened on the right side of the screen. The Reveal Formatting task pane lists all format specifications for the selected text. The items are divided into several groups, including Font, Paragraph, Bullets and Numbering, and Section. You can make formatting changes to the text directly from the Reveal Formatting task pane simply by clicking on the format setting you want to change (the links are shown in blue, underlined text). For example, ***click on the blue underlined word "Font" in the Reveal Formatting task pane.*** Notice that the "Font" window opens. You can now select a new font if you so desire. The Reveal Formatting task pane allows you to quickly see all formatting attached to specific text and, if necessary, to change it.

16. ***Point and click on Cancel in the "Font" window.*** To close the Reveal Formatting task pane, ***click on the "x" (the Close button) at the top of the Reveal Formatting task pane.*** It is just to the right of the words "Reveal Formatting." The Reveal Formatting task pane should now be gone.

17. Press **[CTRL]+[HOME]** to go to the beginning of the document.

18. You will now learn how to use the Clear Formats command. Notice under the heading "1. Objectives" that the sentence "The objectives of this policy are as follows:" is bold and italics; this is a mistake. ***Drag the pointer until this text is highlighted.***

19. ***From the Home ribbon tab, click on the Clear Formatting icon in the Font group*** (see Word 2007 Exhibit 7). This icon looks like an eraser next to a capital "A" and a lowercase "a." Then, ***move the pointer to anywhere in the sentence and click the left mouse button once to make the highlight go away.*** Notice that all of the formatting is now gone. The Clear Formats command is a good way to remove all text formatting quickly and easily.

20. To move the text to the right so it is under "1. Objectives," ***from the Home ribbon tab, click three times on the Increase Indent icon in the Paragraph group*** (see Word 2007 Exhibit 7). This is the icon with a right arrow and some lines on it. The line should now be back in its place.

21. You will now learn how to use the Change Case command. Press **[CTRL]+[HOME]** on the keyboard to go to the beginning of the document.

22. ***Drag the pointer until "World Wide Technology, Inc." in the document's title is highlighted.***

23. *From the Home ribbon tab, point and click on the Change Case icon in the Font group. Click on UPPERCASE.* Notice that the text is now in all capitals. *Click the left mouse button once anywhere in the document to make the highlighting disappear.*

24. *Drag the pointer until the subtitle "alcohol and drug policy" is highlighted. From the Home ribbon tab, click on the Change Case icon in the Font group. Click on "Capitalize Each Word."* Notice that the text is now in title case. *Click the left mouse button once anywhere in the document to make the highlighting go away.* The Change Case command is a convenient way to change the case of text without having to retype it. *Note:* Retyping always increases the risk of introducing errors!

25. Notice that the *A* in *and* in "Alcohol And Drug Policy" is now capitalized, and that a green squiggly line is underneath it. This tells you that Word believes there is a grammar error. *Right-click on the word "And" in the title.* A menu will be displayed. *Point and click on and (this is what Word is suggesting the correction should be).* The word "and" in the title is now lowercase.

26. Press **[CTRL]+[HOME]** on the keyboard to go to the beginning of the document.

27. You will now learn how to use the Find and Replace command. *From the Home ribbon tab, point and click on the Replace icon in the Editing group.* Alternatively, you could press **[CTRL]+[H]**, then *click on Replace.*

28. In the "Find and Replace" window, in the white box next to "Find what:" type **World Wide Technology, Inc.** Then, in the white box next to "Replace with:" type **Johnson Manufacturing.** *Click on the Replace All button in the "Find and Replace" window.* The program will respond by stating that it made four replacements. *Click on OK in that notification window.*

29. *Click on the Close button in the "Find and Replace" window to close the window.* Notice that "World Wide Technology, Inc." has now been changed to "Johnson Manufacturing."

30. You will now learn how to use the Go To command. The Go To command is an easy way to navigate through large and complex documents. Press **[F5].** Notice that the "Find and Replace" window is again displayed on the screen, but this time the Go To tab is selected. In the white box directly under "Enter page number:" type **7** using the keyboard and then *click on Go To in the "Find and Replace" window.* Notice that on page 7, "Reasonable Suspicion Report," is now displayed. (*Note:* If the "Find and Replace" window blocks your view of the text of the document, point at the blue box in the "Find and Replace" window and drag the window lower so you can see the document.) *Click on Close in the "Find and Replace" window.*

31. Suppose that you would like to change the orientation of only one page in a document from Portrait (where the length is greater than the width) to Landscape (where the width is greater than the length). In this example, you will change the layout of only the Reasonable Suspicion Report to Landscape while keeping the rest of the document in Portrait orientation. To do this in Word, you must enter a section break.

32. Your cursor should be on page 7, just above "Johnson Manufacturing Reasonable Suspicion Report." *From the Page Layout ribbon tab, click on Breaks in the Page Setup group.*

33. *Under Section Breaks, click on Next Page.*

34. ***Click on the Draft icon*** in the lower right area of the screen (see Word 2007 Exhibit 7). ***Press the [UP ARROW] key two times.*** Notice that a double dotted line that says "Section Break (Next Page)" is now displayed.

35. The Word 2007 interface allows you to switch views by clicking on one of the view layouts in the lower right of the screen (see Word 2007 Exhibit 7). Print and Draft are two of the most popular layouts. In addition, the Zoom tool just to the right of the Draft view allows you to zoom in or out (increase or decrease the magnification) of your document.

36. With the section break in place, you can now change the format of the page from Portrait to Landscape without changing the orientation of previous pages.

37. ***With the cursor on the "Johnson Manufacturing Reasonable Suspicion Report" page, from the Page Layout ribbon tab, click on Orientation in the Page Setup group. Click on Landscape.*** Notice that the layout of the page has changed.

38. ***Click on the Print Layout icon*** in the lower right of the screen (see Word 2007 Exhibit 7).

39. To confirm that the layout has changed, ***click on the Office button, then point to Print, then click on Print Preview.*** Notice that the layout is now Landscape (the width is greater than the length). Press the **[PAGE UP]** key until you are back to the beginning of the document. Notice that all of the other pages in the document are still in Portrait orientation.

40. ***From the Print Preview ribbon tab, click on the Close Print Preview icon in the preview group*** (this icon is a red X at the far right of the ribbon tab).

41. To print the document, ***click on the Office button, click on Print, then click on OK.***

42. To save the document, ***click on the Office button, point to Save As, then click on Word 97-2003 Document. Under Save in, select the drive or folder*** you would like to save the document in. Then, next to File name:, type **Done—Word 2007 Lesson 5 Document** *and click on Save* to save the document.

43. ***Click on the Office button, then click on Close*** to close the document, or ***click on the Office button and then on Exit Word*** to exit the program.

This concludes Lesson 5.

LESSON 6: USING STYLES

This lesson gives you an introduction to styles. Styles are particularly helpful when you are working with long documents that must be formatted uniformly.

1. Open Windows. ***Double-click on the Microsoft Office Word 2007 icon on the desktop*** to open Word 2007 for Windows. Alternatively, ***click on the Start button, point the cursor to Programs or All Programs, then click on the Microsoft Word 2007 icon.*** (You may also ***point to Microsoft Office and then click on Microsoft Office Word 2007.***) You should now be in a new, clean, blank document. If you are not in a blank document, ***click on the Office button, click on New, then double-click on Blank document.***

2. The first thing you will do is open the "Lesson 6" file from the disk supplied with this text. Ensure that the disk is inserted in the drive, ***click on the Office button, then click on Open.*** The "Open" window should now be displayed. ***Click on the down arrow to the right of the white box next to Look in: and select the drive where the disk is located. Double-click on the Word***

HANDS-ON EXERCISES

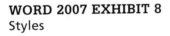

HANDS-ON EXERCISES

Processing File folder. Double-click on the Word 2007 folder. Double-click on the "Lesson 6" file.

3. The text "SARBANES-OXLEY ACT OF 2002" should now be displayed on your screen (see Word 2007 Exhibit 8). In this lesson you will use styles to add uniform formatting to this document. In the Home ribbon tab, notice the Styles group. *Point and click on any text on the page.* Notice in the Styles group on the Home ribbon tab that the Normal box is highlighted in yellow (see Word 2007 Exhibit 8). Currently, all text in this document is in the Normal style.

4. Using your cursor keys or the scroll bar, scroll down through the document. Notice that all of the paragraphs are left-aligned and that the right edge of all the paragraphs is ragged (not justified).

5. *From the Home ribbon tab, click on the Styles Group Dialog Box Launcher icon.* Notice that the Styles task pane now appears on the right side of the screen (see Word 2007 Exhibit 8). In the Styles task pane, *if the white box next to Show Preview is not marked, click on the box so that a green check mark appears* (see Word 2007 Exhibit 8). Notice that a few styles in the Styles task pane are currently being displayed (e.g., Heading 1, Heading 2, and Normal). Also notice that the Normal style has a blue box around it, indicating that your cursor is on text with the Normal style. Finally, notice that there is a paragraph sign after each of these heading names, indicating that these are paragraph styles.

6. Notice at the bottom of the Styles task pane the word Options... in blue; *click on Options.* The "Style Pane Options" window should now be displayed.

7. *In the "Style Pane Options" window under Select styles to show, click the down arrow next to "In current document" and click on "All styles." Then, in the "Style Pane Options" window, click on OK.*

8. Notice that the Styles task pane is now full of additional styles. These are all of the styles that are automatically available in Word 2007. *Click on the down arrow in the Styles task pane to see the full list of styles.*

WORD 2007 EXHIBIT 8
Styles

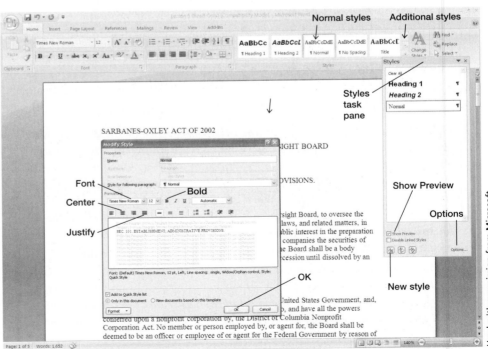

9. To return to the list of just a few styles, ***click on Options in the lower right of the Styles task pane. Under Select styles to show:, click on the down arrow and click on "In current document." Then, in the "Style Pane Options" window, click on OK.***

10. Notice that the short list of styles is again displayed. To access a longer list of styles from the Styles group on the Home ribbon tab, ***click on the down arrow in the Styles group.*** If you select the More icon (the icon that shows a down arrow with a line over it) in the Styles group, you can see all of the styles at one time. Press the **[ESC]** key to close the list.

11. Styles are extremely useful. Assume now that you would like to have all of the text in the document justified. ***Right-click on Normal in the Styles task pane. Left-click on Modify.*** The Modify Style task pane should now be displayed (see Word 2007 Exhibit 8). Using the Modify Style task pane, you can completely change the formatting for any style.

12. ***Click on the Justify icon in the Modify Style task pane*** to change the Normal style from left-aligned to fully justified (see Word 2007 Exhibit 8).

13. ***Click on the down arrow in the "Font" box in the Modify Style task pane and click on Arial*** (you may have to scroll through some fonts to find it). ***Click on the OK button in the Modify Style task pane.*** Notice that Word quickly changed the alignment of all of the text to fully justified and changed the font to Arial.

14. ***Drag the pointer until the full title of the document is highlighted*** (SARBANES-OXLEY ACT OF 2002 TITLE I—PUBLIC COMPANY ACCOUNTING OVERSIGHT BOARD).

15. ***Click on Heading 1 in the Styles task pane.***

16. ***Right-click on Heading 1 in the Styles task pane and select Modify. Then, click on the Center icon. Click the OK button in the Modify Style task pane.***

17. ***Click the left mouse button anywhere in the title to make the highlight disappear.*** Notice that the text of the title shows as Heading 1 in the Styles task pane.

18. ***Point and click anywhere in "SEC. 101. ESTABLISHMENT; ADMINISTRATIVE PROVISIONS." Click on Heading 2 in the Styles task pane.*** Notice that the heading has now changed.

19. ***Point and click anywhere in the subheading "(a) ESTABLISHMENT OF BOARD." Click on the New Style icon at the bottom of the Styles task pane*** (see Word 2007 Exhibit 8).

20. The "Create New Style from Formatting" window should now be displayed. Under Properties, next to Name, type **Heading 3A**; then, ***under Formatting, click on the Bold icon. Click on OK in the "Create New Style from Formatting" window.***

21. Now, go to the following subheadings and format them as Heading 3A by clicking on them and selecting Heading 3A from the Styles task pane:

    (b) STATUS.

    (c) DUTIES OF THE BOARD.

    (d) COMMISSION DETERMINATION.

    (e) BOARD MEMBERSHIP.

    (f) POWERS OF THE BOARD.

    (g) RULES OF THE BOARD.

    (h) ANNUAL REPORT TO THE COMMISSION.

HANDS-ON EXERCISES

Press **[CTRL]+[HOME]** to go to the beginning of the document. Your document is now consistently formatted. Using styles, your documents can also easily be uniformly changed. For example, if you read in your local rules that subheadings for pleadings must be in 15-point Times New Roman font, you could quickly change the subheadings in your document by modifying the heading styles, rather than highlighting each subheading and changing the format manually.

22. To print the document, ***click on the Office button, click on Print, then click on OK.***

23. To save the document, ***click on the Office button and point to Save As. Then click on Word 97-2003 Document. Under Save in, select the drive or folder*** in which you would like to save the document. Then, next to File name:, type **Done—Word 2007 Lesson 6 Document** *and click on Save* to save the document.

24. ***Click on the Office button and then on Close*** to close the document, or ***click on the Office button and then on Exit Word*** to exit the program.

This concludes Lesson 6.

LESSON 7: CREATING A TEMPLATE

This lesson shows you how to create the template shown in Word 2007 Exhibit 9. It explains how to create a template of a letter, how to insert fields, and how to fill out and use a finished template. You will also learn how to add a command to the Quick Access toolbar. The information that will be merged into the letter will be entered from the keyboard. Keep in mind that if you make a mistake at any time, you may press **[CTRL]+[Z]** to undo what you have done.

1. Open Windows. ***Double-click on the Microsoft Office Word 2007 icon on the desktop*** to open Word 2007 for Windows. Alternatively, ***click on the Start button, point the cursor to Programs or All Programs, then click on the Microsoft Word 2007 icon.*** (You can also ***point to Microsoft Office and then click on Microsoft Office Word 2007.)*** You should be in a new, clean, blank

WORD 2007 EXHIBIT 9
Office Letter template

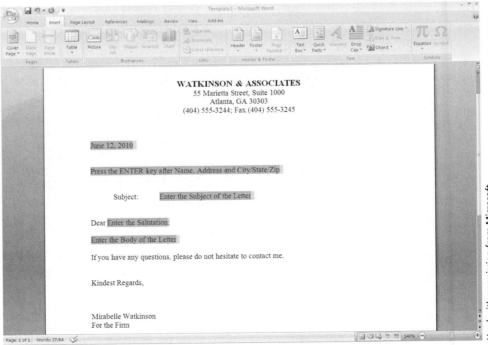

document. If you are not in a blank document, *click on the Office button, click on New, then double-click on Blank document.*

2. *Click on the Office button, then click on New. Under Templates, click on My templates.*

3. *Click on Template under the Create New field in the lower right of the "New" window* (see Word 2007 Exhibit 10).

4. *Click on Blank Document.* Blank Document should now be highlighted. *Click on OK* (see Word 2007 Exhibit 10).

5. You should now have a blank template on your screen. The Windows title should say *Template1—Microsoft Word* in the upper middle of the screen. You will now build the template shown in Word 2007 Exhibit 9.

6. *Also, on the Home ribbon tab, click the Paragraph Group dialog launcher. In the "Paragraph" window, in the Indents and Spacing tab, click the down arrow below Line spacing and select Single.* Make sure the Before and After spacing are both 0 point. Then, *click OK.*

7. *From the Home ribbon tab, click on the Center icon in the Paragraph group. From the Home ribbon tab, click on the Bold icon in the Font group.*

8. *From the Home ribbon tab, click on the Font Size icon from the Font group and select 14 from the list. Click on Font and select Times New Roman.*

9. Type **Watkinson & Associates** and then, *from the Home ribbon tab, click on the Font Size icon and select 12 from the list. Click on the Bold icon from the Font group* to turn off bolding.

10. Press the [**ENTER**] key.

11. Type **55 Marietta Street, Suite 1000** and press the [**ENTER**] key.

12. Type **Atlanta, GA, 30303** and press the [**ENTER**] key.

13. Type **(404) 555–3244; Fax (404) 555–3245** and press the [**ENTER**] key.

14. *From the Home ribbon tab, click on the Align Text Left icon in the Paragraph group.*

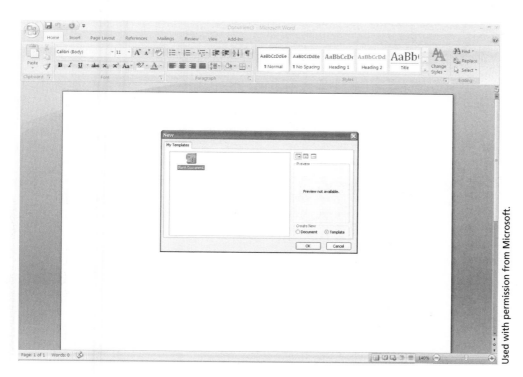

WORD 2007 EXHIBIT 10
Creating a new template

HANDS-ON EXERCISES

15. Press the **[ENTER]** key three times.

16. *From the Insert ribbon tab, click on Quick Parts from the Text group and then click Field.*

17. The "Field" window should now be displayed (see Word 2007 Exhibit 11). The "Field" window has several sections, including Categories: and Field names:. Under Categories:, (All) should be selected.

18. *Click on the down arrow on the Field names: scroll bar until you see the field name Date* (see Word 2007 Exhibit 11). *Click on it.*

19. *From the Field properties list, click on the third option from the top* (the month spelled out, the date, and the year). Notice that the current date is displayed. This field will always display the date on which the template is actually executed, so if the template is executed on January 1, January 1 will be the date shown on the letter. *Click on OK in the "Field" window.*

20. Press the **[ENTER]** key three times.

21. *From the Insert ribbon tab, click on Quick Parts from the Text group and then click Field.*

22. *Click on the down arrow on the Field names: scroll bar until you see "Fill-in" in the Field names: area* (see Word 2007 Exhibit 11). *Click on Fill-in.*

23. In the "Prompt:" box under Field properties:, type **"Type the Name and Address of the Recipient."** *Note:* You must include the quotation marks.

24. *Click on OK in the "Field" window.*

25. You will now see a window on your screen that says **"Type the Name and Address of Recipient."** *Press the ENTER key after Name, Address and City/ State/Zip* (see Word 2007 Exhibit 12). *Click on OK.*

26. Press the **[ENTER]** key three times.

27. Press the **[TAB]** key.

28. Type **Subject:**.

WORD 2007 EXHIBIT 11
Inserting fields in a template

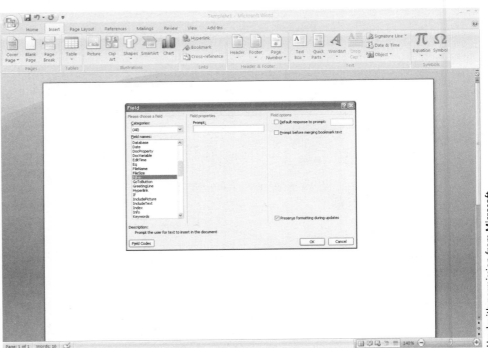

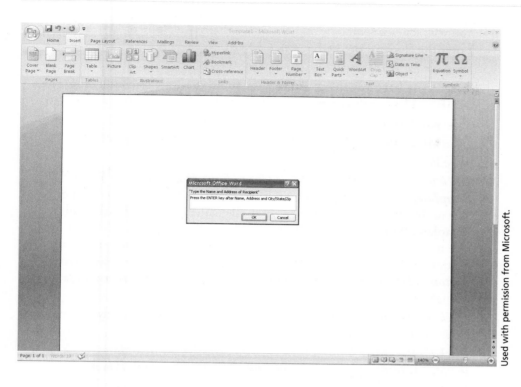

WORD 2007 EXHIBIT 12
Entering a "fill-in" field

HANDS-ON EXERCISES

29. Press the **[TAB]** key.

30. *From the Insert ribbon tab, click on Quick Parts from the Text group and then click on Field.*

31. *Click on the down arrow on the Field names: scroll bar until you see "Fill-in" in the Field names: area. Click on Fill-in.*

32. In the "Prompt:" box, under Field properties:, type **"Type the Subject of the Letter."** *Note:* You must include the quotation marks. *Point and click on OK.*

33. You will now see a window on your screen that says **"Type the Subject of the Letter."** Type **Enter the Subject of the Letter**. *Click on OK.*

34. Press the **[ENTER]** key three times.

35. Type **Dear** and press the **[SPACEBAR]**. Then, *from the Insert ribbon tab, click on Quick Parts from the Text group, then click Field.*

36. *Click on the down arrow on the Field names: scroll bar until you see "Fill-in" in the Field names: area. Click on Fill-in.*

37. In the "Prompt:" box under Field properties:, type **"Salutation"** (*Note:* You must include the quotation marks). *Click on OK.*

38. You will now see a window on your screen that says **"Salutation."** Type **Enter the Salutation.** *Click on OK.*

39. Type **:** [a colon].

40. Press the **[ENTER]** key twice.

41. *From the Insert ribbon tab, click on Quick Parts from the Text group and then click Field.*

42. *Click on the down arrow on the Field names: scroll bar until you see "Fill-in" in the Field names: area. Click on Fill-in.*

43. In the "Prompt:" box under Field properties:, type **"Body of Letter."** *Note:* You must include the quotation marks. *Click on OK.*

44. You will now see a window on your screen that says **"Body of Letter."** Type **Enter the Body of the Letter**. *Click on OK.*

45. Press the [**ENTER**] key twice.

46. Type **If you have any questions, please do not hesitate to contact me.** Press the [**ENTER**] key three times.

47. Type **Kindest regards,** and press the [**ENTER**] key four times.

48. Type **Mirabelle Watkinson** and press the [**ENTER**] key once.

49. Type **For the Firm**.

50. *Click on the Office button, then point to Save As and click on Word Template.* (*Note:* If you do not save this as a Word Template, you will not be able to finish the lesson.) Then, next to File name:, type **Watkinson Letter Template.** Word will save the template to a special template folder; if you save it to another folder, you will not be able to run the template in the next portion of this exercise. *Next to "Save as type:," click on the down arrow button, select Word 97-2003 Template(*.dot), then click on Save* to save the document.

51. *Click on the Office button and then on Close.* You are now ready to type a letter using the template.

52. *Click on the Office button, then click on New. Under Templates, click on My templates. In the "New" window, under the My Templates tab, double-click on Watkinson Letter Template.*

53. The template letter is now running. You will see the Type the Name and Address of the Recipient field on the screen. You will also see the prompt that reminds you to press ENTER after the name, address, and city/state/zip. Type over this prompt.

54. Type **Steven Matthews, Esq.** and press the [**ENTER**] key.

55. Type **Matthews, Smith & Russell** and press the [**ENTER**] key.

56. Type **P.O. Box 12341** and press the [**ENTER**] key.

57. Type **Boston, MA 59920** and then *click on OK.*

58. You will see the Type the Subject of the Letter field on the screen. You will also see the prompt that reminds you to enter the subject of the letter. Type over this prompt.

59. Type **Turner v. Smith, Case No. CV-11-0046** and then *click on OK.*

60. You will now see the Salutation field on the screen. You will also see the prompt that reminds you to enter the salutation. Type over this prompt.

61. Type **Steve** and then *click on OK.*

62. You will now see the Body of Letter field on the screen. You will also see the prompt that reminds you to enter the body of the letter. Type over this prompt.

63. Type **This will confirm our conversation of this date. You indicated that you had no objection to us requesting an additional ten days to respond to your Motion for Summary Judgment.** *Click on OK.* You are now through typing the letter. The completed letter should now be displayed. (*Note:* If another window is displayed prompting you for the name and address of the recipient, simply *click Cancel*; the completed letter should then be displayed.)

64. You are now ready to print the document. First, you will create a Quick Print icon on the Quick Access toolbar. Instead of going to the Office button each time to print, you will be able to print a document from the Quick Access toolbar (see Word 2007 Exhibit 12).

65. *Point and right-click anywhere in the ribbon. Click on Customize Quick Access Toolbar....*

66. The "Word Options" window should now be displayed. *Double-click on Quick Print on the left side of the screen (under Popular Commands), then click Add. Click on OK in the "Word Options" window.*

67. Notice that a Quick Print icon is now displayed in the Quick Access toolbar.

68. *Click on the Quick Print icon on the Quick Access toolbar,* or *click on the Office button, click on Print, then click on OK.*

69. To save the document, *click on the Office button, point to Save As, then click on Word 97-2003 Document. Under Save in, select the drive or folder* in which you would like to save the document. Next to File name:, type **Done— Word 2007 Lesson 7 Document** and *click on Save* to save the document. *Note*: You just saved the output of your template to a separate file named "Done—Word Lesson 7 Document." Your original template ("Watkinson Letter Template") is unaffected by the Lesson 7 document, and is still a clean template ready to be used again and again for any correspondence.

70. *Click on the Office button and then on Close* to close the document, or *click on the Office button and then on Exit Word* to exit the program.

This concludes Lesson 7.

LESSON 8: COMPARING DOCUMENTS

This lesson shows you how to compare documents by simultaneously viewing two documents and by creating a separate blacklined document with the changes. In your law-office career, you will often send someone a digital file for revision, only to find that when the file is returned, the revisions are not apparent. Using the comparison tools in Word 2007, you can see what has changed in the document.

1. Open Windows. *Double-click on the Microsoft Office Word 2007 icon on the desktop* to open Word 2007 for Windows. Alternatively, *click on the Start button, point the cursor to Programs or All Programs, then click on the Microsoft Word 2007 icon.* (You can also *point to Microsoft Office and then click on Microsoft Office Word 2007.)* You should now be in a new, clean, blank document. If you are not in a blank document, *click on the Office button, click on New, then double-click on Blank document.*

2. For the purpose of this lesson, we will assume that your firm drafted an employment contract for a corporate client named Bluebriar Incorporated. Bluebriar is in negotiations with an individual named John Lewis, whom they would like to hire as their vice president of marketing. Your firm is negotiating with John Lewis's attorney regarding the terms and language of the employment contract. The "Lesson 8A" file on the disk supplied with this text is the original document you sent to John Lewis's attorney. The "Lesson 8B" file on the disk is the new file sent back to you by John Lewis's attorney.

3. You will now open both of these files from the disk supplied with this text and then compare them side by side. Ensure that the disk is inserted in the drive, *then click on the Office button, then click on Open.* The "Open" window should now be displayed. *Click on the down arrow to the right of the white box next to Look in: and select the drive where the disk is located. Double-click on the Word Processing Files folder. Double-click on the Word 2007 folder. Double-click on the "Lesson 8A" file.*

4. Follow the same directions to open the "Lesson 8B" file.

5. *From the View ribbon tab, click on View Side by Side in the Window group.* Both documents should now be displayed side by side (see Word 2007 Exhibit 13).

6. Push the [**DOWN ARROW**] key to scroll down through the document. Notice that both documents simultaneously scroll.

7. From the View ribbon tab, notice that the Synchronous Scrolling icon in the Window group is highlighted (see Word 2007 Exhibit 13). To turn this feature off, you would click on this icon. The Synchronous Scrolling icon toggles synchronous scrolling on and off. If you turn off synchronous scrolling and wish to turn it back on, simply realign the windows where you want them, and *click on the Synchronous Scrolling icon.* (*Note:* If the View ribbon tab looks like Word 2007 Exhibit 13, with the Window group collapsed, *point and click on the Window group, and click Synchronous Scrolling.*)

8. You will now learn how to merge the changes into one document. *Click anywhere in Lesson 8A.doc, then click on the Office button and then on Close.*

9. *Do the same to close Lesson 8B.doc.*

10. You should now have no documents open.

11. *From the Review ribbon tab, click on Compare in the Compare group. Then, click on "Compare…"*

12. The "Compare Documents" window should now be displayed (see Word 2007 Exhibit 14). *Under Original document, click on the down arrow; use the Browse… feature to find Lesson 8A.doc, then double-click on it* (see Word 2007 Exhibit 14).

13. *Next, under Revised document, click on the down arrow; use the Browse feature to find "Lesson 8B.doc" and then double-click on it* (see Word 2007 Exhibit 14).

WORD 2007 EXHIBIT 13
Comparing documents
side-by-side

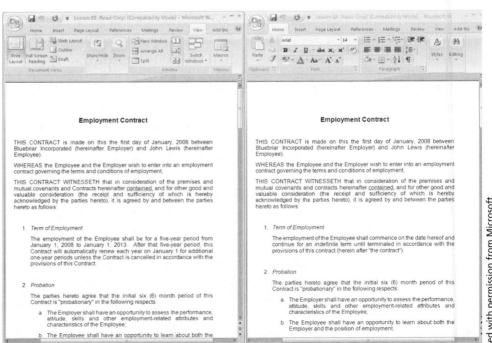

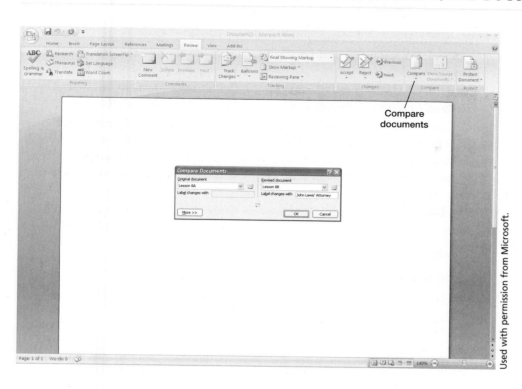

WORD 2007 EXHIBIT 14
Comparing documents—
Legal blackline settings

Compare
documents

14. Next to "Label changes with," type **John Lewis' Attorney** and then *click on OK in the "Compare Documents" window.*

15. Notice that a new document has been created that merges the documents (see Word 2007 Exhibit 15). Scroll through the new document and review all of the changes.

16. The Compare and Merge Document feature is extremely helpful when you are comparing multiple versions of the same file. By right-clicking on any of

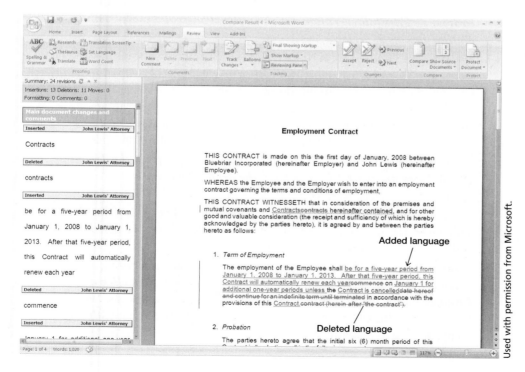

WORD 2007 EXHIBIT 15
Completed blackline
document

the additions or deletions, you can accept or reject the change. This is called Track Changes, and you will learn how to do this in more detail in Lesson 9.

17. To print the document, *click on the Quick Print icon on the Quick Access toolbar,* or *click on the Office button, click on Print, then click on OK.*

18. To save the document, *click on the Office button, point to Save As, and then click on Word 97-2003 Document. Under Save in, select the drive or folder* in which you would like to save the document. Next to File name:, type **Done—Word 2007 Lesson 8 Merged Document** and then *click on Save* to save the document.

19. *Click on the Office button and then on Close* to close the document, or *click on the Office button and then on Exit Word* to exit the program.

This concludes Lesson 8.

LESSON 9: USING TRACK CHANGES

In this lesson, you will learn how to use the Track Changes feature by editing a will, and then accepting and/or rejecting the changes.

1. Open Windows. *Double-click on the Microsoft Office Word 2007 icon on the desktop* to open Word 2007 for Windows. Alternatively, *click on the Start button, point the cursor to Programs or All Programs, then click on the Microsoft Word 2007 icon.* (You can also *point to Microsoft Office and then click on Microsoft Office Word 2007).* You should now be in a new, clean, blank document. If you are not in a blank document, *click on the Office button, click on New, then double-click on Blank document.*

2. The first thing you will do is open the "Lesson 9" file from the disk supplied with this text. Ensure that the disk is inserted in the drive, *click on the Office button, then click on Open.* The "Open" window should now be displayed. *Click on the down arrow to the right of the white box next to Look in: and select the drive where the disk is located. Double-click on the Word Processing Files folder. Double-click on the Word 2007 folder. Double-click on the "Lesson 9" file.*

3. The text "LAST WILL AND TESTAMENT" should now be displayed on your screen (see Word 2007 Exhibit 16). Notice in Word 2007 Exhibit 16 that several revisions have been made to this document. Your client, William Porter, has asked you to use the Track Changes feature to show your supervising attorney the changes he would like to make. Mr. Porter is rather leery of the legal process and wants to make sure your supervising attorney approves of the changes.

4. *From the Review ribbon tab, click on Track Changes from the Tracking group. Click on Track Changes from the drop-down menu* to turn on Track Changes.

5. Make the changes shown in Word 2007 Exhibit 16. Everything that should be added is in red and underlined, and everything that should be deleted is in red and has a line through it.

6. Assume now that you have shown the changes to your supervising attorney. *From the Review ribbon tab, click on Track Changes, then click on Track Changes on the drop-down menu* to turn off Track Changes (see Word 2007 Exhibit 16). This allows you to make changes to the document without having them show up as revisions.

WORD 2007 EXHIBIT 16
Using Track Changes

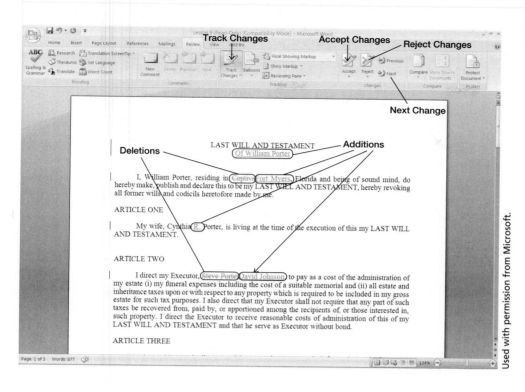

7. *Point and right-click anywhere on the text, "Of William Porter," which you added just under "LAST WILL AND TESTAMENT."* Notice that a menu is displayed that allows you to accept or reject the insertion, among other actions. *Click on Accept Change.* The revision has now been accepted.

8. *From the Review ribbon tab, click on Next in the Changes group*. This should take you to the next change. *From the Review ribbon tab, click on Accept in the Changes group, then click on Accept and Move to Next to accept the change.* Notice that one of the options is "Accept All Changes in Document." This is a quick way to accept all changes in a document without going through each one of them. However, do not select it; we do not want to accept all the changes in this document.

9. Use the Next feature to continue to go to each change and accept the revisions. The only revision you will *not* accept is changing the executor from Steve Porter to David Johnson; reject this change. Assume that the supervising attorney has learned that Mr. Johnson is terminally ill and most likely will not be able to serve as executor, so the client has decided to keep Steve Porter as the executor.

10. To print the document, *click on the Quick Print icon on the Quick Access toolbar,* or *click on the Office button, click on Print, then click on OK*.

11. To save the document, *click on the Office button, then point to Save As, then click on Word 97-2003 Document. Under Save in, select the drive or folder* in which you would like to save the document. Next to File name:, type **Done—Word 2007 Lesson 9 Document** *and then click on Save* to save the document.

12. *Click on the Office button and then on Close* to close the document, or *click on the Office button and then on Exit Word* to exit the program.

This concludes Lesson 9.

▶ ADVANCED LESSONS

LESSON 10: CREATING A MAIL MERGE DOCUMENT

In this lesson, you will create a merge document for an open house that you will send to three clients (see Word 2007 Exhibit 17). First, you will create the data file that will be merged into the letter. Then, you will create the letter itself, and finally, you will merge the two together. Keep in mind that if you make a mistake at any time, you may press **[CTRL]+[Z]** to undo what you have done.

WORD 2007 EXHIBIT 17
Mail merge letter

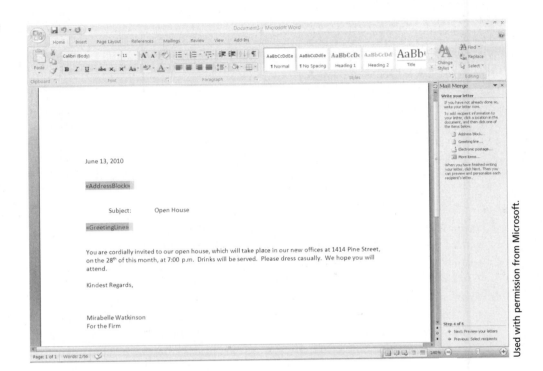

1. Open Windows. ***Double-click on the Microsoft Office Word 2007 icon on the desktop*** to open Word 2007 for Windows. Alternatively, ***click on the Start button, point the cursor to Programs or All Programs, then click on the Microsoft Word 2007 icon.*** (You may also ***point to Microsoft Office and then click on Microsoft Office Word 2007.***) You should now be in a new, clean, blank document. If you are not in a blank document, ***click on the Office button, click on New, then double-click on Blank document.***

2. ***From the Mailings ribbon tab, click on Start Mail Merge from the Start Mail Merge group. From the drop-down menu, select Step by Step Mail Merge Wizard....*** The Mail Merge task pane is now shown to the right of your document.

3. The bottom of the Mail Merge task pane shows that you are on Step 1 of 6. You are asked to **"Select document type."** You are typing a letter, so the default selection, "Letters," is fine. To continue to the next step, ***click on Next: Starting document at the bottom of the Mail Merge task pane under Step 1 of 6.***

4. The bottom of the Mail Merge task pane shows that you are on Step 2 of 6. You are asked to **"Select starting document."** You will be using the current document to type your letter, so the default selection, "Use the current

document," is fine. To continue to the next step, ***click on Next: Select recipients at the bottom of the Mail Merge task pane under Step 2 of 6.***

5. The bottom of the Mail Merge task pane shows that you are on Step 3 of 6. You are asked to **"Select recipients."** You will be typing a new list, so ***click on Type a new list.***

6. ***Under the "Type a new list" section of the Mail Merge task pane, click on Create….***

7. The "New Address List" window is now displayed. You will now fill in the names of the three clients to whom you want to send your open house letter.

8. Type the following. (*Note:* You can use the **[TAB]** key to move between the fields, or you can use the mouse.) Only complete the fields below; skip the fields in the "New Address List" window that we will not be using.

TITLE	
First Name	Jim
Last Name	Woods
Company Name	
Address Line 1	2300 Briarcliff Road
Address Line 2	
City	Atlanta
State	GA
ZIP Code	30306
Country	
Home Phone	
Work Phone	
Email Address	

9. When you have entered all of the information for Jim Woods, ***click on the New Entry button in the "New Address List" window.***

10. Enter the second client in the blank "New Address List" window.

TITLE	
First Name	Jennifer
Last Name	John
Company Name	
Address Line 1	3414 Peachtree Road
Address Line 2	
City	Atlanta
State	GA
ZIP Code	30314
Country	
Home Phone	
Work Phone	
Email Address	

HANDS-ON EXERCISES

11. When you have entered all of the information for Jennifer John, **_click on the New Entry button in the "New Address List" window._**

12. Enter the third client in the blank "New Address List" window.

TITLE	
First Name	Jonathan
Last Name	Phillips
Company Name	
Address Line 1	675 Clifton Road
Address Line 2	
City	Atlanta
State	GA
ZIP Code	30030
Country	
Home Phone	
Work Phone	
Email Address	

13. **When you have entered all of the information for Jonathan Phillips, _click on OK in the "New Address List" window._**

14. The "Save Address List" window is now displayed. You need to save the address list so that it can later be merged with the open-house letter. In the "Save Address List" window, next to File name:, type **Open House List** and then **_click on Save in the "Save Address List" window_** to save the file to the default directory.

15. The "Mail Merge Recipients" window is now displayed (see Word 2007 Exhibit 18). **_Click on the Last Name field in the "Mail Merge Recipients" window_** to sort the list by last name (see Word 2007 Exhibit 18). Notice that the order of the list is now sorted by last name.

16. **_Click on OK in the "Mail Merge Recipients" window._** You are now back at a blank document with the Mail Merge task pane open to the right. The bottom of the Mail Merge task pane indicates that you are still at Step 3 of 6. **_Click on Next: Write your letter at the bottom of the Mail Merge task pane under Step 3 of 6_** to continue to the next step.

17. The bottom of the Mail Merge task pane indicates that you are on Step 4 of 6. In the Mail Merge task pane, **"Write your letter"** is displayed. You are now ready to write the letter. **_On the Home ribbon tab, click the Paragraph Group dialog launcher. In the "Paragraph" window in the Indents and Spacing tab, click the down arrow below Line spacing and select Single._** Make sure the Before and After spacing are both 0 point. Then, **_click OK._**

18. Press the [**ENTER**] key four times.

19. Type the current date and press the [**ENTER**] key three times.

20. **_Click on Address block… in the Mail Merge task pane under "Write your letter."_**

21. The "Insert Address Block" window is now displayed. You will now customize how the address block will appear in the letters.

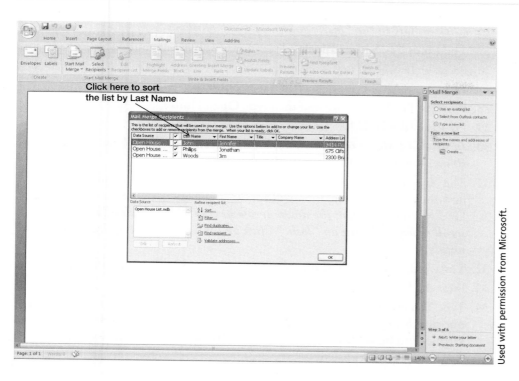

Used with permission from Microsoft.

WORD 2007 EXHIBIT 18
Entering mail merge recipients

22. *In the "Insert Address Block" window, under Insert recipient's name in this format:, click on the second entry, "Joshua Randall Jr." Click on "Insert company name" to deselect it,* because we did not include company names in our data list (see Word 2007 Exhibit 19).

23. *Under Insert postal address:, click on "Never include the country/region in the address"* (see Word 2007 Exhibit 19).

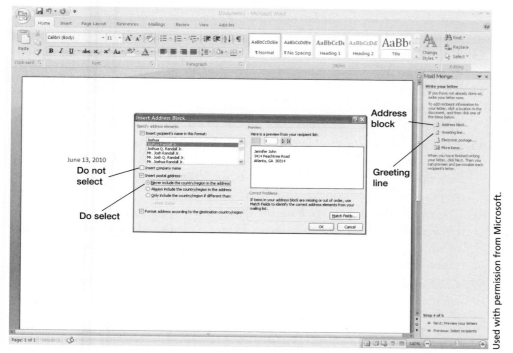

Used with permission from Microsoft.

WORD 2007 EXHIBIT 19
Insert address block

HANDS-ON EXERCISES

24. *Click on OK in the "Insert Address Block" window.*
25. The words **"<<AddressBlock>>"** are now displayed in your document.
26. Press the **[ENTER]** key three times.
27. Press the **[TAB]** key once and then type **Subject:**.
28. Press the **[TAB]** key once and then type **Open House.**
29. Press the **[ENTER]** key twice.
30. *In the Mail Merge task pane, under Write your letter, click on Greeting line…* (see Word 2007 Exhibit 19).
31. The "Insert Greeting Line" window is now displayed. You will now customize how the greeting or salutation will appear in the letter. In the "Insert Greeting Line" window, *click on the down arrow next to "Mr. Randall" and then scroll down and click on "Josh." Click on OK in the "Insert Greeting Line" window.*
32. The words **"<<GreetingLine>>"** are now displayed in your document.
33. Press the **[ENTER]** key three times.
34. Type **You are cordially invited to our open house, which will take place in our new offices at 1414 Pine Street, on the 28th of this month, at 7:00 p.m. Drinks will be served. Please dress casually. We hope you will attend.**
35. Press the **[ENTER]** key twice.
36. Type **Kindest Regards,.**
37. Press the **[ENTER]** key four times.
38. Type **Mirabelle Watkinson**.
39. Press the **[ENTER]** key once and type **For the Firm**.
40. You are now done typing the letter. Your letter should look similar to Word 2007 Exhibit 17. The only thing left to do is merge the recipient list with the form.
41. Under "Step 4 of 6" at the bottom of the Mail Merge task pane, *click on Next: Preview your letters* to continue to the next step.
42. Your first letter is now displayed. *In the Mail Merge task pane, under Preview your letters, click on the button showing two arrows pointing to the right to see the rest of your letters.*
43. To continue to the next step, *click on Next: Complete the merge at the bottom of the Mail Merge task pane under Step 5 of 6.*
44. The Mail Merge task pane now will display **"Complete the merge."** *Click on Print in the Mail Merge task pane under Merge, then click on OK. At the "Merge to Printer" window, click on OK* to print your letters.
45. *Click on Edit individual letters… in the Mail Merge task pane under Merge.* In the "Merge to New Document" window, *click on OK.* Word has now opened a new document with all of the letters in it. (*Note:* At this point, you can edit and personalize each letter if you so desire).
46. To save the document, *click on the Office button, point to Save As, then click on Word 97-2003 Document. Under Save in, select the drive or folder* in which you would like to save the document. Then, next to File name:, type **Open House Letters** and then *click on Save* to save the document.
47. *Click on the Office button and then on Close* to close the personalized letters.

48. You should be back at the mail merge letter. ***Click on the Office button and point to Save As. Click on Word 97-2003 Document. Under Save in, select the drive or folder*** in which you would like to save the document. Next to File name:, type **Open House Mail Merge** and then ***click on Save*** to save the document.

49. ***Click on the Office button and then on Close*** to close the document, or ***click on the Office button and then on Exit Word*** to exit the program.

This concludes Lesson 10.

LESSON 11: CREATING A TABLE OF AUTHORITIES

In this lesson, you will prepare a table of authorities for a reply brief (see Word 2007 Exhibit 22). You will learn how to find cases, mark cases, and then automatically generate a table of authorities.

1. Open Windows. ***Double-click on the Microsoft Office Word 2007 icon on the desktop*** to open Word 2007 for Windows. Alternatively, ***click on the Start button, point the cursor to Programs or All Programs, then click on the Microsoft Word 2007 icon.*** (You may also ***point to Microsoft Office and then click on Microsoft Office Word 2007***). You should now be in a new, clean, blank document. If you are not in a blank document, ***click on the Office button, click on New, then double-click on Blank document.***

2. The first thing you will do is open the "Lesson 11" file from the disk supplied with this text. Ensure that the disk is inserted in the disk drive, ***click on the Office button, then click on Open.*** The "Open" window should now be displayed. ***Click on the down arrow to the right of the white box next to Look in: and select the drive where the disk is located. Double-click on the Word Processing Files folder. Double-click on the Word 2007 folder. Double-click on the "Lesson 11" file.***

3. The text ***"In the Supreme Court of the United States–Ted Sutton, Petitioner, v. State of Alaska, Respondent"*** should now be displayed on your screen.

4. In this exercise you will build the case section of the table of authorities for this reply brief. There are five cases to be included and they are all shown in bold so that you can easily identify them. Your first task will be to mark each of the cases so that Word knows they are to be included; you will then execute the command for Word to build the table.

5. If you are not at the beginning of the document, press **[CTRL]+[HOME]** to go to the beginning.

6. You will now mark the cases. ***From the References ribbon tab, click on Mark Citation from the Table of Authorities group.***

7. The "Mark Citation" window should now be displayed (see Word 2007 Exhibit 20). Notice next to Category: that "Cases" is displayed. This indicates that you will be marking case citations. ***Click on the down arrow next to Cases*** to see that you can also mark citations to be included for statutes, rules, treatises, regulations, and other sources.

8. ***Click on Cases again,*** because you will now start marking cases to be included in the table of authorities.

9. ***In the "Mark Citation" window, click on Next Citation.*** Word looks for terms such as "vs" or "v." when finding citations. The cursor should now be on the "v." in *Ted Sutton, Petitioner, v. State of Alaska.* Because this is the caption

WORD 2007 EXHIBIT 20
Marking a citation for
inclusion in a table of
authorities

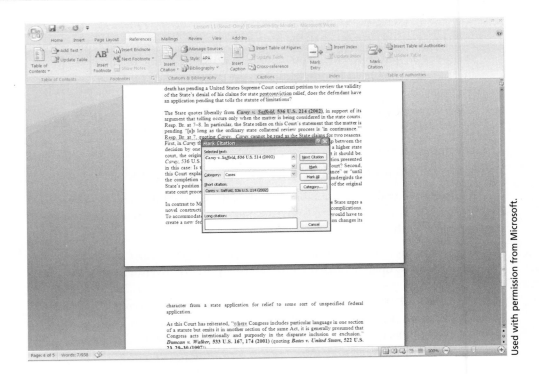

of the current case, we do not want to mark it for inclusion in the table. *Note*:
If the "Mark Citation" window gets in the way and prevents you from seeing
the brief, ***put the cursor on the blue title bar of the "Mark Citation" window
and drag it out of your way.***

10. ***Click on Next Citation in the "Mark Citation" window.*** Again, this is the
    caption of the current case, *Ted Sutton, Petitioner, v. State of Alaska,* so we do
    not want to mark it.

11. ***Click again on Next Citation in the "Mark Citation" window.*** Word has now
    found the case *Carey v. Saffold.* We want to mark this case so that it is included
    in the table of authorities.

12. ***Click once on the* Carey v. Saffold *case.***

13. ***Drag the pointer to highlight Carey v. Saffold, 536 U.S. 214 (2002), then
    click in the white box under Selected text: in the "Mark Citation" window.***
    The case is automatically copied there (see Word 2007 Exhibit 20).

14. ***Click on Mark in the "Mark Citation" window.*** *Note:* When you mark a
    citation, Word changes your view to the Show/Hide paragraph view. It shows
    you that you have embedded table-of-authorities formatting codes in the
    document. To switch out of Show/Hide view, ***from the Home ribbon tab,
    click on the Show/Hide icon in the Paragraph group.*** (It looks like a
    paragraph sign.)

15. ***Click on Next Citation in the "Mark Citation" window.***

16. ***Click once on the* Duncan v. Walker *case.***

17. ***Drag the mouse to highlight* Duncan v. Walker, 533 U.S. 167, 174 (2001)
    and then ***click in the white box under Selected text: in the "Mark Citation"
    window.*** The case is automatically copied there.

18. ***Click on Mark in the "Mark Citation" window.*** Notice that, under Short
    citation: in the "Mark Citation" window, the *Carey* and *Duncan* cases are listed.

Again, if at any time the "Mark Citation" window prevents you from seeing the case you need to highlight, just *click on the blue bar at top of the "Mark Citation" window and drag to the left or right* to move the window out of your way.

19. To switch out of Show/Hide view, *from the Home ribbon tab, click on the Show/Hide icon in the Paragraph group.*

20. *Click on Next Citation in the "Mark Citation" window.*

21. *Click once on the* **Bates v. United States** *case.*

22. *Drag the pointer to highlight* **Bates v. United States, 522 U.S. 23, 29–30 (1997)** *and then click in the white box under Selected text: in the "Mark Citation" window.* The case is automatically copied there.

23. *Click on Mark in the "Mark Citation" window.*

24. *Click on Next Citation in the "Mark Citation" window.*

25. *Click once on the* **Abela v. Martin** *case.*

26. *Drag the pointer to highlight* **Abela v. Martin, 348 F.3d 164 (6th Cir. 2003)** *and then click in the white box under Selected text: in the "Mark Citation" window.* The case is automatically copied there.

27. *Click on Mark in the "Mark Citation" window.*

28. *Click on Next Citation in the "Mark Citation" window.*

29. *Click once on the* **Coates v. Byrd** *case.*

30. *Drag the pointer to highlight* **Coates v. Byrd, 211 F.3d 1225, 1227 (11th Cir. 2000)** *and then click in the white box under Selected text: in the "Mark Citation" window.* The case is automatically copied there.

31. *Click on Mark in the "Mark Citation" window.*

32. *Click on Close in the "Mark Citation" window* to close it.

33. *Click on the Show/Hide paragraph icon on the Home ribbon tab* to make the paragraph marks disappear.

34. Using the cursor keys or the scroll bar, *place the cursor on page 3 of the document two lines under the title "TABLE OF AUTHORITIES"* (see Word 2007 Exhibit 21). You are now ready to generate the table.

35. *From the References ribbon tab, click on the Insert Table of Authorities icon in the Table of Authorities group* (see Word 2007 Exhibit 21).

36. *The "Table of Authorities" window should now be displayed* (see Word 2007 Exhibit 21). *Click on Cases under Category and then click on OK.*

37. Notice that the table of authorities has been prepared and completed, and that the cases and the page numbers where they appear in the document have been included (see Word 2007 Exhibit 22).

38. To print the document, *click on the Quick Print icon on the Quick Access toolbar,* or *click on the Office button, click on Print, then click on OK.*

39. To save the document, *click on the Office button and point to Save As, then click on Word 97-2003 Document. Under Save in, select the drive or folder* in which you would like to save the document. Next to File name:, type **Done—Word 2007 Lesson 11 Document** and *click on Save* to save the document.

40. *Click on the Office button and then on Close* to close the document, or *click on the Office button and then on Exit Word* to exit the program.

This concludes Lesson 11.

HANDS-ON EXERCISES

WORD 2007 EXHIBIT 21
Inserting a table of
authorities

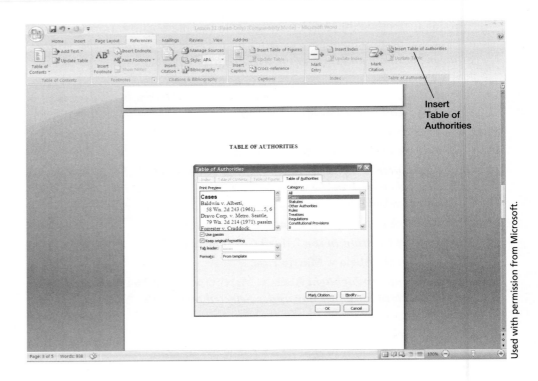

Insert
Table of
Authorities

WORD 2007 EXHIBIT 22
Completed table of
authorities

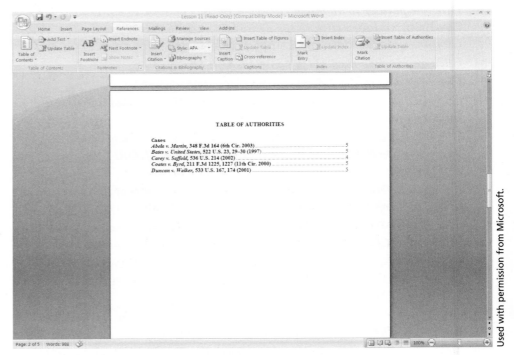

LESSON 12: CREATING A MACRO

In this lesson you will prepare a macro that will automatically type the signature block for a pleading (see Word 2007 Exhibit 23). You will then execute the macro to make sure that it works properly.

1. Open Windows. ***Double-click on the Microsoft Office Word 2007 icon on the desktop*** to open Word 2007 for Windows. Alternatively, ***click on the Start***

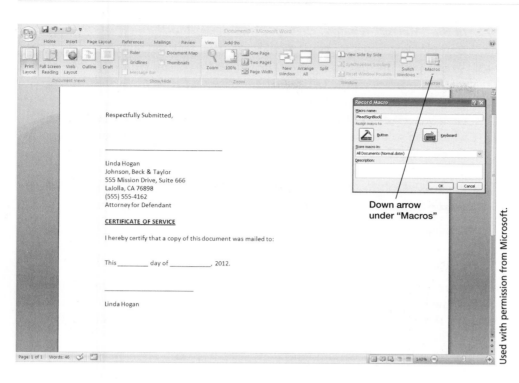

WORD 2007 EXHIBIT 23
Creating a pleading
signature block macro

Down arrow
under "Macros"

HANDS-ON EXERCISES

*button, point to Programs or All Programs, then click on the Microsoft
Word 2007 icon.* (You can also *point to Microsoft Office and then click
on Microsoft Office Word 2007.*) You should now be in a new, clean, blank
document. If you are not in a blank document, *click on the Office button,
click on New, then double-click on Blank document.*

2. The first thing you need to do to create a new macro is to name the macro and
then turn on the Record function. *From the View ribbon tab, click on the
down arrow under Macros in the Macros group* (see Word 2007 Exhibit 23).

3. *Click on Record Macro… on the drop-down menu.*

4. The "Record Macro" window should now be displayed (see Word 2007
Exhibit 23). In the "Record Macro" window, under Macro name:, type
Pleadingsignblock *and then click on OK* (see Word 2007 Exhibit 23).

5. Notice that your cursor looks like a cassette tape. The cassette-tape cursor
indicates that Word is now recording all of your keystrokes and commands.

6. Type the information in Word 2007 Exhibit 23. When you have
completed typing the information, *from the View ribbon tab, click on
the down arrow under Macros in the Macros group* (see Word 2007
Exhibit 23).

7. *Click on Stop Recording on the drop-down menu.*

8. You will now test your macro to see if it works properly. *Click on the Office
button and then on Close* to close the document. At the prompt "Do you want
to save the changes to document?," *click on No.*

9. To open a blank document, *click on the Office button, click on New, then
double-click on Blank document.*

10. To run the macro, *from the View ribbon tab, click on the down arrow under
Macros in the Macros group* (see Word 2007 Exhibit 23).

11. *Click on View Macros.*

12. *In the "Macros" window, click on* **Pleadingsignblock** *and then click on* **Run.** Your pleading signature block should now be in your document.

13. To print the document, *click on the Quick Print icon on the Quick Access toolbar,* or *click on the Office button, click on Print, then click on OK.*

14. To save the document, *click on the Office button, point to Save As, then click on Word 97-2003 Document. Under Save in, select the drive or folder* in which you would like to save the document. Then, next to File name:, type **Done—Word 2007 Lesson 12 Document** *and click on Save* to save the document.

15. *Click on the Office button and then on Close* to close the document, or *click on the Office button and then on Exit Word* to exit the program.

This concludes Lesson 12.

LESSON 13: DRAFTING A WILL

Using the websites at the end of Chapter 2 in the main text, or using a form book from a law library, draft a simple will that would be valid in your state. You will be drafting the will for Thomas Mansell, who is a widower. The will should be dated July 1 of the current year. Mr. Mansell requests the following:

- That his just debts and funeral expenses be paid.
- That his lifelong friend, Elizabeth Smith, receive $50,000 in cash.
- That his local YMCA receive his 100 shares of stock in Google.
- That all of his remaining property (real or personal) descend to his daughter Sharon Mansell.
- That in the event Mr. Mansell and his daughter die simultaneously, for all of his property to descend to Sharon's son Michael Mansell.
- That Elizabeth Smith be appointed the executor of the will; if Ms. Smith predeceases Mr. Mansell, that Mr. Stephen Dear be appointed executor.

Mr. Mansell has also requested that his will be double-spaced and have one-inch margins. He would like the will to look good and be valid in his state.

- Three witnesses will watch the signing of the will: Shelley Stewart, Dennis Gordon, and Gary Fox.
- You will notarize the will.

Print out a hard copy of the will and email it to your instructor.

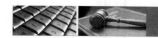

HANDS-ON EXERCISES

ADOBE ACROBAT 9 PRO

I. INTRODUCTION — READ THIS!

Adobe Acrobat lets you view, create, manipulate, and manage files in Adobe's Portable Document Format (PDF). It permits you to present information with a fixed layout similar to paper publication.

II. INSTALLATION INSTRUCTIONS

Note: The Adobe Acrobat (v.9 Pro) software demo is not compatible with Microsoft Office 2010. The Hands-On Exercises should be completed using Microsoft Office 2007.

1. Log in to your CengageBrain.com account.
2. Under "My Courses & Materials," find the Premium Website for Using Computers in the Law Office.
3. *Click Open to go to the Premium Website.*
4. *Under Book Resources, click on the link for Adobe Acrobat 9 Professional.*
5. *Right-click on the link next to Download Now and select Save Target As or Save Link As.*
6. *Choose a folder on your hard drive, such as the Desktop, where you want to save the file, and then click Save.* The files are now being saved to your computer.
7. *In Windows Explorer (Start Button > Computer), open the folder where you saved the file above.*
8. *Double-click the file.*
9. The screen in Installation Exhibit 1 should now be displayed. This process will take a few minutes to complete.
10. Choose the language for the installation and *click OK.*

INSTALLATION EXHIBIT 1

Adobe Acrobat 9 Pro - English, Français, Deutsch - Setup   _ □ ✕

Please wait while the Adobe Acrobat 9 Pro - English, Français, Deutsch Setup is being processed. This will take some time depending on your operating system and hardware.

Processing Adobe Acrobat 9 Pro - English, Français, Deutsch...   1.07 %

NOSSO
powered by nosltd.com   [Pause]   [Resume]   [Exit]

Adobe product screenshots reprinted with permission from Adobe Systems Incorporated.

11. At the next screen, *click Next.*

12. If you have already previously installed Adobe Reader you will see the screen in Installation Exhibit 2. *Click Next.*

INSTALLATION EXHIBIT 2

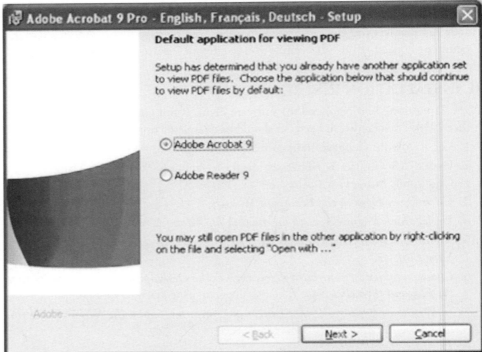

13. At the next screen, *type your name* (and organization, if desired) in the text boxes. *Click the button next to Install the trial version. Click Next.*

14. Choose the "**Typical**" setup type. *Click Next.*

15. At the next screen, choose the default location to install this program by *clicking the Next button.*

16. At the next screen, *click the Install button.*

17. Install is complete. *Click the Finish button.*

Number	Lesson Title	Concepts Covered
BASIC LESSONS		
Lesson 1	Creating a PDF from a Word Document	Using PDFMaker, naming and saving a PDF, converting a Word document into a PDF
Lesson 2	Creating a PDF from a Web Page	Using PDFMaker, naming and saving a PDF, converting a web page into a PDF
INTERMEDIATE LESSONS		
Lesson 3	Combining Multiple Documents into a Single PDF	Combining files, adding files, moving files into desired order, naming and saving a combined PDF
Lesson 4	Creating a Portfolio	Creating a portfolio, editing a portfolio, naming and saving a PDF
ADVANCED LESSON		
Lesson 5	Adding Security to a PDF	Changing the security settings, adding a password

GETTING STARTED
Introduction

Throughout these lessons and exercises, information you need to type into the program will be designated in several different ways:

- Keys to be pressed on the keyboard are designated in brackets, in all caps, and in bold (e.g., press the **[ENTER]** key).
- Movements with the mouse pointer are designated in bold and italics (e.g., ***point to File on the menu bar and click***).
- Words or letters that should be typed are designated in bold (e.g., type **Training Program**).
- Information that is or should be displayed on your computer screen is shown in bold, with quotation marks (e.g., "**Press ENTER to continue.**").

OVERVIEW OF ADOBE ACROBAT

The following tips on using Adobe Acrobat will help you complete these exercises.

Adobe Acrobat Pro 9 is the most commonly used Portable Document Format (PDF) program. A PDF can be used to share files with others who do not have the same software; share files with others regardless of the computer operating system used to view the files; share files that will look the same (layout, fonts) on all computer systems; share files that can be protected from unauthorized viewing, printing, copying, or editing; print files to many different types of printers, and have them all look essentially the same; and create files with hyperlinks and bookmarks that can be electronically shared with others.

When Adobe Acrobat is installed on your computer, it automatically installed PDFMaker, which is used to create PDFs from Microsoft Office applications (Word, Excel, PowerPoint, etc.).

BASIC LESSONS

LESSON 1: CREATING A PDF FROM A WORD DOCUMENT

This lesson shows you how to convert the letter you created in Lesson 1 of the Word-Processing Hands-On Exercises. It explains how to use the PDFMaker application.

1. Open Windows. After it has loaded, ***double-click on the Microsoft Office Word icon on the desktop*** to open Word for Windows. Alternatively, ***click on the Start button, point with the mouse to Programs or All Programs, then click on the Microsoft Word icon*** (or ***point to Microsoft Office, then click on Microsoft Office Word***). You should be in a new, clean, blank document. If you are not in a clean, blank document, ***click on File on the menu bar, click on New, then click on Blank Document.***

2. In this lesson, you will begin by retrieving the document you created in Lesson 1 of the Word 2007 Hands-On Exercises. To open the file, ***click on File from the menu bar and select Open.*** Type **Letter1** and ***click on Open.*** Alternatively, ***scroll until you find the file, using the horizontal scroll bar, point to it, and then click on Open.***

3. ***Click the Acrobat Ribbon tab, then click Create PDF*** (see Adobe Acrobat Exhibit 1).

ADOBE ACROBAT EXHIBIT 1
Converting a Word document to a PDF

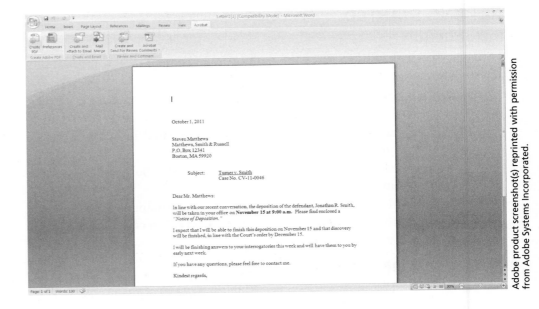

Adobe product screenshot(s) reprinted with permission from Adobe Systems Incorporated.

4. A new dialog box will open, entitled Save Adobe PDF File As. The "File name" box should display the default file name of "Letter1." The Save as type area should display the default file type of "PDF files."

5. The default settings are fine. ***Click on Save.*** The software will then create, display, and save your new PDF file.

LESSON 2: CREATING A PDF FROM A WEB PAGE

This lesson shows you how to create a PDF from a web page. It explains how to select part or all of the web page, and how to create, name, and save the new PDF file.

1. Start Windows.

2. Start your Internet browser. Type **http://www.paralegal.delmar.cengage.com/** in the browser and press the **[ENTER]** key.

3. Your screen should now look similar to Adobe Acrobat Exhibit 2.

ADOBE ACROBAT EXHIBIT 2
Converting a web page to a PDF

From Delmar. *www.paralegal.delmar.cengage.com* © Delmar Learning, a part of Cengage Learning, Inc. Reproduced by permission. www.cengage.com/permissions

4. *Use your cursor keys or mouse to go to the Convert button and click on the drop-down menu.*

5. *Using your cursor keys or mouse, move the cursor to the first option on the drop-down menu, and click Convert Web Page to PDF.*

6. A new box will appear, called "Convert Web Page to Adobe PDF." *Move your cursor to the line marked File name:.* The default setting is the web page's URL. This is probably not the best name for a file, so let's call it "Paralegal Books." The default setting for Save as type: is Adobe PDF (*.pdf). That is fine, so do not change it. See Adobe Acrobat Exhibit 3.

From Delmar. www.paralegal.delmar.cengage.com © Delmar Learning, a part of Cengage Learning, Inc. Reproduced by permission. www.cengage.com/permissions

ADOBE ACROBAT EXHIBIT 3
Saving a PDF

HANDS-ON EXERCISES

7. *Click Save* to create and save your new PDF.

8. You can also choose to save just a portion (or portions) of a web page. We will now discuss how to convert only part of a web page to a PDF.

9. Again, open your Internet browser and type **http://www.paralegal.delmar.cengage.com/** in the browser and press the **[ENTER]** key.

10. Again, your screen should now look similar to Adobe Acrobat Exhibit 2.

11. This time, *move the cursor to the Select button and click on it.* After you do so, *move your cursor around the web page.* As you do, notice that the section of the web page you are pointing to now has a red rectangle (consisting of broken red lines) surrounding it. This shows you the section of the web page selected for conversion to PDF.

12. *Move your cursor to the top of the web page over the Cengage logo.* You will see that portion surrounded by red broken lines (see Adobe Acrobat Exhibit 4). Press the **[ENTER]** key. You will notice that the red broken lines have been replaced by blue lines.

13. To convert the selected portion of the web page, you will follow the same procedure used to create the other PDFs. *Using your cursor keys or mouse, move the cursor to the first option on the drop-down menu, and click on Convert Web Page to PDF.*

14. A new box will appear, called "Convert Web Page to Adobe PDF." *Move your cursor to the line marked File name:.* The default setting is the web page's URL. This is probably not the best name for a file, so let's call it "Paralegal

ADOBE ACROBAT EXHIBIT 4
Selecting a portion of a web page for conversion to a PDF

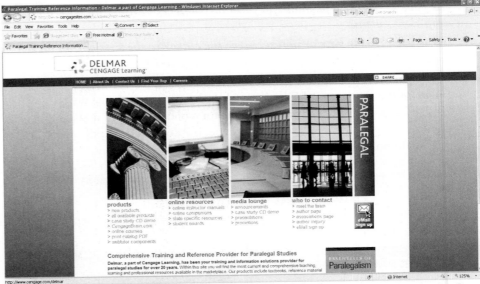

From Delmar. *www.paralegal.delmar.cengage.com* © Delmar Learning, a part of Cengage Learning, Inc. Reproduced by permission. www.cengage.com/permissions

Books-Select." The default setting for Save as type: is Adobe PDF (*.pdf). That is fine, so do not change it. See Adobe Acrobat Exhibit 5.

15. ***Click Save*** to create and save your new PDF.

This concludes Lesson 2.

ADOBE ACROBAT EXHIBIT 5
Saving a PDF

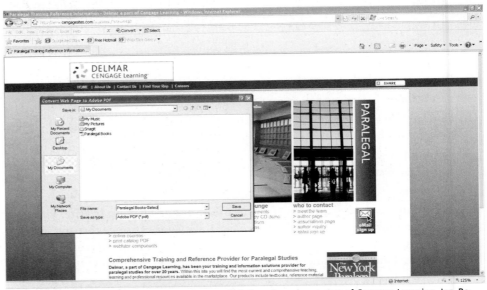

From Delmar. *www.paralegal.delmar.cengage.com* © Delmar Learning, a part of Cengage Learning, Inc. Reproduced by permission. www.cengage.com/permissions

 # INTERMEDIATE LESSONS

LESSON 3: COMBINING MULTIPLE DOCUMENTS INTO A SINGLE PDF

This lesson shows you how to combine separate documents into a single PDF. This lesson assumes that you have completed Lessons 1 and 2 and that you are generally familiar with Adobe Acrobat.

1. ***Double-click on the Adobe Acrobat Pro 9 icon on the desktop*** to open Adobe Acrobat Pro 9. Alternatively, ***click on the Start button, point to Programs or All Programs, then click on Adobe Acrobat Pro 9.*** You should be in a new, clean, empty (blank) document.

2. When you want to combine two or more individual PDFs into a single PDF, you will do so within the Adobe Acrobat Pro 9 program. Look at Adobe Acrobat Exhibit 6, and you will notice the Adobe toolbar. The first icon from

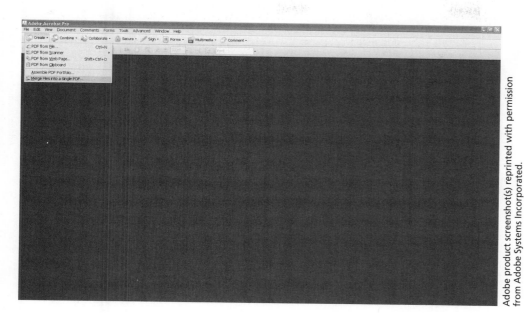

ADOBE ACROBAT EXHIBIT 6
Combining PDFs

Adobe product screenshot(s) reprinted with permission from Adobe Systems Incorporated.

the left is a drop-down menu titled Create. ***Click on Create.*** Notice that the last item on the drop-down menu is Merge Files into a Single PDF …. ***Click on the second icon from the left***, which is a drop-down menu called Combine. ***Click on Combine.*** Notice that the last item on the drop-down menu is Merge Files into a Single PDF. You can use either of these options to combine multiple PDFs into a single PDF. For this lesson, we will use the first drop-down menu, Create.

3. ***Click on Create from the menu bar and select Merge Files into a Single PDF….*** A new window will open, called "Combine Files." You now have to select the individual PDFs to combine into a single PDF. ***First, be sure that the Single PDF button is selected*** (see Adobe Acrobat Exhibit 7). We will work with the other button (PDF Portfolio) in the next lesson. To select the individual files, ***click on Add Files, located at the upper left corner of the "Combine Files" window.*** A drop-down menu will appear (see Adobe Acrobat Exhibit 7).

4. From this drop-down menu, ***click on the first option, Add Files….*** Another window will appear, called "Add Files." Notice that the Files of type: (at the bottom of this window) defaults to **"Adobe PDF Files (*.pdf)"**. Because you want to combine PDFs, the default is fine.

5. You will first select the "Letter1" PDF file you created in Lesson 1 of the Adobe Acrobat Hands-On Exercises. To select the file, ***scroll through the list of your PDFs until you find Letter1. Then, click on Letter1 and select Add Files.***

**ADOBE ACROBAT
EXHIBIT 7**
Combining PDFs

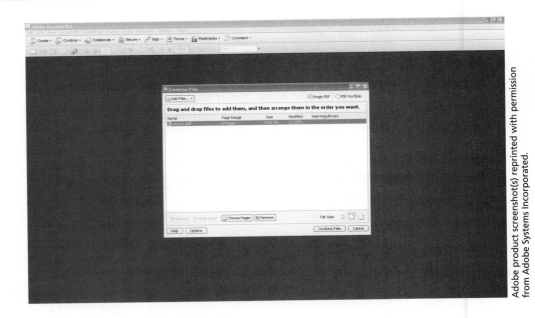

6. You will notice that "Letter1.pdf" is now listed in the "Combine Files" window (see Adobe Acrobat Exhibit 7). Obviously, you will need more than one file if you are to combine them, so you will now add the PDF you created in Lesson 2, "Paralegal Books." To do so, follow the same procedure listed in Steps 3 and 4 of this exercise.

7. Now "Paralegal Books.pdf" is listed in the "Combine Files" window, under Letter1. If you wanted to change the order of the PDFs, you could change it by first *clicking on one of the files to highlight it and then by clicking on either the Move Up or the Move Down button.* Similarly, you could choose to remove a file (by *clicking Remove*). See Adobe Acrobat Exhibit 7.

8. To create the single PDF, *click on the Combine Files button*. A new, single PDF will be created and a new window, called "Save As," will open. Call this file **Combined PDF 1** and *click Save* (see Adobe Acrobat Exhibit 8).

**ADOBE ACROBAT
EXHIBIT 8**
Combining PDFs

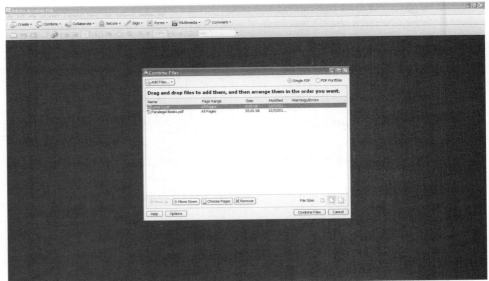

9. Your new PDF has been saved.

10. *Click on File on the menu bar, then on Exit* to exit Adobe Acrobat Pro 9.

This concludes Lesson 3.

LESSON 4: CREATING A PORTFOLIO

This lesson shows you how to combine separate documents into a PDF Portfolio. This lesson assumes that you have completed Lessons 1 through 3 and that you are generally familiar with Adobe Acrobat.

A PDF Portfolio contains multiple files assembled into a single PDF. The files in a PDF Portfolio can be in different formats and created in different applications. For example, you could have a portfolio that includes text documents, email messages, spreadsheets, digital photographs, and PowerPoint presentations.

In this exercise, you will prepare a Portfolio for a negligence case; it will contain a demand letter (Word), a spreadsheet detailing the injured person's damages (Excel), and a photograph of the damaged vehicle (JPEG).

1. *Double-click on the Adobe Acrobat Pro 9 icon on the desktop* to open Adobe Acrobat Pro 9. Alternatively, *click on the Start button, point to Programs or All Programs, then click on Adobe Acrobat Pro 9.* You should be in a new, clean, empty (blank) document.

2. *On the Adobe Acrobat toolbar, click Combine, the second icon from the left.* A drop-down menu will appear. *Click the first menu item, Assemble PDF Portfolio.* You will notice that the current screen disappears and is replaced by a new screen with the message **"Drag files and folders here to add them"** (see Adobe Acrobat Exhibit 9). (*Note:* You could also do this by first *clicking on the Create icon and then on the next-to-last item on the drop-down menu, Assemble PDF Portfolio.*)

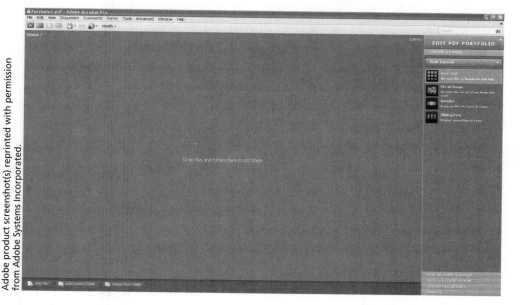

ADOBE ACROBAT EXHIBIT 9
Creating a PDF portfolio

3. You now must open the "Lesson 4" file from the disk supplied with this text. Ensure that the disk is inserted in the disk drive, *click on File on the menu bar, then click on Open.* The "Open" window should now be displayed. *Click on the down arrow to the right of the white box next to Look in: and select the drive where the disk is located. Double-click on the Adobe Acrobat folder. Double-click on the "Lesson 4" file.*

4. You will now see a list of various documents from different programs, including Word and Excel, as well as a photograph (JPEG).

5. *Point, click, and drag the Word file from the "Lesson 4" file to the Adobe Acrobat screen.* You will notice that the document is automatically added to the Portfolio. You should also note that the documents have not been converted to the PDF format; rather, they remain Word documents.

6. *Point, click, and drag the Excel file from the "Lesson 4" file to the Adobe Acrobat screen.* You will notice that the document is automatically added to the Portfolio. You should also note that the documents have not been converted to the PDF format; rather, they remain Excel documents (see Adobe Acrobat Exhibit 10).

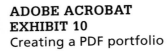

ADOBE ACROBAT EXHIBIT 10
Creating a PDF portfolio

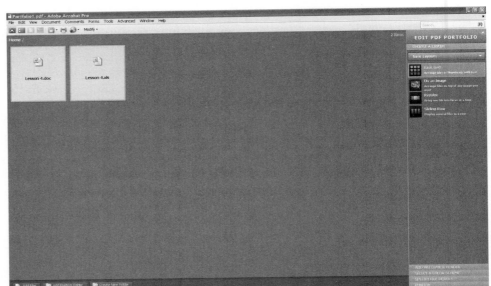

7. *Point, click, and drag the car JPEG file from the "Lesson 4" file to the Adobe Acrobat screen.* You will notice that the document is automatically added to the Portfolio. You should also note that the documents have not been converted to the PDF format; rather, they remain JPEGs.

8. You should now have three items in your Portfolio.

9. Alternately, you could also have added these files to the Portfolio by *clicking Add Files*, which is the first icon on the bottom row of the PDF screen.

10. If you wanted to see a list of the files contained in a Portfolio, you could *click the second icon on the top toolbar. Click that icon now* to see a list of the files that have been added to this Portfolio.

11. To return to the original view of the files, *click the first icon on the top toolbar* (it looks like a house).

12. To save the portfolio, *click File, then Save Portfolio As.* A new window will open called "Save As."

13. In the "File name" box, call this file **Portfolio1**; then *click OK.*

14. You have successfully created, named, and saved a portfolio.

15. *Click on File in the menu bar, and then Exit* to exit Adobe Acrobat Pro 9.

This concludes Lesson 4.

ADVANCED LESSON

LESSON 5: ADDING SECURITY TO A PDF

This lesson shows you how to use the security features of Adobe Acrobat Pro 9 to enhance the security of a PDF. It is essential that PDFs containing confidential or sensitive information have some degree of security, as they are often created and received by individuals who have not met in person and need to know that their information will be viewed only by persons authorized to do so.

1. ***Double-click on the Adobe Acrobat Pro 9 icon on the desktop*** to open Adobe Acrobat Pro 9. Alternatively, ***click on the Start button, point to Programs or All Programs, then click on Adobe Acrobat Pro 9.*** You should be in a new, clean, empty (blank) document.

2. Now you need to open the "Lesson 5" file from the disk supplied with this text. Ensure that the disk is inserted in the disk drive, ***click on File on the menu bar, then click on Open.*** The "Open" window should now be displayed. ***Click on the down arrow to the right of the white box next to Look in: and select the drive where the disk is located. Double-click on the Adobe Acrobat folder. Double-click on the "Lesson 5" file.***

3. You should now have a copy of a demand letter in PDF format.

4. You want to be sure that only authorized persons see this demand letter, so you will enable some of the security features of Adobe Acrobat Pro 9.

5. To do this, ***first click on the Secure icon*** (it looks like a padlock). A drop-down menu will appear. ***Click on the fourth menu item, Show Security Properties.***

6. A new window will open, called "Document Properties." Notice that at the top of the window, next to Security Method:, the No Security option appears. Also, notice that at the bottom of the window, under the heading Document Restrictions Summary, all of the options are Allowed (see Adobe Acrobat Exhibit 11).

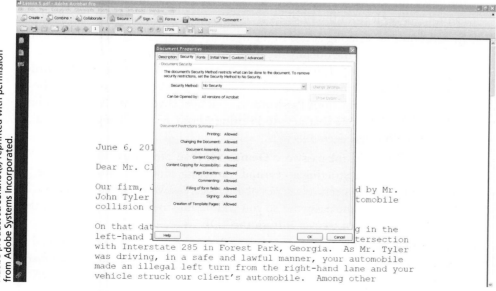

HANDS-ON EXERCISES

**ADOBE ACROBAT
EXHIBIT 11**
Adding security to a PDF

**ADOBE ACROBAT
EXHIBIT 12**
Adding security to a PDF

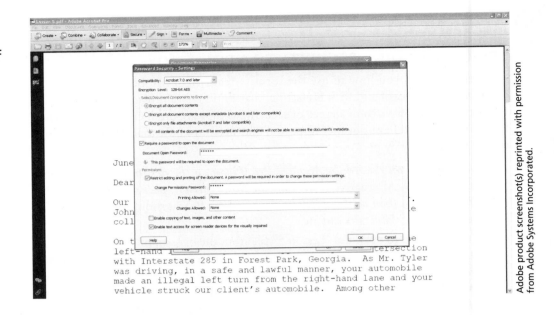

7. ***Click on the drop-down menu next to Security Method: and choose Password Security.*** A new window, called "Password Security – Settings," will open (see Adobe Acrobat Exhibit 12).

8. First, the compatibility setting must be adjusted. This determines what version of Adobe Acrobat a user must have in order to open this PDF. Later versions provide more security than older versions; however, you cannot assume that the user will have the most recent version of Adobe Acrobat. The default setting of Acrobat 7.0 or higher is appropriate, so leave it as is.

9. ***Click the box next to*** **"Require a password to open the document."** Notice that when you do, the text box next to Document Open Password: is no longer shaded (see Adobe Acrobat Exhibit 12).

10. In the text box, type the password **Demand1**. Notice that the password will appear as a series of asterisks. Passwords are case sensitive. Be sure to write down the password so you will be able to find it. If you forget the password, you cannot recover it from the PDF.

11. In addition to restricting access to the document, you can restrict a user's ability to edit and/or print the document. To do so, ***click the box next to*** **"Restrict editing and printing of the document. A password will be required in order to change these permission settings."** Notice that when you do, the text box next to Change Permissions Password: is no longer shaded (see Adobe Acrobat Exhibit 12). Make sure that next to Printing Allowed: and Changes Allowed:, the choice None has been selected.

12. In the text box, type the password **Demand2**. (You cannot use the same password for both restricting access and restricting editing/printing.) Notice that the password appears as a series of asterisks. Passwords are case sensitive. Be sure to write down the password so you will be able to find it. If you forget the password, you cannot recover it from the PDF.

13. After typing the password, ***click OK***. Another window will then open, called "Adobe Acrobat – Confirm Document Open Password." ***Next to the text box called Document Open Password:, retype the password and then click OK.*** This ensures that you have correctly typed the password. Now another window

will open, called "Adobe Acrobat – Confirm Permissions Password." ***Next to the text box called Permissions Password:, retype the password and then click OK.*** This ensures that you have correctly typed the password. If you see additional dialog boxes, just ***click OK.***

14. A new window called "Adobe Acrobat" opens. This box tells you that the security settings you just set will not be applied to the PDF until you save the document. You may continue to change the security settings until you close the document. ***Click OK*** to close this window.

15. You now see the "Document Properties" window again. Notice that Security Method: now says "**Password Security**." ***Click OK.***

16. ***Click the Save icon*** (it looks like a computer disk). Notice that the title of the document now includes "(SECURED)."

17. ***Click File, then click Close*** to close the document.

18. Now you will open the same PDF using the security tools you just enabled. ***Click the Open icon*** (it looks like a file folder) ***and find the "Lesson 5" file, then click OK*** to open it.

19. Notice that when you do so, a new window called "Password" opens. You are required to enter your password to open the PDF. Type your password, **Demand1,** then ***click OK.***

20. Your PDF now appears.

21. ***Click on File in the menu bar, and then on Exit*** to exit Adobe Acrobat Pro 9.

This concludes Lesson 5.

HANDS-ON EXERCISES

HANDS-ON EXERCISES

HOTDOCS 10

I. INTRODUCTION — READ THIS!

HotDocs lets you transform any PDF or word-processor file into an interactive template by marking changeable text with "HotDocs variables." Then the next time you want to generate a completed form or text document, you assemble it from the template you've created.

II. INSTALLATION INSTRUCTIONS

Below are step-by-step instructions for installing HotDocs on your computer. Note that installing this software requires you to restart your system when it is completed.

1. Log in to your CengageBrain.com account.
2. Under "My Courses & Materials," find the Premium Website for Using Computers in the Law Office.
3. *Click Open to go to the Premium Website.*
4. *Locate Book Resources in the left navigation menu.*
5. *Click on the link for HotDocs 10.*
6. A screen requesting your contact information and a "Download Code" should now be displayed. You will need to supply the following download code: **k3gh87ht**
7. *Enter the information necessary to complete the form, including the Download Code, and click Submit.*
8. You will receive an email response from HotDocs Corporation that will include a link for downloading the HotDocs 10 software. *Click on the HotDocs 10 Educational Download link in the email.* A web page will open that includes links for both the 32-bit and 64-bit versions of HotDocs.
9. *Double-click the appropriate file to install HotDocs.* If you are unsure which version of Windows you have, you can check by *right-clicking My Computer, then selecting Properties.* Under **System**, you can view the system type. In Windows 7 and Windows Vista, either **"32-bit operating system"** or **"64-bit operating system"** will be displayed. In Windows XP, if you don't see **"x64 Edition"** listed, you're running the 32-bit version of Windows XP. If **"x64 Edition"** is listed, you're running the 64-bit version of Windows XP. If you are still not sure which version to install, choose the 32-bit version, as that is the more common version. If you choose the incorrect version and the program does not load, you can always try the other version.
10. A screen similar to HotDocs Installation Exhibit 1 should now be displayed. *Click Run.*

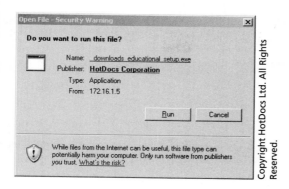

**HOTDOCS
INSTALLATION
EXHIBIT 1**

11. Another "Security Warning" window will open; *click Run.*
12. In the "HotDocs Developer 10 Setup" window, *click Next.*
13. In the "Software License Agreement" window, *click the button next to* **"I accept the terms in the license agreement"** *and click Next.*
14. The screen in HotDocs Installation Exhibit 2 should now be displayed. *Click Next* to install the software in the default directory.
15. Choose the word-processing programs you would like to use with HotDocs and *click Next.*

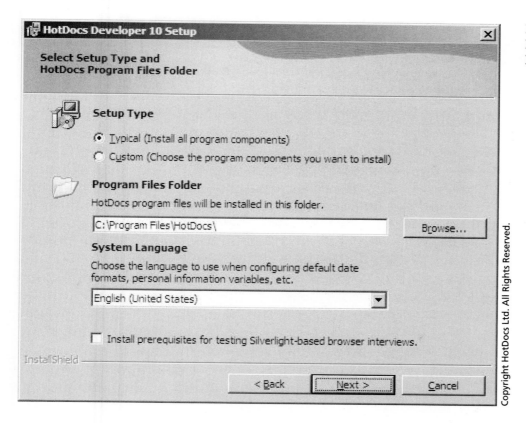

**HOTDOCS
INSTALLATION
EXHIBIT 2**

HANDS-ON EXERCISES

16. The screen in HotDocs Installation Exhibit 3 should now be displayed. Confirm the settings listed and *click Install.*

**HOTDOCS
INSTALLATION
EXHIBIT 3**

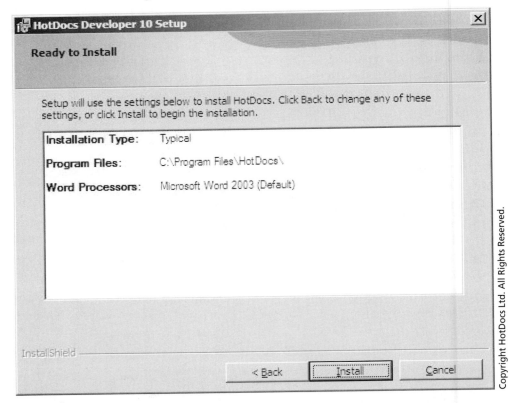

17. The screen in HotDocs Installation Exhibit 4 should now be displayed. *Click Finish* to complete the installation.

**HOTDOCS
INSTALLATION
EXHIBIT 4**

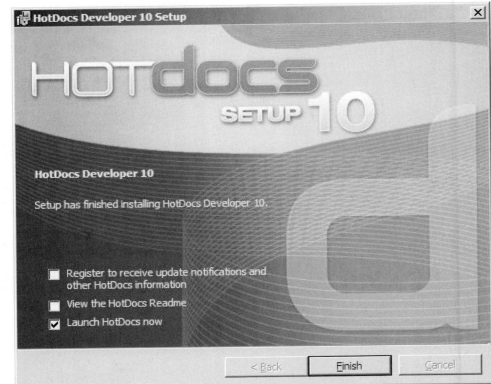

18. HotDocs has now been installed. You can open the appropriate module via the ***Start Button > All Programs > HotDocs10 > HotDocs Developer*** folder.

III. INSTALLATION TECHNICAL SUPPORT

If you have problems installing this software, please contact Delmar Cengage Learning first at http://cengage.com/support. If Delmar Cengage Learning is unable to resolve your installation question, you will need to contact HotDocs Ltd. at http://www.hotdocs.com/Support-Home.aspx or phone (801) 615-2200.

Number	Lesson Title	Concepts Covered
BASIC LESSON		
Lesson 1	Creating a Document from a Text Template	Template libraries; assembling a document from an existing template, editing a document, saving, and printing
INTERMEDIATE LESSON		
Lesson 2	Creating a New Text Template	Creating a new template library, adding templates to a library, finding a document to convert to a template, creating interview questions

GETTING STARTED
Introduction

Throughout these lessons and exercises, information you need to type into the program will be designated in several different ways:

- Keys to be pressed on the keyboard are designated in brackets, in all caps, and in bold (e.g., press the **[ENTER]** key). A key combination, where two or more keys are pressed at once, is designated with a plus sign between the key names (e.g., **[CTRL]+[BACKSPACE]**). You should not type the plus sign.
- Movements with the mouse pointer are designated in bold and italics (e.g., ***point to File on the menu bar and click***).
- Words or letters that should be typed are designated in bold (e.g., type **Training Program**).
- Information that is or should be displayed on your computer screen is shown in bold, with quotation marks (e.g., **"Press ENTER to continue."**).

OVERVIEW OF HOTDOCS 10

Below are some tips on using HotDocs 10 that will help you complete these exercises.

HotDocs can transform any document into an interactive template that can be changed and adapted to suit the requirements of different cases. This allows you to create a single template for a particular use (e.g., a divorce pleading, articles of incorporation) instead of creating new documents from scratch for each client. This is accomplished by answering a series of questions. In these exercises, you will first complete a prepared text template to assemble a new document. You will then create a new template and assemble a new document from that newly formed text template.

BASIC LESSON

LESSON 1: CREATING A DOCUMENT FROM A TEXT TEMPLATE

This lesson shows you how to assemble a document from a text template. It assumes that you already have a viable text template designed for use with the HotDocs software. (In Lesson 2, you will see how to create a text template from scratch and then assemble a new document using that text template.)

1. Open Windows. ***Click on the Start button, point the cursor to Programs or All Programs, then click HotDocs 10, then click HotDocs Developer.*** The Demonstration Templates library will appear on your screen (see HotDocs Exhibit 1).

HOTDOCS EXHIBIT 1

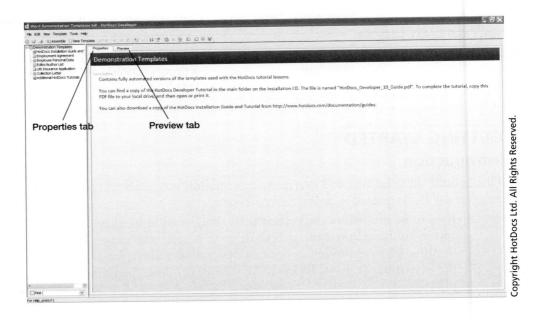

2. In this lesson, you will create an employment agreement using a text template created with HotDocs 10 software. This employment agreement was installed on your computer with the HotDocs 10 software; it is intended as a demonstration template and should not be used for any other purpose.

3. The HotDocs 10 window has two panes. The pane on the left lists the templates contained within the library. Right now, the library contains only the demonstration templates provided with the software. The pane on the right has two tabs; one shows the properties of the selected template and the other shows a preview of the document being assembled.

4. To open the Employment Agreement text template, ***click on Employment Agreement File from the list called Demonstration Templates.*** A list of Interview topics appears in the left panel. The Employment Agreement template will then appear in the right panel. Click on the Preview tab to see the complete template (see HotDocs Exhibit 2).

5. To begin assembling the employment agreement, ***click the Assemble icon on the HotDocs toolbar*** (it looks like a green arrow). Two new windows open. The larger of the two is the Interview. The smaller of the two is called Answer File. As this file does not yet contain any information, the Answer File dialog box shows an untitled answer file. ***Click OK.***

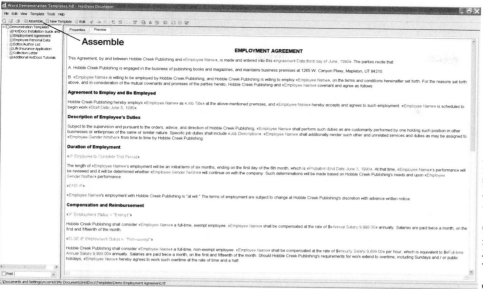

HOTDOCS EXHIBIT 2

6. The larger window now shows the first of the Interview Questions; the answers you supply will populate the fields of the Employment Agreement text template. Notice that on the left side of the window is a list of the interview topics. On the right side are interview questions called Employee Information. For the Employee Name, type **Abigail Shannon**. For Employee Gender, *click the button next to Female* (see HotDocs Exhibit 3). *Click Next* (one blue arrow at the bottom of the window).

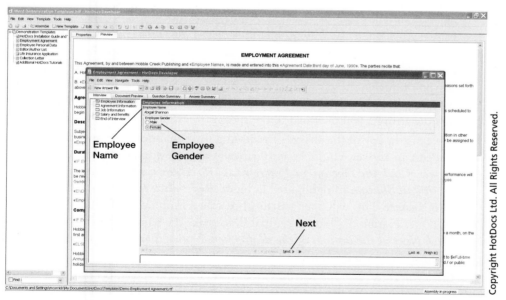

HOTDOCS EXHIBIT 3

7. The next screen has the interview questions regarding the Agreement Information. Under Agreement Date, type **April 29, 2012**. Under Company Representative, *click the button for Stephanie Hanson*; notice that when you do this, the Agreement Date becomes "29 Apr 2012." Leave the Signature Date blank. *Click Next.*

8. The next screen has the interview questions regarding the Job Information. Under Job Title, type **Creative Director**. Under Complete the following sentence: Job duties shall include, type **Oversee advertising and marketing initiatives; manage staff members; prepare budgets.** Under Start Date, type

HOTDOCS EXHIBIT 4

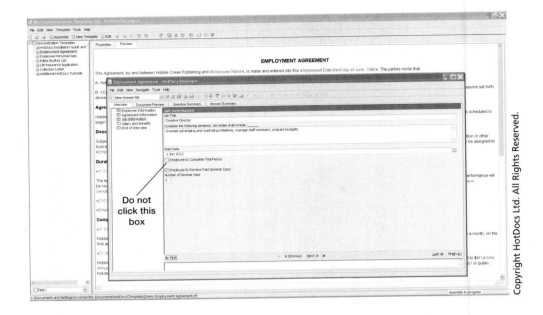

Do not click this box

June 1, 2012. *Do not click the box next to Employee to Complete Trial Period. Do click the box next to Employee to Receive Paid Seminar Days.* When you do this, the Number of Seminar Days box is no longer shaded. Type **2** in that box (see HotDocs Exhibit 4). *Click Next.*

9. The next screen has interview questions regarding Salary and Benefits. *Under Employment Status, click the button next to Exempt.* Notice that now a new text box appears called "Annual Salary." (If you had clicked the "Non-exempt" or "Part-time" boxes, the text box would be titled "Hourly Salary.") Under Annual Salary, type **62,500**. Under Number of Vacation Days, type **10**.

10. Notice that there are four tabs: Interview, the window you have been viewing; Document Preview, which provides a preview of the assembled document at any point during the assembly process; Question Summary, which lists the specific questions contained within the interview; and Answer Summary, which lists the answers you provided to the specific questions.

11. You can edit any of the answers by viewing the Document Preview tab. When you edit an answer, HotDocs automatically edits all questions affected by that answer. *Click the Document Preview tab. Point the cursor to any reference to Abigail Shannon* (highlighted in blue). *Right-click the mouse and click on Edit Answer.* This will open a dialog box called Employee Information (see HotDocs Exhibit 5). Type the initial **E.** to make the name "Abigail E. Shannon." *Click Next at the bottom of the dialog box.* Notice that every reference to the employee now reads "Abigail E. Shannon."

12. *Click the Interview tab again. Click Next.* The next screen is End of Interview. If you failed to answer any questions, you would be prompted to click a button that would take you back to missed question(s). Because we answered all of the questions, we are given the option of sending the assembled document to Microsoft Word. *Click the first option* (it looks like a blue arrow), *then click the box next to Close this window. Click Finish.*

13. Two new windows will open. One is a small dialog box asking if you want to save the answers to this template. It is not necessary to save these answers, so *click Don't Save.* You are then asked if you want to save a copy of the assembled document. *You may click Don't Save.* The second window is a Word copy of the assembled employment agreement. At this point, the employment agreement document is no longer associated with HotDocs. It is

HOTDOCS EXHIBIT 5

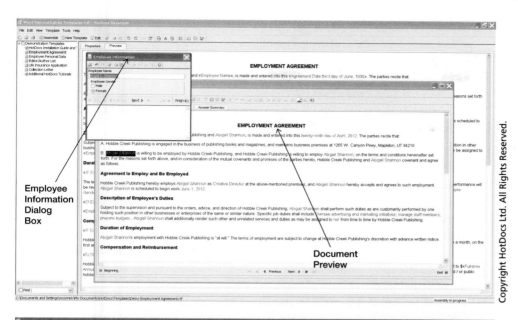

Employee Information Dialog Box

Document Preview

HOTDOCS EXHIBIT 6

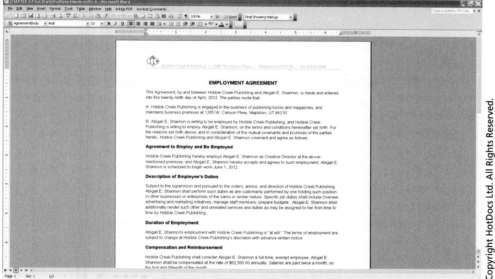

an independent Word document that can be edited, saved, and printed as such (see HotDocs Exhibit 6).

14. On the Employment Agreement Word file, ***click File, then Save As.*** Next to File name, type **Shannon Agreement**. ***Click on Save*** to save the document. ***Then click the X at the top right corner of the screen*** to close the file.

This concludes Lesson 1.

▶ INTERMEDIATE LESSON

LESSON 2: CREATING A NEW TEXT TEMPLATE

This lesson will show you how to create a new text template using the HotDocs 10 software. This lesson assumes that you have completed Lesson 1 and that you are familiar with HotDocs 10.

1. Start Windows. ***Click on the Start button, point the cursor to Programs or All Programs, then click HotDocs 10, then click HotDocs Developer.*** The Demonstration Templates library will appear on your screen.

2. **Click File, then New Library.** The New Library dialog box will appear. Under File name, type **My Training Templates**, then press the **[TAB]** key twice. HotDocs has entered the .hdl suffix to the file name; the program requires this suffix to properly identify the file. Under Title, the program has automatically filled in the title "My Training Templates." This is fine. In the Description box, type **This is the template I created in my Computers in the Law Office class.** Then **click OK.** A new library has been created.

3. Your new library is empty; you need to add a template to it.

4. **Click on the My Training Templates folder.**

5. **Click the New Template icon** (it looks like a rectangle with a star in the upper left corner). The New Template dialog box will open. **Next to Type, select Word RTF Template (.rtf);** this is the appropriate choice for Word users. Under File name, type **Complaint—Breach of Contract**, then press the **[TAB]** key twice. Notice that HotDocs has added the suffix .rtf to the file name. **Click on the text box under Title** and you will see that HotDocs has suggested the title "Complaint—Breach of Contract." This is fine. Under Description, type **This is the template I created for my Computers in the Law Office class.** (See HotDocs Exhibit 7.)

HOTDOCS EXHIBIT 7

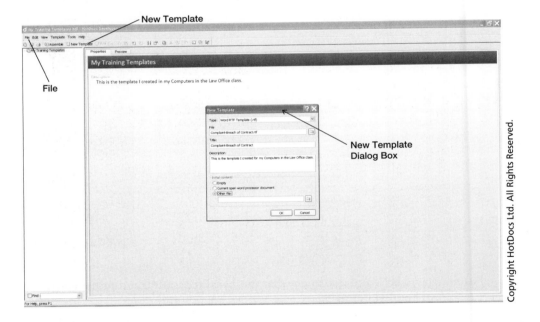

6. **Under Initial contents, click the last button, called Other file, then click the Browse button to the right of the text box.**

7. This opens a new window ("New Template Initial Contents"), which will enable you to choose the text file you will convert to a text template. **Click Look in: and then choose the CD drive for your computer. Click on HotDocs, then click Lesson 2, then click on OK** to return to the New Template dialog box. The document's folder path and file name now appear in the Other file text box.

8. **Click OK.** This creates the new template file and adds it to your library. It also opens the template as a Word document—but notice that a new HotDocs toolbar has been added (see HotDocs Exhibit 8). You will now begin selecting the text fields in this document that are to serve as variables.

9. **Highlight the text "IN THE SUPERIOR COURT OF FULTON COUNTY" at the top of the page, then click the Variable Field button on the HotDocs**

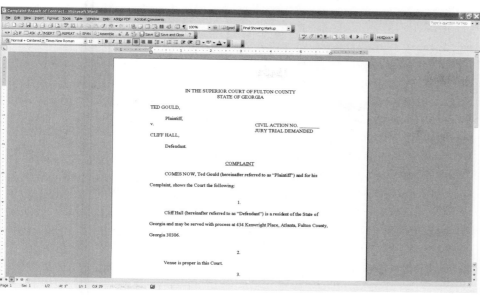

HOTDOCS EXHIBIT 8

toolbar. It is the first icon on the left side of the toolbar and looks like this: <<>>. The Variable Field dialog box will open.

10. ***From the Variable type list, select Text.*** In the Variable text box, type **Court in which complaint is to be filed**. This variable occurs just this one time in the document, so ***click Replace Once.*** Notice that the template now shows that the selected text has been replaced with the description of the variable and that the text now appears in blue (see HotDocs Exhibit 9).

11. You need to follow similar steps to replace the other text variables in the template. ***First, highlight "TED GOULD" and click the Variable Field button at the top left corner of the HotDocs toolbar. In the Variable Field dialog box, choose Text as the Variable type.*** In the Variable text box, type **Name of Plaintiff**. This variable occurs more than once, so ***click Replace Multiple***. You also have the choice of clicking Replace All, which would replace all references to Ted Gould with "Name of Plaintiff"; or using Find Next, which would allow you to review all uses of the variable and decide when to replace it one at a time. We want to replace all references to Ted Gould, so ***click Replace All.***

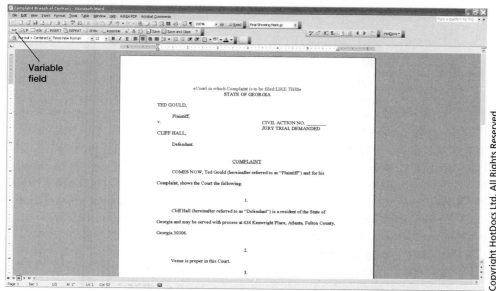

Variable field

HOTDOCS EXHIBIT 9

HANDS-ON EXERCISES

HOTDOCS EXHIBIT 10

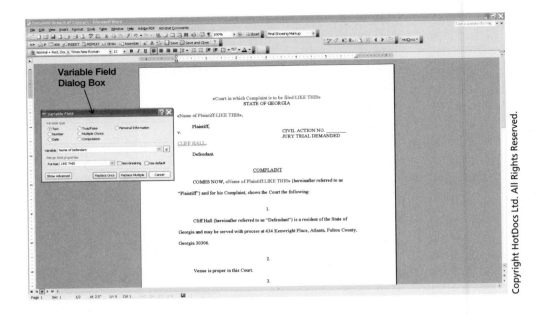

Variable Field Dialog Box

12. Now you will do the same for the defendant. *Highlight "CLIFF HALL" and click the Variable Field button at the top left corner of the HotDocs toolbar. In the Variable Field dialog box, choose Text as the Variable type.* In the Variable text box, type **Name of Defendant**. (See HotDocs Exhibit 10.) This variable occurs more than once, so *click Replace Multiple. Then click Replace All.*

13. Next, *highlight the defendant's address and click the Variable Field button at the top left corner of the HotDocs toolbar. In the Variable Field dialog box, choose Text as the Variable type.* In the Variable text box, type **Defendant's address**. This variable occurs just once, so *click Replace Once.*

14. Next, *highlight "January 1, 2012" and click the Variable Field button at the top left corner of the HotDocs toolbar. In the Variable Field dialog box, choose Date as the Variable type.* In the Variable text box, type **Date contract was created**. This variable occurs just once, so *click Replace Once.*

15. Now *highlight "Ten Thousand Dollars" and click the Variable Field button at the top left corner of the HotDocs toolbar. In the Variable Field dialog box, choose Text as the Variable type.* In the Variable text box, type **Dollar amount of contract**. This variable occurs more than once, so *click Replace Multiple, then click Replace All.*

16. Next, *highlight "June 30, 2012" and click the Variable Field button at the top left corner of the HotDocs toolbar. In the Variable Field dialog box, choose Date as the Variable type.* In the Variable text box, type **Date money was to be repaid**. This variable occurs just once, so *click Replace Once.*

17. Next, *highlight the number "10" in paragraph 3 and click the Variable Field button at the top left corner of the HotDocs toolbar. In the Variable Field dialog box, choose Number as the Variable type.* In the Variable text box, type **Interest rate of loan**. This variable occurs more than once, so *click Replace Multiple, then click Replace All.* (See HotDocs Exhibit 11.)

18. The last variables to be replaced are the pronouns used to refer to the parties in the third person. You need to be sure the complaint does not state "he" when you mean "she." To do this, first *highlight the word "his" in paragraph 5 and click the Variable Field button at the top left corner of the HotDocs toolbar. In the Variable Field dialog box, select Multiple Choice as the Variable type.* Then type **Party gender in the Variable text box**. *Click the Edit Component icon,* which is located at the far right of the text box where you just typed "Party gender." This opens the "Multiple Choice Variable Editor" window.

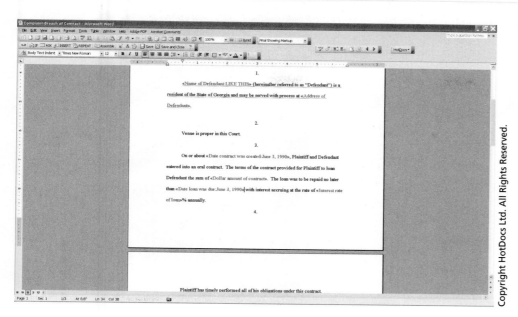

HOTDOCS EXHIBIT 11

19. Type **Male** in the first row of the Option column and **Female** in the second row. ***Click Default Merge Text;*** a drop-down menu of pronouns appears. ***Select "his/her."*** The pronoun "his" appears in the first row and "her" appears in the second row. (See HotDocs Exhibit 12.) ***Then click OK*** to return to the Variable Field dialog box.

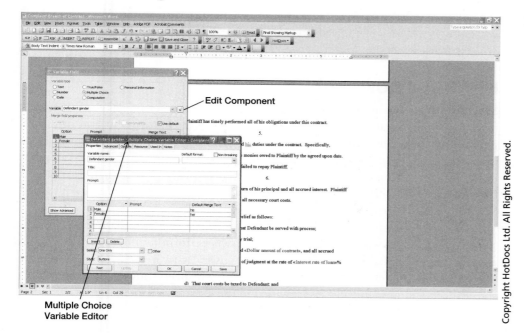

HOTDOCS EXHIBIT 12

Multiple Choice
Variable Editor

20. ***Be sure the Use default box is unchecked.*** This will allow you to use the Merge Text column. ***Click Replace Multiple;*** the Find and Replace dialog box appears.

21. ***Select Find whole words only;*** this will ensure that you only replace the exact word selected (*his*) and not words that contain "his" as part of the word. ***Click Replace All.***

22. ***Click Save and Close on the HotDocs toolbar.***

This concludes Lesson 2.

HANDS-ON EXERCISES

CHAPTER 3

Spreadsheet Software

CHAPTER OBJECTIVES

After completing this chapter, you should be able to do the following:

1. Explain what a spreadsheet is.
2. Describe how rows and columns make up the structure of a spreadsheet.
3. Explain what text, values, and formulas are.
4. Describe the types of graphs commonly found in spreadsheet programs.
5. Explain how copying formulas can simplify the use of a spreadsheet.
6. List and describe the ways in which paralegals can use spreadsheets.

INTRODUCTION

spreadsheet software
Programs that calculate and manipulate numbers using labels, values, and formulas.

Spreadsheet software calculates and manipulates numbers using labels, values, and formulas. Legal organizations use spreadsheets to create department and firm budgets; to calculate child support and alimony payments in domestic relations cases; to prepare amortization schedules, Truth-in-Lending statements, and loan calculations in real estate matters; and to estimate taxes and help prepare tax returns for tax matters. These are just a few of the many uses of spreadsheets for law offices of all types. Spreadsheet software can automate all of these tasks.

As word processors manipulate words, spreadsheets manipulate numbers. Instead of performing word processing, spreadsheets perform number processing. This chapter describes what a spreadsheet is and discusses "what if" analysis, the structure of spreadsheet programs, the fundamentals of spreadsheets, how to plan or create a spreadsheet, and how spreadsheets are used in the legal environment.

WHAT IS A SPREADSHEET?

spreadsheet
A computerized version of an accountant's worksheet or ledger page.

A **spreadsheet** is a computerized version of an accountant's worksheet or ledger page. Spreadsheet software is used to create a spreadsheet, sometimes called a *worksheet*. In the past, accounting professionals primarily used ledger pages, also sometimes called *worksheets*, to track financial information. They would enter financial transactions across the rows and down the columns of the ledger paper. Each column was then added up using a calculator or an adding machine. This process was cumbersome and time-consuming if changes were needed or if errors were found.

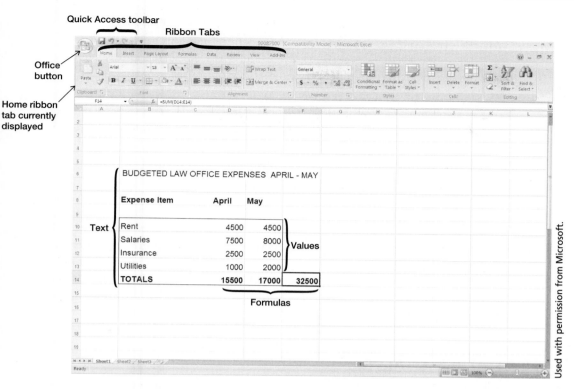

Quick Access toolbar

Ribbon Tabs

Office button

Home ribbon tab currently displayed

EXHIBIT 3–1
A simple spreadsheet using Microsoft Excel 2007

Used with permission from Microsoft.

Spreadsheets, in contrast, are flexible and easy to use. Exhibit 3–1 is a simple spreadsheet showing a small law firm's budgeted expenses for a two-month period. This example introduces basic spreadsheet concepts. More sophisticated and more useful spreadsheets for the legal environment are introduced later in this chapter.

Spreadsheet programs were among the first general business application programs designed to run on personal computers. Spreadsheets are easier to use than manual worksheets, because the data in a spreadsheet can easily be edited and changed. In addition, spreadsheets can calculate totals and perform other mathematical functions automatically. When data are changed in a spreadsheet, the resulting totals are automatically recalculated to reflect the changes made. (Note that data is often a plural word, as shown here.) Spreadsheets have greatly altered the way businesses and legal organizations track and keep numerical data. Reports and computations that once took hours or days now take minutes.

Law firms also enjoy the benefits of spreadsheets. Numerical data are critical in almost all areas of the law. Remember, if it involves money, it involves numbers. For example, many complaints and cases include claims for damages; that is, the people filing the suits often ask for money or some type of monetary relief. Damages calculations can be complex and are often well-suited to spreadsheets; spreadsheets are used extensively in bankruptcy law, tax law, estate law, real estate law, and other areas. Law firms also use spreadsheets administratively to track income and expenses, create budgets, produce financial and accounting records, produce statistical reports about the business, and so on.

Spreadsheet software is easy and flexible to use because it

1. allows all entries to be edited, moved, or copied to other places in the spreadsheet.

2. makes it easy to insert additional columns and rows, even after the spreadsheet has been created.

3. multiplies, divides, adds, and subtracts one entry or many entries.
4. performs complex calculations (e.g., statistical functions, such as standard deviations, averages, and square roots; and financial calculations, such as present value, future value, and internal rate of return).
5. automatically recalculates totals and other calculations when information in a column or a row changes.
6. allows numerical information to be presented in several kinds of graphs and charts.
7. allows information to be saved and retrieved for future use.
8. allows information to be sorted or organized automatically.
9. allows the information in the spreadsheet to be printed.

Microsoft Excel is the spreadsheet program overwhelmingly used by most legal organizations. Versions of Excel that are widely used in the legal environment include Excel 2010, Excel 2007, and Excel 2003. The programs are largely similar except that Excel 2007 and 2010 use a ribbon interface (see Exhibit 3–1) and Excel 2003 uses a largely menu-driven interface. Screen shots from Excel 2007 and Excel 2010 are used throughout this chapter.

"WHAT IF" ANALYSIS

"what if" analysis
A feature of spreadsheets that allows the user to build a spreadsheet and then change the data to reflect alternative planning assumptions or scenarios.

Spreadsheets can also be used for "what if" analysis. **"What if" analysis** refers to the ability to build a spreadsheet and then to change it to reflect alternative planning assumptions or scenarios. As mentioned before, when numerical data are entered into a spreadsheet and later changed, the totals are automatically recalculated. Thus, it is possible to evaluate the effects of a change simply by changing a number. This allows users to hypothesize and evaluate the effects of potential changes easily. For example, in Exhibit 3–1, if the small law firm wanted to evaluate what would happen if rent doubled for the two-month period shown, it could simply change the "4500" rent figure to "9000" and the spreadsheet would automatically recalculate the total. Most businesses are in a state of change at all times, so this feature allows users to prepare for unexpected events.

SPREADSHEET STRUCTURE AND ORGANIZATION

An electronic spreadsheet has many of the same components as its paper ancestor, such as rows and columns. However, it also has many features unique to the electronic format, such as formulas that automatically compute and display the desired information.

Rows and Columns

row
An area that extends across a page horizontally.

column
An area that extends down a page vertically.

Like an accountant's worksheet, a spreadsheet has rows and columns. A **row** is an area that extends across a page horizontally, and a **column** is an area that extends down a page vertically. For example, in Exhibit 3–2, rows are designated by a number (row 1, row 2, etc.), and columns are designated by a capital letter (column A, column B, etc.). Although only 21 rows and 10 columns are shown on the screen in Exhibit 3–2, the spreadsheet actually extends all the way down several thousand rows and all the way across several hundred columns. The exact length of a spreadsheet depends on the spreadsheet program. When the columns go past column Z, the column letters double up (column AA, column AB, etc.).

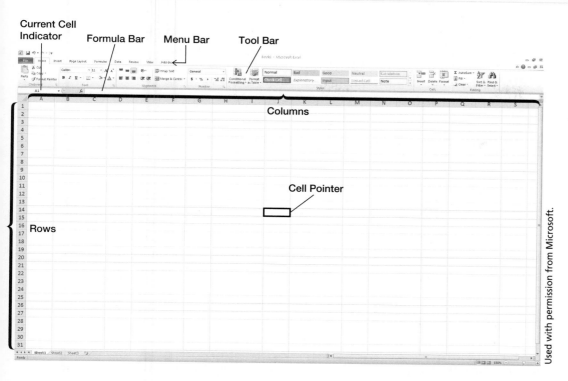

EXHIBIT 3–2
A simple spreadsheet using Microsoft Excel 2010

Cells and Cell Addresses

A **cell** is an intersection between a row and a column (see Exhibit 3–2). Every cell has a **cell address**. A cell address is the row and column location of a cell. The cell address is usually represented by the letter of the column and then the number of the row, such as cell A1 in Exhibit 3–2. Every cell in a spreadsheet has a cell address. Cells hold information such as values (numbers), formulas (mathematical calculations), and text.

The Elements of a Spreadsheet

Most spreadsheet programs have a user interface similar to the one in Exhibit 3–2. After a user loads a spreadsheet program, a blank spreadsheet is displayed. Exhibit 3–2 shows the various elements of a spreadsheet.

Cell Pointer All spreadsheets have a **cell pointer**, or cursor, that indicates which cell is currently selected. The cell pointer is moved by using the arrow or direction keys and can also be moved up and down pages or screens by using the [PAGE UP], [PAGE DOWN], and other keys, depending on the spreadsheet. Most spreadsheet programs also allow the cell pointer to be moved with a mouse. Finally, the cell pointer can be moved using the GO TO command. The GO TO command instructs the spreadsheet to "go to" a certain cell address. In Microsoft Excel 2007 and 2010, the [F5] key is the GO TO command.

Current Cell Indicator and Formula Bar The current cell indicator, sometimes called the *name box*, shows the address of the cell pointer (see Exhibit 3–2). The formula bar, which is just to the right of the current cell indicator, shows the contents of the current cell. Notice in Exhibit 3–2 that the current cell indicator shows "A1" and that there is nothing in the formula bar, because cell A1 is empty. When the cell pointer is on a cell containing text, a value, or a formula, the information in the cell will be shown in the formula bar. The text, value, or formula can be edited by placing the cursor in the formula bar. When the cell pointer is moved, the current cell indicator automatically displays the current cell address.

cell
An intersection between a row and a column in a spreadsheet.

cell address
The row and column location of a cell, usually expressed with column identifier first and row identifier second.

cell pointer
The cursor in a spreadsheet program.

Data Input Area Data are entered into a spreadsheet in the data input area, which is made up of cells.

Status Bar The status bar signifies the current status of the spreadsheet. For example, in Exhibit 3–2, the spreadsheet is in the ready mode, which means that it is ready to accept instructions from a user.

Menus, Toolbars, and Ribbons

Excel 2007 (see Exhibit 3–1) uses a changing ribbon as the interface with the user instead of menus. In Exhibit 3–1 the Home ribbon tab is shown. Available ribbons include: Home, Insert, Page Layout, Formulas, Data, Review, and View. The tools on the ribbon change depending on what tab is selected. Excel 2007 and 2010 also have a small Quick Access toolbar that does not change and that is customizable by the user (see Exhibit 3–1). Excel 2007 uses the Office button and Excel 2010 uses the File tab to access common tasks such as Open, Save, Save As, New, and Close.

Horizontal and Vertical Scroll Bars To bring other parts of the spreadsheet into view, use the horizontal and vertical scroll bars.

Worksheets Most spreadsheet programs allow multiple worksheets in one spreadsheet file. Notice in Exhibit 3–2 that three sheets are available (Sheet 1, Sheet 2, and Sheet 3). Many users find it convenient to have separate worksheets in one file. For example, if your law office had three locations, you could have one spreadsheet file called "budget" with a separate worksheet for each location. The worksheets (Sheet 1, Sheet 2, etc.) can be renamed however you wish, such as Location 1, 2, and 3.

Spreadsheets with WYSIWYG

Most spreadsheets offer a WYSIWYG ("what you see is what you get"; pronounced "wizzy-wig") screen. Exhibits 3–1 and 3–2 are examples of Windows spreadsheet programs with WYSIWYG. The WYSIWYG format allows users to add different fonts or type styles to the spreadsheets and enables application of boxes and other formatting options that can make a spreadsheet easier to read. In addition, all of the formatting appears on the screen exactly as it will print out.

SPREADSHEET FUNDAMENTALS

In this section, you will learn about spreadsheet menus and about inputting text, values, and formulas. Exhibits 3–3A and 3–3B show Quick Reference guides for Excel 2007 and Excel 2010.

Data Input

Data are usually entered into a spreadsheet using a keyboard. Data can be entered more easily and faster if the keyboard has a separate numeric keypad in addition to the direction and cursor keys. This allows you to move the cell pointer with the cursor keys and to enter values and formulas using the numeric keypad.

Three types of data can be entered into a spreadsheet: text, values, and formulas.

Text Descriptive data, called **text**, are entered into a cell. This type of data cannot be used in making calculations. It includes headings, titles, and so forth. For example,

text
Descriptive data, such as headings and titles, used for reference purposes in a spreadsheet.

Excel 2007 Quick Reference Guide

HOME RIBBON

Home button   Quick Access toolbar   Font   Fill color   Font color   Font orientation   Wrap Text   Ribbon Tabs   Number Format   Insert cells   Autofill   Help

Cut   Sum   Sort

Paste   Find/Select

Copy

Format Painter   Bold   Italic   Borders   Format Cells   Left   Right   Merge Center   Increase decimal   Decrease decimal   Delete cells   Clear

Underline   Center   Format Rows/Columns

Dialog Box Launcher

NAVIGATION

UP ONE SCREEN	[Page Up]	TO CELL A1	[CTRL]+[HOME]
DOWN ONE SCREEN	[Page Down]	TO LAST CELL WITH DATA	[CTRL]+[END]
BEGINNING OF A ROW	[Home]	GO TO	[F5]
CELL BELOW CURRENT CELL	[Enter]		

KEYBOARD SHORTCUTS

COPY TEXT	[Ctrl]+[C]	UNDO A COMMAND	[Ctrl]+[Z]
PASTE TEXT	[Ctrl]+[V]	REDO/REPEAT	[Ctrl]+[Y]
CUT TEXT	[Ctrl]+[X]	PRINT A WORKBOOK	[Ctrl]+[P]
BOLD TEXT	[Ctrl]+[B]	SAVE A WORKBOOK	[Ctrl]+[S]
UNDERLINE TEXT	[Ctrl]+[U]	OPEN A WORKBOOK	[Ctrl]+[O]
ITALICS TEXT	[Ctrl]+[I]	FIND/REPLACE	[Ctrl]+[F]
EDIT A CELL	[F2]	ABSOLUTE CELL REFERENCE	[F4]

EXCEL FEATURES   COMMAND STRUCTURE

EXCEL FEATURES	COMMAND STRUCTURE
ABSOLUTE CELL REFERENCE	(=B10*a1); $ signs represent an absolute cell reference, the F4 key will insert the $ signs in a formula.
ADJUSTING COLUMN WIDTH OR ROW HEIGHT	Drag the right border of the column header or the bottom border of the row header. Double-click to Auto Fit the column/row. Or **Home>Cells>Format>Cell Size**
AUTOFILL	Point to the fill handle of the bottom corner of the cell(s), then drag to the destination cells(s).
CHART	**Insert>Charts>**
CLEAR CELL CONTENTS	DEL key or **Home>Editing** group>**Clear, Clear Contents**
CLEAR FORMAT	**Home>Editing>Clear>Clear Formats**
DELETE ROW/COLUMN	**Home>Cells>Delete**
EDIT A CELL	Select the cell and click the Formula bar to edit the contents or press F2
FIND AND REPLACE	**Home>Editing>Find & Select>Find or Replace**
FIT TO ONE PAGE	**Page Layout>Scale to Fit Dialog Box Launcher>Fit To**
FORMAT CELLS	**Home>Font>Font Dialog Box Launcher>** or Right-click **Format Cells**
FORMULA	Select the cell where you want the formula, press = (equal), enter the formula, and press [ENTER] when done (e.g., =a1+a2; =a1*10). Excel performs operations in this order: ( ), :, %, ^, * and /, + and -.
FREEZE PANE	**View>Window>Freeze Panes**
FUNCTIONS	Click **Insert Function** icon next to the Formula Bar; or **Formulas>Function Library>Insert function**
HIDE/UNHIDE A COLUMN	Right-click **Column Header>Hide**; right-click **Header>Unhide**; or **View>Window>Hide**
INSERT ROW/COLUMN	**Home>Cells>insert**
MACRO	**View>Macros>Macros**
PAGE BREAKS FOR PRINTING	**Page Layout>Page Setup>Breaks** or **View>Workbook Views> Page Break Preview;** Drag page break indicator line to where you want the page break to occur.
PASSWORD PROTECT	**Office button, Save>Tools>General Options>Password to Open**
TOTAL A CELL RANGE	Click the cell where you want the total inserted, click the Autosum icon (**Home, Editing, Sum** icon), verify the range, and press [ENTER].
WORKSHEET TAB NAME	Click Sheet1 name and type over it to rename
WRAP TEXT	**Format>Cells>Alignment>Wrap Text**

EXHIBIT 3–3A
Excel 2007 Quick Reference Guide

Excel 2010 Quick Reference Guide

HOME RIBBON

NAVIGATION

Up One Screen	[Page Up]	To Cell A1	[CTRL]+[HOME]
Down One Screen	[Page Down]	To Last Cell with Data	[CTRL]+[END]
Beginning of a Row	[Home]	Go To	[F5]
Cell Below Current Cell	[Enter]		

KEYBOARD SHORTCUTS

Copy Text	[Ctrl]+[C]	Undo a Command	[Ctrl]+[Z]
Paste Text	[Ctrl]+[V]	Redo/Repeat	[Ctrl]+[Y]
Cut Text	[Ctrl]+[X]	Print a Workbook	[Ctrl]+[P]
Bold Text	[Ctrl]+[B]	Save a Workbook	[Ctrl]+[S]
Underline Text	[Ctrl]+[U]	Open a Workbook	[Ctrl]+[O]
Italics Text	[Ctrl]+[I]	Find/Replace	[Ctrl]+[F]
Edit a Cell	[F2]	Absolute Cell Reference	[F4]

EXCEL FEATURES   COMMAND STRUCTURE

EXCEL FEATURES	COMMAND STRUCTURE
Absolute Cell Reference	(=B10*a1); $ signs represent an absolute cell reference, the F4 key will insert the $ signs in a formula.
Adjusting Column Width or Row Height	Drag the right border of the column header or the bottom border of the row header. Double-click to Auto Fit the column/row. Or **Home>Cells>Format>Cell Size**
Autofill	Point to the fill handle of the bottom corner of the cell(s), then drag to the destination cells(s).
Chart	**Insert>Charts>**
Clear Cell Contents	DEL key or **Home>Editing** group>**Clear, Clear Contents**
Clear Format	**Home>Editing>Clear>Clear Formats**
Delete Row/Column	**Home>Cells>Delete**
Edit a Cell	Select the cell and click the Formula bar to edit the contents or press [F2]
Find and Replace	**Home>Editing>Find & Select>Find or Replace**
Fit to One Page	**Page Layout>Scale to Fit Dialog Box Launcher>Fit To**
Format Cells	**Home>Font>Font Dialog Box Launcher>** or Right-click **Format Cells**
Formula	Select the cell where you want the formula, press = (equal), enter the formula, and press [ENTER] when done (e.g., =a1+a2; =a1*10). Excel performs operations in this order: ( ), :, %, ^, * and /, + and -.
Freeze Pane	**View>Window>Freeze Panes**
Functions	Click **Insert Function** icon next to the Formula Bar; or **Formulas>Function Library>Insert function**
Hide/Unhide a Column	Right-click **Column Header>Hide**; right-click **Header>Unhide;** or **View>Window>Hide**
Insert Row/Column	**Home>Cells>insert**
Macro	**View>Macros>Macros**
Page Breaks for Printing	**Page Layout>Page Setup>Breaks** or **View>Workbook Views> Page Break Preview;** Drag page break indicator line to where you want the page break to occur.
Password Protect	**File tab, Save>Tools>General Options>Password to Open**
Total a Cell Range	Click the cell where you want the total inserted, click the Autosum icon (**Home, Editing, Sum** icon), verify the range, and press [ENTER].
Worksheet Tab Name	Click Sheet1 name and type over it to rename
Wrap Text	**Format>Cells>Alignment>Wrap Text**

EXHIBIT 3–3B
Excel 2010 Quick Reference Guide

in Exhibit 3–1, the title "BUDGETED LAW OFFICE EXPENSES APRIL - MAY"; the column headings "Expense Item," "April," and "May"; and the row headings "Rent," "Salaries," "Insurance," "Utilities," and "TOTALS" are all text.

Text is usually entered as a series of words and/or abbreviations, but numbers can also be included, although no calculations can be performed on a number entered as text. For example, instead of writing out May for the column heading in Exhibit 3–1, the number 5 could be substituted, showing that May is the fifth month of the year. The numbers could be entered as text because no calculations will be performed using these cells, which are intended only as column headings.

When a character or letter is typed into a cell, most spreadsheets assume that it is a text entry. Likewise, when a number is typed into a cell, most spreadsheets assume that it is a value or number entry on which calculations can be performed.

The procedure for entering text into a cell is simple. Move the cell pointer to the cell where the text should be placed, then begin typing the text. As the text is being typed, the characters are displayed in the formula bar and in the cell. After you have typed the characters, press the [ENTER] key to enter the text into the cell. Most spreadsheets also allow you to enter data into a cell by pressing either the [ENTER] key or any of the four arrow or direction keys.

Text can be edited later by using the Edit command. The Edit command varies among different spreadsheet programs, but it generally allows a user to correct or change the contents of the cell. The Edit command in Microsoft Excel is [F2]. You can also double-click on a cell to edit it.

Another way to change the contents of an existing cell is to point to the cell to be changed, type new content, and enter the new text into the cell. This deletes the existing content and inserts the new content in the same cell. This procedure can be used for changing text, values, or formulas.

Values Numbers that are entered into a cell and that can be used in making calculations are **values**. In Exhibit 3–1, the amount listed for each expense item is a value. Values can be entered as either positive or negative numbers. Negative values are usually represented with parentheses around them or a negative sign before them. For example, if you wanted to enter negative 20,000, the spreadsheet would show either (20,000) or <–>20,000.

Entering a value in a spreadsheet is similar to entering text. First, point to the cell where the value should be placed, then type the value. As the value is being typed, the characters are usually displayed in the formula bar and in the cell. After you have typed the value, press the [ENTER] key or a cursor key on the keyboard to enter the label into the cell. In Exhibit 3–1, notice that no commas or dollar signs are shown. A separate command is used to enter formatting codes. This is covered later in this chapter.

Formulas Calculations using the values in other cells are performed with **formulas**. For example, in Exhibit 3–4, the entry in cell D14 is a formula (=D10+D11+D12+D13) that adds the values of cells D10, D11, D12, and D13. Because the formula is placed in cell D14, the total is also placed there. The real power of a spreadsheet program is that formulas automatically recalculate totals if a cell value is changed. Thus, if any of the values in D10, D11, D12, or D13 were later changed, the program would automatically recalculate the total in D14.

Formulas can be entered using arithmetic operators or function commands or both.

values
Numbers that are entered into a spreadsheet program for the purpose of making calculations.

formulas
Expressions used in spreadsheet programs to automatically perform calculations on other values.

EXHIBIT 3–4
Entering arithmetic operator formula

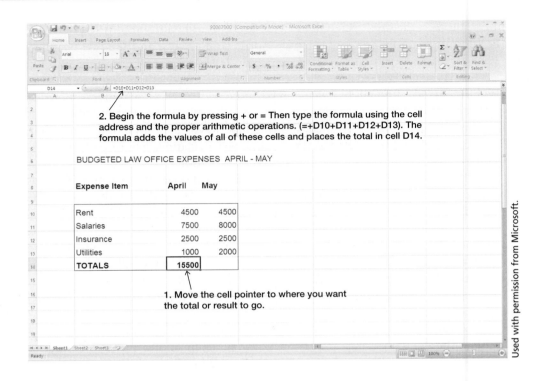

EXHIBIT 3–5
Arithmetic operators

Arithmetic Operator	Name	Formula Example
+	Addition	= C10 + C11 or = 100 + 10
–	Subtraction	= C10 – C11 or = 10 – 10
*	Multiplication	= C10 * C11 or = 100 * 10
/	Division	= C10 / C11 or = 100 / 10

© Cengage Learning 2013

arithmetic operators
Symbols that tell a spreadsheet how to compute values. Examples include addition signs, subtraction signs, and multiplication signs.

Entering Formulas Using Arithmetic Operators One way to enter formulas is to use arithmetic operators and list each cell to be computed separately (see Exhibit 3–4). **Arithmetic operators** tell a spreadsheet how to compute values (see Exhibit 3–5). With this method, you point to the cell where the total should be placed. You then begin by typing an = (equal sign) or a + (plus sign). These tell the spreadsheet that a formula will be entered. When you have typed the formula, press the [ENTER] key or a cursor key to enter it.

In Exhibit 3–4, the formula in cell D14 uses the addition arithmetic operator (+) to tell the spreadsheet program to add the values in cells D10 through D13. This is an example of using an arithmetic operator. Spreadsheets also have arithmetic operators to subtract, multiply, and divide the contents of cells. For example, in Exhibit 3–4, if instead of adding cell D12 you wanted to subtract it, the formula would read =D10+D11–D12+D13, and the total would read 10500.

In most spreadsheets, you have the option of either typing the cell addresses of the cells to be included in the formula (e.g., typing =D10+D11+D12+D13 in Exhibit 3–4) or using the cursor keys to point to the cells to be included in the formula. The second option could be accomplished by simply pointing to the D10 cell, adding an arithmetic operator (+ in this case), and then pointing to the next cell reference to be included in the formula (D11 in this case) until the formula is complete. Spreadsheet novices usually find the pointing method of entering formulas easier.

Arithmetic operators can also be used to add, subtract, multiply, and divide numbers in addition to cells. For example, in addition to a formula using an arithmetic operator to add, subtract, multiply, and divide the values entered into cells (=D10+D11), arithmetic operators can also be used in a formula to add, subtract, multiply, and divide numbers themselves (=100+10). See Exhibit 3–5.

Entering Formulas Using Function Commands

Another way to enter formulas is by using function commands. A **function command** is a predefined or preprogrammed calculation that a spreadsheet can perform.

Function commands are designated by an = (equal sign) followed by the function name. For example, in Exhibit 3–6, the SUM function is used to add cells D10, D11, D12, and D13. Notice that the formula in Exhibit 3–6 reads =SUM(D10:D13). This means "add the contents of cells D10 through D13." This process of dealing with a group of cells is called entering a range (a range is a group of cells). One powerful feature that spreadsheets offer is the ability to work with a group or range of cells at one time.

Many different function commands are available in most spreadsheet programs. Some of the function commands represent long, complex formulas and make them easy to use. Both the arithmetic operators and the function commands yield the same results (compare the totals in Exhibits 3–4 and 3–6). However, for a long formula such as one that adds 100 cells together, to use the arithmetic operator method, you would have to type addition signs between all 100 cell addresses. The function commands make calculating large ranges of cells easy. For example, Exhibit 3–7 shows the Insert Function dialog box. Some of the more common functions are:

- MAX, which computes the largest value within a range of values
- AVERAGE, which computes the average of a range of values
- SUM, which adds numbers in a range and computes the total
- COUNT, which counts the number of cells that contain numbers within a range

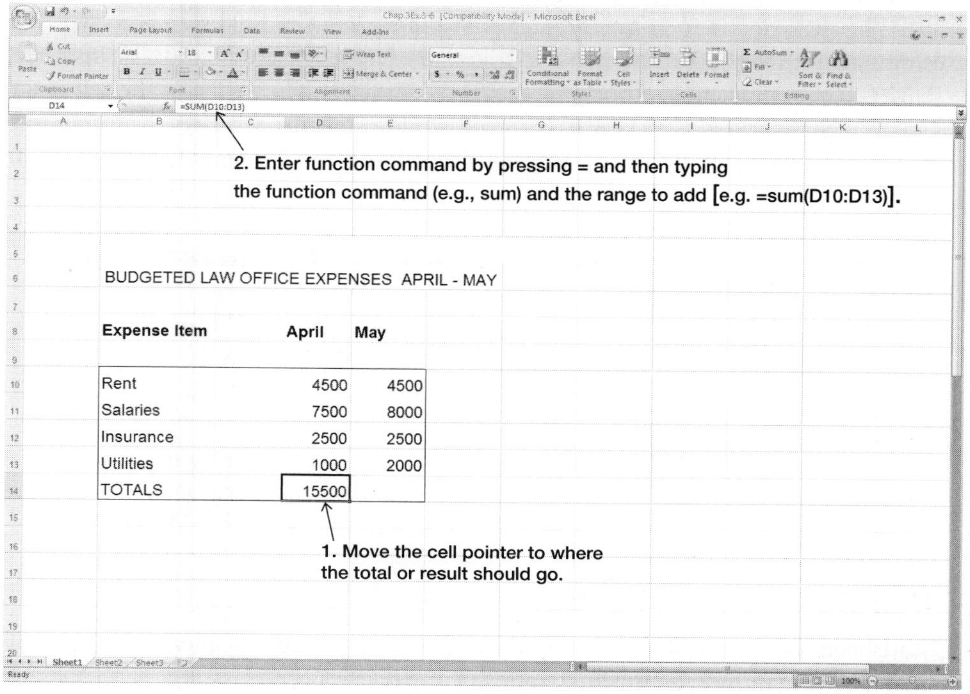

function command
A predefined calculation used in a spreadsheet program to speed up the process of entering complex formulas.

EXHIBIT 3–6
Entering formulas with function command

Used with permission from Microsoft.

EXHIBIT 3–7
Commonly used function commands in Excel

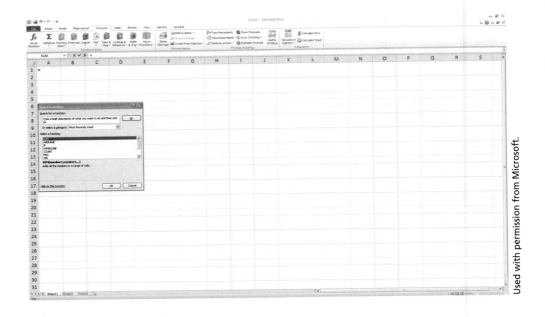

Function commands are entered in nearly the same way as arithmetic operator formulas. Point to the cell where the total should be placed. Next, enter the = sign, followed by the name of the function command and an opening parenthesis. Then, enter the beginning cell address of the range, followed by a colon (:) and the ending cell address of the range. Finally, close the parentheses and press the [ENTER] key to enter the formula into the cell.

A function formula may also be entered using the pointing method. The first step is to go to the cell where the total is to be placed. The next step is to enter the = sign, followed by an opening parenthesis: for example, =SUM(. The next step is to point to the beginning of the range that is to be included and type a colon (:). The colon anchors the range (i.e., it tells the spreadsheet program where the range is to start). The next step is to point to the end of the range. The final step is to type the closing parenthesis and hit the [ENTER] key to execute the command: for instance, =SUM(C10:C13). Using the pointing method is simpler than typing in the cell range for many people and is especially easy for beginning spreadsheet users. Entering formulas is covered in detail in the Excel 2007 and Excel 2010 Hands-On Exercises at Lessons 1, 2, 4, and 6.

Entering Formulas Using Both Arithmetic Operators and Function Commands

Arithmetic operators and function commands can also be used together. For example, if you wanted to add cells C10, C11, C12, and C13 and then divide the total by 2, the formula would read =SUM(C10:C13)/2. This formula uses the SUM function to add the cells together and the division operator to divide the total by 2.

In any case, no matter how a formula is entered, whether by using arithmetic operators or using a function command, if the values change in the cells that are calculated, the spreadsheet will automatically recalculate the totals.

Other Spreadsheet Features

Spreadsheets can perform many functions, including changing cell widths, copying data and formulas, moving formulas, and sorting data.

Changing Cell Width   Every cell has a cell width, sometimes called a column width. The **cell width** refers to the number of characters that can be viewed in a cell. Cells in most spreadsheet programs have a starting value of nine; that is, a cell can display nine characters or numbers. But, of course, the cell width can be adjusted to display more characters or numbers.

Many times you will need to change a cell width to hold either large values (e.g., $200,000,000) or long labels. If a cell width is not large enough to hold the desired value, the cell will be filled with asterisks (*) until you enlarge it. Cell widths can also be shortened if needed. Making cells smaller allows more information to be seen on a page or computer screen at a time. The cell width is easily changed by pointing to the column to be changed and then executing the Column Width command, entering the number of characters the column should hold, and then pressing [ENTER] or clicking on OK.

Another way to change the column width is to use the pointing method. Point to the right border of the heading of the column to be changed. The pointer changes to a double arrow. Drag it to the right to expand the column or to the left to make the column smaller. When the mouse button is released, the column width is automatically changed. Lesson 1 in the Hands-On Exercises covers changing column width in detail.

Copying Data   Spreadsheets have a Copy command that copies information from one part of a spreadsheet to another part or from one spreadsheet to another, while leaving the original intact (see Exhibit 3–8). Point to the cell to be copied and then click Edit > Copy. Then move the cell pointer to the location where the information is to be copied and press [ENTER]. Another way to do this is to place the mouse over the information to be copied, right-click, and click Copy. Then move the pointer to the new location and press [ENTER]. An even more convenient way

> **cell width**
> The number of characters that can be viewed in any given cell in a spreadsheet program.

Step 1
Put cell pointer
on formula to
copy command

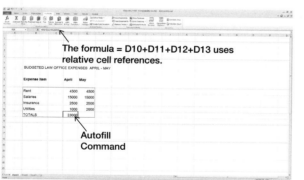

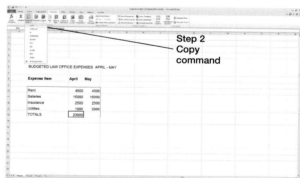

Step 2
Copy
command

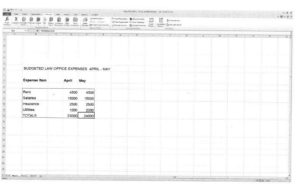

The formula automatically changes when the Copy command is used, because it contains relative cell references

Step 4
Execute

Step 3
Copy to
Destination

EXHIBIT 3–8
Copying formulas-relative cell references

to copy information (as long as the cells are adjacent to one another) is to use the AutoFill command. Notice in the fourth screen in Exhibit 3–8 that the pointer is on cell E14. Notice that there is a small box in the lower right corner of the pointer. To copy data, put the pointer on the cell you want to copy, position the pointer over the "AutoFill" box, drag it to the adjacent cells where the information is to be copied, and release the mouse button. The information is automatically copied. The AutoFill command also works with ranges of cells.

Copying Formulas Copying formulas is a great time-saver. The process for copying formulas is exactly the same as for copying data generally, but it is important that you understand *how* formulas are copied.

Exhibit 3–8 shows an example of copying a formula from D14 to E14. Notice that the utilities expense has increased to 2,000 for the month of May (from 1,000 in April), thus making 24,000 the correct total for May expenses. Also note that even though the formula was copied from D14 to E14, the correct total of 24,000 is shown in E14.

Most new users assume that if the formula in D14, which is =D10+D11+D12+D13, is copied to E14, the formula in cell E14 will read "=D10+D11+D12+D13" and will put the wrong total of 23,000 in the cell. This would happen if a formula used absolute cell references. An **absolute cell reference** is a cell address that does not change when it is copied to a new location. Absolute references can be placed in a formula in most spreadsheets using the dollar sign (e.g., $D$9+$D$10+$D$11+$D$12). This would give the result most people expect.

However, most spreadsheets assume that users want relative cell references. A **relative cell reference** is a cell address that automatically changes to reflect its new location when it is copied. For example, look again at Exhibit 3–8. The formula in D14 is a relative cell reference. So, when it is copied to E14, the spreadsheet automatically changes it to read "=E10+E11+E12+E13." Thus, once a formula is entered, it can be copied time and time again instead of being entered from scratch each time. As with any electronic material, retyping increases the risk of entry errors, so take advantage of any tools that help you avoid retyping or reentering materials.

Suppose a relative cell reference/formula of "=C10+C11" was placed in cell C12. C12 is where the total formula will go. The relative cell reference in C12 actually tells the computer to "go to the cell two rows up from C12 [which is C10] and add the value in it to the value in the cell one row up from C12 [which is C11]." Thus, when a relative cell reference is copied, it just tells the computer how many cells to go up and over. The only thing that changes is where the formula is copied to. So, in our example, if the user copied the formula in C12 to D12, the computer would go to the cell two rows up from D12 (which is D10) and add the value in it to the value in the cell one row up from D12 (which is D11). The formula in Exhibit 3–8 is a relative cell reference.

There are times when you must use an absolute cell reference (see Exhibit 3–9). In Exhibit 3–9, the formulas in cells C7–C10 all use a combined relative cell reference and an absolute cell reference. To calculate cells C7–C10 (the 2012 salary) in Exhibit 3–9, you must take the salary in cells B7–B10 (the 2011 salary) times the salary increase figure in B4 (103.75 percent). Notice in Exhibit 3–9 that cell D7 shows the formula for cell C7. The formula in D7 is B7 (which is a relative cell reference—meaning go one cell over to the left) * (times) $B$4 (the dollar signs mean that this is an absolute cell reference; no matter where this formula is copied to, the application will go one cell over to the left and always multiply it times the value in the cell B4). If a relative cell reference were used for cell C7 it would read B7*B4. This would tell the application to take the cell one row over to the left times the cell three rows up and one column over. This would work fine for cell C7, but if cell C7 were copied to cell

absolute cell reference
A cell address in a spreadsheet program formula that does not change when it is copied to a new location.

relative cell reference
A cell address in a spreadsheet program formula that automatically changes to reflect its new location when it is copied.

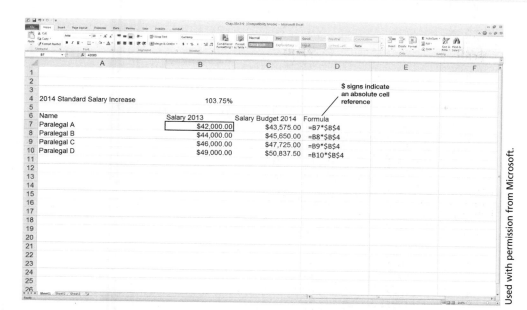

EXHIBIT 3–9
Absolute cell references

C8 (or C9 or C10), the formula would not work anymore. This is because in cell C8 the computer would take the cell one row over to the left (which is B8–that is correct) times the cell three rows up and one column over (which is cell B5). Notice that nothing is entered in cell B5; it is blank. The computer would enter $44,000 ($44,000 * 0 = $0). By the time the formula got to cell C10, the results would be very bad. The formula would take cell B10 (one cell over to the left), $49,000 (which is correct) times cell B7 (three rows up and one column over), $42,000. The result would be $2,058,000 instead of the correct answer of $50,837.50. Thus, the only way for the second part of the formula to work is to always (absolutely) reference cell B4.

Copying formulas with relative cell references is covered in detail in Lesson 1 of the Hands-On Exercises. Copying formulas with absolute cell references is covered in Lesson 4.

Moving Data   Moving data is similar to copying data. First, point to the cell to be moved, select Edit, then select Cut. Then point to the location where the information is to be moved and press [ENTER]. Another way to do this is to point to the cell to be moved, right-click, and then select Cut. You would then move the pointer to the new location and press [ENTER].

Inserting Rows and Columns   It is sometimes necessary to go back and insert additional rows and columns into a spreadsheet. If, for example, you want to insert an expense item (such as an equipment expense item) in Exhibit 3–6, you can do this easily. To insert a row or a column, move the cell pointer to where the new row or column should be inserted. Then execute the Insert Row or Insert Column command. One new row or column is inserted. To insert more than one row or column, drag the pointer down or over the number of rows or columns you want to add, right-click, and select Insert. Use extreme caution when inserting rows and columns after formulas have been created, because it is possible that the existing formulas will not include the new row or column.

Sorting Data   *Sorting* is the process of placing things in a particular order. Spreadsheets, like databases, can sort information. They can sort either values or text in ascending or descending order. In Exhibit 3–10, before sorting, the expense items are

EXHIBIT 3–10
Sorting data

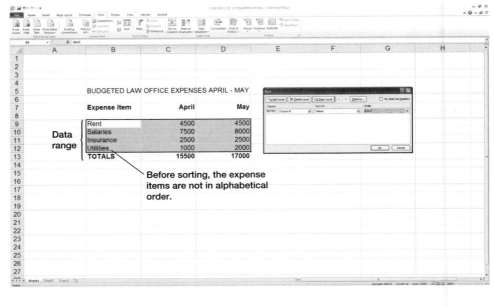

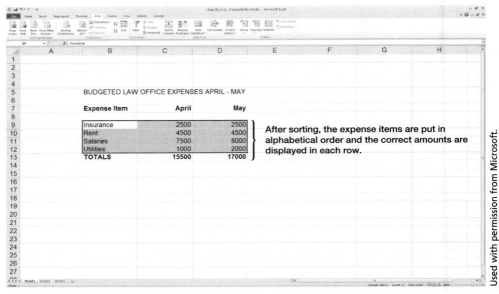

Used with permission from Microsoft.

not in alphabetical order. To sort data, mark the data range of the information to be sorted, execute the Sort command (in Excel you would point to Data and click Sort), and then indicate which column to sort the data on and whether the information is to be sorted in ascending or descending order. In Exhibit 3–10, the data range must include not only the Expense Item column, but also the May and June columns. If the May and June columns were not included in the data range, the spreadsheet would put the expense items in alphabetical order, but would not move the corresponding dollar amounts. In Exhibit 3–10, with the data range properly selected, you would execute the Sort command, instruct the computer to sort the data by Column B, which is the Expense Item, in ascending order, and then select OK. The spreadsheet responds by placing the expense items and corresponding dollar amounts in alphabetical order.

Formatting Cells Most spreadsheet programs allow users to indicate which format or type of values has been entered. For example, in Exhibit 3–10, the values in the spreadsheet should be represented in dollars.

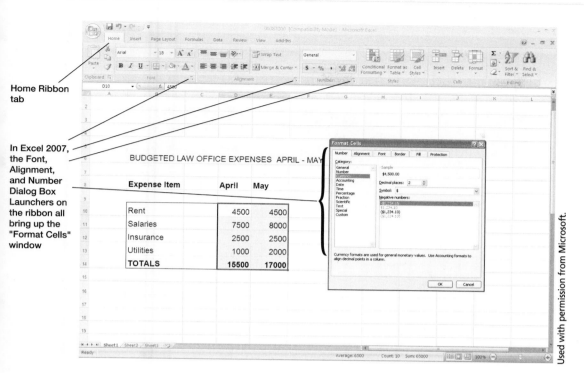

EXHIBIT 3–11
Formatting cells

Home Ribbon tab

In Excel 2007, the Font, Alignment, and Number Dialog Box Launchers on the ribbon all bring up the "Format Cells" window

To change the format of the content of the cells to dollars, drag the pointer over the cells to be changed and execute the Format Cells command. In Exhibit 3–11, notice that when the Format Cells command is initiated, you may select Currency and the desired number of decimal places. After you select OK, the cell values are automatically changed to dollar signs.

Also, notice in Exhibit 3–11 that numbers can be formatted as percentages and other expressions. Most spreadsheets can change the format of cells in many ways, such as alignment, fonts and type sizes, borders, and patterns or backgrounds. Formatting cells is covered in detail in the Hands-On Exercises.

Saving and Retrieving Files Spreadsheets can be saved and retrieved for later use, just as word-processing files and database files can. When working with any program, users should save their work often!

Printing Reports All spreadsheet programs allow the spreadsheets to be printed. Printing large spreadsheets with many columns used to be difficult, because only a limited number of columns could be printed on a page. It often meant taping pages together. Now, however, most spreadsheets and printers allow pages to print in a condensed or compressed mode as well. This means that the data are printed smaller than normal, and it allows more information to be printed on a page. In Exhibit 3–12, notice that one of the options is the Fit to: command. This option allows a print selection to be compressed into a certain number of pages, including into a single page.

Most spreadsheets allow users to change margins, add headers or footers, indicate whether the page should be printed in portrait or landscape mode, and so on. **Portrait** refers to printing down the length of the page, whereas **landscape** refers to printing across the width of the page (see Exhibit 3–12).

Using Macros As we learned in Chapter 2, a macro is a previously saved group of commands or keystrokes that allows you to save commands or procedures so that

portrait
A method of printing that arranges data down the length of a page.

landscape
A method of printing that arranges data across the width of a page.

EXHIBIT 3–12
Page setup print options in Excel

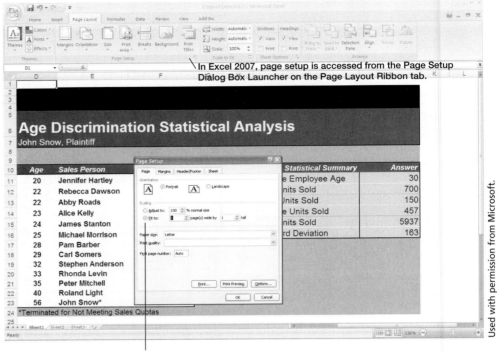

In Excel 2007, page setup is accessed from the Page Setup Dialog Box Launcher on the Page Layout Ribbon tab.

Fit to feature

Used with permission from Microsoft.

they can be used again and again. For example, if you routinely print a spreadsheet each month a certain way, you could write a macro that would automatically save the keystrokes and commands you used to produce that result. This way, you could print the spreadsheet properly by running the macro, instead of reentering all the commands every time you wanted to print it out.

Charting and Graphing   The ability to visualize numerical information in a spreadsheet is beneficial. Most spreadsheet programs have graphing and charting capabilities built into them. After a graph (or chart—we will use the terms *graph* and *chart* interchangeably) has been set up, a link is created between the numerical information in the spreadsheet and the graph (see Exhibit 3–13). When the values in the spreadsheet are changed, the graph automatically reflects those changes.

Most spreadsheet programs have a chart wizard feature that takes the user through a step-by-step process and gives the user many options on how to set up a chart. Creating a chart in an Excel spreadsheet is easy. First, drag the pointer over the data that you want charted (see Exhibit 3–13) and then click on the Chart Wizard.

Many types of graphs and charts are available. The major types of graphs and charts are bar graphs, line graphs, pie charts, and stacked bar graphs. Most spreadsheets support these types of graphs. Graphs are often used in trials to convey complicated numerical data in an easy-to-understand manner. Lesson 2 in the Hands-On Exercises covers creation of a chart.

bar/column graph
A graph consisting of a sequence of bars that illustrate numerical values.

Bar/Column Graph   A **bar/column graph** consists of a sequence of bars that illustrate numerical values. Bar or column graphs are common and can be either horizontal or vertical. Vertical column graphs have columns that go straight up the page (see Exhibit 3–13), and horizontal bar graphs have bars that go across the page. These graphs are best used for comparing values at a specific point in time. For example, the bar graph in Exhibit 3–13 compares the office expenses for the months of April and May.

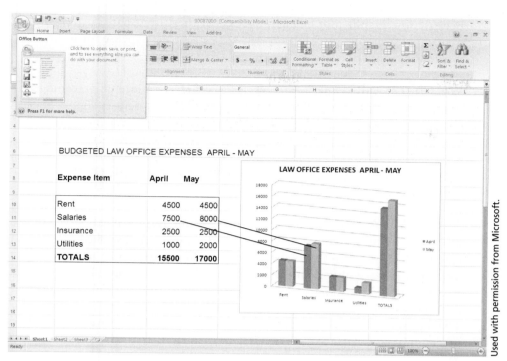

Used with permission from Microsoft.

EXHIBIT 3–13
Linking the values in a spreadsheet with a graph

Bar/column graphs have many uses in legal organizations. A bar graph might be used in a personal injury case to illustrate the large earning potential of a person before an accident and her reduced earning potential after the accident. A bar graph might also be used in a breach of contract case to show the profits a business was making before the breach of contract compared with the reduced profits it made after the breach.

Line Graph   A **line graph** plots the course of a value over time. In the line graph in Exhibit 3–14, each line represents a month's worth of expenses.

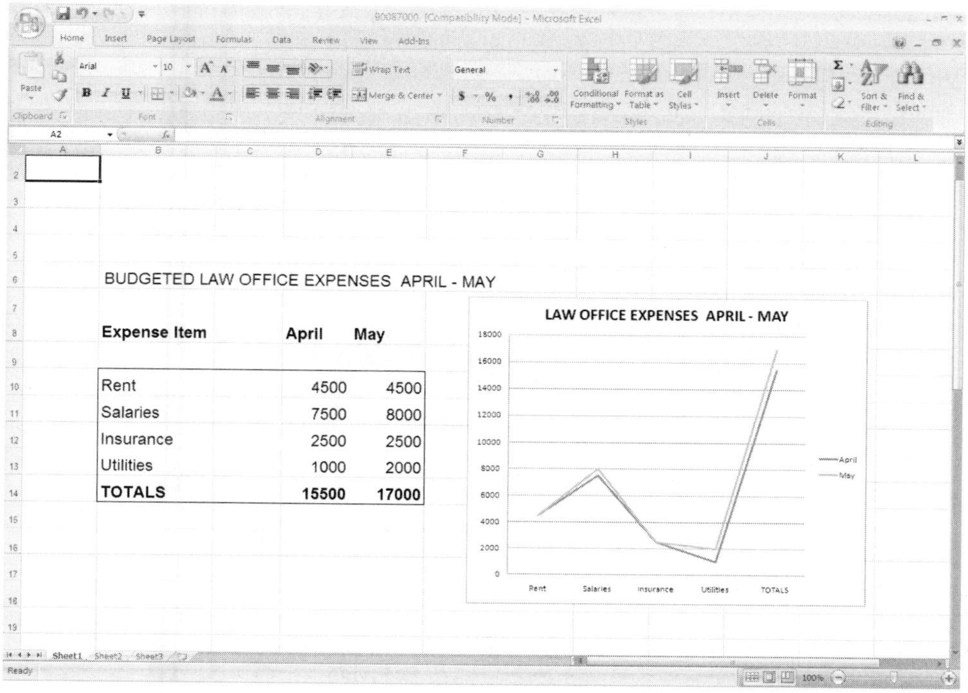

line graph
A graph that plots numerical values as a time line.

EXHIBIT 3–14
Line graph

Used with permission from Microsoft.

Because line graphs plot changes over time, they are useful for plotting trends. For example, in Exhibit 3–14, notice that the expense for utilities rose in the month of May.

pie chart
A chart that represents each value as a piece or percentage of a whole (a total "pie").

Pie Chart   A **pie chart** represents each value as a piece or percentage of a total pie. In Exhibit 3–15, each expense item represents a slice of the pie, with the whole pie representing the total amount of expenses for the month of April. This chart shows that salaries are the biggest piece (or expense) of the pie (that is, of the firm's total expenses). Pie charts are best used for showing the relative contributions of the various pieces that make up a whole.

stacked column graph
A graph that depicts values as separate sections in a single or stacked column.

Stacked Column Graph   A **stacked column graph** compares data by placing columns on top of one another. Like a pie chart, a stacked column graph shows the relative contributions of various elements to a whole. The difference is that rather than showing only a single entity or a single pie, a stacked column can show several. In Exhibit 3–16, each column segment represents a month, and each stack of columns represents an expense item. The stacked column allows users to see the allocation of an expense item over two months.

SPREADSHEET PLANNING

Planning is critical to developing a spreadsheet that accomplishes its intended purpose. Most spreadsheets are more complex than the law-office expense spreadsheet used as an example in this chapter. Most people find it helpful to draft a model of a spreadsheet on paper before actually beginning to enter it in the computer. Some of the most complex aspects of creating a spreadsheet concern the use of formulas. Entering formulas can get complicated quickly, especially when a spreadsheet requires a lot of formulas. Take your time and plan the formulas out carefully.

This section discusses a few rules to keep in mind when planning and using a spreadsheet.

EXHIBIT 3–15
Pie chart graph

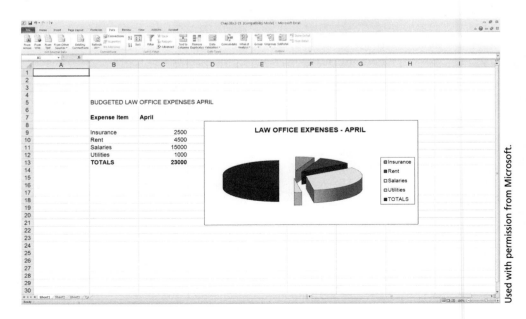

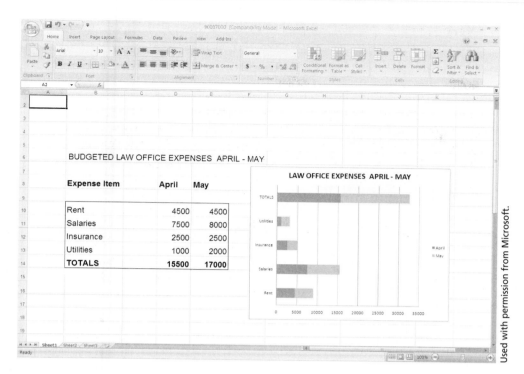

EXHIBIT 3–16
Stacked column graph

Keep Your Spreadsheet Simple

Keep your spreadsheet as simple as possible. Complex spreadsheets are more likely to have errors. In addition, other people may have to use the spreadsheet, and a simple design will keep you from having to spend hours training them to do so. It is also common for even the person who designed a spreadsheet to forget certain aspects of the spreadsheet if she has not worked with it for some time. Finally, use easy-to-understand headings and titles. Say what you mean, and mean what you say. It is confusing to read titles that do not make sense to everyone involved.

Always Document Your Spreadsheet

Always document your spreadsheet well, making notes and narrative statements right in the spreadsheet itself. Always include a section called "Notes" in your spreadsheet. It is common to make assumptions when designing a spreadsheet (such as when entering formulas) and then later forget why or how you made them. Another technique is to add a comment directly to a cell. In Excel and other spreadsheets, you can add explanatory text to a cell itself. The Comment tool is a great way to add specific information about a cell, including any assumptions or justifications you have made regarding the value or formula entered. Users can show or hide comments as they wish, depending on their needs at the time (see Exhibit 3–17). Creating a comment is covered in Lesson 7 of the Hands-On Exercises.

Make a Template of Your Spreadsheet

A template is a blank spreadsheet that has had labels and formulas entered, but has no values filled in. Once a template is made and saved, copies of it can be made and given to other users; then the only thing they will have to do is enter the values.

EXHIBIT 3–17

Adding a comment to a cell in Excel

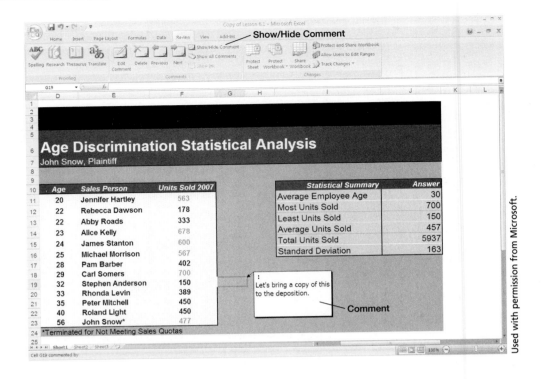

Some software companies also sell a variety of predefined templates. A template saves a user from having to rebuild the same spreadsheet over and over. Users can also access free templates online from software providers and other sources.

Leave Room in the Upper Left Corner

Do not start your spreadsheet in the far corner of the spreadsheet (for example, at cell A1); always leave yourself some room to include additional labels and notes. Start your spreadsheet no closer to the upper left corner than cell C4. This gives you room to add notes, dates, and so forth later on.

Use Cell Widths Wisely

Cell widths should be used wisely. Some people make all their columns 20 characters wide; the problem with this is that they can then see and print only four columns at a time, which makes a spreadsheet difficult to work with. It is better to use narrow columns, which maximize the amount of information you can see and allow the spreadsheet to be printed on one page. For long labels, keep the column width the same size, but wrap the text down to the next line, using the wrap text feature found in most spreadsheets.

Be Careful Inserting Rows and Columns

If you must insert additional rows and columns after a spreadsheet has been designed and entered into the computer, be sure that the formulas you have already entered are adjusted to take the new additions into account. A celebrated lawsuit was filed against Lotus Development Corporation over this problem. A construction firm designed a spreadsheet to allow it to bid on jobs. Staff would enter job costs into the spreadsheet, and the spreadsheet would calculate what the bid on a job should be. Unfortunately, at some point, the spreadsheet user inserted additional rows, and the old formulas did not pick up, or add, the job costs in the new rows. Subsequently, the construction firm bid several hundred thousand dollars too low on a job. The firm sued Lotus, but Lotus won the suit because the user had used the program improperly. Be sure to go back and double-check your formulas!

Rigorously Test Your Spreadsheet

Rigorously test your spreadsheet to make sure it is functioning as intended. It is easy to make a mistake entering a formula, but it is often difficult to recognize and find mistakes. Always enter test data in the spreadsheet, and use a calculator to spot-check that the formulas have been entered properly and are making the calculations correctly. Most spreadsheets have an option that allows you to see the formulas entered instead of the calculations. This is a nice feature when you are checking the logic and formulas of your spreadsheet.

Audit Formulas

To access the Audit Formulas feature, point to the Formulas ribbon tab, then click on Show Formulas in the Formula Auditing group.

Occasionally Read the Spreadsheet Documentation

Most spreadsheet users employ only a fraction of the commands, operators, and function commands that are available in most spreadsheets. Although the commands covered in this book will get you started with spreadsheets, you will find that as you grow more proficient, many sophisticated features will help you solve tough problems. Take the time occasionally to read the Help features and other documentation for your spreadsheet program to learn more about its capacities and functionalities.

SPREADSHEETS IN THE LEGAL ENVIRONMENT

Numerical data are important in the outcome of many types of cases. Remember, if it involves money, it involves numbers. In some lawsuits, parties hire statisticians to research a matter in hopes that the final statistics or numerical data will support their case. Spreadsheets can be used to analyze statistical findings, look for trends, and so forth. Spreadsheet programs, like word processors and database management systems, are extremely flexible, so it is easy to use them to accomplish all types of tasks. Some common applications of spreadsheets in law offices include:

- Tax planning and tax returns
- Estate planning
- Calculations for bankruptcy actions
- Child support calculations
- Alimony payments
- Divorce asset distributions
- Truth-in-Lending statements for real estate transactions
- Amortization schedules
- Loan/payment calculations
- Calculations for collection actions regarding principal and interest due
- Present value and future value calculations regarding damages
- Lost wages and benefits calculations for worker's compensation claims

- Back wages and benefits regarding employment/discrimination actions
- Budgeting
- Accounting-related calculations

Damages Calculations

In many cases, the plaintiff (the person bringing the lawsuit) alleges that he is entitled to money damages—that is, that he should be compensated for whatever injury was sustained. The amount of damages a person should receive is always in dispute. A spreadsheet allows the law-office personnel to test different options or assumptions.

A Simple Damages Calculation Exhibit 3–18 is an example of an easy damages projection. Assume that you represent the plaintiff, John Jones, in an automobile accident case and you must prepare an exhibit for the jury to show the amount of damages the plaintiff is seeking. This spreadsheet simply lists the damage items, the amounts asked for, and a total (i.e., a formula using the SUM function).

A More Complex Damages Calculation (Net Present Value) Spreadsheets can handle complex damages calculations as well, as shown in Exhibit 3–19.

Assume that your firm represents Wendy Jones, who suffered a severe injury on the job and is bringing a worker's compensation claim. Jones is 59 years old and was going to retire at age 65. Assume that because she is now totally disabled, she is entitled to six years of income from her employer. She was making $35,000 a year before she was injured, and on average, she has received increases of about 2 percent every year. Therefore, in the first year following the accident, assume that Jones would have received $35,000, and in every year after that, she would have received a 2 percent increase. Exhibit 3–19 automatically calculates what her gross earnings would have been until retirement, for a total loss of wages of $220,784.23.

Unfortunately, Jones is not entitled to a lump-sum payment of $220,784.23. This is because Jones could take the lump-sum payment, invest it at 6 or 7 or 8 percent, and by the end of the six years have considerably more than she would have earned at her job. Thus, the future payments must be reduced to their present, or current,

EXHIBIT 3–18
Sample damages calculation

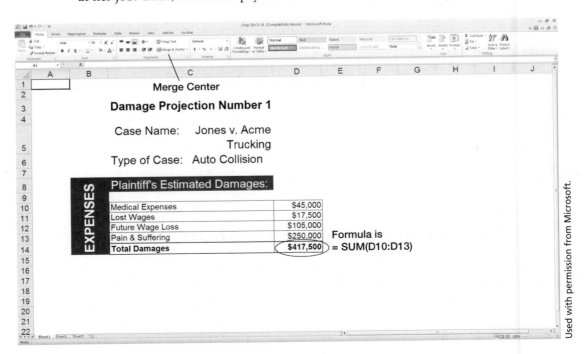

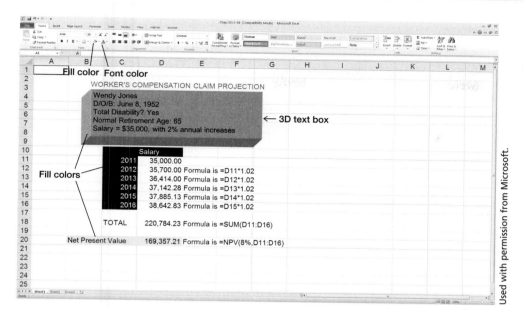

EXHIBIT 3–19
Complex damages
calculation

value. Nearly all spreadsheets have a present value function that accomplishes this task easily. The spreadsheet in Exhibit 3–19 calculates that Jones should be awarded a lump-sum payment of $169,357.21 for future payments worth $220,784.23.

This type of calculation (reducing a payment schedule to a present value) is also useful when considering different settlement offers or options. Notice in Exhibit 3–19 that a number of graphic elements have been added to the spreadsheet. The spreadsheet includes a number of different fill (background) colors and textures, font sizes, styles, and colors. The spreadsheet also includes a text box that has been formatted in three dimensions (3-D). These are all standard features in Excel and other spreadsheets. In Excel 2007, these features can be found on the Insert ribbon tab. Notice in Exhibit 3–18 that an oval has been added to the spreadsheet around the total and that the word "Expenses" appears vertically in the spreadsheet. All of these graphical features are extremely easy to use and can give spreadsheets added visual impact.

Legal Organization Budgeting

Many legal organizations prepare a yearly budget to track expenses and income. The budget is used as a planning tool and as a means of spotting potential problems.

Real Estate Law

Spreadsheets are particularly helpful for legal organizations that practice in the real estate field. An example of spreadsheet use in this field is to create an amortization schedule.

Monthly Payment and Amortization Schedules   Spreadsheets can automatically calculate the monthly payment on a loan and produce an amortization schedule. The loan amortization schedule in Exhibit 3–20 is a template that comes free with Excel. Simply fill in the data in the Loan Information section and the spreadsheet does the rest. To access the template in Excel 2007, click on the Office button, click New, then click under Templates. In Excel 2010, click on the File tab, then click New, then click under Templates.

EXHIBIT 3–20

Loan amortization
schedule

Ready to use
Excel template

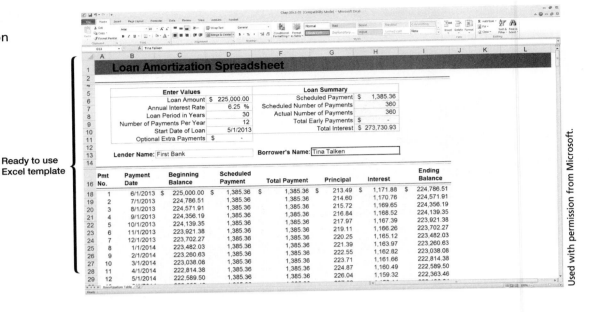

Family Law Cases

Spreadsheets are commonly used to help divide assets in a divorce. When a marriage is dissolved, it is the duty of the court to try to fairly distribute or divide the assets the parties have amassed during the marriage so that neither party gets more than her or his fair share. Spreadsheets are also used to calculate a party's child support obligations. A spreadsheet enables the user to lay out different division-of-asset scenarios or options for consideration. Spreadsheets can also produce lists of assets, family budgets, balance sheets, and income comparisons (such as between husband and wife). These documents are routinely prepared in many divorce cases.

Statistical Analysis

Spreadsheets can also be used to analyze statistics. Most spreadsheets have statistical functions that can help a user analyze a group of values. Suppose your firm represents the plaintiff John Snow, a salesman, in an age-discrimination suit against his former employer. The defendant company states that Snow was terminated because he did not sell enough units of its product. Snow must convince a judge that he was really terminated because the company wanted a younger workforce.

Exhibit 3–21 shows the names and ages of the company's salespersons and the units of product they sold. Looking at the statistical analysis part of the exhibit, notice that the average age of salespersons is 30 (far below Snow's age of 56—it appears that the company may be trying to hire young salespersons). This was arrived at by using the average function (AVG), which automatically totals the values in a range and divides by the number of values.

Now, look at the Most Units Sold cell. The spreadsheet automatically placed the highest value here, using the MAX function. Notice also that the minimum number of units was placed in the Least Units Sold cell, using the MIN function. Also, look at the Average Units Sold cell, which was calculated automatically using the AVG function. (Snow was 20 units above the average units sold—it certainly seems he can make a strong argument for his case.)

Finally, the standard deviation of the values (i.e., the standard deviation from the average of each value) is high, showing that the data vary widely. The formula

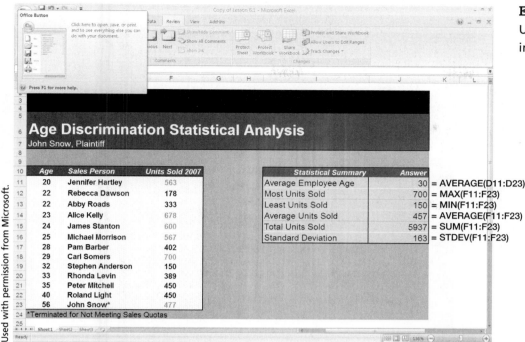

EXHIBIT 3–21
Using statistical functions in spreadsheets

for calculating standard deviations is not simple, but a spreadsheet user can find it by issuing a function command and marking the range. This is an example of how spreadsheets can turn hard tasks into easy ones.

Importing Spreadsheets into Other Programs

Sometimes it is necessary to include numerical information in a word-processing document. For example, you might want to incorporate part of a spreadsheet or a graph into a brief or pleading. In most cases, it is simple to paste a spreadsheet or graph into a word-processing document.

Tracking Investments for Trusts and Estates

Sometimes attorneys or law firms act as trustees or fiduciaries for trusts and estates. Part of this responsibility often involves investing money on behalf of a trust or an estate. Such fiduciaries have a duty not to waste or neglect the trust or estate and to make reasonable investments.

Exhibit 3–22 is an example of a spreadsheet that tracks the progress of stock market investments. By tracking the current prices of the stocks, the firm can get an idea of how the investments are doing and whether it should sell them and buy something else. Notice the use of formulas in Exhibit 3–22. The market value formulas take the number of shares purchased times the current price of the stock. The dollar gain formulas subtract the total purchase price (the number of shares times the purchase price) from the market value. Finally, the percentage gain formulas arrive at results by dividing the dollar gain by the total purchase price.

ETHICAL CONSIDERATIONS

The primary ethical considerations regarding spreadsheets are accuracy and competence.

EXHIBIT 3–22

Using a spreadsheet to track investments for an estate

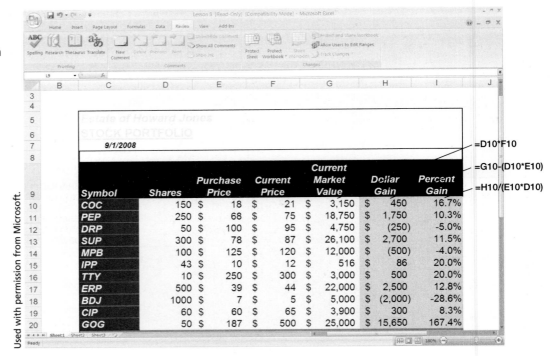

Used with permission from Microsoft.

It is absolutely critical that the spreadsheets the paralegal produces be 100 percent accurate and well tested. If formulas do not correctly manipulate all the data they are supposed to, if formulas have wrong numbers in them, if data are not updated, or if there are any other errors in the spreadsheet, disaster will occur. Unfortunately, often when paralegals work with spreadsheets they are not just working with raw numbers, mathematics, and research—they are working with spreadsheets that relate to actual money and financial projections that have a dollar impact. Thus, errors in a spreadsheet typically have a negative financial impact as well.

These issues are not as much ethical matters (although this is a problem) as they are a malpractice risk. Most spreadsheet users fail to understand the likelihood of spreadsheet errors or the absolute importance of careful quality control of every spreadsheet, no matter how small.

How prevalent are errors in spreadsheets? A number of studies have shown that spreadsheet errors are relatively high. Cell error rates are typically around 5 percent. Thus, for every 20 cells you create, on average, you will have one error. As the total number of cells in a spreadsheet rises, so does the propensity for errors. One auditing firm found that 90 percent of all spreadsheets they reviewed that had 150 or more cells had one or more errors. In many cases the errors were serious. Every study that has been conducted on spreadsheet errors has found them at rates that would be unacceptable in most organizations.

So, what can paralegals do to minimize the potential for errors? They can:

- Double-check all numbers that are entered into a spreadsheet for accuracy.
- Triple-check every single formula in a spreadsheet, including using the Formula Auditing mode to print out all formulas.
- Make comments in specific cells regarding assumptions.
- Create a notes section at the bottom or top of the spreadsheet containing assumptions or other data the reader should be aware of.

- Be extremely careful when adding rows or columns to a spreadsheet in which formulas already exist. Double-check each inserted row or column to make sure it appears in the applicable formulas.
- Have someone else carefully review each spreadsheet, including formulas.
- Before using a new function, completely understand exactly what it does and ensure that it is working 100 percent correctly.
- Use a calculator to spot-check spreadsheets to make sure the formulas are accurate.
- Use the Protect feature to protect cells, particularly formulas, from being changed accidentally (see the following subsections).

If working with a spreadsheet is outside of your knowledge base or comfort zone, ask your supervising attorney to get an expert, such as an accountant or financial analyst, to prepare and/or review the calculations. In the end, it is far cheaper to do this than to discover an error later.

Password Protection

Passwords are an easy way to increase the security of your documents. Password-protecting spreadsheets is easy to do and should always be done if the spreadsheet is going outside of the firm. In Excel 2007, the command sequence is Office button > Save > Tools > General Options > Password to Open. In Excel 2010, the command sequence is File tab > Save > Tools > General Options > Password to Open.

Protecting Cells and Spreadsheets

Protection is a useful security tool for spreadsheet use. When multiple people work with a spreadsheet, it is common for formulas and other data to be accidentally deleted or changed by users. If a formula, for example, is deleted and the recipient tries to correct the problem by writing a new formula, but makes an error, a large problem has been created that could go a long time without being noticed. One way to solve this problem is to use the Protect Cells feature found in most spreadsheets.

In Excel, for example, to protect all or part of a spreadsheet, you must turn on the protection feature. Protection can be turned on from the Review ribbon tab by checking Protect Sheet in the Changes group. *Note*: Cells can be protected against accidental deletion simply by turning on the Protect command (which a user can turn off at a later time) or can be password-protected, in which case protection cannot be turned off unless the user has the password. For example, suppose the creator of a spreadsheet wants to protect certain formulas in an Excel spreadsheet from being accidentally typed over. The spreadsheet creator does not want users to have to type a password if they want to edit the spreadsheet; the creator just wants to protect the formulas from accidental deletion. The spreadsheet creator would use Protect Sheet and leave the password blank. The creator would mark all of the cells that were not locked, using the command right-click, Format Cells > Protection. If a user then wanted to change a formula, he or she could not; instead, the user would get an error message stating that the cell is protected. However, all that user would have to do would be to click Tools > Protection > Unprotect Sheet to turn off the protection feature. The user would then be able to edit the formula. If the spreadsheet creator did not want the user to be able to do this, the creator could use the password feature to lock the spreadsheet cells he or she wanted to keep from being edited.

SUMMARY

Spreadsheet software calculates and manipulates data using labels and formulas. Spreadsheets use rows and columns, which look similar to those on an accountant's paper worksheet. A row is an area that extends across a page horizontally; a column is an area that extends down a page vertically. A cell is an intersection between a row and a column. The cursor, or cell pointer, in a spreadsheet indicates what cell is currently selected.

Three types of data can be entered into a spreadsheet: text, values, and formulas. Text is descriptive data, such as headings and titles, that are entered into a cell; text cannot be used in making calculations. Values are numbers that are entered into a cell and can be used in making calculations. Formulas perform calculations using the values in other cells. Arithmetic operations and function commands are used in constructing formulas; they instruct a spreadsheet how to make the desired calculations.

Copying data places information from one part of a spreadsheet into another part while leaving the original intact. When copying formulas, an absolute cell reference does not change to reflect the new location of the cell pointer. A relative cell reference will automatically change to reflect the new location of the cell pointer.

Most spreadsheets provide a variety of graphing capabilities. A bar graph consists of a sequence of bars that illustrate numerical values. A line graph plots the course of a value over time. A pie chart represents each value as a piece or percentage of a total "pie." A stacked bar graph compares data by placing bars on top of one another.

Paralegals can use spreadsheets to perform and track a huge variety of information, including damages calculations, budget plans and problems, and tax plans and tax return calculations.

KEY TERMS

absolute cell reference
arithmetic operators
bar/column graph
cell
cell address
cell pointer
cell width
column

formulas
function command
landscape
line graph
pie chart
portrait
relative cell reference
row

spreadsheet
spreadsheet software
stacked column graph
text
values
"what if" analysis

INTERNET SITES

Internet sites for this chapter include:

ORGANIZATION	PRODUCT/SERVICE	INTERNET ADDRESS
Microsoft	Microsoft Excel spreadsheet program	www.microsoft.com
Microsoft	Home page for Microsoft, containing a wealth of information, tips, and tricks	www.microsoft.com/excel
Corel Corporation	Quattro Pro spreadsheet	www.corel.com
About.com	General site about spreadsheets, with information and tips	www.spreadsheets.about.com

TEST YOUR KNOWLEDGE

1. An area on a spreadsheet that extends vertically up and down the page is called a _____.

2. An area on a spreadsheet that extends horizontally across a page is called a _____.

3. True or False: An intersection between a row and a column in a spreadsheet is called a *location*.

4. Descriptive data entered in a spreadsheet, such as titles and headings, are called _____.

5. Numbers entered in a spreadsheet are called _____.

6. Expressions used in a spreadsheet program to automatically perform calculations are called _____.

7. True or False: The plus sign, minus sign, multiplication sign, and division sign are examples of function commands.

8. Write two formulas for adding the following cells: A1, A2, and A3.

9. "=SUM," "AVERAGE," and "MAX" are examples of what kind of formulas?

10. Name two kinds of cell references.

11. Name three things that should be kept in mind when planning a spreadsheet.

12. True or False: It is difficult to make errors in spreadsheets because the built-in templates, formulas, and function commands are automatic.

13. One way to keep formulas and cells from being accidentally deleted is to use which command?

ON THE WEB EXERCISES

1. Using the "Internet Sites" listed in this chapter and a general Internet search engine (such as www.google.com or www.yahoo.com), research the issue of errors in spreadsheets. Write a two-page paper on your findings.

2. Go to www.microsoft.com/excel and, under the "Templates" section, view 10 of the many ready-to-use templates for Excel.

3. Research legal-related Excel templates, including tax, real estate, child support, financial planning, estate planning, and related subjects. Write a two-page paper summarizing the types of free and fee-based sites and templates you found.

QUESTIONS AND EXERCISES

1. Using a spreadsheet, track the daily price of any four stocks in which you have an interest for one week. Show the daily beginning stock price, ending stock price, and difference. Calculate the stock's total per-share movement for the week and calculate the stock's average price per share for the week.

2. Using a spreadsheet program, prepare an expense budget for a mythical start-up law firm for one year. Assume that the law firm will have four attorneys (two of whom are partners and two of whom are associates), two paralegals, and two secretaries. Be sure to include leased space, office equipment (computers, copiers, printers, phones, etc.), office supplies, utilities, and miscellaneous expenses.

3. Using a spreadsheet program, summarize the amount of time you spend attending class and studying for your classes for a week. Assume that you will be paid for the time spent studying or attending classes, but that you must present a detailed bill of your activities. The bill must be professional in appearance and be accurately calculated. Assume that you will be paid $60 an hour.

4. Using a spreadsheet program, enter the names, complete addresses, and telephone numbers of 20 relatives and/or friends. The list must be professional in appearance and sorted alphabetically by last name.

5. You have requested a new computer from your law firm in next year's budget. Your managing attorney has asked you to provide a detailed, itemized list of the equipment and the price for each component of the system. Your managing attorney is very frugal, so include a one-page memorandum (with the itemized listing) summarizing why the system you have selected is appropriate.

ETHICS QUESTION

You work in a state that requires use of a spreadsheet in the calculation of child support payments. The attorney you work for does not know how to use a spreadsheet. If the attorney is to take on the representation of a parent in a contested divorce case, what ethical issue(s) may arise?

CourseMate The available CourseMate for this text has an interactive eBook and interactive learning tools, including flash cards, quizzes, and more. To learn more about this resource and access free demo CourseMate resources, go to www.cengagebrain.com, and search for this book. To access CourseMate materials that you have purchased, go to login.cengagebrain.com.

SPREADSHEET SOFTWARE HANDS-ON EXERCISES

 ## *READ THIS FIRST!*

1. Microsoft Excel 2010
2. Microsoft Excel 2007

I. DETERMINING WHICH TUTORIAL TO COMPLETE

To use the Spreadsheet Hands-On Exercises, you must already own or have access to Microsoft Excel 2007 or Excel 2010. If you have one of these programs but do not know which version you are using, it is easy to find out. For Excel 2007, click the Office button, and click Excel Options > Resources; it will tell you what version you are using. For Excel 2010, click the File tab, and click Excel Options > Help; it will tell you what version you are using. You must know the version of the program you are using and select the correct tutorial version or the tutorials will not work correctly.

II. USING THE SPREADSHEET HANDS-ON EXERCISES

The Spreadsheet Hands-On Exercises in this section are easy to use and contain step-by-step instructions. They start with basic spreadsheet skills and proceed to intermediate and advanced levels. If you already have a good working knowledge of Excel, you may be able to proceed directly to the intermediate and advanced exercises. To truly be ready for using spreadsheets in the legal environment, you must be able to accomplish the tasks and exercises in the advanced exercises.

III. ACCESSING THE DATA FILES ON THE CDS THAT COME WITH THE TEXT

Some of the intermediate and advanced Excel Hands-On Exercises use documents on the disk that came with the text. To access these files, put the disk in your computer, select Start, select My Computer, then select the appropriate drive and double-click on the appropriate drive; then double-click on the Excel folder. You should then see a list of Excel files that are available. These files are also available on the Premium Website. To access them, go to your CengageBrain account and click on the link for Premium Website for Cornick's *Using Computers in the Law Office—Basic*. A new window will open. Under Book Level Resources, click the link for Data Files: Excel, then click the link to the desired lesson. When prompted, click Open.

IV. INSTALLATION QUESTIONS

If you have installation questions about loading the Excel data from the disk included with the text, you may contact Technical Support at http://cengage.com/support.

HANDS-ON EXERCISES

MICROSOFT EXCEL 2010 FOR WINDOWS

Number	Lesson Title	Concepts Covered
BASIC LESSONS		
Lesson 1	Building a Budget Spreadsheet—Part 1	[CTRL]+[HOME] command, moving the pointer, entering text and values, adjusting the width of columns, changing the format of a group of cells to currency, using bold, centering text, entering formulas, using the AutoFill/Copy command to copy formulas, and printing and saving a spreadsheet.
Lesson 2	Building a Budget Spreadsheet—Part 2	Opening a file, inserting rows, changing the format of cells to percent, building more formulas, creating a bar chart with the Chart Wizard, printing a selection, and fitting/compressing data to one printed page.
Lesson 3	Building a Damage Projection Spreadsheet	Changing font size, font color, and fill color; using the AutoSum feature; using the wrap text feature; creating borders; and setting decimal points when formatting numbers.
INTERMEDIATE LESSONS		
Lesson 4	Child Support Payment Spreadsheet	Creating a white background, creating formulas that multiply cells, creating formulas that use absolute cell references, and using the AutoFormat feature.
Lesson 5	Loan Amortization Template	Using a template, protecting cells, freezing panes, splitting a screen, hiding columns, and using Format Painter.
Lesson 6	Statistical Functions	Using functions including average, maximum, minimum, and standard deviation; sorting data; checking for metadata; using the format clear command; using conditional formatting; and inserting a picture.
ADVANCED LESSONS		
Lesson 7	Tools and Techniques 1—Marketing Budget	Creating and manipulating a text box, advanced shading techniques, working with a 3-D style text box, creating vertical and diagonal text, creating a cell comment, and using lines and borders.
Lesson 8	Tools and Techniques 2—Stock Portfolio	Using the Merge and Center tool, using the Formula Auditing feature, using the oval tool, and password-protecting a file.

GETTING STARTED

Overview

Microsoft Excel 2010 is a powerful spreadsheet program that allows you to create formulas, "what if" scenarios, graphs, and much more.

Introduction

Throughout these lessons and exercises, information you need to operate the program will be designated in several different ways:

- Keys to be pressed on the keyboard are designated in brackets, in all caps, and in bold (e.g., press the **[ENTER]** key).
- Movements with the mouse pointer are designated in bold and italics (e.g., ***point to File and click***).

- Words or letters that should be typed are designated in bold (e.g., type **Training Program**).

- Information that is or should be displayed on your computer screen is shown in bold, with quotation marks (e.g., **"Press ENTER to continue."**).

- Specific menu items and commands are designated with an initial capital letter (e.g., click Open).

OVERVIEW OF EXCEL 2010

I. WORKSHEET

A. *Entering Commands: The Ribbon*—The primary way of entering commands in Excel 2010 is through the ribbon. The ribbon is a set of commands or tools that change depending on which ribbon is selected (see Excel 2010 Exhibit 1). There are seven ribbon tabs: Home, Insert, Page Layout, Formulas, Data, Review, and View (see Excel 2010 Exhibit 1). Each tab has groups of commands. For example, on the Home tab, the Font group contains a group of commands that govern font choice, font size, bold, italics, underlining, and other attributes (see Excel 2010 Exhibit 1).

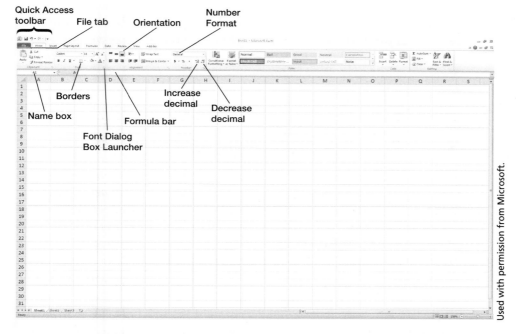

EXCEL 2010 EXHIBIT 1
Excel 2010 interface

B. *File tab*—The File tab (see Excel 2010 Exhibit 1) is where a user accesses commands such as New, Open, Save, and Print. The File tab replaces the Office button used in Excel 2007.

C. *Entering Data*—To enter data, type the text or number in a cell, and press the **[ENTER]** key or one of the arrow (cursor) keys.

D. *Ranges*—A range is a group of contiguous cells. Cell ranges can be created by ***clicking and dragging the pointer*** or holding down the **[SHIFT]** key and using the arrow (cursor) keys.

E. *Format*—Cells can be formatted, including changing the font style, font size, shading, border, cell type (currency, percentage, etc.), alignment, and other attributes by ***clicking the Home ribbon tab, and then clicking one of the dialog box launchers in the Font group, Alignment group, or Number group.*** Each of these dialog box launchers brings up the same "Format Cells" window. You can also enter a number of formatting options directly from the Home tab.

F. *Editing a Cell*—You can edit a cell by ***clicking in the cell and then clicking in the formula bar.*** The formula bar is directly under the ribbon and just to the right of the fx sign (see Excel 2010 Exhibit 1). The formula bar shows the current contents of the selected cell, and it allows you to edit the cell contents. You can also edit the contents of a cell by ***clicking in the cell*** and then pressing the **[F2]** key.

G. *Column Width/Row Height*—You can change the width of a column by ***clicking the line to the right of the column heading.*** (This is the line that separates two columns. When you point to a line, the cursor changes to double-headed vertical arrows.) ***Next, drag the pointer to the right or to the left to increase or decrease the column width, respectively.*** Similarly, you can change the height of a row ***clicking and dragging the horizontal line separating two rows.*** You can also change the width of a column or height of a row by ***clicking somewhere in the column you want to change, clicking the Home tab, and then clicking Format in the Cells group.***

H. *Insert*—You can insert one row or column by ***clicking the Home tab, then clicking the down arrow below the Insert icon in the Cells group, and clicking either Insert Sheet Rows or Insert Sheet Columns.*** You can also insert a number of rows or columns by ***dragging the pointer over the number of rows or columns you want to add, clicking the Home tab, clicking the down arrow below the Insert icon in the Cells group, and then clicking either Insert Sheet Rows or Insert Sheet Columns.*** Finally, you can ***right-click and select Insert from the menu.***

I. *Erase/Delete*—You can erase data by ***dragging the pointer over the area*** and then pressing the **[DEL]** key. You can also erase data by ***dragging the pointer over the area, clicking the Home ribbon tab, clicking the down arrow next to the Clear icon in the Editing group, and then clicking Clear All.*** You can delete whole columns or rows by ***pointing and clicking in a column or row, then clicking on the Home ribbon tab, clicking on the down arrow next to Delete in the Cells group, and then clicking either Delete Sheet Rows or Delete Sheet Columns.*** You can also delete whole columns or rows by ***pointing in the column or row and then right-clicking and selecting Delete.***

J. *Quit*—To quit Excel, ***click on the File tab and then click Exit.***

K. *Copy*—To copy data to adjacent columns or rows, ***click in the cell you wish to copy and then select the AutoFill command,*** which is accessed from the small black box at the bottom right corner of the selected cell. Then, ***drag the pointer to where the data should be placed.*** You can also copy data by ***clicking in the cell, right-clicking, clicking Copy, clicking in the location where the information should be copied,*** and pressing the **[ENTER]** key. Finally, data can be copied by ***clicking and dragging to highlight the information to be copied, clicking the Home tab, and then clicking Copy in the Clipboard group.***

L. *Move*—Move data by ***clicking in the cell, right-clicking, selecting Cut, clicking in the location where the information should be inserted,*** and pressing the **[ENTER]** key. Data can also be moved by ***highlighting the information to be copied, clicking the Home tab, and then clicking Cut in the Clipboard group.*** Then go to the location where the information should be moved, ***click the Home tab, and click Paste in the Clipboard group.***

M. *Saving and Opening Files*—Save a file by **clicking the File tab, then clicking Save or Save As,** and typing the file name. You can also save a file by **clicking the Save icon** (it looks like a floppy disk) on the Quick Access toolbar (see Excel 2010 Exhibit 1). Open a file that was previously saved by **clicking the File tab, clicking Open,** and typing (or clicking) the name of the file to be opened.

N. *Print*—To print a file, **click the File tab, then click Print, and then click Print.**

II. NUMBERS AND FORMULAS

A. *Numbers*—To enter a number in a cell, **click in the cell,** type the number, and press the **[ENTER]** key or an arrow (cursor) key.

B. *Adding Cells (Addition)*—You can add the contents of two or more cells by three different methods:

1. To add the contents of a range of two or more cells:

   a. **Click in the cell where the total should be placed.**

   b. **Click the Home tab, then click the Sum icon in the Editing group** (see Excel 2010 Exhibit 2). The Sum icon looks like an "E." *Note*: To see the name of an icon, point to the icon for a second and the name of the icon will be displayed.

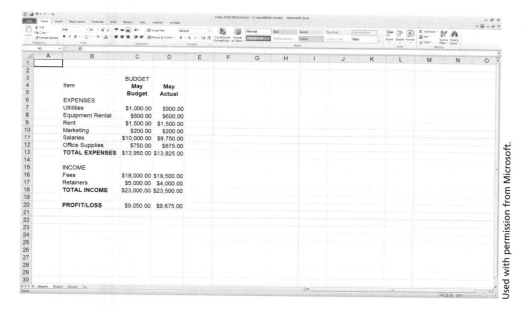

EXCEL 2010 EXHIBIT 2
Budgeting spreadsheet

Used with permission from Microsoft.

   c. Excel guesses which cells you want to add. Press **[ENTER]** if the correct range is automatically selected, or select the correct range by highlighting it (i.e., **clicking and dragging until the range of cells to be added is selected**). Then, press the **[ENTER]** key.

2. To add the contents of two cells, which need not comprise a range:

   a. **Click in the cell where the total should be placed.**

   b. Press **[=]** (the equals sign).

   c. Type the address of the first cell to be added (e.g., B4), or **click in that cell.**

   d. Press **[+]** (the plus sign).

   e. Enter the address of the second cell to be added (or **click in it**).

   f. Press the **[ENTER]** key. (For example, to add the values of cells C4 and C5, you would type **= C4+C5**.)

HANDS-ON EXERCISES

3. To add the contents of a range of two or more cells:

    a. *Click in the cell where the total should be placed.*

    b. Type =**SUM**(.

    c. Enter the address of the first cell to be added (or *click in it*).

    d. Press **:** (a colon).

    e. Enter the address of the second cell to be added (or *click in it*).

    f. Press **)** (a closing parenthesis).

    g. Press the **[ENTER]** key. (For example, to add the values of C4 and C5, the formula would read =**SUM(C4:C5)**.)

C. *Subtracting Cells*—To subtract the contents of one or more cells from those of another:

    1. *Click in the cell where the result should be placed.*

    2. Press [=].

    3. Enter the first cell address (or *click in it*).

    4. Press [–] (the minus sign).

    5. Enter the second cell address (or *click in it*).

    6. Press the **[ENTER]** key. (For example, to subtract the value of C4 from the value of C5, you would type =**C5–C4**.)

D. *Multiplying Cells*—To multiply the contents of two (or more) cells:

    1. *Click in the cell where the result should be placed.*

    2. Press =.

    3. Enter the first cell address (or *click in it*).

    4. Press * (**[SHIFT]**+**[8]**).

    5. Enter the second cell address (or *click in it*).

    6. Press the **[ENTER]** key. (For example, to multiply the value in C4 times the value in C5, you would type =**C5*C4**.)

E. *Dividing Cells*—To divide the contents of two (or more) cells:

    1. *Click in the cell where the result should be placed.*

    2. Press =.

    3. Enter the first cell address (or *click in it*).

    4. Press **/** (the forward slash).

    5. Enter the second cell address (or *click in it*).

    6. Press the **[ENTER]** key. (For example, to divide the value in C4 by the value in C5, you would type =**C4/C5**.)

▶ BASIC LESSONS

LESSON 1: BUILDING A BUDGET SPREADSHEET—PART 1

This lesson shows you how to build the spreadsheet in Excel 2010 Exhibit 3. It explains how to use the **[CTRL]+[HOME]** command; move the cell pointer; enter text, values, and formulas; adjust the width of columns; change the format of cells to currency; use the bold feature; use the AutoFill and Copy features to copy formulas; and print and save a spreadsheet. Keep in mind that if at any time you make a mistake in this lesson, you may press **[CTRL]+[Z]** to undo what you have done.

    1. Open Windows. When it has loaded, *double-click the Microsoft Office Excel 2010 icon on the desktop* to open the program. Alternatively, *click the Start button, point to Programs or All Programs, point to Microsoft Office, and then click Microsoft Excel 2010.* You should be in a clean, blank workbook. If

you are not in a blank workbook, ***click the File tab*** (see Excel 2010 Exhibit 1), ***click on New, and then double-click Blank Workbook.***

2. Notice that the pointer is at cell A1, and the indicator that displays the address of the current cell (called the "name" box in Excel) says **A1**. The "name" box is just under the ribbon and all the way to the left (see Excel 2010 Exhibit 1). Also, notice that you can move the pointer around the spreadsheet using the cursor keys. Go back to cell A1 by pressing the **[CTRL]+[HOME]** keys.

3. Go to cell C3 by ***clicking in cell C3*** or by pressing the **[RIGHT ARROW]** twice, and then pressing the **[DOWN ARROW]** twice.

4. You will now enter the title of the spreadsheet in cell C3. Type **BUDGET** and then press the **[ENTER]** key.

5. Notice that the pointer is now at cell C4.

6. Press the **[UP ARROW]** to go back to cell C3. Notice that BUDGET is left-aligned. To center BUDGET in the cell, ***from the Home tab, click the Center icon in the Alignment group.*** It is the icon with several lines on it that appear centered (see Excel 2010 Exhibit 3). *Note*: If you hover the mouse over an icon on the ribbon for a second, the name of the icon will be displayed. Alternatively, ***from the Home tab, click the Alignment Group Dialog Box Launcher. Next, on the Alignment tab, under the Horizontal field, click the down arrow and select Center. Click OK.***

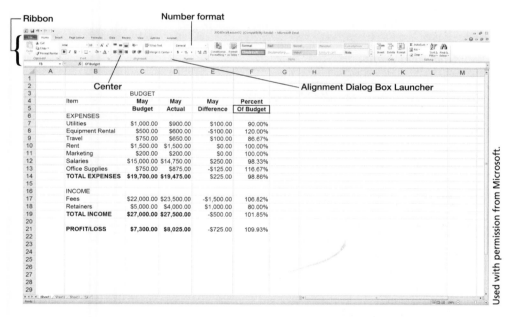

EXCEL 2010 EXHIBIT 3
Expanded budget spreadsheet

7. You should now be ready to enter the budget information. First, move the cell pointer to where the data should go, then type the data, and finally enter the data by pressing the **[ENTER]** key or one of the arrow (cursor) keys. Type the remaining row labels as follows:
Item in B4.
EXPENSES in B6.
Utilities in B7.
Equipment Rental in B8.
Travel in B9.
Rent in B10.
Marketing in B11.
Salaries in B12.

Office Supplies in B13.
TOTAL EXPENSES in B14.
INCOME in B16.
Fees in B17.
Retainers in B18.
TOTAL INCOME in B19.
PROFIT/LOSS in B21.

8. Notice that in column B, some of the data entries (such as "TOTAL EXPENSES" and "Equipment Rental") actually extend into column C. To correct this, you must increase the width of column B. *Put the mouse pointer in the cell lettered B at the top of the screen. Move the pointer to the right edge of the cell.* The pointer should then change to a double-headed vertical arrow and the column width will be displayed in a small box. *Drag the pointer to the right until the column width is 18.00.* Alternatively, you can change the cell width by *placing the cell pointer anywhere in column B; then, from the Home tab, click Format in the Cells group, click Column Width...* , type **18**, and *click OK.*

9. Notice that all of the data entries now fit in the columns. Enter the following:
May in C4.
Budget in C5.
May in D4.
Actual in D5.

10. *Click in cell C4 and drag the pointer over to cell D5* (so that the whole cell range is highlighted)*; then, from the Home tab, click the Center icon in the Alignment group.*

11. You are now ready to enter values into your spreadsheet.

12. *Move the pointer to cell C7.* Type **1000.** Do not type a dollar sign or comma; these will be added later. Press the **[ENTER]** key to enter the value.

13. Enter the following:
500 in C8.
750 in C9.
1500 in C10.
200 in C11.
15000 in C12.
750 in C13.
22000 in C17.
5000 in C18.
900 in D7.
600 in D8.
650 in D9.
1500 in D10.
200 in D11.
14750 in D12.
875 in D13.
23500 in D17.
4000 in D18.

14. The values you entered do not have dollar signs or the commas appropriate to a currency format. You will now learn how to format a range of cells for a particular format (such as the Currency format).

15. *Click in cell C7 and drag the pointer over to cell D21. From the Home tab, click the down arrow next to the "Number Format" box, which should say*

General. Then, click Currency. Then click OK. Notice that dollar signs have been added to all of the values. *Click in any cell to deselect the cell range.*

16. *Click in cell B14 and drag the pointer over to cell D14; then, from the Home tab, click the Bold icon in the Font group.* This will make the TOTAL EXPENSES row appear in bold.

17. *Click in cell B19 and drag the pointer over to cell D19; then, from the Home tab, click the Bold icon in the Font group.* This will make the TOTAL INCOME row appear in bold.

18. *Click in cell B21 and drag the pointer over to cell D21; then, from the Home ribbon tab, click on the Bold icon in the Font group.* This will make the PROFIT/LOSS row appear in bold.

19. Your spreadsheet is nearly complete; all you need to add are the six formulas.

20. *Click in cell C14.*

21. Type **=SUM(** and press **[UP ARROW]** seven times until the cell pointer is at cell C7. Press **.** (a period) to anchor the range.

22. Press the **[DOWN ARROW]** six times, then press **)** (a closing parenthesis), and then press the **[ENTER]** key.

23. Go back to cell C14 and look at the formula in the formula bar. The formula should read =SUM(C7:C13). The total displayed in the cell should read $19,700.00. Note that you also could have typed the formula **=C7+C8+C9+C10+C11+C12+C13.**

24. Enter the following formulas:
    =SUM(D7:D13) in D14.
    =SUM(C17:C18) in C19.
    =SUM(D17:D18) in D19.

25. You now need to enter formulas for the PROFIT/LOSS columns. Enter the following formula in C21:
    =C19–C14 (the total should read $7,300.00)

26. *Go to cell C21 and click the AutoFill command* (it is the small black square at the bottom right of the cell—see Excel 2010 Exhibit 2). *Drag it one column to the right and release the mouse button.* Notice that the formula has been copied. The total should be $8,025.00. Alternatively, *go to cell C21, right-click, click Copy, then move the pointer to cell D21* and press the **[ENTER]** key.

27. The spreadsheet is now complete. To print the spreadsheet, *click the File tab, then click Print, and then click Print.*

28. You will need to save the spreadsheet, because you will use it in Lesson 2. To save the spreadsheet, *click the File tab and then click Save. Under Save in:, select the drive or folder* in which you would like to save the document. Next to File Name, type **Budget1** and *click Save.*

29. To quit Excel, *click the File tab and then click on Exit.*

This concludes Lesson 1.

LESSON 2: BUILDING A BUDGET SPREADSHEET—PART 2

This lesson assumes that you have completed Lesson 1, have saved the spreadsheet created in that lesson, and are generally familiar with the concepts covered in that lesson. Lesson 2 gives you experience in opening a file, inserting a row, formatting numbers as percentages, building additional formulas, creating a bar chart, printing selections, and fitting and compressing data onto one printed page. If you did not exit Excel after Lesson 1, skip steps 1 and 2, and go directly to step 3.

1. Open Windows. ***Double-click on the Microsoft Office Excel 2010 icon on the desktop*** to open the program. Alternatively, ***click the Start button, point to Programs or All Programs, point to Microsoft Office, and then click Microsoft Excel 2010.*** You should now be in a clean, blank workbook.

2. To retrieve the spreadsheet from Lesson 1, ***click on the File tab and then click Open. Next, click the name of your file*** (e.g., **Budget 1**). ***If you do not see it, click through the options under Look in:*** to find the file. When you have found it, ***click on Open.***

3. You will be entering the information shown in Excel 2010 Exhibit 3. Notice in Excel 2010 Exhibit 3 that a line for insurance appears in row 9. You will insert this row first.

4. ***Click in cell B9. From the Home tab, click the down arrow below Insert in the Cells group. On the Insert menu, click Insert Sheet Rows.*** A new row has been added. You could also have ***right-clicked and selected Insert*** to open a dialog box with the option to insert another row.

5. Enter the following:
   Insurance in B9.
   500 in C9.
   450 in D9.

6. Notice that when the new values for insurance were entered, all of the formulas were updated. Because you inserted the additional rows in the middle of the column, the formulas recognized the new numbers and automatically recalculated to reflect them. Be extremely careful when inserting new rows and columns into spreadsheets that have existing formulas. In some cases, the new number will not be reflected in the totals, such as when rows or columns are inserted at the beginning or end of the range that a formula calculates. It is always prudent to go back to each existing formula, examine the formula range, and make sure the new values are included in the formula range.

7. Change the column width of column E to 12 by ***clicking the column heading*** (the letter E) at the top of the screen. ***Move the pointer to the right edge of the column.*** The pointer should change to a double-headed vertical arrow. ***Drag the pointer to the right until the column width is 12.*** Alternatively, you can change the cell width by ***placing the cell pointer anywhere in column E and, from the Home tab, clicking Format in the Cells Group, and selecting Column Width... .*** Then type 12 and ***click OK.***

8. Enter the following:
   May in E4.
   Difference in E5.
   Percent in F4.
   Of Budget in F5.

9. ***Click in cell E4 and drag the pointer over to cell F5*** so that the additional column headings are highlighted. ***Right-click.*** Notice that in addition to a menu, the Mini toolbar appears. It has a number of formatting options on it, including Font, Font size, Bold, and others. ***Click the Bold icon on the Mini toolbar. Point and click the Center icon on the Mini toolbar.***

10. ***Click in cell E14 and drag the pointer over to cell F14. Then, right-click and click on the Bold icon on the Mini toolbar.***

11. ***Click in cell E19 and drag the pointer over to cell F19. Then, right-click and click on Bold icon on the Mini toolbar.***

12. ***Click in cell E21 and drag the pointer over to cell F21. Then, right-click and click on Bold icon on the Mini toolbar.***

13. You are now ready to change the cell formatting for column E to Currency and column F to Percent. ***Click in cell E7 and drag the pointer down to cell E21. Right-click and select Format Cells. From the Number tab in the "Format Cells" window, click Currency and then OK. Click in any cell to get rid of the cell range.***

14. ***Click in cell F7 and drag the pointer down to cell F21. From the Home tab, click the Percent (%) icon in the Number group*** (see Excel 2010 Exhibit 3). ***Then, from the Home tab, click the Increase Decimal icon twice.***

15. ***Click in any cell to get rid of the cell range.***

16. All that is left to do is to enter the formulas for the two new columns. The entries in the May Difference column subtract the actual amount from the budgeted amount for each expense item. A positive amount in this column means that the office was under budget on that item. A negative balance means that the office was over budget on that line item. The Percent Of Budget column divides that actual amount by the budgeted amount. This shows the percentage of the budgeted money that was actually spent for each item.

17. You will first build one formula in the May Difference column, and then copy it. ***Click in cell E7***, type =C7–D7, and press the [ENTER] key.

18. Using the AutoFill command or the Copy command, copy this formula down through cell E14. (To copy, ***right-click and then click Copy; highlight the area where the information should go; then right-click and select Paste and click the icon on the right, Match Destination Formatting.*** Alternatively, you can use the Copy and Paste icons in the Clipboard group on the Home tab.)

19. ***Click in cell E17***, type =D17–C17, and press the [ENTER] key.

20. Using the AutoFill command, copy this formula down through cell E21. Delete the formula in cell E20 by ***clicking in cell E20*** and pressing the [DEL] key.

21. You will now build on the formula in the Percent Of Budget column and copy it. ***Click in cell F7***, type =D7/C7, and press the [ENTER] key.

22. Using the AutoFill command, copy this formula down through cell F21. Delete the formula in cells F15, F16, and F20 by ***clicking in the cell*** and then pressing the [DEL] key.

23. The spreadsheet has now been built. We will now build a bar chart that shows our budgeted expenses compared to our actual expenses (see Excel 2010 Exhibit 4).

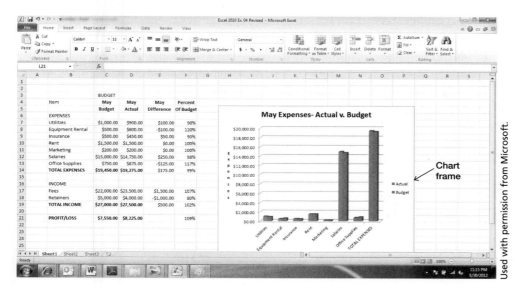

EXCEL 2010 EXHIBIT 4
Completed column grid

24. *Click in cell B7 and then drag the pointer down and over to cell D14.*

25. *From the Insert tab, click Column from the Charts group. Under 3-D Column, click the first option, 3-D Clustered Column* (see Excel 2010 Exhibit 5).

EXCEL 2010 EXHIBIT 5
Creating a column chart

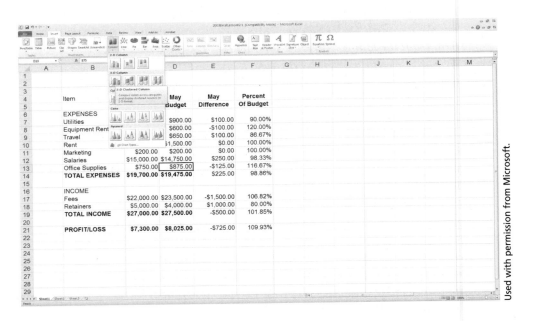

Used with permission from Microsoft.

26. Notice that a draft bar chart has been created. *Click anywhere in the chart frame* (see Excel 2010 Exhibit 4), *and your pointer will turn to a four-headed arrow. Drag the chart across the spreadsheet so the upper left corner of the chart is near cell H4.*

27. *Using the horizontal scroll bar* (see Excel 2010 Exhibit 4), *scroll to the right* so the chart is completely in your screen.

28. *Click the bottom right corner of the chart frame. Your cursor should change to a two-headed arrow that is diagonal. Drag the chart so that the bottom right corner ends near cell P26* (see Excel 2010 Exhibit 4).

29. Notice that new options have been added to the ribbon (e.g., Chart Tools Design, Layout and Format). *Click the Layout ribbon tab under Chart Tools.*

30. *Click Chart Title in the Labels Group, and then select Above Chart.* Notice that a title has been added, Chart Title.

31. *Click on the "Chart Title" text in the bar chart* and press the [DEL] key until the text is gone. Type **May Expenses—Actual v. Budget**. If you would like to move the title—for example, if it is off center—just *click the title frame and drag it* where you would like.

32. *From the Layout tab (under Chart Tools), click Axis Titles in the Labels Group. Click Primary Vertical Axis Title and then select Vertical Title.* Notice that a vertical axis title of "Axis Title" has been added. *Click Axis Title* and use the [DEL] key until the text is gone. Type **Expenses**.

33. To change the legend from Series1 and Series2 to Actual and Budget, *right click on Series1, then click Select Data.* The "Select Data Source" window will open. *Click on Series1 (under Legend Entries (Series)) to highlight it, then click on Edit under the same heading.* The "Edit Series" window will open. Type **Actual** in the text box under Series name:, *then click OK.*

Click on Series2 (under Legend Entries (Series)) to highlight it, then click on Edit under the same heading. The "Edit Series" window will open. Type **Budget** in the text box under Series name:, *then click OK.*

34. To print the chart, *drag the pointer from cell G3 to cell Q27. Then click the File tab and click Print; under Print what, click Selection and then click Print.*

35. You will next print the spreadsheet and the chart on one page. *Click in cell B3 and then drag the pointer until both the spreadsheet and the chart are highlighted* (roughly cell B3 to cell Q27).

36. *Click the Page Layout tab, then click the Page Setup Dialog Box Launcher.* (It is a little box directly under the Print Titles icon in the Page Setup group). The "Page Setup" window should now be displayed. There is another way to bring up this window: *from the Page Setup group of the Page Layout tab, click Margins, then click Custom Margins.*

37. *From the Page tab of the "Page Setup" window, click in the circle next to Fit to: and make sure it says* "**1 page(s) wide by 1 tall**" (it should default to one page). *Then, under Orientation, click on Landscape.*

38. *Click Print and then click Print.* This will compress everything in the print area to one page.

39. To save the spreadsheet, *click the File tab and then click Save As. Under Save in:, select the drive or folder* in which you would like to save the document. Then, next to File Name, type **Budget2** and *click Save.*

40. To quit Excel, *click the File tab and then click Exit.*

This concludes Lesson 2.

LESSON 3: BUILDING A DAMAGE PROJECTION SPREADSHEET

This lesson shows you how to build the damage projection spreadsheet shown in Excel 2010 Exhibit 6. It explains how to increase the size of type, how to wrap text in a cell, how to use the border features, how to use the font and fill color features, how to use the Auto-Sum feature, and how to change the decimal places for a number. This lesson assumes you have successfully completed Lessons 1 and 2. Keep in mind that if at any time you make a mistake in this lesson, you may press **[CTRL]+[Z]** to undo what you have done.

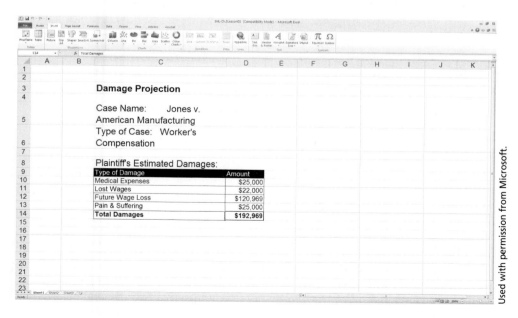

EXCEL 2010 EXHIBIT 6
Damages projection

Used with permission from Microsoft.

1. Open Windows. When it has loaded, *double-click the Microsoft Office Excel 2010 icon on the desktop* to open the program. Alternatively, *click on the Start button, point to Programs or All Programs, point to Microsoft Office, and then click Microsoft Excel 2010.* You should now be in a clean, blank workbook. If you are not in a blank workbook, *click the File tab* (see Excel 2010 Exhibit 1), *then click New, and then double-click Blank Workbook.*

2. To start building the spreadsheet in Excel 2010 Exhibit 6, begin by *increasing size of column C to a width of 37 (Home tab > Cells group > Format > Column Width).*

3. In cell C3, type **Damages Projection.** With the pointer on C3, *click the Bold icon from Font group on the Home tab. Change the size to 14 point by clicking the Font Size box in the Font group on the Home tab;* then type **14.**

4. Type the text shown in cell C5 (see Excel 2010 Exhibit 6). *On the Home tab, click the Font Size box in the Font group and change the type to 14 point.* Notice that the text goes into the next cell. To wrap part of the text down to the next line within the current cell (see Excel Exhibit 6), *from the Home tab, click the Wrap Text icon in the Alignment group* (see Excel 2010 Exhibit 6). The text has now been wrapped down to the next line within the cell C5.

5. Type the text shown in cell C6, make the text 14 point, and wrap the text down so it does not go into cell D6.

6. Type the text shown in cell C8 and make the text 14 point.

7. Type the text and values shown in cells C9 to D13.

8. Type the text shown in cell C14.

9. To enter the formula in cell D14, *click cell D14.* Then, *from the Editing group on the Home tab, click the Sum icon.* Notice that Sum assumed you wanted to add the values in D10 to D13. You could adjust the range by pressing **[SHIFT]+[ARROW]** keys, but the range should be fine as is (i.e., D10 to D13). Press the **[ENTER]** key to enter the formula.

10. *Click in cell C9, drag the mouse pointer to cell D14, and change the font size to 14 point.*

11. *Click in cell C9 and drag the pointer to cell D9. Right-click. On the Mini toolbar, click the down arrow next to the Fill Color icon* (the paint bucket) *and select the black square.* (You also could have clicked the Fill Color icon in the Font group on the Home tab.) The cells are all black; now you just need to change the font color to white to see the text.

12. With cells C9 and D9 still highlighted, *on the Home tab click the down arrow next to the Font Color icon in the Font group, and click on the white square.*

13. *Click in cell C10 and drag the pointer to cell D14. From the Font group on the Home tab, click on the down arrow next to the Border icon.* (It is typically just to the left of the Fill Color icon.) *Click All Borders* (it looks like a windowpane). Notice that there is now a border around every square that was highlighted.

14. *Click in cell C14 and drag the pointer to cell D14. From the Font group on the Home tab, click the down arrow next to the Border icon again. Then click on the Thick Box border* (it looks like a heavy black window frame). Move the pointer and notice that there is now a heavy black border around cells C14 and D14.

15. *Click in cell D10 and drag the pointer to cell D14. From the Number group or the Home tab, click the dollar sign* ($). Notice that two decimal places are shown (e.g., $25,000.00). It is not necessary to show two decimal places in

our projection, so we will change it to zero decimal places. *From the Number group on the Home tab, click the Decrease Decimal icon twice.* Notice that whole dollars are now shown.

16. To print the spreadsheet, *click on the File tab, then click Print, and then click Print.*

17. To save the spreadsheet, *click on the File tab and then click Save. Under Save in:, select the drive or folder* in which you would like to save the document. Then, next to File Name, type *Damages Projection* and *click Save.*

18. To quit Excel, *click on the File tab and then click Exit.*

This concludes Lesson 3.

INTERMEDIATE LESSONS

LESSON 4: CHILD SUPPORT PAYMENT SPREADSHEET

This lesson shows you how to build the child support payment spreadsheet in Excel 2010 Exhibit 7. It explains how to create a white background, create formulas to multiply cells and formulas that use an absolute cell reference, and use the Auto-Format feature. This lesson assumes that you have successfully completed Lessons 1 through 3. Keep in mind that if at any time you make a mistake in this lesson, you may press **[CTRL]+[Z]** to undo what you have done.

HANDS-ON EXERCISES

EXCEL 2010 EXHIBIT 7
Child support payment spreadsheet

Used with permission from Microsoft.

Month	Support Due	Support Paid	Accrued Arrearage	Monthly Interest
CHILD SUPPORT PAYMENTS - HALL v. HALL				
Beginning Balance $2500				
Monthly Payments $500				
Interest=Accrued Arrearage		1%		
Accrued Arrearage= Previous Arrearage + Previous Interest + Support Due - Support Paid				
Beginning Bal Jan. 2014			$2,500.00	$25.00
February	$500.00	$100.00	$2,925.00	$29.25
March	$500.00	$500.00	$2,954.25	$29.54
April	$500.00	$0.00	$3,483.79	$34.84
May	$500.00	$250.00	$3,768.63	$37.69
June	$500.00	$750.00	$3,556.32	$35.56
July	$500.00	$0.00	$4,091.88	$40.92

1. Open Windows. When it has loaded, *double-click the Microsoft Office Excel 2010 icon on the desktop* to open the program. Alternatively, *click the Start button, point to Programs or All Programs, point to Microsoft Office, and then click Microsoft Excel 2010.* You should now be in a clean, blank workbook. If you are not in a blank workbook, *click on the File tab* (see Excel 2010 Exhibit 1), *then click New, and then double-click on Blank Workbook.*

2. When you start to build the spreadsheet in Excel 2010 Exhibit 7, notice that the background is completely white. A completely white background gives you a crisp, clean canvas on which to work and to which you can add colors and graphics.

3. Press **[CTRL]+[A]**. The whole spreadsheet is now selected. ***From the Font group on the Home tab, click the down arrow next to the Fill Color icon, and then click the white square*** (it is all the way in the upper right corner). ***Click in any cell*** to make the highlighting disappear. Notice that the background of the spreadsheet is completely white.

4. Enter the text shown in cell C1; change the font to Bold and the font size to 14 point.

5. Increase the width of column C to 20.

6. Enter the text shown in cells C3 to C6.

7. In cell E5, type **.01** and press the **[ENTER]** key. Change the number format to Percent (zero decimal places).

8. Enter the text shown in cell C7 and in the cell range from D7 to G8. ***Click on C7 and click on bold icon from Font group in Home tab. Click on D7 and drag the pointer to G8, click on Italic icon from font group in Home tab.***

9. Enter the text shown in the cell range from C10 to C16.

10. Enter the numbers (values) shown in cells in D11 to E16.

11. In cell F10, type **1000.**

12. In cell G10, press the [=] key. ***Click in cell F10***, then press **[SHIFT]+[8]** (an asterisk will appear), then ***click in cell E5*** and press the **[F4]** key once. The formula **=F10*$E$5** should be on the screen; press the **[ENTER]** key. The formula multiplies the accrued arrearage (how much the individual is behind on payments) times the interest rate (which is 1 percent). The reason you pressed **[F4]** is that the formula had to be an absolute cell reference; pressing **[F4]** simply put the dollar signs ($) into the formula for you. The dollar signs tell Excel that this is an absolute cell reference, rather than a relative cell reference. In this manner, when you copy the formula to other cells (see below), the accrued arrearage will always be multiplied by the value in E5. Said another way, the second half of this formula (**$E$5**) will not change when the formula is copied to other cells.

13. If you want to find out for yourself why the formula **=F10*E5** will not work once it is copied from cell G10 (where it will work fine), type **=F10*E5** in cell G10, and then copy the formula to cells G11 to G16. Once you have seen the effect of this, delete the changes you made and change the formula in cell G10 to **=F10*$E$5.**

14. To copy the formula from G10 to cells G11 to G16, ***click in cell G10, click the AutoFill handle*** (the little black box at the lower right corner of the cell), ***and drag the mouse pointer down to cell G16.***

15. In cell F11, type **=F10+G10+D11−E11**. The formula adds the accrued amount in the previous month to the previous month's interest and the current support due, and then subtracts the current amount paid.

16. To copy the formula from F11 to cells F12 to F16, ***click in cell F11, click the AutoFill handle, and drag the pointer down to cell F16.***

17. ***Click in cell D10 and drag the pointer to cell G16. Right-click; then click Format Cells. Click the Number tab, click Currency, and then click OK.***

18. Notice that the spreadsheet is very plain. We will use the Cell Styles feature to give the spreadsheet some color. ***Click in cell C7 and drag the pointer to cell G8. From the Styles Group on the Home tab, click the down arrow next to Cell Styles. Click Accent4*** (it is solid purple with white letters).

19. ***Click in cell C9 and drag the pointer to cell G16. From the Styles group on the Home tab, click the down arrow next to Cell Styles. Click***

20%—Accent1. (It is light blue with black letters.) ***Click in any cell to make the highlighting disappear.***

20. To add borders to the spreadsheet, ***click in cell C9 and drag the mouse pointer to cell G16. Then, from the Font group on the Home tab, click the down arrow next to the Border icon. Next, click the All Borders icon*** (it looks like a windowpane).

21. ***Click in cell E5. From the Font group on the Home tab, click the down arrow next to Borders. Then, click Thick Box border.*** Press the **[ENTER]** key. The spreadsheet is now complete and should look like Excel 2010 Exhibit 7.

22. To print the spreadsheet, ***click the File tab, then click Print, and then click Print.***

23. To save the spreadsheet, ***click the File tab and then click Save. Under Save in:, select the drive or folder*** in which you would like to save the document. Then, next to File Name, type **Child Support Payments** and ***click Save.***

24. To quit Excel, ***click the File tab and then click Exit.***

This concludes Lesson 4.

LESSON 5: LOAN AMORTIZATION TEMPLATE

This lesson shows you how to open a loan amortization template and fill it in (see Excel 2010 Exhibit 8). Templates are a great way to simplify complicated spreadsheets. You will also learn how to protect cells, freeze panes, split a screen, hide a column, and use the Format Painter tool. This lesson assumes that you have successfully completed Lessons 1 through 4. Keep in mind that if at any time you make a mistake in this lesson, you may press **[CTRL]+[Z]** to undo what you have done.

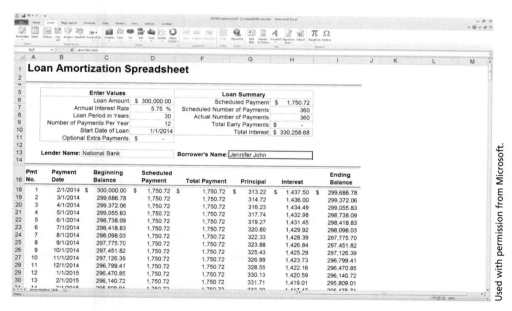

EXCEL 2010 EXHIBIT 8
Loan amortization
template

1. Open Windows. When it has loaded, ***double-click the Microsoft Office Excel 2010 icon on the desktop*** to open the program. Alternatively, ***click the Start button, point to Programs or All Programs, point to Microsoft Office, and then click Microsoft Excel 2010.*** You should now be in a clean, blank workbook.

2. The first thing you will do to complete the template in Excel 2010 Exhibit 8 is to open the "Lesson 5" file from the disk supplied with this text. Ensure that

the disk is inserted in the disk drive. *Click on File on the File tab, then click on Open.* The "Open" window should now be displayed. *Click on the down arrow to the right of the white box next to Look in: and select the drive where the disk is located. Double-click on the Excel Files folder. Double-click on the "Lesson 5" file.* You may also access the file from the Premium Website. To do so, go to your CengageBrain account and *click on the link for Premium Website* for Cornick's *Using Computers in the Law Office—Basic.* A new window will open. *Under Book Level Resources, click the link for Data Files: Excel, then click the link to Lesson 5.* When prompted, *click Open.*

3. You should now have the Loan Amortization Spreadsheet shown in Excel 2010 Exhibit 8 opened, except that your spreadsheet has no data yet.

4. Enter the following information:
Cell D6: **300000**
Cell D7: **5.75**
Cell D8: **20**
Cell D9: **12**
Cell D10: **1/1/2014**
Cell D11: **0** (When you click in Cell D11, a note will appear regarding extra payments; just type **0** (a zero) and press the [**ENTER**] key and the note will disappear.)
Cell C13: **National Bank**
Cell G13: **Jennifer John**

5. Notice that your spreadsheet now appears nearly identical to Excel 2010 Exhibit 8.

6. Notice that in your spreadsheet, just about everything below row 16 is a formula. If a user accidentally deletes one of these formulas, the whole spreadsheet could be affected. You will now turn on the Protection feature and lock some of the cells so they cannot be accidentally deleted.

7. *Right-click in cell D6. Then click Format Cells... . Click the Protection tab in the "Format Cells" window.* Notice that there is no green check mark next to Locked. Cells D6 to D13 and cell G13 are unlocked even when the Protection feature is turned on. When the Protection feature is off, you can change the lock/unlock format of cells by using the *right-click, Format Cells... > Protection* command sequence. Interestingly, when a new blank spreadsheet is opened in Excel, all cells default to "Locked," but this has no effect because the Protection feature is always turned off in a blank workbook.

8. *Click Cancel in the "Format Cells" window* to close the window.

9. Let's open a new spreadsheet so you can see that all cells in Excel start out with the format locked. *Click the File tab, then click New, and then double-click Blank Workbook.*

10. You should now have a new blank spreadsheet displayed. *Right-click in any cell and then click Format Cells... . Next, click the Protection tab.* Notice that the cell is locked. However, the cell is not truly locked until you turn on the Protection feature.

11. *Click Cancel in the "Format Cells" window in the new spreadsheet. Click the File tab and then click Close* to close the file. You should now be back at your amortization spreadsheet.

12. To turn on the Protection feature, *on the Review tab, click Protect Sheet in the Changes group.*

13. The "Protect Sheet" window should now be displayed (see Excel 2010 Exhibit 9). Make sure that the first two selections under Allow all users of this worksheet to: are selected (e.g., Select locked cells and Select Unlocked Cells). Notice that you could enter a password in the white box under Password to unprotect sheet. This would completely lock the spreadsheet (so only unlocked cells could be modified) to users who did not know the password. In this case this is not necessary; it is fine for someone to intentionally change the values at the top of the spreadsheet—we are just using this feature to prevent someone from accidentally changing the formulas below row 16.

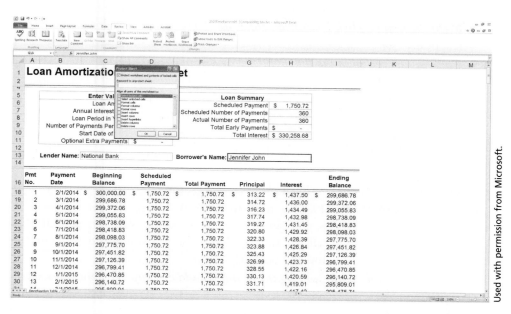

EXCEL 2010 EXHIBIT 9
Protecting cells

Used with permission from Microsoft.

HANDS-ON EXERCISES

14. After the first two items are check-marked under Allow all users of this worksheet to:, *click OK.*

15. *Click in any cell other than D6 to D13 or cell G13* and try to type something in the cell. You should get an error message that says **"The cell [or chart] you are trying to change is protected and therefore read-only."** *Click OK* to close the error window.

16. The whole spreadsheet is now locked, except for cells D6 to D13 and cell G13, because these were not formatted as locked in the template.

17. Now you will turn off the Protection feature because you are still building the spreadsheet. *On the Review tab, click Unprotect Sheet in the Changes group.*

18. You will now use the Format Painter tool to copy the formatting from one set of cells to another set of cells. Notice that cells F13 and G13 do not look like cells B13 and C13. You will copy the format from cells B13 and C13 to cells F13 and G13.

19. *Point in cell B13 and drag the pointer to cell C13. Next, on the Home tab, click the Format Painter icon in the Clipboard group.* (It looks like a paintbrush). Your pointer now should have a paintbrush icon on it.

20. *Click in cell F13, drag the pointer to cell H13, and then let go of the mouse button. Click anywhere to see the cell.* Notice that the formatting has now been copied.

21. Column E in the amortization schedule of the spreadsheet is the "Extra Payment" column. Assume for the purposes of this exercise that you will not have any extra payments and that you do not need this column, but you want to leave the column there in case you need it at a later date. For now, you can hide column E until you need it later.

22. *Right-click on the "E" in the E column heading* (see Excel 2010 Exhibit 9). *From the drop-down menu, click Hide.*

23. *Click in any cell.* The vertical line will disappear. Notice that column E is no longer displayed. The column heading goes from D to F.

24. We will now Unhide column E. *Point on the D column heading and drag the pointer to the F column heading so that both columns are highlighted. Right-click, then click Unhide on the drop-down menu.* Notice that column E reappears.

25. *Click in any cell to make the highlighting disappear.*

26. *Click in cell D18.* Use the [**DOWN ARROW**] key to go to cell D50. Notice that the some column titles, such as "Pmt No.," and "Payment Date," are no longer visible, so it is difficult to know what the numbers mean.

27. Press [**CTRL**]+[**HOME**] to go to the top of the spreadsheet.

28. *Click cell A18.* You will now use the Split Screen command to see the column titles.

29. *On the View tab, click Split in the Window group.*

30. Use the [**DOWN ARROW**] key to go to cell A50. Notice that because you split the screen at row 18, you can still see column titles. Next, use the [**UP ARROW**] key to go to cell A1. You should now see the top portion of your spreadsheet in both the top and bottom screens.

31. *On the View tab, click Split again in the Window group.* The bottom screen is now gone.

32. The Freeze Panes feature is another way to show the column headings when you scroll down a document. The Freeze Panes feature is a convenient way to see both column and row titles at the same time. *Click in cell B18.*

33. *On the View tab, click Freeze Panes in the Window group and then click the first option, Freeze Panes.*

34. Use the [**DOWN ARROW**] key to go to cell B50. Notice that because you froze the screen at cell B18, you can still see column titles. Next, use the [**RIGHT ARROW**] key to go to cell R50. You should still see the "Pmt No." column, including the payment numbers.

35. Press [**CTRL**]+[**HOME**] to go to the beginning of the spreadsheet.

36. *On the View tab, click Freeze Panes in the Window group and then click the first option, Unfreeze Panes.*

37. To print the spreadsheet, *click the File tab, then click Print, and then click Print.*

38. To save the spreadsheet, *click the File tab and then click Save As. Under Save in:, select the drive or folder* in which you would like to save the document. Next to File Name, type **Excel Lesson 5 Spreadsheet DONE** and *click Save.*

39. Templates are a great way to utilize the power of Excel. There are many free templates available on the Internet. Microsoft alone offers more than 100 Excel templates on its website. To access them, *click the File tab, then New.* They are listed to the left under Office.com Templates.

40. To quit Excel, *click the File tab and then click Exit.*

This concludes Lesson 5.

LESSON 6: STATISTICAL FUNCTIONS

This lesson demonstrates how to use and enter statistical formulas such as average, maximum, minimum, and standard deviation. It also shows how to sort data, check for metadata in spreadsheets, use the Format Clear command, use conditional formatting, and insert a clip-art file. When the spreadsheet is complete, it will look like Excel 2010 Exhibit 10. Keep in mind that if at any time you make a mistake in this lesson, you may press **[CTRL]+[Z]** to undo what you have done.

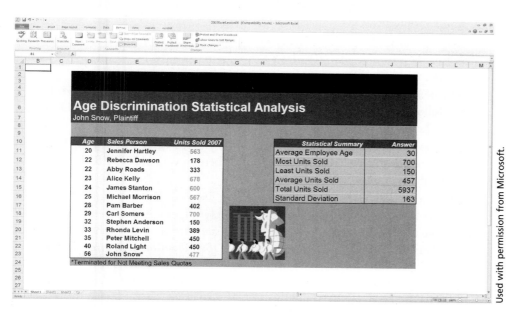

EXCEL 2010 EXHIBIT 10
Statistical spreadsheet

HANDS-ON EXERCISES

1. Open Windows. When it has loaded, ***double-click the Microsoft Office Excel 2010 icon on the desktop*** to open the program. Alternatively, ***click the Start button, point to Programs or All Programs, point to Microsoft Office, and then click Microsoft Excel 2010.*** You should now be in a clean, blank workbook. If you are not in a blank workbook, ***click the File tab*** (see Excel 2010 Exhibit 1), ***then click New, and then double-click on Blank Workbook.***

2. The first thing you will do to complete the template shown in Excel 2010 Exhibit 8 is to open the "Lesson 6" file from the disk supplied with this text. Ensure that the disk is inserted in the disk drive. ***Then, click on File on the File tab, and click on Open.*** The "Open" window should now be displayed. ***Click on the down arrow to the right of the white box next to Look in: and select the drive where the disk is located. Double-click on the Excel Files folder. Double-click on the "Lesson 6" file.*** You may also access this file from the Premium Website. To do so, go to your CengageBrain account and ***click on the link for Premium Website*** for Cornick's *Using Computers in the Law Office—Basic.* A new window will open. ***Under Book Level Resources, click the link for Data Files: Excel, then click the link to Lesson 6.*** When prompted, ***click Open.***

3. You should now see the Age Discrimination Statistical Analysis spreadsheet shown in Excel 2010 Exhibit 10, except your spreadsheet has no formulas in the statistical summary section, the data have not yet been sorted, and there is no clip art yet.

4. You will now enter the formulas in the Statistical Summary section of the spreadsheet. The first formula will calculate the average age of employees of the company. *Click in cell J11.* Type the following formula: **=AVERAGE(D11:D23)** and then press the **[ENTER]** key. The result should be 30. *Note:* Another way to enter the average function is to *go to the Formulas tab and click Insert Function in the Function Library group; next to Or select a category, click the down arrow, then click Statistical, average, and OK.*

5. The next formula will calculate the most units sold. *Click in cell J12.* Type the following formula: **=MAX(F11:F23)** and then press the **[ENTER]** key. The result should be 700.

6. The next formula will calculate the least units sold. *Click in cell J13.* Type the following formula: **=MIN(F11:F23)** and then press the **[ENTER]** key. The result should be 150.

7. The next formula will calculate the average units sold. *Click in cell J14.* Type the following formula: **=AVERAGE(F11:F23)** and then press the **[ENTER]** key. The result should be 457.

8. The next formula will calculate the total units sold. *Click in cell J15.* Type the following formula: **=SUM(F11:F23)** and then press the **[ENTER]** key. The result should be 5937.

9. The last formula will calculate the standard deviation for units sold. The standard deviation is a measure of how widely values are dispersed from the average value (the arithmetic mean). Large standard deviations show that the numbers vary widely from the average. *On the Formulas tab, click Insert Function in the Function Library group. Next to Or select a category, click the down arrow and select Statistical. Then, scroll down the list and click STDEV.P* (see Excel 2010 Exhibit 11). Notice there is a definition for this function. *Click OK in the "Insert Function" window.*

EXCEL 2010 EXHIBIT 11
Entering a standard deviation formula using the insert function command

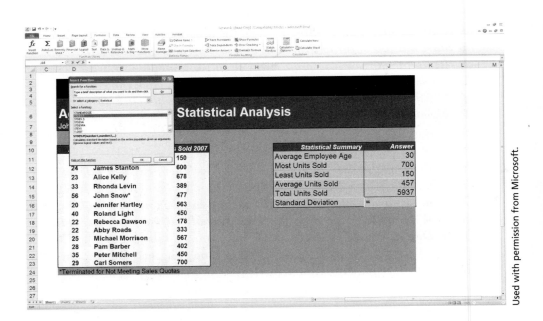

Used with permission from Microsoft.

10. The "Function Arguments" window should now be displayed (see Excel 2010 Exhibit 12). In the "Function Arguments" window, next to Number 1, press **[DEL]** until the box is blank; type **F11:F23** and then *click OK.* The result should be 163.

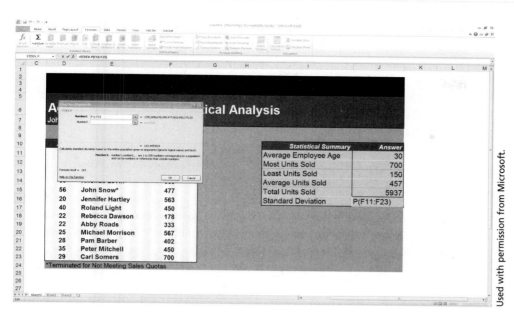

EXCEL 2010 EXHIBIT 12
Entering a standard deviation formula using the functions argument window

11. You will now sort the data based on the age of the employees. ***Click in D11 and then drag the pointer down to F23. From the Data tab, click Sort in the Sort and Filter group.***

12. The "Sort" window should now be displayed (see Excel 2010 Exhibit 13). *Note*: Even though you just want to sort by age, you must select the full data range that includes all of the information, or the age data will be sorted but the other columns and rows will stay where they are. The data will therefore be mismatched (each age will not be matched with the correct person and number of units sold).

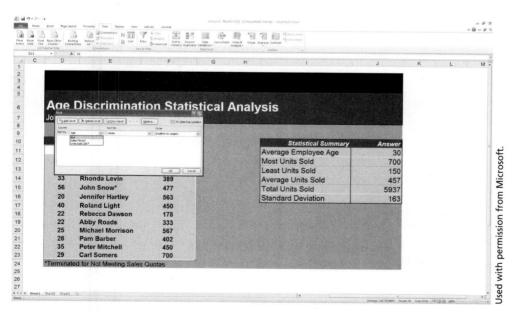

EXCEL 2010 EXHIBIT 13
Sorting data

13. ***In the "Sort" window, click the down arrow next to Sort by, then click Age*** (see Excel 2010 Exhibit 13). Notice that under Order, the default of Smallest to Largest is selected; this is fine, so ***click OK in the "Sort" window.*** The data

should now be sorted according to the age of the individual, with John Snow appearing last in the spreadsheet.

14. You will now ensure that no metadata is included in your document. You must first save the spreadsheet. To save the spreadsheet, *click the File tab and then click Save As. Under Save in:, select the drive or folder* in which you would like to save the document. Next to File Name, type **Excel Lesson 6 Spreadsheet DONE** and *click Save.*

15. Excel 2010 has a special feature called Inspect Document that can extract all metadata from your spreadsheet. *Click the File tab; next to Prepare for Sharing, click Check for Issues, then click Inspect Document* (see Excel 2010 Exhibit 14). Through the "Document Inspector" window, all of the possible places metadata can hide are checked. *Click Inspect.* Some of the categories may have a Remove All button. If you wanted to remove the metadata, you would just click on Remove All for each category. Because this is just an exercise, we do not need to remove the metadata, so go ahead and *click Close* to close the "Document Inspector" window.

EXCEL 2010 EXHIBIT 14
Removing metadata

Used with permission from Microsoft.

16. Sometimes it is helpful to clear a cell or cells of all formatting information at one time. Notice that cell D6, the one titled "Age Discrimination Statistical Analysis," is elaborately formatted, including 24-point font, white letters, red background, and bold text. You will now quickly remove all of the formatting. *Click in cell D6. Then, on the Home tab, click the down arrow next to the Clear icon in the Editing group* (it looks like an eraser—see Excel 2010 Exhibit 15). *Click Clear Formats.* All of the formatting should be gone. Notice in Excel 2010 Exhibit 15 that one of the options when using the Clear command is Clear All. Clicking Clear All will not only clear the formatting, but will also clear the contents of the selected cell(s).

17. Press **[CTRL]+[Z]** (invoking the Undo feature) to restore the original formatting to the cell.

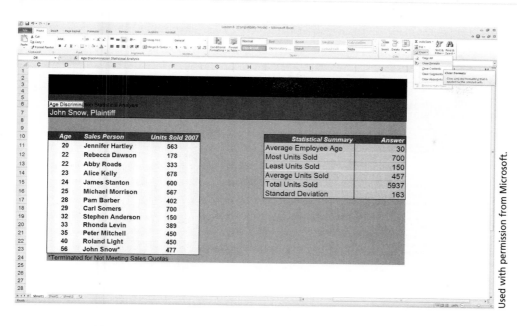

EXCEL 2010 EXHIBIT 15
Clear command

18. Sometimes, particularly in large spreadsheets, it is helpful to have the formatting of a cell change if certain conditions are present. For example, in an actual-versus-budget report, if an item goes over budget by more than 10 percent it might be helpful for that to be bolded so it catches the reader's attention. To accomplish this, you will now learn how to use the Conditional Formatting feature of Excel.

19. Notice that the average sales for the sales team in your spreadsheet is 457. It might be helpful to highlight any salesperson who was over the average. *Click in F11 and then drag the pointer to F23. From the Home tab, click Conditional Formatting in the Styles group* (see Excel 2010 Exhibit 16).

20. *Now, point to the first option, Highlight Cells Rules, and then click the first option again, which is Greater Than* (see Excel 2010 Exhibit 16).

21. The "Greater Than" window should now be displayed (see Excel 2010 Exhibit 17). Press the **[DEL]** key to remove the value under Format Cells that are GREATER THAN:.

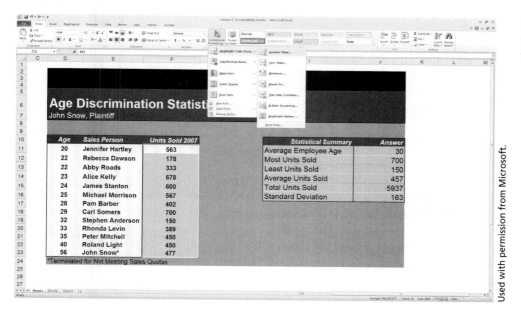

EXCEL 2010 EXHIBIT 16
Creating conditional formatting

EXCEL 2010 EXHIBIT 17
Creating a "Greater
Than" conditional
formatting

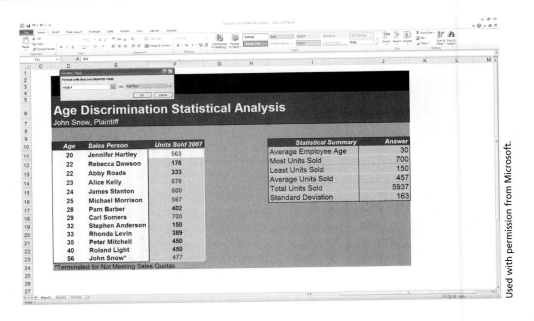

Used with permission from Microsoft.

22. *Click cell J14 on the spreadsheet.* Notice that cell J14 has been entered under Format Cells that are GREATER THAN:. Dollar signs have been added to the cell reference because this is an absolute cell reference.

23. *Click the down arrow next to Light Red Fill with Dark Red Text and select Red Text.* Cells over the average will be shown in red text. *Click OK in the "Greater Than" window.*

24. You will now add clip art to your spreadsheet (assuming that clip art was included when Excel 2010 was installed). *Click in cell I18. Then, from the Insert tab, click Clip Art in the Illustrations group.*

25. The Clip Art task pane will appear to the right of the screen. Under Search For: type **Money** and then *click Go.* You may get a message that asks if you want to include clip art from Microsoft Office Online; *click No.*

26. *Click on the clip art in Excel 2010 Exhibit 10* (a blue bar chart with people in it and a person climbing a dollar sign). The clip art has now been added to your spreadsheet. *Position the clip art where you want it by clicking and dragging it into position.*

27. *Click the "X" in the Clip Art task pane to close the task pane.*

28. To print the spreadsheet, *click the File tab, then click Print, and then click Print.*

29. To save the spreadsheet, *click the File tab and then click Save As.* Choose the directory in which you want to save the file and *click Save.*

30. To quit Excel, *click the File tab and then click Exit.*

This concludes Lesson 6.

▶ ADVANCED LESSONS

LESSON 7: TOOLS AND TECHNIQUES 1—MARKETING BUDGET

In this lesson, you will learn how to create visual impact with spreadsheets. You will learn to create and manipulate a text box, use advanced shading techniques, create a 3-D style text box, create vertical text, create diagonal text, use lines and borders, and

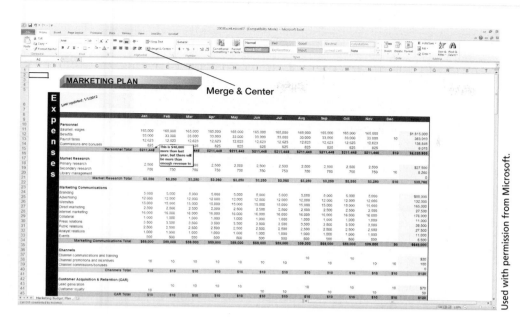

EXCEL 2010 EXHIBIT 18
Creating visual impact in spreadsheets

create a comment. When the spreadsheet is complete, it will look like Excel 2010 Exhibit 18. Keep in mind that if at any time you make a mistake in this lesson, you may press **[CTRL]+[Z]** to undo what you have done.

1. Open Windows. When it has loaded, ***double-click the Microsoft Office Excel 2010 icon on the desktop*** to open the program. Alternatively, ***click the Start button, point to Programs or All Programs, point to Microsoft Office, and then click Microsoft Excel 2010.*** You should now be in a clean, blank workbook.

2. The first thing you will do to complete the spreadsheet in Excel 2010 Exhibit 18 is to open the "Lesson 7" file from the disk supplied with this text. Ensure that the disk is inserted in the disk drive. ***Click on File on the File tab, and then click on Open.*** The "Open" window should now be displayed. ***Click on the down arrow to the right of the white box next to Look in: and select the drive where the disk is located. Double-click on the Excel Files folder. Double-click on the "Lesson 7" file.*** You may also access this file from the Premium Website. To do so, go to your CengageBrain account and ***click on the link for Premium Website*** for Cornick's *Using Computers in the Law Office— Basic.* A new window will open. ***Under Book Level Resources, click the link for Data Files: Excel, then click the link to Lesson 7.*** When prompted, ***click Open.***

3. You should now have the Marketing Plan spreadsheet in Excel 2010 Exhibit 18 opened, except the spreadsheet is missing some of the formatting that gives it visual impact. You will add the formatting to the spreadsheet to make it more visually compelling.

4. You will first add the text box that holds the title "Marketing Plan," as shown in Excel 2010 Exhibit 18. ***From the Insert tab, click Text Box in the Text group.*** Notice that your mouse pointer just turned into an upside down letter "T."

5. ***Point to cell C2 and drag the pointer to about cell F4.*** An outline of a box should now be shown from C2 to F4. This is a *text box.*

6. ***Click inside the text box. Click the Bold icon and change the font size to 20.***

7. Type **MARKETING PLAN.**

EXCEL 2010 EXHIBIT 19
Formatting a shape

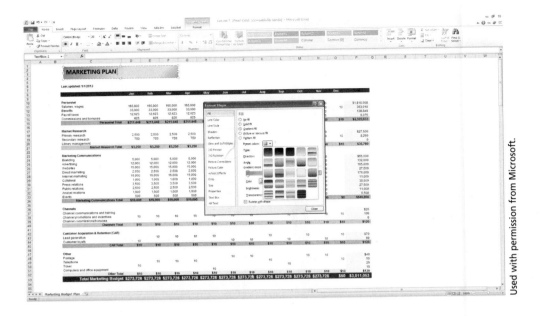

8. *Right-click on the outline of the text box you just created. In the drop-down menu, click Format Shape.* The "Format Shape" window should now be displayed (see Excel 2010 Exhibit 19).

9. *In the "Format Shape" window, notice that Fill is currently selected. Click Gradient fill.*

10. *Click the down arrow next to Preset Colors.* This will open a box with many colors; *click Fog.*

11. *Staying in the "Format Shape" window, point to the down arrow next to Type: and click Linear.*

12. *Still in the "Format Shape" window, click 3-D Format on the left side of the window.* You will now add a 3-D style to the text box. *When the 3-D style choices appear, under Bevel and next to Top, point to the down arrow and click the first selection under Bevel, which is Circle* (see Excel 2010 Exhibit 20).

EXCEL 2010 EXHIBIT 20
Adding 3-D effect to a text box

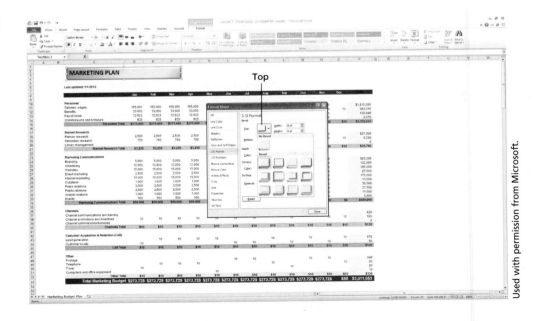

13. *Click Close to close the "Format Shape" window. Click in any other cell so you can see the effect.*

14. You will now create the vertical text in Column B that says "Expenses," as shown in Excel 2010 Exhibit 18. Notice that this is actually one long cell. The first thing you will do is to merge cells B6 through B53 into one cell; you will then add the text and format it to be vertical.

15. *Click in cell B6, drag the pointer down to cell B53, and then let go of the mouse button.*

16. *From the Home tab, click the Merge and Center icon in the Alignment group.* It looks like a box with an "a" in the middle, with left and right arrows around the "a" (see Excel 2010 Exhibit 18). Notice that the selected cells have now been merged into one cell from B6 to B53.

17. With the cursor still in cell B6, *change the Font Size to 22 and click the Bold icon.* Type **Expenses** and press the [**ENTER**] key. The text is shown at the bottom of the cell; you will now correct this.

18. *Right-click anywhere in cell B6; then click Format Cells… .* The "Format Cells" window should now be displayed. *Click the Alignment tab* (see Excel 2010 Exhibit 21).

19. *In the "Format Cells" window, under Orientation, click the box that shows the word* Text *displayed vertically* (see Excel 2010 Exhibit 21).

20. *In the "Format Cells" window, under Vertical, click the down arrow and select Top (Indent).*

21. *Click OK in the "Format Cells" window.* The word "Expenses" should now be displayed vertically down the cell.

22. *With the pointer still in cell B6, on the Home tab, click the down arrow next to the Fill Color icon* (a paint bucket) *in the Font group and then select Black.*

23. *On the Home tab, click the down arrow next to the Font Color icon and select Yellow.*

24. You will next make the text in cell C6 appear diagonally. *Right-click in cell C6; then click Format Cells… .* The "Format Cells" window should now be displayed and the Alignment tab should be selected.

HANDS-ON EXERCISES

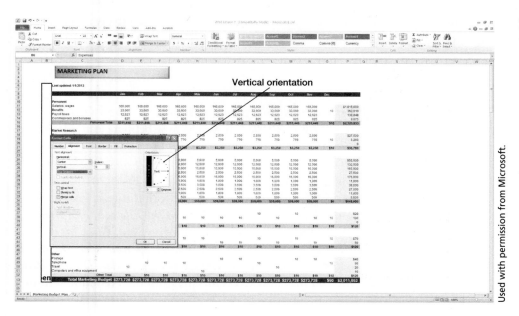

EXCEL 2010 EXHIBIT 21
Creating vertical text

25. *In the "Format Cells" window, under Orientation, click the up arrow next to Degrees until it reads "15 degrees."*

26. *In the "Format Cells" window, click the Fill tab. Click the yellow square; then click OK.*

27. *Click in any cell to make the highlighting disappear.* The words "Last updated 1/1/2008" should now be displayed diagonally in black letters with a yellow background.

28. You will now add the Comment shown in Excel 2010 Exhibit 18. *Right-click in cell D15. On the drop-down menu, click Insert Comment.* Type **This is $40,000 more than last year, but there will be more than enough revenue to cover this.** *Click in any cell to exit the Comment box.*

29. *Hover your cursor over cell D15* so you can see the comment.

30. You will now add borders to the spreadsheet. *Point to cell C53 and drag the pointer to cell P53. Then, on the Home tab, click the down arrow next to the Borders icon in the Font group and click All Borders.* The "Totals" row should now have borders around each cell.

31. *Click in cell C8 and drag the pointer to cell P53. Then, on the Home tab, click the down arrow next to the Borders icon in the Font group, and then click Thick Box border.* A thick border now surrounds the data.

32. To print the spreadsheet, *click the File tab, then click Print, and then click Print.*

33. To save the spreadsheet, *click the File tab and then click Save As. Under Save in:, select the drive or folder* in which you would like to save the document. Next to File Name:, type **Excel Lesson 7 Spreadsheet DONE** and *click Save.*

34. To quit Excel, *click the File tab and then click Exit.*

This concludes Lesson 7.

LESSON 8: TOOLS AND TECHNIQUES 2—STOCK PORTFOLIO

In this lesson, you will continue to learn and apply helpful tools and techniques using Excel. This includes getting additional practice with using the Merge & Center tool, using the formula auditing feature, using the Oval tool, and password-protecting a file. When your spreadsheet is complete, it will look similar to Excel 2010 Exhibit 22. Some of these tools have been covered in previous lessons, and this lesson will help cement your ability to use them effectively. This tutorial assumes that you have completed Lessons 1 through 7, and that you are quite familiar with Excel.

1. Open Windows. When it has loaded, *double-click the Microsoft Office Excel 2010 icon on the desktop* to open the program. Alternatively, *click the Start button, point to Programs or All Programs, point on Microsoft Office, and then click Microsoft Excel 2010.* You should now be in a clean, blank workbook. If you are not in a blank workbook, *click the File tab* (see Excel 2010 Exhibit 1), *then click New, and then double-click Blank Workbook.*

2. The first thing you will do to complete the spreadsheet in Excel 2010 Exhibit 22 is to open the "Lesson 8" file from the disk supplied with this text. Ensure that the disk is inserted in the disk drive. *Click on File on the File tab, and then click on Open.* The "Open" window should now be displayed. *Click on the down arrow to the right of the white box next to Look in: and select the drive where the disk is located. Double-click on the Excel Files folder. Double-click on the "Lesson 8" file.* You may also access this file from the Premium Website.

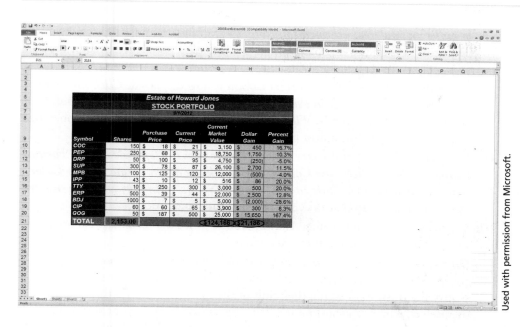

EXCEL 2010 EXHIBIT 22
Stock portfolio

Used with permission from Microsoft.

To do so, go to your CengageBrain account and *click on the link for Premium Website* for Cornick's *Using Computers in the Law Office—Basic.* A new window will open. *Under Book Level Resources, click the link for Data Files: Excel, then click the link to Lesson 8.* When prompted, *click Open.*

3. You should now have the stock portfolio spreadsheet shown in Excel 2010 Exhibit 22 opened, except the spreadsheet will be missing two rows of data and some of the formatting. You will add the rows and formatting to the spreadsheet.

4. *Use the Merge and Center icon on the Home tab in the Alignment group to merge cells C5 to I5.*

5. *Use the Merge and Center icon on the toolbar to merge cells C6 to I6.*

6. *Use the Merge and Center icon to merge cells C7 to I7.*

7. Make sure the titles are aligned as shown in Excel 2010 Exhibit 22 *(use the Left and Center Align icons on the Home tab in the Alignment group).*

8. *Use the Fill Color icon on the Home tab, in the Font group, to make the fill color for cell C5 dark blue* (or any color you choose).

9. *Use the Fill Color icon to make the fill color for cell C6 purple* (any light purple is fine).

10. *Use the Fill Color icon to make the fill color for cell C7 gray* (any light gray is fine).

11. The cell range from C8 to I8 is a text graphic box (similar to a text box, except that it is just more difficult to see). *Right-click the box and select Format Shape. Then, in the Fill section, click Gradient fill; next to Preset Color, click on the first one, Early Sunset* (just hover your cursor over a color and the name will be displayed). *Under Direction, click the first option, Linear Diagonal; then click Close to close the "Format Shape" window.*

12. *Use the Borders icon on the Home tab, in the Font group, to give cells D10 to I21 a border of All Borders.*

13. *From the Insert tab, click Shapes in the Illustrations group. Under Basic Shapes, click the Oval tool* (it should be the second shape). *Start in the upper left corner of cell G21 and drag the pointer to the lower right corner of G21*

HANDS-ON EXERCISES

to make an oval around the total. *Note:* You can slightly move the oval by using the cursor keys on the keyboard to nudge it into place so it is centered in the cell.

14. The color of the oval must now be corrected. Notice that the ribbon has changed: the Drawing Tools Format ribbon is now displayed. ***Click the down arrow next to Shape Fill in the Shape Styles group of the Drawing Tools Format tab. Then, click No Fill.*** The oval is now surrounding the number, but the line color of the oval must be changed.

15. ***Right-click the oval and select Format Shape. On the left side of the "Format Shape" window, click Line Color. Then, click the down arrow next to Color, click Black, and click Close in the "Format Shape" window.*** Make an oval in cell H21 identical to that in cell G21 using the same process.

16. You will now use the Formula Auditing mode to see the formulas that are in the spreadsheet and to ensure they are accurate.

17. ***On the Formulas tab, click Show Formulas in the Formula Auditing group.*** Scroll over to the right and look at all of the cells in your spreadsheet. Notice that instead of seeing the result of the formulas, you see the formulas themselves. This is a great tool for checking the accuracy of your spreadsheets. Look at your formulas and make sure they are correct. When you are sure your formulas are accurate, ***turn off the Formula Auditing mode by clicking on Show Formulas again.***

18. You will now learn how to password-protect your spreadsheet files. ***Click the File tab and then click Save As. In the "Save As" window, click Tools*** (it is in the lower portion of the window) and then ***click General Options... .*** Under File Sharing and next to Password to open, type **A** and ***click OK.*** At the "Confirm Password" window, type **A**, and then ***click OK.*** At the "Save As" window, ***click Save*** to save the file to My Documents (or the folder of your choice—you must remember where you save it). You will then get a prompt that asks you whether you want to increase the security of the document by conversion to Office Open XML Format. Because this is just an exercise, ***click No.***

19. If you get a compatibility prompt, just ***click Continue.***

20. ***Click the File tab and then click Close to close the file.***

21. ***Now, click the File tab, and under Recent Documents click on the file you just saved.***

22. The "Password" window should now be displayed. Type **A** in the "Password" window. (The password is case sensitive, so if you typed a capital A when you created the password, you must type a capital A to open the document.) ***Click OK.*** The file should now be displayed.

23. You can turn off a password in the same way. ***Click the File tab, and then Save As. In the "Save As" window, click Tools and then click on General Options... .*** Under File Sharing and next to Password to open, use the [DEL] key to remove the asterisk. ***Then, click OK and click Save.*** At the "**Do you want to replace the existing file?**" prompt, ***click Yes.***

24. If you get a compatibility prompt, just ***click Continue.***

25. Close the file and then reopen it, and you will see that you no longer need a password to open it.

26. To print the spreadsheet, ***click the File tab, then click Print, and then click Print.***

27. To quit Excel, ***click the File tab and then click Exit.***

This concludes the Excel 2010 Hands-On Exercises.

HANDS-ON EXERCISES

MICROSOFT EXCEL 2007 FOR WINDOWS

Number	Lesson Title	Concepts Covered
BASIC LESSONS		
Lesson 1	Building a Budget Spreadsheet, Part 1	[CTRL]+[HOME] command, moving the pointer, entering text and values, adjusting the width of columns, changing the format of a group of cells to currency, using bold, centering text, entering formulas, using the AutoFill/ Copy command to copy formulas, printing and saving a spreadsheet
Lesson 2	Building a Budget Spreadsheet, Part 2	Opening a file, inserting rows, changing the format of cells to percent, building more formulas, creating a bar chart with the Chart Wizard, printing a selection, fitting/ compressing data to one printed page
Lesson 3	Building a Damage Projection Spreadsheet	Changing font size, font color, using the AutoSum feature, using the wrap text feature, creating borders, setting decimal points when formatting numbers
INTERMEDIATE LESSONS		
Lesson 4	Child Support Payment Spreadsheet	Creating a white background, creating formulas that multiply cells, creating formulas that use absolute cell references, using the AutoFormat feature
Lesson 5	Loan Amortization Template	Using a template, protecting cells, freezing panes, splitting a screen, hiding columns, using Format Painter
Lesson 6	Statistical Functions	Using functions including average, maximum, minimum, and standard deviation; sorting data; checking for metadata; using the Format Clear command; using conditional formatting; inserting a picture
ADVANCED LESSONS		
Lesson 7	Tools and Techniques 1—Marketing Budget	Creating and manipulating a text box, advanced shading techniques, working with a 3-D style text box, creating vertical and diagonal text, creating a cell comment, using lines and borders
Lesson 8	Tools and Techniques 2—Stock Portfolio	Using the Merge and Center tool, using the Formula Auditing feature, using the oval tool, password-protecting a file

GETTING STARTED
Overview

Microsoft Excel 2007 is a powerful spreadsheet program that allows you to create formulas, "what if" scenarios, graphs, and much more.

Introduction

Throughout these lessons and exercises, information you need to operate the program will be designated in several different ways:

- Keys to be pressed on the keyboard are designated in brackets, in all caps, and in bold (e.g., press the **[ENTER]** key).
- Movements with the mouse pointer are designated in bold and italics (e.g., ***point to File and click***).
- Words or letters that should be typed are designated in bold (e.g., type **Training Program**).
- Information that is or should be displayed on your computer screen is shown in bold, with quotation marks (e.g., "**Press ENTER to continue.**").
- Specific menu items and commands are designated with an initial capital letter (e.g., click Open).

OVERVIEW OF EXCEL 2007
I. Worksheet

A. *Entering Commands: The Ribbon*—The primary way of entering commands in Excel 2007 is through the ribbon. The ribbon is a set of commands or tools that change depending on which ribbon is selected (see Excel 2007 Exhibit 1). There are seven ribbon tabs: Home, Insert, Page Layout, Formulas, Data, Review, and View (see Excel 2007 Exhibit 1). Each tab has groups of commands. For example, on the Home tab, the Font group contains a group of commands

EXCEL 2007 EXHIBIT 1
Excel 2007 interface

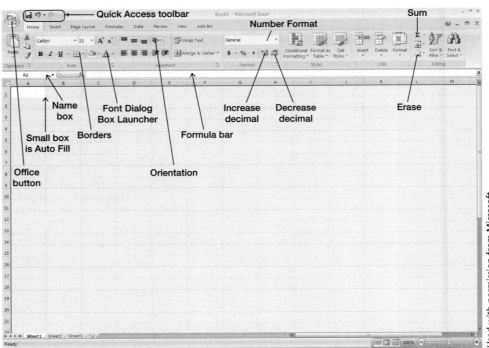

Used with permission from Microsoft.

that relate to font choice, font size, bold, italics, underlining, and other attributes (see Excel 2007 Exhibit 1).

B. *Office Button*—The Office button (see Excel 2007 Exhibit 1) is where a user accesses commands such as New, Open, Save, and Print. The Office button replaces the File menu that was used in previous versions of Excel.

C. *Entering Data*—To enter data, type the text or number in a cell, then press the **[ENTER]** key or one of the arrow (cursor) keys.

D. *Ranges*—A *range* is a group of contiguous cells. Cell ranges can be created by ***clicking and dragging the pointer*** or holding the **[SHIFT]** key down and using the arrow (cursor) keys.

E. *Format*—Cells can be formatted, including changing the font style, font size, shading, border, cell type (currency, percentage, etc.), alignment, and other attributes. To do this, ***click the Home ribbon tab, then click one of the Dialog Box Launchers in the Font group, Alignment group, or Number group.*** Each of these dialog box launchers brings up the same "Format Cells" window. You can also enter a number of formatting options directly from the Home tab.

F. *Editing a Cell*—You can edit a cell by ***clicking in the cell and then clicking in the formula bar.*** The formula bar is directly under the ribbon and just to the right of the **fx** sign (see Excel 2007 Exhibit 1). The formula bar shows the current contents of the selected cell, and it allows you to edit the cell contents. You can also edit the contents of a cell by ***clicking in the cell*** and then pressing the **[F2]** key.

G. *Column Width/Row Height*—You can change the width of a column by ***clicking the line to the right of the column heading***. (This is the line that separates two columns. When you point to a line, the cursor changes to a double-headed vertical arrow.) ***Drag the pointer to the right or left to increase or decrease the column width, respectively.*** Similarly, you can change the height of a row by ***clicking and dragging the horizontal line separating two rows***. You can also change the width of a column or height of a row by ***clicking somewhere in the column you want to change, clicking the Home tab, then clicking Format in the Cells group.***

H. *Insert*—You can insert one row or column by ***clicking the Home tab, then clicking the down arrow below the Insert icon in the Cells group, and clicking either Insert Sheet Rows or Insert Sheet Columns.*** You can also insert a number of rows or columns by ***dragging the pointer over the number of rows or columns you want to add, clicking the Home tab, clicking the down arrow below the Insert icon in the Cells group, and then clicking either Insert Sheet Rows or Insert Sheet Columns.*** Finally, you can ***right-click and select Insert from the menu.***

I. *Erase/Delete*—You can erase data by ***dragging the pointer over the area*** and then pressing the **[DEL]** key. You can also erase data by ***dragging the pointer over the area, clicking the Home ribbon tab, clicking the down arrow next to the Clear icon in the Editing group, and then clicking Clear All.*** You can delete whole columns or rows by ***pointing and clicking in a column or row, then clicking on the Home ribbon tab, clicking on the down arrow next to Delete in the Cells group, and then clicking either Delete Sheet Rows or Delete Sheet Columns.*** You can also delete whole columns or rows by ***pointing in the column or row and then right-clicking and selecting Delete.***

J. *Quit*—To quit Excel, ***click on the Office button and then click Exit Excel.***

K. *Copy*—To copy data to adjacent columns or rows, ***click in the cell you wish to copy and then select the AutoFill command,*** which is accessed from the small black box at the bottom right corner of the selected cell. ***Drag the pointer to where the data should be placed.*** You can also copy data by ***clicking in the cell, right-clicking, clicking Copy, clicking in the location where the information should be copied,*** and pressing the **[ENTER]** key. Finally, data can be copied by ***clicking and dragging to highlight the information to be copied, clicking the Home tab, then clicking Copy in the Clipboard group.***

L. *Move*—Move data by ***clicking in the cell, right-clicking, selecting Cut, clicking in the location where the information should be inserted,*** and pressing the **[ENTER]** key. Data can also be moved by ***highlighting the information to be copied, clicking the Home tab, then clicking Cut in the Clipboard group.*** Then go to the location where the information should be moved, ***click the Home tab, then click Paste in the Clipboard group.***

M. *Saving and Opening Files*—Save a file by ***clicking the Office button, then clicking Save or Save As,*** and typing the file name. You can also save a file by ***clicking the Save icon*** (it looks like a floppy disk) on the Quick Access toolbar (see Excel 2007 Exhibit 1). Open a file that was previously saved by ***clicking the Office button, clicking Open,*** and typing (or clicking) the name of the file to be opened.

N. *Print*—You can print a file by ***clicking the Office button, then Print, then OK.***

II. Numbers and Formulas

A. *Numbers*—To enter a number in a cell, click in the cell, type the number, and press the **[ENTER]** key or an arrow (cursor) key.

B. *Adding Cells (Addition)*—You can add the contents of two or more cells by three different methods:

  1. To add the contents of a range of two or more cells:

    a. Click in the cell where the total should be placed.

    b. ***Click the Home tab, then click the Sum icon in the Editing group*** (see Excel 2007 Exhibit 2). The Sum icon looks like a Greek letter "E." *Note*: To see the name of an icon, point to the icon for a second and the name of the icon will be displayed.

    c. Excel guesses which cells you want to add. Press **[ENTER]** if the correct range has been automatically selected, or select the correct range by highlighting it (i.e., ***click and drag until the range of cells to be added is selected***). Then press **[ENTER]**.

  2. To add the contents of two cells, which need not comprise a range:

    a. ***Click in the cell where the total should be placed.***

    b. Press = (the equals sign).

    c. Type the address of the first cell to be added (e.g., B4); alternatively, ***click in that cell.***

    d. Press + (the plus sign).

    e. Enter the address of the second cell to be added (or ***click in that cell***).

    f. Press the **[ENTER]** key. (For example, to add the values of cells C4 and C5, you would type **=C4+C5**.)

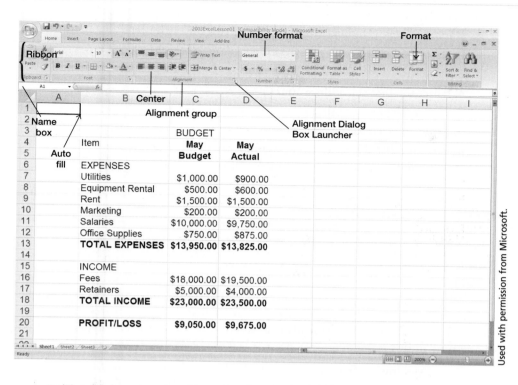

EXCEL 2007 EXHIBIT 2
Budgeting spreadsheet

3. To add the contents of a range of two or more cells:

   a. *Click in the cell where the total should be placed.*

   b. Type **=SUM(.**

   c. Enter the address of the first cell to be added (or *click in that cell*).

   d. Type **:** (a colon).

   e. Enter the address of the second cell to be added (or *click in it*).

   f. Type **)** (a closing parenthesis).

   g. Press the **[ENTER]** key. (For example, to add the values of C4 and C5, the formula would read **=SUM(C4:C5)**.)

C. *Subtracting Cells*—To subtract the contents of one or more cells from those of another:

   1. *Click in the cell where the result should be placed.*

   2. Press **=.**

   3. Enter the first cell address (or *click in it*).

   4. Press **–** (a minus sign).

   5. Enter the second cell address (or *click in it*).

   6. Press the **[ENTER]** key. (For example, to subtract the value of C4 from the value of C5, you would type **=C5–C4**.)

D. *Multiplying Cells*—To multiply the contents of two (or more) cells:

   1. *Click in the cell where the result should be placed.*

   2. Press **=.**

   3. Enter the first cell address (or *click in it*).

   4. Press ***** (**[SHIFT]+[8]**).

   5. Enter the second cell address (or *click in it*).

   6. Press the **[ENTER]** key. (For example, to multiply the value in C4 times the value in C5, you would type **=C5*C4**.)

E. *Dividing Cells*—To divide the contents of two (or more) cells:

1. ***Click in the cell where the result should be placed.***
2. Press =.
3. Enter the first cell address (or ***click in it***).
4. Press **/** (the forward slash).
5. Enter the second cell address (or ***click in it***).
6. Press the **[ENTER]** key. (For example, to divide the value in C4 by the value in C5, you would type **=C4/C5**.)

BASIC LESSONS

LESSON 1: BUILDING A BUDGET SPREADSHEET, PART 1

This lesson shows you how to build the spreadsheet in Excel 2007 Exhibit 2. It explains how to use the [CTRL]+[HOME] command; move the cell pointer; enter text, values, and formulas; adjust the width of columns; change the format of cells to currency; use the bold feature, use the AutoFill and Copy features to copy formulas; and print and save a spreadsheet. Keep in mind that if you make a mistake at any time in this lesson, you may press **[CTRL]+[Z]** to undo what you have done.

1. Open Windows. After it has loaded, ***double-click the Microsoft Office Excel 2007 icon on the desktop*** to open the program. Alternatively, ***click the Start button, point to Programs or All Programs, point to Microsoft Office, then click Microsoft Office Excel 2007.*** You should be in a new, clean, blank workbook. If you are not in a blank workbook, ***click the Office button*** (see Excel 2007 Exhibit 1), ***click on New, then double-click Blank Workbook.***

2. Notice that the pointer is at cell A1, and the indicator that displays the address of the current cell (called the "name" box in Excel) says A1. The "name" box is just under the ribbon and all the way to the left (see Excel 2007 Exhibit 2). Also, notice that you can move the pointer around the spreadsheet using the cursor keys. Go back to cell A1 by pressing the **[CTRL]+[HOME]** keys.

3. Go to cell C3 by ***clicking in cell C3*** or by pressing the **[RIGHT ARROW]** key twice, then pressing the **[DOWN ARROW]** key twice.

4. You will now enter the title of the spreadsheet in cell C3. Type **BUDGET** and then press the **[ENTER]** key.

5. Notice that the pointer is now at cell C4.

6. Press the **[UP ARROW]** key to go back to cell C3. Notice that BUDGET is left-aligned. To center BUDGET in the cell, ***from the Home tab, click the Center icon in the Alignment group.*** It is the icon with several lines on it that appear centered (see Excel 2007 Exhibit 3). *Note*: If you hover the mouse over an icon on the ribbon for a second, the name of the icon will be displayed. Alternatively, ***from the Home tab, click the Alignment Group Dialog Box Launcher. On the Alignment tab, under the Horizontal field, click the down arrow and select Center. Click OK.***

7. You should now be ready to enter the budget information. First, move the cell pointer to where the data should go, then type the data, and finally enter the data by pressing the **[ENTER]** key or one of the arrow (cursor) keys. Type the remaining row labels as follows:
   Item in B4.
   EXPENSES in B6.

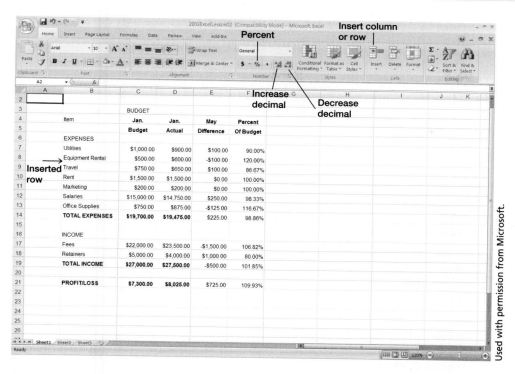

EXCEL 2007 EXHIBIT 3
Expanded budget
spreadsheet

Utilities in B7.
Equipment Rental in B8.
Rent in B9.
Marketing in B10.
Salaries in B11.
Office Supplies in B12.
TOTAL EXPENSES in B13.
INCOME in B15.
Fees in B16.
Retainers in B17.
TOTAL INCOME in B18.
PROFIT/LOSS in B20.

8. Notice in column B that some of the data entries (such as "EXPENSES" and "Equipment Rental") actually extend into column C. To correct this, you must increase the width of column B. ***Put the mouse pointer in the cell lettered B at the top of the screen. Move the pointer to the right edge of the cell.*** The pointer should then change to a double-headed vertical arrow and the column width will be displayed in a small box. ***Drag the pointer to the right until the column width is 18.00.*** Alternatively, you can change the cell width by ***placing the cell pointer anywhere in column B. Then, from the Home tab, click Format in the Cells group, then click Column Width...,*** type **18**, and ***click OK.***

9. Notice that all of the data entries now fit in the columns. Enter the following:
Jan in C4.
Budget in C5.
Jan in D4.
Actual in D5.

10. *Click in cell C4 and drag the pointer over to cell D5* (so that the whole cell range is highlighted)*; then, from the Home tab, click the Center icon in the Alignment group.*

11. You are now ready to enter values into your spreadsheet.

12. *Move the pointer to cell C7.* Type **1000.** Do not type a dollar sign or comma; these will be added later. Press the [**ENTER**] key to enter the value.

13. Enter the following:

    500 in C8.
    1500 in C9.
    200 in C10.
    10000 in C11.
    750 in C12.
    18000 in C16.
    5000 in C17.
    900 in D7.
    600 in D8.
    1500 in D9.
    200 in D10.
    9750 in D11.
    875 in D12.
    19500 in D16.
    4000 in D17.

14. The values you entered do not have dollar signs or the commas appropriate to a currency format. You will now learn how to format a range of cells for a particular format (such as the Currency format).

15. *Click in cell C7 and drag the pointer over to cell D20. From the Home tab, click the down arrow next to the "Number Format" box, which should say "General." Click Currency. Then click OK.* Notice that dollar signs have been added to all of the values. *Click in any cell to deselect the cell range.*

16. *Click in cell B13 and drag the pointer over to cell D13. Then, from the Home tab, click the Bold icon in the Font group.* This will make the TOTAL EXPENSES row appear in bold.

17. *Click in cell B18 and drag the pointer over to cell D18. Then, from the Home tab, click the Bold icon in the Font group.* This will make the TOTAL INCOME row appear in bold.

18. *Click in cell B20 and drag the pointer over to cell D20. Then, from the Home tab, click on the Bold icon in the Font group.* This will make the PROFIT/LOSS row appear in bold.

19. Your spreadsheet is nearly complete; all you need to add are the six formulas.

20. *Click in cell C13.*

21. Type **=SUM(** and press the [**UP ARROW**] key six times until the cell pointer is at cell C7. Press **.** (a period) to anchor the range.

22. Press the [**DOWN ARROW**] key five times, then press **)** (a closing parenthesis). Press the [**ENTER**] key.

23. Go back to cell C13 and look at the formula in the formula bar. The formula should read "**=SUM(C7:C12)**". The total displayed in the cell should read $13,950.00. Note that you also could have typed the formula **=C7+C8+C9+C10+C11+C12.**

24. Enter the following formulas:
    =SUM(D7:D12) in D13.
    =SUM(C16:C17) in C18.
    =SUM(D16:D17) in D18.

25. You now need to enter formulas for the PROFIT/LOSS columns. In C20, enter **=C18–C13** (the total should read $9,050.00).

26. *Go to cell C20 and click the AutoFill command* (it is the small black square at the bottom right of the cell). *Drag it one column to the right and release the mouse button.* Notice that the formula has been copied. The total should be $9,675.00. Alternatively, *go to cell C20, right-click, click Copy, move the pointer to cell D20,* and press the [**ENTER**] key.

27. The spreadsheet is now complete. To print the spreadsheet, *click the Office button, then click Print, then click OK.*

28. You will need to save the spreadsheet, because you will use it in Lesson 2. To save the spreadsheet, *click the Office button and then click Save. Under Save in:, select the drive or folder* in which you would like to save the document. Next to File name:, type **Budget1** and *click Save.*

29. To exit Excel, *click the Office button and then click on Exit Excel.*

This concludes Lesson 1.

LESSON 2: BUILDING A BUDGET SPREADSHEET, PART 2

This lesson assumes that you have completed Lesson 1, have saved the spreadsheet from that lesson, and are generally familiar with the concepts covered in that lesson. Lesson 2 gives you experience in opening a file, inserting a row, formatting numbers as percentages, building additional formulas, creating a bar chart, printing selections, and fitting and compressing data onto one printed page. If you did not exit Excel after Lesson 1, skip Steps 1 and 2 in this lesson and go directly to Step 3.

1. Open Windows. *Double-click on the Microsoft Office Excel 2007 icon on the desktop* to open the program. Alternatively, *click the Start button, point to Programs or All Programs, point to Microsoft Office, then click Microsoft Office Excel 2007.* You should now be in a new, clean, blank workbook.

2. To retrieve the spreadsheet from Lesson 1, *click on the Office button and then click Open. Next, click the name of your file* (e.g., **Budget 1**). If you do not see it, *click through the options under Look in: to find the file.* When you have found it, *click on Open.*

3. You will be entering the information shown in Excel 2007 Exhibit 3. Notice in Excel 2007 Exhibit 3 that a line for travel appears in row 9. You will insert this row first.

4. *Click in cell B9. From the Home tab, click the down arrow below Insert in the Cells group. On the Insert menu, click Insert Sheet Rows.* A new row is added. You could also *right-click and select Insert* to open a dialog box with the option to insert another row.

5. Enter the following:
   Travel in B9.
   750 in C9.
   650 in D9.

6. Notice that when the new values for travel were entered, all of the formulas were updated. Because you inserted the additional row in the middle of the column, the formulas recognized the new numbers and automatically recalculated to reflect them. Be extremely careful when inserting new rows and columns into spreadsheets that have existing formulas. In some cases, the new number will not be reflected in the totals, such as when rows or columns are inserted at the beginning or end of the range that a formula calculates. It is always prudent to go back to each existing formula, examine the formula range, and make sure the new values are included in the formula range.

7. Change the column width of column E to 12 by *clicking the column heading* (the letter E) at the top of the screen. *Move the pointer to the right edge of the column.* The pointer should change to a double-headed vertical arrow. *Drag the pointer to the right until the column width is 12.* Alternatively, you can change the cell width by *placing the cell pointer anywhere in column E and, from the Home tab, clicking Format in the Cells Group and selecting Column Width... ;* then type **12** and *click OK.*

8. Enter the following:
   May in E4.
   Difference in E5.
   Percent in F4.
   Of Budget in F5.

9. *Click in cell E4 and drag the pointer over to cell F5* so that the additional column headings are highlighted. *Right-click. Notice that in addition to a menu, the Mini toolbar appears.* It has a number of formatting options on it, including Font, Font size, Bold, and others. *Click the Bold icon on the Mini toolbar. Point and click the Center icon on the Mini toolbar.*

10. *Click in cell E14 and drag the pointer over to cell F14. Right-click and then click on the Bold icon on the Mini toolbar.*

11. *Click in cell E19 and drag the pointer over to cell F19. Right-click and then select the Bold icon on the Mini toolbar.*

12. *Click in cell E21 and drag the pointer over to cell F21. Right-click and then select the Bold icon on the Mini toolbar.*

13. You are now ready to change the cell formatting for column E to Currency and column F to Percent. *Click in cell E7 and drag the pointer down to cell E21. Right-click and select Format Cells. From the Number tab in the "Format Cells" window, click Currency and then OK. Click in any cell to get rid of the cell range.*

14. *Click in cell F7 and drag the pointer down to cell F21. From the Home tab, click the Percent Style (%) icon in the Number group* (see Excel 2007 Exhibit 3). *Then, from the Home tab, click the Increase Decimal icon twice in the Number group.*

15. *Click in any cell to get rid of the cell range.*

16. All that is left to do is enter the formulas for the two new columns. The entries in the May Difference column subtract the actual amount from the budgeted amount for each expense item. A positive amount in this column means that the office was under budget on that line item. A negative balance means that the office was over budget on that line item. The Percent Of Budget column divides that actual amount by the budgeted amount. This shows the percentage of the budgeted money that was actually spent for each item.

17. You will first build one formula in the May Difference column, and then copy it. *Click in cell E7,* type **=C7−D7**, and press the **[ENTER]** key.

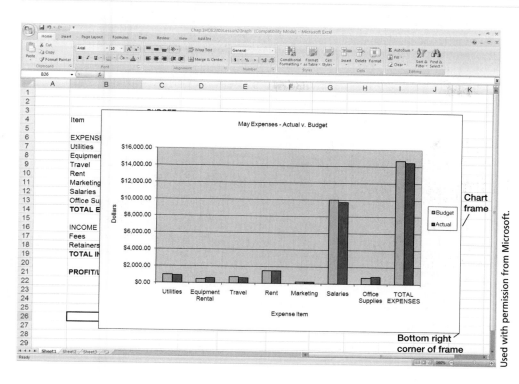

Used with permission from Microsoft.

HANDS-ON EXERCISES

18. Using the AutoFill command or the Copy command, copy this formula down through cell E14. (To copy, *right-click and then click Copy; highlight the area where the information should go; then right-click and select Paste.* Alternatively, you can use the Copy and Paste icons in the Clipboard group on the Home tab.)

19. *Click in cell E17,* type **=C17–D17**, and press the **[ENTER]** key.

20. Using the AutoFill command, copy this formula down through cell E21. Delete the formula in cell E20 by *clicking in cell E20* and pressing the **[DEL]** key.

21. You will now build on the formula in the Percent Of Budget column and copy it. *Click in cell F7,* type **=D7/C7**, and press the **[ENTER]** key.

22. Using the AutoFill command, copy this formula down through cell F21. Delete the formula in cells F15, F16, and F20 by *clicking in the cell* and then pressing the **[DEL]** key.

23. The spreadsheet has now been built. You will now build a column chart that shows budgeted expenses compared to actual expenses (see Excel 2007 Exhibit 4).

24. *Click in cell B7, then drag the pointer down and over to cell D14.*

25. *From the Insert tab, click Column from the Charts group. Under 3-D Column, click the first option, 3-D Clustered Column* (see Excel 2007 Exhibit 5).

26. Notice that a draft column chart has been created. *Click anywhere in the chart frame* (see Excel 2007 Exhibit 4). Your pointer will turn to a four-headed arrow. *Drag the chart across the spreadsheet so the upper left corner of the chart is near cell B4.*

27. *Using the horizontal scroll bar* (see Excel 2007 Exhibit 4), *scroll to the right* so the chart is completely in your screen.

28. *Click the bottom right corner of the chart frame.* Your cursor should change to a two-headed arrow that is diagonal. *Drag the chart so that the bottom right corner ends near cell H22* (see Excel 2007 Exhibit 4).

EXCEL 2007 EXHIBIT 5
Creating a column chart

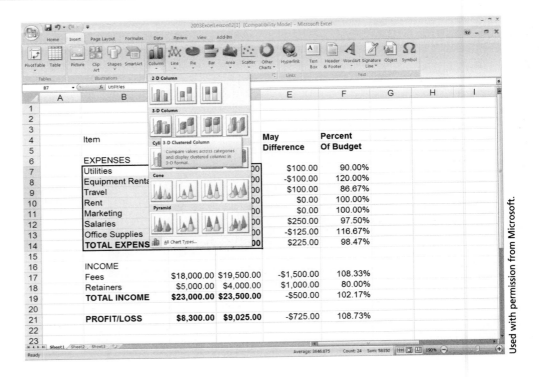

Used with permission from Microsoft.

29. Notice that new options have been added to the ribbon (e.g., Chart Tools Design, Layout, and Format). *Click the Layout ribbon tab under Chart Tools.*

30. *Click Chart Title in the Labels group, then select Above Chart.* Notice that a title has been added, "Chart Title."

31. *Point and click on the "Chart Title" text in the bar chart* and press the **[DEL]** key until the text is gone. Type **May Expenses—Actual v. Budget**. If you would like to move the title—for example, if it is off-center—*just click the title frame and drag it where you would like.*

32. *From the Layout tab (under Chart Tools), click Axis Titles in the Labels group. Click Primary Horizontal Axis Title and then select Title Below Axis.* Notice that a horizontal axis title of "Axis Title" has been added. *Click Axis Title* and use the **[DEL]** key until the text is gone. Type **Expenses**.

33. To change the legend from Series1 and Series2 to Actual and Budget, *right-click on Series1, then click Select Data.* The "Select Data Source" window will open. *Click on Series1 (under Legend Entries (Series)) to highlight it, then click on Edit under the same heading.* The "Edit Series" window will open. Type **Actual** in the text box under Series name:, *then click OK. Click on Series2 (under Legend Entries (Series)) to highlight it, then click on Edit under the same heading.* The "Edit Series" window will open. Type **Budget** in the text box under Series name:, *then click OK. Click OK in the "Select Data Source" window.*

34. To print the chart, *drag the pointer from cell G3 to cell Q27. Click the Office button and click Print; then, under Print what, click Selection and then click OK.*

35. You will next print the spreadsheet and the chart on one page. *Click in cell B3 and drag the pointer until both the spreadsheet and the chart are highlighted* (roughly cell B3 to cell Q27).

36. *Click the Page Layout tab, then click the Page Setup Dialog Box Launcher.* (It is a little box directly under the Print Titles icon in the Page Setup group). The "Page Setup" window should now be displayed. There is another way to bring up this window: *from the Page Setup group of the Page Layout tab, click Margins, and then click Custom Margins.*

37. *From the Page tab of the "Page Setup" window, click in the circle next to Fit To: and make sure it says "1 page(s) wide by 1 tall"* (it should default to one page). *Then, under Orientation, click on Landscape.*

38. *Click Print and then click OK.* This will compress everything in the print area to one page.

39. To save the spreadsheet, *click the Office button and then click Save As. Under Save in:, select the drive or folder* in which you would like to save the document. Next to File name:, type **Budget2** and *click Save.*

40. To exit Excel, *click the Office button and then click Exit Excel.*

This concludes Lesson 2.

LESSON 3: BUILDING A DAMAGE PROJECTION SPREADSHEET

This lesson shows you how to build the damage projection spreadsheet shown in Excel 2007 Exhibit 6. It explains how to increase the size of type, how to wrap text in a cell, how to use the border features, how to use the font and fill color features, how to use the AutoSum feature, and how to change the decimal places for a number. This lesson assumes that you have successfully completed Lessons 1 and 2. Keep in mind that if you make a mistake at any time in this lesson, you may press **[CTRL]+[Z]** to undo what you have done.

EXCEL 2007 EXHIBIT 6
Damages projection

1. Open Windows. *Double-click the Microsoft Office Excel 2007 icon on the desktop* to open the program. Alternatively, *click on the Start button, point to Programs or All Programs, point to Microsoft Office, then click Microsoft Office Excel 2007.* You should now be in a new, clean, blank workbook. If you are not in a blank workbook, *click the Office button* (see Excel 2007 Exhibit 1), *then click New and double-click Blank Workbook.*

2. To start building the spreadsheet in Excel 2007 Exhibit 6, begin by increasing the size of column C to a width of 37 *(Home tab > Cells group > Format > Column Width).*

3. In cell C3, type **Damage Projection.** With the pointer on C3, *click the Bold icon from the Font group on the Home tab.* Change the size to 14 point by *clicking the Font Size box in the Font group on the Home tab* and typing **14**.

4. Type the text shown in cell C5 (see Excel 2007 Exhibit 6). *Click the Font Size box in the Font group on the Home tab and change the type to 14 point.* Notice that the text goes into the next cell. To wrap part of the text down to the next line within the current cell (see Excel Exhibit 6), *from the Home tab, click the Wrap Text icon in the Alignment group* (see Excel 2007 Exhibit 6). The text now wraps down to the next line within cell C5.

5. Type the text shown in cell C6, make the text 14 point, and wrap the text down so it does not go into cell D6.

6. Type the text shown in cell C8 and make the text 14 point.

7. Type the text and values shown in cells C9 to D13.

8. Type the text shown in cell C14.

9. To enter the formula in cell D14, *click cell D14.* Then, *from the Editing group on the Home tab, click the Sum icon* (see Excel 2007 Exhibit 6). Notice that when you clicked Sum, Excel assumed that you wanted to add the values in D10 to D13. You could adjust the range by pressing the **[SHIFT]+[ARROW]** keys, but the range should be fine as is (i.e., D10 to D13). Press the **[ENTER]** key to enter the formula.

10. *Click in cell C9, drag the mouse pointer to cell D14,* and change the font size to 14 point.

11. *Click in cell C9 and drag the mouse pointer to cell D9. Right-click. On the Mini toolbar, click the down arrow next to the Fill Color icon (the paint bucket) and select the black square.* (You could also click the Fill Color icon in the Font group on the Home tab.) The cells are all black; now you just need to change the font color to white to see the text.

12. With cells C9 and D9 still highlighted, *on the Home tab, click the down arrow next to the Font Color icon in the Font group, and click on the white square.*

13. *Click in cell C10 and drag the mouse pointer to cell D14. From the Font group on the Home tab, click on the down arrow next to the Border icon.* (It is typically just to the left of the Fill Color icon—see Excel 2007 Exhibit 6). Then, *click All Borders* (it looks like a windowpane). Notice that there is now a border around every square that was highlighted.

14. *Click in cell C14 and drag the mouse pointer to cell D14. From the Font group on the Home tab, click the down arrow next to the Border icon again.* Then *click on the Thick Box Border* (it looks like a heavy black window frame). Move the pointer and notice that there is now a heavy black border around cells C14 and D14. *From the Font group on the Home tab, click on the Bold icon again.*

15. *Click in cell D10 and drag the pointer to cell D14. From the Number group on the Home tab, click the dollar sign ($).* Notice that two decimal places are shown (e.g., 25,000.00). It is not necessary to show two decimal places in this projection, so you will now change it to zero decimal places. *From the Number group on the Home tab, click the Decrease Decimal icon twice.* Notice that whole dollars are now shown.

16. To print the spreadsheet, *click the Office button, click Print and then click OK.*

17. To save the spreadsheet, *click on the Office button and then click Save. Under Save in:, select the drive or folder* in which you would like to save the document. Next to File name:, type **Damage Projection** and *click Save.*

18. To exit Excel, *click the Office button and then click Exit Excel.*

This concludes Lesson 3.

▶ INTERMEDIATE LESSONS

LESSON 4: CHILD SUPPORT PAYMENT SPREADSHEET

This lesson shows you how to build the child support payment spreadsheet in Excel 2007 Exhibit 7. It explains how to create a white background, how to create formulas to multiply cells and formulas that use an absolute cell reference, and how to use the AutoFormat feature. This lesson assumes that you have successfully completed Lessons 1 through 3. Keep in mind that if you make a mistake at any time in this lesson, you may press **[CTRL]+[Z]** to undo what you have done.

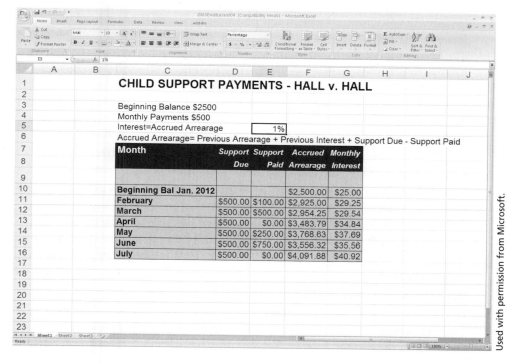

EXCEL 2007 EXHIBIT 7
Child support payment spreadsheet

Used with permission from Microsoft.

HANDS-ON EXERCISES

1. Open Windows. *Double-click the Microsoft Office Excel 2007 icon on the desktop* to open the program. Alternatively, *click the Start button, point to Programs or All Programs, point to Microsoft Office, and then click Microsoft Office Excel 2007.* You should now be in a new, clean, blank workbook. If you are not in a blank workbook, *point and click the Office button* (see Excel 2007 Exhibit 1), *then click New, then double-click on Blank Workbook.*

2. When you start to build the spreadsheet in Excel 2007 Exhibit 7, notice that the background is completely white. A completely white background gives you a crisp, clean canvas on which to work and to which you can add colors and graphics.

3. Press **[CTRL]+[A].** The whole spreadsheet is now selected. *From the Font group on the Home tab, click the down arrow next to the Fill Color icon, then click the white square* (it is all the way in the upper right corner). *Click*

in any cell to make the highlighting disappear. Notice that the background of the spreadsheet is completely white.

4. Enter the text shown in cell C1, then change the font to Bold and the font size to 14 point.

5. Increase the width of column C to 20.

6. Enter the text shown in cells C3 to C6.

7. In cell E5, type **.01** and press [**ENTER**]. Change the number format to Percent (zero decimal places).

8. Enter the text shown in cells C7 and in the cell range from D7 to G8. *Click on C7 and click on the bold icon from the Font group in the Home tab. Click on D7 and drag the pointer to G8, then click on the Italic icon from the Font group in the Home tab.*

9. Enter the text shown in the cell range from C10 to C16.

10. Enter the numbers (values) shown in cells in D11 to E16.

11. In cell F10, type **2500.**

12. In cell G10, type = (an equals sign), *click in cell F10*, then press [**SHIFT**]+[**8**] (an asterisk will appear). *Click in cell E5* and press the [**F4**] key once. The formula **=F10*$E$5** should be on the screen; press the [**ENTER**] key. This formula multiplies the accrued arrearage (how much the individual is behind on payments) times the interest rate (which is 1 percent). The reason you pressed [**F4**] is that the formula had to be an absolute cell reference; pressing [**F4**] simply put the dollar signs ($) into the formula for you. The dollar signs tell Excel that this is an absolute cell reference rather than a relative cell reference. Hence, when you copy the formula to other cells (see following steps), the accrued arrearage will always be multiplied by the value in E5. Said another way, the second half of this formula ($E$5) will not change when the formula is copied to other cells.

13. If you want to find out for yourself why the formula **=F10*E5** will not work once it is copied from cell G10 (where it will work fine), type **=F10*E5** in cell G10 and then copy the formula to cells G11 to G16. Once you have seen the effect of this, delete the changes you made and change the formula in cell G10 to **=F10*$E$5.**

14. To copy the formula from G10 to cells G11 to G16, *click in cell G10, click the AutoFill handle* (the little black box at the lower right corner of the cell) *and drag the mouse pointer down to cell G16.*

15. In cell F11, type **=F10+G10+D11–E11.** Press the [**ENTER**] key. This formula adds the accrued amount in the previous month with the previous month's interest and the current support due, and then subtracts the current amount paid.

16. To copy the formula from F11 to cells F12 to F16, *click in cell F11, click the AutoFill handle, and drag the mouse pointer down to cell F16.*

17. *Click in cell D10 and drag the mouse pointer to cell G16. Right-click, then click Format Cells. Click the Number tab, click Currency, then click OK.*

18. Notice that the spreadsheet is very plain. We will use the Cell Styles feature to give the spreadsheet some color. *Click in cell C7 and drag the mouse pointer to cell G8. From the Styles Group on the Home tab, click the down arrow next to Cell Styles. Click Accent4* (it is solid purple with white letters).

19. *Click in cell C9 and drag the mouse pointer to cell G16. From the Styles group on the Home tab, click the down arrow next to Cell Styles. Click 20%—Accent1. (It is light blue with black letters.) Click in any cell to make the highlighting disappear.*

20. To add borders to the spreadsheet, *click in cell C9 and drag the mouse pointer to cell G16. From the Font group on the Home tab, click the down arrow*

next to the Border icon. Next, click the All Borders icon (it looks like a windowpane).

21. *Click in cell E5. From the Font group on the Home tab, click the down arrow next to Borders. Click Thick Box Border.* Press the **[ENTER]** key. The spreadsheet is now complete and should look like Excel 2007 Exhibit 7.

22. To print the spreadsheet, *click the Office button, click Print, then click OK.*

23. To save the spreadsheet, *click the Office button and then click Save. Under Save in:, select the drive or folder* in which you would like to save the document. Next to File name:, type **Child Support Payments** and *click Save.*

24. To exit Excel, *click on the Office button and then click Exit Excel.*

This concludes Lesson 4.

LESSON 5: LOAN AMORTIZATION TEMPLATE

This lesson shows you how to open a loan amortization template and fill it in (see Excel 2007 Exhibit 8). Templates are a great way to simplify complicated spreadsheets. You will also learn how to protect cells, freeze panes, split a screen, hide a column, and use the Format Painter tool. This lesson assumes that you have successfully completed Lessons 1 through 4. Keep in mind that if you make a mistake at any time in this lesson, you may press **[CTRL]+[Z]** to undo what you have done.

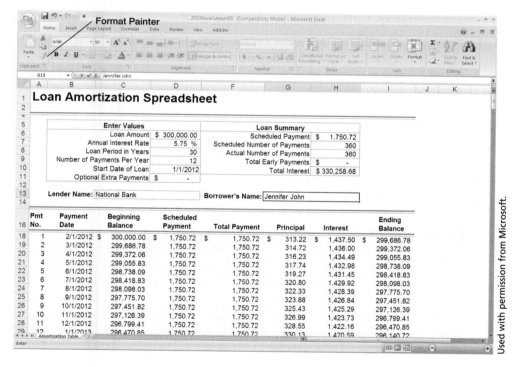

EXCEL 2007 EXHIBIT 8
Loan amortization template

1. Open Windows. *Double-click the Microsoft Office Excel 2007 icon on the desktop* to open the program. Alternatively, *click the Start button, point to Programs or All Programs, point to Microsoft Office, then click Microsoft Office Excel 2007.* You should now be in a new, clean, blank workbook.

2. The first thing you will do to complete the template in Excel 2007 Exhibit 8 is open the "Lesson 5" file from the disk supplied with this text. Ensure that the disk is inserted in the disk drive, *click on File on the Office button, then click on Open.* The "Open" window should now be displayed. *Click on the down arrow to the right of the white box next to Look in: and select the drive*

where the disk is located. Point and double-click on the Excel Files folder.
Double-click on the Excel 2007 folder. Double-click on the "Lesson 5" file.

3. You should now have the loan amortization spreadsheet shown in Excel 2007
   Exhibit 8 open. However, your spreadsheet has no data yet.

4. Enter the following information:
   Cell D6: **300000**
   Cell D7: **5.75**
   Cell D8: **30**
   Cell D9: **12**
   Cell D10: **1/1/2012**
   Cell D11: **0**

(When you click in Cell D11, a note will appear regarding extra payments; just type a
zero and press [**ENTER**] and the note will disappear.)

   Cell C13: **National Bank**
   Cell G13: **Jennifer John**

5. Notice that your spreadsheet now appears nearly identical to Excel 2007
   Exhibit 8.

6. Notice in your spreadsheet that just about everything below row 16 is a
   formula. If a user accidentally deletes one of these formulas, the whole
   spreadsheet could be affected. You will now turn on the Protection feature and
   lock some of the cells so they cannot be accidentally deleted.

7. *Right-click in cell D6. Then click Format Cells … . Click the Protection*
   tab in the "Format Cells" window. Notice that there is no green check mark
   next to Locked. Cells D6 to D13 and cell G13 are unlocked even when the
   Protection feature is turned on. When the Protection feature is off, you can
   change the lock/unlock format of cells by using the *right-click, Format Cells >*
   Protection command sequence. Interestingly, when a new blank spreadsheet
   is open in Excel, all cells default to Locked, but this has no effect because the
   Protection feature is always turned off in a blank workbook.

8. *Click Cancel in the "Format Cells" window to close the window.*

9. Let's open a new spreadsheet so you can see that all cells in Excel start out with
   the format locked. *Click the Office button, then click New, then double-click*
   Blank Workbook.

10. You should now have a new, blank spreadsheet displayed. *Right-click in any*
    cell and then click Format Cells… . Click the Protection tab. Notice that
    the cell is locked. However, the cell is not truly locked until you turn on the
    Protection feature.

11. *Click Cancel in the "Format Cells" window in the new spreadsheet. Click the*
    Office button and then click Close to close the file. You should now be back at
    your loan amortization spreadsheet.

12. To turn on the Protection feature, *on the Review tab, click Protect Sheet in*
    the Changes group.

13. The "Protect Sheet" window should now be displayed (see Excel 2007
    Exhibit 9). Make sure that the first two selections under Allow all users of
    this worksheet to: are selected (e.g., Select locked cells and Select unlocked
    cells). Notice that you could enter a password in the white box under
    Password to unprotect the sheet. This would completely lock the spreadsheet
    (so that only unlocked cells could be modified) to users who did not know
    the password. In this instance, this is not necessary; it is fine for someone
    to intentionally change the values at the top of the spreadsheet. We are

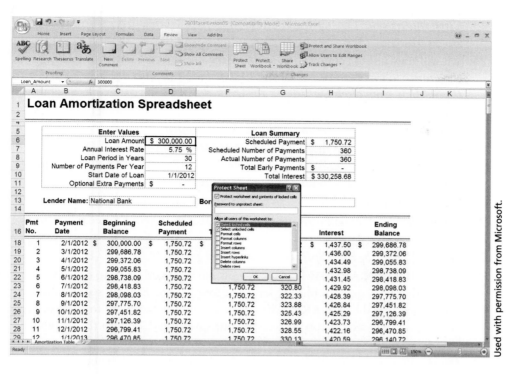

EXCEL 2007 EXHIBIT 9
Protecting cells

just using this feature to prevent someone from accidentally changing the formulas below row 16.

14. After the first two items are check-marked under Allow all users of this worksheet to:, *click OK.*

15. *Now click in any cell other than D6 to D13 or cell G13 and try to type something in the cell.* You should get an error message that says "**The cell or chart that you are trying to change is protected and therefore read-only.**" *Click OK* to close the error window.

16. The whole spreadsheet is now locked, except for cells D6 to D13 and cell G13, because these were not formatted as locked in the template.

17. Now you will turn off the Protection feature because you are still building the spreadsheet. *On the Review tab, click Unprotect Sheet in the Changes group.*

18. You will now use the Format Painter tool to copy the formatting from one set of cells to another set of cells. Notice that cells F13 and G13 do not look like cells B13 and C13. You will copy the format from cells B13 and C13 to cells F13 and G13.

19. *Point in cell B13 and drag the mouse pointer to cell C13. On the Home tab, click the Format Painter icon in the Clipboard group.* (It looks like a paintbrush). Your pointer now should have a paintbrush icon on it.

20. *Click in cell F13, drag the mouse to cell H13, and then let go of the mouse button. Click anywhere to see the cell.* Notice that the formatting has now been copied.

21. Column E in the amortization schedule of the spreadsheet is the "Extra Payment" column. Assume for the purposes of this exercise that you will not have any extra payments and that you do not need this column, but you want to leave the column there in case you need it at a later date. For now, you can hide column E (and unhide it if you need it later).

22. *Point and right-click on the "E" in the E column heading. From the drop-down menu, click Hide.*

23. *Click in any cell.* The vertical line will disappear. Notice that column E is no longer displayed. The column headings go from D to F.

24. We will now unhide column E. *Point on the D column heading and drag the mouse to the F column heading so that both columns are highlighted. Right-click, then click Unhide on the drop-down menu.* Notice that column E reappears.

25. *Click in any cell to make the highlighting disappear.*

26. *Click in cell D18.* Use the [**DOWN ARROW**] key to go to cell D50. Notice that some column titles, such as "Pmt No.," and "Payment Date," are no longer visible, so it is difficult to know what the numbers mean.

27. Press [**CTRL**]+[**HOME**] to go to the top of the spreadsheet.

28. *Click cell A18.* You will now use the Split Screen command to see the column titles.

29. *On the View tab, click Split in the Window group.*

30. Use the [**DOWN ARROW**] cursor key on the keyboard to go to cell A50. Notice that because you split the screen at row 18, you can still see column titles. Next, use the [**UP ARROW**] cursor key on the keyboard to go to cell A1. You should now see the top portion of your spreadsheet in both the top and bottom screens.

31. *On the View tab, click Split again in the Window group.* The bottom screen is now gone.

32. The Freeze Panes feature is another way to show the column headings when you scroll down a document. The Freeze Panes feature is a convenient way to see both column and row titles at the same time. *Click in cell B18.*

33. *On the View tab, click Freeze Panes in the Window group and then click the first option, Freeze Panes.*

34. Use the [**DOWN ARROW**] key to go to cell B50. Notice that because you froze the screen at cell B18, you can still see column titles. Next, use the [**RIGHT ARROW**] key to go to cell R50. You should still see the "Pmt No." column, including the payment numbers.

35. Press [**CTRL**]+[**HOME**] to go to the beginning of the spreadsheet.

36. *On the View tab, click Freeze Panes in the Window group and then click the first option, Unfreeze Panes.*

37. To print the spreadsheet, *click the Office button, click Print, then click OK.*

38. To save the spreadsheet, *click the Office button and then click Save As. Under Save in: select the drive or folder in which you would like to save the document.* Next to File name:, type **Excel Lesson 5 Spreadsheet DONE** and *click Save.*

39. Templates are a great way to utilize the power of Excel. Many free templates are available on the Internet. Microsoft alone offers more than 100 Excel templates on its website. To access them, *click the Office button, then New.* They are listed to the left under Microsoft Office Online.

40. To exit Excel, *click on the Office button and then click Exit Excel.*

This concludes Lesson 5.

LESSON 6: STATISTICAL FUNCTIONS

This lesson demonstrates how to use and enter statistical formulas such as average, maximum, minimum, and standard deviation. It also shows how to sort data, check

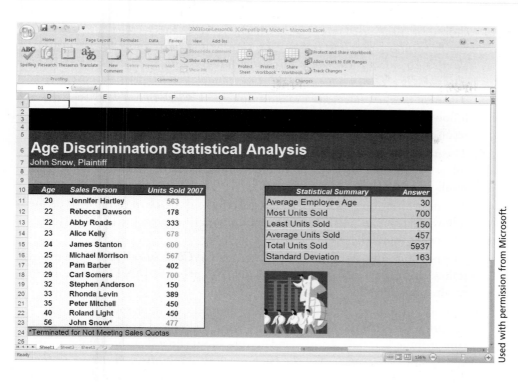

Used with permission from Microsoft.

EXCEL 2007 EXHIBIT 10
Statistical spreadsheet

HANDS-ON EXERCISES

for metadata in spreadsheets, how to use the Format Clear command, how to use conditional formatting, and how to insert a clip-art file. When the spreadsheet is complete, it will look like Excel 2007 Exhibit 10. Keep in mind that if you make a mistake at any time in this lesson, you may press **[CTRL]+[Z]** to undo what you have done.

1. Open Windows. ***Double-click the Microsoft Office Excel 2007 icon on the desktop*** to open the program. Alternatively, ***click the Start button, point to Programs or All Programs, point to Microsoft Office, then click Microsoft Office Excel 2007.*** You should now be in a new, clean, blank workbook. If you are not in a blank workbook, ***click the Office button*** (see Excel 2007 Exhibit 1), ***then click New, then double-click on Blank Workbook.***

2. The first thing you will do to complete the template shown in Excel 2007 Exhibit 10 is open the "Lesson 6" file from the disk supplied with this text. Ensure that the disk is inserted in the disk drive, ***click on File on the Office button, then click on Open.*** The "Open" window should now be displayed. ***Click on the down arrow to the right of the white box next to Look in: and select the drive where the disk is located. Double-click on the Excel Files folder. Double-click on the Excel 2007 folder. Double-click on the "Lesson 6" file.***

3. You should now see the Age Discrimination Statistical Analysis spreadsheet shown in Excel 2007 Exhibit 10; however, your spreadsheet has no formulas in the statistical summary section, the data have not yet been sorted, and there is no clip art yet.

4. You will now enter the formulas in the statistical summary section of the spreadsheet. The first formula will calculate the average age of employees of the company. ***Click in cell J11.*** Type the following formula: **=AVERAGE(D11:D23)** and then press the **[ENTER]** key. The result

should be 30. *Note:* Here is another way to enter the average function: ***on the Formulas tab, click Insert Function in the Function Library group; next to Or select a category, click the down arrow, then click Statistical > AVERAGE > OK.***

5. The next formula calculates the most units sold. ***Click in cell J12.*** Type the following formula: **=MAX(F11:F23)** and then press the **[ENTER]** key. The result should be 700.

6. The next formula calculates the least units sold. ***Click in cell J13.*** Type the following formula: **=MIN(F11:F23)** and then press the **[ENTER]** key. The result should be 150.

7. The next formula calculates the average units sold. ***Click in cell J14.*** Type the following formula: **=AVERAGE(F11:F23)** and then press the **[ENTER]** key. The result should be 457.

8. The next formula calculates the total units sold. ***Click in cell J15.*** Type the following formula: **=SUM(F11:F23)** and then press the **[ENTER]** key. The result should be 5937.

9. The last formula calculates the standard deviation for units sold. *Standard deviation* is a measure of how widely values are dispersed from the average value (the arithmetic mean). Large standard deviations show that the numbers vary widely from the average. ***On the Formulas tab, click Insert Function in the Function Library group. Next to Or select a category, click the down arrow and select Statistical. Scroll down the list and click STDEVP*** (see Excel 2007 Exhibit 11). Notice that there is a definition for this function. ***Click OK in the "Insert Function" window.***

10. The "Function Arguments" window should now be displayed. In the "Function Arguments" window, next to Number 1, press **[DEL]** until the box is blank. Type **F11:F23,** then ***click OK*** (see Excel 2007 Exhibit 12). The result should be 163.

EXCEL 2007 EXHIBIT 11
Entering a standard deviation formula using the insert function command

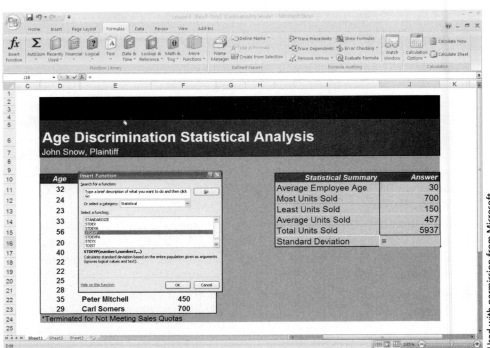

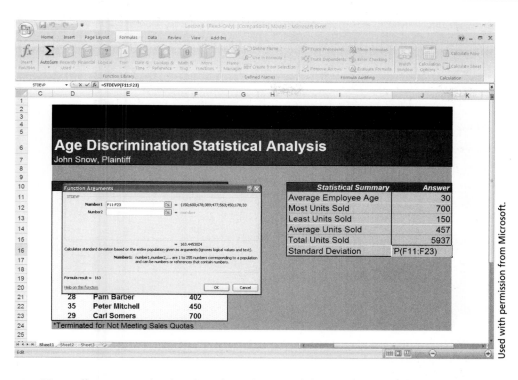

EXCEL 2007 EXHIBIT 12
Entering a standard
deviation formula using
the functions argument
window

11. You will now sort the data based on the age of the employees. ***Click in D11 and then drag the mouse down to F23. From the Data tab, click Sort in the Sort & Filter group.***

12. The "Sort" window should now be displayed (see Excel 2007 Exhibit 13). *Note*: Even though you just want to sort by age, you must select the full data range that includes all of the information, or the age data will be sorted but the other columns and rows will stay where they are. The data will therefore be mismatched (each age will not be matched with the correct person and number of units sold).

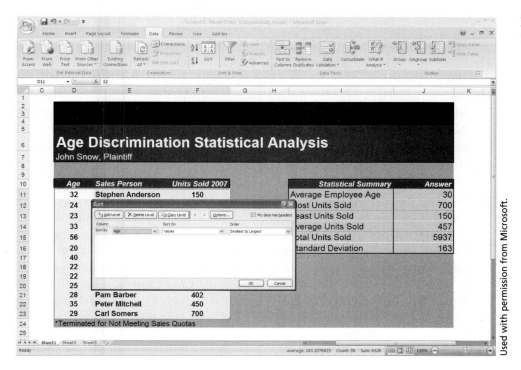

EXCEL 2007 EXHIBIT 13
Sorting data

EXCEL 2007 EXHIBIT 14
Removing metadata

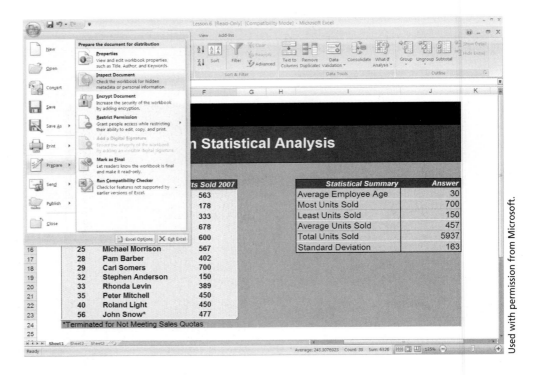

13. *In the "Sort" window, click the down arrow next to Sort by, then click Age* (see Excel 2007 Exhibit 13). Notice that under Order, the default of Smallest to Largest is selected; this is fine, so *click OK in the "Sort" window.* The data should now be sorted according to the age of the individual, with John Snow appearing last in the spreadsheet.

14. You will now ensure that no metadata is included in your document. You must first save the spreadsheet. To save the spreadsheet, *click the Office button and then click Save As. Under Save in:, select the drive or folder* in which you would like to save the document. Next to File name:, type **Excel Lesson 6 Spreadsheet DONE** and *click Save.*

15. Excel 2007 has a special feature called Inspect Document that can extract all metadata from your spreadsheet. *Click the Office button, click Prepare, then click Inspect Document* (see Excel 2007 Exhibit 14). Through the "Document Inspector" window, all of the possible places metadata can hide are checked. *Click Inspect.* Some of the categories may have a Remove All button. If you wanted to remove the metadata, you would just click on Remove All for each category. Because this is just an exercise, we do not need to remove the metadata, so go ahead and *click Close* to close the "Document Inspector" window.

16. Sometimes it is helpful to clear a cell or cells of all formatting information at one time. Notice that cell D6, the one titled "Age Discrimination Statistical Analysis," is elaborately formatted, including 24-point font, white letters, red background, and bold text. You will now quickly remove all of that formatting. *Click in cell D6. Then, on the Home tab, click the down arrow next to the Clear icon in the Editing group* (it looks like an eraser—see Excel 2007 Exhibit 15). *Click Clear Formats.* All of the formatting should disappear. Notice in Excel 2007 Exhibit 15 that one of the options when using the Clear commands is Clear All. Clicking Clear All will not only clear the formatting, but will also clear the contents of the selected cell(s).

17. Press **[CTRL]+[Z]** (the Undo feature) to restore the original formatting to the cell.

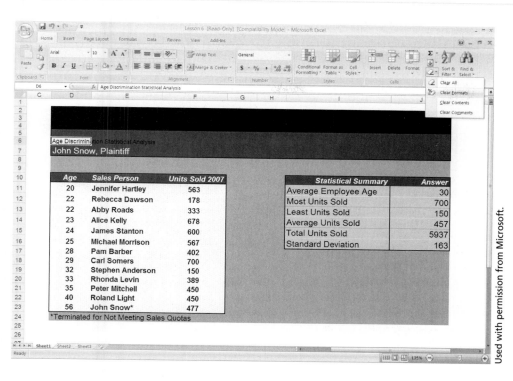

EXCEL 2007 EXHIBIT 15
Clear command

18. Sometimes, particularly in large spreadsheets, it is helpful to have the formatting of a cell change if certain conditions are present. For example, in an actual-versus-budget report, if an item goes over budget by more than 10 percent it might be helpful for that to be bolded so it catches the reader's attention. To accomplish this, you will now learn how to use the Conditional Formatting feature of Excel.

19. Notice that the average sales for the sales team in your spreadsheet is 457. It might be helpful to highlight any salesperson who was over the average. ***Click in F11 and then drag the mouse to F23. Then, from the Home tab, click Conditional Formatting in the Styles group*** (see Excel 2007 Exhibit 16).

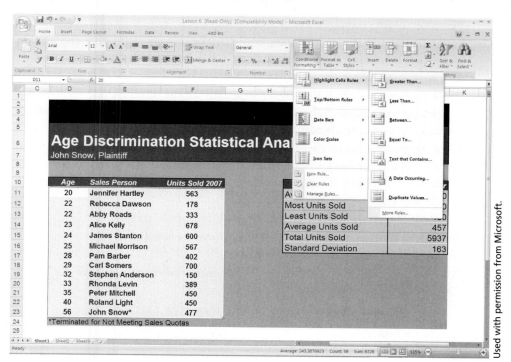

EXCEL 2007 EXHIBIT 16
Creating conditional formatting

HANDS-ON EXERCISES

EXCEL 2007 EXHIBIT 17
Creating a "Greater Than" conditional formatting

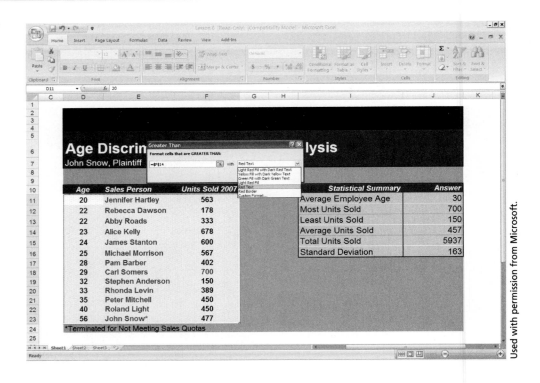

20. *Point to the first option, Highlight Cells Rules, and then click the first option again, which is Greater Than...* (see Excel 2007 Exhibit 16).

21. The "Greater Than" window should now be displayed (see Excel 2007 Exhibit 17). Press the **[DEL]** key to remove the value under Format cells that are GREATER THAN:.

22. *Click cell J14.* Notice that cell J14 has been entered under Format cells that are GREATER THAN:. Dollar signs have been added to the cell reference because this is an absolute cell reference.

23. *Click the down arrow next to Light Red Fill with Dark Red Text and select Red Text.* Cells over the average will be shown in red text. *Click OK in the "Greater Than" window.*

24. You will now add clip art to your spreadsheet (we are assuming that clip art was included when Excel 2007 was installed). *Click in cell I18. From the Insert tab, click Clip Art in the Illustrations group.*

25. The Clip Art task pane will appear to the right of the screen. Under Search for, type **Money** and then *click Go.* You may get a message that asks if you want to include clip art from Microsoft Office Online; *click No.*

26. *Click on the clip art in Excel 2007 Exhibit 10* (a blue bar chart with people in it and a person climbing a dollar sign). The clip art has now been added to your spreadsheet. *Position the clip art where you want it by clicking and dragging it into position.*

27. *Click the X in the Clip Art task pane* to close the task pane.

28. To print the spreadsheet, *click the Office button, click Print, then click OK.*

29. To save the spreadsheet, *click the Office button and then click Save As.* Choose the directory in which you want to save the file and *click Save.*

30. To exit Excel, *click the Office button and then click Exit Excel.*

This concludes Lesson 6.

ADVANCED LESSONS

LESSON 7: TOOLS AND TECHNIQUES 1—MARKETING BUDGET

In this lesson you will learn how to create visual impact with spreadsheets. You will learn to create and manipulate a text box, use advanced shading techniques, create a 3-D style text box, create vertical text, create diagonal text, use lines and borders, and create a comment. When the spreadsheet is complete, it will look like Excel 2007 Exhibit 18. Keep in mind that if you make a mistake at any time in this lesson, you may press **[CTRL]+[Z]** to undo what you have done.

1. Open Windows. ***Double-click the Microsoft Office Excel 2007 icon on the desktop*** to open the program. Alternatively, ***click the Start button, point to Programs or All Programs, point to Microsoft Office, then click Microsoft Office Excel 2007.*** You should now be in a new, clean, blank workbook.

2. The first thing you will do to complete the spreadsheet in Excel 2007 Exhibit 18 is open the "Lesson 7" file from the disk supplied with this text. Ensure that the disk is inserted in the disk drive, ***click on the Office button, click on File, then click on Open.*** The "Open" window should now be displayed. ***Click on the down arrow to the right of the white box next to Look in: and select the drive where the disk is located. Double-click on the Excel Files folder. Double-click on the Excel 2007 folder. Double-click on the "Lesson 7" file.***

3. You should now have the Marketing Plan spreadsheet in Excel 2007 Exhibit 18 open, except that your spreadsheet is missing some of the formatting that gives it visual impact. You will add the formatting to the spreadsheet to make it more visually compelling.

4. You will first add the text box that holds the title "Marketing Plan," as shown in Excel 2007 Exhibit 18. ***From the Insert tab, click Text Box in the Text group.*** Notice that your mouse pointer just turned into an upside-down letter "T."

HANDS-ON EXERCISES

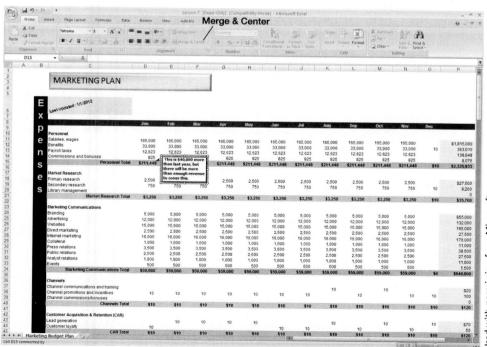

EXCEL 2007 EXHIBIT 18
Creating visual impact in spreadsheets

Used with permission from Microsoft.

EXCEL 2007 EXHIBIT 19
Formatting a shape

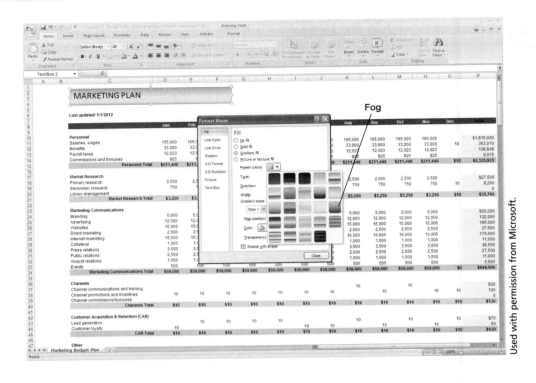

5. *Point to cell C2 and drag the mouse to about cell F4.* An outline of a box should now be shown from C2 to F4. This is a *text box.*

6. *Click inside the text box. Click the Bold icon and change the font size to 20.*

7. Type **MARKETING PLAN.**

8. *Right-click on the outline of the text box you just created. In the drop-down menu, click Format Shape.* The "Format Shape" window should now be displayed (see Excel 2007 Exhibit 19).

9. *In the "Format Shape" window, notice that Fill is currently selected. Click Gradient fill.*

10. *Click the down arrow next to Preset colors:.* This will open a box with many colors; *click Fog.*

11. *Staying in the "Format Shape" window, point to the down arrow next to Direction and click the first option, which is Linear Diagonal.*

12. *Still in the "Format Shape" window, click 3-D Format on the left side of the window.* You will now add a 3-D style to the text box. When the 3-D style choices appear, under Bevel and next to Top, *point to the down arrow and click the first selection under Bevel, which is Circle* (see Excel 2007 Exhibit 20).

13. *Click Close to close the "Format Shape" window. Click in any other cell so you can see the effect.*

14. You will now create the vertical text in Column B that says "Expenses," as shown in Excel 2007 Exhibit 18. Notice that this is actually one long cell. The first thing you will do is merge cells B6 through B53 into one cell; you will then add the text and format it to be vertical.

15. *Click in cell B6, drag the mouse down to cell B53, and then let go of the mouse button.*

16. *From the Home tab, click the Merge & Center icon in the Alignment group.* It looks like a box with an "a" in the middle, with left and right arrows around

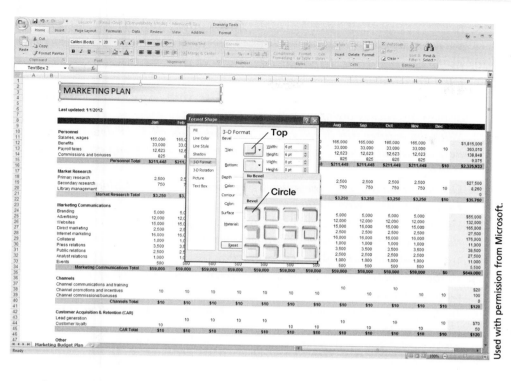

EXCEL 2007 EXHIBIT 20
Adding 3-D effect to a
text box

the "a" (see Excel 2007 Exhibit 18). Notice that the selected cells have now been merged into one cell stretching from B6 to B53.

17. With the cursor still in cell B6, *change the font size to 22 and click the Bold icon.* Type **Expenses** and press the **[ENTER]** key. The text is shown at the bottom of the cell; you will now correct this.

18. *Point and right-click anywhere in cell B6, then click Format Cells.* The "Format Cells" window should now be displayed. *Click the Alignment tab* (see Excel 2007 Exhibit 21).

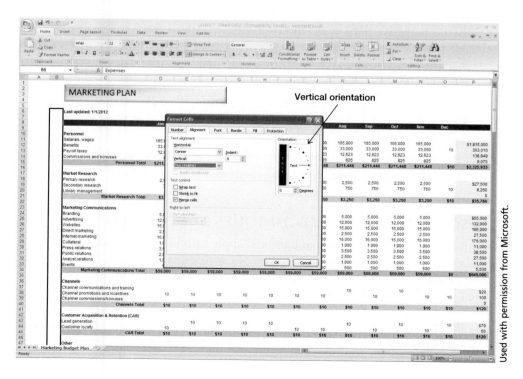

EXCEL 2007 EXHIBIT 21
Creating vertical text

HANDS-ON EXERCISES

19. *In the "Format Cells" window under Orientation, click the box that shows the word Text displayed vertically* (see Excel 2007 Exhibit 21).

20. *In the "Format Cells" window under Vertical, click the down arrow and select Top (Indent).*

21. *Click OK in the "Format Cells" window.* The word "Expenses" should now be displayed vertically down the cell.

22. *With the pointer still in cell B6, on the Home tab, click the down arrow next to the Fill Color (a paint bucket) icon in the Font group and then select Black.*

23. *On the Home tab, click the down arrow next to the Font Color icon in the Font group and select Yellow.*

24. You will next make the text in cell C6 appear diagonally. *Right-click in cell C6, then click Format Cells.* The "Format Cells" window should now be displayed and the Alignment tab should be selected.

25. *In the "Format Cells" window under Orientation, click the up arrow next to Degrees until it reads 15.*

26. *In the "Format Cells" window, click the Fill tab. Click the yellow square, then click OK.*

27. *Click in any cell to make the highlighting disappear.* The words "Last updated: 1/1/2012" should now be displayed diagonally in black letters on a yellow background.

28. You will now add the comment shown in Excel 2007 Exhibit 18. *Right-click in cell D15. On the drop-down menu, click Insert Comment.* Press **[BACKSPACE]** twice to delete the colon, and then type **This is $40,000 more than last year, but there will be more than enough revenue to cover this.** *Click in any cell to exit the "Comment" box.*

29. *Hover your mouse over cell D15* so you can see the comment.

30. You will now add borders to the spreadsheet. *Point to cell C53 and drag the mouse to cell P53. On the Home tab, click the down arrow next to the Borders icon in the Font group and click All Borders.* The "Totals" row should now have borders around each cell.

31. *Click in cell C8 and drag the mouse to cell P53. On the Home tab, click the down arrow next to the Borders icon in the Font group, then click Thick Box Border.* A thick border now surrounds the data.

32. To print the spreadsheet, *click the Office button, click Print, then click OK.*

33. To save the spreadsheet, *click the Office button and then click Save As. Under Save in: select the drive or folder* in which you would like to save the document. Next to File name:, type **Excel Lesson 7 Spreadsheet DONE** *and click Save.*

34. To exit Excel, *click the Office button and then click Exit Excel.*

This concludes Lesson 7.

LESSON 8: TOOLS AND TECHNIQUES 2—STOCK PORTFOLIO

In this lesson, you will continue to learn and apply helpful tools and techniques using Excel. This includes getting additional practice with using the Merge & Center tool, using the formula auditing feature, using the Oval tool, and password-protecting a file. When your spreadsheet is complete, it will look similar to Excel 2007 Exhibit 22. Some of these tools have been covered in previous lessons, and this lesson will help reinforce your ability to use them effectively. This tutorial assumes that you have completed Lessons 1 through 7, and that you are quite familiar with Excel.

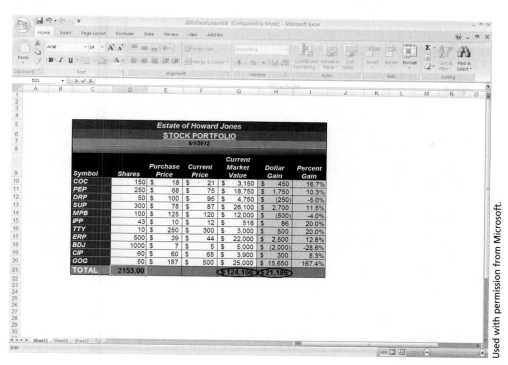

EXCEL 2007 EXHIBIT 22
Stock portfolio

Used with permission from Microsoft.

1. Open Windows. ***Double-click the Microsoft Office Excel 2007 icon on the desktop*** to open the program. Alternatively, ***click the Start button, point to Programs or All Programs, point on Microsoft Office, then click Microsoft Office Excel 2007.*** You should now be in a new, clean, blank workbook. If you are not in a blank workbook, ***click the Office button*** (see Excel 2007 Exhibit 1), ***then click New, then double-click Blank Workbook.***

2. The first thing you will do to complete the spreadsheet in Excel 2007 Exhibit 22 is open the "Lesson 8" file from the disk supplied with this text. Ensure that the disk is inserted in the disk drive, ***click on File on the Office button, then click on Open.*** The "Open" window should now be displayed. ***Click on the down arrow to the right of the white box next to Look in: and select the drive where the disk is located. Double-click on the Excel Files folder. Double-click on the Excel 2007 folder. Double-click on the "Lesson 8" file.***

3. You should now have the stock portfolio spreadsheet shown in Excel 2007 Exhibit 22 open, except that your spreadsheet will be missing two rows of data and some of the formatting. You will add the rows and formatting to the spreadsheet.

4. ***On the Home tab, use the Merge & Center icon in the Alignment group to merge cells C5 to I5.***

5. ***Use the Merge & Center icon to merge cells C6 to I6.***

6. ***Use the Merge & Center icon to merge cells C7 to I7.***

7. Make sure the titles are aligned as shown in Excel 2007 Exhibit 22 ***(on the Home tab, use the Left and Center Align icons in the Alignment group).***

8. ***On the Home tab, use the Fill Color icon in the Font group to make the fill color for cell C5 dark blue*** (or any color you choose).

9. ***Use the Fill Color icon to make the fill color for cell C6 purple*** (any light purple is fine).

10. *Use the Fill Color icon to make the fill color for cell C7 gray* (any light gray is fine).

11. The cell range from C8 to I8 is a text graphic box (similar to a text box—it is just more difficult to see). *Right-click the box and select Format Shape. Then, in the Fill section, click Gradient fill. Next to Preset Colors, click on the first one, Early Sunset* (just hover your cursor over a color and the name will be displayed). *Under Direction, click the first option, Linear Diagonal, then click Close to close the "Format Shape" window.*

12. *On the Home tab, use the Borders icon in the Font group to give cells D10 to I21 a border of All Borders.*

13. *From the Insert tab, click Shapes in the Illustrations group. Under Basic Shapes, click the Oval tool* (it should be the second shape). *Start in the upper left corner of cell G21 and drag the mouse to the lower right corner of G21 to make an oval around the total. Note:* You can slightly move the oval by using the cursor keys on the keyboard to nudge it into place so it is centered in the cell.

14. The color of the oval must now be corrected. Notice that the ribbon has changed and that the Drawing Tools Format ribbon is now displayed. *Click the down arrow next to Shape Fill in the Shape Styles group of the Drawing Tools Format tab. Click No Fill.* The oval now surrounds the number, but the line color of the oval must be changed.

15. *Right-click the oval and select Format Shape. On the left side of the "Format Shape" window, click Line Color. Click the down arrow next to Color, click Black, then click Close in the "Format Shape" window. Make an oval in cell H21 identical to that in cell G21, using the same process.*

16. You will now use the Formula Auditing mode to inspect the formulas in the spreadsheet and ensure that they are accurate.

17. *On the Formulas tab, click Show Formulas in the Formula Auditing group.* Scroll over to the right and look at all of the cells in your spreadsheet. Notice that instead of seeing the result of the formulas, you see the formulas themselves. This is a great tool for checking the accuracy of your spreadsheets. Look at your formulas and make sure they are correct. When you are sure your formulas are accurate, *turn off the Formula Auditing mode by clicking on Show Formulas again.*

18. You will now learn how to password-protect your spreadsheet files. *Click the Office button and then click Save As. In the "Save As" window, click Tools* (it is in the lower portion of the window), *then click General Options.* Under File sharing and next to Password to open, type **A. Click OK.** At the "Confirm Password" window, type **A**, then *click OK.* At the "Save As" window, *click Save* to save the file to My Documents (or the folder of your choice—you must remember where you save it). You will then get a prompt that asks whether you want to increase the security of the document by conversion to Office Open XML Format. Because this is just an exercise, *click No.*

19. If you get a compatibility prompt, just *click Continue.*

20. *Click the Office button, then click Close* to close the file.

21. *Now, click the Office button, and under Recent Documents click on the file you just saved.*

22. The "Password" window should now be displayed. Type **A** in the "Password" window. (The password is case-sensitive, so if you typed a capital A when you

created the password, you must type a capital A to open the document.) ***Click OK.*** The file should now be displayed.

23. You can turn off a password in the same way. ***Click the Office button and then Save As. In the "Save As" window, click Tools, then click on General Options.*** Under File sharing and next to Password to open, use the [**DEL**] key to remove the asterisk. ***Click OK and then click Save.*** At the "**Do you want to replace the existing file?**" prompt, ***point and click Yes.***

24. If you get a compatibility prompt, just ***click Continue.***

25. Close the file and then reopen it, and you will see that you no longer need a password to open it.

26. To print the spreadsheet, ***click the Office button, click Print, then click OK.***

27. To exit Excel, ***click the Office button and then click Exit Excel.***

This concludes the Excel 2007 Hands-On Exercises.

CHAPTER 4

Legal Timekeeping and Billing Software

CHAPTER OBJECTIVES

After completing this chapter, you should be able to do the following:

1. Explain what timekeeping and billing are.
2. Explain the computerized timekeeping and billing process.
3. Describe the different types of legal fee agreements.
4. Identify why accurate billings are important to law firms.
5. List the basic features and functions of timekeeping and billing programs.
6. Describe how timeslips are entered into a timekeeping and billing system.
7. Explain how management reports generated from a timekeeping and billing system can help a firm.
8. Explain what electronic billing is.
9. Describe the factors for determining whether a fee is reasonable.

INTRODUCTION

timekeeping
Tracking time for the purpose of billing clients.

A lawyer's time is the only thing he or she has to sell. Therefore, it is important to keep accurate records of how that time is spent. In the legal environment, the process of tracking time for the purpose of billing clients is called **timekeeping**. In addition to being paid for their time, attorneys must also be reimbursed for the expenses that they incur on each case (such as for postage, copies, court filing fees, expert witness costs, and so forth).

billing
The process of issuing invoices (bills) to collect monies for legal services performed and for expenses incurred.

In the legal environment, the process of issuing bills to collect monies for legal services performed and for expenses incurred is called **billing**. This chapter introduces the principles of legal timekeeping and billing, compares manual and computerized billing systems, describes the computerized timekeeping and billing process, introduces the kinds of fee agreements attorneys and clients enter into, describes what a good billing system is intended to accomplish, shows how computerized timekeeping and billing software can improve efficiency and accuracy in this process, and discusses ethical issues related to timekeeping and billing.

INTRODUCTION TO TIMEKEEPING AND BILLING

Law firms, like all businesses, must generate income. As with other businesses, the running of law firms has a management side. One important management duty that law offices perform is to track the time and expenses of their staff and then generate accurate billings for clients so that law-office staff can be paid. Attorneys spend their time advising clients, talking to witnesses, drafting documents, taking depositions, appearing in court, and undertaking other activities on behalf of their clients. All these activities must be tracked so that clients can be accurately billed for the work the attorneys do. In addition, the expenses attorneys incur on behalf of their clients must be tracked so that the attorneys can be reimbursed. Expenses incurred on behalf of clients include the cost of making photocopies of documents for a client's file, the cost of mailing letters and other documents, travel expenses incurred while working on a client's case, court filing fees, deposition transcription costs, and much more.

If time and expenses were not tracked, law firms could not generate bills, get paid, or adequately run the business. Although timekeeping and billing are not glamorous, they are necessary to the survival of nearly all law firms. Firms that do not put a priority on billing clients, on a regular and accurate basis, will most likely not be around long. It is simply bad business practice to work 70 hours a week, bill for 50 hours, and be paid for 30 hours.

The timekeeping and billing problem becomes even worse when large law firms have to track the time and expenses of hundreds of attorneys and hundreds of paralegals. A good timekeeping and billing system is an absolute necessity.

Why Do Paralegals Need to Know Timekeeping and Billing?

Paralegals need to know about timekeeping and billing for several reasons. In many private law practices, paralegals are required to track their time so it can be charged to the case(s) they are working on. Many law practices that use this system require paralegals to bill a minimum number of hours each year. It is important to remember that private law firms are fundamentally businesses—and like any other business, they need to make money, operate at a profit, and earn money for their owners. Therefore, the billing of time to a firm's clients is crucial to its operations and success as a business. It is not uncommon for a firm to require each paralegal to bill between 26 and 35 hours a week (1,352 and 1,820 hours annually). Paralegals may be terminated from their jobs if they fail to bill the required number of hours. Thus, it is necessary for paralegals to understand how timekeeping and billing work.

In addition, paralegals are sometimes put in charge of the timekeeping and billing system, including managing the timekeeping process and generating bills. This usually occurs in smaller law offices. In those situations, it is important for the paralegals not only to know the process, but also to know how to actually run and operate the system.

MANUAL VERSUS COMPUTERIZED BILLING SYSTEMS

Before legal billing software came along, bills were generated manually, using typewriters or word processors. The manual method was cumbersome and slow, commonly issued bills that contained mathematical errors, and often produced billings that were outdated or inaccurate. This was especially true of large firms with hundreds of clients.

Long ago, it was common for law firms to send out bills only when they needed to pay their own bills (rent, staff salaries, etc.). Attorneys often sat down with a client's file months after work had been performed and tried to remember what they did on the case and how much time it took to do it. Of course, these billings were very inaccurate; it is extremely hard to remember this type of information after the fact, even by the end of a day, let alone after weeks or months. In addition, with manual

timeslip

A slip of paper or
computer record that
records information about
the legal services legal
professionals provide to
each client.

methods, the billing process took hours or days to complete, especially if a large number of bills were being done.

The more traditional way of handling manual billing is to send out bills based on timeslips that each attorney or paralegal fills out every day. A **timeslip** is a piece of paper or a computer entry that legal professionals use to record information about the legal services they provide to each client. Most timeslips contain information such as the name of the case worked on, the date a service was provided, a description of the service, and so on (see Exhibit 4–1). In addition to tracking time, all law firms

PC—Phone Conference	R—Review	Time Conversion	
LR—Legal Research	OC—Office Conference	6 Minutes 0.1 Hour	36 Minutes 0.6 Hour
L—Letter	T—Travel	12 Minutes 0.2 Hour	42 Minutes 0.7 Hour
D—Dictation	CT—Court Hearing	15 Minutes 0.25 Hour	45 Minutes 0.75 Hour
		18 Minutes 0.3 Hour	48 Minutes 0.8 Hour
		24 Minutes 0.4 Hour	54 Minutes 0.9 Hour
		30 Minutes 0.5 Hour	60 Minutes 1.0 Hour

Date	Client/Case	File No.	Services Performed	Attorney	Time Hours & Tenths	
5-7	Smith v. United Sales	118294	Summarized 6 depositions; Client; Δ (Defendant) Helen; Δ Barney, Δ Rose; Witness Forrest & Johnson	BJP	6.	5
5-8	Marcel v. True Oil	118003	PC w/Client Re: Settlement offer; Discussions w/Attorney; Memo to file Re: offer	BJP		3
5-8	Johnson v. State	118118	PC w/Client's Mother, PC w/Client; LR Re: Bail; Memo to file; R correspondence	BJP		75
5-8	Potential claim of Watkins v. Leslie Grocery	Not Assigned Yet	OC w/Client; (New client); Reviewed facts; Received medical records Re; accident; Conf. w/atty	BJP	1.	50
5-8	Smith v. United Sales	118294	Computerized searches on depositions for attorney	BJP		75
5-8	Jay Tiller Bankruptcy	118319	PC w/Creditor, Bank One; Memo to file; Client; LJ to Client	BJP		3
5-8	Potential Claim of Watkins v. Leslie Grocery	—	LR Slip & Fall cases generally; Standard of care	BJP	1.	00
5-8	Marcel v. True Oil	118003	Conf. w/atty. & Client Re: Settlement; Drafted & prepared LJ to Δs Re: Settlement offer	BJP	1.	10
5-8	Jay Tiller Bankruptcy	118319	Drafted Bankruptcy petition; OC w/Client; List of Debts; Fin. Stmt; Conf. w/atty	BJP	1.	00
5-8	Smith v. United Sales	118294	Drafted and prepared depo notice to Witness Spring	BJP		25
5-9	Seeley Real Estate Matter	118300	Ran amortization schedule to attach to 'Contract for Deed'	BJP		25

EXHIBIT 4–1

Typical manual timeslip/Time record form

Johnson, Beck & Taylor
Expense Slip

Expense Type & Code
1 Photocopies	4 Filing Fees	7 Facsimile	10 Travel
2 Postage	5 Witness Fees	8 Lodging	11 Overnight Delivery
3 Long Distance	6 Westlaw/Lexis	9 Meals	12 Other _____

Date   4-5-08   Case Name: Smith v. United   File No.   118294
Expense Code: 1   Quantity 20 pages   Amount File rate   (Billable) Nonbillable
Expense Code: 2   Quantity 4 packages   Amount $4.66   (Billable) Nonbillable
Expense Code: Quantity sent   Amount   Billable Nonbillable
Name of Person Making Expense Slip: JBP

Description of Expense(s) Incurred:
Copies and postage re: Motion to compel 4/5
_____
_____
_____
_____

© Cengage Learning 2013

EXHIBIT 4–2
Expense slip

---

must also track expenses. An **expense slip** is a record of each expense item a firm incurs on behalf of a client (see Exhibit 4–2). Some common expenses include:

- copying costs
- court reporter fees
- electronic legal research (Westlaw/Lexis)
- expert witness fees
- filing fees
- overnight delivery charges
- postage
- travel expenses
- witness/subpoena fees

When a member of a firm incurs an expense for a client, such as by making copies of documents, using postage to send out material, or making a long-distance telephone call, an expense slip is filled out. Then, usually on a monthly basis, manual billings are sent out, based on the timeslips and expense slips that have been collected. Although billings based on timeslips are more accurate than those based on memory, the billing process itself is still quite tedious and slow when done manually.

Computerized billing systems solve many of these problems. Exactly how much time a computerized time and billing program saves over a manual system is somewhat debatable, but a study by one attorney found that manual billing systems can take up to three times longer than computerized methods to produce bills every billing cycle (i.e., every time billings are sent, whether it be biweekly, monthly, or according to some other schedule).

Generally, timekeepers still must record what they do with their time on a timeslip, whether the billing system is manual or computerized. A **timekeeper** is anyone who bills out his or her time; this includes partners, associates, and paralegals. Usually, the information from paper timeslips is entered into the legal billing software

expense slip
A record of each expense item a firm incurs on behalf of the client.

timekeeper
Anyone who bills for time, including partners, associates, and paralegals.

on a daily basis. However, there is a growing trend for attorneys and paralegals to enter their time directly into the computerized timekeeping and billing system without using a separate timeslip at all. This is particularly true in law offices where all timekeepers are connected to a local area network. It is common for firms using computerized billing systems to produce monthly or even weekly bills, according to the wishes of the client.

In addition to alleviating cash-flow problems, most legal billing software produces reports that management can use to help operate the law-firm business (this is covered in more detail later in the chapter). Computerized timekeeping and billing systems also produce billings that are more accurate than those produced by manual methods, because all mathematical computations are performed automatically by the computer.

THE COMPUTERIZED TIMEKEEPING AND BILLING PROCESS

Timekeeping and billing software packages differ greatly from one another. However, the computerized timekeeping and billing process for most billing packages is as shown in Exhibit 4–3.

1. The Client and the Attorney Reach Agreement on Legal Fees

An attorney can bill for services in many different ways. At the outset of most cases, the client and the attorney reach an agreement regarding how much the attorney will charge for her or his services. Preferably, the agreement is in writing in the form of a

EXHIBIT 4–3

Computerized timekeeping and billing cycle

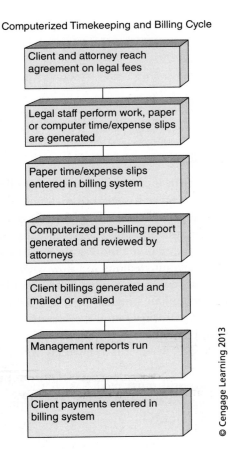

Computerized Timekeeping and Billing Cycle

- Client and attorney reach agreement on legal fees
- Legal staff perform work, paper or computer time/expense slips are generated
- Paper time/expense slips entered in billing system
- Computerized pre-billing report generated and reviewed by attorneys
- Client billings generated and mailed or emailed
- Management reports run
- Client payments entered in billing system

© Cengage Learning 2013

contract. After the legal fee has been agreed on, the new matter is set up in the computerized billing package by entering the client's name and address, the type of case it is, the type of legal fee that has been agreed on, and any other relevant information the law office has identified for inclusion.

2. Legal Staff Perform Services and Prepare Timeslips

When attorneys or paralegals perform work on a legal matter for a client, they fill out a timeslip to track the exact services (either using a manual timeslip form or entering the information directly into the computer). Many timekeeping and billing programs also support data entry from a handheld computer or personal digital assistant (PDA). Expense slips are also generated this way.

3. Timeslips and Expense Slips Are Entered into the Billing System

If manual timeslips are used, the information they contain must be entered into the billing system. Usually the information is typed into the computer in roughly the same format as it appears on the timeslip. It is essential that the information be accurately entered into the computer. In addition, expense slips are entered into the computer to track the expenses the firm has incurred on behalf of a client.

4. A Pre-Billing Report Is Generated and Reviewed

After legal services have been performed and recorded in the time and billing software, the next step is for a **pre-billing report** to be generated. This is done before the final client bills are produced. A pre-billing report is a rough draft of the billings that eventually will be sent to clients (see Exhibit 4–4). The pre-billing report is given to the attorney in charge of the case for review or to a billing committee to make sure the billings are accurate.

pre-billing report
A rough draft compilation of billings.

Attorneys may choose to discount bills for a variety of reasons, including thinking the task should have taken less time than it actually did. Discounts are also given for good customers, because of the client's hardship, for professional courtesy or for friends, or because the billing looks unreasonable. This can, however, be very frustrating to a paralegal who has his or her time cut back. Typically, only the amount that is actually billed is counted against the target or minimum number of billable hours a paralegal is expected to work.

5. Client Billings Are Generated and Mailed or Emailed

Formal client billings (invoices) are generated by the billing system (see Exhibit 4–5). Most timekeeping and billing programs can produce many different billing formats. The computer automatically prints the bills, and they are subsequently mailed or emailed to the clients. Also, most computerized billing systems can now produce some form of electronic billing (see discussion later in this chapter) or can produce PDF files to be emailed.

6. Management Reports Are Generated

In most computerized timekeeping and billing programs, a wide variety of management reports may be generated. Management reports are not used for billing clients; rather, they are used to evaluate the effectiveness of a firm. For example, most programs generate a report that shows how much time is nonbillable (i.e., not chargeable to clients). If a firm has a lot of nonbillable time, it might indicate that the firm is not productive and is losing valuable time from its timekeepers.

EXHIBIT 4–4

Pre-billing report

JOHNSON, BECK & TAYLOR

8/01	Pre-billing Report	Page 1

Refrigeration, Inc.
Miscellaneous Corporate Matters
Case Number: Refrig-002
P.O. Box 10083
500 East Fifth Street

Los Angeles, CA 90014
Phone: (213) 555-9342

Corporate Matters
Monthly
Trust Balance: $2,825
Case Rate: $125
Case Attorney: MJB

Previous Bill Owed $470.20

—Legal Fees—

7/6	MJB	Telephone conference with Stevenson re: June minutes	.50 hr	$62.50
7/7	MJB	Preparation of June minutes; prepared for review at next meeting of the board of directors	1.00 ~~1.50~~ hr	$125.00 MJB ~~$187.50~~
7/9	MJB	Conference with Stevenson at home	.25 hr	none
			1.75	$187.50 MJB
		Total Legal Fees	~~2.25~~ hr	~~$250.00~~

—Costs Advanced—

7/7	MJB	Photocopy documents; June 2005 minutes (for board meeting)	$.25 ea	
			100 items	$25.00
		Total Costs Advanced		**$25.00**

Continued on Page Two

© Cengage Learning 2013

Management reports can also be used to make management decisions, such as that particular types of cases are no longer profitable, the firm needs to raise hourly rates, or other such finance-related decisions.

7. Client Payments Are Entered into the Billing System

Finally, payments made as a result of billings must be recorded or entered into the billing system, giving clients proper credit for the payments they have made.

The Billing Cycle

The timekeeping and billing process is a recurring cycle. Once bills are produced and payments are made for a period, the process starts over if more work is performed on a case. The timeslips for the new period are entered, bills are generated, and so forth. Once a year or so, old timeslips should be purged or deleted from the computer. Without the outdated information, the computer can operate faster.

In essence, manual systems go through the same process or cycle as do computerized systems, except that the pre-billing reports, final billings, and payments are all generated and recorded by hand. However, most manual systems do not have the capability to produce management reports.

```
                    JOHNSON, BECK & TAYLOR
                      555 Flowers Street, Suite 200
                     Los Angeles, California 90038
                          (213) 555-2342

Mary Smith                              Billing Date: 8/02
Refrigeration, Inc.
P.O. Box 10083                          Acct. Number: 4345AS3234
500 East Fifth Street                   Previous Bal. in Trust
                                        $2,825.00
Los Angeles, CA 90014

              RE: Refrigeration Miscellaneous Corporate Matters
```

DATE	PROFESSIONAL SERVICES	INDIV.	TIME	
7/6	Telephone conference with Stevenson re: June minutes	MJB	.50	$62.50
7/7	Preparation of June minutes: prepared for review at next meeting of the board of directors	MJB	1.00	$125.00
7/9	Conference with Stevenson at home	MJB	.25	$-0-
TOTAL FOR THE ABOVE SERVICES			**1.75**	**$187.50**

DATE	EXPENSES	
7/7	Photocopy documents; June minutes (for board meeting)	$25.00
TOTAL FOR ABOVE EXPENSES		**$25.00**
TOTAL BILLING		**$212.50**
CURRENT BALANCE IN TRUST		**$2,612.50**

EXHIBIT 4–5
Final client billing

© Cengage Learning 2013

KINDS OF LEGAL FEE AGREEMENTS

All bills are, of course, based on the fees the law firm charges. Legal fees can be charged and structured in many different ways. The kind of legal fee depends on the type of case or client matter, the specific circumstances of each particular client, and the law practice's preference for certain types of fee arrangements. Fee agreements may specify hourly rates, contingency fees, flat fees, or retainer fees.

Regardless of the type of agreement, a fee agreement should also specify what legal procedures, if any, the attorney is *not* obligated to provide to the client. For example, in Exhibit 4–6, paragraph 3 specifically excludes representation on appeal from this fee agreement. Another example of legal services commonly excluded is collection activities to collect the money awarded by the court or in a settlement. Of course, these activities may always be the subject of another (separate) fee agreement. If there is ambiguity in a fee agreement, the client will generally get the benefit of the doubt: Courts will assume that the legal professional drafted the fee agreement and included all the rights and privileges desired.

Hourly Rate Fees

Hourly rate agreements are the most common. An **hourly rate fee** is a fee for legal services that is billed to the client by the hour at an agreed-upon rate. For example, suppose a client hires an attorney to draft a business contract. The client agrees to pay $250 for every hour the attorney spends drafting the contract and advising the client. If the attorney spent four hours working on the contract, the client would owe the attorney $1,000 ($250 times 4 hours equals $1,000).

hourly rate fee
A fee for legal services that is billed to the client by the hour at an agreed upon rate.

Hourly Rate Contract for Legal Services

This contract for legal services is entered into by and between H. Thomas Weber (hereinafter "Client") and Johnson, Beck & Taylor (hereinafter "Attorneys") on this _____ day of December, 201__. The following terms and conditions constitute the entirety of the agreement between Attorneys and Client and said agreement supersedes and is wholly separate and apart from any previous written or oral agreements.

1. Client hereby agrees to employ Attorneys and Attorneys hereby agree to represent Client in connection with a contract dispute in Jefferson County District Court of Client's claim against Westbridge Manufacturing.

2. Client agrees to pay a retainer fee of $5,000.00, which will be held in Attorney's trust account until earned.

3. Client agrees to pay associate attorneys at $250.00 per hour, partners at $350.00 per hour, paralegals at $100.00 per hour and senior paralegals at $115.00 per hour for legal services rendered regarding the matter in paragraph (1). Attorneys are not hereby obligated to take an appeal from any judgment at the trial court level; if an occasion for an appeal arises, Attorneys and Client hereby expressly agree that employment for such an appeal must be arranged by a separate contract between Attorneys and Client.

4. Client agrees to reimburse Attorneys for all expenses incurred in connection with said matter, and Client agrees to advance all expenses requested by Attorneys during the duration of this contract. Client understands that he is ultimately responsible for the payment of all expenses incurred in connection with this matter.

5. Client understands that Attorneys will bill Client periodically (usually on a monthly or quarterly basis, depending on how quickly the case moves through the system) for copying costs at the rate of $.25 per copy, postage and handling costs, long-distance telephone costs, travel costs, and other costs, and that Client is obligated to make payments upon said billing for said fees and expenses described at paragraphs (2), (3) and (4) above, or otherwise satisfy said fees and expenses. Attorneys will also bill Client for all deposition costs incurred and Client is solely responsible for said deposition costs and Client will be required to advance the sum of **$10,000.00** (or more as necessary) for trial costs (including subpoenas, travel costs, and preparation costs) once the case is set for trial.

6. Client understands and agrees that this litigation may take two to five years or longer to complete and that he will make himself available for Attorneys to confer with and generally to assist Attorneys in said matter. Client agrees he will not discuss the matter of his litigation with any unauthorized person at any time or in any way. Client understands and agrees that Attorneys may withdraw from representation of Client upon proper notice. Client further understands that he can apply for judicial review and approval of this fee agreement if he so desires.

7. Client agrees that associate counsel may be employed at the discretion of Attorneys and that any attorney so employed may be designated to appear on Client's behalf and undertake Client's representation in this matter and such representation shall be upon the same terms as set out herein. **Client understands that Attorneys cannot and do not guarantee any particular or certain relief and expressly state that they cannot promise or guarantee Client will receive any money damages or money settlement.**

The undersigned hereby voluntarily executes this agreement with a full understanding of same and without coercion or duress. All agreements contained herein are severable and in the event any of them shall be deemed to be invalid by any competent court, this contract shall be interpreted as if such invalid agreements or covenants were not contained herein. Client acknowledges receiving a fully executed copy of this contract.

Date _____

Date _____   Johnson, Beck & Taylor _____

NOTE: THIS IS ONLY AN EXAMPLE AND IS NOT INTENDED TO BE A FORM. CHECK WITH YOUR STATE BAR FOR A PROPER FORM.

Hourly rate language {applies to paragraph 3}

© Cengage Learning 2013

EXHIBIT 4–6
Attorney/paralegal hourly rate contract

Hourly rate agreements can be complicated. Law offices have several specific types of hourly rate contracts, including:

- attorney or paralegal hourly rate
- client hourly rate
- blended hourly rate fee
- activity hourly rate

Some law practices use a combination of these as the basis of client billings.

Attorney or Paralegal Hourly Rate The attorney's or paralegal's level of expertise and experience in a particular area determines the **attorney or paralegal hourly rate**. Exhibit 4–6 is an example of this type of contract. If a partner worked on a case, his or her hourly rate charge might be considerably more than an associate's or paralegal's hourly rate charge. Partners typically can bill from $300 to $600 or more an hour, compared with associates, who might bill $200 to $350 an hour. Paralegals typically charge from $65 to $135 (or more) per hour. The difference in price is based on the expertise and experience of the individual working on the case, her or his job title, and locally acceptable rates. In this type of fee agreement, it is possible for a client to be billed at several different rates in a given period if several attorneys or paralegals work on a matter, as they may all charge different rates.

Client Hourly Rate The **client hourly rate** method is based on only one hourly charge for the client, regardless of which attorney works on the case and what is done on the case. For example, if an insurance company hired a law practice to represent it, the insurance company and the law practice might negotiate a client rate of $200 per hour for attorneys and $85 an hour for paralegals. This means that no matter which attorney or paralegal works on the case, whether the attorney or paralegal has 1 year's or 20 years' experience, and regardless of what the attorney or paralegal does (e.g., making routine phone calls or appearing in court), the insurance company will be charged $200 an hour for attorney time or $85 an hour for paralegal time.

Blended Hourly Rate Fee An hourly rate that is set taking into account the blend or mix of law office staff working on a matter is a **blended hourly rate fee**. *one rate* The "mix" includes the associates, partners, and sometimes paralegals working on the matter. Some states allow the "blend" to include only associates and partners, whereas other states allow paralegals to be included. The advantage to this is that billing is simpler, because there is one rate for all paralegal and attorney time spent on the case. The bill is easier for the law office to produce and easier for the client to read. Some states allow paralegals to have their own "blend," which results in one rate for all paralegals (whether experienced or inexperienced, senior or junior, etc.) who work on the matter.

Activity Hourly Rate An **activity hourly rate** is based on the different hourly rates attaching to the type of service or activity actually performed. For example, offices using this approach might bill legal staff time to clients as follows:

Court appearances	$350 per hour
Legal research by attorneys	$225 per hour
Drafting by attorneys	$175 per hour
Telephone calls by attorneys	$150 per hour
Legal research by paralegals	$ 80 per hour
Drafting by paralegals	$ 70 per hour

This sliding-scale hourly fee is based on the difficulty of an activity.

Contingency Fees

A **contingency fee** agreement entitles the attorney to a certain percentage of the total amount of money awarded to the client. If no money is recovered, the attorney collects no legal fees, but is still entitled to be reimbursed for all expenses incurred (see Exhibit 4–7). Contingency fees are typically used by law firms that represent plaintiffs in personal injury, worker's compensation, civil rights, medical malpractice, and other types of cases in which monetary damages may be awarded. The individual

attorney or paralegal hourly rate
A fee based on the attorney's or paralegal's level of expertise and experience in a particular area.

client hourly rate
A fee based on a single hourly charge for the client, regardless of which attorney works on the case and what she or he does on the case.

blended hourly rate fee
A single hourly rate that is set by taking into account the mix of attorneys working on the matter.

activity hourly rate
A fee based on hourly rates that vary depending on the type of service or activity performed and the degree of difficulty of the activity.

contingency fee
A fee collected if the attorney successfully represents the client; typically a percentage of the total recovery.

Contingency Fee Contract for Legal Services

Date:
Name: D.O.B.
Address: Phone:

1. I hereby employ **Johnson, Beck & Taylor** (hereinafter "attorneys") to perform legal services in connection with the following matter as described below:
Personal injury claims arising out of an automobile accident which occurred January 12, 2012, on Interstate I-70.
2. I agree to pay a nonrefundable retainer fee of $2,500; plus,
3. I agree attorneys will receive 20% of any recovery, if prior to filing suit;
I agree attorneys will receive 25% of any recovery, if prior to pretrial conference;
I agree attorneys will receive 33% of any recovery, if after first trial begins;
I agree attorneys will receive 33% of any recovery, if after appeal or second trial begins.
Attorneys are not hereby obligated to take an appeal from any judgment at the trial court level; if an occasion for an appeal arises, attorneys and client hereby expressly agree that employment for such an appeal will be arranged by a separate contract between these parties. Further, I agree that attorneys will be entitled to the applicable above-mentioned percentage of recovery minus whatever a court may award, if I am a prevailing party and the court awards fees following my request therefore.
4. As to the expenses of litigation: I agree to reimburse attorneys for all expenses incurred in connection with said matter, and any expenses not fully paid as incurred may be deducted from my portion of any recovery. I agree to advance any and all expenses requested by attorneys during the duration of this contract. I agree to make an advance of expenses upon execution of this contract in the amount of $1500.00. I understand that these litigation expenses do not pertain to the retainer fee or percentage of any recovery, and I am ultimately responsible for the payment of all litigation expenses.
5. I understand that attorneys will bill client periodically, and that client is obligated to make payments upon said billing for said fees and expenses described at paragraphs (2), and (4), or otherwise satisfy said fees and expenses.
6. I understand and agree that this litigation may take 2 to 5 years, or longer to complete, and that I will make myself available to attorneys to confer with, and generally to assist attorneys in said matter. I will not discuss the matter of my litigation with any unauthorized person at any time in any way. I understand and agree that attorneys may withdraw from representation of client at any time upon proper notice.
7. I agree that associate counsel may be employed at the discretion of Johnson, Beck & Taylor, and that any attorney so employed may be designated to appear on my behalf and undertake my representation in this matter and such representation shall be upon the same terms as set out herein. Attorneys have **not** guaranteed, nor can they guarantee, any particular or certain relief.
The undersigned herewith executes this agreement with a full understanding of same, without coercion or duress, and understands the same to be the only agreement between the parties with regard to the above matter, and that if any other terms are to be added to this contract, the same will not be binding, unless and until they are reduced to writing and signed by all parties to this contract. I acknowledge receiving a fully executed copy of this contract. Further, the undersigned Client understands that said Client is entitled to apply for judicial review and approval of this fee agreement, if Client so desires.

Date

Date   Johnson, Beck & Taylor

NOTE: THIS IS ONLY AN EXAMPLE AND IS NOT INTENDED TO BE A FORM. CHECK WITH YOUR STATE BAR FOR A PROPER FORM.

© Cengage Learning 2013

Contingency fee language (bracket label)

EXHIBIT 4–7
Contingency fee contract

who would like to bring the lawsuit usually has little or no money to pay legal fees up front. Contingency fees typically range from 20 percent to 50 percent.

Contingency fee agreements must be in writing. Exhibit 4–7 shows a sample contingency fee contract. Some states put a cap (a maximum percentage) on what an attorney can collect for claims in areas such as worker's compensation and medical malpractice. For example, some states prohibit attorneys from receiving more than a 25 percent contingency fee in a worker's compensation case.

By their nature, contingency fees are risky because if no money is recovered, the attorney receives no fee. However, even if no money is recovered, the client must still pay legal expenses such as filing fees and photocopying. Contingency fees and hourly fees also may be used together. When clients agree to this arrangement, some offices reduce their hourly fee and/or lessen the percentage of the contingency portion of the fee.

Flat Fees

A **flat fee** (sometimes called a *fixed fee*) is a fee for specific legal services that is billed as a specific dollar amount. Some offices have a set fee for handling certain types of matters, such as preparing a will or handling an uncontested divorce, a name change, or a bankruptcy. For example, suppose a client agreed to pay an attorney a flat fee of $500 to prepare a will. No matter how many hours the attorney spends preparing the will, the fee is still $500. Flat fee agreements are usually used when a legal matter is simple, straightforward, and involves few risks.

flat fee
A fee for specific legal services that is billed as a fixed amount.

Retainer Fees

The word *retainer* has several meanings in the legal environment. Generally, retainer fees are monies paid by the client at the beginning of a case or matter. However, there are many types of retainers. When an attorney or paralegal uses the term *retainer*, it could mean a retainer for general representation, a case retainer, a pure retainer, or a cash advance. In addition, all retainer fees are either earned or unearned.

Earned versus Unearned Retainers

There is a *very* important difference between an earned retainer and an unearned retainer. An **earned retainer** means that the law office or attorney has done work to earn the money and is entitled to deposit the money in the office's or attorney's **operating account**. Firms use monies from the operating account to pay the attorney's or law office's operating expenses, such as salaries and rent.

An **unearned retainer** is money that is paid up front by the client as an advance against the attorney's future fees and expenses; it is a kind of down payment. Until the money is actually earned by the attorney or law office, it belongs to the client. According to ethical rules, unearned retainers may *not* be deposited in the attorney's or law office's normal operating (checking) account. Unearned retainers must be deposited into a separate trust account and can be transferred into the firm's operating account only as they are earned.

A **trust or escrow account** is a separate bank account, apart from a law office's or attorney's operating account, where unearned client funds are deposited. As an attorney or law office begins to earn money by providing legal services to the client, the attorney can bill the client and move the earned portion from the trust account to his or her own law office operating account.

The written contract should set out whether the retainer is earned or unearned. However, in some instances the contract may be vague on this point. Typically, when a contract refers to a nonrefundable retainer, this means an earned retainer.

Additionally, in many contracts, flat-fee rates, as discussed earlier, are said to be nonrefundable and thus are treated as earned. However, some state ethical rules regulate this area heavily: Some hold that all flat fees are a retainer, so they are considered unearned and must be placed in trust until they are "earned out." Hence, whether a retainer is earned or unearned will depend on your state's ethical rules and on the written contract.

earned retainer
The money the law office or attorney has earned and is entitled to deposit in the office's or attorney's own bank account.

operating account
Bank account used by a law firm for the deposit of earned fees and payment of law-firm expenses.

unearned retainer
Money that is paid up front by the client as an advance against the attorney's future fees and expenses. Until the money is actually earned by the attorney or law office, it actually belongs to the client.

trust or escrow account
A bank account, separate and apart from a law office's or attorney's operating bank account, where unearned client funds are deposited.

Where Does the Interest Go? All bank accounts earn interest, even if the interest is not paid to the account holder. The money in a trust account belongs to the client, but the account is in the name of the law firm. So, who gets the interest? The law firm cannot keep interest earned on client funds. It might seem that the easy answer is to pay the interest to the client, especially if the amount held in trust is large enough or is held in the trust account long enough. However, that is not usually either possible or feasible.

The problem is twofold: First, the amount of interest that any individual client might earn is typically very small. (Remember that, in most instances, a single trust account contains funds belonging to many clients.) Second, it costs money to calculate and remit the exact amount of interest that might be owed to each client. For example, it might cost a firm $20 to send a client a check for less than $1.00. So, who gets the interest?

The answer is IOLTA, which stands for "Interest on Law Office Trust Accounts." Banks participating in the IOLTA program take the interest earned by trust accounts and pay that money to the state IOLTA program. The money is then used to fund or support legal aid or indigent defense programs in the state.

cash advance
Unearned monies that are paid before services are rendered, to cover the attorney's future fees and expenses.

Cash Advance Retainer One type of retainer is a **cash advance**: this money is unearned and is an advance against the attorney's future fees and expenses. Until the attorney does the work to earn the money, it actually belongs to the client. The cash advance is a typical type of unearned retainer.

For example, suppose a client wishes to hire an attorney to litigate a contract dispute. The attorney agrees to represent the client only if the client agrees to pay $200 per hour with a $10,000 cash advance against fees and expenses. The attorney must deposit the $10,000 in a trust account. If the attorney deposits the cash advance in her own account (whether it is the firm's account or the attorney's own personal account), the attorney has violated several ethical rules. As the attorney works on the case and bills the client for fees and expenses, the attorney will write checks out of the trust account for the amounts of those billings. The attorney must tell the client that money is being withdrawn and keep an accurate balance of how much the client has left in trust. So, if after a month the attorney has billed the client for $500, the attorney would write a check for $500 from the trust account, deposit the $500 in the attorney's or the firm's own bank account, and inform the client that the remaining retainer (trust balance) is $9,500. If the case ended at this point, the client would be entitled to a refund of the $9,500 remaining in trust.

retainer for general representation
A retainer is typically used when a client such as a corporation or school board requires continuing legal services throughout the year.

Retainer for General Representation Another type of retainer is a **retainer for general representation**. This type of retainer is typically used when a client such as a corporation requires continuing legal services throughout the year. The client pays a specific amount, typically up front or on a prearranged schedule, to receive these ongoing services. For example, suppose a small school board would like to be able to contact an attorney at any time with general legal questions. The attorney and the school board could enter into this type of agreement for a fee of $7,500 every 6 months. The school board could contact the attorney at any time and ask general questions, but the attorney would never receive more (or less) than $7,500 for the six-month period regardless of how often they did so.

Retainers for general representation allow the client to negotiate and anticipate what the fee will be for the year. This type of agreement usually covers only general legal advice, and does not include matters such as litigation. Depending on the specific arrangements between the client and the attorney, and on the specific state's rules of ethics, many retainers for general representation are viewed as being earned, since the client can call at any time and get legal advice. Retainers for general representation resemble a flat-fee agreement. The difference is that in a flat-fee agreement, the attorney or law office is contracting to do a specific thing for a client, such as prepare a will or file a bankruptcy. In the case of a retainer for general representation, the attorney is agreeing to make himself available to the client for all nonlitigation needs.

Case Retainer Another type of retainer is a **case retainer**, which is a fee that is billed at the beginning of a matter, is not refundable to the client, and is usually paid to the office at the beginning of the case as an incentive for the office to take the case. For example, a client comes to an attorney with a criminal matter. The attorney agrees to take the case only if the client agrees to pay a case retainer of $1,000 up front plus $200 an hour for every hour worked on the case. The $1,000 is paid to the attorney as an incentive to take the case and thus is earned. The $200 per hour is a client hourly rate charge. Because the case retainer is earned, the attorney can immediately deposit it in the office's own bank account.

Another example of use of a case retainer is a case involving a contingency fee. Suppose a client comes to an attorney asking her to file an employment discrimination case. The attorney agrees to accept the case only if the client agrees to a 30 percent contingency fee and a nonrefundable or case retainer of $1,000. Again, the earned retainer is an incentive for the attorney to take the case and can be deposited in the attorney's or the office's own bank account.

Pure Retainer A rather rare type of retainer is a **pure retainer**. A pure retainer obligates the law office to be available to represent the client throughout the time period agreed upon. The part that distinguishes a pure retainer from a retainer for general representation is that the office typically must agree not to represent any of the client's competitors and not to undertake any type of representation adverse to the client. Some clients, typically major corporations, think that listing the name of a prestigious law firm as counsel has a business value that they are willing to pay for.

Retainers for general representation, case retainers, and pure retainers are usually earned retainers, and a cash advance is an unearned retainer. However, *the language of the contract determines whether amounts paid to attorneys up front are earned or unearned.* The earned/unearned distinction is extremely important and is yet another reason all fee agreements should be in writing.

> **case retainer**
> A fee that is billed at the beginning of a matter, is not refundable to the client, and is usually paid at the beginning of the case as an incentive for the office to take the case.

> **pure retainer**
> A fee that obligates the office to be available to represent the client throughout the agreed-upon time period.

Value Billing

Recently, much has been written in the legal press about why private law practices should stop billing by the hour and use a different billing method. The reasons for the change from hourly billing include:

- The client never knows during any stage of the work how much the total legal fee will be.
- Clients sometimes avoid calling (or otherwise communicating with) paralegals and attorneys because they know they will be charged for the time, even if it is a simple phone call.
- Clients have trouble seeing the relationship between what is performed by the paralegal or attorney and the enormous fees that can be incurred.
- Hourly billing encourages lawyers and paralegals to be inefficient (i.e., the longer it takes to perform a job, the more revenue they earn).
- Many law offices force attorneys and paralegals to bill a quota number of hours a year, which puts a tremendous amount of pressure on the individual paralegal and attorney.

Value billing has been proposed as an alternative to the traditional system. The **value billing** concept uses a type of fee agreement that is based not on the time required to perform the work, but on the basis of the perceived value of the services to the client. Value billing typically requires that the attorney and client reach a consensus on the amount of fees to be charged. Because of increased competition in the legal environment and because of the power of the client as a buyer of legal services, clients are demanding that they have a say in how much they are going to pay for legal services, what type(s) of service will be provided, and what quality of legal services they will get for that price.

LEGAL EXPENSES

Under most ethical canons, attorneys must charge for the expenses they incur on behalf of a client. Expenses include the costs of photocopies, postage for mailing letters and documents regarding a case, long-distance telephone calls regarding the case, and so forth. Legal expenses for cases that are litigated or filed in court can sometimes be very high. They include court reporter fees (fees charged by a court reporter to transcribe hearings, oral statements, trial testimony, etc.) and expert witness fees (fees charged, usually by the hour, by subject matter experts to give testimony), just to name two.

TIMEKEEPING AND BILLING FOR PARALEGALS

Many law offices are still firmly wedded to the billable hour concept, and thus set billable hour quotas that paralegals must meet. As indicated previously, an average number of billable hours for paralegals ranges from 1,400 to 1,800 hours annually. Historically, this was not the case. In the late 1950s, 1,300 billable hours was thought to be realistic. The minimum number of billable hours varies greatly depending on the location and size of the law office and on the types of cases it handles.

Recording Time

A **billable hour** consists of 60 minutes of legal services. Clients expect to receive a full 60 minutes of legal services when they are billed for one hour. Interruptions, calls home, and checking personal email are not billable. It is imperative that legal professionals take great care when billing clients for their time.

There are several different ways to actually record and/or track your time. One method is to bill time in tenths of an hour, with 0.5 being a half-hour and 1.0 being an hour. Every six minutes is a tenth of the hour, so you would be billing for six-minute intervals. Billing in tenths works out as follows:

0–6 minutes	= 0.1 hour
7–12 minutes	= 0.2 hour
13–18 minutes	= 0.3 hour
19–24 minutes	= 0.4 hour
25–30 minutes	= 0.5 hour
31–36 minutes	= 0.6 hour
37–42 minutes	= 0.7 hour
43–48 minutes	= 0.8 hour
49–54 minutes	= 0.9 hour
55–60 minutes	= 1.0 hour

As an alternative, some offices bill using a quarter of an hour as the smallest increment of time, as follows:

$$0\text{–}15 \text{ minutes } = 0.25 \text{ hour}$$
$$16\text{–}30 \text{ minutes } = 0.50 \text{ hour}$$
$$31\text{–}45 \text{ minutes } = 0.75 \text{ hour}$$
$$46\text{–}60 \text{ minutes } = 1.0 \text{ hour}$$

Although the quarterly basis is easier to use, it is not as accurate as the tenth-of-an-hour system. Suppose you took a five-minute phone call from a client and your average billing rate was $70 an hour. Using the tenth-of-an-hour system, the fee for the phone call would be $7.00 (0.1 hour times $70 equals $7.00). However, using the quarterly system, the fee for the phone call would be $17.50, since 0.25 is the least possible billable interval (0.25 times $70 equals $17.50), or more than twice as much.

It is important that you include as much detail as possible when completing your time records, that the language be clear and easily understandable, and that the time record itself be legible. Clients are usually more willing to pay a bill when they know exactly what service was performed for them. For example, compare these bill excerpts:

1. Telephone conference—0.50 hr., $35.00.
2. Telephone conference with client on Plaintiff's Request for Production of Documents regarding whether client has copies of the draft contracts at issue—0.50 hr., $35.00.

Most clients prefer the latter, as they are able to see, and hopefully remember, exactly what specific services they received. Which of these bills would *you* rather receive?

Timekeeping Practices

If the average paralegal is required to bill between 1,400 and 1,800 hours a year, it is very important that he or she take the timekeeping function extremely seriously. The following are some suggestions regarding time tracking.

- *Find out how many hours you must bill annually, monthly, and weekly up front, and track where you are in relationship to the quota.* One of the first things you should do when you start a new paralegal job is find out how many billable hours you must submit. If the office requires that you bill 1,400 hours a year, budget this on a monthly and weekly basis, and keep track of where you are so that you will not have to try to make it all up at the end of the year.
- *Find out when timesheets are due.* Find out exactly what day of the week timesheets are due, so that you can submit yours on time.
- *Keep copies of your timesheets.* Always keep a copy of your timesheet for your own file in case the original is lost or misplaced. Having a copy also allows you to go back and calculate the number of billable hours you have put in to date.
- *Record your time contemporaneously on a daily basis.* One of the biggest mistakes you can make is to not record your time as you go along during the day. If you wait until the end of the day and then try to remember all the things you did, there is absolutely no way you will be able to accurately reconstruct everything. In the end, you will be the one who suffers, doing work you did not get credit for. Keep a timesheet handy and fill it out as you go along.
- *Record your actual time spent; do not discount your time.* Do not discount your time because you think you should have been able to perform a job faster.

If it took you four hours to finish an assignment and you worked the whole four hours, there is no reason to discount the time. If the supervising attorneys think a discount is warranted, they can decide to do so, but it is not up to you to do that. However, if you made a mistake or had a problem that you do not think the client should be billed for, tell your supervising attorney, and let him or her help you make the decision.

- *Be aware if billable hours are related to bonuses or merit pay increases.* Be aware of how billable hours are used. In some law offices, billable hours are used in allocating bonuses and merit increases, and may be considered in performance evaluations, so know up front how your office uses the tally.
- *Be ethical.* Always be honest and ethical in the way you fill out your timesheets. Padding your timesheets is unethical and simply wrong. Eventually, wrongdoing regarding timekeeping, billing, or handling client funds will become apparent.
- *Be aware of things that keep you from billing time.* Be aware of distractions and things that decrease your productivity, such as:
  - People who lay their troubles at your feet or who are constantly taking your attention away from your work. An appropriate approach is to say, "I would really like to hear about it at lunch, but right now I am very busy."
  - Time wasted trying to track down other people or trying to find information you need.
  - Constant interruptions, including phone calls. If you really need to get something done, go someplace where you can get the work done and tell others to hold your calls. However, check in every once in a while to return client phone calls. Client calls should be returned as soon as possible (note also that calls with clients probably constitute billable time!).

Billing for Paralegal Time—Paralegal Profitability

Many law offices bill for paralegal time as well as for attorney time. Many clients prefer this, because the paralegal hourly rates are much lower than the attorney hourly rates. The average actual billing rate for paralegals ranges from $65 to $135 per hour.

For example, assume that an associate attorney and a paralegal can both prepare discovery documents in a case and that the task will take seven hours. If the paralegal bills at $75 an hour and the associate bills at $150 an hour, the cost to the client if the paralegal does the job is $525, whereas the cost if the associate drafts the discovery is $1,050. Thus, the client will have saved $525 simply by allowing the paralegal to do the job. The client would still have to pay for the attorney's time to review the paralegal's work, but that cost would be minimal. This strategy represents substantial savings to clients.

The question of whether law offices can bill for paralegal time was considered by the U.S. Supreme Court in *Missouri v. Jenkins,* 491 U.S. 274 (1989). In that case, the plaintiff was successful on several counts in a civil rights lawsuit and was attempting to recover attorney's fees from the defendant under a federal statute. The statutory language provided that the prevailing party could recover "reasonable attorney's fees" from the other party. The plaintiff argued for recovery for the time that paralegals spent working on the case as well as for the time that attorneys spent. The defendant argued that paralegal time was not "attorney's fees." Alternatively, the defendants argued that if they did have to pay something for paralegal time, they should have to pay only about $15 an hour, which represented the overhead costs to the office for a paralegal.

The Court noted that paralegals carry out many useful tasks under the direction of attorneys and found that "reasonable attorney's fees" refers to the reasonable fee for work produced, whether it be by attorneys or paralegals. The Court also found that under the federal statute, paralegal time should not be compensated for at the overhead cost to the office, but should be paid at the prevailing market rates in the area for paralegal time. The Court noted that the prevailing rate for paralegals in that part of the country at that time was about $40 an hour and held that the office was entitled to receive that amount for paralegal hours worked on the case. Thus, it is clear that offices can bill for paralegal time if they choose to do so. The case also reminds us that purely clerical tasks or secretarial tasks cannot be billed at the paralegal rate— or any other rate.

Although the *Missouri v. Jenkins* case was a landmark decision for paralegals, the opinion involved the interpretation of a specific statute, the Civil Rights Act. Fee questions arise in many different situations, and if another court is deciding a fee question other than in the context of the Civil Rights Act, it may reach a different decision. Since *Missouri v. Jenkins* was decided, many courts in many different jurisdictions have allowed the recovery of paralegal time at the prevailing local rate. In addition, courts have also found that billing for an attorney's time spent on a matter is not reasonable (for purposes of court awarded fees) if the tasks performed "are normally performed by paralegals." Thus, many courts have recognized the unique niche that paralegals fill in the legal field.

FUNCTIONS OF A SUCCESSFUL BILLING SYSTEM

An often forgotten requirement for any billing system is that it must please the firm's customers or clients: The quality of the billing system is determined in large part by whether the firm's clients are satisfied with the billings and whether they pay the bills that are sent to them. One of the quickest ways for a firm to lose a good client is by mishandling the client's money in some way, by overbilling the client, or by giving the client the impression that its money is being used unjustly or unfairly. In addition, mishandling a client's money is a top reason that attorneys are disciplined. A good billing system, whether or not it is computerized, must do several things, including accurately track each client's account, provide regular billings, and itemize the services performed. In short, a billing system should satisfy the law office customers so that they are willing to make timely payments.

Accurately Track How Much a Client Has Paid the Firm

A successful billing system must be able to accurately track how much clients have paid the firm, and whether the payments were made in cash, through a trust account, or otherwise. Although this may seem easy, it often is not. Consider how you feel when a creditor either loses one of your payments or misapplies it in some manner. This is especially important for a law firm because in many instances large sums of money are involved. Payments can be lost, not entered into the billing system, or applied to the wrong client's account. It is important that the firm take great care with what goes into and comes out of the billing system, and that the information be accurate.

Send Regular Billings

We all expect to receive regular billings for routine things, such as credit card balances, utility use, and so forth. This makes budgeting and financial planning much easier. Likewise, most clients like to receive timely billings, at least monthly.

Imagine the frustration of a client who receives a quarterly billing that is four or five times more expensive than expected. Regular billings will alert clients to how they are being billed and how much they need to budget for legal services. In addition, if a client sees timely bills that are higher than were planned for, he can tell the firm how to proceed so as to limit future bills before costs are incurred. This at least gives the client the option of cutting back on legal services instead of having to overspend and get angry at the firm for not communicating the charges on a timely basis.

Provide Client Billings That Are Fair and Respectful

Billings that are fair and courteous are essential to a good billing system. If a client believes that the firm is overcharging for services or that the billings are curt and unprofessional, the client may simply not pay a bill, or may delay payment. If you ever speak to a client regarding a bill, always be courteous and respectful, and try to understand the situation from the client's point of view. If a dispute arises, simply make notes on the client's side of the story, relay the information to the attorney in charge of the matter, and let the attorney resolve the situation.

Provide Client Billings That Identify What Services Have Been Provided

It is important for the client to know exactly what services she received and what the bill covers. Bills that just say "For Services Rendered" are for the most part a thing of the past. Although the format of the bill will depend on the client, it is recommended that invoices indicate exactly what service was performed, by whom, on what date, for how long, and for what charge. With an itemized record, the client can see exactly what the firm is doing and how hard the staff is working, and may thus be more willing to pay the bill.

Provide Client Billings That Are Clear

Finally, billings should be clear and free of legalese. They should be easy to read and contain the information a client wants to see. Payments on billings that are complicated and hard to understand are often held up while the client tries to decipher the bill.

COMPUTERIZED TIMEKEEPING AND BILLING: SOFTWARE

Many different billing and timekeeping programs are available. As with most software applications, competing programs offer a wide range of diverse features, structures, and prices. Some programs just do timekeeping and billing; others offer functionalities in a variety of related areas such as general ledger, accounts payable, accounts receivable, payroll, trust accounting, docket control and calendaring, and case management. Programs are available for all sizes and types of law firms. Some timekeeping and billing software packages are designed for particular sizes of law firms, usually designated as large (100 to a thousand attorneys), medium (25 to 100 attorneys), and small (1 to 25 attorneys).

This text only covers the basics of timekeeping and billing software; the manner in which any particular package handles these functions will depend on the package. In this section you will learn to understand the fundamentals of computerized timekeeping and billing: the main menu and the primary tasks that most timekeeping and billing programs perform; the client information screen and how client records are set up in timekeeping and billing programs; how time and expense slips are entered into the billing system; how client bills are produced; and what management reports most systems can run (such as case/client lists, aged accounts receivable reports, and timekeeper productivity reports). This text also touches on the nature of and systems involved in electronic billing.

Main Menu/Fundamental Tasks of Timekeeping and Billing Programs

Exhibit 4–8 shows the main menu of Tabs3, a popular timekeeping and billing program. Exhibit 4–8 is a good example of the functions found in most timekeeping and billing programs. These include entering and maintaining client accounts and preferences, entering time records, tracking attorneys' fees, entering and tracking expenses, recording client payments, managing client trust funds (some programs do this and others do not), managing and tracking client accounts, generating and managing pre-bills and final bills/statements, tracking accounts receivable, and producing management reports. Some of these tasks and activities are discussed in more detail in this chapter, but these are the general functions that most timekeeping and billing programs provide.

Entering Client-Related Information

Before timekeeping data can be entered into the computer or a bill can be generated for a client, certain information regarding the client must be entered into the

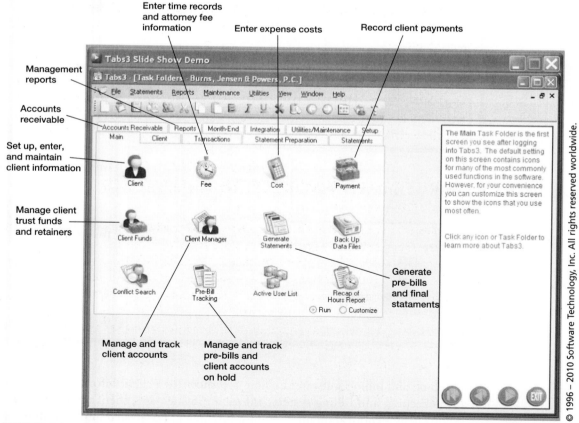

EXHIBIT 4–8
Timekeeping and billing program main menu

EXHIBIT 4–9
Client information screens

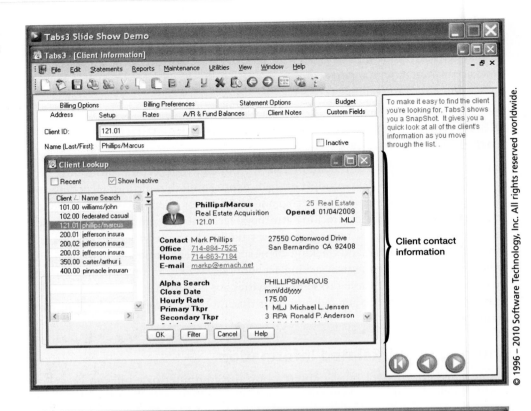

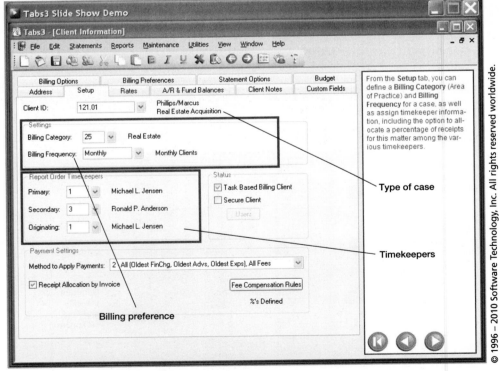

timekeeping and billing software. Exhibit 4–9 shows two client information screens in a timekeeping and billing system. Information such as a client's name and address and client identification number must be entered. Fee-related information must also be entered, such as how the case will be billed and whether the fee is an hourly rate, a flat fee, or another type of fee, and who is the primary timekeeper for the file (see Exhibit 4–9). Most legal billing programs are very flexible regarding how cases are to be billed. Notice in the second screen of Exhibit 4–9 that the billing frequency for this particular client is monthly. This can be changed depending on how often the client wants to be billed. The Billing Preferences option allows a firm to set up different billing formats for each client. Some clients may want complete details and a description of every action that was performed on their behalf—who performed it, how long it took, and so forth. Other clients may want only a very brief description of what services were performed. Bill preference options allow you to control this type of information.

Exhibit 4–10 shows the accounts receivable and fund balances screen for a client. This client information screen gives an overall view of the client's account and billing status, as well as information related to any funds the client may have in trust.

Time Record Data Entry

Once the basic information about a firm's clients has been entered into the timekeeping and billing software, specific timekeeping information can be entered into the computer. Many timekeepers now enter their own timeslips directly into the computer. Time records can also be entered remotely, using a laptop, handheld computer, or PDA. The timekeeper enters the information into the PDA offsite, such as at a courthouse or deposition; then, when she gets back to the office, she synchronizes the PDA with the main computer and billing program. Alternatively, a timekeeper may complete a manual timeslip and have a clerk enter it into the computer.

Exhibit 4–11 shows a typical time record entry screen. In the Timekeeper field, the timekeeper's initials (or name) are entered. (Remember, a timekeeper is anyone who bills for his or her time.) In Exhibit 4–11, the timekeeper's name is Michael

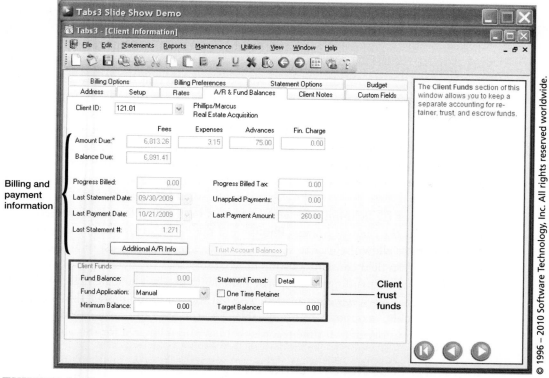

EXHIBIT 4–10

Client information—Accounts receivable and fund balances screen

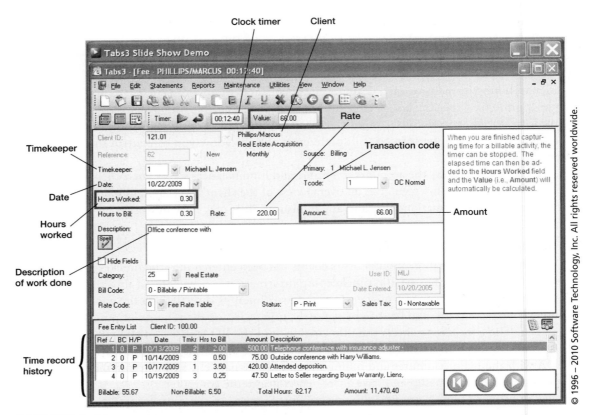

EXHIBIT 4–11
Entering a time record

Jensen. Many programs allow the user to "pop up" a list of all the possible time-keepers in a firm. Notice the clock/timer feature in Exhibit 4–11. It shows that the timekeeper has been performing a task for the client for 12 minutes and 40 seconds. Many timekeeping and billing programs allow users to interactively turn on a clock or meter as they are providing legal services to clients so that they know exactly how much time they have spent on a matter. Exhibit 4–11 also shows the current hours worked on the project (three-tenths of an hour), the rate at which the client is being billed ($220 an hour), and the current amount being charged to the client for the task. The Tcode field in Exhibit 4–11 accepts transaction codes; in this example, the code is 1, which in this system represents an office conference. Other standard transaction codes represent legal research, court appearances, depositions, drafting, and so forth.

The Client ID field indicates which client is to be billed for this time record. In Exhibit 4–11, the client is Marcus Phillips and the matter is a real estate acquisition. Most programs allow the user to select a client's account from a list of active clients. The Description field contains a listing of what services were performed. This can be detailed or brief, depending on the particular client's needs. The Date field, obviously, shows when the services were provided. The bill code in Exhibit 4–11 shows that the service is billable, as opposed to nonbillable. The time record screen in Exhibit 4–11 even shows a history of past time records that have been entered for this client.

Expense/Cost Record Data Entry

The data entry screen for entering expense or cost records is nearly the same as the time record data entry screen in most programs. It will include areas for entering a client ID, date, transaction code (for example, fax costs), and units (such as the number of pages faxed). Many programs also display an expense history, similar to the history of past time records shown at the bottom of Exhibit 4–11.

Pre-Billing and Final Statements

Generating bills is the most important aspect of any timekeeping and billing program. In general, the timekeeping and billing program takes all the time and expense slips for a period, assembles them by client, and calculates the amount due for each slip for each client. It then includes any past due balances and client payments, and calculates a total amount due for that period for each client.

Once all the timeslips and expense slips for a period have been entered into the timekeeping and billing system, usually the next step in preparing client bills is to generate a pre-billing report. Most programs give you the option to produce either drafts (pre-bills) or final bills. The pre-billing tracking screen shows when pre-bills for the selected clients were run and gives you the option of putting a "hold" on the account or going ahead and issuing final statements.

One of the first steps in generating pre-bills or bills is to select which time records and expense slips to include. Users can also select time and expense records by client ID, timekeeper, billing frequency, location, or status of files, among other things (see first screen of Exhibit 4–12).

Once the pre-billing report has been generated, it is up to the individual time-keepers or decision makers to decide if changes should be made to the bills. It is usually fairly simple to make changes in bills and to correct any mistakes. Once the information is accurate, the final step is to generate the actual client billings.

In many programs, the format of a bill is set up in the client information screen (see second screen of Exhibit 4–12). Law firms use many different formats to bill clients. For example, some bill formats contain only general information about the services provided, whereas other formats show greater detail. The look and format of billings depend on the law firm, its clients, the type of law practiced, and so forth. Thus, it is important that any timekeeping and billing package be flexible as to client billing formats and have a variety of formats easily available.

Producing detailed bills takes work. It requires timekeepers to prepare accurate, current timeslips of what work they have done. This seems easy enough, but it is not. It is sometimes difficult to convince timekeepers to write down each service they perform for each client. However, most clients strongly prefer detailed billings. So, although itemized billings are sometimes inconvenient for the timekeepers and take longer to produce, if the bill is paid in the end, the extra work has "paid off."

Management Reports

Almost all timekeeping and billing software packages can produce a wide variety of management reports (see Exhibit 4–13). **Management reports** are used to help law office managers analyze whether the office is operating efficiently and effectively. Management reports can be used to track problems an office may be experiencing and to help devise ways to correct any problems. The following subsections explain some common management reports and how law office staff use them.

management reports
Reports used to help managers analyze whether the office is operating in an efficient, effective, and profitable manner.

Case/Client List   Most billing packages allow the user to produce a case or client list. An accurate list of all active cases is very important when a firm is trying to effectively manage a large caseload. Most reports list clients not only by name, but also by the appropriate account number (called the client identification number by some programs). This cross-listing is useful when trying to locate a client's identification number.

EXHIBIT 4–12
Generating final bills

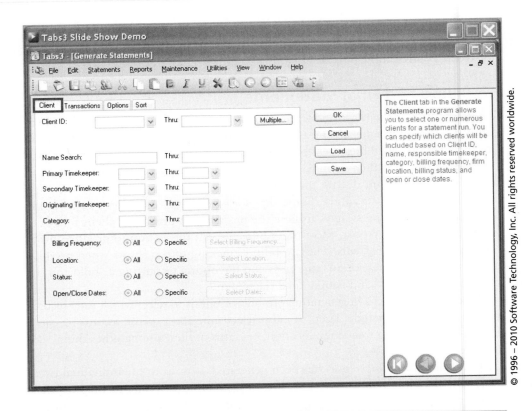

aged accounts receivable report

A report showing all cases that have outstanding balances due and how much these balances are past due.

Aged Accounts Receivable Report   The **aged accounts receivable report** shows all clients that have outstanding balances owed to the office and how long these balances are past due. This report allows management to clearly see which clients are not paying and how old the balances are. This report also is helpful for identifying and following up with clients who are slow to pay their bills.

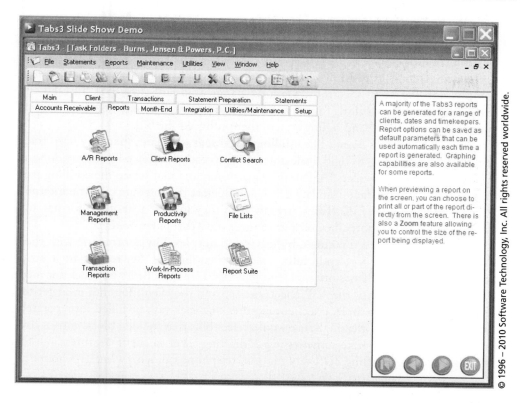

EXHIBIT 4–13
Management reports

Most programs allow such a report to be run according to the type of case. Thus, management can see what types of cases (criminal, divorce, tax, etc.) have the most aged accounts. If one particular type of case has more than its share of aged accounts, it might be more profitable to stop taking such cases. So, from a management perspective, this can be a very important and useful report.

Note that aged account information should not appear on bills sent to clients. Bills with balances that are more than 30 days old should simply say "past due."

Timekeeper Productivity Report   The amount of billable and nonbillable time being spent by each timekeeper is shown in the **timekeeper productivity report**. This report can be used to identify which timekeepers are the most diligent or productive. Most packages allow a productivity report to be run for a quarter or a whole year.

Case Type Productivity Report   The **case type productivity report** shows which types of cases (criminal, personal injury, bankruptcies, etc.) are bringing in the most revenue. Obviously, this report shows which types of cases are the most profitable and which are the least profitable. Management can use this report to decide which areas of law to concentrate on to become more profitable.

Electronic Billing

When using **electronic billing**, law firms bill clients in a fashion that conforms to standard billing codes and uses a standard electronic format, using such means as the Internet. Many large clients, such as Fortune 1000 corporations and other businesses, demand that law firms bill them using electronic means. For large clients, electronic billing is a big improvement over traditional paper billing, although it introduces a certain amount of rigidity and places some administrative burden on the law firm.

timekeeper productivity report
A report showing how much billable and nonbillable time is being spent by each timekeeper.

case type productivity report
A report showing which types of cases (e.g., criminal, personal injury, bankruptcy, etc.) are the most profitable.

electronic billing
Client billing that uses a standard electronic format, using such means as the Internet, and conforms to standard billing codes.

Electronic billing is actually a term of art; it does not mean, for example, just sending a bill as a PDF or Microsoft Word email attachment to the client. Rather, electronic billing means sending bills that conform to the Uniform Task-Based Management System (UTBMS, a standard way of referring to timekeeper tasks) and comply with the Legal Electronic Data Exchange Standard (LEDES). LEDES is a standardized, uniform billing format in which to output billing data to clients regardless of the timekeeping and billing system that produced the bill.

Some timekeepers do not like e-billing because it mandates that they keep track of their time according to rigid, inflexible UTBMS codes. Many e-billing vendors are application service providers (ASPs), third-party vendors that set up the e-billing part of the system, receive data from law firms, and operate the software over the Internet. Clients are able to see bills (from any law firm they use) in a standard format and then customize the reports they output to meet their particular needs.

Some clients are even taking e-billing to the next level by contracting with their own ASP clearinghouses to audit bills, to ensure that the bills they receive are in strict compliance with the client's internal requirements. If the law firm's bill does not meet the client's requirements, the ASP rejects the bill and the client does not even get the electronic data. For example, if a client requires that each task be billed for separately (itemized), the client's clearinghouse would reject bills that include block entries covering three or four separate activities (e.g., "drafting letter to client; legal research for discovery motion, drafting discovery motion; telephone call with witness: 5 hours").

INTEGRATING TIMEKEEPING AND BILLING, ACCOUNTING, AND CASE MANAGEMENT

In a fully automated legal organization, the "back office" computer system will have at least three main components: (1) timekeeping and billing software, (2) accounting software, and (3) case management software. Timekeeping and billing have already been discussed in this chapter. Accounting software handles the financial side of the legal organization: receiving and applying money, making deposits, issuing checks, paying taxes, tracking aged accounts receivable, writing payroll checks, and the like. Case management software helps a legal organization provide services to clients by tracking client cases; tracking schedules, appointments, deadlines, and things to be done in cases; and tracking case-related information such as opposing parties and opposing counsel. For example, when a new client comes to a legal organization with a matter to be handled, case management software would be used to set up the new case, including client name, client address, client matter/case name, type of case, things to be done, and so forth. The same client will have to be set up in the time and billing system (to receive bills, have monies applied correctly, etc.), by entry of such data as client name, client matter, and when payments are made and recorded in the time and billing system. The legal organization's accounting software will need to know this so that deposits can be made, accounts receivable balances adjusted, and so on. The point is that all of these back-office systems have to be able to communicate with each other and share information; otherwise there will be much duplication of effort, and the possibility of error will increase greatly because of repetitive data entry.

Software manufacturers typically handle integration in one of three ways. (1) Separate software programs (from different manufacturers) exchange information among themselves (this is becoming much more common, but does not always work as promised). (2) One manufacturer makes a product that handles all of the back-office needs of the legal organization (this is also fairly common). (3) Integration is ignored and the legal organization must duplicate its efforts. It should be fairly clear that it is most efficient to design legal organization computer systems that are integrated and share information seamlessly across functions.

WHAT TO LOOK FOR IN TIMEKEEPING AND BILLING SOFTWARE

As with most software, no single timekeeping and billing program is best for all attorneys and all firms. Attorneys bill clients in very different formats and ways. The size of the firm also plays a role in choosing the right package. A timekeeping and billing package that works for a five-member law firm may not work well for a fifty-member firm.

Although paralegals do not always play a part in deciding which timekeeping and billing package to purchase, often they are consulted. (They may even be charged with the task of researching the software available and making recommendations!) When considering purchasing timekeeping and billing software, keep in mind that the billing program should do the following:

1. Be flexible, allowing the firm to charge different hourly rates, mix different fee arrangements, and so on.
2. Provide a wide variety of billing formats for different types of clients. An inflexible program that allows only one or two billing formats is usually not a good idea.
3. Be easy to use. Programs that allow users to look up information instead of memorizing keystrokes are almost always easier and more convenient to use.
4. Give the user the flexibility to bill each client whenever the user wishes, instead of having to bill all clients at one time.
5. Allow users to define a list of timekeepers and activities. Such programs are almost always easier and faster to use than programs that have predefined lists.
6. Include plenty of room for a description of the legal service provided. Some programs allow only one or two lines, which is often inadequate for recording a complicated entry.
7. Permit users to edit timeslips or expense slips instead of reentering slips that have mistakes in them.
8. Offer plenty of management reports and formats to help management operate the firm.
9. Utilize a robust security system, such as passwords, to keep unauthorized or unwanted users from accessing the system. Some programs have different levels of security; for example, a secretary might have access to the password that allows him to enter data, but not to the password to run bills or management reports. Security is an important aspect of any system.
10. Have the ability to integrate with accounting and case management software.
11. Include the ability to comply with the UTBMS and LEDES protocols.

THE ETHICS OF TIMEKEEPING AND BILLING

More ethical complaints related to timekeeping and billing are filed against attorneys and law offices than all other types of complaints combined. It is important that paralegals completely understand the ethics of timekeeping and billing. In years past, timekeeping and billing complaints were viewed simply as "misunderstandings" between the client and the law office. More recently, state bars have come to see timekeeping and billing disputes as having major ethical implications for attorneys. In fact, such disputes were often not simply misunderstandings; law offices were sometimes flagrantly violating ethical rules regarding money and financial issues.

Timekeeping and billing complaints by clients do not just lead to ethical complaints against attorneys. They may also turn into the basis for criminal fraud charges filed against attorneys and paralegals.

Ethical Considerations Regarding Legal Fee Agreements

We should stress several important ethical considerations regarding fee agreements. The first is that *all fee agreements should be in writing*, especially when a contingency fee is involved. Second, contingency fees should not be used in criminal or domestic relations matters. Third, only a reasonable fee can be collected. Disputes regarding attorney handling of fees are taken seriously and can lead to adverse ethical findings or worse.

Fee Agreements Should Be in Writing

It is highly recommended that, as a matter of course, all fee arrangements be in writing. The days of a handshake cementing an agreement between an attorney and a client are long gone. There is no substitute for reducing all fee agreements to writing. If the firm and the client have a dispute over fees, the document will clarify the understanding between the parties.

Why is it so important for legal fee agreements to be in writing?

1. Clients file more ethical complaints against attorneys and law offices for fee disputes than for any other type of dispute or problem.
2. The client and the attorney may (will) forget what the exact fee agreement was unless it is reduced to writing.
3. In a factual dispute regarding a fee between a client and an attorney, the evidence is typically construed in the light most favorable to the client.

Contingency Fee Agreements Must Be in Writing When a contingency fee is involved, most jurisdictions state that the agreement *must* be in writing for the office to collect the fees. The primary reason that a contingency fee agreement must be in writing is that in many cases, large sums of money are recovered; the difference between 20 percent and 30 percent may be tens of thousands of dollars. Contingency agreements are risky for the attorney, and they simply must be reduced to writing so that the client and the attorney both know what the proper percentage of fees should be. It also is important that the contingency agreement state—and the client understand—that even if there is no recovery in the case, the client must still pay for expenses.

Contingency Fees Are Not Allowed in Criminal and Domestic Relations Proceedings in Some Jurisdictions Many jurisdictions prohibit contingency fees in criminal and domestic relations proceedings as a matter of public policy. For example, assume that an attorney agrees to represent a client in a criminal matter. The client agrees to pay the attorney $10,000 if the client is found not guilty, but the attorney will receive nothing if the client is found guilty. This is an unethical contingency fee agreement. It rewards the attorney not for efforts, but for results that are not entirely within the attorney's control; thus, the attorney may be tempted or pressured to engage in unethical or even criminal pursuits to ensure the desired verdict.

To avoid such possibilities and protect the public interest, contingency fees in these types of cases are prohibited.

Only a "Reasonable" Fee Can Be Collected

It is important to keep in mind that no matter what the contract or legal fee agreement is with a client, attorneys and paralegals can receive only a "reasonable" fee. Unfortunately, there is no absolute standard for determining reasonableness, except that reasonableness will be determined on a case-by-case basis. However, most states have set out a number of factors to be considered in determining reasonableness:

1. The time and labor required, including the novelty and difficulty of the questions involved, and the skill required to perform the legal services.
2. The likelihood that acceptance of the legal matter will preclude the lawyer from accepting other cases.
3. The customary fee in the area for such legal services.
4. The outcome of the matter, including the amount involved.
5. Any time limitations imposed by the client or by the circumstances.
6. The type, nature, and length of the professional relationship with the client.
7. The ability of the lawyer involved, including experience, reputation, and ability.
8. Whether the type of fee was fixed or contingent.

Rules of Many State Bars Provide for Oversight/Arbitration on Fee Issues

One of the ways in which state bar associations and courts have dealt with the plethora of fee disputes is by providing for immediate and informal review and/or arbitration of fee disputes. Many state ethical rules and court rules provide that clients have the right, at any time, to request that the judge in the case or an attorney representing the state bar review the reasonableness of the attorney's fees. In many states, the attorney is required to inform the client of this right. In those states, the judge or attorney hearing the matter has the right to set the fee and determine what is reasonable under the particular facts and circumstances of the case.

Fraud and Criminal Charges

Charging an unreasonable fee is no longer simply a matter of ethics. Attorneys and paralegals have been criminally charged with fraud for intentionally recording time and sending bills for legal services that were never provided. Criminal fraud is a false representation of a present or past fact made by the defendant, upon which the victim relies, and which results in the victim suffering damages.

Criminal charges for fraud are not filed against attorneys and paralegals when there is simply a disagreement over what constitutes a reasonable fee. Criminal charges are filed when an attorney or paralegal acts intentionally to defraud clients. This usually happens when the attorney or paralegal bills for time when he or she did not really work on the case, or in instances in which the office intentionally billed a grossly overstated hourly rate far above the market rate.

Interestingly, many of the most recent criminal cases are being brought against well-respected law offices (both large and small) specializing in insurance defense and corporate work. Some insurance companies and corporations, as a matter of course when a case has been concluded, hire an audit firm or independent attorney to go back and audit the legal billings and files to be sure they were billed accurately. In some instances, these audits have concluded that intentional criminal fraud was perpetrated, and the cases were referred to prosecutors who filed criminal charges. No matter what type of firm is involved, intentionally overstating bills can lead to very big problems.

Ethical Problems

The general subject of timekeeping and billing brings up a wide variety of ethical issues and considerations, only a few of which are mentioned here. No matter what kind of timekeeping and billing system your office uses, whether it be manual or computerized, it is critically important that the underlying agreement between the law office and the client be in writing. Second, ethical rules state that only a "reasonable" fee can be collected from clients. It is very important that bills be accurately produced the first time and that no errors occur, so that only a "reasonable" fee is collected. Data entry is absolutely crucial to timekeeping and billing. If a timeslip is entered twice so that a client is billed twice for the same service, if a payment is not recorded to a client's account, or if a client is overcharged for legal services, the firm could lose that client or be faced with an ethical complaint. Thousands of ethical complaints are filed every year against attorneys regarding timekeeping and billing practices, so it is of utmost importance that this function be handled properly.

Several difficult ethical problems regarding timekeeping and billing are explored in this section, although they have no definite answers or solutions. The rule in deciding ethical questions such as these is to use your common sense and notions of fairness and honesty.

Can You Bill More than One Client for the Same Time?   From time to time a paralegal or attorney has the opportunity to bill more than one client for the same time period. This is known as double billing. For instance, while you are monitoring the opposing side's inspection of your client's documents in case A, you are drafting discovery for case B. Another example: while travelling to attend an interview with a witness in case A, you work on case B.

If you were the client, would you think it is fair for the attorney to charge full price for travel time related to your case while also billing another case? Reasonable approaches are to bill only the case you are actively working on, to split the time between the cases, or to bill the case you are actively working on at the regular hourly rate and bill the case you are inactively working on at a greatly reduced rate. Be fair and honest; your clients as well as judges and others looking at your time records will respect you for it.

When Billing by the Hour, Is There an Ethical Obligation to Be Efficient?   Does the firm have to have a form file, rather than researching each document anew each time? Must an office use a computer to save time? These types of ethical questions are decided on a case-by-case basis. The point is that billing by the hour rewards people for working slowly: the more slowly they work, the more they are paid.

Common sense tells you that if you were the client, you would want your legal staff to be efficient and not to "milk" you for money. The real issue is whether the attorney or paralegal acted so inefficiently and charged so much, when compared with what a similar attorney or paralegal with similar qualifications would charge in the same community, that the fee is clearly unreasonable. When judges rule on the reasonableness of fees, there is no doubt that they will consider what a reasonably efficient attorney or paralegal in the same circumstances would have charged. Use your common sense and be honest and efficient, because someone in your office might have to justify your time and charges someday.

Should You Bill for Clerical or Secretarial Duties?

Law offices cannot bill clients for clerical or secretarial time or tasks. These tasks are viewed as overhead costs, a normal part of doing business. An easy, but unethical, way to bill more hours is for a paralegal to bill time to clients for clerical functions such as copying documents or filing materials. Paralegals clearly should not bill for time spent performing these types of clerical tasks. Paralegals bill time for professional services, not for clerical functions. If you are unsure about whether a task is clerical, ask your supervising attorney, or record the time initially and point it out to the supervising attorney and let him or her decide.

Should You Bill for the Mistakes of the Law Office?

This is another tough problem. People make mistakes all the time. Clients generally feel that they should not have to pay for mistakes; after all, the reason they went to an attorney in the first place was to get an expert to handle their situation. This decision should be left for each law office to decide, but generally the practice of billing for mistakes is discouraged.

Must a Task Be Assigned to Less Expensive Support Staff When Possible?

Common sense and efficiency will tell you that tasks should be delegated as low as possible. Clients should not have to pay for attorney time when the task could be completed by an experienced paralegal. In addition, this arrangement is more profitable for the law office, because higher-paid persons are freed to do tasks for which they can bill clients at their normal rates.

SUMMARY

In the legal environment, the process of tracking time for the purpose of billing clients is called timekeeping. The process of issuing bills for the purpose of collecting monies for legal services performed and for expenses is called billing. Timekeeping and billing software is the second most popular kind of software for law offices, right after word processing.

The computerized timekeeping and billing process or cycle includes the following steps: the client and the attorney reach an agreement with regard to how fees will be calculated; the attorney performs legal services and prepares manual or computer timeslips; paper timeslips and expense slips are entered into the timekeeping and billing software; a pre-billing report is generated; client billings are generated; management reports are generated; and client payments are entered into the computer.

Many types of fee arrangements are available, including hourly rate fees, contingency fees, flat fees, and retainers.

Every timekeeping and billing program has a screen where relevant information about each client is entered. The client information screen usually shows and receives client information such as name, address, identification number, fee arrangements, bill formatting options, and the like.

The data entry screen is where timeslips and expense slips are entered into the computer. Computerized timeslip entry screens look much like manual timeslips.

Generating accurate and timely client bills is an important function of any timekeeping and billing system. Many timekeeping and billing programs allow users to choose from among several different billing formats.

Management reports are used to help management analyze whether a law firm is operating efficiently and effectively. Many programs allow you to generate a case or client list, aged accounts receivable report, timekeeping productivity report, case type productivity report, and more.

Many ethical complaints are filed against attorneys due to timekeeping and billing issues. It is important to have written fee agreements, bill honestly and accurately, and bill only reasonable fees.

KEY TERMS

activity hourly rate
aged accounts receivable report
attorney or paralegal hourly rate
billable hour
billing
blended hourly rate fee
case retainer
case type productivity report
cash advance
client hourly rate

contingency fee
earned retainer
electronic billing
expense slip
flat fee
hourly rate fee
management reports
operating account
pre-billing report
pure retainer

retainer for general representation
timekeeper
timekeeper productivity report
timekeeping
timeslip
trust or escrow account
unearned retainer
value billing

INTERNET SITES

Internet sites for this chapter include:

ORGANIZATION	PRODUCT/SERVICE	INTERNET ADDRESS
Abacus Data Systems, Inc.	Abacus Silver, timekeeping, billing, accounting and case management software	www.abacuslaw.com
Aderant	CMS Open Billing	www.cmsopen.com
IOLTA	Information about IOLTA and IOLTA programs	www.iolta.org
Juris	Juris legal timekeeping and billing software	www.juris.com
LEDES	Legal Electronic Data Exchange Standard (LEDES)	www.ledes.org
LexisNexis	PC LAW legal timekeeping and billing software	www.pclaw.com
Micro Craft, Inc.	Verdict Time & Billing	www.micro-craft.net
Omega Legal Systems	Omega Billing & Accounting	www.omegalegal.com
Orion Law Management Systems	Timekeeping and billing software	www.Orionlaw.com
Perfect Law Software	Timekeeping and billing software and comprehensive back-office systems	www.perfectlaw.com
ProVantage Software, Inc.	Timekeeping and billing software and comprehensive back-office systems	www.provantagesoftware.com
Rainmaker Software, Inc.	Rainmaker Gold timekeeping and billing software	www.rainmakerlegal.com
Sage Software	Timeslips legal timekeeping and billing software	www.timeslips.com
Software Technology, Inc.	Tabs3 legal timekeeping and billing software	www.Tabs3.com
Thomson	Elite Enterprise and Prolaw time-keeping and billing software systems	www.elite.com

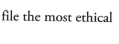

TEST YOUR KNOWLEDGE

1. What is the difference between timekeeping and billing?
2. Name four types of hourly rates.
3. When a lawyer takes a percentage of the recovery in the case, it is called a _____ fee.
4. True or False: It is strongly recommended that all fee arrangements be in writing.
5. True or False: A flat-fee agreement must be in writing.
6. A retainer that can be deposited in the firm's or attorney's operating checking account is called a(n) _____ retainer.
7. True or False: An account where unearned client monies are deposited is called a trust fund.
8. A retainer for general representation is a(n) _____ retainer.
9. A case retainer is a(n) _____ retainer.
10. A cash advance retainer is a(n) _____ retainer.
11. For what activity do clients file the most ethical complaints against lawyers?
12. True or False: A contingency agreement can be used in all kinds of cases.
13. True or False: If a client signs a contract with an attorney and the fee turns out to be clearly excessive, it doesn't matter, because a contract was signed and the contract prevails.
14. Name four of the eight factors that courts use to determine if a fee is unreasonable.
15. True or False: Paralegals can bill for time spent doing photocopying and other clerical tasks.
16. Define electronic billing.
17. True or False: Integrated programs that include timekeeping and billing, accounting, and other features do not really offer the modern law office much advantage.

ON THE WEB EXERCISES

1. Using the "Internet Sites" listed in this chapter or a general Internet search engine (such as www.google.com or www.yahoo.com), research three timekeeping and billing programs. Compare the features, price, training options, and other information about the products and write a three-page paper on your findings, including which program you liked the best and why.
2. Using the "Internet Sites" listed in this chapter or a general Internet search engine (such as www.google.com or www.yahoo.com), research legal electronic billing. Write a three-page paper on the results of your research. Include what it is; how it works; what, if any, problems there are regarding implementation of electronic billing; and what benefits clients and legal organizations derive from electronic billing.
3. Using the "Internet Sites" listed in this chapter or a general Internet search engine (such as www.google.com or www.yahoo.com), find a minimum of three articles on legal timekeeping and billing. Write a one-page summary of each article.
4. Visit five state bar association websites and find three articles on either legal timekeeping, billing, or legal fees.
5. Go to the Georgia Bar Association's website at www.gabar.org and use the Search tool to find a sample contingency fee agreement. Go to several other state bar association websites and try to find another sample contingency fee or hourly rate contract agreements.
6. Visit the National Association of Legal Assistants website at www.nala.org and review the latest NALA National Utilization and Compensation Survey Report. Read and print out the section related to paralegal billing rates. If you have difficulty finding it, try using the "Search" feature on the website. If you still have trouble finding it, use www.google.com and search on the full title.
7. Go to the ABA Law Practice Management Section home page at www.abanet.org and find two articles on timekeeping, billing, fees, and finance-related matters. Summarize the articles in a two-page paper.

QUESTIONS AND EXERCISES

1. You are a new paralegal and have worked for a medium-sized law office for three months. It has been a tremendous experience for you, as you learned how the office does business; its policies and procedures; what type of service you are expected to give to clients; where resources are; and how to use resources, such as the office's computer systems, law library, copy machines, and form files. Although it has taken time for you to learn these things, you have also been productive and have received several compliments on the quality of your work.

   One day, you read in the office's staff manual that all paralegals are required to bill 1,500 hours annually or face possible discipline. You immediately contact your supervisor and ask whether, as a new paralegal, you will be expected to bill this amount. Your supervisor responds, "Of course. You were told that when you were hired." You immediately begin gathering copies of your timesheets to compile your total. You also request that the billing department send you the total numbers of hours you have billed to date. When you get the report from billing, you panic; you have billed only 300 hours. What do you do now, and how could you have avoided this unfortunate situation?

2. On June 30, a billing goes out to Susan Simon, one of the clients whose cases you have been working on. Ms. Simon calls you a few days later and complains about the amount of time shown on the bill. She is extremely rude and discourteous. Ms. Simon flatly states that she thinks she is being overbilled. How do you handle the phone call?

3. You are interviewing a new client. The client wants to hire your office to help negotiate the purchase of a small business. The seller has proposed $20,000. The new client would be willing to pay this amount, although she thinks it is a bit high, but she does not feel comfortable negotiating with the seller and would rather have an attorney involved in the deal for her protection. However, she is suspicious of paralegals and attorneys and is especially concerned about how much it will cost to get the representation she needs. You inform the client that the attorney will be the one who actually talks to her about the fee issue, but that typically this type of case is taken on an hourly basis and that the attorney will be able to give her only a very broad estimate of what the total matter will cost. The client states that this would be unacceptable to her because she "does not have a lot of money to pay overpriced attorneys." The client also states that she would like this matter settled as soon as possible. You must prepare a memorandum to the attorney outlining the issue and possible solutions. What type of fee arrangement would you suggest to the attorney? Please keep in mind the client's anxieties and her particular needs.

4. Recently, your office has found a niche in representing spouses collecting on past-due child support. In most cases, your clients have little money to pay you with and are financially strapped, because they no longer have the income of their former spouses to support their children and have not been receiving the child support. In some cases, large amounts of money are owed, but finding the former spouses has proven difficult. Your supervising attorney decides that the best way to handle these types of cases is on a one-third contingency basis. Your supervising attorney asks for your comments. How do you respond?

5. Yesterday was a hectic day. Although you wanted to record your time earlier, you just could not get to it. Record your time now, using a spreadsheet. Build the spreadsheet so it has columns for the date, client/case name, timekeeper, services rendered, billable time, and nonbillable time. For each activity listed, decide whether it is billable or not billable. Record your time, first using tenths of hours.
   You should also fill out expense slips for items that should be charged back to clients. Build the spreadsheet to include date, client/case name, type of expense, and cost. The firm charges 25 cents each for copies and 50 cents per page to send a fax. Assume that long-distance phone calls cost 25 cents a minute. Total the cost of each expense slip. As best you can recall, this is how your day went:

   8:00 a.m.–8:12 a.m.: Got a cup of coffee, talked to other law office staff members, reviewed your schedule/things-to-do sheet for the day, and reviewed the email in your inbox.

   8:13 a.m.–8:25 a.m.: Talked to your supervising attorney (Lisa Mitchell) about some research she needs done on the grounds to support a motion to dismiss *Johnson v. Cuttingham Steel*. Ms. Mitchell also asked you to find a bankruptcy statute she needs for *Halvert v. Shawnee Savings & Loan*.

   8:26 a.m.–8:37 a.m.: A paralegal from another office calls to remind you that the paralegal association you belong to is having a meeting at noon and that you are running the meeting.

8:38 a.m.–8:40 a.m.: One of your least favorite clients, John Hamilton, calls to ask you when he is supposed to be at your office to prepare for his deposition tomorrow. You access the weekly schedule electronically and read him the information he needs.

8:40 a.m.–8:50 a.m.: You find the information you need for the motion to dismiss in *Johnson v. Cuttingham Steel* in a motion in another case you helped to prepare last month. The research is still current, and Ms. Mitchell is pleased that you found it so fast. You note that it took you two hours to research this issue when you did it the first time. You copy the material Ms. Mitchell needs (five pages) and put it on her desk, and also send it to her electronically.

8:55 a.m.–9:30 a.m.: You speak with a witness you have been trying to contact in *Menly v. Menly*. The call is long-distance. The call lasts 15 minutes and writing the memo to the file documenting the call takes 15 minutes.

9:30 a.m.–9:54 a.m.: Ms. Mitchell asks you to contact the attorney in *Glass v. Huron* regarding a discovery question. You spend 10 minutes on hold. The call is long-distance but you get an answer to Ms. Mitchell's question.

10:00 a.m.–10:15 a.m.: Coffee break and talk with attorney about the ballgame.

10:15 a.m.–10:45 a.m.: One of the secretaries informs you that you must interview a new client, Richard Sherman. The person who was supposed to see Mr. Sherman got delayed. Mr. Sherman comes to your office regarding a simple adoption. However, in talking to Mr. Sherman you find out that he also needs someone to incorporate a small business that he is getting ready to open. You gladly tell him that your office has a department that handles this type of matter. You take down the basic information regarding both matters. You tell the client that you will prepare a memo regarding these matters to the appropriate attorney and that one of the office's attorneys will contact him within two days to further discuss the matter. You also copy 10 pages of information that Mr. Sherman brought.

10:45 a.m.–10:54 a.m.: One of the secretaries asks you to cover her phone for her while she takes a quick break. Because the secretary always helps you when you ask for it, you gladly cover the phone for a few minutes. Ms. Mitchell asks you to send a fax regarding *Stewart v. Layhorn Glass*, so you use this time to send the six-page fax.

10:55 a.m.–12:00 noon: Yesterday Ms. Mitchell asked you to organize some exhibits in *Ranking v. Siefkin*. The deadline was noon today. You finally have some free time to organize the exhibits.

12:00 noon–1:00 p.m.: Lunch.

1:00 p.m.–2:00 p.m.: You work on a pro bono criminal case for a client whom Ms. Mitchell is representing on appeal. In an effort to become familiar with the case, you read some of the transcripts from the trial.

2:00 p.m.–3:30 p.m.: Ms. Mitchell hands you a new case and says that your firm will be representing the defendant, Maude Pinchum. She asks you to read the petition and client file, analyze the case, and draft interrogatories to send to the plaintiff. You spend the rest of the day working on this case.

3:30 p.m.–3:45 p.m.: Make personal phone calls.

3:45 p.m.–5:00 p.m.: Continue working on Pinchum case.

ETHICS QUESTION

It is the first day of your new job as a paralegal. As you perform your first job assignment, you discover that it is taking longer than you think it should. You do not want your boss to think that you are incompetent or lazy, so when you submit the bill for your time, you report only half the time you actually spent on the assignment. What ethical issues, if any, are raised by this scenario?

TABS3 BILLING SOFTWARE

 ## *READ THIS FIRST!*

I. INTRODUCTION–READ THIS!

The Tabs3 timekeeping and billing program demonstration version is a full working version of the program with a few limitations. The main limitation is that only a limited number of clients can be entered into the program. The demonstration version does *not* time out (quit working after a set number of days).

II. USING THE TABS3 HANDS-ON EXERCISES

The Tabs3 Hands-On Exercises are easy to use and contain step-by-step instructions. Each lesson builds on the previous exercise, so please complete the Hands-On Exercises in order. Tabs3 is a user-friendly program, so using the program should be intuitive. Tabs3 also comes with sample data, so you should be able to try many features of the program.

III. INSTALLATION INSTRUCTIONS

Below are step-by-step instructions for loading the Tabs3 timekeeping and billing demonstration version on your computer.

1. Insert the disk supplied with this text into your computer.
2. When prompted with **"What do you want Windows to do?"** *select "Open folder to view files using Windows Explorer," then click OK.* If your computer does not automatically recognize that you have inserted a disk, *double-click the My Computer icon, then double-click the drive where the disk is.*
3. *Double-click the Tabs3 folder. Then double-click the launch.exe file.* This will start the Tabs3 installation wizard.

4. The screen in Tabs3 Installation Exhibit 1 should now be displayed. ***Click "Next."***

TABS3 INSTALLATION EXHIBIT 1

5. Your screen will look like Tabs3 Installation Exhibit 2. ***Click* "Install Tabs3 Trial Software."**

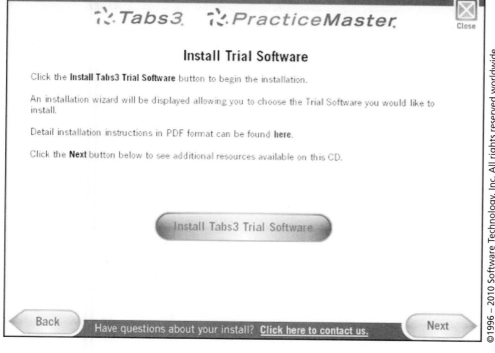

TABS3 INSTALLATION EXHIBIT 2

6. The Tabs3 Trial Software Setup window should now be displayed. (See Installation Exhibit 3.) ***Click Next.***

TABS3 INSTALLATION EXHIBIT 3

7. Your screen will look like Tabs3 Installation Exhibit 4. Review the license agreement, then ***click Yes.***

TABS3 INSTALLATION EXHIBIT 4

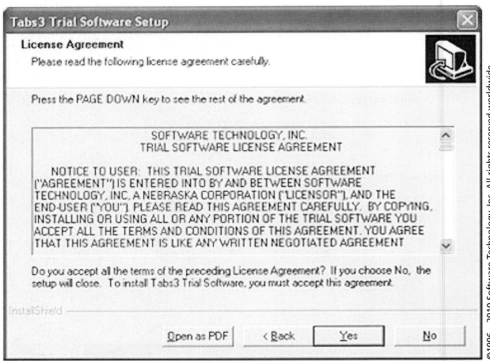

8. Your screen will look like Tabs3 Installation Exhibit 5. ***Click Next.***

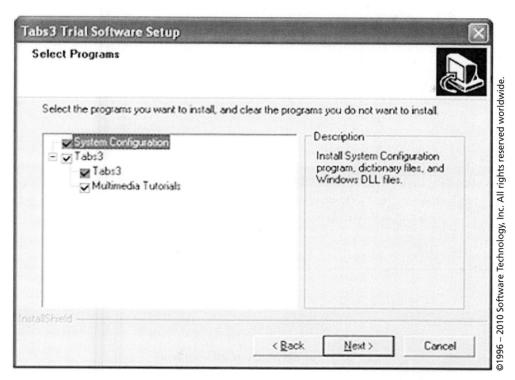

**TABS3 INSTALLATION
EXHIBIT 5**

9. Your screen will look like Tabs3 Installation Exhibit 6. ***Click Next.***

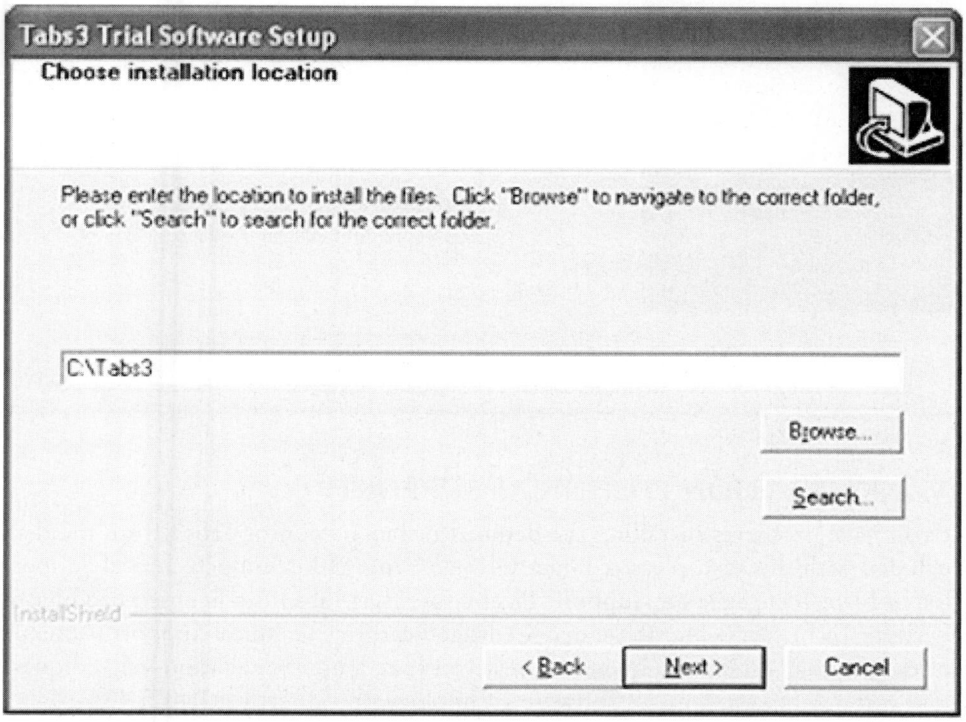

**TABS3 INSTALLATION
EXHIBIT 6**

HANDS-ON EXERCISES

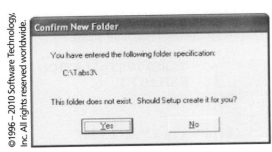

**TABS3 INSTALLATION
EXHIBIT 7**

10. You may be asked to confirm the creation of a new folder (see Tabs3 Installation Exhibit 7). ***Click Yes.***

11. You may be asked if you wish to install starter data. ***Click Yes*** (see Tabs3 Installation Exhibit 8).

12. Installation is complete. Your screen will look like Tabs3 Installation Exhibit 9. ***Click Finish.***

**TABS3 INSTALLATION
EXHIBIT 8**

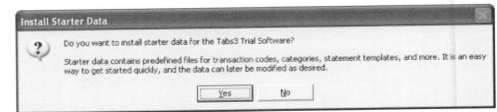

**TABS3 INSTALLATION
EXHIBIT 9**

IV. INSTALLATION TECHNICAL SUPPORT

If you have problems installing the demonstration version of Tabs3 from the disk included with this text, please contact Delmar Cengage Learning Technical Support first at http://cengage.com/support. Please note that Tabs3 is a licensed product of Software Technology, Inc. If Delmar Cengage Learning Technical Support is unable to resolve your installation question, or if you have a non-installation–related question, you will need to contact Software Technology, Inc. directly at (402) 423-1440.

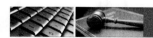
HANDS-ON EXERCISES

TABS3 BILLING SOFTWARE

Number	Lesson Title	Concepts Covered
BASIC LESSONS		
Lesson 1	Introduction to Tabs3	An introduction to the Tabs3 interface
Lesson 2	Entering a New Client	Entering a new client into Tabs3, including entering contact data, setup, rates, billing, and statement information
INTERMEDIATE LESSONS		
Lesson 3	Entering Fee/Time Records	Entering several different types of fee/time record entries
Lesson 4	Entering Cost/Expense Records and Using the Fee Timer Feature	Entering several different types of cost/expense records and learning how to use the Fee Timer feature
Lesson 5	Generating and Printing Draft and Final Statements	Generate and print draft statements and final statements; update statements
Lesson 6	Entering a Payment	Enter and apply a payment
ADVANCED LESSON		
Lesson 7	Processing and Printing Reports	Process and print a number of management, productivity, and client reports

GETTING STARTED
Introduction

Throughout these lessons and exercises, information you need to type into the software will be designated in several different ways:

- Keys to be pressed on the keyboard are designated in brackets, in all caps, and in bold (e.g., press the **[ENTER]** key).
- Movements with the cursor are designated in bold and italics (e.g., ***point to File on the menu bar and click***).
- Words or letters that should be typed are designated in bold (e.g., type **Training Program**).
- Information that is or should be displayed on your computer screen is shown in bold, with quotation marks (e.g., **"Press ENTER to continue."**).
- Specific menu items and commands are designated with an initial capital letter (e.g., click Open).

OVERVIEW OF TABS3

Tabs3 is a full-featured time, accounting, and billing system. Software Technology, Inc., also produces additional modules that integrate with the billing software, including general ledger software, accounts payable software, trust accounting software, Tabs3 and GLS Report Writers, and PracticeManager case management software. This tutorial covers only the billing software. Tabs3 Exhibit 1 shows the main Tabs3 window with task folders displayed. With Tabs3, you can enter new clients, fee/time records, expense entries, and payments; run billing/management

TABS3 EXHIBIT 1
Tabs3 window with task folders

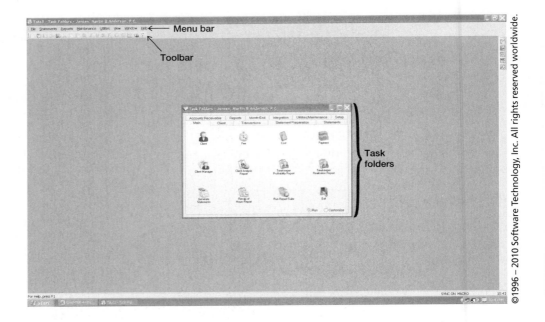

Menu bar

Toolbar

Task folders

reports; and control a firm's overall billing system. Tabs3 is robust and offers many advanced billing features, and it is also easy to use. By the end of the exercises, you should have a good understanding of the basics of legal time entry and billing with Tabs3.

 # BASIC LESSONS

LESSON 1: INTRODUCTION TO TABS3

This lesson introduces you to Tabs3. It explains basic information about the Tabs3 interface, including an overview of clients, fees, costs, payments, generating bills and statements, and running reports.

Before you start, install the Tabs3 trial version on your computer by following the instructions entitled "Tabs3 Hands-On Exercises—Read This First!" *Note:* The Tabs3 Billing Software trial version does *not* time out (quit working after a set number of days). The main limitation of the trial version is that only 30 clients can be entered into the software.

1. Open Windows. After it has loaded, ***double-click Tabs3 with Sample Data on the desktop,*** or ***click the Start button on the Windows desktop, point to Programs or All Programs, point to the Tabs3 & PracticeMaster group, point to Trial Software with Sample Data, then click Tabs3 with Sample Data.*** Tabs3 will then open with sample data already present in the software. *Note:* If a message about the integration between Tabs3 and PracticeMaster is displayed, you have opened the trial software without sample data. ***Click OK, then click Close in the "Tip of the Day" window.*** Press [**CTRL**]+[**S**] to save customization settings, ***click the Close icon*** (the red square with a white "X") to exit the software, and then try again to open the program.

2. The "Tip of the Day" window should now be displayed. ***Click Close in the "Tip of the Day" window.*** *Note:* If you do not want to see the Tip of the Day, ***select the "Do not show tips at startup" box before clicking Close.***

3. The screen in Tabs3 Exhibit 2 should now be displayed. The Tabs3 window states that sample data is being used and that the system date in use with the

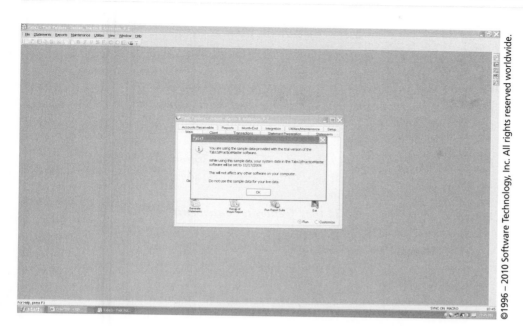

TABS3 EXHIBIT 2
Sample data/date notice

HANDS-ON EXERCISES

sample data is set to 11/17/2009. This date will not affect any other software
on your computer.

4. ***Click OK in the "Tabs3" window.*** The screen in Tabs3 Exhibit 1 should now
be displayed. Notice the "Task Folders—Jensen, Martin & Anderson, P.C."
window (hereinafter referred to as the "Task Folders" window) in the middle of
the screen in Tabs3 Exhibit 1. *Note:* Sample data for the fictitious law firm of
Jensen, Martin & Anderson, P.C. are used throughout this tutorial.

5. Notice in Tabs3 Exhibit 1 that the Main tab in the "Task Folders" window
is currently displayed (other tabs include Client, Transactions, Statements,
Reports, etc.). The icons change depending on which tab is selected.

6. ***Click the Client icon in the "Task Folders" window.***

7. A blank "Client Information" window should now be displayed. This is where
you enter information about a client, such as name, contact information, billing
options, setup options, statement options, and so on. In Lesson 2 you will set
up a new client using this window.

8. ***Click the Close icon*** (the red square with a white "X") ***at the upper right of the
"Client Information" window.*** *Note:* To have the computer display the name
of an icon, just hover the cursor over the icon for a second; the name will be
displayed.

9. ***Click Fee in the "Task Folders" window.***

10. The "Fee Entry" window should now be displayed. This is where client
time/fee entries (time records) are entered into Tabs3. In this window,
the user designates the client to be billed, timekeeper, date of the record,
transaction code (the activity), number of hours worked, a description of
the activity, and other data. In Lesson 3, you will enter a number of fee
records into Tabs3.

11. ***Click the Close icon in the upper right of the "Fee Entry" window.***

12. ***Click Cost in the "Task Folders" window.***

13. The "Rapid Cost Entry" window should now be displayed. This is where client
cost entries (cost records or expenses) are entered into Tabs3. These include
costs such as photocopying, courier fees, transcription fees, and travel expenses.

In this window the user designates the client to be billed, the date the cost was incurred, a description of the cost, and related information. In Lesson 4, you will enter a number of cost records into Tabs3.

14. ***Click the Close icon in the upper right of the "Rapid Cost Entry" window.***

15. ***Click Generate Statements in the "Task Folders" window.***

16. The "Generate Statements" window should now be displayed. This is where users designate which clients to bill.

17. ***Click the Transactions tab in the "Generate Statements" window.*** This is where users control what type of fees, expenses, advances, and payments are billed/credited to a client.

18. ***Click the Options tab in the "Generate Statements" window.*** This is where users select whether to produce draft (pre-billing) statements or final statements, and assign beginning statement numbers, individual billing thresholds (e.g., only producing statements that are more than $100), and related options.

19. ***Click the Close icon at the upper right of the "Generate Statements" window.***

20. ***Click Payment in the "Task Folders" window.***

21. The "Rapid Payment Entry" window should now be displayed. This is where users can enter and apply payments to client invoices and accounts.

22. ***Click the Close icon at the upper right of the "Rapid Payment Entry" window.***

23. ***Click the Client tab in the "Task Folders" window.*** Notice that the icons have now changed.

24. ***Click each of the tabs in the "Task Folders" window to see all of the icons listed.***

25. ***Click back to the Main tab in the "Task Folders" window.***

26. ***Click File on the menu bar and then click Exit.***

This concludes Lesson 1.

LESSON 2: ENTERING A NEW CLIENT

In this lesson you will learn how to enter a new client into Tabs3. In doing so, you will explore the many options users have to set up a client with respect to billing and payments.

1. Open Windows. ***Double-click Tabs3 with Sample Data on the desktop, or click the Start button on the Windows desktop, point to Programs or All Programs, point to the Tabs3 & PracticeMaster group, point to Trial Software with Sample Data, then click Tabs3 with Sample Data.*** Tabs3 will then open with sample data already present in the software.

2. The "Tip of the Day" window may now be displayed. ***Click Close in the "Tip of the Day" window.***

3. ***Click OK in the "Tabs3" window*** to acknowledge the 11/17/2009 date.

4. ***Click Client in the "Task Folders" window.*** The "Client Information" window should now be displayed (see Tabs3 Exhibit 3). Notice that the Address tab is selected.

5. Your cursor should be in the Client ID field. ***Click the New icon on the toolbar*** (see Tabs3 Exhibit 3). Tabs3 automatically generates the next Client ID number, which is 851.00.

TABS3 EXHIBIT 3
Entering a new client in the Address tab of the "Client Information" window

HANDS-ON EXERCISES

6. Enter the following information in the Address tab of the "Client Information" window (see Tabs3 Exhibit 3). *Note:* You can press the [**TAB**] key to move forward through the fields, or press [**SHIFT**]+[**TAB**] to move backward through the fields. If a field is left blank in the following list, just skip it.

FIELD	INFORMATION TO BE ENTERED
Name (Last/First):	**Richards/Sherry**
Work Description:	**Richards v. EZ Pest Control**
Name Search:	**Richards/Sherry**
Address Line 1:	**2000 Clayton Boulevard**
Address Line 2:	
Address Line 3:	
City:	**Atlanta**
State:	**GA**
Zip:	**30303**
Country:	
Location:	
Date Opened:	**11/17/2009**
Date Closed:	**mm/dd/yyyy**
Contact:	
Office:	**888-555-5429**
Home:	**888-555-3999**
Fax:	
Cellular:	**888-555-5567**
E-mail:	**srichards@aom.com**

7. **Click the Setup tab in the "Client Information" window** (see Tabs3 Exhibit 4).

TABS3 EXHIBIT 4
Entering a new client—
Setup options

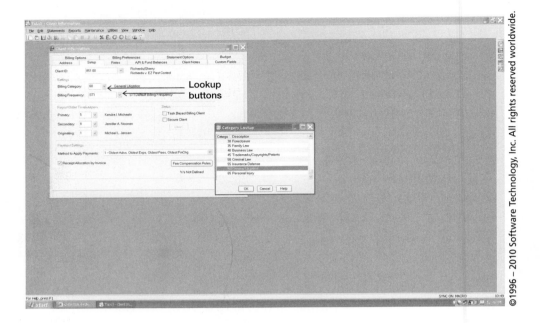

8. **Click the Lookup button.** (It is the down arrow to the right of the Billing Category field.) The "Category Lookup" window should now be displayed (see Tabs3 Exhibit 4). **Scroll down, click 60 General Litigation, then click OK in the "Category Lookup" window.**

9. **Click the Lookup button** (down arrow) **to the right of Billing Frequency:.** The "Billing Frequency Lookup" window should now be displayed. Notice that you can select Bill on Demand, Monthly, Quarterly, etc. We will use the default setting of STI, so just **click Cancel in the "Billing Frequency Lookup" window.**

10. **Under Report Order Timekeepers, click the Lookup button** (down arrow) **next to Primary:.** The "Timekeeper Lookup" window should now be displayed.

11. **Double-click Kendra I. Michaels.** The primary timekeeper is the attorney who is responsible for the case; in this example the primary timekeeper is an associate.

12. **Under Report Order Timekeepers, click the Lookup button** (down arrow) **next to Secondary:.** The "Timekeeper Lookup" window should again be displayed.

13. **Double-click on Jennifer A. Noonan.** The secondary timekeeper is the support staff person who is responsible for the case; in this example, the secondary timekeeper is a paralegal. (*Note:* The *originating timekeeper* is the person who brought the client to the firm. We will leave the originating timekeeper as Michael L. Jensen.)

14. **Click the Rates tab in the "Client Information" window** (see Tabs3 Exhibit 5). Notice that the screen has a number of options for customizing the billing rate for a client. In this example, the Billing Rate Code that will be used is "1 - Timekeeper Rate 1" (see Tabs3 Exhibit 5). This indicates that each timekeeper's Hourly Rate 1 will be used as the default billing rate.

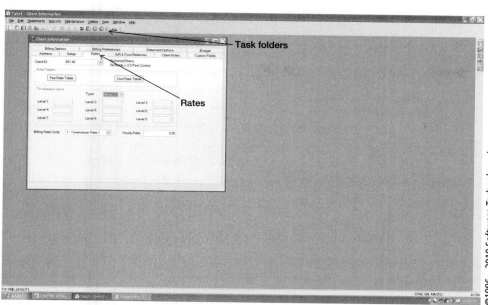

TABS3 EXHIBIT 5
Entering a new client—
Rates options

15. You will now look at what the Timekeeper Rate 1 amount is for Kendra I. Michaels and Jennifer A. Noonan. ***Click the Task Folders icon on the toolbar*** (see Tabs3 Exhibit 5). The "Task Folders" window should now be displayed.

16. ***Click the Setup tab in the "Task Folders" window.***

17. ***Click Timekeeper on the Setup tab.***

18. ***In the "Miscellaneous" window, click the Lookup button next to Timekeeper:*** (see Tabs3 Exhibit 6).

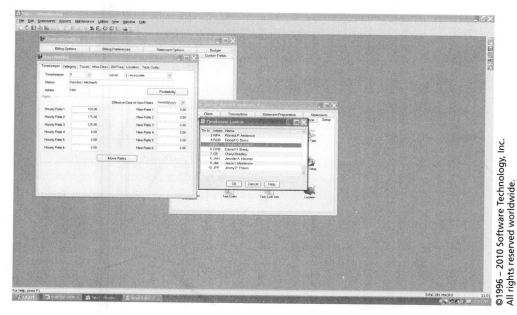

TABS3 EXHIBIT 6
Hourly rates for Kendra
I. Michaels

19. ***Double-click Kendra I. Michaels.*** Notice that the amount in her Hourly Rate 1: field is $150.00.

20. ***In the "Miscellaneous" window, click the Lookup button next to Timekeeper.***

21. ***Double-click Jennifer A. Noonan.*** Notice that the amount in her Hourly Rate 1: field as a paralegal is $100.00.

22. ***Click the Close icon at the upper right of the "Miscellaneous" window.***

23. ***Click anywhere in the "Client Information" window.*** *(Note:* To move a window, just **click and drag the title bar at the top of the window**).

24. ***Click the A/R & Fund Balances tab in the "Client Information" window.*** Once fees, expenses, and billings have been entered, this tab will contain current balances for the client.

25. ***Click the Client Notes tab in the "Client Information" window.***

26. ***Put your cursor in the Client Notes field.*** Type **Client says she wants to be billed monthly, but will generally pay the balance owed every 60 days.** (see Tabs3 Exhibit 7).

TABS3 EXHIBIT 7
Entering a new client—
Client Notes

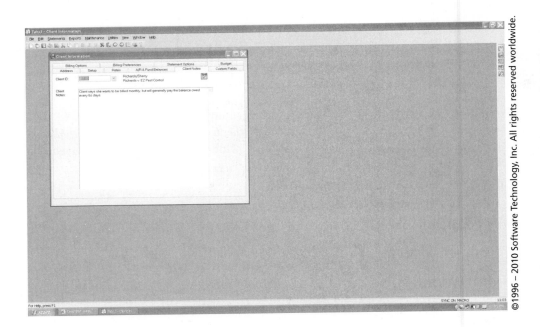

27. ***Click the Billing Options tab in the "Client Information" window.*** This window is where users can set up a billing threshold, a courtesy discount, sales tax, or a finance charge. This client does not have or need any special billing options.

28. ***Click the Billing Preferences tab in the "Client Information" window.*** This window is where users can set up additional billing requirements for the client, such as special billing instructions or a secondary billing address. Again, this client has no special needs.

29. ***Click the Statement Options tab in the "Client Information" window.*** This window allows users to set up and customize the billing templates for the client. The default options are fine for this client.

30. ***Click the Budget and Custom Fields tabs in the "Client Information" window*** to see what these tabs look like. You will not enter any information in these tabs.

31. ***Click the Save icon on the toolbar*** (it looks like a floppy disk).

32. ***Click the Close icon at the upper right of the "Client Information" window.***

33. To make sure the client has been entered into Tabs3, ***click the Main tab in the "Task Folders" window, then click the Client icon.***

34. *In the "Client Information" window, click the down arrow next to the Client ID: field.* The Client Lookup screen should now be displayed.

35. *Double-click on 851.00 richards/sherry.* The information for *Sherry Richards* and *Richards v. EZ Pest Control* should now be displayed.

36. *Click the Close icon at the upper right of the "Client Information" window.*

37. *Click File on the menu bar and then click Exit.*

This concludes Lesson 2.

 # INTERMEDIATE LESSONS

LESSON 3: ENTERING FEE/TIME RECORDS

In this lesson, you will learn how to enter time records into Tabs3.

1. Open Windows. *Double-click Tabs3 with Sample Data on the desktop, or click the Start button on the Windows desktop, point to Programs or All Programs, point to the Tabs3 & PracticeMaster group, point to Trial Software with Sample Data, then click Tabs3 with Sample Data.* Tabs3 will then open with sample data already entered into the program.

2. The "Tip of the Day" window may now be displayed. *Click Close in the "Tip of the Day" window.*

3. *Click OK in the "Tabs3" window* to acknowledge the 11/17/2009 date.

4. *Click Fee in the "Task Folders" window.*

5. *Click the Detail/Rapid icon on the toolbar in the "Fee Entry" window* (*not* the main toolbar—see Tabs3 Exhibit 8). Notice that fewer fields are now displayed. The Detail/Rapid icon toggles between a detail fee entry window that has several fields, and a rapid data entry window that has fewer fields.

6. Your cursor should already be in the Client ID: field, with the last Client ID number, 851.00, listed. Press the **[TAB]** key to go to the Reference: field.

7. Press the **[TAB]** key to go to the Timekeeper: field.

8. *Click the Lookup button next to the Timekeeper: field. Double-click on Jennifer A. Noonan.*

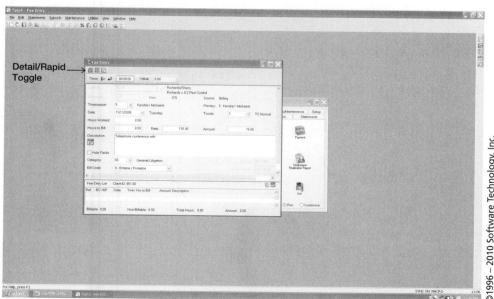

Detail/Rapid
Toggle →

TABS3 EXHIBIT 8
Entering a fee/time record

HANDS-ON EXERCISES

9. At the Date: field, press the [TAB] key to accept the default date of 11/17/2009.

10. ***Click the Lookup button next to the Tcode: (transaction code) field.*** The "Tcode Lookup" window should now be displayed. ***Double-click on 3 TC Telephone conference with.***

11. In the Hours Worked: field, type **.50** and then press the [TAB] key.

12. The cursor should now be in the Amount: field with 50.00 highlighted. Press the [TAB] key.

13. The cursor should now be in the Description: field. At the end of **"Telephone conference with"** type **client.** and then press the [TAB] key.

14. ***Click the Save icon on the main toolbar.*** A blank fee/time record is now displayed.

15. Enter and save each of the following fee/time records:

FIELD	INFORMATION TO BE ENTERED
Client ID:	**851.00**
Reference:	
Timekeeper:	**5**
Date:	**11/17/2009**
Tcode:	**8**
Hours Worked:	**6.00**
Hours to Bill:	**6.00**
Rate:	**150.00**
Amount:	**900.00**
Description:	**Draft and revise Response to Motion for Summary Judgment.**
Category:	**60**
Bill Code:	**0 – Billable / Printable**

FIELD	INFORMATION TO BE ENTERED
Client ID:	**851.00**
Reference:	
Timekeeper:	**8**
Date:	**11/17/2009**
Tcode:	**10**
Hours Worked:	**3.00**
Hours to Bill:	**3.00**
Rate:	**100.00**
Amount:	**300.00**
Description:	**Legal research—relevant case law in support of Response to Motion for Summary Judgment.**
Category:	**60**
Bill Code:	**0 – Billable / Printable**

FIELD	INFORMATION TO BE ENTERED
Client ID:	851.00
Reference:	
Timekeeper:	2
Date:	11/18/2009
Tcode:	3
Hours Worked:	1.00
Hours to Bill:	1.00
Rate:	225.00
Amount:	225.00
Description:	**Telephone conference with expert witness**
Category:	60
Bill Code:	0 – Billable / Printable

FIELD	INFORMATION TO BE ENTERED
Client ID:	851.00
Reference:	
Timekeeper:	8
Date:	11/18/2009
Tcode:	3
Hours Worked:	1.00
Hours to Bill:	1.00
Rate:	100.00
Amount:	100.00
Description:	**Telephone conference with client regarding Response to Motion for Summary Judgment**
Category:	60
Bill Code:	0 – Billable / Printable

16. *Click the Save icon on the main toolbar.*

17. Notice in the bottom of the "Fee" window that you can see the prior fee/time records you have entered. *Click the Close icon at the upper right of the "Fee – Richards/Sherry" window.*

18. The "Fee Verification List" window should now be displayed. This feature can print a report summarizing all of the entries you just made. This is not necessary for the small number of time records you just entered, so *click the Close icon in the "Fee Verification List" window.*

19. *Click File on the menu bar and then click Exit.*

This concludes Lesson 3.

HANDS-ON EXERCISES

LESSON 4: ENTERING COST/EXPENSE RECORDS AND USING THE FEE TIMER FEATURE

In this lesson, you will learn how to enter cost/expense records into Tabs3 and how to use the Fee Timer feature.

1. Open Windows. *Double-click Tabs3 with Sample Data on the desktop,* or *click the Start button on the Windows desktop, point to Programs or All Programs, point to Tabs3 & PracticeMaster group, point to Trial Software with Sample Data, then click Tabs3 with Sample Data.* Tabs3 will then open with sample data already present in the software.

2. The "Tip of the Day" window may now be displayed. *Click Close in the "Tip of the Day" window.*

3. *Click OK in the "Tabs3" window* to acknowledge the 11/17/2009 date.

4. *Click Cost in the "Task Folders" window.*

5. The "Rapid Cost Entry" window should now be displayed (see Tabs3 Exhibit 9).

TABS3 EXHIBIT 9
Entering a cost/expense record

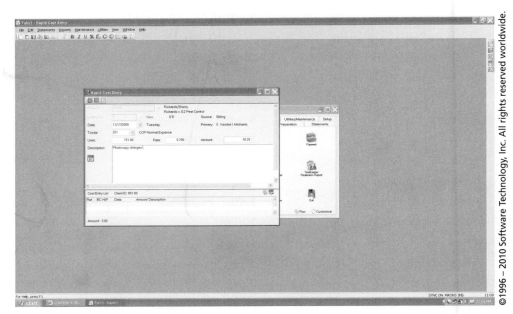

6. Your cursor should be in the Client ID: field with **851.00** filled in. Press the **[TAB]** key to accept the entry.

7. Press the **[TAB]** key again to go to the Date: field.

8. Press the **[TAB]** key to accept the default date of 11/17/2009.

9. *Click the Lookup button next to the Tcode: field. Scroll and double-click on "251 COP Photocopy charges."*

10. In the Units: field, type **151** (151 copies at the firm default rate of 20 cents a copy). Press the **[TAB]** key.

11. The calculation in the Amount: field is $30.20. Press the **[TAB]** key.

12. In the Description: field, enter **Photocopy charges—Response to Motion for Summary Judgment.**

13. *Click the Save icon on the main toolbar.*

14. Enter and save each of the following cost/expense records:

FIELD	INFORMATION TO BE ENTERED
Client ID:	851.00
Reference:	
Date:	11/17/2009
Tcode:	102
Units:	1.00
Rate:	
Amount:	20.00
Description:	Courier fee—info re: Response to Motion for Summary Judgment

FIELD	INFORMATION TO BE ENTERED
Client ID:	851.00
Reference:	
Date:	11/17/2009
Tcode:	106
Units:	1.00
Rate:	
Amount:	50
Description:	Online legal research—Response to Motion for Summary Judgment

FIELD	INFORMATION TO BE ENTERED
Client ID:	851.00
Reference:	
Date:	11/17/2009
Tcode:	107
Units:	1.00
Rate:	
Amount:	375.00
Description:	Transcription fees—defendant's deposition

15. *Click the Save icon on the main toolbar.*

16. *Click the Close icon* (the red square with a white "X") *at the upper right of the "Rapid Cost Entry" window.*

17. *Click on the Close icon at the upper right of the "Cost Verification List" window.*

18. You will now learn how to use the Fee Timer feature in Tabs3. *Click Fee in the "Task Folder" window.* The "Fee Entry" window should now be displayed.

19. *Click the green triangle just to the right of the word* "Timer" *in the "Fee Entry" window.* This is the Start Timer icon. Notice that the timer begins to count. The timer is now timing how long it takes you to complete a task such as making a phone call or drafting a letter.

20. Fill in the rest of the following information in the "Fee Entry" window:

FIELD	INFORMATION TO BE ENTERED
Client ID:	851.00
Reference:	
Timekeeper:	5
Date:	11/15/2009
Tcode:	3
Hours Worked:	0.00
Hours to Bill:	0.00
Rate:	150
Amount:	0.00
Description:	Telephone conference with counsel
Category:	60
Bill Code:	0 – Billable / Printable

21. *Click the red square next to Timer: on the Fee Entry toolbar to stop the timer.* (Assuming it took you less than a few minutes to enter the fee information, the value should be $15.00).

22. *Click the Save icon on the main toolbar.*

23. A window should now be displayed asking you if you want to **"Add timer to Hours?"** *Click Yes.*

24. *At the window that displays* **"Add to Amount?"**, *click Yes.* Notice at the bottom of the screen that the entry has been added and a cost of $15.00 has been recorded.

25. *Click the Close icon at the upper right of the "Fee-Richards/Sherry" window.*

26. *Click the Close icon at the upper right of the "Fee Verification List" window.*

27. *Click File on the menu bar and then click Exit.*

This concludes Lesson 4.

LESSON 5: GENERATING AND PRINTING DRAFT AND FINAL STATEMENTS

In this lesson, you will learn how to generate and print draft and final statements in Tabs3.

1. Open Windows. *Double-click Tabs3 with Sample Data on the desktop,* or *click the Start button on the Windows desktop, point to Programs or All Programs, point to the Tabs3 & PracticeMaster group, point to Trial Software with Sample Data, then click Tabs3 with Sample Data.* Tabs3 will then open with sample data already present in the software.

2. The "Tip of the Day" window may now be displayed. *Click Close in the "Tip of the Day" window.*

3. *Click OK in the "Tabs3" window* to acknowledge the 11/17/2009 date.

4. *Click Generate Statements in the "Task Folders" window.*

5. In the Client ID: field, type **851** and then press the [**TAB**] key. At the Thru: field, press the [**TAB**] key again.

6. *Click the Options tab in the "Generate Statements" window.* Notice that the default entry for Statement Type: is "Draft." Because you want to print a draft statement for Sherry Richards, leave it as is.

7. *Click the Lookup button next to Statement Date: and select* **November 18, 2009.** *(Note:* Statements are usually done at the end of the month, but this client has asked for a special mid-month bill.)

8. *Click OK in the "Generate Statements" window.*

9. *In the "Generate Statements" window, click the Lookup button under Selected Printer: to select a printer and then click Printer:.*

10. *Click OK in the "Generate Statements" window. (Note:* You can also save the statement as a PDF or text file, or print it to the DropBox for easy attachment to an email).

11. The draft statement should look similar to Tabs3 Exhibit 10. Normally, the timekeeper responsible for the case reviews and approves the draft statement. The next steps instruct you how to mark a statement as having been reviewed, how to run the statement as final, and how to update a statement.

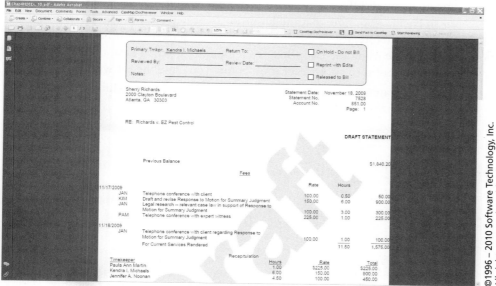

TABS3 EXHIBIT 10
Draft statement for *Richards v. EZ Pest Control*

12. *Click the Close icon at the upper right of the "Generate Statements" window.*

13. *Click Statements on the menu bar* (see Tabs3 Exhibit 11).

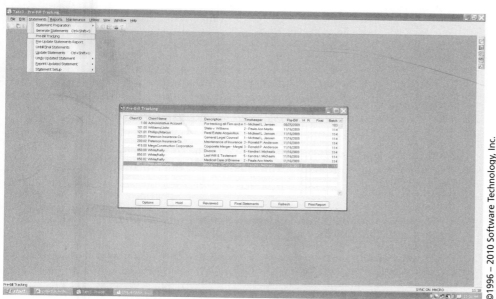

TABS3 EXHIBIT 11
Pre-billing tracking

HANDS-ON EXERCISES

14. *Click Pre-Bill Tracking.* The "Pre-Bill Tracking" window should now be displayed (see Tabs3 Exhibit 11).

15. *Double-click "851.00, Richards/Sherry, Richards v. EZ Pest Control."* Notice that a check mark appears in the "R" column. This means that the statement has been reviewed and is ready for a final statement.

16. *Click Final Statements in the "Pre-Bill Tracking" window.*

17. The "Generate Statements" window is now displayed. *Click the Options tab in the "Generate Statements" window.* Change the statement date to **11/18/2009**.

18. *Click OK in the "Generate Statements" window.*

19. *In the "Generate Statements" window, click the Lookup button under Selected Printer: to select a printer. Then click Printer.*

20. *Click OK in the "Generate Statements" window.* (*Note:* You can also save the statement as a PDF or text file, or print it to the DropBox for easy attachment to an email. Also, note that the DropBox is cleared each time the software is closed. Therefore, if you are waiting to print statements or other documents for class and are using the DropBox as a temporary holding area, the files must be printed or saved to another location before you close the software.)

21. The final statement produced should be similar to Tabs3 Exhibit 12.

TABS3 EXHIBIT 12
Final statement—Sherry Richards

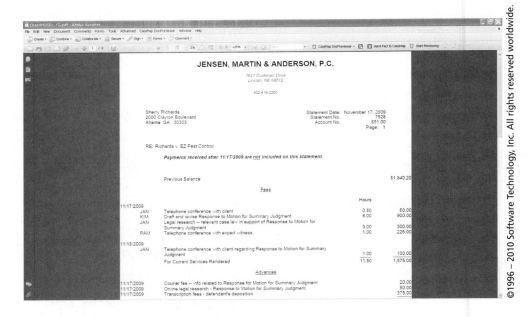

22. *Click the Close icon at the upper right of the "Generate Statements" window.*

23. *Click the Close icon at the upper right of the "Pre-Bill Tracking" window.*

24. The final stage in the billing process in Tabs3 is to run the Update Statements program. In Tabs3, changes can be made to the final statements until the Update Statements program is run. The Update Statements program updates accounts receivable and billed productivity information, and moves work-in-process transactions into the archive.

25. *Click the Statements tab (not the Statement Preparation tab) in the "Task Folders" window. Click Update Statements.*

26. A warning window will be displayed asking if you would like to back up your data first. *Click No. Note:* When using the full version of the software and running bills in an office setting, you will want to click Yes to create a backup.

27. In the "Update Statements" window, in the Client ID: field, type **851** in the first box, and press the [**TAB**] key. *Click OK.*

28. When the "Update Statements Status" window indicates that **"Statements are now updated,"** *click OK in the "Update Statements Status" window.*

29. *Click the Close icon at the upper right of the "Update Statements" window.*

30. *In the "Update Statements Verification List" window, click Cancel.*

31. *In the "Task Folders" window, click the Main tab, then click Client.*

32. *In the "Client Information" window, click the A/R & Fund Balances tab.* Notice that you can see the total balance due and the amount due for fees, expenses, and advances. The billing process has been successful.

33. *Click the Close icon at the upper right of the "Client Information" window.*

34. *Click File on the menu bar and then click Exit.*

This concludes Lesson 5.

LESSON 6: ENTERING A PAYMENT

In this lesson, you will learn how to enter a payment and apply it to a client's accounts receivable balance.

1. Open Windows. *Double-click Tabs3 with Sample Data on the desktop,* or *click the Start button on the Windows desktop, point to Programs or All Programs, point to the Tabs3 & PracticeMaster Technology group, point to Trial Software with Sample Data, then click Tabs3 with Sample Data.* Tabs3 will then open with sample data already present in the software.

2. The "Tip of the Day" window may now be displayed. *Click Close in the "Tip of the Day" window.*

3. *Click OK in the "Tabs3" window* to acknowledge the 11/17/2009 date.

4. *Click Payment in the "Task Folders" window.* The "Rapid Payment Entry" window should now be displayed (see Tabs3 Exhibit 13).

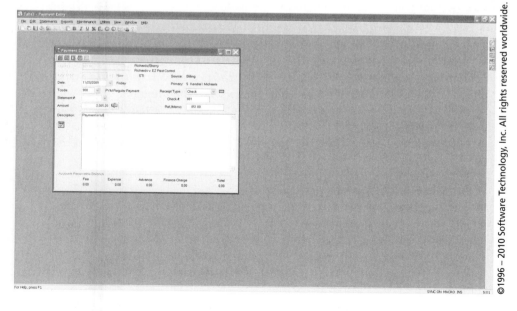

TABS3 EXHIBIT 13
Recording a payment

5. The cursor should be in the Client ID: field with **851.00** already entered. Press the [**TAB**] key to go to the Reference: field.

6. Press the [**TAB**] key to go to the Date: field.

7. Enter **11/20/2009** in the Date: field.

8. Press the [**TAB**] key to go to the Tcode: field. A Tcode of **900** should be entered in the field.

9. Press the [**TAB**] key to go to the Statement: field.

10. Press the [**TAB**] key to go to the Amount: field. In the Amount: field, type **2065.20**

11. Press the [**TAB**] key to go to the Description: field. In the Description: field, type **Payment in full.**

12. Press the [**TAB**] key to go to the Receipt Type: field.

13. Press the [**TAB**] key to accept the default value of Check.

14. In the Check #: field, **enter 881** as the check number.

15. *Click the Save icon on the main toolbar.* The "Unapplied Payment Options - Client 851.00" window is now displayed. *Click OK.*

16. *Click the Close icon* (the red square with a white "X") *at the upper right of the "Rapid Payment Entry" window.*

17. *Click the Close icon at the upper right of the "Payment Verification List" window.*

18. *In the "Task Folders" window, click Client.*

19. The number **851** should be displayed in the Client ID: field. *Click the A/R & Fund Balances tab in the "Client Information" window.* Notice that the Amount Due: is $0.00 and the Last Payment Amount: is $2,065.20.

20. *Click the Close icon at the upper right of the "Client Information" window.*

21. *Click File on the menu bar and then click Exit.*

This concludes Lesson 6.

 # ADVANCED LESSON

LESSON 7: PROCESSING AND PRINTING REPORTS

In this lesson, you will learn how to process and print several reports using Tabs3.

1. Open Windows. *Double-click Tabs3 with Sample Data on the desktop,* or *click the Start button on the Windows desktop, point to Programs or All Programs, point to the Tabs3 & PracticeMaster group, point to Trial Software with Sample Data, then click Tabs3 with Sample Data.* Tabs3 will then open with sample data already entered into the program.

2. The "Tip of the Day" window may now be displayed. *Click Close in the "Tip of the Day" window.*

3. *Click OK in the "Tabs3" window* to acknowledge the 11/17/2009 date.

4. *Click the Reports tab in the "Task Folders" window.*

5. *Click Productivity Reports.*

6. *Click Category Productivity.*

7. The default values for the report are all fine, so *click OK in the "Category Productivity Report" window.*

8. *In the "Print Category Productivity Report" window, click the Lookup button under Selected Printer: to select a printer; then select Printer:.*

9. *Click OK in the "Print Category Productivity Report" window.* (*Note:* You can also save the statement as a PDF or text file, or print it to the DropBox for easy attachment to an email.)

10. The report breaks out hours worked, billed hours, and other information by category (case type) for the reporting period of August to November 2009.

11. ***Click the Close icon*** (the red square with a white "X") ***at the upper right of the "Category Productivity Report" window.***

12. ***Click Productivity Reports in the Reports tab of the "Task Folders" window.***

13. Print the Timekeeper Productivity report.

14. Print the Timekeeper Analysis Report.

15. Print the Client Analysis Report.

16. ***At the Reports tab of the "Task Folders" window, click Management Reports.***

17. Print the Client Realization Report.

18. Print the Timekeeper Realization Report.

19. Print the Timekeeper Profitability Report.

20. ***At the Reports tab of the "Task Folders" window, click A/R Reports.***

21. ***Print the Collections Report.***

22. ***Print the A/R by Invoice Report.***

23. ***Close all of the open windows.***

24. ***Click File on the menu bar and then click Exit.***

This concludes the Tabs3 Hands-On Exercises.

CHAPTER 5

Database Management Systems

CHAPTER OBJECTIVES

After completing Chapter 5, you should be able to do the following:

1. Define a database.
2. Explain what a field is.
3. Define a record and a table.
4. Explain relational and logical operators.
5. List how databases can be used in the legal environment.
6. Explain how to plan a database.
7. Define a relational database.
8. Discuss database management-related ethical considerations.

database management system
Application software that manages a database by storing, searching, sorting, and organizing data.

database
A collection of related data items. Databases are created because the information contained in them must be accessed, organized, and used.

INTRODUCTION

All businesses, including legal organizations, must maintain and track information. Businesses routinely use database management systems (DBMSs) to collect and analyze information. A **database management system** is application software that stores, searches, sorts, and organizes data. A **database** is a collection of pieces of related data. For example, a database can be anything from a list of appointments, to a card catalog in a library, to an address book. These databases, whether or not they are on a computer, contain related information: appointments, listings of books, and addresses, respectively. They are organized by the date of the appointment; by the subject, title, and/or author of the book; and by the name of the person. A DBMS allows users to track and organize this kind of information using a computer. This chapter explains what a database is and how one is structured, provides an overview of DBMS functions, introduces database management fundamentals, describes types of DBMSs, and discusses how a DBMS can be used in the legal environment.

WHAT IS A DATABASE?

DBMSs are used in millions of businesses to manage and track vital information. They are powerful and flexible and can be used for thousands of different purposes. For example, a law firm might use a DBMS to track its clients' names and addresses, and a manufacturer might use a DBMS to track its inventory of parts and finished products. A DBMS can not only store or hold information, but can also organize that information in a relevant manner. For example, the law firm might need an alphabetical list of its clients' names and addresses to be used for reference purposes. The manufacturer, in contrast, might use a DBMS to give it an inventory list of products by completion date. It is sometimes easy to think of databases simply as organized lists or catalogs of information.

Exhibit 5–1 is a database that shows a legal organization's client list. A client database tracks the name, address, and other information for each client that an attorney or law firm represents. Notice that a row exists for each individual client. Many things can be done with the client database in Exhibit 5–1.

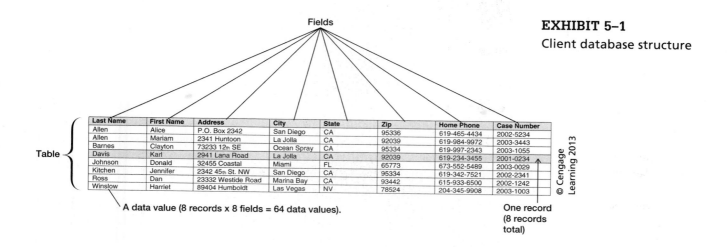

EXHIBIT 5–1
Client database structure

Last Name	First Name	Address	City	State	Zip	Home Phone	Case Number
Allen	Alice	P.O. Box 2342	San Diego	CA	95336	619-465-4434	2002-5234
Allen	Mariam	2341 Huntoon	La Jolla	CA	92039	619-984-9972	2003-3443
Barnes	Clayton	73233 12th SE	Ocean Spray	CA	95334	619-997-2343	2003-1055
Davis	Karl	2941 Lana Road	La Jolla	CA	92039	619-234-3455	2001-0234
Johnson	Donald	32455 Coastal	Miami	FL	65773	673-552-5489	2003-0029
Kitchen	Jennifer	2342 45th St. NW	San Diego	CA	95334	619-342-7521	2002-2341
Ross	Dan	23332 Westide Road	Marina Bay	CA	93442	615-933-6500	2002-1242
Winslow	Harriet	89404 Humboldt	Las Vegas	NV	78524	204-345-9908	2003-1003

Fields

Table

A data value (8 records x 8 fields = 64 data values).

One record (8 records total)

© Cengage Learning 2013

1. A complete directory of the firm's clients, including names, addresses, and phone numbers, can be printed for the law office's staff to use when drafting correspondence and for general reference purposes. To make the directory easy to use, it can be sorted alphabetically by the clients' last names (as shown in Exhibit 5–1).

2. Information about new clients can easily be entered into the database.

3. Client data can be easily changed if a client moves or gets a new phone number.

4. Mailing labels can be printed for sending out firm newsletters, brochures, or other announcements. The labels can be sorted in numerical order according to zip code, so that all the pieces going to a single zip code are together (cheaper postal rates are available for mailings that are presorted).

5. Targeted mailings can be sent to clients in a specific state or area. If a multi-state law firm wanted to send a mailing to only California residents, this could be done by searching for only CA in the State column of the database. The database would then retrieve only the names and addresses of clients who live in California.

Organizations in the legal environment use databases to track many kinds of information. Legal organizations use DBMSs to track specific information about a particular case, such as tracking many thousands of documents in large cases. This process is called *litigation support*. Each document is entered into a litigation support system, which is another kind of DBMS.

A DBMS allows users to manipulate data as they wish. For example, if a legal organization wanted a list displaying only its clients' names and home phone numbers on a report (and no other information), a new query report could be developed to display this information (see Exhibit 5–2) while still leaving the underlying data in Exhibit 5–1 unchanged. Even though a vast amount of information is entered into a database, that information does not have to be printed out in every report. Information in a database is used as needed. Users can use or print only the information they want at any given time. All the other information is still left intact, unharmed, in the database.

Database software is flexible, powerful, and convenient to use and operate because it allows users to:

Store and retrieve information easily
Arrange and rearrange data over and over without affecting the data itself
Update and change information
Add information
Search for information
Sort and organize information
Print information in many different formats

Legal organizations and paralegals create databases for a wide variety of purposes in addition to litigation support, including opposing attorney databases, forms database, class action database, judges database, legal research database, conflict of interest database, factual database (for a specific case), expert witness database, library catalog database, active file database, inactive file database, licensed software database, marketing database, trial database, and many others.

Microsoft Access (a relational database program) controls a significant portion of the legal database market. Two versions of Access are widely used today, Access 2007 and Access 2010. As in Word and Excel, Access users issue commands by accessing tools on ribbons that change depending on which ribbon tab is selected (see Exhibit 5–2). Access is a common database program used typically for "small" databases that

EXHIBIT 5–2

New query and report

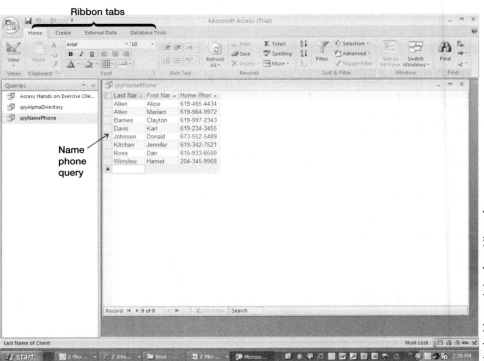

may contain hundreds or even several thousand records. However, for large databases that contain millions of records, Access would not be used.

Depending on the size of the legal organization, paralegals may be used in different roles relating to database management. For example, in a small legal organization a paralegal might be completely responsible for the design and implementation of a complete database system, whether it be for litigation support, for administrative purposes, or for some other reason. In larger legal organizations that have complex litigation support/database needs, paralegals may answer questions and give assistance to a professional programmer who is hired to actually design the database. In addition, in large legal organizations, paralegals typically play a vital role in entering data into litigation support databases.

DATABASE STRUCTURE

Databases are organized into tables, records, fields, and data values.

Table

A database is made up of tables that contain related information and the tools necessary to manipulate the data. A **table** is a collection of related information stored in rows and columns. The entirety of the data in Exhibit 5–1 is a table.

A table stores information about a particular topic. The table in Exhibit 5–1 stores contact information about a law office's clients. Many databases have more than one table. For example, the law-firm database in Exhibit 5–3 has four separate tables. Each table contains information about a particular topic: the Client table contains client contact information, the Case File table contains information about each case (case name, court, judge, case type, etc.), the Opposing Attorney table contains contact information for opposing counsel, and the Case Evidence table contains a detailed listing of the pieces of the evidence in each case. Having additional tables simplifies and speeds up querying the database and in some ways makes the database

table
A collection of related information stored in rows and columns.

✓ of database program

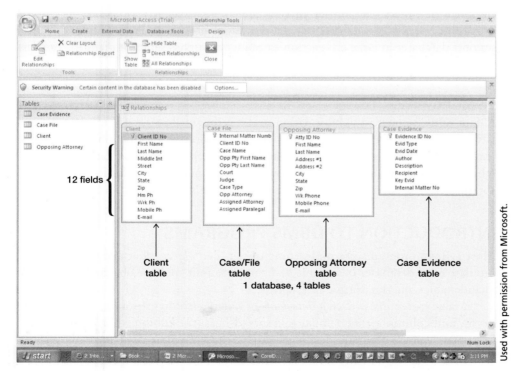

EXHIBIT 5–3
A database with multiple tables—Access 2007

Used with permission from Microsoft.

easier to manipulate, since instead of having one file with everything dumped in it the user has broken up the information into smaller subunits while still having the various information elements connected or related to each other. Tables and table design are a crucial part of designing effective databases.

Fields

A **field** is a column in a table that contains a category of information. For example, Exhibit 5–1 shows eight fields in the table:

1. Last Name
2. First Name
3. Address
4. City
5. State
6. Zip
7. Home Phone
8. Work Phone

In Exhibit 5–3 there are twelve fields in the Client table, eleven fields in the Case File table, eleven fields in the Opposing Attorney table, and eight fields in the Case Evidence table. The fields within any given database will be different. For example, in a docket control database used to control a legal organization's deadlines and appointments, the fields might include date of event, event description, case name, and place of event. All databases must have fields to input and collect the data. Large databases commonly have hundreds of fields in which to enter information. It is common for some DBMSs to refer to fields as *columns*.

Record

A **record** is a collection of fields treated as a unit. It is essentially one row in a table. In Exhibit 5–1, each record has all the information for one client entry—that is, the complete set of field data for one entry. A total of eight records, or clients, are entered in Exhibit 5–1. Large databases may have millions of records. For example, litigation support databases in large class action cases involving thousands of plaintiffs can easily have millions of records.

Data Value

A **data value** is one item of information, and it is the smallest piece of information in a table. For example, in Exhibit 5–1, each individual piece of information is a data value (e.g., "Winslow," "Harriett," "Allen," "San Diego," etc.). There are 64 data values in Exhibit 5–1. Multiply the number of records times the number of fields for each table to compute the total number of data values (e.g., 8 records times 8 fields = 64 data values).

INTRODUCTION TO DBMS PROGRAMS

Most DBMS programs use tools, sometimes called *objects*, that allow users to manipulate each database. In Exhibit 5–4 there are four tools or objects listed. These include tables, queries, forms, and reports.

A table (sometimes called a *data table* or *datasheet*) stores the data in the database in row and column format similar to a spreadsheet (see Exhibit 5–5). Tables are the heart of a database program. Each database file can have more than one table. Exhibit 5–5 shows the Datasheet view of a table in Microsoft Access.

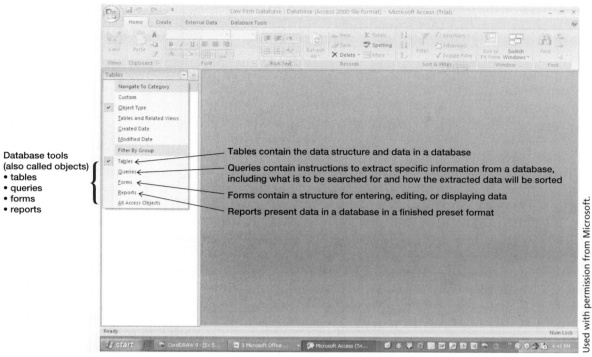

Database tools
(also called objects)
• tables
• queries
• forms
• reports

Tables contain the data structure and data in a database

Queries contain instructions to extract specific information from a database, including what is to be searched for and how the extracted data will be sorted

Forms contain a structure for entering, editing, or displaying data

Reports present data in a database in a finished preset format

Used with permission from Microsoft.

EXHIBIT 5–4

Access 2007 tools/objects—Tables, queries, forms, and documents

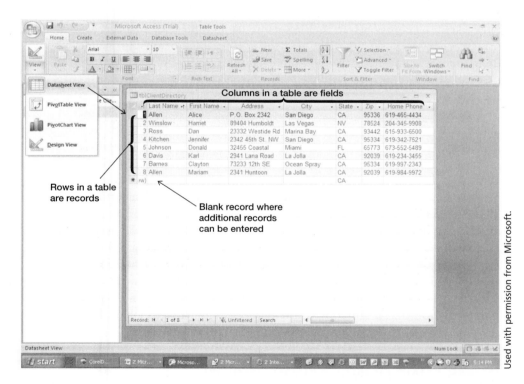

Columns in a table are fields

Rows in a table
are records

Blank record where
additional records
can be entered

Used with permission from Microsoft.

EXHIBIT 5–5

A table in the datasheet
view in Access 2007

A **form** allows a user to view, enter, and edit data in a special, or custom, format designed by the user. Notice in Exhibit 5–6 that the user created a special on-screen form in which to enter and view data. Although information can be entered directly into a table in the Datasheet view (see Exhibit 5–5), many users find it easier to enter

form

Allows a user to view,
enter, and edit data in a
custom format designed
by the user.

EXHIBIT 5–6

A custom-designed entry form

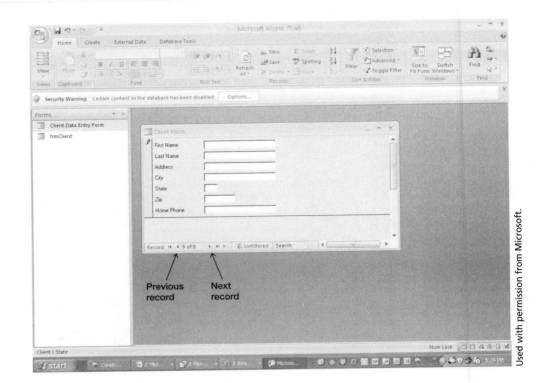

Used with permission from Microsoft.

(handwritten margin note) Specific view of data. Allows user to answer specific questions.

query

Extracts data from a table based on criteria designed by the user. A query allows a user to search for and sort only the information the user is looking for at that time.

report

Prints data from a table or query as designed by the user. While forms are designed to be used on the screen, reports are designed to be printed.

data into a form such as the one in Exhibit 5–6. Notice in Exhibit 5–5 that the client's last name comes before the first name. In Exhibit 5–6 the order was changed for data entry purposes, and First Name of Client comes before Last Name. This was done to make data entry easier and more logical. Also, notice in Exhibit 5–6 that the user can go to the next record by clicking on the next record arrow or go backward through the records.

A **query** extracts data from a table based on criteria designed by the user. A query allows a user to search for and sort only the information the user is looking for at that time. The first screen in Exhibit 5–7 shows a query in the design view and the second screen shows the results of the query. Queries create a specific view of data and allow the user to answer specific questions. In Exhibit 5–7 the question that is being answered by the query is "What clients of the law firm reside in San Diego?" Once a user creates a query, the user can save it and then use it whenever they need. After a query has been created (see the first screen in Exhibit 5–7), the user must run or execute the query to see the results (see the second screen in Exhibit 5–7).

A **report** prints data from a table or query as designed by the user. Whereas forms are designed to be used on the screen, reports are designed to be printed (see Exhibit 5–8). A report consists of information that is pulled from tables or queries, as well as information that is stored with the report design, such as labels, headings, and graphics.

DBMS FUNCTIONS: AN OVERVIEW

Every DBMS program has its own set of commands and its own structure. However, the topics covered herein are universal to all DBMSs. These programs have been around since the inception of computers and contain hundreds of different commands and functions, but good database design is critical to all, from the simplest to the most complex database.

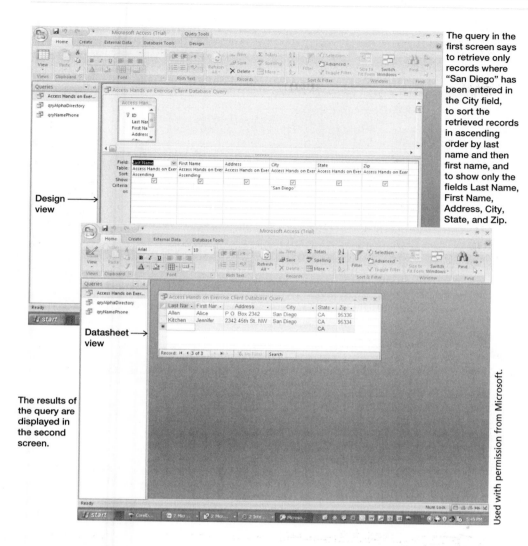

EXHIBIT 5–7

A query in Design view and the same query in Datasheet view

The query in the first screen says to retrieve only records where "San Diego" has been entered in the City field, to sort the retrieved records in ascending order by last name and then first name, and to show only the fields Last Name, First Name, Address, City, State, and Zip.

Design view

Datasheet view

The results of the query are displayed in the second screen.

DATABASE PLANNING AND DESIGN

Database planning and design is a critical step in building an effective and competent database that meets the needs of the user. This section provides an overview of the design process and then goes into detail regarding database planning fundamentals.

Database Design and Implementation Process Overview

To design a well-thought-out database that truly meets the needs of the user, the steps shown in Exhibit 5–9 are recommended. Databases that are not carefully designed often contain logic mistakes and reasoning errors, causing the database not to meet the user's needs. They take much longer to complete, as the mistakes have to be corrected through trial and error. The larger the database, the more time and effort should go into its planning. It would be logical to assume that a database with tens of thousands of records might take months to plan, whereas a database with a few records, tables, queries, and reports might take a few hours to plan.

Identify the Problem A database is created to solve a problem or to fulfill a need. For example, before the client database in Exhibit 5–1 was created, a manual card file may have existed showing the names and addresses of all clients.

1st step

EXHIBIT 5–8

A report in Design view and Report view

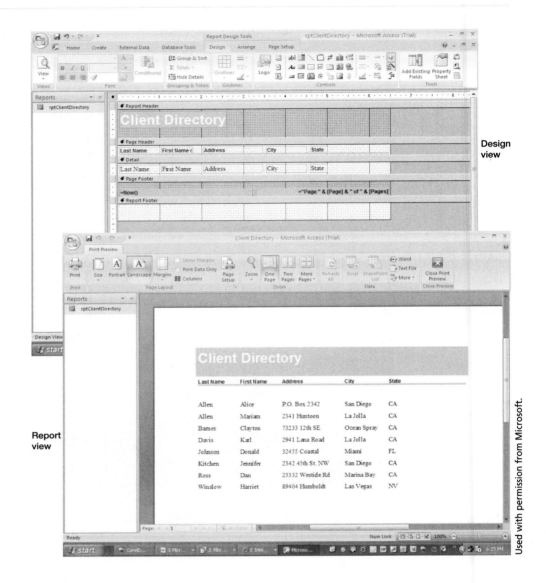

Design view

Report view

Used with permission from Microsoft.

Unfortunately, everyone in the office had to have his or her own card file. This was a problem, because any changes had to be entered on all the card files, which represented tremendous duplication.

Determine What Users Need from the Database It is critical to accurately determine exactly how users will utilize the finished database and to accurately document what the users' needs are. To do this correctly the database designer must spend time with the end users to determine their existing and future needs. Possible alternatives for meeting the users' needs must be considered. In the client database example, a firm might determine that if a computerized database is created, the information could be kept by one person; any changes can be made by that one person; and the information could be accessed by all staff using a shared network directory that all staff have access to, or placed on a firm intranet.

It is also important to think in advance about who will be using the database. What problems does each of the users want to solve by creating the database? In analyzing and evaluating the problem, it is good to have the perspective of multiple people. A group of people tends to see problems and solutions from multiple angles, which greatly adds to the evaluation process and brainstorming of new ideas and

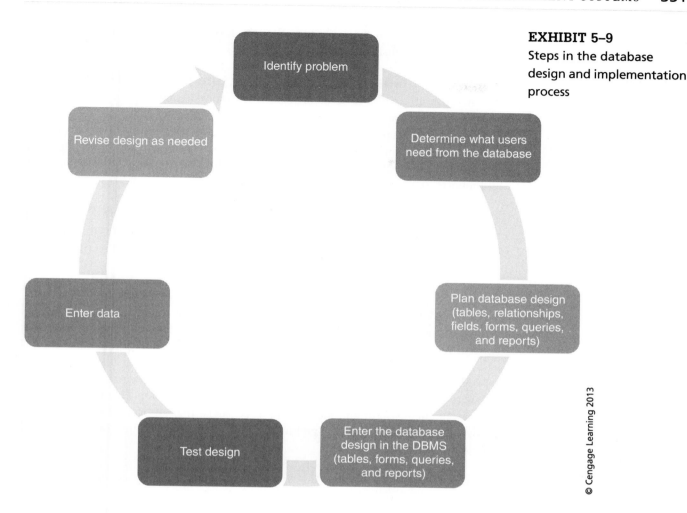

© Cengage Learning 2013

EXHIBIT 5-9
Steps in the database design and implementation process

new answers. The importance of truly understanding the needs of the user cannot be overstated. If the end database does not meet the needs of the user, all the time and money spent in building and populating it has been wasted.

Plan the Database Design Many people outline the database design on paper or in a word processor before creating it directly in the DBMS. Among other things, you should think about the following:

- *What problems do I want to solve?* In thinking about a database design, it is a good idea to start at the end (what do I want the end product to look like?) and then work backward.

- *What tables do I need and how will they be related to each other?* Decide how you will structure the data into groups and how the groups will be related so no information is duplicated from one table to the other.

- *What specific information do I want to track or store?* Decide what fields you need to include.

- *How will I want to see the data?* Determine what queries you will need to develop to search and sort the data to solve your problems.

- *How will I use the information?* What are the different reports you will need to solve your problems?

Planning the database design includes carefully designing the fields needed for each table; the layout and design of each table; the relationships between the tables (discussed later in the chapter); and all of the forms, queries, and reports the users will need for the finished system.

Enter the Database Design and Structure into the DBMS Once the user has an outline of a database design, it is time to actually begin creating or designing the database in the DBMS. The first task is to give the database a name. The database name should reflect exactly the kind of information that it will store. For example, Client Directory specifically identifies the type of database being stored in the example. Entering the database design, including creating tables, forms, queries, and reports, is included in detail later in this chapter.

Test Design After a database design has been entered into the DBMS (including the tables, forms, queries, and reports), the user should test it. This can be done by entering a few records into the database and then executing the forms, queries, and reports to see if the database is producing the desired information. It is always a good idea to test the database before entering hundreds or thousands of records.

Enter Data Once the design of the database has been tested and put through its paces and the users have evaluated whether the design in fact meets their needs, it is time to enter the data. The data entry phase of the implementation process is critical. Data entry is covered in detail later in this chapter, but the old adage of "garbage in—garbage out" applies when entering data. If data are haphazardly entered in the database using inconsistent methods, then all searches and reports on the data will likewise be inconsistent and incomplete. It is crucial that all data be entered consistently and that careful planning go into the data entry process to minimize errors and problems later.

Revise Design as Needed Once the database design process has taken place, the structure entered, the testing done, and the data entered, any revising should hopefully be very limited. It is extremely difficult and time-consuming to revise a database, even a simple one, at this stage. However, as users utilize the system and time goes by, new queries, reports, and uses may be identified, calling for changes to the system. For any database to continue to meet the needs of the user, the database should be reviewed and revised from time to time.

Database Planning Fundamentals

As indicated previously, planning and critical thinking about what a database is going to accomplish is very important. If, for example, you were planning the client database in Exhibit 5–1, you would write down all the information you wanted to track about a client. The particular information that is tracked depends on the legal organization and how it operates. In addition to tracking the name, address, phone number, and case number of a client, a firm might want to track information about the client's case. This might include the type of case (e.g., criminal, personal injury, etc.); whether the client paid a retainer and, if so, how much it was; and so forth. It is also a good idea to have others review your design. For example, if you are designing a database to track witnesses for a case, it is strongly recommended that the managing attorney on the case review the design to help troubleshoot it and to determine if there are any problems.

Example of a Poorly Planned Database Good design is critical to any database. Planning a database involves more than just writing down fields for information that must be tracked. You must think carefully about how the information will be used (i.e., how you want the information to be searched, sorted, and printed

A. Poorly planned client database

Name	Address
Clayton Barnes	73233 12th SE
Harriet Winslow	89404 Humboldt
Jennifer Kitchen	2342 45th St. NW
Karl Davis	2941 Lane
Mariam Allen	2341 Huntoon

B. Well-planned client database

Last Name	First Name	Address
Allen	Mariam	2341 Huntoon
Barnes	Clayton	73233 12th SE
Davis	Karl	2941 Lane
Kitchen	Jennifer	2342 45th St. NW
Winslow	Harriet	89404 Humboldt

EXHIBIT 5–10

Poorly planned and well-planned databases

© Cengage Learning 2013

in the end). If this is not done well, the database will be error-ridden and will not work properly. For example, assume the client database is intended to be used to produce a list that is sorted using the client's last name. If the database were designed with only one name field, Name, and all 500 records were entered into the database as in Exhibit 5–10, with the first name first and then the last name (e.g., Harriet Winslow), the database would not accomplish the intended purpose, because most DBMSs use the first letters entered in a field to alphabetize or sort a list. Instead of having a list alphabetized by last name, you would have a useless client list that could be alphabetized only by first name. In this example, the database would have to be redesigned, and all the information would have to be reentered to solve the problem. Users must also be careful when designing a database with dates in it. If the DBMS can designate a field as a date field, then there is not much problem. However, if the user enters a date, such as month/day/year (e.g., 07/03/2008), in a text field or tries to enter a date in a numeric field, it can cause problems. Many databases cannot sort or search dates properly using this design.

Rules for Planning a Database Keep the following rules or ideas in mind when planning a database:

1. *Getting Started*—Many times, a computerized database design is based on a manual system or an outdated computer system. Start the process by enumerating what you like and dislike about the prior (or existing) method. In the client database example, the legal organization might have previously used a manual card system for keeping track of clients. This would be a good starting point for designing the computerized version.

2. *Plan Ahead*—Plan for the future. If you think you might need an extra field later, add it now for safety. For example, in the client database, if you think you eventually might want a field for a fax number, mobile phone number, Internet site, or email address, include it now even though you might not use it right away. Some users enter two or three blank fields so they can go back, name them, and add information to them later. Try to anticipate your future needs. It is difficult to change a table's structure once it is filled with data.

3. ***Do Not Put Too Many Fields into One Table***—Each table should be simple and cover just one topic. A common mistake is to put too many fields and too much information into one table. Most databases, such as Access and others, are relational databases, which are covered later in the chapter. Relational databases can have multiple tables in one database with relationships among the fields in the different tables that operate as if they were in one table. Notice in Exhibit 5–3 that each of the four tables has a specific purpose and no one table has more than twelve fields in it. The tables in Exhibit 5–3 have been carefully designed so that no one table has too much information in it or contains unrelated information.

4. ***Do Not Repeat Fields***—Another common mistake is for users to try to make each table look like a stand-alone report. For example, if a user wanted to track the status of each case in the client database (e.g., whether the case is ready for trial, in discovery, on appeal, etc.) it would not be necessary to recreate first name, last name, and case number in the new table. Because this information is already contained in the client database table, the user could relate the two tables together and thus easily create a report or form that includes this information any time (as long as each table has at least one field in common with another table).

5. ***Keep Fields in Logical Order***—When you create the table design and design the data entry form (the screen that you see when you enter the records), make sure the fields are put in a logical order that flows well. For example, in the client database, you would not want the last name field to be followed by the zip code field in the data entry form. Make sure the form corresponds to how you will be entering the information into the records. In Exhibit 5–5, the order of the fields is roughly the same as the information in a manual Rolodex system.

6. ***Allow Plenty of Space for Each Field***—If you have to enter a maximum field length (i.e., the maximum number of characters you can enter into a field), leave plenty of space. For instance, if you allowed for only five digits in a zip code field, you would have a problem, as many businesses use the full nine-digit hyphenated zip code. Again, careful planning is critical.

7. ***Separate Data into Small Fields***—It is almost always better to separate data into small fields than to place multiple kinds of information in large fields. The preceding example of a poor design that used one name field (Name) instead of two smaller name fields (Last Name and First Name) shows what can happen. Also, always separate city, state, and zip code. In the future, you might want to sort or search using these specific fields.

8. ***Make Field Names as Small as Possible***—When you print data, large field names get in the way, especially when the data the field contains have only a few characters. Although this can be adjusted, it is better to use smaller names whenever possible.

9. ***Anticipate How the Database Will Be Used***—Before you design the database, think about how the information will be searched, how it will be sorted, and what format your reports and printouts will take. Most databases that fail do so because this rule was not followed.

10. ***Always Test the Design***—No matter how good you think a design is, always test it before you put in hundreds of records, only to find out the design is faulty.

Carpenters have a saying, "Measure twice and cut once," which means before you cut a board, measure the distance once and then measure it again for accuracy, so that when you actually cut the board, it is the right length. The same analogy applies here. Design and redesign the database; otherwise, the database may not do what you intend it to do.

CREATING A TABLE

Creating a table is the core of database management. Tables hold all of the data that users enter. Creating a table in most DBMSs is straightfoward. Tables that are efficient and meet all of the needs of the users take planning and attention to detail. Exhibit 5–11 shows a table being created in Design view for the client directory example. Users can switch between Design view (Exhibit 5–11) and Datasheet view (Exhibit 5–5) quickly and easily. Most DBMSs also have a wizard or automated feature that can help the user quickly and easily create a table. Many DBMSs come with a variety of standard templates, tables, and databases that have already been set up for users. These typically include time and billing, expense tracking, resource scheduling, and other applications. In addition, Microsoft Access has a direct link to a template website that has additional database templates. Looking at these designs is sometimes helpful in designing your own databases.

Field Names

Each field in the database must have a field name. Each field name must be unique and should reasonably describe the information that will be placed in it. Exhibit 5–11 shows a listing of the fields in the client information database. To create a field in the database in Exhibit 5–11, and create some basic information for each field, the user simply types the name in the Field Name box, enters the data type and description, and presses [TAB] to go to the next field. The user continues until all the fields are entered. In addition to entering the basic information, the user can also enter a number of types of highly customized information, such as field size, default values, lookups, and whether a field is required.

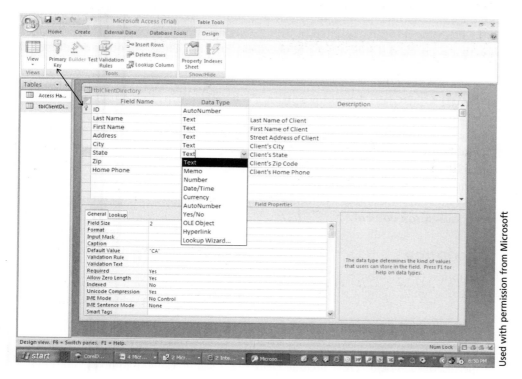

EXHIBIT 5–11

Creating a table in Design view

Data Type

In all databases, the user must tell the DBMS what kind of information will be held in each field. Fields can hold several different kinds of data. In Exhibit 5–11, notice that a field can hold text, memo, numbers, dates and times, currency, an automatic number, Yes/No, and other types of information. The following is a description of the main data types.

Text Text fields hold text, numbers, and symbols. Notice in Exhibit 5–11 that most of the fields are shown as text in the data type.

Memo This type of field holds text, but there is no maximum field length set, so the user can type an infinite amount of text in the field.

Number A number field contains only numbers. Most databases can perform complex mathematical computations on information entered into number fields; typically, only numbers can be entered into number fields.

Dates/Times A date/time field holds dates and times, as the name implies. It is often necessary to sort information by date, and this feature makes it possible to do so. Some DBMSs require the user to indicate how the information should be formatted (e.g., 1/1/14, January 1, 2014, Jan 1, 14, etc.).

Currency The currency data type formats the numbers with dollar signs and treats the information as money. For example, if the client directory contained a field for the amount of retainer the client paid, this field would have a data type of currency.

AutoNumber An autonumber data type automatically generates a new consecutive number for the field when a new record is entered. For example, in Exhibit 5–11 notice that there is a field for a client ID number. It will be populated with a unique internal identification number (AutoNumber) that will be generated automatically by the DBMS for each client.

Yes/No A yes/no data type allows the user to indicate only yes or no in the field. In some DBMSs, this is represented by either a yes or a no appearing in the field or by a box that is checked if it is yes or not checked if it is no. There are other data types as well in some DBMSs.

Lookup Options A **lookup option** is a list of options that a user must choose from when entering information into a table (see Exhibit 5–11, "Lookup Wizard"). An example would be entering a client's state in the client database example; a list of state abbreviations will be displayed on the screen and the user can select from one of the fifty state abbreviation options. Lookup options are extremely helpful in trying to control accuracy and data integrity as data is being entered into the database. The process of trying to control what information is entered into a database is sometimes called **validation control.**

> **lookup option**
> A list of options that a user must choose from when entering information into a table.

> **validation control**
> The process of controlling and limiting what information is entered into a database for the purpose of ensuring accuracy.

Description

Description (see Exhibit 5–11) simply allows the user to enter additional information to describe what the field will hold.

General

The General tab in the lower area of Exhibit 5–11 has several options for defining the properties of each field. These include Field Size, Default Value, Required, and others.

Field Size Notice in Exhibit 5–11 that the State field is currently selected. Notice in the General tab at the bottom of Exhibit 5–11 that the user has entered a field size of 2. This means that the field can contain only two characters. This makes sense because the user wants the person entering the data to enter two-character state abbreviations instead of typing the Full Name of each state, which takes more time.

Default Value Default value means that a preset or standard value will be entered into the field unless it is changed by the user. This speeds up data entry. Notice in Exhibit 5–11 that the Default Value for the field is CA. This means that when a new client is being entered, CA will automatically be displayed in the State field. The user can either accept the default value or overwrite it.

Required This means that the field is mandatory and must be filled in for the record to be added to the database. In Exhibit 5–11, State is shown as a required field.

ENTERING AND EDITING DATA

The physical typing of data into databases is not difficult. However, entering the data so they are accurate, consistent, and in line with how the database was designed is more challenging. The larger the database, the more complex the database, and the more people entering the data, the more difficult it is to get information accurately entered into a database. Consider that even if the design of the database is brilliant (the tables, records, and fields will absolutely meet the users' needs), the queries are carefully crafted and designed, and the reports are beautifully formatted, if the data entry is poorly done (inconsistent, inaccurate, and haphazardly done)—nothing else will matter and the database will fail. The data entry must be done accurately, and in the end accuracy will play a significant role in whether the database accomplishes its purposes. The data entry must also exactly match how the queries will be performed, or the queries will come back incomplete and will fail to return all of the data they should.

Data can usually either be entered directly into the table in Datasheet view (see Exhibit 5–5) or be entered using a form (see Exhibit 5–6). To enter data, the user simply opens the table in Datasheet view or in a form and begins entering data. Most DBMSs allow users to go to the next field by either pressing the [TAB] key or using the mouse.

To edit or modify a field or record, the user goes to the record in either the table (Datasheet view) or in a form and edits the information. In large databases (with tens of thousands of records), finding a specific record may not be easy. To find a specific record, a user may want to use the Find icon, which in many DBMSs is the binoculars (see Exhibit 5–12). In Exhibit 5–12, the user has selected the binoculars, typed in "Barnes" in the Find What: field, selected a table in Look In, and chosen Any Part of Field in the Match field. The Match dropdown list allows the following options:

- *Whole Field*—This finds fields where the specified text is the only thing in that field. For example, "Barnes" would not find "Barnes and Noble."
- *Start of Field*—This finds fields that begin with the specific text. For example, "Barnes" would find "Barnes" and "Barnes and Noble," but not "J. Barnes."
- *Any Part of Field*—This finds fields that contain the specific text in any way. "Barnes" would find "Barnes," "Barnes and Noble," "Noble and Barnes" and "J. Barnes."

It is typically easier to find something when Any Part of Field is selected because the DBMS will find the data in any part of a field and an exact match is not required. The down side is that Any Part of Field is more likely to find irrelevant fields as well.

EXHIBIT 5–12

Using the Find feature
(binoculars)

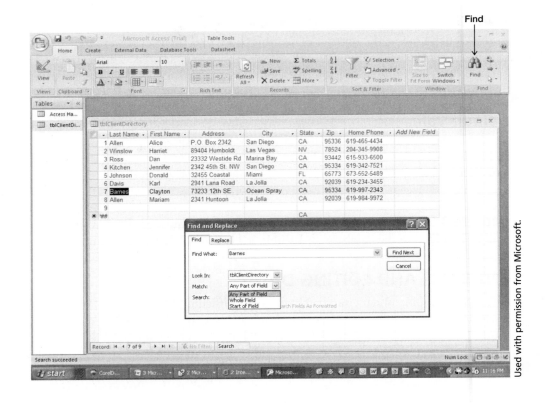

Users can also delete entire records that are no longer needed and can copy and move information from one record to another.

CREATING FORMS

It is possible to do all data entry using Datasheet view commands (see Exhibit 5–5), but it is usually not the best way. Unless the field widths are set very wide, the entries probably will not be entirely visible and the user will frequently have to scroll horizontally while information is being entered. With a form (see Exhibit 5–6), data entry can be accomplished much more easily. The user can allot as much space as needed for each field, information can be entered into multiple tables, and it is easier to see what record is being worked on because only one record is shown at a time (see Exhibit 5–6). The Datasheet view is also cluttered with all of the previous records (see Exhibit 5–5). To create a form, the user simply indicates how the form should look and what fields to include in the form. Most DBMSs also have a wizard or automated feature that can help the user quickly and easily create a form.

SEARCHING, SORTING, AND QUERYING THE DATABASE

The most powerful tools for manipulating a database include searching for specific information and sorting and organizing the information according to the specific needs of the user. This section gives you an overview of searching and sorting databases, and then provides specific examples.

Overview of Searching Databases

A user can ask a DBMS to display all the information or parts of the information that was entered into a database. For example, suppose in Exhibit 5–13 the user wanted

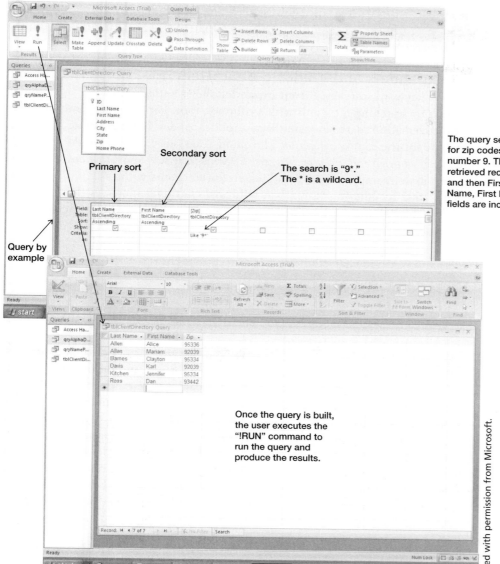

Used with permission from Microsoft.

EXHIBIT 5–13
Creating a query

The query searches the database for zip codes that begin with the number 9. The query sorts the retrieved records by Last Name and then First Name. Only Last Name, First Name, and Zip Code fields are included in the query.

Once the query is built, the user executes the "!RUN" command to run the query and produce the results.

to know all clients that had a zip code that began with the number 9, the user wanted the information sorted by last name and then first name, and these were the only fields the user wanted displayed. The first screen in Exhibit 5–13 shows the query that was built and the second screen shows the results. Users can query a database using several different methods, including structured query languages, query by example, root expanders and wildcard characters, relational operators, and logical operators (also called Boolean operators).

Structured Query Languages
DBMSs search and retrieve information in different ways. Some DBMSs have a sophisticated structured query language for searching databases. A **structured query language (SQL)** uses words in proper syntax to search for and retrieve data in a database. In many ways, an SQL is much like regular programming languages. SQLs are somewhat complicated because the user must learn the proper command words and syntax, but they are also very powerful. SQLs are generally used in large, sophisticated DBMSs.

structured query language (SQL)
A database programming language used to search for and retrieve information in some DBMSs.

Query by Example Many DBMSs allow for a method of searching and retrieving data called **query by example** (QBE—see Exhibit 5–13). Using this method, a user interactively builds a query that will search and sort a database.

Root Expanders and Wildcard Characters These are two methods used to enlarge keyword searches. A **root expander** allows a user to increase the scope of the search by searching for words with a common root. For example, some databases use the exclamation mark character (!) as a root expander. If a user wanted to search a database for the root of *litigation,* she could enter "litig!". This would search for words such as *litigation, litigate, litigates, litigated, litigator,* and *litigators.* Or, in the client database example, a user could search for all clients with case numbers starting with 2002 by entering "2002!". A **wildcard character** increases the scope of a search by replacing one of the characters in a word. A common wildcard character is the asterisk (*) (see Exhibit 5–13). For example, a user could search for *run* and *ran* by entering "r*n" in the search. Different databases use different symbols for root expanders and wildcard characters, but the concepts are the same.

Root Expanders and Wildcard Characters

    ! Root expander: Retrieves all roots of the word
    * Wildcard characters: Searches for all characters in the wildcard position

Relational Operators Data relationships are expressed by **relational operators**. For instance, if the client database included a field for the amount of retainer paid, and a user wanted to find all the clients who had paid a retainer fee of $999 or more, this could be done using a relational operator. The user would enter ">999" in the criteria part of the query in the "Retainer Amount" field. The ">" symbol is a relational operator that means *greater than.* The computer would respond by displaying the records that fit the search criterion. Relational operators include equal to, greater than, less than, greater than or equal to, less than or equal to, and not equal to. They are frequently used to search fields containing numbers and dates. For example, if the user wanted all dates greater than or equal to 6/1/2008, he would search using the following relational operators: ">=6/1/2008."

Relational Operators

>	Greater than
<	Less than
=	Equal to
<>	Not equal to
>=	Greater than or equal to
<=	Less than or equal to

Boolean/Logical Operators To instruct a database to look for more than one criterion, a **Boolean operator** (sometimes called a logical operator) is used. Boolean operators include: AND, OR, and NOT. Many database searches are based on the principles of Boolean logic. Boolean logic refers to the interrelationship between search terms and is named for the British mathematician George Boole. Exhibit 5–14 explains the general concepts of Boolean operators. Boolean operators expand or limit searches depending on the specific needs of the user at the time.

Overview of Sorting Databases

It is helpful for the data in a DBMS to be arranged or sorted in a specific manner. Several different sorting options are routinely used in DBMSs, including ascending and descending sorting, and primary and secondary sorting.

Boolean/Logical Operators	Search Example	Description
OR	house OR home	The search will retrieve records in which EITHER of the search terms is present. The search will return the records: 1. Sam's **house** 2. Sam's **home**  Because either "house" or "home" could be relevant to the search, both must be included to make the search comprehensive. The more terms you include in the search, the more records you will retrieve.
AND	real estate AND property	The search will retrieve ONLY records in which BOTH search terms are present. The search will return the record: 1. He owned personal **property** in Delaware and operated a **real estate** business in New Hampshire. 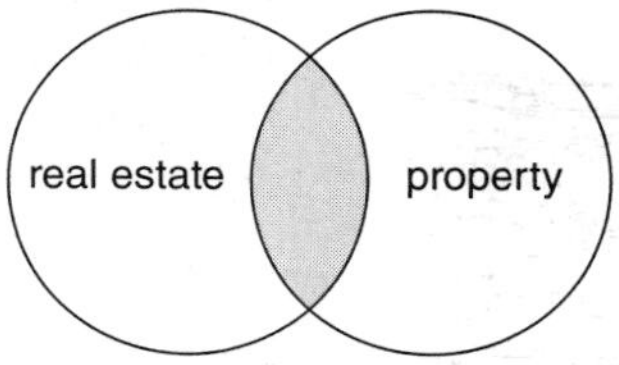 The AND search logically states "I only want records that have BOTH search terms present." If only one search term is present, the record will not be retrieved. The more search terms you have in an AND search, the fewer records you will retrieve.
NOT	property NOT real estate	The search will ONLY retrieve records in which ONE term is present. The search will return the record: 1. He owned personal **property.**  The search logically stated "I only want to see records where property is used AND real estate is NOT." No records are retrieved in which the word "real estate" appears, even if the word "property" appears there too. NOT logic excludes records from the search.

EXHIBIT 5–14

Boolean/logical operators

ascending sort

A sort criterion that places data in ascending order from beginning to end, from A to Z, or from low numbers to high numbers.

descending sort

A sort criterion that places data in descending order from end to beginning, from Z to A, or from high numbers to low numbers.

primary sort

The first sort criterion that a DBMS uses to sort information.

secondary sort

The second sort criterion that a DBMS uses to sort information.

Ascending and Descending Sorts When data are sorted, the information must be placed in either ascending or descending order. **Ascending sorts** place data in ascending order from beginning to end, or from low numbers to high numbers. When words are sorted in ascending order, it means that they are placed in alphabetical order (i.e., from *A* to *Z*). When numbers are sorted in ascending order, it means that they are placed in numerical order, with smaller numbers coming before larger numbers (i.e., first *1*, then *2*, then *3*, etc.). Descending order is just the opposite of ascending order. **Descending sorts** place data in descending order from ending to beginning or from high numbers to low numbers. Words that are sorted in descending order are placed in reverse alphabetical order (i.e., from *Z* to *A*). Numbers that are sorted in descending order are placed with large numbers coming before small numbers (i.e., from *10* to *1*).

Primary and Secondary Sorts A **primary sort**, as the name implies, is the primary (or first) sort criterion that a DBMS executes. A **secondary sort** is the second sort criterion that a DBMS executes. For example, in Exhibit 5–13 in the client database, there are two clients with the name Allen—Alice Allen and Mariam Allen. To sort the database correctly (i.e., alphabetically), in Exhibit 5–13 the user must use both a primary and a secondary sort. The primary sort criterion (which is ascending) is on the Last Name field. This tells the DBMS to sort the clients' last names alphabetically. If the user used only a primary sort (with one sort criterion), then the DBMS could put Mariam Allen before Alice Allen, which would be incorrect (see Exhibit 5–13). To correct this problem, the user would include another, or secondary, sort on First Name. The primary and secondary sorts working together would then sort the data accurately.

Examples of Searching, Sorting, and Querying Databases

DBMSs give users many options to search and sort the database, including the Find feature, the filter feature, the ascending and descending sort features, and queries.

Find As indicated earlier, when you want to locate one specific record quickly, the Find feature (the binocular icon, see Exhibit 5–15) is the best way to locate the information.

Filter The Filter By Selection feature is a good way to quickly narrow down the records displayed. A filter is faster than building a query, because it can be executed directly in a table, but it cannot be saved. For example, in Exhibit 5–15, notice that the cursor is on the third record (Barnes, Clayton) in CA (the State field). To quickly display only the records with CA in the State field, click the Filter icon and only those records will be displayed (see the second screen in Exhibit 5–15). To remove the filter, click the mouse on the Toggle Filter icon and the data will be displayed in the original format (shown in the top screen in Exhibit 5–15).

Ascending and Descending Sorts The ascending and descending sort icons work much like the Filter feature. For example, to see the data in Exhibit 5–15 sorted by city, alphabetically, simply click the mouse in any record in the City field and then click the Ascending Sort icon. The data would be sorted alphabetically in ascending order. The Descending Sort icon sorts the cities in descending order according to City when that feature is selected.

Queries Creating a query is the most powerful way of searching and sorting a database. A query allows a user to select or pull out only the information that she is looking for and to organize and sort the information any way she would like (see

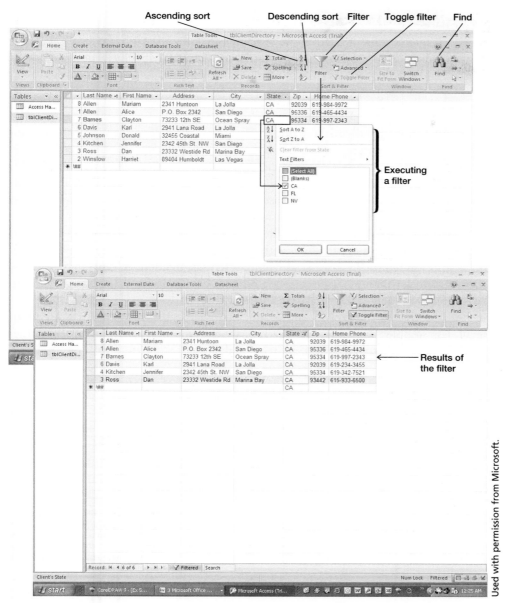

EXHIBIT 5–15
Find, filters, and ascending/descending sorts

Exhibit 5–13). Queries are an extremely powerful and versatile way to manipulate databases. Most DBMSs have a wizard or automated feature that can help the user quickly create queries.

CREATING REPORTS

Most DBMS programs have a **report writer** feature that allows the user complete control over how data are printed, what information is printed (searched for, selected, and retrieved), how that information is organized (sorted), and what format the data are printed in.

The top section of Exhibit 5–8 shows the Design view in Reports and the bottom section shows the report in Report view mode. To create a report, the user simply designs how the report should appear and what fields to include in the form. Most DBMSs have a wizard or automated feature that can help the user easily create a custom report. The user can also reference queries to control how the information is searched and sorted.

report writer
Allows the user complete control over how data in the database are printed without affecting the data in the database.

TYPES OF DBMSS

Several different types of DBMSs are available, including flat-file databases and relational databases. Each type of DBMS has its own unique capabilities and method of processing data.

Flat File

flat-file DBMS
A DBMS that can work with only one database table at a time.

[handwritten note: or in single file. Cannot link/ or merge]

A **flat-file DBMS** handles data in one database or in a single file at a time and cannot link or merge data entered in one database with information in another database (see Exhibit 5–16). For example, if the client database was entered into a flat-file DBMS, you could not merge it with another database, such as a case list database that tracks information about the firm's active cases, including the name of a case (e.g., *Johnson v. Sanders*), the case number, the client's first name and last name, the court where the case was filed, the judge assigned to the case, and the current status of the case. This is true even if some of the fields were the same in both databases (see Exhibit 5–16). If the firm wanted such a case list, it would have to be maintained separately from the client list. If, for example, a client's case number changed, the change would have to be entered into each of the databases separately.

Although a flat-file DBMS cannot link separate databases together, it is useful for small, less complex databases. Flat-file DBMSs are rare; most DBMSs on the market now, including Microsoft Access, are relational.

EXHIBIT 5–16

Flat-file and relational databases

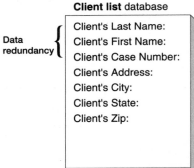

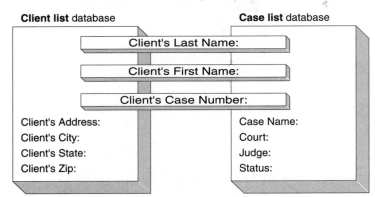

A. Flat-file database
In a flat-file database, files are separate.

Client list database

- Client's Last Name:
- Client's First Name:
- Client's Case Number:
- Client's Address:
- Client's City:
- Client's State:
- Client's Zip:

Data redundancy

Case list database

- Client's Last Name:
- Client's First Name:
- Client's Case Number:
- Case Name:
- Court:
- Judge:
- Status:

In a flat-file DBMS, two separate databases would have to be created and maintained. Duplicate data would then be created (client's last name, first name, and case number).

B. Relational database
In a relational database, files are related.

Client list database

Client's Last Name:
Client's First Name:
Client's Case Number:

- Client's Address:
- Client's City:
- Client's State:
- Client's Zip:

Case list database

- Case Name:
- Court:
- Judge:
- Status:

In a relational DBMS, there is 1 database but there are 2 tables in the database. Data need only be entered and maintained in one place, because the tables are related to one another.

© Cengage Learning 2013

Relational

A **relational DBMS** can handle data across multiple tables at the same time, so that the tables are connected, or related. Relational DBMSs allow users to remove data redundancy (duplicate data) from databases by dividing the data into many subject-based tables. Then, using relationships, the divided information is put back together. This is accomplished by placing common fields, called "keys," in tables that are related.

In Exhibit 5–3 the concept of having multiple tables in one database was presented. In that example a law office not only wanted to track client contact information, but also wanted to track case file information, case evidence, and information about opposing attorneys, all in one database. Instead of having all of the fields in one table, the fields were divided into four logical subject tables. Each table had a different subject matter. Exhibit 5–3, however, is incomplete because the tables are not linked together; they are all standing alone and as such they cannot share information.

Exhibit 5–17 shows the proper relationships among the tables. Notice in Exhibit 5–17 that each table has a small key symbol next to one field in the table. This is called a **primary key**. The primary key is a field that uniquely identifies each record. Exhibit 5–11 shows the primary key for the Client Directory database. Most tables have at least one field that is selected as the primary key. The data in the primary key field must be unique for each record. For example, a social security number would be a likely primary key in many databases because it is unique for each person. Notice in Exhibit 5–17 that the primary key for each table is different and that each primary key is a unique ID or internal number.

There are three types of relationships among tables in a relational database: one-to-one, one-to-many, and many-to-many (see Exhibit 5–18). In a **one-to-one relationship**, each record in the first table contains a field value that corresponds to and matches the field value in one record in another table. In a **one-to-many relationship**, one record in one table can have many matching records in another table. The table on the "one" side is typically called the *parent* table and the other is

relational DBMS
A DBMS that can work with multiple tables at a time, so long as at least one common field occurs in each table.

primary key
A field that uniquely identifies each record.

one-to-one relationship
Each record in the first table contains a field value that corresponds and matches the field value in one record in the other table.

one-to-many relationship
One record in one table can have many matching records in another table. The table on the "one" side is called the "parent" table and the other is called the "child" table.

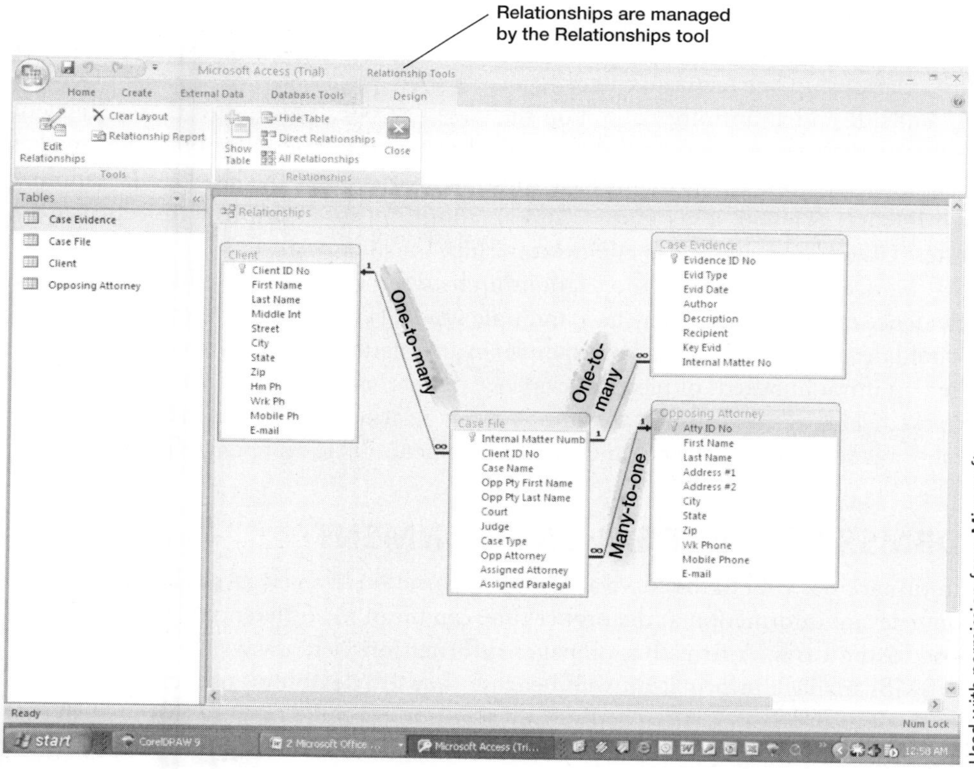

Relationships are managed by the Relationships tool

EXHIBIT 5–17
Creating relationships between tables

EXHIBIT 5–18

Three ways to relate information in tables

RELATIONSHIP TYPE	Description
ONE-TO-ONE	This is an association between two tables in which each record in the first table contains a field value that corresponds to and matches the field value in one record in the other table. This relationship is more like a lookup tool, in which each record in one of the tables has a matching record in the other table.
ONE-TO-MANY	This is the most common type of relationship. One record in one table can have many matching records in another table. The table on the "one" side is typically called the *parent* table and the other is called the *child* table. To represent a one-to-many relationship in a database design, the primary key takes on the "one" side of the relationship and adds it as an additional field or fields to the table on the "many" side of the relationship.
MANY-TO-MANY	This is an association between two tables where one record in either table can relate to many records in the other table. The many-to-many relationship is not permitted in relational databases as such; instead, a third table is used, called a "junction table," that serves as a bridge between the two tables.

© Cengage Learning 2013

many-to-many relationship

One record in either table can relate to many records in the other table. The many-to-many relationship is not permitted in most relational databases.

called the *child* table. In a **many-to-many relationship,** one record in either table can relate to many records in the other table. The many-to-many relationship is not permitted in most relational databases. If this type of design is needed, a third table, called a *junction table*, is used to be a bridge between the two tables. Advanced database relationships go beyond the scope of this text; suffice it to say that database relationships are complex and specific courses are taught in this one area of learning. This does, however, give you a brief overview of the subject.

Notice in Exhibit 5–17 that there is a small 1 and an infinity symbol (an "8" on its side) depicting each of the relationships. Notice further in Exhibit 5–17 that the relationship between the Client table and the Case File table shows a "1" on the Client side and an infinity symbol on the Case File side. This means that each client a law office has can have multiple (or an infinite number of) Case Files. This makes sense, because one client might have multiple matters that the law firm is handling for it, such as a will, a tax matter, and an adoption, for example. This represents a one- (Client) to-many (Case File) relationship.

Notice in Exhibit 5–17 the relationship between the Case File table and the Case Evidence table. Each case may have multiple types of evidence an attorney or paralegal would need or want to track. For example, in any matter involving litigation there may be tens if not hundreds of pieces of evidence (letters, emails, reports, etc.) that must be tracked. This again illustrates the one-to-many relationship. In this instance the Case File table represents the "one" and the Case Evidence table represents the "many."

DBMSS IN THE LEGAL ENVIRONMENT

Information is vital to the survival of any organization in the legal environment. Having relevant information at the proper time can mean the difference between winning and losing cases. A firm that manages information well always has an advantage. DBMSs manage information well because they are flexible to use, can store thousands of records, can retrieve and sort information precisely the way a firm needs it at any given time, and can print reports in many different formats.

The practice of law is information intensive. One role of a paralegal is to assist attorneys in managing information. In any legal matter, information has a tendency to get backed up and out of control. In almost all cases, attorneys have a duty to share information (documents, witness testimony, etc.) with the other attorney or party in a lawsuit. The process of sharing information in a lawsuit is called *discovery.* During the discovery stage of a lawsuit, attorneys send written questions, called *interrogatories,* to the other party; take oral examinations, called *depositions,* of witnesses; and also request documents of the other party by filing a *request for production of documents.* Throughout the discovery stage and throughout the trial of a case, information is being distributed between the parties and must be tracked and organized. A database can be used to perform this litigation support function.

In addition to managing documents regarding cases, law firms must manage information about their clients, business, personnel, and so forth. Depending on the law firm, paralegals may be required to set up and design databases, enter data into a database, perform searches and sorts, and print reports. They can use DBMSs to manage many types of information, ranging from legal research data to marketing data.

Legal Research Database

Every firm in the legal environment must at one time or another perform legal research. Because firms often handle certain kinds of cases and issues over and over, it is helpful to have an index showing what items have already been researched in prior cases and to have an index of unpublished opinions. Firms can easily keep an index of this information using a DBMS. For example, a firm's legal research database might contain fields such as these (see Exhibit 5–19):

1. Research Topic (to identify the general topic researched)
2. Subtopic (to further delineate and explain the specific issue involved)
3. Case Name (to identify what case the research was conducted for)
4. Document Name (to identify what document to look for in the file)
5. Document Date (also to help identify the appropriate document in the file)

A legal research database can help a paralegal track often-used case law.

Conflict of Interest Database

Attorneys are bound by ethical rules not to participate in matters where they have a conflict of interest. For example, an attorney might have a conflict of interest if at one time the attorney represented a client's interest and then at a later time had to sue or take adverse action against the former client.

Legal Research Database				
Research Topic	Subtopic	Case Name	DOC Name	DOC Date
ANTITRUST	Generally	*Smith v. Jones*	Mot. Sum. Judg	4/3/2007
ANTITRUST	St. Act. Doct.	*Dunn v. Jones*	Mot. Sum. Judg	6/1/2006
APPEALS	Stnd. of Rev.	*Bud v. John*	Brief. Appell.	1/23/2007
APPEALS	Jurisdiction	*King v. Head*	Brief. Appell.	6/30/2006
DAMAGES	Present Value	*Copp v. USD 201*	Mot. New Trial	3/2/2008

© Cengage Learning 2013

EXHIBIT 5-19
Legal research database

When attorneys represent a large number of clients, it is often difficult to remember every client. Thus, it is possible for an attorney to have a conflict of interest but simply not remember the former client. Some insurance companies that issue malpractice insurance to attorneys require that a conflict of interest database be maintained as a way to limit malpractice claims. A database can easily track such conflicts. A typical conflict of interest database might have fields such as the following:

1. Client's First Name
2. Client's Last Name
3. Client's Social Security Number
4. Client's Employer
5. Case Name or Matter
6. Date Case Handled
7. Adverse Party
8. Other Parties

When a new client comes into the office, the database can be searched for all possible conflicts against the new client, the new client's employer, adverse parties, or other parties, or for other possible conflicts.

Dead-File Database

All cases and legal matters must eventually come to an end. Cases that have been decided and are no longer being worked must be terminated or put on inactive status. In most offices, a terminated file will be shipped off to a storage facility or microfilmed. In any case, an index of what files have been terminated and where they have been stored must be kept so that the files can later be found and retrieved if necessary. Some paralegals must track this information. A DBMS can easily handle this job.

A dead-file database usually contains fields such as these:

1. Case Name
2. Case Number
3. Location (where file is stored)
4. Dead-File Number (sometimes the files are stored by number instead of by case name)
5. Type of Case

Expert Witness Database

An expert witness is an individual who is a specialist or possesses a high degree of learning in a specific field or matter. Attorneys often hire expert witnesses to testify about a case or matter. Medical doctors often have a great deal of knowledge about specific types of injuries, depending on their specialty, and are sometimes called as expert witnesses to testify about a plaintiff's injuries in personal injury cases. In fact, a defendant in a personal injury case might also call an expert witness to try to attack the credibility of the plaintiff's expert.

Because attorneys regularly hire expert witnesses, it is sometimes necessary for paralegals to keep a list of expert witnesses, what their specialties are, and how to contact them. When an attorney needs an expert for a case, all the paralegal has to do is search for the particular specialty needed in the Specialty field, and the name of an expert will be displayed.

An expert witness database might contain fields concerning the expert witness such as the following:

1. Last Name
2. First Name
3. Address
4. City
5. State
6. Zip
7. Home Phone
8. Work Phone
9. Mobile Phone
10. Email Address
11. Specialty
12. Hourly Fee

Active Case List Database

An active case list is a list of all cases or matters that a firm or an attorney has pending. Usually the list will have fields such as these:

1. Client's Last Name
2. Client's First Name
3. Adverse Party's Last Name
4. Case Number
5. Attorney in Charge (i.e., for the office)
6. Court

An active case list database could also be used to give an attorney a list of all his cases. For example, a report could be generated that retrieved only the cases that had the initials "SLP" in the Attorney in Charge field. The attorney could then use this list to keep track of all his active cases.

Docket Control Database

Docket control means to handle and manage an attorney's appointments, meetings, deadlines, court appearances, and so forth (see Exhibit 5–20). Paralegals often perform this task.

A docket control database tracks this data using a DBMS. Most docket control databases will have fields such as the ones listed here:

1. Date of Event
2. Event
3. Case Name
4. Place of Event
5. First Warning (i.e., a reminder a few days *before* the event, notifying the firm of the approaching deadline or event)
6. Second Warning

In Exhibit 5–20, the events were sorted in ascending order according to their dates. The warning date fields are used to give the attorney a few days' notice before an event is to take place.

Docket Control Database					
Date of Event	**Event**	**Case Name**	**Place of Event**	**First Warning**	**Second Warning**
01/13/2014	Trial	*Black v. Neal*	Court #3	01/02/2014	01/10/2014
01/24/2014	Appt/Sanders	*Smit v. Jones*	Office	01/02/2014	01/20/2014
01/30/2014	Depo/Defend.	*King v. Hill*	Def. Off.	01/15/2014	01/25/2014
02/01/2014	Setlmnt. Mtg	*Berg v. Rob*	J. Black's	01/20/2014	01/28/2014
02/03/2014	Deadin-MSJ	*Hope v. Hope*	Office	01/25/2014	01/30/2014
03/01/2014	Trial	*Doe v. Doe*	Court #12	01/02/2014	02/01/2014

© Cengage Learning 2013

EXHIBIT 5–20
Docket control database

A report could also be generated that retrieved only a certain type of event, such as all the trials set for an attorney or office for a year. This could be accomplished by retrieving only those entries with the word *trial* in the Event field.

Library Catalog Database

Almost all offices in the legal environment have a library of law-related books. It is often necessary for the office to have a card catalog to track the books in and out of the library and to keep inventory records. A firm's law library might want the collection sorted alphabetically by the titles of the books. It also would be helpful to produce an author index (by sorting the database alphabetically based on the authors' names) or a subject index (by sorting the database alphabetically based on the subjects).

A library catalog database typically has fields such as these:

1. Title
2. Author
3. Subject
4. Date Published
5. Library Number

Litigation Support Database

A litigation support database tracks documents and possible evidence in a particular case. A typical litigation support database will have the following fields:

1. Document Type
2. Document Name
3. Document Number (i.e., a number that the firm assigns to that document)
4. Document Date
5. Subject Matter
6. Document Author
7. Individual Who Received the Document
8. Notes

A litigation support database is used to search and retrieve whatever particular information an attorney needs at any given time. When thousands of documents are being tracked, a computerized database is almost a necessity for tracking down specific documents.

As indicated earlier in the chapter, databases and Microsoft Access in particular are used by paralegals for litigation support purposes. Litigation support is an important task for which legal organizations use databases and paralegals.

Collective Experience Database

Some firms have a database that contains the collective experience of the attorneys in the firm as it relates to judges the attorneys must appear before, expert witnesses, and others. Some judges have peculiar likes, dislikes, or requirements about certain types of cases or certain tendencies that a firm might want to remember when similar cases come up in the future. For example, a particular judge might like personal injury cases, but dislike labor law cases. If an attorney has a choice of where to file a case, this information might be important. An attorney might also like to have a database regarding expert witnesses, with information such as how to attack the credibility of certain experts and what prior cases the firm has encountered an expert in, so as to prepare for future encounters.

Lawyer Information Database

Some firms use a lawyer information database to track the names, addresses, telephone numbers, and areas of practice of other attorneys. Such a database can be helpful when returning phone calls or when trying to find a co-counsel in a case. Attorneys often bring in another attorney, called a co-counsel, who specializes in a particular area to help them represent a client. A database such as this makes tracking other attorneys' specialties easy and gives an ongoing list of attorney specialties.

Marketing Database

Many firms maintain a marketing database that tracks how clients are referred to them and where clients come from, in an attempt to understand where they should be marketing their services. This information is usually gained from a questionnaire that is given to new clients. Such a questionnaire might ask how the client came to the attorney's office, whether by means of a referral from another attorney, from the firm's Internet site or banner ad, a referral from a past client, a newspaper article, the Yellow Pages, and so forth. This type of database allows firms to track which other attorneys or past clients are referring clients to them, so that the referring parties might be thanked or encouraged to keep doing this. This type of database also allows a firm to track which marketing efforts are working and which are not. Such a database might include fields about new clients such as the following:

1. First Name
2. Last Name
3. Address
4. City
5. State
6. Zip
7. Home Phone
8. Referral Source
9. Date
10. Other Comments

Trial Database

Trial databases are used to prepare for a trial. The purpose is to organize the file and documents in order to integrate every kind of evidence, including depositions, interrogatories, and documents, into one database. The following fields might be used:

1. Type of Evidence
2. Date of Evidence

3. Author
4. To (name of recipient of documentary evidence)
5. Summary or Notes
6. Subject
7. Witnesses
8. Present Location of Evidence
9. Media Type (hard copy, image, etc.)

ETHICAL CONSIDERATIONS

Several ethical considerations arise when discussing database management in the legal environment, including checking for conflicts of interests when accepting new cases (DBMSs excel at checking conflicts), accurately and competently designing databases, accurately entering data, consistently and competently searching databases, and confidentiality.

Conflicts of Interest

An attorney and a law office have an ethical duty to avoid conflicts of interest. A conflict of interest occurs when an attorney or a paralegal has competing personal or professional interests with a client's case that would preclude her from acting impartially toward the client. Conflict of interest problems typically occur when a law office, attorney, paralegal previously worked for a client who is now an adverse party in a current case.

Because many legal organizations and attorneys represent a large number of clients, it is often difficult for them to clearly identify the client or clients so that they can determine whether a conflict of interest actually exists. It is very possible for an attorney to have a conflict of interest but simply not remember a former client. For example, suppose an attorney represents a woman in a personal injury case and then eight years later the woman's husband comes in for representation in a divorce action against her. The attorney would arguably have a conflict of interest but simply not remember the prior representation of the woman. Thus, it is the responsibility of the legal organization and attorney to set up a system so that conflicts such as this do not happen. Many legal organizations use a conflict of interest database to do this (see earlier in the chapter for the design of such a database). They maintain a list of all of the organization's clients, former clients, and adverse parties and check the database before a new case is accepted to make sure there is no conflict.

Design of Client Databases

As mentioned earlier, accurate design of client databases is critical to their success or failure. One of the ethics rules discussed earlier in this text states that attorneys and law offices must represent clients competently.

If a paralegal sets up a database with a poor design and bills the client for the amount of time it took to design and enter the information in it, and if the database then fails to produce the information needed due to poor design, this will probably hurt the client's case. Such a situation certainly brings up some ethics problems. The most powerful DBMS in the world will not solve a vague or poorly defined problem and will not prevent the failure of a poorly designed database. It is extremely important for the user to understand *exactly* what problem the database should solve *before* he begins to design it.

Data Entry Consistency and Errors

Data must be entered in a database with as much accuracy as humanly possible. Data entry errors are not just errors or misspellings in a database; they equate to the old adage "garbage in—garbage out" and also impact the ethical duty of competence. For instance, suppose a paralegal is in charge of a client database project, including supervising three data entry operators who are entering information about evidentiary documents into a litigation support database for a case. Suppose one of the fields in the database is Document Type. Assume the paralegal has not given the data entry operators any guidance as to how to enter information. Suppose data entry operator 1 enters letters (correspondence) in the Document Type field as "LTR"; data entry operator 2 enters letters as "LT"; and data entry operator 3 enters letters sometimes as "Correspondence" (which is sometimes misspelled), sometimes as "LTS," sometimes as "Letters," and sometimes as nothing at all. Now, suppose the paralegal is sitting in a courtroom, the lead attorney for the firm is cross-examining an important witness, and the witness refers to a crucial letter that the lead attorney must immediately have to effectively cross-examine the important witness. The paralegal, sitting at the counsel table, searches the database for a list of all letters using the search criterion "LETTERS," and the database retrieves two records, neither of which is remotely close to the letter the witness is referring to. The lead attorney must continue with his examination as the paralegal frantically searches for the document. The client's case suffers, the client is unhappy, the lead attorney is hampered in his cross-examination and is frustrated, and the paralegal has failed to carry out an assignment properly. The point is that data-entry consistency and accuracy are extremely important, and if garbage is put into the computer, that is what it will output.

Search Criteria Accurately searching databases is as important as effectively designing the database and accurately entering the data. When entering search criteria, the user must be sure that the information is entered accurately and must understand how to search. Again, if the user enters a search criterion that will not retrieve what the attorney is looking for because the search is inaccurate or not well conceived, then the database is worthless, and all the time it took to develop it was wasted.

Confidentiality As with all client information a legal organization collects, the ethical duty to keep that information confidential is paramount. Client databases and the duty to keep those databases confidential represent a real ethical consideration for any legal organization. Consider that in one (litigation support) database, all of the evidentiary documents, summaries of the documents, and every piece of information about the client could reside on one CD-ROM. It is absolutely critical that any database with client-related information be securely maintained: both from a physical standpoint, in that only limited individuals have access to the computer, the CD-ROM, or the access rights (over a network) to the database; and that the database is adequately protected with passwords and other electronic security devices (firewalls for extranets, etc.). Consideration must also be given to adequately securing legal organization administrative databases. Think what would happen if a comprehensive client/case matter list for a large legal organization was backed up and the backup tape was casually discarded and then obtained by a competitor. Databases are wonderful for collecting, organizing, and searching information, but because they can contain so much useful information, legal professionals must clearly recognize the duty to keep the information absolutely confidential. They must also realize the catastrophic result if it is made public and take actions to make sure it never happens.

SUMMARY

A database is a collection of related items. A database management system is an application that manages a database by storing, searching, sorting, and organizing data. A table in a database is a collection of related information stored in rows and columns. Many databases have more than one table. A field is a column in a table; each field contains a category of information. A record is a collection of fields that is treated as a unit. Large databases may have millions of records. A data value is the smallest piece of information in a table.

Four tools or objects are found in most DBMSs: tables, forms, queries, and reports. A table stores the information in the database. A form gives the user a custom format with which to view, enter, or edit the data. A query extracts specific data from a database and sorts the extracted data as required. A report prints data from a table or query in final format that can be used by the user.

The database design and implementation process includes (1) identifying the problem; (2) determining exactly what the user needs from the database; (3) planning the database design, including planning the tables, table relationships, and fields; (4) entering the database design in the DBMS; (5) testing the design; (6) entering the data; and (7) revising the design as needed.

Careful database planning includes not having too many fields in one table, not repeating fields, and not having redundant information. The job of entering data in the database in a uniform and consistent manner is crucial. Inconsistent data entry leads to searches, queries, and reports that are incomplete and error ridden. When searching databases, root expanders (!) and wildcard characters (*) can increase the scope of a search. Relational operators such as ">" (greater than) and "<" (less than) can be used in database searching. Boolean/logical operators such as "AND," "OR," and "NOT" can also be used in database searches.

When sorting data, the primary sort is the first sort criterion entered and the secondary sort is the second level of sorting. Ascending sorts manipulate the data so the data order is A to Z or 1 to 10. Descending sorts are just the opposite.

Relational databases handle and manipulate data across multiple tables. Using this method, users can divide their data into many subject-based tables. Then, using relationships, the divided information is put back together into one coherent group of information. Most tables have a primary key designated that uniquely identifies each record. There are three data relationships in relational databases: one-to-one, one-to-many, and many-to-many. In the one-to-one relationship, each record in the first table contains a field value that corresponds to and matches the field value in one record in the other table. In the one-to-many relationship, one record in one table can have many matching records in another table. The table on the "one" side is called the parent table and the other is called the child table. In the many-to-many relationship, one record in either table can relate to many records in the other table. The many-to-many relationship is not permitted in most relational databases.

KEY TERMS

ascending sort	many-to-many relationship	report
Boolean/logical operator	one-to-many relationship	report writer
database	one-to-one relationship	root expander
database management system	primary key	secondary sort
data value	primary sort	structured query language (SQL)
descending sort	query	table
field	query by example (QBE)	validation control
flat-file DBMS	record	wildcard character
form	relational DBMS	
look up option	relational operator	

INTERNET SITES

Internet sites for this chapter include the following:

ORGANIZATION	PRODUCT/SERVICE	INTERNET ADDRESS
Microsoft	Microsoft Access database	www.microsoft.com
Microsoft Access home page	A wealth of information for Access users, including database templates, tips, tricks, user group lists, and much more	www.microsoft.com/office/access
Corel Corporation	Paradox database	www.corel.com
IBM	Approach database	www.IBM.com/Lotus
About, Inc.	A general site that contains information about database design	databases.about.com

TEST YOUR KNOWLEDGE

1. True or False: An application program that stores and searches data is called a database.

2. A is a collection of related information stored in rows and columns.

3. Typically, relational databases have table(s):
   a. Zero
   b. One
   c. Multiple

4. A is a column in a table and contains a category of information.

5. A is a row in a table and is treated as a unit.

6. The smallest individual piece of information in a database is called a .

7. True or False: A form holds the data in a database.

8. True or False: A query extracts data from a table.

9. Name the four tools or objects found in most DBMSs.

10. True or False: Good database design is about the person designing the system, not about the end user.

11. One of the single most important factors of having a good database is data entry.

12. The old adage is accurate when it comes to data entry. The data coming out of the system is only as good as what was entered.

13. Define what a lookup option in a database is.

14. What is validation control?

15. True or False: Uniform data entry is not important because queries can be written to make up for whatever deficiencies there are in data entry.

16. When using the Find tool, which search option is the most expansive: Whole Field, Start of Field, or Any Part of Field?

17. Name two relational operators.

18. Name one of three Boolean operators.

19. A is a field that uniquely identifies each record.

20. When one record in one table can relate to many records in another table, the relationship is called _____.

ON THE WEB EXERCISES

1. Using a general Internet search engine (such as google.com or yahoo.com) or a general computing magazine, research the latest features in database management programs and write a one-page summary of your findings.

2. Using a general Internet search engine (such as google.com or yahoo.com) or the sites at the end of the chapter, research basic database design and write a three-page paper on what you found.

3. The business world literally runs on databases. Using a general Internet search engine (such as google.com or yahoo.com), research the largest databases in the world. What are they, what do they do, what would life be like if we did not have them, how important are they, and how complex are they? Write a two-page report on your findings.

4. Using a general Internet search engine (such as google.com or yahoo.com), research the database design process. Write a two-page paper on your findings.

QUESTIONS AND EXERCISES

1. Using a word processor or a legal pad, design your own contact database of addresses, phone, mobile phone, email, and other such information for friends and family. Include what tables and fields you would include in your design.

2. Using a word processor or legal pad, design a database that will track something that you collect, such as DVDs, CD-ROMs, MP3s, or other items. Design the table(s), fields, and at least one report you would like the system to output.

3. Using Exhibit 5–9, follow the steps in the process and design any database that will solve a problem that you have encountered. Document the design process in a paper that is at least three pages long and that explains how you worked through the design of the system.

4. Design a relational database for a legal organization that will track contact information for each client, the status of each client's case, a current list of upcoming events for each case, a list of witnesses for each case, and information on how to contact the witnesses. Prepare the database design on paper first by making a list of the fields for each table.

5. Design and implement your own expert witness database in a DBMS. Think of at least 10 fields that your database can track.

6. Your supervising attorney asks you to type up a list of the documents in a case that he has to try. There are approximately 50 documents. The list must contain the date of each document, who it is to, the type of document it is, the subject of the document, and a short description of the contents. The attorney indicates it is up to you to decide whether you will use a word processor, a spreadsheet, or a DBMS. Discuss the strengths and weaknesses of using each and state which one you would use and why. Is there any additional information you would like from the attorney?

7. You have been asked to prepare a list of personal and real property in a complex divorce action. Approximately two thousand pieces of information will have to be entered. Key issues in the divorce include what the total value of the property is, how each piece of property was acquired (was it the husband's before marriage, the wife's before marriage, acquired during the marriage, given as a gift, etc.), when the property was acquired, whether there is a mortgage or loan on the item, whether your client is willing to give up the property or wants to keep it, and where the item is now. Plan and design a database to accomplish this.

ETHICS QUESTION

A law firm has just installed the latest and greatest law-office database program. The attorneys and paralegals diligently attended all of the training classes required to master the new software program. All client and case matter information was uploaded into the new program. However, when inputting data, one of the paralegals entered the wrong date for a court hearing on an opposing party's motion for summary judgment. The opposing party won its motion by default because the law firm failed to appear on behalf of its client. What ethical issues, if any, are raised by this scenario?

The available CourseMate for this text has an interactive eBook and interactive learning tools, including flash cards, quizzes, and more. To learn more about this resource and access free demo CourseMate resources, go to www.cengagebrain.com, and search for this book. To access CourseMate materials that you have purchased, go to login.cengagebrain.com.

HANDS-ON EXERCISES

HANDS-ON EXERCISES

DATABASE HANDS-ON EXERCISES

 ### READ THIS FIRST!

1. Microsoft Access 2010
2. Microsoft Access 2007

I. DETERMINING WHICH TUTORIAL TO COMPLETE

To use the Database Hands-On Exercises, you must already own or have available to you Microsoft Access 2010 or Access 2007. If you have one of the programs but do not know the version you are using, it is easy to find out. For Access 2010, click the File tab, then click Help. For Access 2007, click the File tab, click Access Options, and then look under the title "Resources." It should then tell you what version of the program you are using. You must know the version of the program you are using and select the correct tutorial version or the tutorials will not work correctly.

II. USING THE DATABASE HANDS-ON EXERCISES

The Database Hands-On Exercises in this section are easy to use and contain step-by-step instructions. They start with basic database skills and proceed to intermediate and advanced levels. To truly be ready to use databases in the legal environment, you must be able to accomplish the tasks and exercises in the advanced exercises.

III. ACCESSING THE HANDS-ON EXERCISES FILES THAT COME WITH THE TEXT

Lesson 6 of the Hands-On Exercises uses a document on the disk that comes with the text. To access the document, put the disk in your computer, select Start, click My Computer, then select the appropriate drive and double-click on the appropriate drive; then double-click on the Access Database Files folder. You will see one database file entitled "Lesson 6 Law Firm Database." *Note:* In Access 2010, once the file is loaded you will need to immediately use the Save As command to save the file to another drive, such as your hard drive. These files are also available on the Premium Website. To access them, go to your CengageBrain account and click on the link for Premium Website for Cornick's Using Computers in the Law Office—Basic. A new window will open. Under Book Level Resources, click the link for Data Files: Access, then click the link to the desired lesson. When prompted, click Open.

IV. INSTALLATION QUESTIONS

If you have installation questions regarding opening the Access database file, you may contact Technical Support at http://cengage.com/support.

HANDS-ON EXERCISES

MICROSOFT ACCESS 2010 FOR WINDOWS

Number	Lesson Title	Concepts Covered
BASIC LESSONS		
Lesson 1	Creating a Table—Client Database	How to create a new table/database, create and design fields, create a primary key, move between the Table Design view and the Datasheet view, enter a record, and save the database.
Lesson 2	Creating a Form and Entering Data—Client Database	How to create a form, enter data in the form, view the Datasheet view of the form, and close a form.
Lesson 3	Querying a Database—Client Database	How to use the Ascending Sort icon, create a query that searches and sorts the database, modify a query, use a primary and secondary sort option, run a query, and print a query.
INTERMEDIATE LESSONS		
Lesson 4	Creating a Report—Client Database	How to create and print a report.
Lesson 5	Creating a Litigation Support Database	How to build a litigation support database that tracks documents in a case; creating the fields, entering the data, running helpful sorts and filters to search the data, running a query, running a report, and printing a report.
ADVANCED LESSONS		
Lesson 6	Working with a Comprehensive Law-Office Relational Database	Working with a true relational database, including working with multiple tables, assigning relationships among tables, and writing queries and reports that access data from multiple tables.

HANDS-ON EXERCISES

GETTING STARTED
Introduction

Throughout these lessons and exercises, information you need to type into the program will be designated in several different ways:

- Keys to be pressed on the keyboard are designated in brackets, in all caps, and in bold (e.g., press the [**ENTER**] key).
- Movements with the mouse pointer or cursor are designated in bold and italics (e.g., ***point to File and click***).
- Words or letters that should be typed are designated in bold (e.g., type **Training Program**).
- Information that is or should be displayed on your computer screen is shown in bold, with quotation marks (e.g., **"Press ENTER to continue."**).
- Specific menu items and commands are designated with an initial capital letter (e.g., click Open).

OVERVIEW OF ACCESS 2010

Access 2010 is a relational database management application. Access 2010 Exhibit 1 shows the Access interface. Notice the ribbon across the top of the screen (see Access 2010 Exhibit 1). The ribbon has several tabs across the top; these are called "ribbon tabs" or sometimes just "tabs." When a different tab is selected, the tools and commands on the ribbon change. In Access 2010 Exhibit 1, the Create ribbon tab is selected. Notice that the Create ribbon tab in Access 2010 Exhibit 1 has six groups, including the Templates, Tables, Queries, Forms, Reports, and Macros & Code groups. At the very top to the left of the screen is the Quick Access toolbar, a toolbar that can be customized by the user. In the top left of the screen is the File tab. The File tab allows the user to open files, save files, create new files, and print documents, among other things. On the left side of the screen is the Navigation pane. The Navigation pane can be configured in different ways, but in Access 2010 Exhibit 1 the user has all of the objects for the database displayed for easy access. This includes all of the user's tables, queries, forms, and reports.

ACCESS 2010 EXHIBIT 1
Access 2010 screen

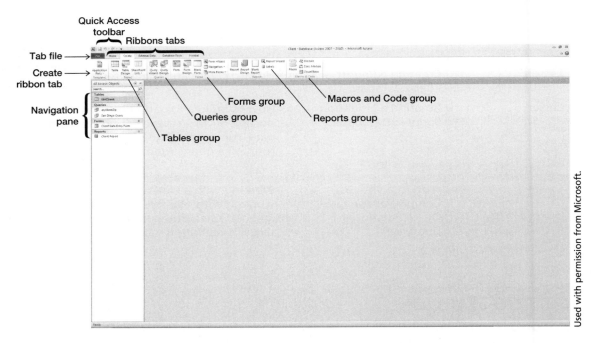

Used with permission from Microsoft.

Additional information about Access 2010 will be provided as you complete the exercises. By the end of the exercises you should have a good understanding of the basics of Access 2010.

 ## BASIC LESSONS

LESSON 1: CREATING A TABLE—CLIENT DATABASE

This lesson shows you how to build the table shown in Access 2010 Exhibit 3. It explains how to create a new table/database, create new fields, create a primary key, move between the Table Design view and the Datasheet view, and save the database. Keep in mind that if you make a mistake in this lesson, you may press **[CTRL]+[Z]** to undo what you have done. Note, however, that in some cases this command will not work (e.g., when you delete a record, it is permanently deleted).

    1. Open Windows. When it has loaded, ***double-click on the Microsoft Office Access 2010 icon on the desktop*** to open Access 2010 for Windows. Alternatively, ***click on the Start button, point to Programs or All Programs,***

*and then click on the Microsoft Access 2010 icon (or **point to Microsoft Office and then click Microsoft Access 2010).***

2. When Access 2010 opens, the File tab screen is displayed. This screen offers the user a number of templates that can be accessed to speed the creation of databases in Access.

3. Just under the **"Available Templates"** title are several different database templates. ***Click Blank database.***

4. Notice that the right side of the screen now says **"Blank Database."** ***Click under File Name,*** use the **[DEL]** key to delete the current title, and type **Client**. To save the new database in the default directory, ***click Create.*** To browse where you would like to save the new database, ***click the Browse icon*** (it looks like an open file folder with an arrow) ***just to the right of the file name. Then, select the directory or folder you would like to save the file to,*** type **Client** next to File name, ***and click OK. Finally, click Create.*** See Access 2010 Exhibit 2.

ACCESS 2010 EXHIBIT 2
Creating a new table in Datasheet view

Used with permission from Microsoft.

HANDS-ON EXERCISES

5. You should now have a blank table in Datasheet view displayed on your screen. Notice that the Table Tools—Fields ribbon tab is currently shown. ***Click the Home ribbon tab, then click the down arrow under View, and then click Design View.***

6. The "Save As" window should now be displayed. Type **tblClient** under "**Table Name:**" and then ***click OK.***

7. The Design View of your table (tblClient) should now be on your screen. Your screen should be similar to Access 2010 Exhibit 3, except that the table on your screen will be blank. You will now begin to build the structure of a client database by entering the fields shown in Access 2010 Exhibit 3.

8. Notice that Access has entered a default field name of "ID" in the first row of your table (see Access 2010 Exhibit 3). It is useful to have an ID number for each client, so press the **[TAB]** key three times to move to the next row. Notice also in the ID field that the data type is **"AutoNumber."** This means that Access will automatically create a unique ID number for each client.

9. With your pointer in the second row of the first column, Field Name, type **Last Name** and then press the **[TAB]** key.

**ACCESS 2010
EXHIBIT 3**
Creating fields
in a table

Save

View

Primary
key

Fields in
the table

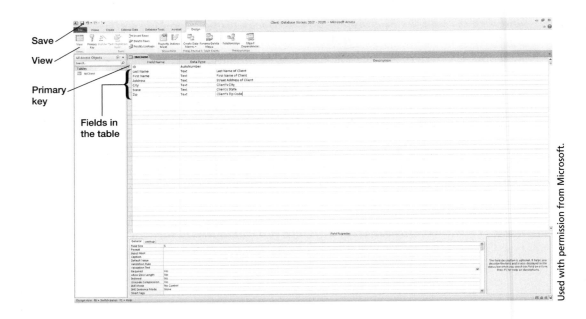

10. Your pointer should now be in the Data Type column and **"Text"** should be displayed in the field. If you click the down arrow next to **"Text,"** you can see the different data types that Access offers. By selecting the data type, you tell Access what kind of information will be stored in the field. Because text will be stored in the Last Name field, press the **[TAB]** key to go to the Description column.

11. In the Description column, type **Last Name of Client.**

12. Notice at the bottom of the screen, under Field Properties, that there are two tabs, General and Lookup. The General tab should be displayed. It allows you to change the field size (the number of characters that may be entered into the field) and other items as well. Notice that the default field size is 255; this is too long. ***Click on "255"*** and delete it using the **[BACKSPACE]** key on your keyboard. Type **50.**

13. Next to the Required field under the General tab, ***click No. Then, click the down arrow next to No, and click Yes.*** See Access 2010 Exhibit 3. This will require the user to enter this field when entering new data. The other options are fine, so you do not have to change them.

14. The Last Name field is now complete. ***Click in the third row, directly under Last Name.***

15. Using the same procedure as above, type the following information into the table:

Field Name	Data Type	Description	Field Size	Required
First Name	Text	First Name of Client	50	Yes
Address	Text	Street Address of Client	50	Yes
City	Text	Client's City	25	Yes
State	Text	Client's State	2	Yes
Zip	Text	Client's Zip Code	5	Yes

16. Your screen should look similar to Access 2010 Exhibit 3.

17. ***Click the General tab under Field Properties.***

18. Once all of the information has been entered, ***click on the Save icon*** (it looks like a floppy disk) ***on the Quick Access toolbar to save your data.***

19. Notice that a small key icon is displayed next to the ID field. This indicates that the ID field is the primary key (the field that uniquely identifies each record) for this table.

20. You are currently in the Table Design View. Design view means that you are looking at the *design* of the table and not the data in the table itself. You will now change your view to Datasheet view. Once data has been entered into the table, you can see the data in the Datasheet view.

21. ***From the Views group on the Design ribbon tab, click the down arrow under the View icon*** (see Access 2010 Exhibit 3), ***then select Datasheet View***. *Note*: To see the name of any icon, just hover the mouse pointer over the icon for a second and the name of the icon will appear.

22. You should now see all of your fields displayed horizontally across the screen (see Access 2010 Exhibit 4). You can toggle back and forth between Design View and Datasheet View by clicking on the View icon.

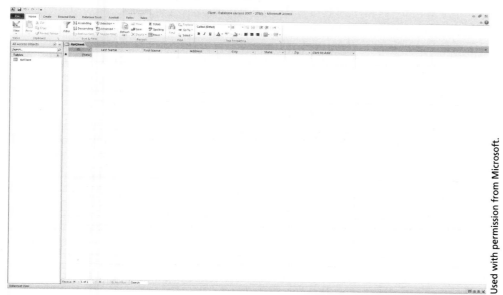

**ACCESS 2010
EXHIBIT 4**
Table Datasheet view

Used with permission from Microsoft.

23. Press the **[TAB]** key to go to the Last Name field.

24. Enter the following information (to go to the next field, press the **[TAB]** key).

ID	Last Name	First Name	Address	City	State	Zip
	Sullivan	Susan	P.O. Box 2342	San Diego	CA	95336

25. Although you can use Table Datasheet view to enter new records, it is not always the best way to enter data. In the next lesson, we will create a form to enter new records.

26. ***Click the Save icon on the Quick Access toolbar to save your data.***

27. ***Click the File tab and then click Exit to exit the program.***

This concludes Lesson 1.

LESSON 2: CREATING A FORM AND ENTERING DATA—CLIENT DATABASE

In this lesson, you will create a form from which you can enter data into the database. You will then enter the rest of the data into the client database using the form you created.

1. Open Windows. When it has loaded, ***double-click on the Microsoft Office Access 2010 icon on the desktop*** to open Access 2010 for Windows. Alternatively, ***click the Start button, point to Programs or All Programs, and then click the Microsoft Access 2010 icon*** (or ***point to Microsoft Office and then click on Microsoft Access 2010).***

2. ***Click the File tab*** (see Access 2010 Exhibit 1). ***Then, under Recent, click the name of the client file you created in Lesson 1 (Client.accdb).***

3. If a security warning (for example, **"Security Warning: Some active content has been disabled. Click for more details."**) is displayed just under the ribbon, ***click Enable Content next to the Security Warning.*** There is no security problem, because you know the content came from a trustworthy source, as you are the one who created the file.

4. Notice that the file called "tblClient" that you created in Lesson 1 is listed on the Navigation pane.

5. You are now ready to create a data entry form that will assist you in entering the data into the "tblClient" file.

6. ***Click the Create ribbon tab, then click Form in the Forms group.*** Access should return a default data entry form similar to the one shown in Exhibit 5 (see Access 2010 Exhibit 5).

ACCESS 2010 EXHIBIT 5
Corrected data entry form

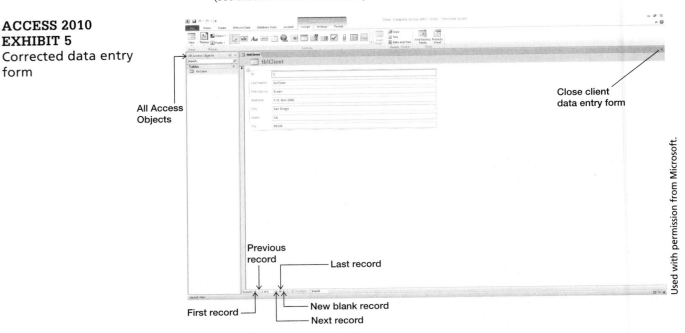

All Access Objects

Close client data entry form

Previous record

Last record

First record

New blank record

Next record

7. Access gives you many options for easy formatting of your form. Notice on the ribbon that a new tab appeared called Form Layout Tools, and that **"Form Layout Tools – Design"** is selected. ***Click the down arrow in the Themes group on the Design ribbon tab*** (see Access 2010 Exhibit 5) to look at the Themes options for your form (see Access 2010 Exhibit 5). ***Click on one of the Themes options that you like.***

8. ***Click on the Save icon*** (it looks like a floppy disk) ***on the Quick Access toolbar to save your form.*** In the "Save As" window, under Form Name, type **Client Data Entry Form** and then ***click OK.***

9. ***Click All Access Objects in the Navigation pane*** (see Access 2010 Exhibit 5) ***and then, under Navigate to Category, click Object Type.*** Notice on the

Navigation pane that you can now see "tblClient" under Tables and "Client Data Entry Form" under Forms. Any time you add new objects to your database, they will be shown in the Navigation pane.

10. Notice that the first record you entered is now displayed (Sullivan, Susan).

11. Access placed the fields in the data entry form in the same way they were entered in the table. In this instance, Last Name is before First Name in the form. It would be more logical and easier for first name to be first. This is easy to correct.

12. First, *click on Views and select Design View. Click anywhere in the First Name field of your form, then drag it (by holding the left mouse button) to just above the Last Name field and let go of the mouse button.* The First Name field should now be shown above the Last Name field. Although this corrected the physical layout on the screen, the tab order (where the pointer moves when you press the [TAB] key to go to the next field) must also be checked to make sure it changed as well.

13. *Click on Tab Order in the Tools group. In the "Tab Order" window, make sure First Name is above Last Name.* If it is, proceed to the next step. If it is not, *click just to the left of First Name in the "Tab Order" window to select the First Name row, and then drag the line to just above the Last Name.*

14. *Click OK to close the "Tab Order" window.*

15. To make the changes active, you need to save the form, exit the form, and then reopen the form. *Click the Save icon on the Quick Access toolbar. Then, click the Close Client Data Entry Form icon* (the black "X") *to the right of the title "tblclient"* (see Access 2010 Exhibit 5). *Next, double-click the client data entry form (under Forms on the Navigation pane) to reopen the form.*

16. Press the [TAB] key three times. Notice that the tab order is correct (ID, then First Name, then Last Name). (*Note*: If the order is not correct, you can *right-click on Client Data Entry Form under Forms on the Navigation pane, and click Layout view. Click the Form Layout Tools—Arrange tab* to once again readjust the tab order, and then save, exit, and reopen the client data entry form).

17. Press the [TAB] key seven times to go to the next record (Record 2). Alternatively, you can go to the next record or the previous record by *clicking on the Greater Than and Less Than icons at the bottom of the page*, or by pressing the [PAGE UP] or [PAGE DOWN] keys on the keyboard (see Access 2010 Exhibit 5).

18. Enter the following records into the database. You can go between fields by pressing the [TAB] or [SHIFT]+[TAB] keys, or by *clicking with the mouse.* When you are on the last field, you can go to the next record by pressing the [TAB] key.

Record 2	
First Name	**Harriet**
Last Name	**Winslow**
Address	**89404 Humboldt Road**
City	**Las Vegas**
State	**NV**
Zip	**78524**

Record 3	
First Name	**Dan**
Last Name	**Ross**
Address	**23332 West Road**
City	**Marina Bay**
State	**CA**
Zip	**93442**

Record 4	
First Name	**Jennifer**
Last Name	**Kitchen**
Address	**2342 45th Street NW**
City	**San Diego**
State	**CA**
Zip	**95334**

Record 5	
First Name	**Donald**
Last Name	**Johnson**
Address	**32455 Coastal Drive**
City	**Miami**
State	**FL**
Zip	**35773**

19. When you have finished entering all of the data, ***click the Save icon on the Quick Access toolbar.***

20. ***Click the Close Client Data Entry Form icon*** (see Access 2010 Exhibit 5).

21. ***Double-click "tblClient" under Tables on the Navigation pane.***

22. The Datasheet view of your table is now displayed (see Access 2010 Exhibit 6). You should now see all of your data displayed horizontally across the screen. *Note*: If you cannot see all of the data in a field, just ***click in the column heading on the vertical line that separates each field and drag it to the right to make the field larger*** (see Access 2010 Exhibit 6).

23. ***Click the File tab, then click Print, and then click the Print icon to print the document.***

24. ***Click the Save icon on the Quick Access toolbar.***

25. ***Click the File tab and then click Exit to exit the program.***

This concludes Lesson 2.

LESSON 3: QUERYING A DATABASE—CLIENT DATABASE

In this lesson, you will learn how to use the Ascending Sort icon on the toolbar, create a query that searches and sorts the database, modify a query, use a primary and secondary sort option, run a query, and print a query using the database you created in Lessons 1 and 2.

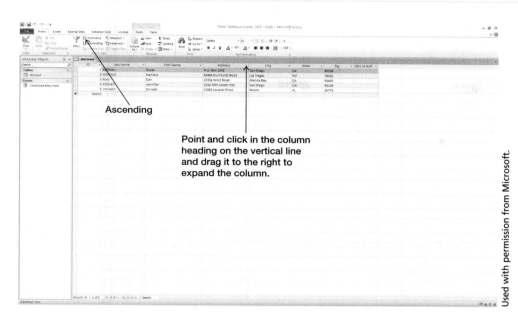

ACCESS 2010
EXHIBIT 6
Datasheet view of the table

Ascending

Point and click in the column heading on the vertical line and drag it to the right to expand the column.

Used with permission from Microsoft.

1. Open Windows. When it has loaded, ***double-click the Microsoft Office Access 2010 icon on the desktop*** to open Access 2010 for Windows. Alternatively, ***click the Start button, point to Programs or All Programs, and then click the Microsoft Access 2010 icon*** (or ***point to Microsoft Office and then click on Microsoft Access 2010).***

2. ***Click the File tab*** (see Access 2010 Exhibit 1). ***Click Recent, then click the name of the client file you created in Lessons 1 and 2 (Client.accdb).***

3. If a security warning (for example, **"Security Warning: Some active content has been disabled. Click for more details."**) is displayed just under the ribbon, ***click Enable Content next to the Security Warning.*** There is no security problem, because you know the content came from a trustworthy source, as you are the one who created the file.

4. Notice that the "tblClient" file you created in Lesson 1 and the client data entry form you created in Lesson 2 are listed on the Navigation pane.

5. ***Double-click on "tblClient" under Tables in the Navigation pane.***

6. You should now see your data displayed in the Datasheet View.

7. Notice that the data is not sorted. To quickly and easily sort the data, ***click on any record in the Last Name field; then, on the Home ribbon tab, click the Sort Ascending icon in the Sort & Filter group.*** (The icon looks like the letter "A" on top of the letter "Z" with a down arrow next to them—see Access 2010 Exhibit 6). *Note:* Point to any icon for a second and the name of the icon will be displayed. Your records should now be sorted alphabetically by last name.

8. ***Click the Save icon on the Quick Access toolbar.***

9. ***Click the Close tblClient icon*** (the black "X").

10. ***Click the Create ribbon tab, and then click Query Wizard in the Queries group.***

11. In the "New Query" window, the Simple Query Wizard selection should be highlighted, so ***click OK.***

**ACCESS 2010
EXHIBIT 7**
Creating a query with
the Query wizard

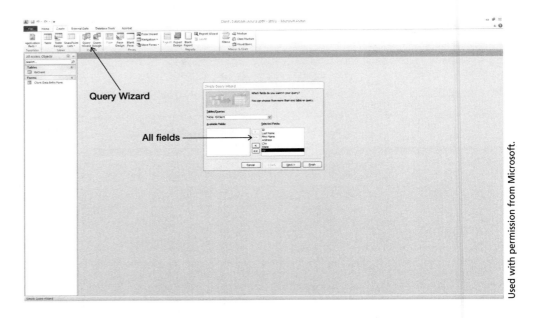

12. You should now have the "Simple Query Wizard" window on your screen (see Access 2010 Exhibit 7). ***Click >>*** (two "greater than" signs). This will select all of the fields for the query (see Access 2010 Exhibit 7).

13. ***Click on Next.***

14. You will then be asked **"What title do you want for your query?"** Type **San Diego Query**. ***Then, click Modify the query design and click on Finish.***

15. The query is then displayed on your screen (in Query Design View). You will now make the modifications shown in Access 2010 Exhibit 8. You will use the Query Design View mode to make the revisions. Notice that each column shows one of the fields in the table.

16. ***Click the Show row under the ID column*** (the first column). There should now be an **empty box (no check mark).** This is because we do not want this to show on our query (see Access 2010 Exhibit 8).

**ACCESS 2010
EXHIBIT 8**
Modifying a query in
Design view

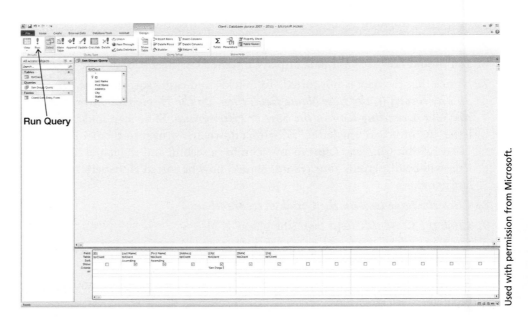

17. ***Click the Sort row under the Last Name column. Now, click the down arrow button and click Ascending*** (see Access 2010 Exhibit 8). This tells Access that the primary sort for the database will be on the Last Name field.

18. ***Click the Sort row under the First Name column. Now, click the down arrow button and click Ascending*** (see Access 2010 Exhibit 8). This tells Access that the secondary sort for the database will be on the First Name field. This is necessary because if we had two clients with the same last name, we would then want Access to sort the data based on the client's first name.

19. ***Click the Criteria row under City.*** Type **"San Diego"** (*Note*: You *must* type the quotation marks—see Access 2010 Exhibit 8).

20. This tells Access to select only those clients that have "San Diego" entered in the City field.

21. ***Click the Save icon on the Quick Access toolbar.*** This will save the query.

22. ***Click the Run command on the toolbar*** (the icon that looks like a red exclamation mark). This will run the query.

23. Two records should now be displayed on your screen: Jennifer Kitchen and Susan Sullivan (see Access 2010 Exhibit 9). Notice also that **"San Diego Query"** is now listed under Queries in the Navigation pane.

ACCESS 2010 EXHIBIT 9
Results of the San Diego query

Used with permission from Microsoft.

24. ***Click the File tab, then Print, and then click Print or Quick Print to print the query results.***

25. ***Click the Save icon on the Quick Access toolbar.***

26. ***Click Close San Diego Query*** (the black "X").

27. ***Click the File tab and then click Exit to exit the program.***

This concludes Lesson 3.

 INTERMEDIATE LESSONS

LESSON 4: CREATING A REPORT—CLIENT DATABASE

In this lesson you will create and print a report using the database you created in Lessons 1–3.

1. Open Windows. When it has loaded, ***double-click the Microsoft Office Access 2010 icon on the desktop*** to open Access 2010 for Windows. Alternatively, ***click the Start button, point to Programs or All Programs, and then click the Microsoft Access 2010 icon*** (or ***point to Microsoft Office and then click Microsoft Access 2010).***

2. ***Click the File tab*** (see Access 2010 Exhibit 1). ***Then click Recent and click on the name of the client file you created in Lessons 1 and 2 (Client. accdb).***

3. If a security warning (for example, **"Security Warning: Some active content has been disabled. Click for more details."**) is displayed just under the ribbon, ***click Enable Content next to the Security Warning.*** There is no security problem, because you know the content came from a trustworthy source, as you are the one who created the file.

4. Notice that the "tblClient" file you created in Lesson 1, the client data entry form you created in Lesson 2, and the San Diego query you created in Lesson 3 are listed on the Navigation pane.

5. ***Click the Create ribbon tab and then click Report Wizard in the Reports group.***

6. You should now have the "Report Wizard" window on your screen.

7. Under Tables/Queries in the "Report Wizard" window, ***click the down arrow icon and make sure that Table:tbl Client is selected.*** (*Note*: If **"Query: San Diego Sort"** is selected, your report will run, but it will only pull the records for clients living in San Diego. This is how users can combine queries and reports. Because we want a list of all clients, make sure the "Table:tbl Client" file is selected).

8. ***Click the >> icon*** (two "greater than" signs). This will select all of the fields for our report (see Access 2010 Exhibit 10). ***Click Next.***

9. You will then be asked **"Do you want to add any grouping levels?"** You do not, so ***click Next.***

Report Wizard

**ACCESS 2010
EXHIBIT 10**
Creating a report with
the Report Wizard

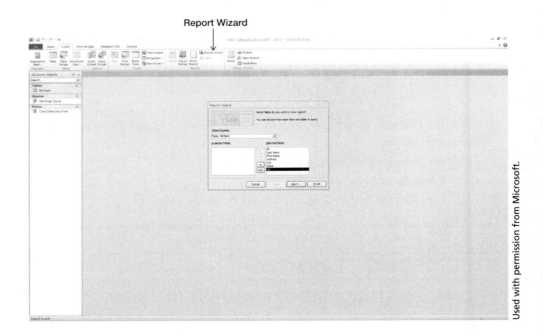

Used with permission from Microsoft.

10. You will then be asked **"What sort order do you want for your records?"** *Click on the down arrow button on the 1 field and then select Last Name* (see Access 2010 Exhibit 11). Notice that it defaults to an ascending sort.

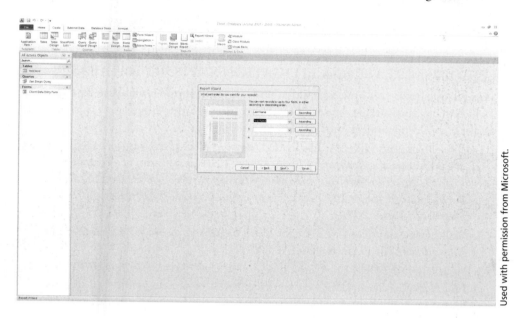

Used with permission from Microsoft.

**ACCESS 2010
EXHIBIT 11**
Sorting a report in the Report Wizard

11. *Click the down arrow button next to the 2 field, and then select First Name* (see Access 2010 Exhibit 11).

12. *Select Next.*

13. You will then be asked how you would like to lay out the report. *Click Tabular under Layout and Portrait under Orientation, then select Next.*

14. You are then asked **"What title do you want for the report?"** Type **Client Report.** You want to preview the report, so *click Finish.*

15. The report with the five clients is displayed on your screen (see Access 2010 Exhibit 12).

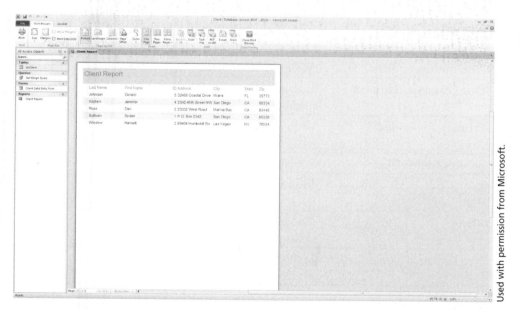

Used with permission from Microsoft.

**ACCESS 2010
EXHIBIT 12**
Print Preview of client report

16. *Click the File tab, then click Print, and then click Print to print the document.*

17. *Click the Save icon on the Quick Access toolbar.*

18. *Click the Close icon* (the black "X").

19. *Click the File tab and then click Exit to exit the program.*

This concludes Lesson 4.

LESSON 5: CREATING A LITIGATION SUPPORT DATABASE

This lesson shows you how to build a new litigation support database from scratch, including creating a table, entering fields, creating a form, entering data, sorting the database, building a query, and producing a report.

1. Open Windows. When it has loaded, *double-click the Microsoft Office Access 2010 icon on the desktop* to open Access 2010 for Windows. Alternatively, *click the Start button, point to Programs or All Programs, and then click the Microsoft Access 2010 icon* (or *point to Microsoft Office and then click Microsoft Access 2010).*

2. Make sure you are on the File tab. *Click on Blank database just under the New Blank Database section.*

3. Notice that the right side of the screen now says **"Blank database."** *Click under File Name,* use the **[DEL]** key to delete the current title, and type **Litigation Support**. To save the new database in the default directory, *click Create.*

4. You should now have a blank table on the screen.

5. On the Home tab, *click View in the Views group to go to Design View.*

6. The "Save As" window should now be displayed. Under Table Name, type **Documents** and then *click OK.*

7. Notice that Access has created a field named "ID" and designated it as an AutoNumber data type. Press the **[TAB]** key three times to accept this and move to the second row.

8. Enter the following fields/information into the table:

Field Name	Data Type	Description	Field Size	Required
Doc Name	Text	Name of document	50	Yes
Doc Type	Text	Type of document	50	Yes
Doc Date	Date/Time	Date of document	—	Yes
Doc Author	Text	Author of document	50	Yes
Doc Number	Number	Internal document ID number	Long Integer	Yes
Primary Recipient	Text	Who the document was sent to	50	Yes
Subject Matter	Text	Subject of document	75	Yes
Issue Code	Number	Internal code	Long Integer	No
Notes	Memo	Coder's notes about document	—	No
Key Evidence	Yes/No	Is this a key piece of evidence in the case?	—	Yes

9. *Click Doc Type again in the Field Name column, then click the Lookup tab* (just to the right of the General tab). Access 2010 Exhibit 13 shows the changes you will be making to the Lookup tab for the Doc Type field.

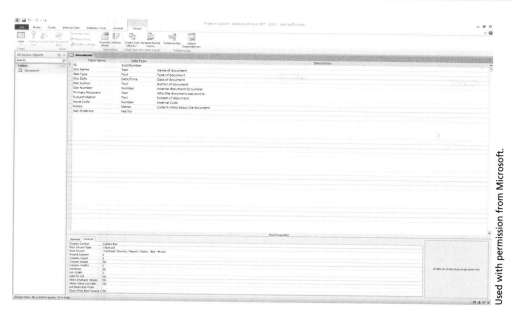

**ACCESS 2010
EXHIBIT 13**
Creating fields for
a litigation support
database

10. *Under the Lookup tab to the right of Display Control, click Text Box. Click
    the down arrow to the right of Text Box. Click Combo Box.* Notice that a
    number of other options are now available on the "Lookup" tab (see Access
    2010 Exhibit 13).

11. *To the right of Row Source Type, click Table/Query. Click the down arrow to
    the right of Table/Query. Click Value List.*

12. *Click the blank box to the right of Row Source* and type **"Contract"**,
    "Invoice", **"Report"**, **"Notes"**, **"Bid"**, and **"Photo"**. *Note:* You *must* type
    the quotation marks (see Access 2010 Exhibit 13). When you enter data into
    the table (either directly or with a form), these choices will appear in a drop-
    down box for you to select; this is a good way of creating data uniformity and
    consistency.

13. *Click in the blank box to the right of Column Widths,* then type **1"** (you
    must include the quotation mark).

14. *Click Auto next to List Width,* use the **[DEL]** key to delete "Auto," and then
    type **1"** (you must include the quotation mark).

15. *Click the Save icon on the Quick Access toolbar.*

16. You are currently in Design View. The Table Tools – Design ribbon tab should
    already be displayed. *Click View in the Views group to go to Datasheet View.*

17. *Click on the Close icon* (the black "X") *in the Field List task pane on the
    right side of the screen.*

18. You should now see the fields you just created displayed horizontally across the
    screen. To see all of your fields, you will need to use the scroll bar at the bottom
    of the screen or your cursor keys. You can toggle back and forth between Design
    view and Datasheet view by clicking on the View icon on the Home ribbon tab.

19. *Click the Save icon on the Quick Access toolbar.*

20. *Click the Close Documents icon* (the black "X").

21. You are now ready to create a data entry form for entering data into the table.
    You must first *click Documents under Tables and click under All Access
    Objects* so that Access knows the table with which the new form will be
    associated.

22. *Click the Create ribbon tab, and then click Form in the Forms group.*

**ACCESS 2010
EXHIBIT 14**
Litigation support data
entry form

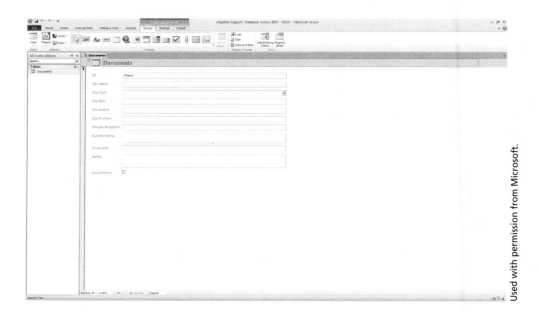

23. The form should now be displayed on your screen. Your screen should look similar to Access 2010 Exhibit 14. The default form is fine, and no modifications are necessary. If you would like to change the colors of the form, do so by selecting one of the AutoFormats on the ribbon.

24. *Click the Save icon on the Quick Access toolbar.* The "Save As" window should now be displayed. Under Form Name, type **Doc Data Entry Form Richards v EZ Pest Control** and then *click OK.* You are currently in Layout view. To switch to Form view so you can enter data into the table/form, *click the down arrow under the View icon on the ribbon* (the Form Layout Tools – Format ribbon tab should already be selected), *and then click Form View.*

25. Enter the records from the table on page 375 into the database. You can go between fields by pressing the **[TAB]** or **[SHIFT]+[TAB]** keys, or by pointing and clicking with the mouse. Notice in the Doc Type field that there is a drop-down menu with choices you can select. Because it is a "combo box," you can also enter text into the field, but for this exercise, we will just select entries from the drop-down menu. Notice also in the Key Evidence field that if the document is a key piece of evidence, you just need to click in the box and a check mark will appear. When you are at the last field, you can go to the next record by pressing the **[TAB]** key. You can also go between records by pressing the **[PAGE UP]** or **[PAGE DOWN]** keys or by *pointing and clicking on the "greater than" and "less than" symbols at the bottom of the page.*

26. When you have finished entering all of the data, *click the Save icon on the Quick Access toolbar.*

27. *Click the Close Doc Data Entry Form Richards v EZ Pest Control* (the black "X").

28. *Click All Access Objects on the Navigation pane and click Object Type.* You can now see the "Documents" table under Tables and "Doc Data Entry Form Richards v . . ." under Forms.

29. *Double-click Documents under Tables in the Navigation pane.*

30. You should now see your fields displayed horizontally across the screen (although, due to the length of the entries, you may not be able to see all of the data). Use the scroll bar at the bottom of the screen to scroll left and right to see all of the fields (see Access 2010 Exhibit 15).

31. *Click on the Save icon on the Quick Access toolbar.*

Doc Name	Doc Type	Doc Date	Doc Author	Doc No	Primary Recipient	Subject Matter	Issue Code	Notes	Key Evidence
HUD Settlement Statement	Contract	06/01/2014	Sherry Richards, Bill Lee	501	Sherry Richards	Sale of house	1	Includes pest inspection cost of $300	Yes
EZ Pest Agreement for Termite Inspection	Contract	05/01/2014	John Lincoln, Bill Lee	502	Sherry Richards	Agreement to inspect the house for termites	1	The contract states that EZ Pest will conduct a thorough examination of the property.	Yes
EZ Pest Invoice for Pest Inspection	Invoice	05/15/2014	John Lincoln, EZ Pest	503	Sherry Richards	Invoice for pest inspection	1	Shows total due $300 and that it was paid on 5/20/2014	No
EZ Pest Inspection Report	Report	05/15/2014	John Lincoln, EZ Pest	504	Sherry Richards	Inspection Report	2	The report states "No visible evidence of infestation from wood destroying insects was observed." Signed by John Lincoln.	Yes
EZ Pest Inspection Report Notes	Notes	05/07/2014	John Lincoln	505	John Lincoln	Notes of John Lincoln taken to assist in preparation of Inspection Report	2	John Lincoln's notes do not show that he actually checked the east side of the house where termites were later found.	Yes
Bid from Stewart Construction	Bid	11/01/2014	Tim Stewart	506	Sherry Richards	Bid to rebuild the east side where the termites destroyed house	3	Bid of $50,000 to repair the termite damage on the east side.	Yes
Photograph of east side of house	Photo	10/01/2014	Sherry Richards	507	Sherry Richards	Photograph of house	3	Photograph showing east side of house behind vinyl siding showing frame of house nearly eaten through.	Yes

Ascending sort

Filter by selection

Find

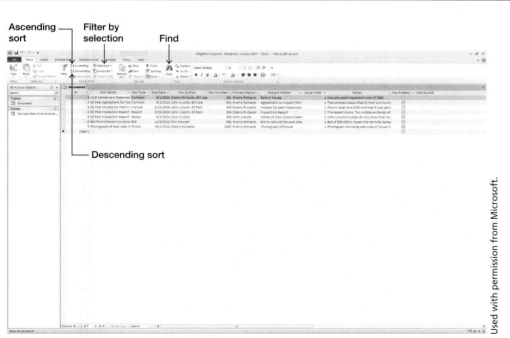

Descending sort

ACCESS 2010 EXHIBIT 15
Datasheet view of data in the documents table

HANDS-ON EXERCISES

32. You will next see some different views of the data (without damaging the integrity of the data).

33. *Click any record in the Doc Name field. Then, on the Home ribbon tab, click the Sort Ascending icon in the Sort & Filter group* (it looks like the letter "A" on top of the letter "Z" with a down arrow next to them). (*Note:* Point to any icon on the toolbar for a second and the name of the icon will be displayed.) Your records should now be sorted alphabetically by document name.

34. *Click any record in the Doc Date field and then click the Sort Descending icon on the toolbar.* The documents are now sorted in date order, with the most recent first.

35. *Click any record in the Subject Matter field, and then click the Find icon in the Find group on the Home ribbon tab* (it looks like binoculars). The "Find and Replace" window should be displayed. Next to Find What:, type **vinyl siding** and then, next to Look In:, *click the down arrow and select Current document.* (This will allow you to search all fields in the Document table, not just the Subject Matter field.) *Next to Match, click the down arrow, click Any Part of Field, and then click Find Next.* Notice that the pointer went to document 507 and found where "vinyl siding" was entered. *Click Cancel to make the "Find and Replace" window disappear.*

36. *Click Document 501 and click in the Primary Recipient field.* Notice that "Sherry Richards" is in the field. *Click the Filter by Selection icon in the Sort & Filter group in the Home ribbon tab* (it looks like a silver funnel with a lightning bolt—see Access 2010 Exhibit 15), *then click Text Filters and then Equals. . .* and type **Sherry Richards** in the Custom Filter. Notice that only documents with Sherry Richards as the primary recipient are left. (The other documents are still in the database; Access just temporarily removed them from the current view.)

37. To bring back all of the documents, remove the filter by *clicking the Toggle Filter icon in the Sort & Filter group on the Home ribbon tab.* Notice that all of the documents are back.

38. To put the documents back in the order in which you entered them, simply *click in the Doc Number field and click the Sort Ascending icon.*

39. *Click the Save icon on the Quick Access toolbar.*

40. *Click the Close Documents icon* (the black "X").

41. You will now run a query to select only documents that have Issue Code 2 in them, and where Sherry Richards was the recipient. The Documents table under Tables on the Navigation pane should still be selected. *Click the Create ribbon tab, then click Query Wizard in the Queries group.*

42. You should now have the "New Query" window displayed on your screen. Simple Query Wizard should be selected, *so click OK.*

43. You should now have the "Simple Query Wizard" window on your screen. *Click >>* (two "greater than" signs). This will select all of the fields for your query.

44. *Click Next.*

45. You will then be asked **"Would you like a detail or a summary query?"** *Click Detail* (shows every field of every record). *Click Next.*

46. You will then be asked **"What title do you want for your query?"** Type **qry Richards Issue Code 1**. *Then, click Modify the query design and click Finish.*

47. The query is displayed on your screen. Notice that each column shows one of the fields in the table.

48. *Click in the Show row in the ID column* (the first column). There should now be an **empty box (no check mark)**. This is because we do not want this to show on our query.

49. ***Click in the Sort row under Doc Number. Now, click the down arrow and click Ascending.*** This tells Access that the primary sort for the database will be on this field.

50. ***Click in the Criteria row under Issue Code,*** **then type 1.** (*Note*: **Do not type anything else in the criteria for this field—just type the number 1.**)

51. ***Click in the Criteria row under Primary Recipient*** and type **"Sherry Richards."** (*Note:* You *must* type the quotation marks for this field.) This tells Access to select only those records that meet both of these selection/search criteria.

52. ***Click the Run icon in the Results group on the Query Tools – Design ribbon tab*** (the icon that looks like a red exclamation mark). This will run the query. Document 501 should be displayed.

53. ***Click the Save icon on the Quick Access toolbar.***

54. ***Click the down arrow just under the View icon in the Views group on the Home ribbon tab and then select Design view. Click back and forth between Design view and Datasheet view.*** Notice that you can make changes to the query in Design view, and then run the query and correct any problems that you may have had in your query.

55. In Datasheet view, ***click the File tab and then click Print and then Print or Quick Print.*** Notice that the whole record did not print.

56. ***Click the Save icon on the Quick Access toolbar.***

57. ***Click the Close qry Richards Issue Code 1 icon*** (the black "X").

58. ***Click the Create ribbon tab, and then click Report Wizard.*** You should now have the "Report Wizard" window on your screen.

59. ***Click under Tables/Queries on the down arrow button and select Query: qry Richards Issue Code 1.***

60. ***Click the >> icon*** (two "greater than" signs). This will select all of the fields for our report. ***Click Next.***

61. You will then be asked **"Do you want to add any grouping levels?"** ***Click Next.***

62. You will then be asked **"What sort order do you want for your report?"** ***Click Next.***

63. You will then be asked **"How would you like to lay out your report?"** ***Click Justified, then click Landscape, and then select Next.***

64. You are then asked **"What title would you like for the report?"** Type **Sherry Richards Primary Recipient—Issue Code 1 Report.**

65. ***Click Finish.***

66. The report should now be displayed on your screen.

67. ***Click the File tab, then click Print, and then click Print or Quick Print to print the document.***

68. ***Click the Save icon on the Quick Access toolbar.***

69. ***Click the Close Sherry Richards Primary Recipient—Issue Code 1 Report icon*** (the black "X").

70. ***Click the File tab and then click Exit Access to exit the program.***

This concludes Lesson 5.

ADVANCED LESSON

LESSON 6: WORKING WITH A COMPREHENSIVE LAW-OFFICE RELATIONAL DATABASE

In this lesson, you will work with a true relational database, including working with multiple tables, assigning relationships among tables, and writing queries and reports

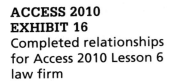

that access data from multiple tables. This lesson assumes that you have read Chapter 5 on database management systems, and that you have completed Lessons 1–5. To begin, you will open the Access Lesson 6 Law Firm Database from the disk supplied with this text, and work with a database with four related tables in it.

1. Open Windows. When it has loaded, ***double-click the Microsoft Office Access 2010 icon on the desktop*** to open Access 2010 for Windows. Alternatively, ***click the Start button, point to Programs or All Programs, and then click the Microsoft Access 2010 icon*** (or ***point to Microsoft Office and then click Microsoft Access 2010).***

2. The first thing you will do is to open the "Lesson 6 Law Firm Database" file from the disk supplied with this text. Ensure that the disk is inserted in the disk drive, ***click on File on the menu bar, and then click on Open.*** The "Open" window should now be displayed. ***Click on the down arrow to the right of the white box next to Look in: and select the drive where the disk is located. Double-click on the Access Database Files folder. Double-click on the "Lesson 6 Law Firm Database" file.*** You may also access this data file from the Premium website.

3. At the security warning (**"Security Warning: Some active content has been disabled. Click for more details."**) just under the ribbon, ***click Enable Content next to the Security Warning.*** There is no security problem, because you know the content comes from a trustworthy source.

4. ***Click Tables on the Navigation pane. Click All Access Objects.*** This will allow you to see all of the objects in the database that have already been created.

5. In this lesson you are working with a true relational law-office database. In the previous lessons, you have only worked with databases with one table. Notice that four tables are listed: Case Evidence, Case File, Client, and Opposing Attorney. You will now get an overview of the tables and create a relationship between two tables.

6. ***Click the Database Tools ribbon tab, then click Relationships in the Show/ Hide group.***

7. Your screen should now be similar to Access 2010 Exhibit 16, except that there is no relationship between the Case File table and the Case Evidence table.

8. Look carefully at the four tables. The subject matter of the Client table is just the client. It includes a client ID number and client contact information only.

ACCESS 2010 EXHIBIT 16
Completed relationships for Access 2010 Lesson 6 law firm

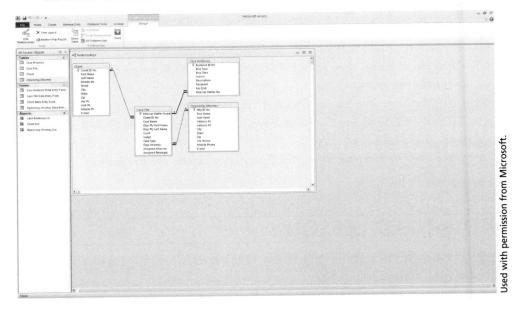

The Case File table includes broad data about the legal subject matter of the case, including an internal matter number, the case name, court, judge, case type, and assigned attorney and paralegal. The Opposing Attorney table just tracks contact information for opposing counsel on cases. The Case Evidence table tracks specific pieces of evidence in each case. This type of structure, including multiple tables that hold a variety of client- and case-related information, can be found in legal organizations just about anywhere.

9. Each table in a relational database must be connected to another table or the tables will not be able to share information. For example, the Case Evidence table is not connected to any other table. The table can reside in the database and the user can enter information into it, but it will be a stand-alone table. For example, if you wanted to print a report that had the contact information for each client and a listing of all of the case evidence for the client, you would not be able to do so without creating a relationship between the tables. You will now create a one-to-many relationship between the Case File table and the Case Evidence table using the Internal Matter Number field as the conduit.

10. ***Click in the Internal Matter Number field in the Case File table, then drag it to the Internal Matter No field in the Case Evidence table and let go.*** The "Edit Relationships" window should now be displayed (see Access 2010 Exhibit 17).

11. In the "Edit Relationships" window, ***click Enforce Referential Integrity, click Cascade Update Related Fields, then click Cascade Delete Related Records*** (see Access 2010 Exhibit 17). At the bottom of the "Edit Relationships" window, it should now say **"Relationship Type: One-To-Many."** That is because each case file can have many pieces of evidence that should be tracked in the Case Evidence table.

12. In the "Edit Relationships" window, ***click Join Type.*** . (see Access 2010 Exhibit 17). In the "Join Properties" window, make sure that option 1, **"Only include rows where the joined fields from both tables are equal,"** is selected. ***Then, click OK in the "Join Properties" window.***

13. In the "Edit Relationships" window, ***click Create.*** Your relationships window should now look like Access 2010 Exhibit 16.

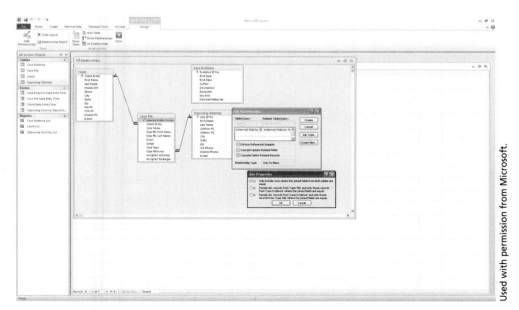

ACCESS 2010 EXHIBIT 17
The "Edit Relationships" window

14. *Click Close on the Relationship Tools – Design ribbon tab (in the Relationships group).*

15. You will now build a query that pulls information from three of the tables.

16. *Click the Create ribbon tab, and then click Query Wizard in the Queries group.*

17. The "New Query" window should now be displayed. **"Simple Query Wizard"** should be highlighted, so just *click OK.*

18. The screen should now say **"Which fields do you want in your query?"** Under Tables/Queries, *click the down arrow and select Table: Client.* Notice that now the fields for the Client table are shown under Available Fields. *Click Last Name and then click > to add the field under Selected Fields.* You will now build the query by selecting the tables and fields exactly as shown below. This should be done carefully, because you must skip around among the different tables to build the query correctly.

    In addition to the Last Name field you have already selected, enter the following:

TABLE	FIELD TO SELECT
Client	First Name
Case File	Case Name
Case File	Case Type
Case File	Court
Case File	Judge
Opposing Attorney	Last Name
Case File	Assigned Attorney
Case File	Assigned Paralegal

    When completed, your screen should look similar to Access 2010 Exhibit 18.

19. *Click Next.*

20. You will then be asked **"Would you like a detail or a summary query?"** The Detail (shows every field of every record) option should already be selected, so just *click Next.*

ACCESS 2010 EXHIBIT 18
Building a query with multiple tables in the Query Wizard

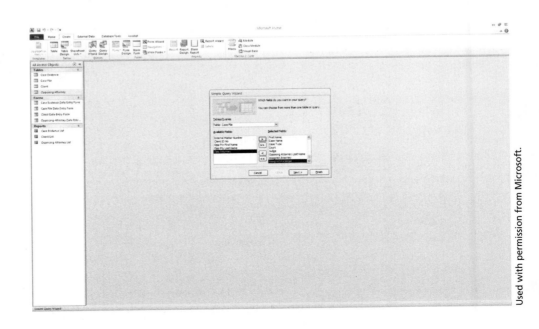

21. You will then be asked **"What title do you want for your query?"** Type **Case List Query**. *Then, click Modify the query design and click Finish.*

22. The query is displayed on your screen in Design view. Notice that each column shows one of the fields and that the table that it is drawn from is shown in the Table row (see Access 2010 Exhibit 19).

23. *Click on the Sort row in the first column (Client_Last Name) and then click the down arrow and click Ascending* (see Access 2010 Exhibit 19). This tells Access that the primary sort for the database will be on this field.

24. *Click the Sort row in the second column (First Name), and then click the down arrow button and click Ascending* (see Access 2010 Exhibit 19). This tells Access that the secondary sort for the database will be on this field.

25. *Click the Run icon* (it looks like a bright red exclamation mark) *in the Results group on the Query Tools – Design ribbon tab.* Your query should look similar to Access 2010 Exhibit 20.

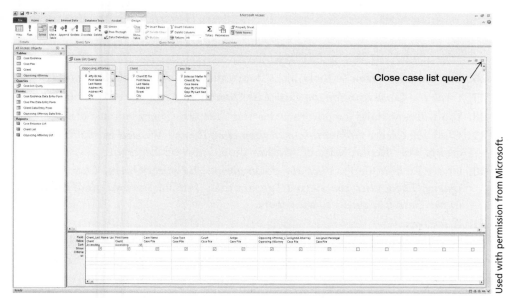

ACCESS 2010 EXHIBIT 19
Modifying the case list query in Query Design view

Used with permission from Microsoft.

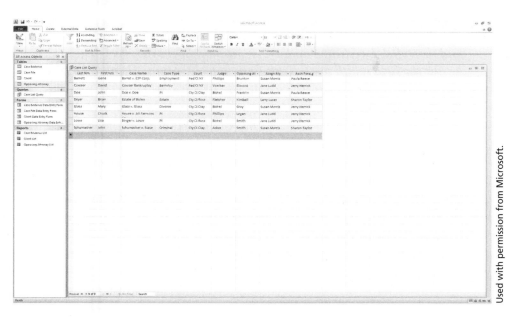

ACCESS 2010 EXHIBIT 20
Completed case list query in Datasheet view

Used with permission from Microsoft.

HANDS-ON EXERCISES

**ACCESS 2010
EXHIBIT 21**
Finalized case list report

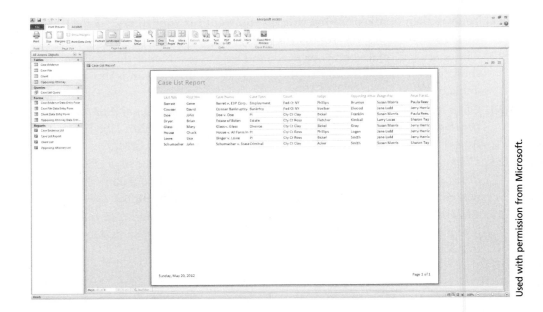

26. *Click the Save icon* (it looks like a floppy disk) *on the Quick Access toolbar.*

27. *Click the Close icon for the Case List Query* (see Access 2010 Exhibit 20).

28. You will now build a report that uses the Case List Query you just created.

29. *Click the Create ribbon tab, and then click Report Wizard in the Reports group.* The "Report Wizard" window should now be displayed.

30. Under Tables/Queries, *click the down arrow and select Query: Case List Query. Then, click the >>* (two "greater than" symbols) *to add all of the fields in the Case List query to the report.*

31. *Click Next.*

32. You will then be asked **"How do you want to view your data?"** *Click Next.*

33. You will then be asked **"Do you want to add any grouping levels?"** *Click Next.*

34. You will then be asked **"What sort order do you want for detail records?"** Because the query is already sorting the data, *click Next.*

35. You are now asked **"How would you like to lay out your report?"** *Click Block and then click Landscape under Orientation. Leave the check mark in the Adjust the field width so all fields fit on a page option. Then, select Next.*

36. You are then asked **"What title would you like for the report?"** Type **Case List Report,** leave the Preview the report option selected, and *click Finish.*

37. The report should now be displayed on your screen. It should look similar to Access 2010 Exhibit 21.

38. *Click the Print icon on the ribbon tab in the Print group. Then, click OK to print the document.*

39. *Click Close Print Preview on the ribbon tab in the Close Preview group.*

40. *Click the Save icon on the Quick Access toolbar.*

41. *Click the Close icon for the Case List Report* (the black "X").

42. *Click the File tab and then click Exit to exit the program.*

This concludes the Access 2010 Hands-On Exercises.

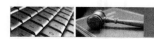

HANDS-ON EXERCISES

MICROSOFT ACCESS 2007 FOR WINDOWS

Number	Lesson Title	Concepts Covered
BASIC LESSONS		
Lesson 1	Creating a Table—Client Database	How to create a new table/database, create and design fields, create a primary key, move between the Table Design View and the Datasheet View, enter a record, and save the database.
Lesson 2	Creating a Form and Entering Data—Client Database	How to create a form, enter data in the form, view the Datasheet View of the form, and close a form.
Lesson 3	Querying a Database—Client Database	How to use the Ascending Sort icon on the ribbon, create a query that searches and sorts the database, modify a query, use a primary and secondary sort option, run a query, and print a query.
INTERMEDIATE LESSONS		
Lesson 4	Creating a Report—Client Database	How to create and print a report.
Lesson 5	Creating a Litigation Support Database	How to build a litigation support database that tracks documents in a case; creating the fields, entering the data, running helpful sorts and filters to search the data, running a query, running a report, and printing a report.
ADVANCED LESSONS		
Lesson 6	Working with a Comprehensive Law-Office Relational Database	Working with a true relational database, including working with multiple tables, assigning relationships among tables, and writing queries and reports that access data from multiple tables.

GETTING STARTED

Introduction

Throughout these lessons and exercises, information you need to type into the program will be designated in several different ways:

- Keys to be pressed on the keyboard are designated in brackets, in all caps, and in bold (e.g., press the **[ENTER]** key).
- Movements with the mouse pointer are designated in bold and italics (e.g., **_point to File and click_**).
- Words or letters that should be typed are designated in bold (e.g., type **Training Program**).
- Information that is or should be displayed on your computer screen is shown in bold, with quotation marks (e.g., **"Press ENTER to continue."**).
- Specific menu items and commands are designated with an initial capital letter (e.g., click Open).

OVERVIEW OF ACCESS 2007

Access 2007 is a relational database management application. Access 2007 Exhibit 1 shows the Access interface. Notice the ribbon across the top of the screen. The ribbon has several tabs across the top; these are called "ribbon tabs" or sometimes just "tabs."

**ACCESS 2007
EXHIBIT 1**

Access 2007 screen

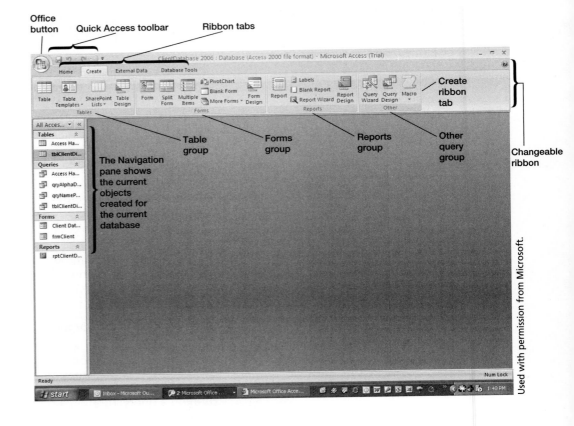

When a different tab is selected, the tools and commands on the ribbon change. In Access 2007 Exhibit 1, the Create ribbon tab is selected. Notice that the Create ribbon tab in Access 2007 Exhibit 1 has four groups, including the Tables, Forms, Reports, and Other groups (which includes queries). At the very top to the left of the screen is the Quick Access toolbar, a toolbar that can be customized by the user. In the top left of the screen is the Office button. The Office button allows the user to open files, save files, create new files, and print documents, among other things. On the left side of the screen is the Navigation pane. The Navigation pane can be configured in different ways, but in Access 2007 Exhibit 1 the user has all of the objects for the database displayed for easy access. This includes all of the user's tables, queries, forms, and reports.

Additional information about Access 2007 will be provided as you complete the exercises. By the end of the exercises you should have a good understanding of the basics of Access 2007.

▶ BASIC LESSONS

LESSON 1: CREATING A TABLE—CLIENT DATABASE

This lesson shows you how to build the table shown in Access 2007 Exhibit 3. It explains how to create a new table/database, create new fields, create a primary key, move between the Table Design View and the Datasheet View, and save the database. Keep in mind that if you make a mistake in this lesson, you may press [CTRL]+[Z] to undo what you have done, but note that in some cases this command will not work (e.g., when you delete a record, it is permanently deleted).

1. Open Windows. When it has loaded, ***double-click on the Microsoft Office Access 2007 icon on the desktop*** to open Access 2007 for Windows. Alternatively, ***click on the Start button, point to Programs or All Programs, and then click on the Microsoft Access 2007 icon*** (or ***point to Microsoft Office and then click Microsoft Office Access 2007).***

2. When Access 2007 opens, the Getting Started with Microsoft Office Access screen is displayed. This screen offers the user a number of templates that can be accessed to speed the creation of databases in Access.

3. Just under the **"Getting Started with Microsoft Office Access"** title is the New Blank Database section. ***Click Blank Database . . . just under the New Blank Database section.***

4. Notice that the right side of the screen now says **"Blank Database." *Click under File Name,*** use the **[DEL]** key to delete the current title, and type **Client.** To save the new database in the default directory, ***click Create.*** To browse where you would like to save the new database, ***click the Browse icon*** (it looks like an open file folder with an arrow) just to the right of the file name. Then, select the directory or folder you would like to save the file to, type **Client** next to **"File name," *and then click OK. Finally, click Create.***

5. You should now have a blank table in Datasheet View displayed on your screen (see Access 2007 Exhibit 2). Notice that the Table Tools—Datasheet ribbon tab is currently shown (see Access 2007 Exhibit 2). From the Views group on the Datasheet ribbon tab, ***click the down arrow under View, and then click Design View.***

6. The "Save As" window should now be displayed. Type **tblClient** under Table Name and then ***click OK.***

7. The Design View of your table (tblClient) should now be on your screen. Your screen should be similar to Access 2007 Exhibit 3, except that the table on

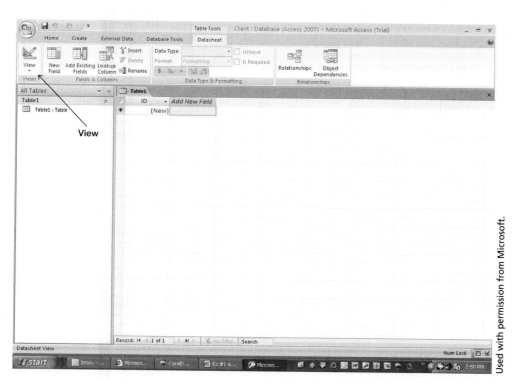

ACCESS 2007 EXHIBIT 2
Creating a new table in Datasheet view

**ACCESS 2007
EXHIBIT 3**
Creating fields in a table

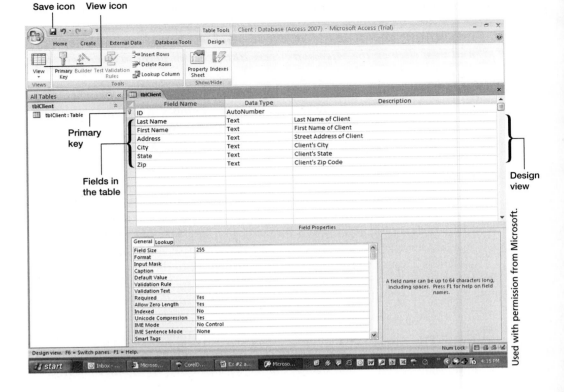

your screen will be blank. You will now begin to build the structure of a client database by entering the fields shown in Access 2007 Exhibit 3.

8. Notice that Access has entered a default field name of "ID" in the first row of your table (see Access 2007 Exhibit 3). It is useful to have an ID number for each client, so press the **[TAB]** key three times to move to the next row. Notice also in the ID field that the data type is **"AutoNumber."** This means that Access will automatically create a unique ID number for each client.

9. With your pointer in the second row of the first column, Field Name, type **Last Name** and then press the **[TAB]** key.

10. Your pointer should now be in the Data Type column and **"Text"** should be displayed in the field. If you click the down arrow next to **"Text,"** you can see the different data types that Access has. By selecting the data type, you tell Access what kind of information will be stored in the field. Because text will be stored in the Last Name field, press the **[TAB]** key to go to the Description column.

11. In the Description column, type **Last Name of Client.**

12. Notice at the bottom of the screen under Field Properties that there are two tabs, General and Look Up. The General tab should be displayed. It allows you to change the field size (the number of characters that may be entered into the field) and other items as well.

13. Next to the Required field under the General tab, *click No. Then, click the down arrow next to No, and then click Yes.* This will require the user to enter this field when entering new data. The default field size and the other options are fine, so you do not have to change them.

14. The Last Name field is now complete. *Click in the third row, directly under Last Name.*

15. Type the following information into the table:

Field Name	Data Type	Description	Field Size	Required
First Name	Text	First Name of Client	50	Yes
Address	Text	Street Address of Client	50	Yes
City	Text	Client's City	25	Yes
State	Text	Client's State	2	Yes
Zip	Text	Client's Zip Code	9	Yes

16. Your screen should look similar to Access 2007 Exhibit 3.

17. *Click back on the General tab under Field Properties.*

18. Once all of the information has been entered, *click on the Save icon* (it looks like a floppy disk) *on the Quick Access toolbar to save your data.*

19. Notice that a small key icon is displayed next to the ID field. This indicates that the ID field is the primary key (the field that uniquely identifies each record) for this table.

20. You are currently in the Table Design View. Design View means that you are looking at the *design* of the table and not the data in the table itself. You will now change your view to Datasheet View. Once data have been entered into the table, you can see the data in the Datasheet View.

21. *From the Views group on the Design ribbon tab, click the down arrow under the View icon* (see Access 2007 Exhibit 3), *and then select Datasheet View.* *Note*: To see the name of any icon, just hover the mouse pointer over the icon for a second and the name of the icon will appear.

22. You should now see all of your fields displayed horizontally across the screen (see Access 2007 Exhibit 4). You can toggle back and forth between Design View and Datasheet View by clicking on the View icon.

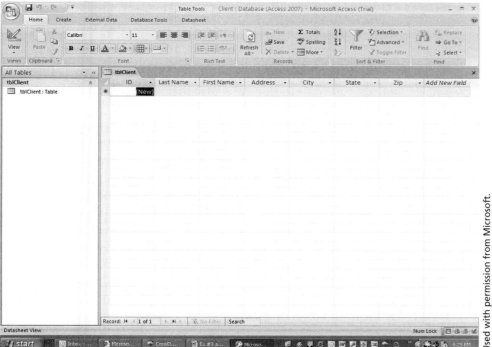

ACCESS 2007 EXHIBIT 4
Table Datasheet view

23. Press the [**TAB**] key to go to the Last Name field.

24. Enter the following information (to go to the next field press the [**TAB**] key).

ID	Last Name	First Name	Address	City	State	Zip
	Allen	Alice	P.O. Box 2342	San Diego	CA	95336

25. Although you can use Table Datasheet View to enter new records, it is not always the best way to enter data. In the next lesson, we will create a form to enter new records.

26. *Click the Save icon on the Quick Access toolbar to save your data.*

27. *Click the Office Button and then click Exit Access to exit the program.*
This concludes Lesson 1.

LESSON 2: CREATING A FORM AND ENTERING DATA—CLIENT DATABASE

In this lesson, you will create a form from which you can enter data into the database. You will then enter the rest of the data into the client database using the form you created.

1. Open Windows. When it has loaded, *double-click on the Microsoft Office Access 2007 icon on the desktop* to open Access 2007 for Windows. Alternatively, *click the Start button, point to Programs or All Programs, and then click the Microsoft Access 2007 icon* (or *point to Microsoft Office and then click on Microsoft Office Access 2007).*

2. *Click the Office button* (see Access 2007 Exhibit 1). *Then, under Recent Documents, click the name of the client file you created in Lesson 1 (Client. accdb).*

3. If a security warning (for example, **"Security Warning: Certain content in the database has been disabled"**) is displayed just under the ribbon, *click Options next to the security warning. Then, in the "Microsoft Office Security Options" window, click Enable this Content and then click OK.* There is no security problem, because you know the content came from a trustworthy source, as you are the one who created the file.

4. Notice that the file called "tblClient:Table" that you created in Lesson 1 is listed on the Navigation pane.

5. You are now ready to create a data entry form that will assist you in entering the data into the "tblClient:Table" file.

6. *Click the Create ribbon tab, then click Form in the Forms group.* Access should return a default data entry form for you (see Access 2007 Exhibit 5).

7. Access gives you many options to easily format your form. Notice on the ribbon that a new tab appeared called Form Layout Tools, and that **"Form Layout Tools – Format"** is selected. *Click the down arrow in the AutoFormat group on the Format ribbon tab* (see Access 2007 Exhibit 5) to look at the AutoFormat options for your form. You can click on the More icon in the AutoFormat group to see all of the options at one time (see Access 2007 Exhibit 5). *Click on one of the AutoFormat options that you like.*

8. *Click on the Save icon* (it looks like a floppy disk) *on the Quick Access toolbar to save your form.* In the "Save As" window, under Form Name, type **Client Data Entry Form** and then *click OK.*

9. *Click All Tables in the Navigation pane* (see Access 2007 Exhibit 5) *and then, under Navigate to Category, click Object Type.* Notice on the Navigation

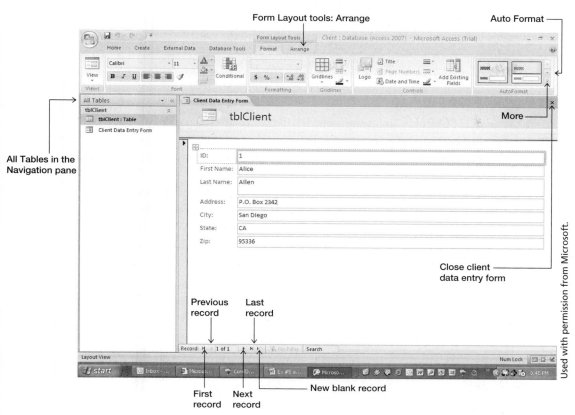

**ACCESS 2007
EXHIBIT 5**
Corrected data entry
form

pane that you can now see "tblClient" under Tables and "Client Data Entry Form" under Forms. Any time you add new objects to your database, they will be shown in the Navigation pane.

10. Notice that the first record you entered is now displayed (Allen, Alice).

11. Access placed the fields in the data entry form in the same way they were entered in the table. In this instance, Last Name is before First Name in the form. It would be more logical and easier for first name to be first. This is easy to correct. *Note: Switch to layout view (click down arrow under view icon on the toolbar).*

12. *Click anywhere in the First Name field of your form, then drag it (by holding the left mouse button) to just above the Last Name field and let go of the mouse button.* The First Name field should now be shown above the Last Name field. Although this corrected the physical layout on the screen, the tab order (where the pointer moves when you press the [**TAB**] key to go to the next field) must also be checked to make sure it changed as well.

13. *Click on the Form Layout Tools – Arrange ribbon tab* (see Access 2007 Exhibit 5). *Then, click on Tab Order in the Control Layout group. In the "Tab Order" window, make sure First Name is above Last Name.* If it is, proceed to the next step. If it is not, *click just to the left of First Name in the "Tab Order" window to select the First Name row, and then drag the line to just above the Last Name.*

14. *Click OK to close the "Tab Order" window.*

15. To make the changes active, you need to save the form, exit the form, and then reopen the form. *Click the Save icon on the Quick Access toolbar. Then, click the Close Client Data Entry Form icon* (the black X) *to the right of the title "tblclient"* (see Access 2007 Exhibit 5). *Next, double-click the Client Data Entry Form (under Forms on the Navigation pane) to reopen the form.*

16. Press the [TAB] key three times. Notice that the tab order is correct (ID, then First Name, then Last Name). (*Note*: If the order is not correct, you can *right-click on Client Data Entry Form under Forms on the Navigation pane, and click Layout View. Then you can click the Form Layout Tools—Arrange tab* to once again readjust the tab order, and then *save, exit, and reopen the Client Data Entry Form).*

17. Press the [TAB] key four times, which will take you to the next record (Record 2). In addition, you can go to the next record or the previous record by *clicking on the Greater Than and Less Than icons at the bottom of the page*, or by pressing the [PAGE UP] or [PAGE DOWN] keys on the keyboard (see Access 2007 Exhibit 5).

18. Enter the following records into the database. You can go between fields by pressing the [TAB] or [SHIFT]+[TAB] keys, or by *clicking with the mouse.* When you are on the last field you can go to the next record by pressing [TAB].

Record 2	
First Name	Harriet
Last Name	Winslow
Address	89404 Humboldt
City	Las Vegas
State	NV
Zip	78524

Record 3	
First Name	Dan
Last Name	Ross
Address	23332 Westide Road
City	Marina Bay
State	CA
Zip	93442

Record 4	
First Name	Jennifer
Last Name	Kitchen
Address	2342 45th St. NW
City	San Diego
State	CA
Zip	95334

Record 5	
First Name	Donald
Last Name	Johnson
Address	32455 Coastal
City	Miami
State	FL
Zip	65773

19. When you have finished entering all of the data, ***click the Save icon on the Quick Access toolbar.***

20. ***Click the Close Client Data Entry Form icon*** (see Access 2007 Exhibit 5).

21. ***Double-click tblClient under Tables on the Navigation pane.***

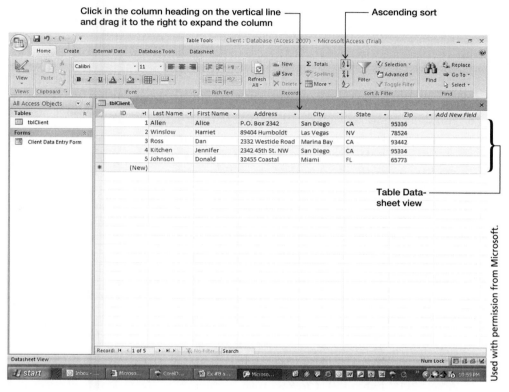

Click in the column heading on the vertical line and drag it to the right to expand the column — Ascending sort

Table Datasheet view

Used with permission from Microsoft.

ACCESS 2007 EXHIBIT 6
Datasheet view of the table

22. The Datasheet View of your table is now displayed (see Access 2007 Exhibit 6). You should now see all of your data displayed horizontally across the screen. *Note*: If you cannot see all of the data in a field, just ***click in the column heading on the vertical line that separates each field and drag it to the right*** to make the field larger (see Access 2007 Exhibit 6).

23. ***Click the Office button, then click Print, and then click OK to print the document.***

24. ***Click the Save icon on the Quick Access toolbar.***

25. ***Click the Office button and then click Exit Access to exit the program.***

This concludes Lesson 2.

LESSON 3: QUERYING A DATABASE—CLIENT DATABASE

In this lesson, you will learn how to use the Ascending Sort icon on the toolbar, create a query that searches and sorts the database, modify a query, use a primary and secondary sort option, run a query, and print a query using the database you created in Lessons 1 and 2.

1. Open Windows. When it has loaded, ***double-click the Microsoft Office Access 2007 icon on the desktop*** to open Access 2007 for Windows. Alternatively, ***click the Start button, point to Programs or All Programs, and then click the Microsoft Access 2007 icon*** (or ***point to Microsoft Office and then click on Microsoft Office Access 2007***).

2. *Click the Office button* (see Access 2007 Exhibit 1). *Then, under Recent Documents, click the name of the client file you created in Lessons 1 and 2 (Client.accdb).*

3. If a security warning (for example, **"Security Warning: Certain content in the database has been disabled"**) is displayed just under the ribbon, *click Options... next to the security warning. Then, in the "Microsoft Office Security Options" window, click Enable this Content and then click OK.* There is no security problem, because you know the content came from a trustworthy source, as you are the one who created the file.

4. Notice that the "tblClient:Table" file you created in Lesson 1 and the client data entry form you created in Lesson 2 are listed on the Navigation pane.

5. *Double-click on tblClient under Tables in the Navigation pane.*

6. You should now see your data displayed in the Datasheet View.

7. Notice that the data are not sorted. To quickly and easily sort the data, *click on any record in the Last Name field and then, on the Home ribbon tab, click the Sort Ascending icon in the Sort & Filter group.* (The icon looks like the letter "A" on top of the letter "Z" with a down arrow next to them—see Access 2007 Exhibit 6). *Note:* Point to any icon for a second and the name of the icon will be displayed. Your records should now be sorted alphabetically by last name.

8. *Click the Save icon on the Quick Access toolbar.*

9. *Click the Close tblClient icon* (the black "X").

10. *Click the Create ribbon tab, and then click Query Wizard in the Other group.*

11. *In the "New Query" window, the Simple Query Wizard selection should be highlighted, so click OK.*

12. You should now have the "Simple Query Wizard" window on your screen (see Access 2007 Exhibit 7). *Click >>* (two "greater than" signs). This will select all of the fields for the query (see Access 2007 Exhibit 7).

13. *Click on Next.*

14. You will then be asked **"What title do you want for your query?"** Type **San Diego Query**. *Then, click Modify the query design, and then click on Finish.*

15. The query is then displayed on your screen (in Query Design View). You will now make the modifications shown in Access 2007 Exhibit 8. You will use the Query Design View mode to make the revisions. Notice that each column shows one of the fields in the table.

16. *Click the Show row under the ID column* (the first column). There should now be **an empty box (no check mark).** This is because we do not want this to show on our query (see Access 2007 Exhibit 8).

17. *Click the Sort row under the Last Name column. Now, click the down arrow button and click Ascending* (see Access 2007 Exhibit 8). This tells Access that the primary sort for the database will be on the Last Name field.

18. *Click the Sort row under the First Name column. Now, click the down arrow button and click Ascending* (see Access 2007 Exhibit 8). This tells Access that the secondary sort for the database will be on the First Name field. This is necessary because if we had two clients with the same last name, we would then want Access to sort the data based on the client's first name.

Query Wizard icon

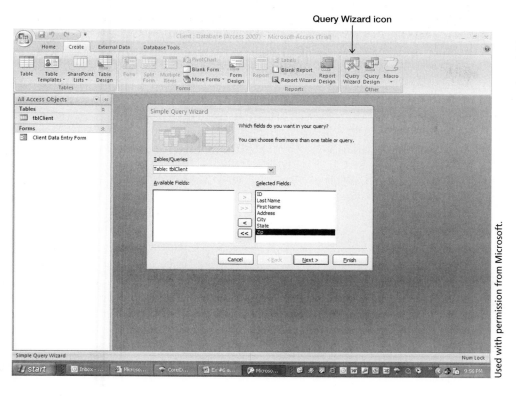

ACCESS 2007
EXHIBIT 7
Creating a query with
the Query Wizard

Run Query icon

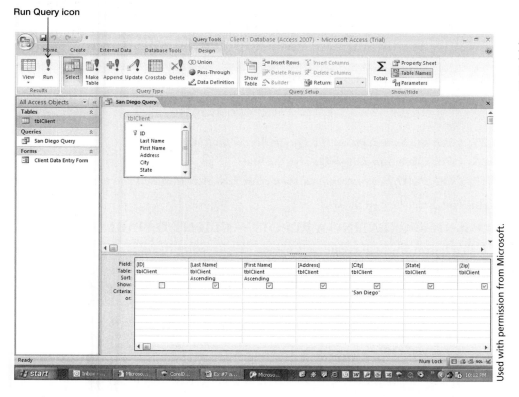

ACCESS 2007
EXHIBIT 8
Modifying a query in
Design view

19. **Click the Criteria row under City.** Type **"San Diego"** (*Note: You must type the quotation marks*—see Access 2007 Exhibit 8).

20. This tells Access to select only those clients that have "San Diego" entered in the City field.

21. *Click the Save icon on the Quick Access toolbar.* This will save the query.

22. *Click the Run command on the toolbar* (the icon that looks like a red exclamation mark). This will run the query.

**ACCESS 2007
EXHIBIT 9**
Results of the San Diego query

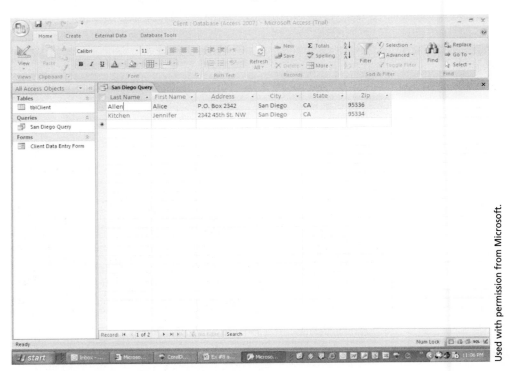

23. Two records should now be displayed on your screen, Alice Allen and Jennifer Kitchen (see Access 2007 Exhibit 9).

24. *Click the Office button, then Print, and then click OK* to print the query results.

25. *Click the Save icon on the Quick Access toolbar.*

26. *Click Close San Diego Query* (the black "X").

27. *Click the Office button and then click Exit Access to exit the program.*

This concludes Lesson 3.

LESSON 4: CREATING A REPORT—CLIENT DATABASE

In this lesson you will create and print a report using the database you created in Lessons 1–3.

1. Open Windows. When it has loaded, *double-click the Microsoft Office Access 2007 icon on the desktop* to open Access 2007 for Windows. Alternatively, *click the Start button, point to Programs or All Programs, and then click the Microsoft Access 2007 icon* (or *point to Microsoft Office and then click Microsoft Office Access 2007).*

2. *Click the Office button* (see Access 2007 Exhibit 1). *Then, under Recent Documents, click on the name of the client file you created in Lessons 1 and 2 (Client.accdb).*

3. If a security warning (for example, **"Security Warning: Certain content in the database has been disabled"**) is displayed just under the ribbon, *click Options… next to the security warning. Then, in the "Microsoft Office Security Options" window, click Enable this Content and then click OK.*

Report Wizard

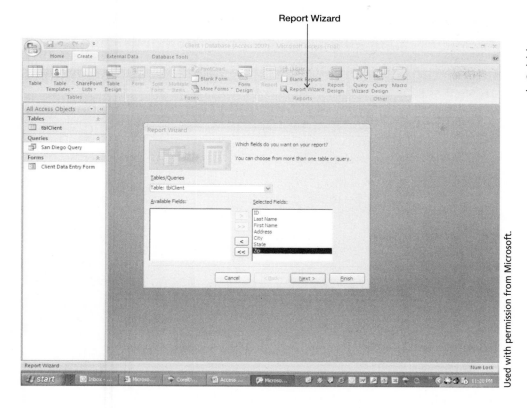

**ACCESS 2007
EXHIBIT 10**
Creating a report with
the Report Wizard

There is no security problem, because you know the content came from a
trustworthy source, as you are the one who created the file.

4. Notice that the "tblClient:Table" file you created in Lesson 1, the client data
entry form you created in Lesson 2, and the San Diego query you created in
Lesson 3 are listed on the Navigation pane.

5. *Click the Create ribbon tab and then click Report Wizard in the Reports
group.*

6. You should now have the "Report Wizard" window on your screen.

7. Under Tables/Queries in the "Report Wizard" window, *click the down arrow
icon and make sure that* **"Table:tbl Client"** *is selected.* (*Note*: If **"Query: San
Diego Sort"** is selected, your report will run, but it will only pull the records
for clients living in San Diego. This is how users can combine queries and
reports. Because we want a list of all clients, make sure the "Table:tbl Client"
file is selected).

8. *Click the >> icon* (two "greater than" signs). This will select all of the fields for
our report (see Access 2007 Exhibit 10). *Then, click Next.*

9. You will then be asked **"Do you want to add any grouping levels?"** You do
not, so *click Next.*

10. You will then be asked **"What sort order do you want for your report?"** *Click
on the down arrow button on the 1 field and then select Last Name* (see
Access 2007 Exhibit 11). Notice that it defaults to an ascending sort.

11. *Click the down arrow button next to the 2 field, and then select First Name*
(see Access 2007 Exhibit 11).

12. *Select Next.*

13. You will then be asked how you would like to lay out the report. *Click Tabular
and then select Next.*

**ACCESS 2007
EXHIBIT 11**
Sorting a report in the
Report Wizard

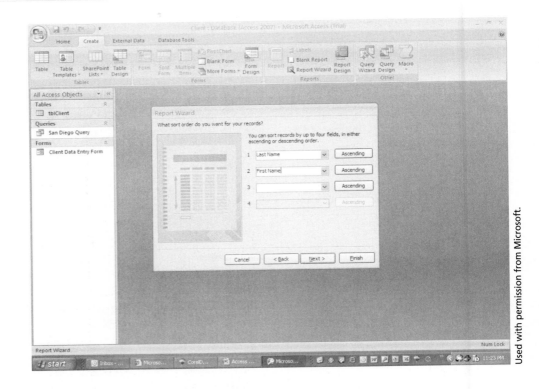

14. You will then be asked **"What style would you like?"** *Click Trek and then select Next.*

15. You are then asked **"What title do you want for your report?"** Type **Client Report.** You want to preview the report, so *click Finish.*

16. The report with the five clients is then displayed on your screen (see Access 2007 Exhibit 12).

17. *Click the Office button, then click Print, and then click OK to print the document.*

**ACCESS 2007
EXHIBIT 12**
Print preview of client
report

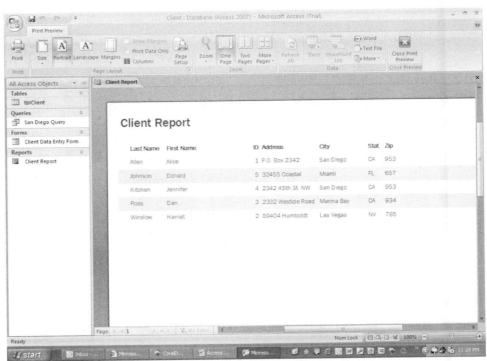

18. *Click the Save icon on the Quick Access toolbar.*
19. *Click the Close icon* (the black "X").
20. *Click the Office button and then click Exit Access to exit the program.*

This concludes Lesson 4.

LESSON 5: CREATING A LITIGATION SUPPORT DATABASE

This lesson shows you how to build a new litigation support database from scratch, including creating a table, entering fields, creating a form, entering data, sorting the database, building a query, and producing a report.

1. Open Windows. When it has loaded, *double-click the Microsoft Office Access 2007 icon on the desktop* to open Access 2007 for Windows. Alternatively, *click the Start button, point to Programs or All Programs, and then click the Microsoft Access 2007 icon* (or *point to Microsoft Office and then click Microsoft Office Access 2007*).

2. *Click on Blank Database. . . just under the New Blank Database section.*

3. Notice that the right side of the screen now says **"Blank Database."** *Click under File Name,* use the **[DEL]** key to delete the current title, and type **Litigation Support**. To save the new database in the default directory, *click Create.* To browse to where you would like to save the new database, *click the Browse icon* (it looks like an open file folder with an arrow) *just to the right of the file name. Then, select the directory or folder you would like to save the file to,* type **Litigation support** next to **"File name,"** *and then click OK. Finally, click Create.*

4. You should now have a blank table on the screen.

5. The Table Tools – Datasheet ribbon tab should already be displayed. *Click View in the Views group to go to Design View.*

6. The "Save As" window should now be displayed. Under Table Name, type **Documents** and then *click OK.*

7. Notice that Access has created a field named "ID" and designated it as an AutoNumber data type. Press the **[TAB]** key three times to accept this and move to the second row.

8. Enter the following fields/information into the table:

Field Name	Data Type	Description	Field Size	Required
Doc Name	Text	Name of document	50	Yes
Doc Type	Text	Type of document	50	Yes
Doc Date	Date/Time	Date of document	—	Yes
Doc Author	Text	Author of document	50	Yes
Doc Number	Number	Internal document ID number	Long Integer	Yes
Primary Recipient	Text	Who the document was to	50	Yes
Subject Matter	Text	Subject of document	75	Yes
Issue Code	Number	Internal code	Long Integer	No
Notes	Memo	Coder's notes about document	—	No
Key Evidence	Yes/No	Is this a key piece of evidence in the case?	—	Yes

ACCESS 2007 EXHIBIT 13
Creating fields for a litigation support database

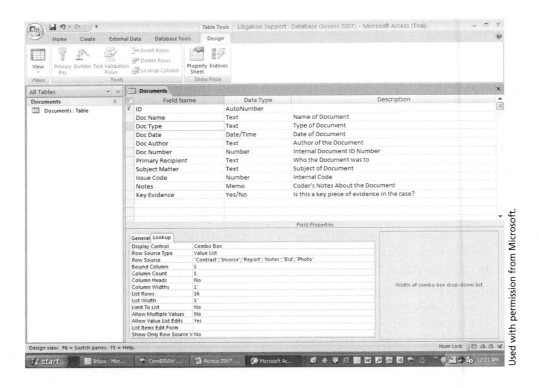

9. *Click Doc Type again in the Field Name column. Then, click the Lookup tab* (just to the right of the General tab). Access 2007 Exhibit 13 shows the changes you will be making to the Lookup tab for the Doc Type field.

10. *Under the Lookup tab to the right of Display Control, click Text Box. Click the down arrow to the right of Text Box. Click Combo Box.* Notice that a number of other options are now available on the Lookup tab (see Access 2007 Exhibit 13).

11. *To the right of Row Source Type, click Table/Query. Click the down arrow to the right of Table/Query. Click Value List.*

12. *Click the blank box to the right of Row Source* and type **"Contract"; "Invoice"; "Report"; "Notes"; "Bid"; "Photo."** *Note: You must type the quotation marks* (see Access 2007 Exhibit 13). When you enter data into the table (either directly or with a form), these choices will appear in a drop-down box for you to select; this is a good way of creating data uniformity and consistency.

13. *Click in the blank box to the right of Column Widths,* then type **1"** (you must include the quotation mark).

14. *Click Auto next to List Width.* Use the **[DEL]** key to delete "Auto," and then type **1"** (you must include the quotation mark).

15. *Click the Save icon on the Quick Access toolbar.*

16. You are currently in Table Design View. The Table Tools – Design ribbon tab should already be displayed. *Click View in the Views group* to go to Datasheet View.

17. *Click on the Close icon ("X") in the Field List task pane on the right side of the screen.*

18. You should now see the fields you just created displayed horizontally across the screen. To see all of your fields, you will need to use the scroll bar at the bottom

of the screen or your cursor keys. You can toggle back and forth between Design View and Datasheet View by *clicking on the View icon on the Home ribbon tab.*

19. *Click the Save icon on the Quick Access toolbar.*

20. *Click the Close Documents icon* (the black "X").

21. You are now ready to create a data entry form for entering data into the table. You must first *click Documents:Table under All Tables and under Documents* so that Access knows the table with which the new form will be associated.

22. *Click the Create ribbon tab, and then click Form in the Forms group.*

23. The form should now be displayed on your screen. Your screen should look similar to Access 2007 Exhibit 14. The default form is fine, and no modifications are necessary. If you would like to change the colors of the form, do so by selecting one of the AutoFormats on the ribbon.

24. *Click the Save icon on the Quick Access toolbar.* The "Save As" window should now be displayed. Under Form Name, type **Doc Data Entry Form Smith vs EZ Pest Control** and then *click OK.* You are currently in Layout View. To switch to Form View so you can enter data into the table/form, *click the down arrow under the View icon on the ribbon* (the Form Layout Tools – Format ribbon tab should already be selected), *and then click Form View.*

25. Enter the records from the table into the database. You can go between fields by pressing the **[TAB]** or **[SHIFT]+[TAB]** keys, or by pointing and clicking with the mouse. Notice in the Doc Type field that there is a drop-down menu with choices you can select. Because it is a "combo box," you can also enter text into the field, but for this exercise, we will just select entries from the drop-down menu. Notice also in the Key Evidence field that if the document is a key piece of evidence, you just need to click in the box and a check mark will appear. When you are at the last field you can go to the next record by pressing **[TAB]**. You can also go between records by pressing the **[PAGE UP]** or **[PAGE**

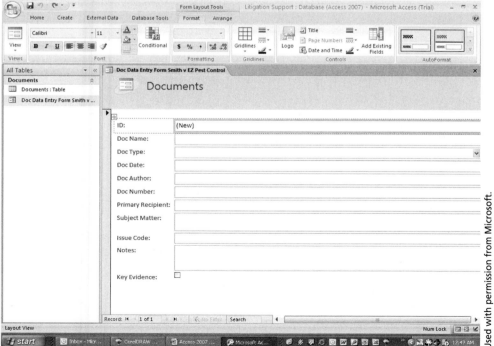

**ACCESS 2007
EXHIBIT 14**
Litigation support data entry form

Doc Name	Doc Type	Doc Date	Doc Author	Doc No	Primary Recipient	Subject Matter	Issue Code	Notes	Key Evidence
HUD Settlement Statement	Contract	06/01/2007	Judy Smith, Bill Lee	501	Judy Smith	Sale of house	1	Includes pest inspection cost of $300	Yes
EZ Pest Agreement for Termite Inspection	Contract	05/01/2007	John Lincoln, EZ Pest	502	Judy Smith	Agreement to inspect the house for termites	1	The contract states that EZ Pest will conduct a thorough examination of the property.	Yes
EZ Pest Invoice for Pest Inspection	Invoice	05/15/2007	John Lincoln, EZ Pest	503	Judy Smith	Invoice for pest inspection	1	Shows total due $300 and that it was paid on 5/20/2007	No
EZ Pest Inspection Report	Report	05/15/2007	John Lincoln, EZ Pest	504	Judy Smith	Inspection Report	2	The report states "No visible evidence of infestation from wood destroying insects was observed." Signed by John Lincoln.	Yes
EZ Pest Inspection Report Notes	Notes	05/07/2007	John Lincoln, EZ Pest	505	John Lincoln	Notes of John Lincoln taken to assist in preparation of Inspection Report	2	John Lincoln's notes do not show that he actually checked the east side of the house where termites were later found.	Yes
Bid from Stewart Construction	Bid	11/01/2007	Tim Stewart	506	Judy Smith	Bid to rebuild the east side where the termites destroyed house	3	Bid of $50,000 to repair the termite damage on the east side.	Yes
Photograph of east side of house	Photo	10/01/2007	Judy Smith	507	Judy Smith	Photograph of house	3	Photograph showing east side of house behind vinyl siding showing frame of house nearly eaten through.	Yes

DOWN] keys or by pointing and clicking on the "greater than" and "less than" symbols at the bottom of the page.

26. When you have finished entering all of the data, ***click the Save icon on the Quick Access toolbar.***

27. ***Click the Close Doc Data Entry Form Smith v EZ Pest Control*** (the black "X").

28. ***Click All Tables on the Navigation pane and click Object Type.*** You can now see the "Documents" table under Tables and "Doc Data Entry Form Smith v . . ." ***under Forms.***

29. ***Double-click Documents under Tables in the Navigation pane.***

30. You should now see your fields displayed horizontally across the screen (although, due to the length of the entries, you may not be able to see all of the data). Use the scroll bar at the bottom of the screen to scroll left and right to see all of the fields (see Access 2007 Exhibit 15).

31. ***Click on the Save icon on the Quick Access toolbar.***

32. You will next see some different views of the data (without damaging the integrity of the data).

33. ***Click any record in the Doc Name field. Then, on the Home ribbon tab, click the Sort Ascending icon in the Sort & Filter group*** (it looks like the letter "A" on top of the letter "Z" with a down arrow next to them). (*Note:* Point to any icon on the toolbar for a second and the name of the icon will be displayed.) Your records should now be sorted alphabetically by document name.

34. ***Click any record in the Doc Date field and then click the Sort Descending icon on the toolbar.*** The documents are now sorted in date order, with the most recent first.

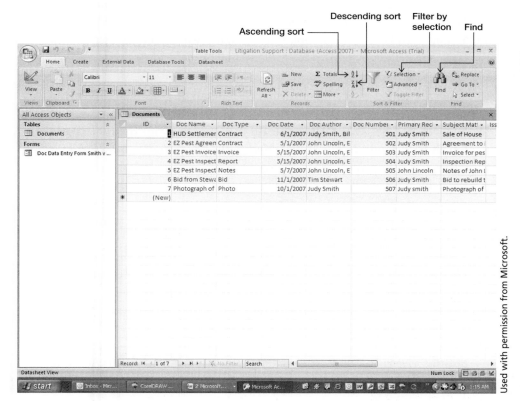

**ACCESS 2007
EXHIBIT 15**
Datasheet view of data in the documents table

35. *Click any record in the Subject Matter field, and then click the Find icon in the Find group on the Home ribbon tab* (it looks like binoculars). The "Find and Replace" window should be displayed. Next to Find What, type **vinyl siding** and then, next to Look In, *click the down arrow and select Documents.* (This will allow you to search all fields in the Document table, not just the Subject Matter field.) *Then, next to Match, click the down arrow, click Any Part of Field, and then click Find Next.* Notice that the pointer went to document 507 and found where "vinyl siding" was entered. *Click Cancel to make the "Find and Replace" window disappear.*

36. *Click Document 502 and click in the Primary Recipient field.* Notice that "Judy Smith" is in the field. *Click the Filter by Selection icon in the Sort & Filter group in the Home ribbon tab* (it looks like a silver funnel with a lightning bolt—see Access 2007 Exhibit 15), *then click Equals "Judy Smith."* Notice that only documents with Judy Smith as the primary recipient are left. (The other documents are still in the database; Access just temporarily removed them from the current view.)

37. To bring back all of the documents, remove the filter by *clicking the Toggle Filter icon in the Sort & Filter group on the Home ribbon tab.* Notice that all of the documents are back.

38. To put the documents back in the order in which you entered them, simply *click in the Doc Number field and click the Sort Ascending icon.*

39. *Click the Save icon on the Quick Access toolbar.*

40. *Click the Close Documents icon* (the black "X").

41. You will now run a query to select only documents that have Issue Code 2 in them, and where Judy Smith was the recipient. The Documents table under Tables on the Navigation pane should still be selected. *Click the Create ribbon tab, then click Query Wizard in the Other group.*

42. You should now have the "New Query" window displayed on your screen. Simple Query Wizard should be selected, *so click OK.*

43. You should now have the "Simple Query Wizard" window on your screen. *Click >>* (two "greater than" signs). This will select all of the fields for your query.

44. *Click Next.*

45. You will then be asked **"Would you like a detail or a summary query?"** *Click Detail* (shows every field of every record). *Click Next.*

46. You will then be asked **"What title do you want for your query?"** Type **qry Smith Issue Code 2**. *Then, click Modify the query design and click Finish.*

47. The query is displayed on your screen. Notice that each column shows one of the fields in the table.

48. *Click in the Show row in the ID column* (the first column). There should now be an empty box (no check mark). This is because we do not want this to show on our query.

49. *Click in the Sort row under Doc Number. Now, click the down arrow and click Ascending.* This tells Access that the primary sort for the database will be on this field.

50. *Click in the Criteria row under Issue Code,* then type **2**. (*Note: Do not* type anything else in the criteria for this field—just type the number 2.)

51. *Then, click in the Criteria row under Primary Recipient* and type "**Judy Smith.**" (*Note:* You *must* type the quotes for this field.) This tells Access to select only those records that meet both of these selection/search criteria.

52. ***Click the Run icon in the Results group on the Query Tools – Design ribbon tab*** (the icon that looks like a red exclamation mark). This will run the query. Document 504 should be displayed.

53. ***Click the Save icon on the Quick Access toolbar.***

54. ***Click the down arrow just under the View icon in the Views group on the Home ribbon tab and then select Design View. Click back and forth between Design View and Datasheet View.*** Notice that you can make changes to the query in Design View, and then run the query and correct any problems that you may have had in your query.

55. In Datasheet View, ***click the Office button, and then click Print and OK.*** Notice that the whole record did not print.

56. ***Click the Save icon on the Quick Access toolbar.***

57. ***Click the Close "qry Smith Issue Code 2" icon*** (the black "X").

58. ***Click the Create ribbon tab, and then click Report Wizard.*** You should now have the "Report Wizard" window on your screen.

59. ***Click under Tables/Queries on the down arrow button and select "Query: qry Smith Issue Code 2."***

60. ***Click the >> icon*** (two "greater than" signs). This will select all of the fields for our report. ***Click Next.***

61. You will then be asked **"Do you want to add any grouping levels?"** ***Click Next.***

62. You will then be asked **"What sort order do you want for your report?"** ***Click Next.***

63. You will then be asked **"How would you like to lay out your report?"** ***Click Justified, then click Landscape, and then select Next.***

64. You will then be asked **"What style would you like?"** ***Click Civic and then select Next.***

65. You are then asked **"What title do you want for your report?"** Type **Judy Smith Primary Recipient—Issue Code 2 Report.**

66. ***Click Finish.***

67. The report should now be displayed on your screen.

68. ***Click the Office button, then click Print, and then click OK to print the document.***

69. ***Click the Save icon on the Quick Access toolbar.***

70. ***Click the Close Judy Smith Primary Recipient—Issue Code 2 Report icon*** (the black "X").

71. ***Click the Office button and then click Exit Access to exit the program.***

This concludes Lesson 5.

LESSON 6: WORKING WITH A COMPREHENSIVE LAW-OFFICE RELATIONAL DATABASE

In this lesson, you will work with a true relational database, including working with multiple tables, assigning relationships among tables, and writing queries and reports that access data from multiple tables. This lesson assumes that you have read Chapter 5–Database Management Systems, and that you have completed Lessons 1–5. To begin, you will open the Access Lesson 6 Law Firm Database from disk supplied with the text and work with a database with four related tables in it.

1. Open Windows. When it has loaded, ***double-click the Microsoft Office Access 2007 icon on the desktop*** to open Access 2007 for Windows. Alternatively,

rows where the joined fields from both tables are equal," is selected. ***Then, click OK in the "Join Properties" window.***

13. ***In the "Edit Relationships" window, click Create.*** Your relationships window should now look like Access 2007 Exhibit 16.

14. ***Click Close on the Relationship Tools—Design ribbon tab (in the Relationships group.)***

15. You will now build a query that pulls information from three of the tables.

16. ***Click the Create ribbon tab, and then click Query Wizard in the Other group.***

17. The "New Query" window should now be displayed. **"Simple Query Wizard"** should be highlighted, so just ***click OK.***

18. The screen should now say **"Which fields do you want in your query?"** Under Tables/Queries, ***click the down arrow and select Table: Client.*** Notice that now the fields for the Client table are shown under Available Fields. ***Click Last Name and then click > to add the field under Selected Fields.*** You will now build the query by selecting the tables and fields exactly as shown below. This should be done carefully, because you must skip around among the different tables to build the query correctly.

In addition to the Last Name field you have already selected, enter the following:

TABLE	FIELD TO SELECT
Client	First Name
Case File	Case Name
Case File	Case Type
Case File	Court
Case File	Judge
Opposing Attorney	Last Name
Case File	Assigned Attorney
Case File	Assigned Paralegal

When completed, your screen should look similar to Access 2007 Exhibit 18. Note that the last selected field (Assigned Paralegal) is not shown on Access 2007 Exhibit 18, but it is still present in the query.

19. ***Click Next.***

20. You will then be asked **"Would you like a detail or a summary query?"** The Detail (shows every field of every record) option should already be selected, so just ***click Next.***

21. You will then be asked **"What title do you want for your query?"** Type **Case List Query**. ***Then, click Modify the query design and click Finish.***

22. The query is displayed on your screen in Design View. Notice that each column shows one of the fields and that the table that it is drawn from is shown in the Table row (see Access 2007 Exhibit 19).

23. ***Click on the Sort row in the first column (Client_Last Name:Las) and then click the down arrow and click Ascending*** (see Access 2007 Exhibit 19)***.*** This tells Access that the primary sort for the database will be on this field.

24. ***Click the Sort row in the second column (First Name), and then click the down arrow button and click Ascending*** (see Access 2007 Exhibit 19)***.*** This tells Access that the secondary sort for the database will be on this field.

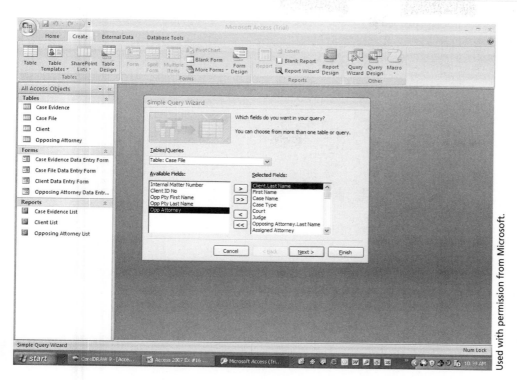

Used with permission from Microsoft.

**ACCESS 2007
EXHIBIT 18**
Building a query with
multiple tables in the
Query Wizard

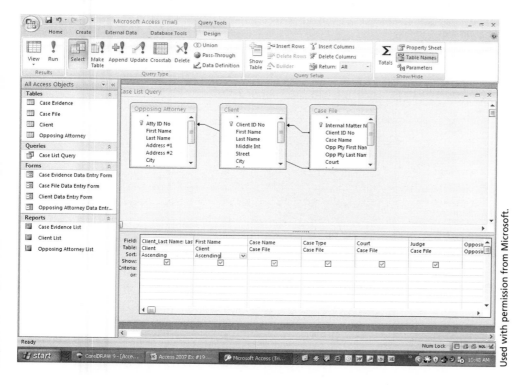

Used with permission from Microsoft.

**ACCESS 2007
EXHIBIT 19**
Modifying the case list
query in Query Design
view

25. *Click the !Run icon* (it looks like a bright red exclamation mark) *in the Results group on the Query Tools – Design ribbon tab.* Your query should look similar to Access 2007 Exhibit 20.

26. *Click the Save icon* (it look like a floppy disk) *on the Quick Access toolbar.*

27. *Click the Close icon for the Case List query* (see Access 2007 Exhibit 20).

ACCESS 2007
EXHIBIT 20
Completed case list
query in Datasheet view

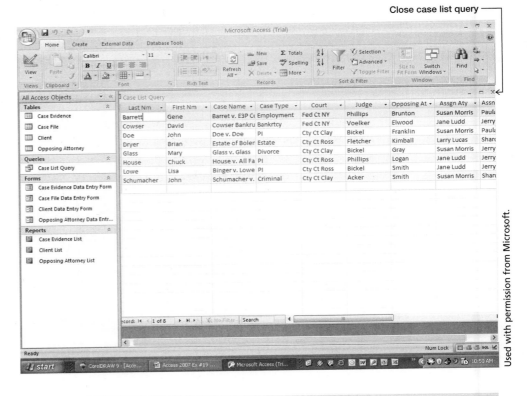

Used with permission from Microsoft.

ACCESS 2007
EXHIBIT 21
Finalized case list report

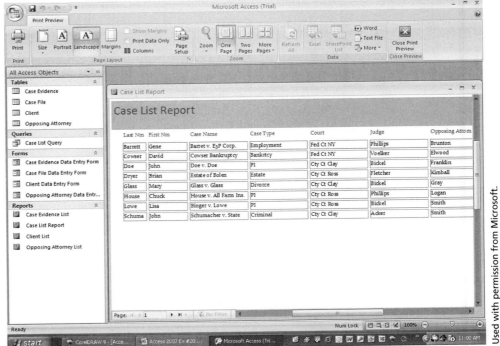

Used with permission from Microsoft.

28. You will now build a report that uses the Case List query you just created.

29. ***Click the Create ribbon tab, and then click Report Wizard in the Reports group.*** The "Report Wizard" window should now be displayed.

30. Under Tables/Queries, ***click the down arrow and select Query: Case List Query. Then, click the >> (two "greater than" symbols) to add all of the fields in the Case List Query to the report.***

31. *Click Next.*

32. You will then be asked **"How do you want to view your data?"** *Click Next.*

33. You will then be asked **"Do you want to add any grouping levels?"** *Click Next.*

34. You will then be asked **"What sort order do you want for detail records?"** Because the query is already sorting the data, *click Next.*

35. You are now asked **"How would you like to lay out your report?"** *Click Block and then click Landscape under Orientation. Leave the check mark in the Adjust the field width so all fields fit on a page option. Then, select Next.*

36. You will then be asked **"What style would you like?"** *Click Flow, then click Next.*

37. You are then asked **"What title would you like for the report?"** Type **Case List Report,** leave the Preview the report option selected, and *click Finish.*

38. The report should now be displayed on your screen. It should look similar to Access 2007 Exhibit 21.

39. *Click the Print icon on the ribbon tab in the Print group. Then, click OK to print the document.*

40. *Click Close Print Preview on the ribbon tab in the Close Preview group.*

41. *Click the Save icon on the Quick Access toolbar.*

42. *Click the Close icon for the Case List Report* (the black "X").

43. *Click the Office button and then click Exit Access to exit the program.*

This concludes the Access 2007 Hands-On Exercises.

CHAPTER 6

The Electronic Courthouse, Automated Courtroom, and Presentation Graphics

CHAPTER OBJECTIVES

After completing this chapter, you should be able to do the following:

1. Explain what the "electronic courthouse" is.
2. Describe how an automated courtroom works.
3. Describe what presentation software does.
4. Explain how presentation software can be used in the legal environment.

INTRODUCTION

The courthouses of the past, with paper files and manual systems, have changed. Electronic courthouses, which allow electronic filing of court documents and access to court records, dockets, files, and other data via the Internet, are a reality in many jurisdictions. Courtrooms have changed as well. In many jurisdictions, automated courtrooms have evidence display systems, which include computers and monitors for the judge, attorneys, court reporter, jurors, and the public. In these automated courtrooms, presentation graphics and trial presentation software are used to present evidence to the court and jurors electronically, using computers and monitors. The presentations can include text, photographs, video, animation, sound, clip art, re-creations of scenes or actions, and much more.

THE ELECTRONIC COURTHOUSE

The notion of the local courthouse as a place to which legal professionals must mail documents, or where they must hand-file documents and access court records and court files using manual methods, is rapidly disappearing. In many jurisdictions, legal professionals can now instantly file motions, briefs, and other documents electronically, and can instantly access court dockets and court records using the Internet. With electronic filing, courts accept electronic versions of legal documents via the Internet or other electronic means instead of requiring a hard copy of the document to be physically presented.

The federal district and bankruptcy courts have been on the cutting edge of this technology for several years. As of this writing, the Case Management/Electronic Case Filing (CM/ECF) system is used in more than 98 percent of the federal courts:

93 district courts, 93 bankruptcy courts, the Court of International Trade, the Court of Federal Claims, and 10 of the United States Courts of Appeals. To date, more than 27 million cases have been put on the CM/ECF system. More than 250,000 legal professionals have filed documents using the Internet and CM/ECF. The plan is for all United States courts to convert to use of CM/ECF in the near future.

Filing documents using the system is easy. The user logs onto a court's website with a court-issued password, enters some general information about the case and the document to be filed, and then submits the document to be filed in Portable Document Format (PDF). Once the PDF file is received, a notice of receipt is generated and sent to the user. Other parties to the action then automatically receive an email notifying them of the filing. The CM/ECF system also gives courts the option to make filed documents accessible to the public over the Internet.

Another federal system, the Public Access to Court Electronic Records (PACER) program, allows the public to access court-related information (see Exhibit 6–1). PACER is an electronic public access service that allows users to obtain a variety of docket and case-related information regarding federal courts using the Internet. Links to all courts are provided from the PACER website. To access PACER, a user must register with the PACER Service Center, have an Internet connection, and log into the system. There is also a small charge for the service. PACER allows users to request information about an individual or case, including:

- Party and participant listings, including attorneys and judges
- General case-related data, including the nature of the lawsuit, the cause(s) of action alleged, and the amount of damages requested
- A chronology of events/docket items in the case
- The case status
- Judgment(s) and appeals

Using PACER, a person can also access the United States Case/Party Index, which allows one to search for party names throughout much of the federal court system.

Although the federal court system is rapidly nearing the end of its electronic courthouse implementation project, it may take some years for all the states to catch up. Some states have completed the move to electronic systems, but many are still

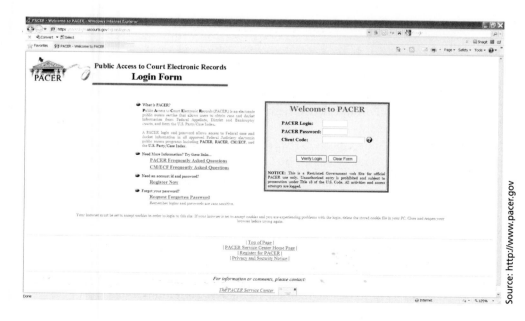

EXHIBIT 6–1

Public Access to Court Electronic Records (PACER)

Source: http://www.pacer.gov

EXHIBIT 6–2
Internet Access to the
Oklahoma State Courts
Network

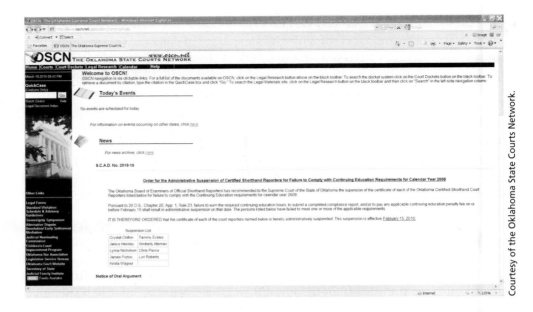

Courtesy of the Oklahoma State Courts Network.

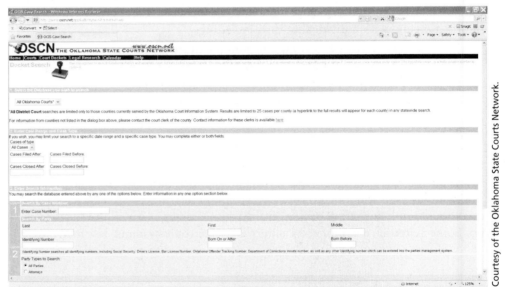

Courtesy of the Oklahoma State Courts Network.

moving through the implementation stage. Traditional roadblocks to these types of systems include cost, standardization issues, security, and obtaining the hardware and software needed to support electronic filing. Like the federal court system, many state courts have selected Portable Document Format (PDF) as their standard for filing documents electronically.

The Oklahoma State Courts Network (www.oscn.net) is a good example of state implementation of this technology. The Oklahoma State Courts Network allows users to access court dockets statewide, including the Oklahoma Supreme Court, the Court of Criminal Appeals, the Court of Civil Appeals, and 77 district courts (see Exhibit 6–2).

Electronic services such as Westlaw and LexisNexis also have access to some court dockets and can electronically track document filings in cases and access court records. Some of these services even automatically alert the legal professional (electronically) to new filings in cases, at intervals such as once a week or twice a week. Although a legal organization must pay the vendor for these services (as opposed to getting them free when states or courts implement the program), many legal organizations find it worth the cost.

THE AUTOMATED COURTROOM

In addition to automating access to the courthouse, many courts are also automating their courtrooms. Most automated courtrooms include evidence display systems, videoconferencing, and real-time court reporting.

An **evidence display system** typically provides networked computer monitors to the judge, jurors, court reporter, clerk, attorneys, and the public. The master controls are located at the judge's bench so that he or she can control all monitors, sound systems, and/or cameras in the courtroom. The attorneys and/or judge can use the evidence display system to display properly admitted evidence such as images, photographs, video images, animations, and others. Most systems also include a **document camera**, an overhead projector that uses a camera to display hard-copy documents that have not been imaged.

Many evidence display systems also support videoconferencing. With this capability, if a judge approves the use, a witness could testify at a trial without being physically present in the courtroom.

Another extremely useful courtroom technology is real-time court reporting. With this system, a witness's testimony, as transcribed by a court reporter, becomes available within a few seconds after utterance of the testimony. The testimony can be displayed on the courtroom monitors or transmitted to the judge, jurors, or attorneys on a real-time basis.

It is now routine for trial attorneys to present opening statements and closing arguments, cross-examine witnesses, and display evidence using electronic means such as presentation graphics software or trial presentation software. These presentations are made in front of the jury using automated courtroom equipment.

The automated courtroom thus offers many advantages over a manual one. Electronic presentations and evidence can be viewed by everyone in the courtroom simultaneously (so that everyone can see the same thing at the same time). Electronic presentation of evidence can simplify complex subjects and add to the ability of judges, jurors, and others to comprehend and understand the issues and facts in a case. For years, educators have known that people remember far more of what they see than of what they merely hear. Combining these two sensory modes enhances both comprehension and understanding of the material presented.

The automated courtroom is also more convenient than manual methods and actually saves court time. For example, if an attorney images all of her exhibits to be admitted for trial, they can then be electronically displayed; there is no need to rely on or shuffle through hard-copy documents, which can be lost or damaged. Computer software that automatically tracks trial exhibits, in addition to displaying them using the evidence display system, can also save time for everyone involved. In some courts, criminal defendants who are too hostile to appear in court can view the proceedings offsite via a live video/audio feed. Using presentation graphics and trial presentation programs, legal professionals are able to get the most out of automated courtroom equipment.

OVERVIEW OF PRESENTATION AND TRIAL PRESENTATION SOFTWARE

Presentation software allows users to create visually interesting electronic presentations. Many legal professionals use generic presentation graphics programs, such as Microsoft PowerPoint, to create presentations for trials, such as exhibits, graphs, and charts, as well as presentations for internal training purposes or public seminars. Using presentation software, one can combine a number of elements to create visually interesting presentations, including text, color, video, animation, clip art, graphs,

---

evidence display system
Technology that provides networked computer monitors to a judge, jury, court reporter, clerk, attorneys, and the public.

document camera
An overhead projector that uses a camera to display hard-copy documents that have not been imaged.

charts, and sound. A user builds a presentation by organizing evidence, transcripts, images, photographs, and other materials into individual slides; the software then gives the user the options of showing all the slides at one time, or controlling the timing of presentation with a remote control. Most presentation programs can also create outlines and speaker's notes.

In addition to generic presentation programs, there are **trial presentation programs** that have been specifically designed to meet the needs of practicing attorneys, particularly those who try cases to juries and courts. TrialDirector and Sanction are examples of trial presentation programs designed specifically for the legal market.

Trial presentation programs can do much more than just display electronic slides. Some trial presentation programs can manage documents, including maintaining document abstracts and tracking: who admitted the document (plaintiff or defendant); the Bates number of the document; the date the document was admitted into evidence; the witness who was on the stand when the document was admitted; the status of the document, including whether introduction of the document was objected to; and other information (see Exhibit 6–3). Even in relatively small cases, managing and tracking all the documents in a trial can be difficult and time-consuming. Trial presentation programs can automate that process in addition to displaying electronic documents.

Trial presentation programs can manage complex tasks, such as combining video/audio, graphs, and documents into a single slide or presenting these materials individually (see Exhibit 6–4). Trial presentation software also can synchronize the playback of video/audio with a transcript of prior testimony, so that a factfinder can not only read the words of the transcript, but can also see and hear the witness speaking the words. Trial presentation programs can also display presentations in applications such as Microsoft PowerPoint.

Notably, trial presentation programs can access data nonsequentially. PowerPoint works well when everything is linear and goes straight from beginning to end. However, most trials do not proceed this way. Attorneys need to be able to produce a particular document on a moment's notice. Trial presentation programs can access data quickly and conveniently, unlike PowerPoint. In addition, most trial presentation programs have the ability to search the trial database and access data quickly and efficiently. Generally speaking, trial presentation programs are quite powerful and are better suited to most trial purposes than generic presentation programs.

trial presentation programs
Presentation graphics programs specifically designed to meet the needs of trial attorneys.

EXHIBIT 6–3
Some trial presentation programs can manage documents.

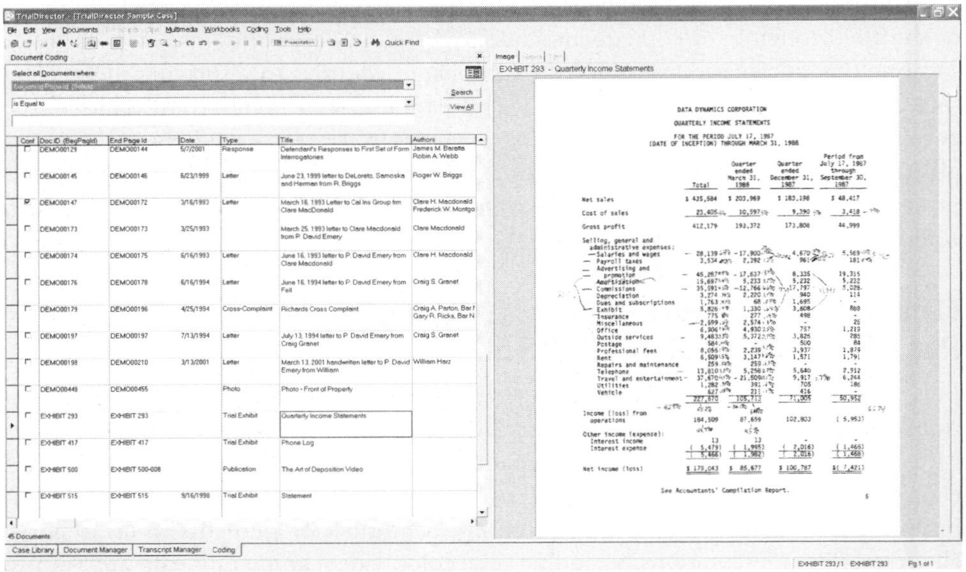

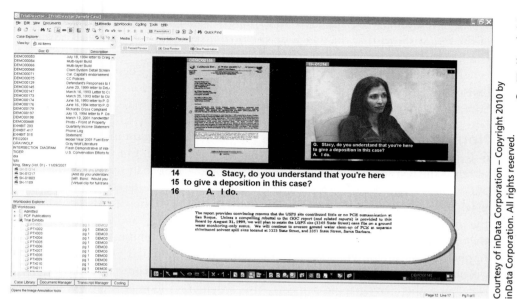

EXHIBIT 6–4
Trial presentation software can manage both video and documentary material.

CREATING LEGAL PRESENTATIONS WITH MICROSOFT POWERPOINT

It is quite easy to create legal presentations with general presentation software like Microsoft PowerPoint. In this chapter, we walk through the process of creating an opening statement for a case using the interface of Microsoft PowerPoint 2007.

The Screen and Views

Exhibit 6–5 shows the title page for the opening statement presentation. Notice that, as in any Microsoft Office 2007 program, the ribbon bar, Office button, title bar, and

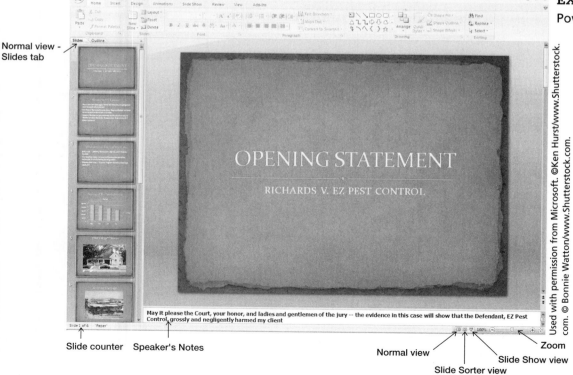

EXHIBIT 6–5
PowerPoint 2007 slide

Quick Access toolbar are displayed. In Exhibit 6–5, the slide counter in the lower left of the screen shows that the user is on the first of six slides. This helpful feature lets you know at all times where you are in the presentation.

Three icons are displayed at the lower right of the screen. These three icons represent the different ways the user can view or see this presentation: Normal view, Slide Sorter view, and Slide Show view.

Normal View   The Normal view for this particular program is shown in Exhibit 6–6. The **normal view** shows the slide that is being created. On the left side of the screen is the text for all the slides in this presentation. Notice in Exhibit 6–5 that the Slides tab is selected. In Normal view, you can select either Slides or the Outline display mode (see the upper left of Exhibit 6–6). Exhibit 6–6 shows the second slide of the presentation; this time the slide is shown in Normal view and the Outline tab in the upper left of the window is selected. The outline portion of the screen, as the name implies, shows an outline of the presentation. Notice in Exhibit 6–6 that the outline portion of the screen shows some of the same information contained in the current slide but without any graphic elements. Also, Exhibit 6–5 shows a section of the screen (under the slide) where you can enter speaker's notes about that particular slide. These can be printed out for reference purposes when you are ready to give the presentation. Speaker's notes can be created for each slide of the presentation.

Slide Sorter View   The **slide sorter view** shows the slides in the presentation, but in a greatly reduced format. The slide sorter view is typically used to review and/or change the order of slides. For example, to move slide 8 in front of slide 3, you would simply click on slide 8 and drag it in front of slide 3. The program will automatically renumber the slides, but you must manually recheck and change cross-references on other slides when you do this. Slide Sorter view gives you a big picture of the presentation and allows you to easily organize or reorganize the presentation.

normal view
PowerPoint screen that shows the slide that is being created, an outline of the total presentation, and speaker's notes for the slide currently displayed.

slide sorter view
PowerPoint screen that shows the slides in the presentation, but in a greatly reduced format; typically used to review and/or change the order of slides.

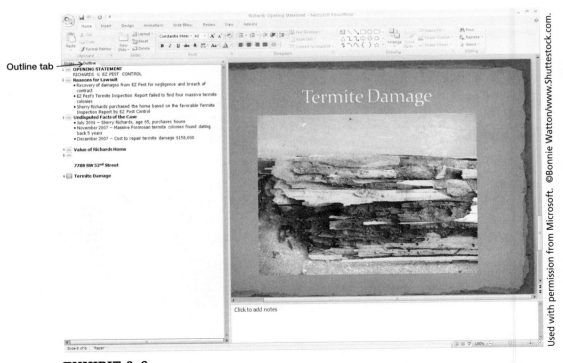

EXHIBIT 6–6
Microsoft PowerPoint Normal view—Outline display mode

Slide Show View The **slide show view** is used during a presentation or when you are developing a presentation and want to learn how the audience will actually see the slide. The only thing shown on the screen is the slide itself. The program interface, outline, and speaker's notes are not shown.

Backgrounds, Adding Slides, and Formatting a Presentation

The first step in creating a presentation is to select the background. The **background** is the design on which the other elements of the presentation (words, clip art, etc.) will be placed. It is similar to the canvas of a painting. PowerPoint comes with several predesigned backgrounds that you can choose from. You can also create your own backgrounds or select backgrounds from Microsoft Office Online.

The next step in creating a presentation is to add slides. PowerPoint 2007 has a New Slide command, found on the Home ribbon (see Exhibit 6–7). The New Slide command gives you a menu of different formats for creating a slide (see Exhibit 6–7). These automatic formats make it easy to select a format and then quickly begin entering the information.

Photographs, Clip Art, Word Art

PowerPoint allows you to include clip art, photographs, and word art in presentations. **Clip art** is predrawn art. Be careful when considering the use of clip art in trial and legal presentations; some clip art actually diminishes the professional appearance of the presentation. Make sure that what you choose is appropriate, well executed, and (most importantly) enhances the impact or comprehensibility of your presentation; never throw in images just for the sake of having a picture.

Notice that the presentation in Exhibit 6–8 includes several clear, high-impact photographs. High-quality photographs can enhance the professionalism of a presentation and create strong visual impact. Word art may also be useful for highlighting material, or for creating a consistent visual theme throughout a presentation. **Word art**

---

slide show view
PowerPoint screen used during a presentation or when the user wants to preview how the audience will actually see the slide. Only the current slide is shown on the screen. The program interface, menus, outline view, and speaker's notes are not shown.

background
The design on which the other elements of the presentation (words, clip art, etc.) are placed.

clip art
Predrawn art.

word art
Feature that allows users to add special formatting to text.

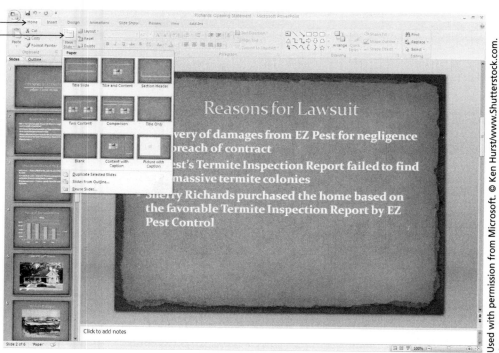

Home tab
New Slide command

Used with permission from Microsoft. © Ken Hurst/www.Shutterstock.com.
©Bonnie Watton/www.Shutterstock.com.

EXHIBIT 6–7
Options for adding a new slide

EXHIBIT 6–8
Photographs in
PowerPoint

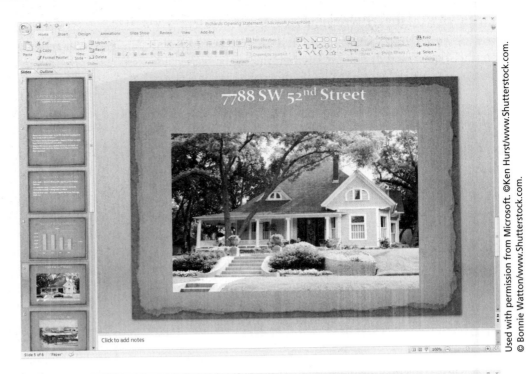

EXHIBIT 6–9
Graph in PowerPoint

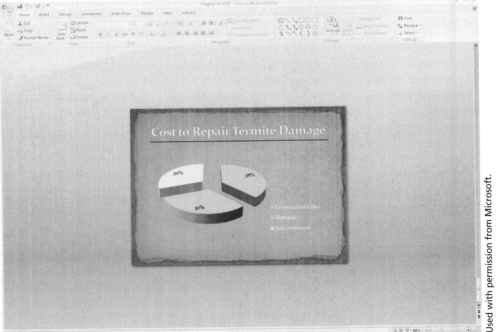

features allow you to add special formatting to text, including three-dimensional (3-D) designs.

Graphs/Charts

PowerPoint allows you to create graphs and charts, either as stand-alone elements (such as a graph for a case) or as part of a presentation. Notice in Exhibit 6–9 that the graph has the same background as the rest of the presentation and that it is in 3-D. Power-Point provides a wide variety of graph and chart formats to choose from, including column charts, bar graphs, and pie charts.

Multimedia, Transition, and Animation Effects

Multimedia effects, such as sound files and video clips, can also be added to presentations, so that sound and video will run whenever the slide is displayed. This can add interest and excitement to a presentation. (It also engages more sensory modalities, so that factfinders are more likely to comprehend and remember the material.)

Another option is a **slide transition** effect, which controls how the program proceeds from one slide to another. For example, you could move from slide 2 to slide 3 and make slide 3 appear on the screen much like horizontal blinds being drawn, with each piece sliding onto the screen individually until the slide is complete. *Animation* refers to other effects, such as how bullet points appear on the screen. You could make bullet points and text "fly" onto the screen individually, either automatically or when the mouse button is pushed. Animation is similar to slide transitions, but it happens within a slide instead of between slides. Again, be careful in using transition and animation effects so as to not diminish the professionalism (or comprehensibility) of the presentation. Always remember that the reason for using any effect is to enhance the impact, interest, and comprehensibility of your presentation, not to show off technological capabilities.

slide transition
Effects that control how the program proceeds from one slide to another.

Displaying a Presentation

PowerPoint allows a presentation to be output in many different formats. These include slide show presentations; printing the presentation in black and white or color; printing it as overhead transparency slides; or exporting it into web-based learning software. In addition, you can print the slides, an outline, speaker's notes, or a combination of these items.

COURTROOM PRESENTATION TIPS

In some legal organizations, the creation of presentations for trials falls to paralegals. Creating and designing trial presentations is different from creating other presentations. In addition, often a paralegal actually operates the computer and presentation/equipment during trial, to allow the attorney(s) to concentrate on litigation. This section offers a variety of tips and tricks related to preparing and showing courtroom presentations.

Test All Computer Equipment in Advance and Have Staff Support

It is impossible to overstate the importance of having the technology used at trial actually work when it is supposed to. If the courtroom is equipped with its own technology, such as a projector and screen, then users only have to ensure that they have the proper cables and other hardware to interface with the court's equipment. If the court is not properly or adequately equipped, then users will have to supply and set up all of the necessary equipment, such as a portable projector, screen, and speakers. Other necessary equipment might include a laptop computer, cables, extension cords, and a printer/scanner/copier.

It is crucial that you test and retest *all* of the hardware and software—in the configuration in which you plan to use it—to make sure that it works. Leave nothing to chance, and have backup equipment available if at all possible. Little things, such as testing electrical outlets, are critical; just because they are there doesn't mean they work. Never add or include new or untested equipment at the last minute; leave yourself enough time to work out any possible kinks. Thoroughly check out the courtroom in advance of the trial, if possible, so that you understand the complete layout of the room and what problems could potentially arise.

Possible complications include incompatible computer platforms, insufficient electrical connections, slow or spotty Internet or wireless connections, awkward or obstructed lines of sight for the factfinders, poor lighting, display monitors that are too small or poorly placed, and inadequate sound systems, among many, many others. The more of these obstacles you can predict and plan for (or work around), the better off your team will be.

Always Rehearse

Always rehearse, many times, before putting on a presentation to a judge or jury. This is particularly critical if a support person (such as a paralegal) will be running the hardware and/or software. It takes time to prepare trial presentations and to work out all the kinks and problems. In addition, even if the technology works, in the end it really comes down to the presenter and how well that person presents the information to the judge or jury. For the presentation to be effective, everything must work together and flow well—and that takes time and practice.

Don't Keep Judges or Juries Waiting—Bring Powerful Technology

Always make sure the software you are using can run adequately on the computer hardware you are using. Judges and juries get extremely impatient when a user's computer constantly shows the Windows "hourglass" icon. The new class of trial presentation software, in particular, has hefty computing needs in terms of both active and storage memory. Always use a computer with more than enough horsepower to get the job done. (Of course, you will have thoroughly tested your setup and presentation(s) before you get to trial, so you should know well ahead of time if there are problems in this area.)

Always Have a Backup Plan

Always have a backup plan—*always*, every time. It is a sad fact that hard disks crash, CDs and DVDs get scratched, software freezes, computers get unplugged, cables wear out, bright lights wash out computer screens, operator errors occur, and information gets accidentally deleted. It is critical that you always have a backup plan in case the technology fails. Something—anything—is better than nothing. A presentation that is printed out and can be copied and handed to the judge or jurors is better than no presentation at all.

Keep It Simple—Don't Overload Slides with Too Much Information

Presentations should be professional, clean, and simple. A common mistake is to put too many bullet points on a single slide. This makes the slide difficult to read. In addition, the font size of slide text should be relatively large, because some jurors may have trouble reading small fonts. Ambient lighting, such as from overhead fixtures or glare from courtroom windows, can wreak havoc with visibility, especially if the display monitors are undersized or poorly placed. Know ahead of time what you will be dealing with and prepare the presentation accordingly.

Use Color Conservatively

It is fine to include some color, but presentation designs should be conservative and professional—no loud, extravagant colors, and not too many colors. Color should be used to enhance the presentation, not distract the viewers.

Use Animation, Sound, and Clip Art Cautiously

Use animation, sound clips, and clip art cautiously in trial presentations. Because they often have a cartoonish quality, they tend to diminish the quality and professionalism of a presentation. It is easy for these elements to come off as cheap, cheesy, or just in poor taste. The acid test for any element is whether it enhances the comprehensibility, interest, and overall impact of the presentation.

Use Images, Maps, Video, and Charts/Graphs When Possible

Include graphical elements, such as images (photographs), maps, video, and charts/graphs, in a presentation whenever possible. They add excitement and diversity to text and many times make it easier for jurors to understand the concept you are trying to convey.

Video testimony is particularly important. For example, if a witness states something in open court that is different from the testimony he or she gave in a video deposition, the ability to play the video deposition in front of the jury and impeach the witness's current testimony is priceless.

Scan Key Documents and Use Markup Tools

Scan the key documents in a case, so that you can include them as part of a complete presentation. If documents are in electronic form, you can use presentation software to mark or highlight important passages for easy identification by the factfinder.

Include Timelines

Timelines are critical in just about every case that goes to trial. They explain what happened, in chronological order. Attorneys often present things out of sequence for specific reasons, and witnesses often jump around in their testimony or are unclear regarding dates and times. Hence, timelines are crucial for bringing everything in a case together for a jury.

Allow Extra Time to Pass Security Checkpoints

If you have ever tried to take a laptop computer onto an airplane, you may have an idea of what it will take to get through courthouse security with computers, projectors, speakers, and other equipment. Be sure to give yourself enough time to physically get the equipment into the courthouse and set up in the courtroom.

ETHICAL CONSIDERATIONS

Ethical considerations regarding trial and presentation software and graphics revolve around competency and rules of evidence. It is important, when putting together anything that will be used in a client's case, to make sure that it is well thought out and competently executed. It is certainly not unusual for a paralegal to be asked to create a chart, graph, table, exhibit, or even a full presentation for trial. It is extremely important that these be prepared with a high degree of accuracy and competency.

In addition, anything that is presented at trial or to a factfinder will be subject to the rules of evidence and could be objected to by the opposing party. Charts, graphs, and tables may be viewed as **demonstrative evidence**. Examples of demonstrative evidence include maps, diagrams, models, charts, and illustrations. The admissibility of demonstrative evidence is largely controlled by the rules of evidence and the judge

demonstrative evidence
All evidence other than testimony.

sitting on the case. Arguments between attorneys regarding a piece of demonstrative evidence often concern whether it fairly and reasonably depicts the subject matter it covers. Thus, the heart of admissibility of demonstrative evidence depends on the accuracy, quality, and competency of the exhibit itself.

SUMMARY

Electronic courthouses, where legal professionals file documents electronically and have instant access to court information, are becoming a reality. Automated courtrooms with computers and monitors for all participants are also a reality.

Presentation software allows users to create visually interesting electronic presentations. Presentation graphics programs are used in legal organizations for creating internal training programs, public seminars, and presentations for clients, and developing trial presentations. Some of these programs are generic business presentation programs. A trial presentation program is specifically designed to meet the needs of practicing attorneys, particularly those who try cases to juries and courts.

Most presentation graphics programs have several views and display presentations to work with. Creating new presentations entails creating a background design; adding slides; adding and formatting text; adding photographs, clip art, and word art; adding graphs and charts; and creating multimedia effects and transition/animation effects.

Designing and presenting trial presentations to judges and juries takes a great deal of preparation and thought. Tips for doing this well include testing computer equipment in advance, always having a backup plan, and always rehearsing presentations. To create professional, effective presentations, keep slides simple and uncluttered; use color conservatively; use animation, sound, and clip art cautiously; use images, maps, video, and charts/graphs as much as possible; scan key documents; use markup tools; and include timelines.

KEY TERMS

background
clip art
demonstrative evidence
document camera

evidence display system
normal view
slide show view
slide sorter view

slide transition
trial presentation programs
word art

INTERNET SITES

Internet sites for this chapter include:

ORGANIZATION	SOFTWARE PRODUCT	WORLD WIDE WEB ADDRESS
Adobe Acrobat	PDF file creation program	www.adobe.com
Case Management/Electronic Case Files	The federal courts' case management and electronic case files system	www.uscourts.gov
Corel Corp.	Presentations X3 presentation program	www.corel.com
Doar	Trial presentation services vendor	www.doar.com
Idea, Inc.	Trial Pro	www.trialpro.com
InData Software	TrialDirector trial presentation software	www.indatacorp.com
LexisNexis	TimeMap (timeline creation software)	www.casemap.com
Microsoft Corp.	PowerPoint presentation software	www.microsoft.com

Public Access to Court Electronic Records	PACER (electronic public access to federal court information)	pacer.psc.uscourts.gov
Verdict Systems	Sanction trial presentation software	www.verdictsystems.com

TEST YOUR KNOWLEDGE

1. True or False: Only a few courts, cases, or attorneys participate in the federal courts' Case Management/Electronic Case Filing system.
2. What standard do most courts use for submission of electronic documents?
3. What is a document camera?

4. True or False: Trial presentation programs and generic presentation programs such as Microsoft PowerPoint have the same features.
5. Why should you be careful when using clip art and sound files in trial presentations?
6. Name four things to remember when using presentation programs in the courtroom.

ON THE WEB EXERCISES

1. Use a general search engine, such as Google or Yahoo!, to find several articles regarding use of computer presentation programs in the courtroom or before a jury. Write a two-page paper summarizing your research.
2. Use the Internet sites listed in this chapter and/or a general search engine (such as Google or

Yahoo!) to find two trial presentation programs. Compare the prices, features, support, and training available. Download trial versions of the programs if you can. Write a two-page memo summarizing your research and findings. Identify the program that you think is best and explain why.

QUESTIONS AND EXERCISES

1. Contact an attorney, paralegal, or court staff member in your area and interview that person regarding his or her experiences using technology

in the courtroom, electronic filing, or accessing electronic court records. Write a two-page memo summarizing your interview.

ETHICS QUESTION

You are working with trial presentation software to prepare a brief video clip of an opposing party's deposition. As you are creating the clip, you notice that if you stop the clip one second sooner, the opposing witness

appears to be scowling. You would like to present the opposing witness in a less than flattering light. What ethical issues, if any, arise from this scenario?

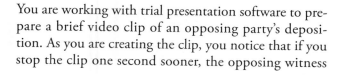

The available CourseMate for this text has an interactive eBook and interactive learning tools, including flash cards, quizzes, and more. To learn more about this resource and access free demo CourseMate resources, go to www.cengagebrain.com, and search for this book. To access CourseMate materials that you have purchased, go to login.cengagebrain.com.

HANDS-ON EXERCISES

FEATURED SOFTWARE
Microsoft PowerPoint 2010
Microsoft PowerPoint 2007

PRESENTATION SOFTWARE

 READ THIS FIRST!

1. Microsoft PowerPoint 2010
2. Microsoft PowerPoint 2007

I. DETERMINING WHICH TUTORIAL TO COMPLETE

To use the PowerPoint Hands-On Exercises, you must already own or have access to Microsoft PowerPoint 2007 or PowerPoint 2010. If you have one of these programs but do not know the version you are using, it is easy to find out. For PowerPoint 2007, click the Office button in the upper left of the screen, click PowerPoint Options, and then click Resources to see what version of the program you are using. For PowerPoint 2010, click the File tab in the upper left of the screen, click PowerPoint Options, and then click Resources to see what version of the program you are using. You must know the version of the program you are using and select the correct tutorial version or the tutorials will not work correctly.

II. USING THE POWERPOINT HANDS-ON EXERCISES

The PowerPoint Hands-On Exercises in this section are easy to use and contain step-by-step instructions. They start with basic skills and proceed to intermediate and advanced levels. If you already have a good working knowledge of PowerPoint, you may be able to proceed directly to the intermediate and advanced exercises. To truly be ready for using presentation software in the legal environment, you must be able to accomplish the tasks and exercises in the more advanced exercises.

III. ACCESSING THE DATA

Some of the advanced PowerPoint Hands-On Exercises use documents on the disk provided with this text. To access these files, put the disk in your computer and click Start; then click My Computer, double-click on the appropriate drive, and double-click the PowerPoint Files folder. You should then see the presentation available for these exercises. These files are also available on the Premium Website. To access them, go to your CengageBrain account and click on the link for Premium Website for Cornick's *Using Computers in the Law Office—Basic*. A new window will open. Under Book Level Resources, click the link for Data Files: PowerPoint, then click the link to the desired lesson. When prompted, click Open.

IV. INSTALLATION QUESTIONS

If you have installation questions regarding installing the exercise data file from the disk, you may contact Technical Support at http://cengage.com/support.

HANDS-ON EXERCISES

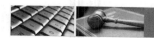 **HANDS-ON EXERCISES**

MICROSOFT POWERPOINT 2010

Number	Lesson Title	Concepts Covered
BASIC LESSONS		
Lesson 1	Creating a Presentation	Selecting a presentation design, entering text, entering speaker's notes, and saving a file
Lesson 2	Creating Additional Slides	Inserting a new slide; selecting a slide layout; viewing a slide in Slide Show, Outline, and Slide Sorter views; and creating additional slides
INTERMEDIATE LESSONS		
Lesson 3	Creating a Graph	Creating and entering data in a chart
ADVANCED LESSONS		
Lesson 4	Finalizing the Presentation	Creating transition effects, creating animation effects, and viewing a final presentation

GETTING STARTED
Overview

Microsoft PowerPoint 2010 is a presentation graphics program. It allows you to create presentations, charts, graphs, tables, and much more. PowerPoint 2010 is an easy-to-use program. Please note that you will be creating a presentation for an opening statement presentation.

Introduction

Throughout these lessons and exercises, information you need to operate the program will be designated in several different ways:

- Keys to be pressed on the keyboard are designated in brackets, in all caps, and in bold (e.g., press the **[ENTER]** key).
- Movements with the mouse pointer are designated in bold and italics (e.g., *point to File and click*).
- Words or letters that should be typed are designated in bold (type **Training Program**).
- Information that is or should be displayed on your computer screen is shown in bold, with quotation marks (e.g., "**Press ENTER to continue.**").
- Specific menu items and commands are designated with an initial capital letter (e.g., click Open).

LESSON 1: CREATING A PRESENTATION

In this lesson, you will start PowerPoint 2010, select a background design for the opening statement presentation, enter the first slide, view your slide, and save your presentation.

1. Start Windows. After it has loaded, *double-click the Microsoft PowerPoint 2010 icon on the desktop* to start the program. Alternatively, *click the Start button, point to Programs or All Programs, click Microsoft Office and then click on Microsoft PowerPoint 2010.*

2. A blank presentation should be on your screen. *Click the File tab in the upper left corner of the screen, then click New.* The "New Presentation" window should now be displayed.

3. *On the left side, under Available Templates and Themes, click Themes. Scroll down and select Paper. Click Create.*

4. A blank title screen should now be displayed.

5. *Click* **"Click to add title."** Notice that you are now allowed to type your own title. Type **OPENING STATEMENT** (see PowerPoint 2010 Exhibit 1).

POWERPOINT 2010 EXHIBIT 1

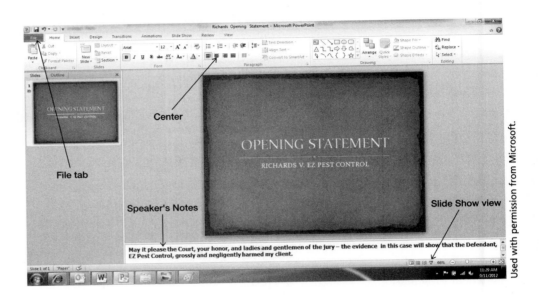

Used with permission from Microsoft.

6. *On the Home ribbon tab, click the Center icon in the Paragraph group.*

7. *Click* **"Click to add subtitle."** Type **RICHARDS V. EZ PEST CONTROL** (see PowerPoint 2010 Exhibit 1).

8. *On the Home ribbon tab, click the Center icon in the Paragraph group.*

9. The slide is now created.

10. To view your slide, *click the Slide Show icon in the lower right of your screen* (PowerPoint 2010 Exhibit 1). *Note:* You will see four icons in the lower right of the screen (for Normal view, Slide Sorter view, Reading view, and Slide Show view). The Slide Show icon is all the way to the right. Remember, if you point to any icon and hold the mouse pointer there for a second, the title of the icon will be displayed.

11. You should now see your slide displayed full screen on your computer. Notice that the dark background with the light-colored letters makes your slide very readable. This is how your audience will see your slide.

12. Press **[ESC]** to return to editing your presentation.

13. Notice that at the bottom of the screen, under the current slide, it says **"Click to add notes."** This is the Speaker's Notes section of the screen. Speaker's Notes are not shown in Slide Show view, but they can be printed so that the presenter has talking points from which to speak.

14. *Click anywhere in the Speaker's Notes section.* Now, type **May it please the Court, your honor, and ladies and gentlemen of the jury – the evidence in this case will show that the Defendant, EZ Pest Control, grossly and negligently harmed my client.** (See PowerPoint Exhibit 1).

15. ***Click the Slide Show icon in the lower right of the screen again.*** Notice that speaker's notes do not appear.

16. Press **[ESC]** to return to editing your presentation.

17. It is a good idea to save your presentation often. To save your presentation, ***click the File tab and then click Save.***

18. Type **Richards Opening Statement,** *then click Save* to save the file in the default directory. Be sure to remember where the file is saved so that you can retrieve it in the next lesson.

This concludes Lesson 1. To exit PowerPoint, ***click the File tab and then click Exit.*** To go directly to Lesson 2, stay at the current screen.

LESSON 2: CREATING ADDITIONAL SLIDES

In this lesson, you will add more slides to the presentation you created in Lesson 1, and you will look at the presentation using several views. If you did not exit Power-Point from Lesson 1, go to Step 3.

1. Start Windows. When it has loaded, ***double-click the Microsoft Office PowerPoint 2010 icon on the desktop*** to start PowerPoint 2010 for Windows. Alternatively, ***click the Start button, point to Programs or All Programs, and then click the Microsoft PowerPoint 2010 icon*** (or ***point to Microsoft Office and then click Microsoft PowerPoint 2010).*** You should be in a clean, blank document.

2. ***Click the File tab, then click Open.*** The "Open" window should now be displayed. ***Navigate to the folder where the file is located. Click Richards Opening Statement and then click Open.*** Alternatively, if you click the File tab, recently used files appear on the right side of the menu. Locate your file and then ***click on it.***

3. You should have the "Richards Opening Statement" slide on your screen. Notice in the lower left of the screen that it says **"Slide 1 of 1."** This shows you what slide number you are on.

4. To create a new slide, ***on the Home ribbon tab, click the down arrow next to New Slide in the Slides group.*** Notice that the program offers you a number of different layouts.

5. ***Click the Title and Content option.***

6. A new slide is displayed on your screen. The top part of the slide should say **"Click to add title"** and the bottom section of the slide (next to a bullet) should say **"Click to add text."** There should also be graphics in the center of the screen.

7. ***Click** "Click to add title."* Type **Reasons for Lawsuit** (see PowerPoint 2010 Exhibit 2).

8. ***On the Home ribbon tab, click the Center icon in the Paragraph group.***

9. ***Click** "Click to add text."* Type **Recovery of damages from EZ Pest for negligence and breach of contract** and press the **[ENTER]** key. Notice that an additional bullet has been created.

10. Type **EZ Pest's Termite Inspection Report failed to find four massive termite colonies** and then press the **[ENTER]** key.

11. Type **Sherry Richards purchased the home based on the favorable termite report by EZ Pest Control** and press the **[ENTER]** key.

12. The slide is now created (see PowerPoint Exhibit 2).

13. To view your slide, ***click the Slide Show icon.***

**POWERPOINT 2010
EXHIBIT 2**

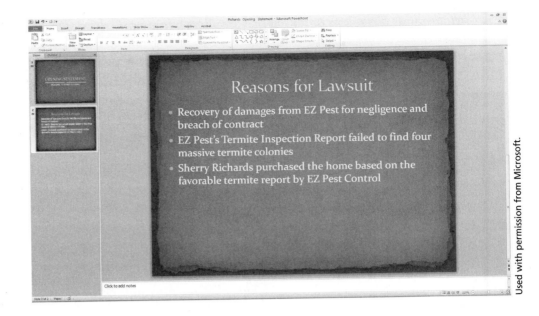

14. You should now see your slide displayed full screen on your computer. With the slide running in Slide Show view, press the **[Page Up]** key and notice that the first slide is now shown on your screen. Press the **[Page Down]** key and notice that you are back at the second slide.

15. Press the **[ESC]** key to return to Normal view.

16. You will now look at your presentation using other views. Notice on the left side of the screen that small versions of both of your slides are displayed (see PowerPoint 2010 Exhibit 2). Notice that, just above the slides, the Slides tab is selected.

17. ***Click the Outline tab just to the right of the Slides tab.***

18. The Outline view is now displayed; notice that you can read the words on both of your slides (see PowerPoint 2010 Exhibit 3).

**POWERPOINT 2010
EXHIBIT 3**

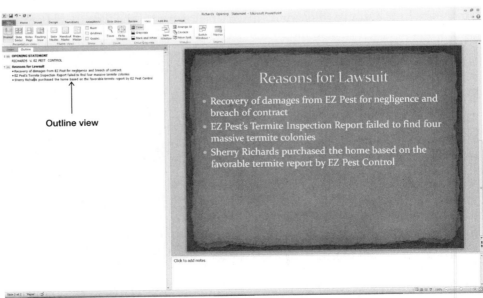

Outline view

19. ***Click the Slides tab just to the left of the Outline tab*** to go back to the Slides view.

20. You will now view your slides using the Slide Sorter view. ***Click the Slide Sorter view icon.*** The Slide Sorter view icon is at the bottom right of the screen; it is the second of the four "View" icons, and has a picture of four small squares (see PowerPoint 2010 Exhibit 1).

21. Notice that you can see all of your slides on the screen at the same time (see PowerPoint 2010 Exhibit 4). This is helpful for getting an overview of your presentation and arranging and rearranging your slide order.

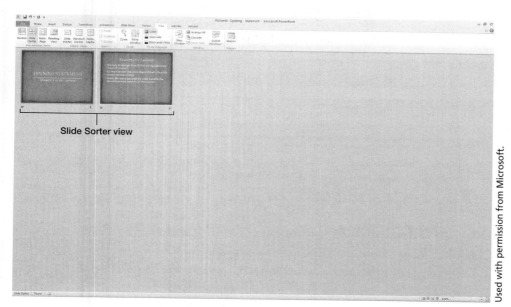

Slide Sorter view

Used with permission from Microsoft.

**POWERPOINT 2010
EXHIBIT 4**

HANDS-ON EXERCISES

22. While you are in Slide Sorter view, ***point to the second slide, click and drag the mouse pointer (holding down the mouse button) to the left of the first slide, and then release the mouse button.*** Notice that the order of the slides is now changed.

23. Press **[CTRL]+[Z]** to undo the move and put the slides back into their original order.

24. ***Click the Normal view icon in the lower right of your screen*** (see PowerPoint 2010 Exhibit 1).

25. You should now have the "OPENING STATEMENT" slide on your screen. If you are not there, use the **[PAGE UP]** key to go there.

26. You are now ready to create another slide. ***On the Home ribbon tab, click the down arrow next to New Slide in the Slides group. Click the Title and Content option.***

27. A new slide should now be displayed on your screen. The top of the slide should say **"Click to add title"** and there should be two columns (left and right) that say **"Click to add text."** There should also be some icons in the middle of the screen.

28. ***Click*** **"Click to add title."** Type **Undisputed Facts of the Case** (see PowerPoint 2010 Exhibit 5).

29. ***On the Home ribbon tab, click the Center icon in the Paragraph group.***

**POWERPOINT 2010
EXHIBIT 5**

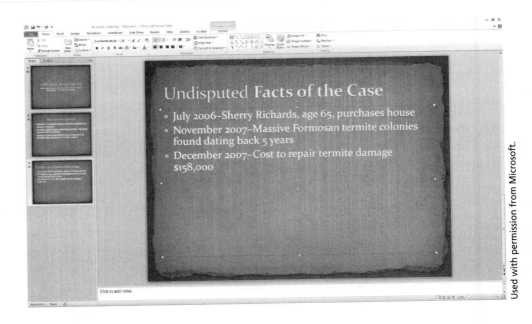

30. *Click* **"Click to add text."** Type **July 2006–Sherry Richards, age 65, purchases house** and press the **[ENTER]** key.

31. Type **November 2007–Massive Formosan termite colonies found dating back 5 years** and press the **[ENTER]** key.

32. Type **December 2007–Cost to repair termite damage $158,000**.

33. Your presentation now has three slides in it.

34. To save your presentation, *click the Save icon on the Quick Access toolbar.* (It looks like a floppy disk and is in the upper left of the screen.)

This concludes Lesson 2. To exit PowerPoint, *click the File tab and then click Exit.* To go to Lesson 3, stay on the current screen.

▶ INTERMEDIATE LESSON

LESSON 3: CREATING A GRAPH

In this lesson, you will add a slide with a graph into the training program presentation. If you did not exit PowerPoint from Lesson 2, go to Step 4.

1. Start Windows. When it has loaded, *double-click the Microsoft Office PowerPoint 2010 icon on the desktop* to start PowerPoint 2010 for Windows. Alternatively, *click the Start button, point to Programs or All Programs, and then click the Microsoft PowerPoint 2010 icon* (or *point to Microsoft Office and then click Microsoft PowerPoint 2010).* You should be in a clean, blank document.

2. *Click the File tab and then click Open.* The "Open" window should now be displayed. *Navigate to the folder where the file is located. Click Richards Opening Statement, then click Open.* Alternatively, if you click the File tab, recently used files appear on the right side of the menu. Locate your file and then *click on it.*

3. You should have the "Richards Opening Statement" slide on your screen. Push the **[PAGE DOWN]** key until you are on the third slide, "Undisputed Facts of the Case."

4. You are now ready to create another slide. *On the Home ribbon tab, click the down arrow next to New Slide in the Slides group.*

5. *Click on the Title and Content option.* A new slide is displayed on your screen.

6. The top part of the slide should say **"Click to add title"** and the bottom section of the slide should say **"Click to add text."** In addition, there are a number of graphical icons in the middle of the screen; one of them is a bar chart.

7. *Click on "Click to add title."* Type **Value of Richards Home.** *From the Home ribbon tab, click on the Center icon in the Paragraph group* (see PowerPoint 2010 Exhibit 6).

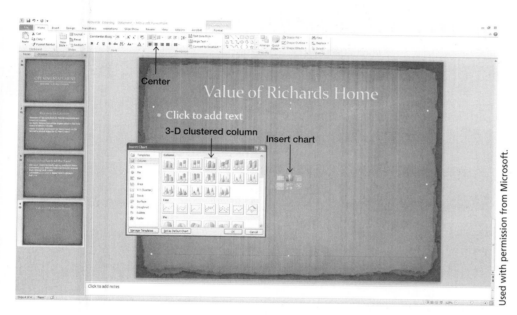

**POWERPOINT 2010
EXHIBIT 6**

HANDS-ON EXERCISES

8. Notice that, in the lower middle of the new slide, there are six graphical icons. *Click on the Insert Chart icon* (it is in the middle on the first row—it looks like a multicolored vertical bar chart).

9. The "Insert Chart" window is displayed (see PowerPoint 2010 Exhibit 6). *Click on Column under Templates on the left side of the window. Then, click on the 3-D Clustered Column chart* (see PowerPoint 2010 Exhibit 6—it is on the first row, fourth chart from the left).

10. *Click on OK.*

11. A default chart is displayed on the left and a default spreadsheet is displayed on the right (see PowerPoint 2010 Exhibit 7).

12. You will now add some data and new titles, and also delete some data.

13. Type over the existing data in the spreadsheet for columns A and B as set out in PowerPoint Exhibit 8 (do not do anything with columns C and D yet).

14. You will now delete columns C and D, as they are not necessary. *Point to cell C1 and (holding the mouse pointer down) drag to the right so that cell D5 is highlighted.*

15. *Right-click in the highlighted area, point to Delete, then click Table Columns.*

16. Your spreadsheet and chart should look similar to PowerPoint 2010 Exhibit 8.

POWERPOINT 2010 EXHIBIT 7

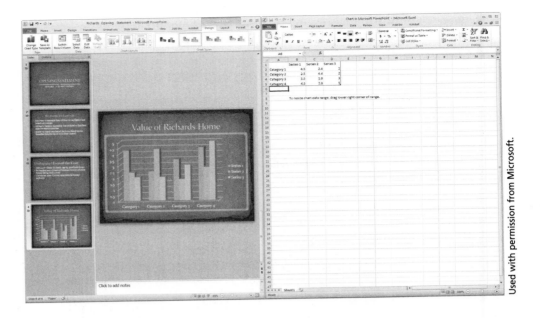

Used with permission from Microsoft.

POWERPOINT 2010 EXHIBIT 8

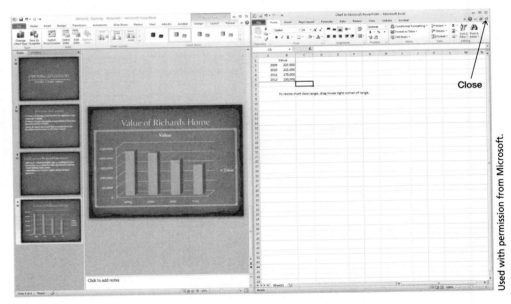

Used with permission from Microsoft.

17. *In the spreadsheet window, click the Close icon* (the "X" in the upper right corner; see PowerPoint 2010 Exhibit 8).

18. The chart should now be displayed (see PowerPoint 2010 Exhibit 9).

19. PowerPoint 2010 gives you many premade chart styles and colors to choose from.

20. *On the Chart Tools – Design ribbon tab, click the More icon in the Chart Styles group* (see PowerPoint 2010 Exhibit 9). *Note*: You can only access the Chart Tools ribbon when the chart is selected, so *click the chart if you do not see the Chart Tools ribbon*.

21. Notice that a wide variety of chart styles is now displayed. *Click any of the charts in the last row;* these are the 3-D sculpted options.

22. The chart is now complete. To view your chart full screen, *click the Slide Show icon.*

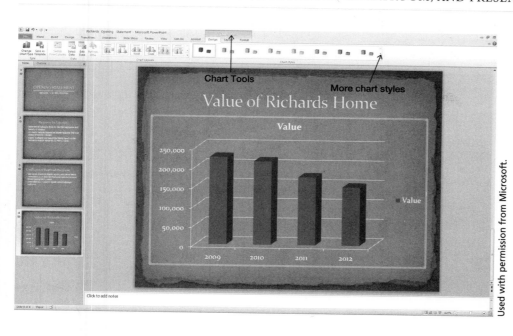

Used with permission from Microsoft.

23. Press the [**ESC**] key.

24. To save your presentation, ***click the Save icon*** (it looks like a floppy disk) ***on the Quick Access toolbar.***

This concludes Lesson 3. To exit PowerPoint, ***click the File tab and then click Exit.*** To go to Lesson 4, stay on the current screen.

 # ADVANCED LESSON

LESSON 4: FINALIZING THE PRESENTATION

In this lesson, you will add more slides to the opening statement presentation, duplicate a slide, enter slide transition effects, create animation effects, and show your presentation. If you did not exit PowerPoint from Lesson 3, go to step 3.

1. Start Windows. When it has loaded, ***double-click the Microsoft Office PowerPoint 2010 icon on the desktop*** to start PowerPoint 2010 for Windows. Alternatively, ***click the Start button, point to Programs or All Programs, and then click the Microsoft PowerPoint 2010 icon*** (or ***point to Microsoft Office and then click Microsoft PowerPoint 2010).*** You should be in a clean, blank document.

2. ***Click the File tab, then click Open.*** The "Open" window should now be displayed. ***Navigate to the folder where the file is located. Click Richards Opening Statement and then click Open.***

3. You should have the "Opening Statement" slide on your screen. Push the [**PAGE DOWN**] key until you are at the fourth slide, which is the bar chart.

4. You are now ready to create another slide. ***On the Home ribbon tab, click the down arrow next to New Slide in the Slides group.***

5. ***Click the Title and Content option.*** A new slide should be displayed on your screen.

6. The top part of the slide should say "**Click to add title**" and the bottom section of the slide should say "**Click to add text.**"

7. ***Click*** "**Click to add title**" and then type **7788 SW 52nd Street**. ***On the Home ribbon tab, click the Center icon in the Paragraph group.***

HANDS-ON EXERCISES

**POWERPOINT 2010
EXHIBIT 10**

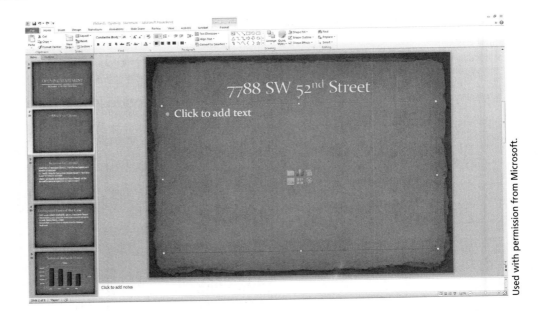

8. *In the lower box, where it says "Click to add text", click on Insert Picture from File.* (It is the first icon on the bottom left; see PowerPoint 2010 Exhibit 10.) You will now add a photograph to the presentation.

9. The "Insert Picture" window should now be displayed. Navigate to the drive where the disk that accompanied this text is located.

10. *Double-click the PowerPoint Files folder, then double-click the "Lesson 4 house" file (JPEG).*

11. *Click on the photograph of the house, then click Insert.* **Your screen should now look like PowerPoint 2010 Exhibit 11. If you need to change the size of the image, you can** *click on one of the sides of the image and drag the image to the desired size.*

12. You will now add another slide. *On the Home ribbon tab, click the down arrow next to New Slide in the Slides group.*

**POWERPOINT 2010
EXHIBIT 11**

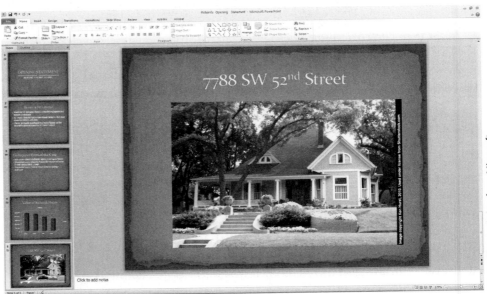

13. ***Click the Title and Content option.*** A new slide should be displayed on your screen.

14. The top part of the slide should say **"Click to add title"** and the bottom section of the slide should say **"Click to add text."**

15. ***Click "Click to add title"*** and type **Termite Damage**. *On the Home ribbon tab, click the Center icon in the Paragraph group.*

16. ***In the lower box, where it says "Click to add text", click on Insert Picture from File.*** (It is the first icon on the bottom left; see PowerPoint 2010 Exhibit 10.) You will now add a photograph to the presentation.

17. The "Insert Picture" window should now be displayed. Navigate to the drive where the disk that accompanied this text is located.

18. ***Double-click the PowerPoint Files folder, then double-click the "Lesson 4 termite damage" file (JPEG).***

19. ***Click on the photograph of the termite damage, then click Insert.*** Your screen should now look like PowerPoint 2010 Exhibit 12. If you need to change the size of the image, you can ***click on one of the sides of the image and drag the image to the desired size.***

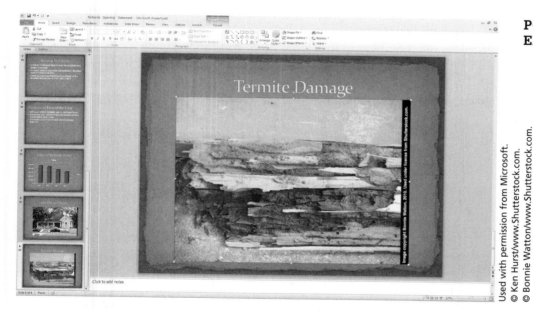

POWERPOINT 2010 EXHIBIT 12

20. Now that you have now created all of your slides, you are ready to begin finalizing the presentation. Press **[CTRL]+[HOME]** to go to the first slide in the presentation.

21. ***Click the Slide Sorter view at the bottom left of the screen.*** Notice that you can see all six of your slides on the screen.

22. You will now enter transition effects (effects that take place when you move from one slide to another) and animation effects (effects that take place during display of a single slide).

23. ***Click on the first slide, "Richards Opening Statement."***

24. ***Click the Transitions ribbon tab.*** You should see the Transition to This Slide group (see PowerPoint 2010 Exhibit 13).

**POWERPOINT 2010
EXHIBIT 13**

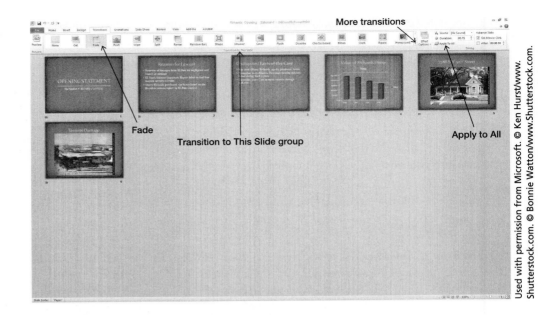

Fade

Transition to This Slide group

More transitions

Apply to All

25. ***Click the More icon in the Transition to This Slide group.*** Notice that many types of slide transitions are available.

26. Press the **[ESC]** key to make the "More transitions" list disappear.

27. ***Click the Fade transition effect in the Transition to This Slide group, then click the Effect Options and click Smoothly.*** Notice that after you selected it, your slide displayed the transition effect. Fade Smoothly is a professional-appearing transition effect that is not distracting, so it is a good one to use in the legal setting.

28. ***Click Apply To All in the Transition to This Slide group.*** This will apply the Fade Smoothly effect to all of the slides in the presentation. Notice that little symbols now appear under all of your slides in the slide sorter; this shows that they have transition effects associated with them.

29. Notice that in the Timing group, under Advance Slide, **"On Mouse Click"** is selected. This means that the slide will automatically move to the next slide only when the mouse is clicked. You could set it to move to the next slide automatically after a given amount of time, but the current selection is fine for this presentation.

30. ***Click the Slide Show icon at the bottom right of the screen*** to see your presentation, including the transition effects. ***Click the mouse button to proceed through the presentation and back to the Slide Sorter screen.***

31. You will now create an animation effect that determines how the slides with bullet points appear on the screen.

32. ***Double-click the second slide, "Reasons for Lawsuit."***

33. ***Click anywhere in the lower half of the screen.***

34. ***On the Animations ribbon tab, click Fade, then click the Effect Options and click By Paragraph*** (see PowerPoint 2010 Exhibit 14).

35. ***Repeat this same process for slide 3.***

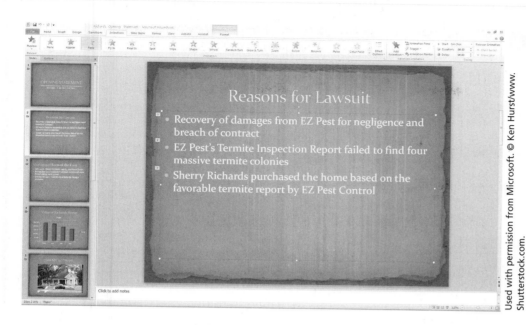

**POWERPOINT 2010
EXHIBIT 14**

HANDS-ON EXERCISES

36. You are now ready to view your presentation. Press the **[PAGE UP]** key to go to the first slide in the presentation.

37. *Click the Slide Show icon at the bottom right of the screen.*

38. Your first slide is now shown full-screen size. To proceed to the next slide, press the **[SPACE BAR]** or *click the left mouse button.* Keep pressing the **[SPACE BAR]** or *clicking the left mouse button* to proceed with the presentation. Notice on the slides with bullets that you must press the **[SPACE BAR]** or *click the mouse* to go to the next bullet; this is the animation effect you created.

39. When you get to the end of the presentation, press the **[SPACE BAR]** or *click the left mouse button* to go back to editing the presentation.

40. To print your presentation, *click the File tab, point to Print, and then click Print.*

41. To save your presentation, *click the Save icon* (it looks like a floppy disk) *on the Quick Access toolbar.*

42. *Click the File tab and then click Close.*

This concludes the PowerPoint 2010 Hands-On Exercises. To exit PowerPoint, *click the File tab, then click Exit.*

 **HANDS-ON EXERCISES**

MICROSOFT POWERPOINT 2007

Number	Lesson Title	Concepts Covered
BASIC LESSONS		
Lesson 1	Creating a Presentation	Selecting a presentation design; entering text; entering speaker's notes; saving a file
Lesson 2	Creating Additional Slides	Inserting a new slide; selecting a slide layout; viewing a slide in Slide Show, Outline, and Slide Sorter views; creating additional slides
INTERMEDIATE LESSON		
Lesson 3	Creating a Graph	Creating a chart; entering data in a chart
ADVANCED LESSON		
Lesson 4	Finalizing the Presentation	Creating transition effects; creating animation effects; viewing a final presentation

GETTING STARTED
Overview

Microsoft PowerPoint 2007 is a presentation graphics program. It allows you to create presentations, charts, graphs, tables, and much more. PowerPoint 2007 is easy to learn and easy to use. Please note that you will be creating a presentation for an opening statement.

Introduction

Throughout these lessons and exercises, information you need to type into the software will be designated in several different ways:

- Keys to be pressed on the keyboard are designated in brackets, in all caps, and in bold (e.g., press the **[ENTER]** key).
- Movements with the mouse pointer are designated in bold and italics (e.g., *point to File on the menu bar and click*).
- Words or letters that should be typed are designated in bold (e.g., type **Training Program**).
- Information that is or should be displayed on your computer screen is shown in bold, with quotation marks (e.g., **"Press ENTER to continue."**).
- Specific menu items and commands are designated with an initial capital letter (e.g., click Open).

 BASIC LESSONS

LESSON 1: CREATING A PRESENTATION

In this lesson, you will start PowerPoint 2007, select a background design for the opening statement presentation, enter the first slide, view your slide, and save your presentation.

1. Start Windows. After it has loaded, ***double-click the Microsoft PowerPoint 2007 icon on the desktop*** to start the program. Alternatively, ***click the Start button, point to Programs or All Programs, click Microsoft Office, then click on Microsoft Office PowerPoint 2007.***

2. A blank presentation should appear on your screen. ***Click the Office button in the upper left corner of the screen, then click New.*** The "New Presentation" window should now be displayed.

3. ***On the left side, under Templates, click Installed Themes. Scroll down and select Paper. Click Create.***

4. A blank title screen should now be displayed.

5. ***Click "Click to add title."*** Notice that you are now allowed to type your own title. Type **OPENING STATEMENT** (see PowerPoint 2007 Exhibit 1).

6. ***On the Home ribbon tab, click the Center icon in the Paragraph group.***

7. ***Click "Click to add subtitle."*** Type **RICHARDS V. EZ PEST CONTROL** (see PowerPoint 2007 Exhibit 1).

8. ***On the Home ribbon tab, click the Center icon in the Paragraph group.***

9. The slide is now created.

10. To view your slide, ***click the Slide Show icon in the lower right of the screen*** (PowerPoint 2007 Exhibit 1). *Note:* You will see three icons in the lower right of the screen (for Normal view, Slide Sorter view, and Slide Show view). The Slide Show icon is all the way to the right. Remember, if you point to any icon and hold the mouse pointer there for a second, the title of the icon will be displayed.

11. You should now see your slide displayed full screen on your computer. Notice that the dark background with the light-colored letters makes your slide very readable. This is how your audience will see your slide.

12. Press the [**ESC**] key to return to editing your presentation.

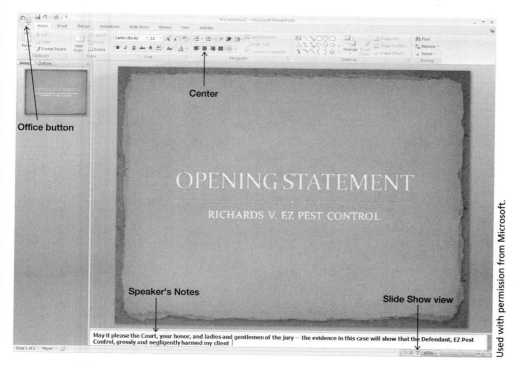

POWERPOINT 2007 EXHIBIT 1

HANDS-ON EXERCISES

13. Notice that at the bottom of the screen, under the current slide, it says **"Click to add notes."** This is the speaker's notes section of the screen. Speaker's notes are not shown in Slide Show view, but they can be printed so that the presenter has talking points to which to refer.

14. ***Click anywhere in the speaker's notes section.*** Type **May it please the Court, your honor, and ladies and gentlemen of the jury—the evidence in this case will show that the Defendant, EZ Pest Control, grossly and negligently harmed my client** (see PowerPoint 2007 Exhibit 1).

15. ***Click the Slide Show icon in the lower right of the screen again.*** Notice that the speaker's notes do not appear.

16. Press the **[ESC]** key to return to editing your presentation.

17. It is a good idea to save your work often. To save your presentation, ***click the Office button and then click Save.***

18. Type **Richards Opening Statement**, ***then click Save*** to save the file in the default directory. Be sure to remember where the file is saved so that you can retrieve it for the next lesson.

This concludes Lesson 1. To exit PowerPoint, ***click the Office button and then click Exit PowerPoint.*** To go to Lesson 2, stay at the current screen.

LESSON 2: CREATING ADDITIONAL SLIDES

In this lesson, you will create additional slides for the opening statement presentation you created in Lesson 1, and you will look at the presentation using several views. If you did not exit PowerPoint from Lesson 1, go to Step 3 in the following instructions.

1. Start Windows. ***Double-click the Microsoft Office PowerPoint 2007 icon on the desktop*** to start PowerPoint 2007 for Windows. Alternatively, ***click the Start button, point to Programs or All Programs, then click the Microsoft PowerPoint 2007 icon*** (or ***point to Microsoft Office and then click Microsoft Office PowerPoint 2007***). You should be in a clean, blank document.

2. ***Click the Office button, then click Open.*** The "Open" window should now be displayed. Navigate to the folder where the file is located. ***Click Richards Opening Statement, then click Open.*** Alternatively, if you click the Office button, recently used files appear on the right side of the menu. Locate your file, then ***click on it.***

3. You should have the "Opening Statement" slide on your screen. Notice in the lower left of the screen that it says **"Slide 1 of 1."** This shows you what slide number you are on.

4. To create a new slide, ***on the Home ribbon tab, click the down arrow next to New Slide in the Slides group.*** Notice that the program offers a number of different layouts.

5. ***Click the Title and Content option.***

6. A new slide is displayed on your screen. The top part of the slide should say **"Click to add title"** and the bottom section of the slide (next to a bullet) should say **"Click to add text."** There should also be graphics in the center of the screen.

7. ***Click "Click to add title."*** Type **Reasons for Lawsuit** (see PowerPoint 2007 Exhibit 2).

8. ***On the Home ribbon tab, click the Center icon in the Paragraph group.***

9. ***Click "Click to add text."*** Type **Recovery of damages from EZ Pest for negligence and breach of contract** and press the **[ENTER]** key. Notice that an additional bullet has been created.

10. Type **EZ Pest's Termite Inspection Report failed to find four massive termite colonies** and then press the **[ENTER]** key.

11. Type **Sherry Richards purchased the home based on the favorable Termite Inspection Report by EZ Pest Control** and press the **[ENTER]** key.

12. The slide is now created (see PowerPoint Exhibit 2).

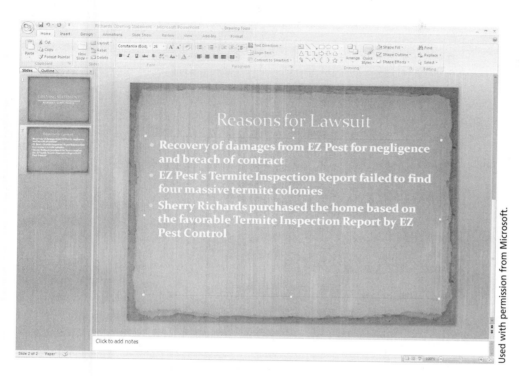

Used with permission from Microsoft.

POWERPOINT 2007 EXHIBIT 2

13. To view your slide, *click the Slide Show icon.*

14. You should now see your slide displayed full screen on your computer. With the slide running in Slide Show view, press the **[PAGE UP]** key and notice that the first slide is now shown on your screen. Press the **[PAGE DOWN]** key and notice that you are back at the second slide.

15. Press the **[ESC]** key to return to Normal view.

16. You will now look at your presentation using other views. Notice on the left side of the screen that small versions of both of your slides are displayed (see PowerPoint 2007 Exhibit 2). Notice, just above the slides, that the Slides tab is selected.

17. *Click the Outline tab just to the right of the Slides tab.*

18. The Outline view is now displayed; notice that you can read the words on both of your slides (see PowerPoint 2007 Exhibit 3).

19. *Click the Slides tab just to the left of the Outline tab* to go back to the Slides view.

20. You will now view your slides using the Slide Sorter view. *Click the Slide Sorter view icon.* The Slide Sorter view icon is at the bottom right of the screen; it is the second of the three View icons, and has a picture of four small squares (see PowerPoint 2007 Exhibit 1).

21. Notice that you can now see all of your slides on the screen at the same time (see PowerPoint 2007 Exhibit 4). This is helpful for getting an overview of your presentation and arranging and rearranging the slide order.

HANDS-ON EXERCISES

**POWERPOINT 2007
EXHIBIT 3**

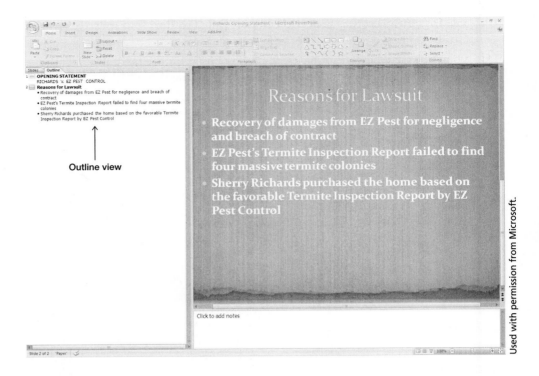

Outline view

**POWERPOINT 2007
EXHIBIT 4**

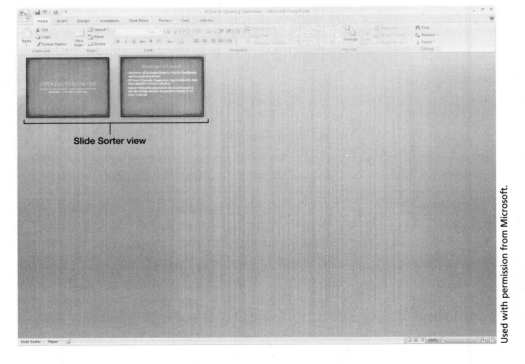

Slide Sorter view

22. While you are in Slide Sorter view, *point to the second slide, click on it, and (holding down the mouse button) drag the mouse pointer to the left of the first slide. Release the mouse button.* Notice that the order of the slides has been changed.

23. Press **[CTRL]+[Z]** to undo the move and put the slides back into their original order.

24. ***Click the Normal view icon in the lower right of your screen*** (see PowerPoint 2007 Exhibit 1).

25. You should now have the "Opening Statement" slide on your screen. If you are not there, use the **[PAGE DOWN]** key to go there.

26. You are now ready to create another slide. ***On the Home ribbon tab, click the down arrow next to New Slide in the Slides group. Click the Title and Content option.***

27. A new slide is displayed on your screen. The top part of the slide should say **"Click to add title"** and the bottom section of the slide (next to a bullet) should say **"Click to add text."** There should also be graphics in the center of the screen.

28. ***Click*** **"Click to add title."** Type **Undisputed Facts of the Case** (see PowerPoint 2007 Exhibit 5).

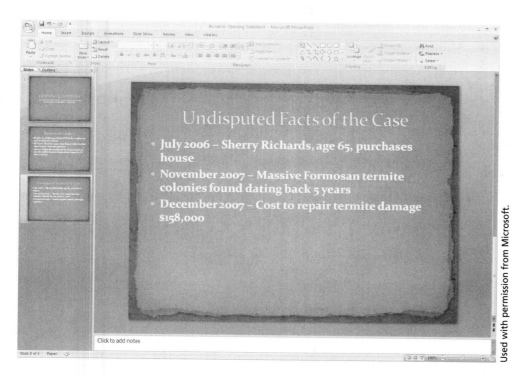

**POWERPOINT 2007
EXHIBIT 5**

Used with permission from Microsoft.

29. ***On the Home ribbon tab, click the Center icon in the Paragraph group.***

30. ***Click*** **"Click to add text."** Type **July 2006 – Sherry Richards, age 65, purchases house** and press the **[ENTER]** key.

31. Type **November 2007 – Massive Formosan termite colonies found dating back 5 years** and press the **[ENTER]** key.

32. Type **December 2007 – Cost to repair termite damage $158,000**.

33. Your presentation now has three slides in it.

34. To save your presentation, ***click the Save icon on the Quick Access toolbar.*** (It looks like a floppy disk and is in the upper left of the screen.)

This concludes Lesson 2. To exit PowerPoint, ***click the Office button, then click Exit PowerPoint.*** To go to Lesson 3, stay at the current screen.

▶ INTERMEDIATE LESSON

LESSON 3: CREATING A GRAPH

In this lesson, you will add a slide with a graph to the opening statement presentation. If you did not exit PowerPoint after completing Lesson 2, go to Step 4 in the following instructions.

1. Start Windows. *Double-click the Microsoft Office PowerPoint 2007 icon on the desktop* to start PowerPoint 2007 for Windows. Alternatively, *click the Start button, point to Programs or All Programs, then click the Microsoft PowerPoint 2007 icon* (or *point to Microsoft Office and then click Microsoft Office PowerPoint 2007*). You should be in a clean, blank document.

2. *Click the Office button, then click Open.* The "Open" window should now be displayed. Navigate to the folder where the file is located. *Click Richards Opening Statement and then click Open.* Alternatively, if you click the Office button, recently used files appear on the right side of the menu. Locate your file and then *click on it.*

3. You should have the "Opening Statement" slide on your screen. Push the [**PAGE DOWN**] key until you are on the third slide, "Undisputed Facts of the Case."

4. You are now ready to create another slide. *On the Home ribbon tab, click the down arrow next to New Slide in the Slides group.*

5. *Click on the Title and Content option.* A new slide is displayed on your screen.

6. The top part of the slide should say **"Click to add title"** and the bottom section of the slide should say **"Click to add text."** In addition, there are a number of graphical icons in the middle of the screen; one of them is a bar chart.

7. *Click on* "**Click to add title.**" Type **Value of Richards Home** and then press the [**ENTER**] key (see PowerPoint 2007 Exhibit 6). *On the Home ribbon tab, click on the Center icon in the Paragraph group.*

POWERPOINT 2007 EXHIBIT 6

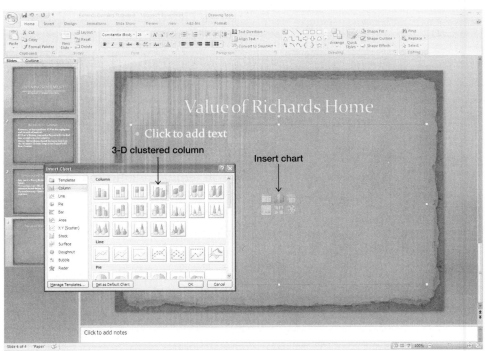

8. Notice that, in the lower middle of the new slide, there are six graphical icons. ***Click on the Insert Chart icon*** (it is in the middle on the first row—it looks like a multicolored vertical bar chart).

9. The "Insert Chart" window is displayed (see PowerPoint 2007 Exhibit 6). ***Click on Column under Templates on the left side of the window, then click on the 3-D Clustered Column chart*** (e.g., see PowerPoint 2007 Exhibit 6—it is on the first row, fourth chart from the left).

10. ***Click on OK.***

11. A default chart is displayed on the left and a default spreadsheet is displayed on the right (see PowerPoint 2007 Exhibit 7).

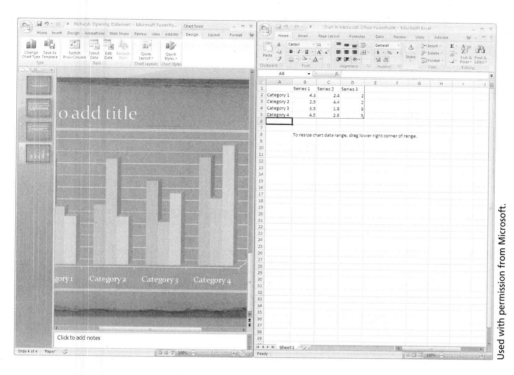

Used with permission from Microsoft.

POWERPOINT 2007 EXHIBIT 7

12. You will now add some data and new titles, and also delete some data.

13. Type over the existing data in the spreadsheet for columns A and B as follows (do not do anything with columns C and D yet):

	A	B	C	D
	2009	2010	2011	2012
Value	225,000	215,000	175,000	150,000

14. You will now delete columns C and D, because they are not necessary. ***Point to cell C1 and (holding the mouse pointer down) drag to the right so that cell D7 is highlighted.***

15. ***Right-click in the highlighted area, point to Delete, then click Table Columns.***

16. A Microsoft Office Excel window will appear saying that the worksheet contains one or more invalid references; ***click OK.***

17. Your spreadsheet and chart should look similar to PowerPoint 2007 Exhibit 8.

18. ***In the spreadsheet part of the "Chart" window, click the Close icon*** (the X in the upper right corner; see PowerPoint 2007 Exhibit 8).

**POWERPOINT 2007
EXHIBIT 8**

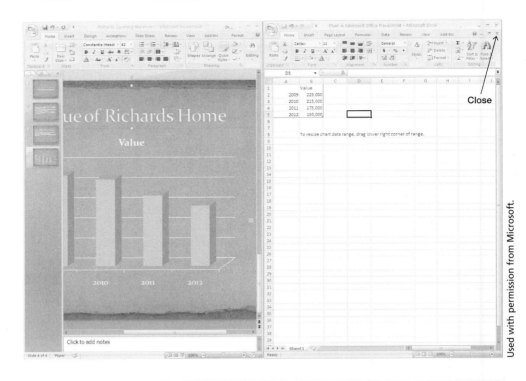

Close

Used with permission from Microsoft.

**POWERPOINT 2007
EXHIBIT 9**

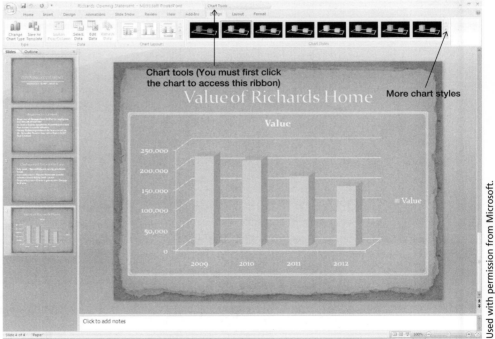

Chart tools (You must first click the chart to access this ribbon)

More chart styles

Used with permission from Microsoft.

19. The chart should now be displayed (see PowerPoint 2007 Exhibit 9).

20. PowerPoint 2007 offers many premade chart styles and colors to choose from.

21. ***On the Chart Tools – Design ribbon tab, click the More icon in the Chart Styles group*** (see PowerPoint 2007 Exhibit 9). *Note*: You can access the Chart Tools ribbon only when a chart is selected, so ***click the chart if you do not see the Chart Tools ribbon***.

22. A wide variety of chart styles is now displayed. ***Click any of the charts in the last row;*** these are the 3-D sculpted options.

23. The chart is now complete. To view your chart full-screen, ***click the Slide Show icon.***

24. Press the **[ESC]** key.

25. To save your presentation, ***click the Save icon*** (it looks like a floppy disk) ***on the Quick Access toolbar.***

This concludes Lesson 3. To exit PowerPoint, ***click the Office button, then click Exit PowerPoint.*** To go to Lesson 4, stay at the current screen.

▶ ADVANCED LESSON

LESSON 4: FINALIZING THE PRESENTATION

In this lesson, you will add more slides to the opening statement presentation, duplicate a slide, enter slide transition effects, create animation effects, and show your presentation. If you did not exit PowerPoint from Lesson 3, go to step 3 in the following instructions.

1. Start Windows. ***Double-click the Microsoft Office PowerPoint 2007 icon on the desktop*** to start PowerPoint 2007 for Windows. Alternatively, ***click the Start button, point to Programs or All Programs, then click the Microsoft PowerPoint 2007 icon*** (or ***point to Microsoft Office and then click Microsoft Office PowerPoint 2007***). You should be in a clean, blank document.

2. ***Click the Office button, then click Open.*** The "Open" window should now be displayed. Navigate to the folder where the file is located. ***Click Richards Opening Statement and then click Open.***

3. You should have the "Opening Statement" slide on your screen. Push the **[PAGE DOWN]** key until you are at the fourth slide, which is the bar chart.

4. You are now ready to create another slide. ***On the Home ribbon tab, click the down arrow next to New Slide in the Slides group.***

5. ***Click the Title and Content option.*** A new slide should be displayed on your screen.

6. The top part of the slide should say **"Click to add title"** and the bottom section of the slide should say **"Click to add text."**

7. ***Click*** **"Click to add title"** and then type **7788 SW 52nd Street**.

8. ***In the lower box, where it says*** **"Click to add text,"** ***click on Insert Picture from File.*** (It is the first icon on the bottom left; see PowerPoint 2007 Exhibit 10.) You will now add a photograph to the presentation.

9. The "Insert Picture" window should now be displayed. Navigate to the drive where the disk that accompanied this text is located.

10. ***Double-click the PowerPoint Files folder, double-click the PowerPoint 2007 folder, and then double-click the "Lesson 4 house" (JPEG).***

11. ***Click on the photograph of the house, then click Insert.*** Your screen should now look like PowerPoint 2007 Exhibit 11. If you need to change the size of the image, ***click on one of the sides of the image and drag the image to the desired size.***

12. You will now add another slide. ***On the Home ribbon tab, click the down arrow next to New Slide in the Slides group.***

13. ***Click the Title and Content option.*** A new slide should be displayed on your screen.

**POWERPOINT 2007
EXHIBIT 10**

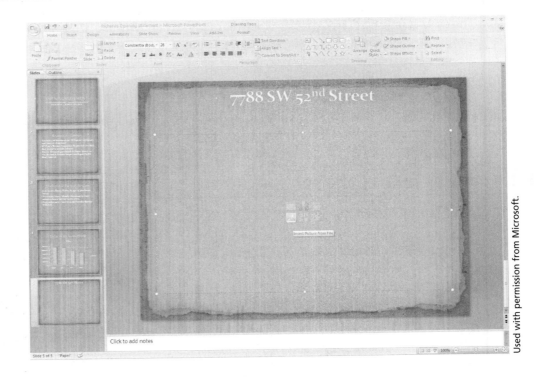

Used with permission from Microsoft.

**POWERPOINT 2007
EXHIBIT 11**

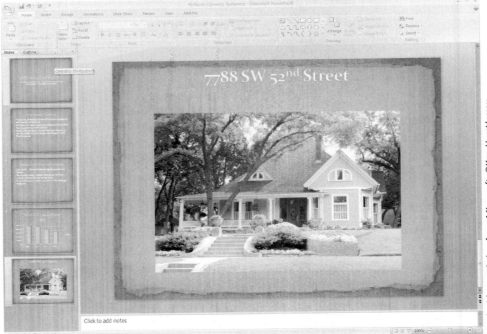

Used with permission from Microsoft. ©Ken Hurst/www.
Shutterstock.com.

14. The top part of the slide should say **"Click to add title"** and the bottom section of the slide should say **"Click to add text."**

15. *Click* "Click to add title" and type **Termite Damage**.

16. *In the lower box, where it says* **"Click to add text,"** *click on Insert Picture from File.* (It is the first icon on the bottom left; see PowerPoint 2007 Exhibit 10.) You will now add another photograph to the presentation.

17. The "Insert Picture" window should now be displayed. Navigate to the drive where the disk that accompanied this text is located.

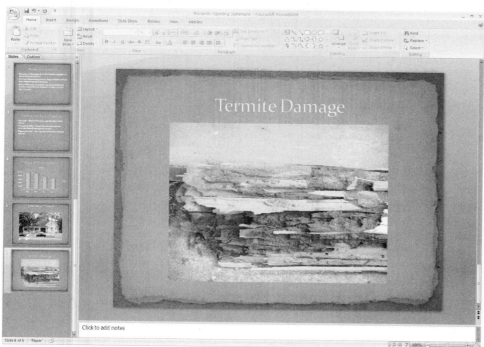

**POWERPOINT 2007
EXHIBIT 12**

HANDS-ON EXERCISES

18. *Double-click the PowerPoint Files folder, double-click the PowerPoint 2007 folder, and then double-click the "Lesson 4 termite damage" (JPEG) file.*

19. *Click on the photograph of termite damage, then click Insert.* Your screen should now look like PowerPoint 2007 Exhibit 12. If you need to change the size of the image, *click on one of the sides of the image and drag the image to the desired size.*

20. Now that you have created all of your slides, you are ready to begin finalizing the presentation. Press **[CTRL]+[HOME]** to go to the first slide in the presentation.

21. *Click the Slide Sorter view icon at the bottom right of the screen.* Notice that you can see all six of your slides on the screen.

22. You will now apply transition effects (effects that take place when you move from one slide to another) and animation effects (effects that take place during display of a single slide).

23. *Click on the first slide, "Richards Opening Statement."*

24. *Click the Animations ribbon tab.* You should see the Transition to This Slide group (see PowerPoint 2007 Exhibit 13). On the left side of the Transition to This Slide group are the various transition choices. To the right are the settings available for each transition.

25. *On the Animations ribbon tab, click the More icon in the Transition to This Slide group.* Notice that many types of slide transitions are available.

26. Press the **[ESC]** key to make the "More transitions" list disappear.

27. *On the Animation ribbon tab, click the Fade Smoothly transition effect in the Transition to This Slide group.* Notice that after you selected it, your slide displayed the transition effect. Fade Smoothly is a professional-appearing transition effect that is not distracting, so it is a good one to use in the legal setting.

28. *On the Animations ribbon tab, click the down arrow next to Transition Speed: Fast and then click Medium.*

**POWERPOINT 2007
EXHIBIT 13**

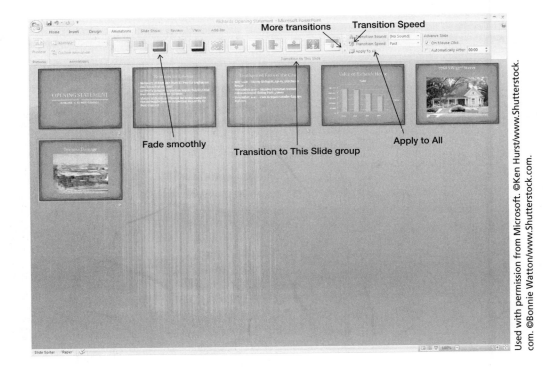

Used with permission from Microsoft. ©Ken Hurst/www.Shutterstock. com. ©Bonnie Watton/www.Shutterstock.com.

29. *On the Animations ribbon tab, click Apply to All in the Transition to This Slide group.* This will apply the Fade Smoothly effect to all of the slides in your presentation. Notice that little symbols now appear under all of your slides in the slide sorter; this shows that they have transition effects associated with them.

30. Notice that in the Transition to This Slide group, under Advance Slide, "On Mouse Click" is selected. This means that the presentation will automatically move to the next slide only when the mouse is clicked. You could set it to move to the next slide automatically after a given amount of time, but the current selection is fine for this presentation.

31. *Click the Slide Show icon at the bottom right of the screen* to see your presentation, including the transition effects. *Click the mouse button to proceed through the presentation and go back to the Slide Sorter screen.*

32. You will now create an animation effect that determines how the slides with bullet points appear on the screen.

33. *Double-click the second slide, "Reasons for Lawsuit."*

34. *Click anywhere in the lower half of the screen.*

35. *On the Animations ribbon tab, click the down arrow next to Animate: No Transition in the Animation group* (see PowerPoint 2007 Exhibit 14).

36. *Under Fade, click By 1st Level Paragraphs.* Notice that the animation effect is then demonstrated.

37. *Repeat this same process for slide 3.*

38. You are now ready to view your presentation. Press the **[PAGE UP]** key to go to the first slide in the presentation.

39. *Click the Slide Show icon at the bottom right of the screen.*

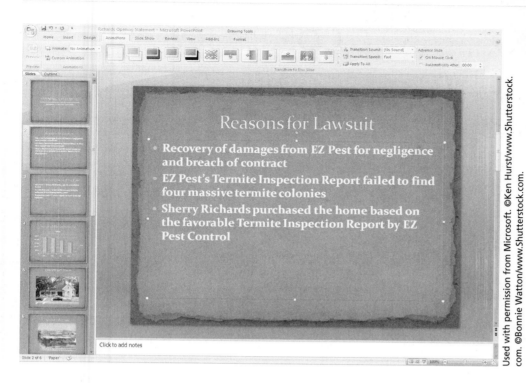

Used with permission from Microsoft. ©Ken Hurst/www.Shutterstock.com. ©Bonnie Watton/www.Shutterstock.com.

**POWERPOINT 2007
EXHIBIT 14**

40. Your first slide is now shown at full-screen size. To proceed to the next slide, press the **[SPACE BAR]** or *click the left mouse button.* Keep pressing the **[SPACE BAR]** or clicking the left mouse button to proceed with the presentation. Notice that, on the slides with bullets, you must press the **[SPACE BAR]** or click the mouse to go to the next bullet; this is the animation effect you created.

41. When you get to the end of the presentation, press the **[SPACE BAR]** or *click the left mouse button* to go back to editing the presentation.

42. To print your presentation, *click the Office button, point to Print, and click OK.*

43. To save your presentation, *click the Save icon* (it looks like a floppy disk) *on the Quick Access toolbar.*

44. *Click the Office button and then click Close.*

This concludes the PowerPoint 2007 Hands-On Exercises. To exit PowerPoint, *click the Office button, then click Exit PowerPoint.*

GLOSSARY

absolute cell reference   A cell address in a spreadsheet program formula that does not change when it is copied to a new location.

access rights   Network security measure that limits a user's access to only those directories and programs that the user is authorized to use.

access time   The amount of time it takes to transfer data between a storage device and RAM.

activity hourly rate   A fee based on hourly rates that vary depending on the type of service or activity performed and the degree of difficulty of the activity.

aged accounts receivable report   A report showing all cases that have outstanding balances due and how much these balances are past due.

antivirus and antispyware utilities   Programs that attempt to prevent virus and spyware programs from getting into the computer system; most also function to locate and remove any viruses or spyware that do manage to get into the computer.

application service provider (ASP)   A company that provides software or a service application through the Internet directly to the user's computer.

application software   Instructions (programs) that tell the computer to perform a specific function or task, such as word processing.

arithmetic operators   Symbols that tell a spreadsheet how to compute values. Examples include addition signs, subtraction signs, and multiplication signs.

ascending sort   A sort criterion that places data in ascending order from beginning to end, from A to Z, or from low numbers to high numbers.

attorney or paralegal hourly rate   A fee based on the attorney's or paralegal's level of expertise and experience in a particular area.

automatic page numbering   Word-processor feature that automatically numbers the pages of a document for the user; also renumbers pages as material is moved, added, or deleted.

auxiliary storage device   A device that stores information so that it can be retrieved for later use. Auxiliary storage devices retain data after power to the computer has been turned off. Auxiliary storage devices include flash drives, hard disk drives, and others.

background   The design on which the other elements of the presentation (words, clip art, etc.) are placed.

backing up   Making a copy of a user's computer files.

backup utility   Program that creates a copy of a user's hard disk or other storage device. The backup copy can be restored if the hard disk is damaged or lost.

bar code scanner   Device that reads the special lines of bar codes. Can be used to track documents in litigation, or physical objects such as office furniture and equipment.

bar/column graph   A graph consisting of a sequence of bars that illustrate numerical values.

billable hour   Sixty minutes of legal services.

billing   The process of issuing invoices (bills) to collect monies for legal services performed and for expenses incurred.

blended hourly rate fee   A single hourly rate that is set by taking into account the mix of attorneys working on the matter.

Boolean/logical operator   A symbol that instructs a DBMS to search for more than one criterion. Examples include AND, OR, and NOT.

cable modem   A data modem that is designed to work over cable TV lines.

case retainer   A fee that is billed at the beginning of a matter, is not refundable to the client, and is usually paid at the beginning of the case as an incentive for the office to take the case.

case type productivity report   A report showing which types of cases (e.g., criminal, personal injury, bankruptcy, etc.) are the most profitable.

cash advance   Unearned monies that are paid before services are rendered, to cover the attorney's future fees and expenses.

cell   An intersection between a row and a column in a spreadsheet.

cell address   The row and column location of a cell, usually expressed with column identifier first and row identifier second.

cell pointer   The cursor in a spreadsheet program.

cell width   The number of characters that can be viewed in any given cell in a spreadsheet program.

central processing unit (CPU)   The part of a computer that contains the processor chip and main memory. The CPU organizes and manipulates information, in addition to coordinating with peripheral devices.

centralized word-processing system   A system in which all the word-processing documents for an organization are input or typed in a single location or by one department (i.e., a word-processing department).

client hourly rate A fee based on a single hourly charge for the client, regardless of which attorney works on the case and what she or he does on the case.

client/server network A network that uses a server (or servers) to enhance the function and meet the needs of the other computers on the network.

clip art Predrawn art.

cloud computing The ability to use one computer to access information stored on a different computer or server.

column An area that extends down a page vertically.

comment Word-processor feature that allows a user to annotate and create notes in a document without changing the text of the document.

compare documents Word-processor feature that allows a user to compare and contrast two documents, either side by side or by blacklining (usually through the creation of a third document showing differences).

compression utility Program that reorganizes a file so that the file takes up less room when it is saved. Many large files that are downloaded from the Internet are routinely compressed to reduce the time needed for the download.

computer An electronic device that accepts input data, processes data, outputs data, and stores data electronically; types include desktop, laptop, handheld, tablet, and file server.

computer virus A destructive computer program that may be designed to delete data, corrupt files, or do other damage; may also be self-replicating, using an "infected" computer to transmit itself to other computers.

contingency fee A fee collected if the attorney successfully represents the client; typically a percentage of the total recovery.

data value One item of information, which is the smallest piece of information in a table.

database A collection of related data items. Databases are created because the information contained in them must be accessed, organized, and used.

database management system Application software that manages a database by storing, searching, sorting, and organizing data.

decentralized word-processing system A system in which individuals or separate departments in an organization perform their own word processing.

demonstrative evidence All evidence other than testimony.

descending sort A sort criterion that places data in descending order from end to beginning, from Z to A, or from high numbers to low numbers.

disaster recovery plan A prewritten plan of action to be followed if a disaster befalls the legal organization.

document assembly software Powerful computer program that creates standardized templates and forms.

document camera An overhead projector that uses a camera to display hard-copy documents that have not been imaged.

document management software Program that organizes, controls, distributes, and allows for extensive searching of electronic documents, typically in a networked environment.

double indenting Word-processor feature (also found in other types of programs) that indents text an equal distance from the left and right margins.

DSL (Digital Subscriber Line) A type of digital phone line that allows both data and voice to be transmitted on the same line, simultaneously if desired. Transmission speed is fairly fast.

earned retainer The money the law office or attorney has earned and is entitled to deposit in the office's or attorney's own bank account.

electronic billing Client billing that uses a standard electronic format, using such means as the Internet, and conforms to standard billing codes.

electronic filing Supplying electronic versions of legal documents to a court, via the Internet or other electronic means, when the court does not require the hard copy of the document.

encryption Process of running a message through an encoder that uses an encrypting key to alter the characters in the message. Unless the person wanting to read the message has the encryption key needed to decode it, the message appears unreadable.

endnote Material that is printed at the end of a chapter or document; marked in text by a numbered referent.

evidence display system Technology that provides networked computer monitors to a judge, jury, court reporter, clerk, attorneys, and the public.

expense slip A record of each expense item a firm incurs on behalf of the client.

extranet A secure web-based site that allows clients to access information about their cases and collaborate with the legal professionals who are providing legal services to them.

field A column in a table that contains a category of information.

firewall Security measure that allows users from inside an organization to access the Internet but keeps outside users from entering the computer or LAN.

flat fee A fee for specific legal services that is billed as a fixed amount.

flat-file DBMS A DBMS that can work with only one database table at a time.

footer Text that appears at the bottom of each page of a document.

footnote Material that is printed at the bottom of a page; marked in text by a numbered referent.

form Allows a user to view, enter, and edit data in a custom format designed by the user.

formulas Expressions used in spreadsheet programs to automatically perform calculations on other values.

function command A predefined calculation used in a spreadsheet program to speed up the process of entering complex formulas.

gigahertz (GHz) Measure of the clock speed of a computer.

hard disk drive A reliable and fast auxiliary storage device that stores data on a rigid magnetic disk; may be built into the computer (internal) or a freestanding peripheral device (external).

hardware   The physical equipment of a computer system, as opposed to programs or software.

header   A title or heading that appears at the top of each page of a document.

hourly rate fee   A fee for legal services that is billed to the client by the hour at an agreed upon rate.

imaging   Scanning a document into a computer so the user can see an exact picture of the document on the computer.

input   Data or information that is entered or transferred into a computer (including by keyboard, mouse, scanner, voice, etc.).

input devices   Devices used to enter information into a computer; include the mouse, keyboards, scanners, voice recognition devices, digital cameras, and others.

Internet   One of the world's largest computer networks; actually a "network of networks." It allows hundreds of millions of users around the world to share information.

intranet   An internal network designed to provide and disseminate information to internal staff; most mimic the look and feel of the World Wide Web.

landscape   A method of printing that arranges data across the width of a page.

license agreement   Contract setting out the user's rights and restrictions on how a piece of software can be used.

line graph   A graph that plots numerical values as a time line.

local area network (LAN)   A multiuser system linking computers that are in close proximity for the purpose of communication.

lookup option   A list of options that a user must choose from when entering information into a table.

macro   Word-processor feature that records the user's keystrokes, saves those keystrokes, and then allows the user to play those keystrokes back.

magnetic tape system   Storage device that records data on magnetic tape.

main memory   The part of the CPU that stores information that the computer is processing. Main memory consists of read-only memory and random-access memory.

management reports   Reports used to help managers analyze whether the office is operating in an efficient, effective, and profitable manner.

many-to-many relationship   One record in either table can relate to many records in the other table. The many-to-many relationship is not permitted in most relational databases.

memory chips   Parts of a computer that store or hold information.

merging   The process of combining a form with a list of variables to automatically produce a document; sometimes called document generation.

metadata   Electronically stored information that may identify the origin, date, author, usage, comments, or other information about a file; "data about data."

modem   A device that allows computers in different locations to communicate using a telephone line.

monitor   Screen that displays computer output.

mouse   An input device used to move the cursor on the monitor. The cursor moves in the same direction as the mouse is moved.

network operating system   System that handles communication tasks between the computers on a network.

normal view   PowerPoint screen that shows the slide that is being created, an outline of the total presentation, and speaker's notes for the slide currently displayed.

one-to-many relationship   One record in one table can have many matching records in another table. The table on the "one" side is called the "parent" table and the other is called the "child" table.

one-to-one relationship   Each record in the first table contains a field value that corresponds and matches the field value in one record in the other table.

operating account   Bank account used by a law firm for the deposit of earned fees and payment of law-firm expenses.

operating system software (program)   A set of instructions that tell the computer how to operate its own circuitry and manage its components; also controls how the computer communicates with input, output, and auxiliary storage devices. Allows the user to manage the computer.

optical character recognition (OCR)   A technology that allows the text of documents to be read or scanned into a computer so the text of the document can be searched or brought into a word processor to be edited.

optical storage devices   Devices that use laser beams to write data onto small plastic disks. Optical storage devices can record hundreds of megabytes of data on a single disk.

output   Information or computer results that are produced or transmitted from a computer to a user as a result of the computer's operations (including to monitor, printer, etc.).

output device   Peripheral device that provides a user with the data a computer has generated, accessed, or manipulated.

paperless office   Firm in which all hard-copy documents are converted into electronic form(s) for storage, processing, and distribution.

password   Code entered into a computer system or software that acts as a key, allowing the user to access the system and the information it contains.

peer-to-peer network   A computer network in which each computer acts both as a server and a client.

peripheral devices   Pieces of equipment that are connected to a computer to perform specific functions, such as storing information (auxiliary storage devices), inputting information (input devices), outputting information (output devices), and communicating with other computers (communication devices).

pie chart   A chart that represents each value as a piece or percentage of a whole (a total "pie").

Portable Document Format (PDF)   A file format developed by Adobe Systems, Inc., for sharing files independently of the application that created the file or the computer's operating system.

portrait   A method of printing that arranges data down the length of a page.

power-on password   Password that the computer immediately prompts the user to enter after the machine has been turned on, but before the computer has completely booted the operating system software. If the user does not know the password, the system will not start and the computer will be unusable.

pre-billing report   A rough draft compilation of billings.

primary file   A file that contains the information that remains the same (the constant) in a document that is used more than once; usually referred to as a *form* or *template* in a merge document.

primary key   A field that uniquely identifies each record.

primary sort   The first sort criterion that a DBMS uses to sort information.

processor chip   The part of the computer that performs the actual arithmetic computations and logic functions.

project management software   Application program that allows the user to track the sequence and timing of the separate activities of a larger project or task.

pure retainer   A fee that obligates the office to be available to represent the client throughout the agreed-upon time period.

query   Extracts data from a table based on criteria designed by the user. A query allows a user to search for and sort only the information the user is looking for at that time.

query by example (QBE)   A method of querying a database where the user interactively builds a query that will search and sort a database.

random-access memory (RAM)   A part of main memory that is temporary and volatile in nature; it is erased every time the computer's power is turned off. Application programs and data are loaded into RAM when the computer is processing the data.

read-only memory (ROM)   A part of main memory that contains permanent information a computer uses to operate itself. ROM can be read, but cannot be written to.

record   A collection of fields that are treated as a unit. It is essentially one row in a table.

relational DBMS   A DBMS that can work with multiple tables at a time, so long as at least one common field occurs in each table.

relational operator   A symbol that expresses data relationships in a database when performing searches. Examples include greater than, less than, and equal to symbols.

relative cell reference   A cell address in a spreadsheet program formula that automatically changes to reflect its new location when it is copied.

removable drive   A small portable device that stores a large amount of data; often used to transfer information between computers.

report   Prints data from a table or query as designed by the user. While forms are designed to be used on the screen, reports are designed to be printed.

report writer   Allows the user complete control over how data in the database are printed without affecting the data in the database.

retainer for general representation   A retainer is typically used when a client such as a corporation or school board requires continuing legal services throughout the year.

root expander   A search technique that increases the scope of a database search by searching for words with a common root.

row   An area that extends across a page horizontally.

secondary file   The file that contains the information that varies (the *variable*) in a merge document.

secondary sort   The second sort criterion that a DBMS uses to sort information.

single-user system   A computer that can accommodate only one person at a time and is not linked to other systems or computers.

slide show view   PowerPoint screen used during a presentation or when the user wants to preview how the audience will actually see the slide. Only the current slide is shown on the screen. The program interface, menus, outline view, and speaker's notes are not shown.

slide sorter view   PowerPoint screen that shows the slides in the presentation, but in a greatly reduced format; typically used to review and/or change the order of slides.

slide transition   Effects that control how the program proceeds from one slide to another.

social media   Online platforms that enable people to communicate easily to share information and resources, including text, audio, video, and images.

software   Computer programs that instruct the computer hardware how to function and perform tasks.

sound card   A device that enhances the sounds that come out of a computer and/or enables speakers attached to a computer to function. Nearly all computers now come with a sound card.

speech recognition   The ability of a computer to understand spoken words.

spreadsheet   A computerized version of an accountant's worksheet or ledger page.

spreadsheet software   Programs that calculate and manipulate numbers using labels, values, and formulas.

spyware   A general term for software that tracks a user's movement on the Internet for advertising and marketing purposes, collects personal information about the user, or changes the configuration of the user's computer without the user's consent.

stacked column graph   A graph that depicts values as separate sections in a single or stacked column.

storage   Retention of electronic information for future use (using storage devices such as hard disks, CD-ROMs, DVDs, flash drives, and other media).

storage capacity   The maximum amount of data that can be stored on a device.

structured query language (SQL)   A database programming language used to search for and retrieve information in some DBMSs.

style   A named set of formatting characteristics that users can apply to text.

table   A collection of related information stored in rows and columns.

table of authorities   Automated word-processor feature that allows the program to generate an accurate list of case and statute citations (authorities), along with the page number(s) on which each cite appears.

text   Descriptive data, such as headings and titles, used for reference purposes in a spreadsheet.

timekeeper   Anyone who bills for time, including partners, associates, and paralegals.

timekeeper productivity report   A report showing how much billable and non billable time is being spent by each timekeeper.

timekeeping   Tracking time for the purpose of billing clients.

timeslip   A slip of paper or computer record that records information about the legal services legal professionals provide to each client.

track changes   Word-processor feature that allows reviewers to make or recommend changes to a document; these changes can later be either accepted or rejected by the original author.

trial presentation programs   Presentation graphics programs specifically designed to meet the needs of trial attorneys.

trust or escrow account   A bank account, separate and apart from a law office's or attorney's operating bank account, where unearned client funds are deposited.

unearned retainer   Money that is paid up front by the client as an advance against the attorney's future fees and expenses. Until the money is actually earned by the attorney or law office, it actually belongs to the client.

utility software   Instructions that help users with the housekeeping and maintenance tasks a computer requires; helps manage either the hardware or software aspects of a computer.

validation control   The process of controlling and limiting what information is entered into a database for the purpose of ensuring accuracy.

value billing   A type of fee agreement that is based not on the time required to perform the work, but on the basis of the perceived value of the services to the client.

values   Numbers that are entered into a spreadsheet program for the purpose of making calculations.

video adapter card   Piece of hardware that acts as an interface between the monitor and the computer.

videoconferencing   A private broadcast between two or more remote locations, with live image transmission, display, and sound. Uses data communications to conduct long-distance, face-to-face meetings.

Voice over Internet Protocol (VoIP)   Functionality that allows users to make telephone calls using a broadband Internet connection instead of a regular phone line.

"what if" analysis   A feature of spreadsheets that allows the user to build a spreadsheet and then change the data to reflect alternative planning assumptions or scenarios.

wide area network (WAN)   A multiuser system linking computers that may be located thousands of miles apart.

wildcard character   A search technique that increases the scope of a database search by replacing one character in a word.

Windows   A graphical operating system developed by Microsoft for IBM-compatible computers. Various versions of Windows include Windows XP, Windows Vista, and Windows 7.

wireless modem   Modems that many mobile phones and handheld computers now use to connect to the **Internet**.

wireless networking   System that allows computers on the network to communicate with each other using wireless antennas coordinated through a wired access point.

word art   Feature that allows users to add special formatting to text.

word-processing software   Program used to edit, manipulate, and revise text to create documents.

INDEX

Note: Page numbers followed by *e* indicate exhibits.

track changes feature, 44,
   87–89, 128–129
trial database, 351–352
trial presentation programs, 414
trial presentation software
   courtroom presentation tips,
      419–421
   ethical considerations,
      421–422
   Microsoft Powerpoint,
      415–419
   overview, 413–414
trial software, 19
TrialDirector, 414
trust account interest earned,
   274
trust or escrow account, 273
trusts and estates, 191
Twitter, 21
typographical errors, 53

U

unauthorized practice of law,
   53–54
unearned retainer, 273, 274
Uniform Task-Based
      Management System
      (UTBMS), 288
upper left corner, 186
USB drive, 5
utility software, 12, 14

V

validation control, 336
validation of information, 54
value billing, 275–276

values, 173
variables, 46, 51
VHS tape, 5
video adapter card, 7
video evidence, 7
videoconferencing, 8
virus protection, 15e
viruses, 25
voice input systems, 7
voice over Internet protocol
   (VoIP), 8–9

W

web-based networks, 11
weblogs, 17
Westlaw (ASP), 16, 20, 412
"what if" analysis, 168
whole-paragraph functions,
   38–40
Wi-Fi computing, 26
wide area networks (WAN), 11
wildcard character, 340
wills, drafting, 98, 140
Windows operating system,
   13–14
WinZip, 14
wireless modem, 8
wireless networking, 10
Word. *See* Microsoft Word
word art, 417–418
word processing. *See also* Corel
      WordPerfect; Microsoft
      Word
   and Adobe Acrobat, 47
   centralized and decentralized,
      33–34

comments feature, 42–43
compare documents feature,
   42–43
document assembly, 46,
   50–52
electronic distribution of
   documents, 40
ethical considerations, 52–54
file formats, 46
hidden codes, 45
macros, 40–42
merging documents, 46
PDF file creation, 47–49
printing, 40
software, 33
table of authorities, 44
tables, 40
track changes feature, 44
training and templates, 46–47
whole-paragraph functions,
   38–40
worksheets, 166, 170,
   199–201, 230–232.
   See also Microsoft
   Excel; spreadsheets and
   spreadsheet software
WYSIWYG, 170

Z

zip drives, 5

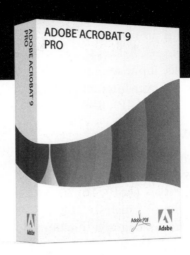
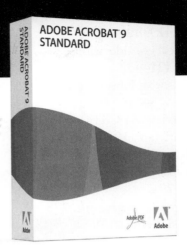